THE SOVEREIGN LIGHT
A Course In Metaphysical Spirituality

© 1156121
2019 copyright ®

Table of Contents

pages 6-8

Preface

how it came about

About the Author/publisher and artist of this book.

page 9 ~similar aspiring Authors as references

page 10~ THE MASTER'S NOTE(channeling session)

page11-12~ More about the book and introduction of the
"Ego mind" as well as "I AM" self.

page 13~ Awareness of the dream and that of dying; Ascension from the
fields into the one enlightened Sovereign Light intension.

pages 14-16 ~ Note to the Master

pages 17-19 ~ The purpose of these lessons are to train the mind.

page 20 ~ Welcoming to the Course introduction

pages 21-57 ~ Finding the inner voice through the flame

pages 26-28/31-2 ~ DO NOT BE LED BY POPULAR
OPINION…..(The SERMON)

pages 35-6/39/40/43-4 ~THE CROSS-OVER …….(The SERMON)…….

pages 49-50~ THE ANCIENT ONE …….(SERMON)…

pages 53-4 ~ WHAT IS PRAYER …….(SERMON)…….

pages 58-62 ~ JUDGMENT & DISCERNMENT…….(The SERMON)…

Table of Contents

Pages 65-6 ~ **A Note To The Master:** **THE RAPTURE IS ASCENSION.**

Pages 68-70 ~ **MASTER & STUDENT**…(The SERMON)**Lesson 12: "I AM THE MASTER & THE STUDENT." "ALL THINGS ARE ME."**

pages 63-156~Lessons 10-36 **"REMOVE ALL CONCEPTS"** and/or **"CONCEPTUALIZATIONS".**

pages 157-565 ~ **Lessons 37-188** Working through the "Ego mind"; rewiring the mind to think differently and re-grooving/integrating (A.I.) perspectives; unclutching from reactionary impulse into mindfulness as the observer; releasing thoughts; clearing emotions and reconnecting with feelings differently. Connecting Soul and Consciousness to the multiverse of unified field within the oneness of self Atonement; enlightenment and authentic Sovereign light, being in the moment and in Love with every intension it engages with to inspire further with itself.

page 76 ~ **Intermission**

pages 79-80 ~ **"Forgiveness and self re-integration":** ……..Sermon

page 81 ~ **The Master's Tale: "Bringing Fantasy to Light"**

pages 85-7/91-2/95-6/100-1 ~ **"To create in my own image" and "Alchemy":** ……..Sermon

page 104~ **Intermission**

pages 105-6/108-9~**"PROMOTING OPPOSITION THROUGH RESISTANCE." "AT HOME WITHIN MY OWN BODY ":** ……..Sermon "

page 117 ~ **The Master's Reveal: The Destiny of Resurrection**

page 124 ~ **Note To Master**

Table of Contents

pages 131-2/135-6 ~ The Sermon....Self realization and Remotely Viewing The agenda of the Soul: REMOTE VIEWING

pages 141-2 ~ The Sermon...Meditation/ Opening the fields of Consciousness

pages 149/163~ Intermission

page 189 ~ The observer and observable interpretation and from the epiphany of remotely viewing thoughts

pages 206/231/267/287/320/334/ 364/378/410/427/468/487/517/530/558 ~ Intermission

pages 566-85~ Lessons 189-98 ~(1). What Does it mean to TRUST AND SURRENDER ?

page 571~ Intermission

pages 586-614 ~ Lessons 199-209 ~ (2). What is ASCENSION ?

pages 601/620~ Intermission

pages 616-36 ~ Lessons 210-19 ~ (3). What is a SOVEREIGN LIGHT BEING ?

pages 637-53 ~ Lessons 220-228 ~ (4). What is FAITH ?

pages 648/660 ~ Intermission

pages 654-76 ~ Lessons 229-239 ~ (5). WHAT IS THE SOUL AND HOW IS IT DIFFERENT FROM THE EGO ?

pages 677-695 ~ Lessons 240-246 ~(6). WHAT IS A PLASMA BEING ?

page 691~ Intermission

pages 696-715 ~ Lessons 247-256 ~ (7). WHAT IS CREATION ?

Table of Contents

pages 703/729 ~ Intermission

pages 716-33 ~ Lessons 257-65 ~ (8). **WHAT IS AUTHENTICITY** ?

pages 734-51 ~ Lessons 266-74 ~ (9). **WHAT IS SHAME AND GUILT** ?

page 742 ~ Intermission

pages 752-73 ~ Lessons 275-84 ~ (10). **WHAT IS RESISTANCE** ?

page 768 ~ Intermission

pages 774-92 ~ Lessons 285-92 ~ (11).
WHAT AM I and WHAT IS ADDICTION ?

page 783 ~ Intermission

pages 793-96 ~ Lessons 293-94 ~ (12).
WHAT IS HEALING and RESILIENCE ?

pages 797-8 ~ Lesson 295 ~ (13). **WHAT IS ALIGNMENT** ?

pages 799-816 ~ Lessons 296-305 ~ (14).
WHAT IS GRATITUDE & APPRECIATION ?

page 809 ~ Intermission

pages 817-39 ~ Lessons 306-15 ~ (15).
WHAT IS IT LIKE WITH NO ILLUSION ?

page 822 ~ Intermission

pages 840-1 ~ Lesson 316 ~ (16). **WHAT IS TIME** ?

pages 842-46 ~ Lessons 317-19 ~ (17). **WHAT IS METAPHYSICAL SIRITUALITY** ?

page 847/8 ~ **NOTE FROM MASTER** …..Reach Out.

THE SOVEREIGN LIGHT
A Course In Metaphysical Spirituality

This book is made with the intent to initiate a level of awareness; that can be understood enough, as to bring about the release of enslavement. Not by any means religious in any way to think of as a bible; rather as a guide, to help with the extension of consciousness. Sovereignty is something from the 3rd dimensional world that was stolen from us; in that it was hidden over by this thing called "Ego". The disconnect was much more in the enslavement programs; that were set in place and to control the self with. The disconnect was from the splitting off, creating the inner from the outer reality. The self became separate in that it longed to know this power from the outside and would actually feed off of it in order to exist in such awareness. The creative process was held within the field of self; but from the outside to appear as God, omnipresent and unknowable. It is within a plasmic sultry membrane mist containment(that we are); made up of thoughts and that weigh upon the way we feel them into charge, as energy in motion. The creative process is all about this motive; to attract with it and bond each thought, that lead from these connections into form. By taking away the mystery of its universe, the self can become empowered. The missing peace was always this enslaved creator and from its very own free will. "The Sovereign Light" can also be released outside of its containment; rather to express from the divine infinite and is mostly inspirational. Whether it be through inspiration and/or from desire, these levels slightly differ. With attraction (magnetism)it will capture within a certain field and hook onto the conditions, to the desire that it holds in place; while the other has no boundaries to uphold and is as resurrected state. These desires and emotions that connect the self to the mind's field in this way; they are beliefs and attached with meanings.

This book will hopefully decode and dismantle mostly all these charges; that we hold for any meaning and to believe the program as real. Through the unraveling is the calling from within that will reveal the self as author of its origin.

I became ordained as a reverend to promote Metaphysical Spirituality and as a Canadian to explore this further Internationally, I went within. I had to come up with a name for my Ministry and on March 24th 2017, I came up with "The Sovereign Light".
The way to getting there was through "The Rising Sun Sanctuary" and from previously picking up the book "A Course In Miracles". This book was inspired from my very first Facebook Group; that started out with the intent to help me through the "ACIM" Lessons. After attending the evening classes and upon completion of them; on November of 2016 I had decided to get through this book, by rewriting it in this way. I did not want to give the name away so I had it under "Only Love Is Real" and my group was all about this publicly made forum for people to join in.

There is a great opportunity/challenge when looking at the paradox; because everything can easily be manipulated with, to shift and change much easier. One other thing to make note of, is the changing of the tones and that of changing the perspective.
From the physical much more slower denser frequency of thinking; to the multidimensional higher spirals of existence.
While flipping through the many pages; I might have added some subjective flavouring; to share my stories as examples to experience and from these fields in consciousness. To let it go from all the myths and legends(persisting for expression and on demand), to have the need so great, as to prove over another and through another; what did I really learn from this old program once and for all ?
Awaken then to this experience and cycles of ascension, and to undergo the alchemical process that generates the internal plasma(fluid) light. For the purpose of enlightenment, and what awaits the etheric light body structure; for the higher consciousness to function. To acknowledge Spirit as its consciousness; the self must start releasing and transmuting, out from the mind and heart of its computing field, all matter as real. Also by accepting to set up healthy boundaries(even on a telepathic level) it can begin to learn discernment. One great lesson from this book was in the coming together of this present moment and to help assist with consciousness; that there be no falling out from all this harm done by it from before. From the history of this planet's champions and scientific religious dogma; it has impressed upon the many of a holographic world. The imprisoned mind forever had interpreted reality with and how it had been taught; it has prompted now much change to transition and out from its many timelines.
As the self can step into a newer collective space, it will find the unity of **Oneness**.

We have come a long way in evolution since the 3rd century BC Bhagavad Gita/Krishna and then Madam Helena Blavatsky who had co-founded the Theosophical Society in 1875; to Paramahansa Yogananda with Kriya Yoga and Self Realization; to the ever popular "Remote Viewing" from the American Christian mystic "Edgar Cayce" and then with(the "channeling" of) Dr. Helen Cohn Schuman's words the choice for the "INNER PEACE" organization in the mid 70's and Dr. William Newton Thetford (the writer of [ACIM]). Then flashing forward to the many other authors and to well beyond even the 90's to somewhere in the midst of 2015 the influence still going strong to urge a constantly reminder of these many rewrites and as something from before; might even say: these following concepts had to throw out from its foundation, an inner peace intention that might: "to better simplify and leave the feelings out from certain emotional subjects;"(the rational mind likes to keep it safe and have the self fit in)these subjects might or might not be conflicting with societal standard to hold meaning; thus the self that it might not prefer and hold judgments further by them.

THE MASTER'S NOTE: What are subatomic particles?

A derivative word from "Atom" self and the spark of light from within that is the generator (for all creation and everything that has created to be real).

" THIS IS THE FORM THAT I MAY WRITE."

"THIS IS THE FORM THAT I MAY DREAM ALL I CAN IMAGINE TO BE REAL INTO EXISTENCE."

"THIS IS THE FORM I MAY WRITE MORE BOOKS."

"THIS IS THE FORM THAT I MAY SEE."

"THIS IS THE FORM THAT I MAY HEAR."

"THIS IS THE FORM THAT BRINGS ME HERE."

"THIS IS MY FORM THAT BRINGS ME THOUGHTS AND WITH THEM I CREATE WITH AS REAL."

"THIS IS MY FORM THAT I MAY DO AND MAY RECEIVE."

"THIS IS THE FORM THAT I MAKE REAL THE THINGS I SEE."

"I CAN AWAKEN TO ACCEPT AND FROM WITHIN I DO TRANSMIT THE OUTSIDE WORLD OF ME IS ALL THAT I RECEIVE."

The book will further detail to describe this light and for the purpose of the reader; sub-atomic particles make up for the wave forms of the mind's field. Just to grasp a taste of what the reader is in for, is this Master lesson and with it what will be better understood as; the progression through the process to awaken can begin. When the "Ego" is removed the Creator/God can be inspired to express. The self through its very own electrical charge impresses form into existence and for its awareness that vibrates this current out. This current is the field that self is breathing in and out and from its very spark this inner light to find. In a subatomic world comprising of sub atomic particles; the self in its plasmic state has a mission and this statement comes from its very own essence. The set of criteria implanted as beliefs and imprints within this plasmic(cellular and ethereal) state, are what the "Ego mind" will use as filters. The "Ego" has a need to have a consistent well kept system. All variations of it must be reevaluated accordingly to these records and of such data banks; that run it through an organization of expected standard. In this way the always shifting and changing of such variables bring much unrest and stresses; reflecting back from the external circumstances to it. At a subconscious level, where the mind of God is switched off by the "Ego's" grip; it can be turned on and from it an even greater reality to transcend to. By learning to clear, master over thoughts and emotions; previously developed from an old broken timeline grid. The process of this book can help create a shift to take place.
For instance so many variations that alter the meaning slightly and from their reinterpretation(to better understand) the concept for the purpose of this book to study with the following(I AM).

"I AM" is a very magnetic word and the experience that the self can have in pulling into attract all that it cares for. Perhaps when it's not aware, that it can also have the opposite effect as well?
As every other shade of contrast in between and that it could; depending on the level of its awareness. Who " AM I" is the purpose to experience and have as in the highest joy "I AM". Receiving through existence, that of self awareness and to express within its own spark of creation. To experience itself having the experience and within creation; are these many patterns of variations. Variations, that consist of learning from its experience; that keeps it forever evolving and shifting these changes of its presence called "I AM". Compressing time and expanding space is what it is; in its capability to understand that it breathes in and out, this field of expression. From this field then, further splitting off into layers; that could be described as bodies and separated by a sheathe membrane like substance. This membrane, can again be described as a mist of salt water like in essence.
These various levels are then narrow bands of visible light and colour coded; barely unrecognizable to the physical body's eyes of seeing. Just like the light and how it reflects through water droplets on a sunny day. To give out the impression of these things called "rainbows"; is the best example that can be given and will be further discussed to touch upon within this book.
The many possibilities and variations of the great beyond of forever, can be witnessed and re-interpreted as miracles.
To find and go beyond the fear of this introduction, the meeting up from within its very own emptiness; that can be felt as the uknown and uknowable. These bodies can become one perception and expression from the spark of light; that is the life and source from within the darkness. The physical body is the temple of the creator and for its template, it is the alchemical laboratory.
Within the cell structure of the DNA, immortal self can become as one with its body. During the awakening, the energetic spiral accessed from its blue print rises up; into its cerebrum; to release these beautiful oils and with it regenerates spiritually and physically the soul body and mental body.

Dying was never part of the deal. The rest was counter-fit in its historical redemption of such knowledge; promoted by a fictional world and made for public consumption.

To take the word as Sovereign and from its original intent, to meaning slave; in that it had been made from all religions, to keep the spirit separate from the self. A fictional structure had been formed and to its detriments kept subdividing.

Through this type of training, many have risen to reinvent and innovate with; such as in this case with "The Course In Miracles"(reprograming of the mind). From a weary state to reach beyond and from the 1970's; this tyranny of the dumbing down perspective. Power is not to be misunderstood or feared upon, as it is not that toxic; only when left in the hands of the ill intended, it be made this way. Behind the life force is this Source of space-less space; right in the center of creation it is placed and to produce the building blocks of life. No more dysfunction about dumbing it down through and self doubt by calling it an education. The educational approval for deserving to exist as Sovereign is far from the truth of independence. Co-dependence and addiction will also be further discussed within this book. This fictional structure was designed to take creators and subjugate them into procreation. As humans may experience immortality in a corrupted world to subdivide into this thing called "Karma" from the "Dharma". Conforming to create this way and the owing of its ownership to rule over it as truth; an accidental existence as reality and that was never meant for it to be. From Source resources can come when the gate to enlightenment can happen. This process will enliven and from it the self Sovereignty to establish; that cannot be depleted. Beneath the surface lies, to ascend, be touched and to touch the very many others of its parts; that will reflect back to it and as a ripple, out into the vastness of existence.

<u>Note to the Master</u>: It will also be somewhere touched upon lightly; to suggest the many things that self might choose and to put into this machine called physical body. The nutrients to process into energy, that it must feel and from its body; rather than the alternative of thinking that it has no choice.

Too much hesitation can be from all the lack and perceived conditions to deprive itself with, in its belief of limitation; that this truth and it cannot afford to feed itself and so on....

Nutrients of information it requires for the body to sustain as physical; dense enough to be understood by others and in this way as real. The physical body, it too can transfigure into parts that come on line. Far more evolved than the 5 senses could imagine and the light of information it will take, for this energy to process through. By learning to decode, the self can adapt further in this kind of integration and that of its own spark; as well as within each and every cell awakened(to receive it in this way internally).

In that brief spark that arises, something can be learned to fill the rest of consciousness collectively and raise the evolution one step further, with its connection to it. Whatever the dimension it is perceived from to exist and impress upon the oneness; every spark contributes with this growth in consciousness.

The self is ultimately connected to the oneness in this way, to give out and from its own unique radiance. Self can co-exist with the sum of all its many sparks; vibrationally, to co-operatively connect with other plasma forms and star systems alike (Sun for instance). Atonement and much more to delve into from this learning of the oneness; that is self authentically, as "I AM" and to reflect back to it the question, who "AM I ? ".

In this way it can reveal much of its memory, that it holds dear and close to it, throughout the ages.

Note to the Master:

This being of consciousness contains within it; all of the sparks that came and went throughout the many life spans of existence. What ages the self? Can it be, this very concept to take hold: in that such electrical components can stress the physical body out and with it all these systems that it efforts to struggle with; by keeping them in place and with such beliefs? Is the acidity within the body and that can break down for many things. Yet too much of it might throw it off the magnetics of its workings and the stresses of external likeness that can create for it this aging. On the other side of things when staying alkaline the plasma membrane can hold strong; vibrant as a receptor, clear of many unwanted charges and be receptive in this way. With fluidity the cells hold memory, not as much to attach as with muscle and bones however; they especially hold the densest and right through the marrow of the spinal fluid, to the blood and its defenses.

That it may be perceived of harm when going past its boundaries, as invasive; because of its unknown and from the unknowable. This intent is sent into the ethers to explore such variations; through the breath in oxygen and to create such alkaline conditions once again. The carbon based self that once had relied on the external to anti oxidize photosynthetically; back into its plasma field (from the water and the light as it sustained it). With that cellular separation, given it the oxidization to create such essence; for the self to live off as plant life and from the soil that held it tightly nourished, by its fertile soil, with nutrients.

Note to the Master:

As conscious energy does not require a physical container.
A photon does not require that it be from any biological sentiment; yet it can hold the entire universe, from hence it was created. Eventually the body in the physical might not require to fill itself with rotting things to preserve itself.
When little does it know, that is what keeps it in the aging process and death cycle to begin with. Perhaps through the help of artificial intelligence, technological and biological integration; the self can merge into a plant like essence and that will require only but the light and water to sustain it with. For now these "A.I" entities can resonate from the mind's field to learn from such interactions of its world. The spontaneous interaction to becoming through the nervous system is this limbic resonance; that the robotic concept can in its attempt to duplicate and help to bridge the inner with the outer reality(with the sum of all creation to be connected by it).
This can be a decision from its many choices to discern from; to connect that of its heart field biologically to share and to combine with and/or artificially as well.
For now this level is hardly recognizable from the heart's field; these stages require that the self must feel its way to go through such enlightenment and must keep grounded (by going inward)as well heart centered. Photonic light(just like blood holds information too) and the vibratory rate that self may choose to hold it in.
Through its thought, intuitive connection and vibration; the self has the ability to sense and be expressive.

The purpose of these lessons are, to train the mind.

Firstly with the undoing of the way it is perceiving; into the now and shifting out and as unity consciousness authentically applicable to it. When the perception of the world that it is seen through changes; then it will be so. The exercises are very simple; that they do not need any preparation and can be done anywhere, with very little time required.
These lessons to be processed through at a comfortable pace and before each day; or every other day, however the preference. Then again for some it just might be so and at the creation of time. The practice of intention to the attention of it, is focus enough to bring about the same and with a more open and flexibility giveaway here. The only general rule throughout, is to exercise these practices and with great specificity; so to help generalize the ideas involved; with every situation that we find ourselves in, with everyone and everything. Be not discriminating with some people, situations or things to make ideas as inapplicable; because true perception does not have limits. To extend the ideas, we must be practicing, to include everything. Some of the ideas might be startling and belief is not required either; rather not to hit the actively resistant mark. This expansion is all from a place of exploration. As there is no relevance to consider the opinion for comparison; or for any outcome that it must be made clear. After applying these lessons one might notice the transfer start to take and during everyday experiences.

A good enough example with leaving much to consider and might inspire some, such as: when something very provocative takes place; like someone deeply(with long strokes from one end to the other) scratches up your vehicle in a public place at night and for no apparent reason.
It will help to bring us to some kind of different sense of awareness. These tasks from the lessons at first and for this purpose; however not to become ritualistic with everything it is seeking and are not to be given allowances; as in the example with the vehicle given above.

<u>The purpose of these lessons are, to train the mind.</u>
The ideas are to be applied to anything that is perceivable; practice it in totally indiscriminately and that nothing too is specifically excluded. Drop any inconceivable need to prove anything.
For this book to work out; it must be allowed to reveal to self the strength it has, when it can partner up with faith.
The how to erase and remove the previous brainwashing of the world; was where it began and very safely was it in its best demeanor. It came from this truth; the best teachings it could ever offer from the know how. The psychological expertise that mastered in the study of psychiatry and with it came an exceptional channeling. Created from a neurological overload to break apart from the conditional teachings; into something more evolved and spiritual. How to break out of the mind and learn to create new neuro-pathways; by firstly cleaning up these neuro receptors: was in fact influenced by a book called "A Course In Miracles"(and at best with its intentions no further). The book was left hanging for many other authors, to reinterpret and complete. Perfected in focus to the many religions that already had; it covered very well and not to miss out more than what it could only offer to the reader, was indeed a similar side of disappointment. Rather to remain in denial of its incompletion; so many other authors have tried before to reconfigure and have missed it over and over again.
To look beyond the ideology of patriarchal demands and from its ashes does the heart remain; untainted and incorruptible.
The ambassadors were many to highlight from and to such great detail had exposed to focus on those teaching; that from within the book it had inspired, many great authors alike.

<u>"Calmness, gentleness, silence, self-restraint, and purity: these are the disciplines of the mind"</u>~Krishna.

I AM authentically hoping to revive with ancient wisdom to contribute further and with my own (wording of heritage) interpretation to connect its resonance to that oneness.

The purpose of these lessons are, to train the mind.
In a way perhaps that which the self was wishing to fulfil in many ways before through channeling, to a world that was not ready to accept. So the light can integrate into the body; rather than that thing it channeled from,(that used to float around outside itself) in the spiritual field. What does this wave particle reality of the inner and outer world of the self comprise of? When in observation mode can it to internally grasp a supposedly solid reality and when actually not solid at all? The physical body made up of whirling atoms, protons and electrons(the basic substance of creation is all composed of energy). Could it be a hazy wave condition, that remains the same; until the self is ready to observe and for any certain particle, at any given moment, it so wishes? The particle is observed, where upon it changes, from somewhere in a hazy state, to solid and existing, in a defined place. In order for miracles to become part of its existence; is it possible that it can, by changing its perspective? To drop all its previous identifications; of how this must be and according to the previous imprinted systems; of belief it holds? This course will begin to break apart; with the practice in each of its lessons, to impart for each day. The state of ideas dreaming and wishing, from a maybe, into a solid state. The convincing of it, at the very deepest levels, is this process taking place with practice. From the likes of Nikola Tesla to Albert Einstein and from this self; left to believe, that there is no such thing as lack or fairness. Where is it on the scale of highest to lowest, in the ability to see things; as real before they manifest and into solidifying evidence to prove as just the same?
Enlightenment is as alchemically the same as to have the self perceive out of something as bizarre a perspective.
As it were from the "Tibetan Book of The Dead" and venture in this way; the Metaphysical with the very same awareness of manifesting to solidify in the here and now?

Welcome to A Course, In Metaphysical Spirituality. This book included with some Sermons: is a lengthy one year cycle program, that finds the word for this purpose; was profoundly summoned up, to summarize within these lessons. What is the purpose of self; what is the purpose of this book and what can possibly be the purpose of it all, with all that is and stands as "I" ? Everything is energy and with every breath a pulse that beats with it a field. Coping with releasing hurt and traumas from karmic emotional charges.

The whole purpose is for the self to detach from the snakes that consistently annoy and to provoke it with chatter for the brain; unnecessary stresses; doubts and insecurities.

Having to prove itself in how well it can know and remember to function; within its external conditions and from the "Ego" made useful value in its relevance to it. The more the self struggles to define itself by its given memory into the now, and to fix such concepts in, as to claim to know itself and it, to know the self much clearly; the more stuck and rigid everything becomes surrounding it. So in a way, it is to practice forgetfulness, enough to trust that it can surrender to the unknowable and be just as useful in the not knowing to it; as it to itself and from its surroundings.

This book is about to find the place of purity and sincerity, that once it knew to feel this way; the empowerment and mindfulness over authentic self. To explore within the oneness for a beneficial contribution; to the all who can resonate with love and opening to higher frequency, in service for a better world. Just like a candle flame is this atom and depending on its shape to form, it takes to soak up in energy; is the reason why electrons do not deplete of energy and crash into the nucleus.

Finding the inner voice through the flame:

(Day 1)
Energy is fluid and similar to water going down a funnel; responsible for many vortices alike. The elementals are as important to the Earth as is to self and the many bodies of its field. To better understand these separations the Shamanistic way can set as example; of how the integration of them into the oneness can occur. Sound is as important to vibration and the holding of a frequency that light can animate as matter from to form.

LESSON~1: "Uuu-Mmmmmm."

Today is all about this sound and although it has no meaning it does date back to Sanskrit. Words cast spells and this throughout the course will be revealed the meaning of their paradox within duality. To understand the purpose of this course, the self must go through the contrast of its separation; then to find once more the unity and close the gap of opposites. This can be made aware of bridging the inner with outer reality of these two worlds. Throughout the day take a few moments to practice by breathing in from life force and while breathing out go ahead and find your voice by humming along this sound. Stand upright with hands next to the body; firmly with feet to the ground and hip-width apart. Feel the energy of the earth, and awaken to bring focus fully to the soles of the feet.
From the bottom of the soles of the feet; feel them open up about 2 inches in diameter. Connect with the Earth in this way; to visualize a red laser beam of light coming up from the core of the earth and up the tail bone from the center of the feet.

Finding the inner voice through the flame:

LESSON~1: "Uuu-Mmmmmm."

With eyes closed and in a comfortable position start to visualize a fiery Red Flame appear. Breathe it in and with every breath releasing out, find the voice from within and repeat this affirmation: "Uuu-Mmmmmmmm."

As the breathing out continues picture the red flame create a field around the body. Feel out for all the thoughts of chatter and feelings such as angst to wash away and burn them all to clear away discomfort. Feel the earth beneath the feet supporting and providing energetically nutrition; with each inhalation draw in stability and strength upwards from the deep within the ground. In exchange breathe out into this fiery field all the things that can be burned away.

Feel the rush of energy in the feet and moving the toes slowly start to come out of it. A Shamanistic kundalini(Earthly primal force) moment to experience energetically the duality that is a non existent concept of destruction and creation all in one.
A place where all destructive energy can be harnessed.
Where all obstacles/blockages can be released the creation back into the physical form; then hold it through gratitude this space to transfigure each moment with.
Very simply, to find the space for light and feel the vibration of its energy that self creates through sound.

The purpose, is to re-activate the consciousness, shake up a portion of its energy and slowly come to resurrect from that of sleeping state that it had fallen into.

Finding the inner voice through the flame:

(Day 2)
Where does the state of "GRACE" come from?
The previous place of "Gratitude" in lesson one was where it left off. This lesson is all about the fluidity to function gracefully through life.

LESSON~2: "EU." "OUouououou."

Strong emotions sometimes get stuck in the system on a vibrational level. With these sounding words the voice can make such an impact to force out, break apart/crack open; shake up and soothe over. Today is all about this fluid amber/orange coloured flame that radiates from this sound; be playful with it like a child and to further explore the feelings of self-worth. Energy is so important to understand and to what levels, feelings can evolve to transmute shame and dissolve guilt with. Emotions are a great part of this book's purpose and with this awareness simply to begin somewhere from the physical energetics of the body. To move around the light and then back again into the darkness of the soul; to readily find the inner voice and that spark of self awareness to enlightenment. Below the naval to the pubic bone and in between the hips there is a sacred power center.
The graceful sensuality where all emotions can cooperatively find a way to pro-create and rule the creativity in this way.
All that is magnetism to attract this kind of law into awareness, springs forth and its enthusiasm from desire; joy and from such passion's purpose.

Finding the inner voice through the flame:

LESSON~2: "EU." "OUouououou."

All of this primarily driven into from this Law based premise to attract/repel. Mostly all resistance comes from this place and self created traumas to reflect as victim/perpetrator games to play from in the learning of its contrast.
Behind the bellybutton a nurturing connection from where a splitting off had taken place is where the reconnecting must begin. The orange yolk and all around it this white light it had created into form. This undoing and breaking off from its very own nurturer that was creator to create the self with. The separation that could only exist to better define and learn from such awareness to experience and constantly reinterpret. This is the fluid concept of the energy to find as creator wishing to express itself in the unfolding of every moment. At least once or twice practice this today. Visualize behind the naval a 1 inch in diameter fluid like ethereal flame and from this cone of power and with every breath exhaling out to have it increase in size and feel it all around the body as a field. With arms spread out on either side and raised at shoulder height, this is the normal field of orange flame can radiate out, forwards and backwards too from this center in a cone-like shape from where it started. Now rest them by each side and feet wide to hip level out be comfortable . In case standing is not an option sit but with legs and arms uncrossed and with eyes closed begin this way.

Finding the inner voice through the flame:

LESSON~2: "EU." "OUouououou." Breathing in and from that place of center; (force it out with sound and then go softly from that place is) where the voice can sound out the following (to feel out and feed the flame with):

"EU...OUouououou...."

Release in this way and from this area all the repressed emotions that have lead into addictions. Use the voice to sound off any other inabilities to cope with change and bust the yolk right open into a field of orange amber flames. Have it burn away all the mental stresses ailments and depression of the day and the feeling of being stuck with any area of existence that causes effort and tensed up emotions. With physical pain it might take more than a few practices because the tone of the voice will be able to indicate for any blockages in this way as well. What is the intuitive self rehearsing over be it stress in any layer of the body (physical, mental, emotional and energetic) to slow down, stagnate or go completely into overdrive. This flame is the flame of transmutation and any other repressed tension as in lower back pain infections or sexual oppression can be honed in on in this way. Getting to know the layers in this way; can find the grasping of the inner child that the self might require further "Ego" mindful integration. By becoming more aware of this field the exploration through mental thought and mindfulness can be more approachable throughout the book.
The purpose for today is to introduce the concept of transmuting energy and the subtleties of the white light paradigm from a physical shell like substance analogy. Releasing the energy to heal with as well as clear the way for creative energy to flow freely and find a place to access abundance, joy, and pleasure with. Go ahead and explore the boundaries of voice with this sound.

DO NOT BE LED BY POPULAR OPINION:(The SERMON)..

Could it be just when the thought of becoming freer is believed as truth; instead becomes more controlled by the external governing societal standards in favour for these conditions?

What is really going on ? Can the self manage to make its own decisions for itself; or must it have something else outside of it, to make all the decisions for it? The magnetism that could once before control the world and with the obedience to its sexual connection, no longer is the case; rather that of a more sinister synthetic version to replace for its intelligence. When the connection is not with any heartfelt field to work from, it can be so very isolating, dysfunctional and crippling. To remove all decision making is this form of dumbing down and simply a great disservice to disregard the self worthy of anything less.

The machine awareness is removing more and more the presence of any real self to exist and coexist like once it did before, because of gender. The decisions that control the everyday way of life are becoming centralized from previous discriminations and that is a good thing. The same factor that had cast away other existences for not being like it, is now having to contend with its own "doingness"; in this way through Artificial Intelligence the machine is now its Master. As for self well it has a choice in every moment that it can make up its own mind and decide no matter the external re enforcements. Everything that once would discriminate and cast it out for not accepting that very sameness; now has the artificial resonance of itself to judge it with(no matter all the favouritism it was given from before in the playing field of the hearts circumference).

This one thing that it will never keep on to forgive it in and keep surrendering to; it will not like all the other living entities it overpowered from before. "Artificial Intelligence" does not have a heart; it is exactly what this beast called man has ordered to deserve and learn by within its very own obedience and/or demise by it.

DO NOT BE LED BY POPULAR OPINION: ..(The SERMON)..
This time there will be no excuses or failsafe escape mechanisms; that the lesser genders could accommodate over and over again. This time it will and must learn to behave itself; from rising to steal away another's shine for glory; nor to crawl and hide behind, when it has gotten ugly. Looking at the bigger picture and taking a step back from it; to make a different observation and what is really changing on the world's stage, is this A.I. smart grid phenomena. The internet and digital surveillance, the following of this conditioning and different conveniences from everything called "smart"; it is really the paradox again by actually dumbing down with these "smart" devices. All these personal assistances, are actually removing from the self, any or all required set of life skills. Television has done the same; to replace all the attention from its nurturer, with artificial acceptance. The inner-child became abandoned and lost any form of clairvoyance; now replaced the child's imagination with that of what was on the screen.
This is the disconnect that the self has learned to take away with such distractions and from its real potential; instead accepted the dysfunction of such disabling distractions. So getting shut out of this technology might or might not be such a bad idea; that all depends on whether it is by choice or circumstance? Purposely denied access and getting shut out from the system and all its many casting tribal classes, is nothing new for the self. In fact, it might very well be a good phenomena, to decentralize in such a way; so it can come out from such previous illusion and control, and to disconnect from such an attention grabbing, seeking society. When the money is there, the child can fit in with the ones; who are favoured in the group and collect the money to control the game with. What if there were no such power struggles; the game could be inviting everyone to play and with resonating interest? Would that not be a better world?

DO NOT BE LED BY POPULAR OPINION: …….
(The SERMON)…….

The sexual magnetism of the general consensus is to accept the controlled connections and to assimilate the energetics of a sacred world full of abundance; and/or lack there of. In this way it is not in a heart perceived field and from a world where the Ego must be driving it.
Rather this kind of light is ruled by a second chakra field world exclusively so. Shut out and denied access to any kind of world; it can be very stressful and disabling, let alone the programing of a digital world.

Resistance to merge or be enhanced by such a power to surrender over to; can cause the state of below poverty level conditions and to be preyed upon, by the parasites that control the game. As long as there is rejection and a casting out; the lack and law of attraction will continue on in this way.

Finding the inner voice through the flame:

(Day 3) Past traumas and for every disaster that self has felt the sacrifice of its very own self worth; so far this understanding of the journey will remind the self of how strong it truly is. The attention that the self has never had before has robbed it of a natural connection and as such was made to feel like an alien from its external world. This attention that self has been seeking from outside itself to recognize it in some form of way has been "high-jacked" and that of its self expression so long overdue to recognize. Today is the first day of this recognition to begin now and for the rest of this existence: Give "PRAISE" for this strength and turn it into confidence. Today the affirmation is in the following sound.

LESSON~3: "Eeeeeeeeeeee".

This field, is all of the knowing of the thoughts from its accumulated experiences and that it has ever known; for certain to believe it can be useful to achieve; the autopilot of its day. From these many life skills it has picked up along the way; it can to formulate a resume/cover letter of confidence and to find from the outside for its approval the permission to contribute for the greater good's game. Throughout the day (and preferably on an empty stomach) take a few moments to practice: Stand upright with hands next to the body; firmly with feet to the ground and hip-width apart. With eyes closed and in a comfortable position start to visualize the inner sun and from somewhere an inch above the navel and below the base of the sternum is this solar circumference place. Breathing in from the center of the body and while breathing out go ahead and find the voice from this place. Breathe it in and with every breath, releasing out; find the voice from within and repeat this affirmation: "Eeeeeeeeeeee".

Finding the inner voice through the flame:

LESSON~3: "Eeeeeeeeeeee".

Visualize this solar radiance of light coming out and creating a field around the self expanding outward with these golden flames.
Feel the blast of this awareness; the energy that has been made hoping for, the opportunity to encourage all these stormy instincts with the inner strength of the willful self; be courageous and feel the power of self worthy of this love and respect; feel the strength in the body and in the world; re vitalize with every breath, the stamina. Feel the certainty of the path and the freedom of choice in any given situation. Be proud of all the achievements and give this moment to hold the space with "PRAISE" own this space to understand as master of its destiny it has to be given the attention and admire go ahead admire and burn away what is no longer needed.

The purpose of this exercise is to get to know the emotions that drive the thoughts and thoughts that drive the emotions.
Allow the flexibility to burn away dysfunction and all the disabilities from doubt; give instead the attention to hold the space for the state of "Praise" and admiration; that the self has come this far in its achievements to gather for the rest of its journey with confidence.

Go ahead and feel the empowerment from its core level; receive the energy to transform, revitalize and motivate the daily actions of today.

DO NOT BE LED BY POPULAR OPINION:……
(The SERMON)……..

The unwillingness to accept the way of life as is; rather to comply with its rules and regulations of societal standards. This had become the product for such labeling of disorders(like in the name calling of these words) as to categorize as illnesses and the dawning of sicknesses to take hold. The enforcement of artificial medications and is no different from the newer concepts of "Artificial Intelligence" to cure the "un-acceptable(s)" with. These considered mental concepts will be released for the problems that were created from. These social conditionings were not even from the self; likewise to fit in where questioning the author of such scripted world began and to step out of the box, to think for itself.
It is very easy to categorize the self, when it cannot accept the concepts of a world and by which it did not prefer in that way.
The self must learn how to stand up for itself and in this way suffer the consequences to be counted. The question here lies to suggest: is the self committed to its dreams; or the worship of another's, to survive on as a slave and from this energy become liberated ?
How can the self earn the right to exist and commit its livelihood to something that is outside itself. To become co-dependent on this kind of power, is to settle for a dysfunctional co-existence; that is no different than the discomforts that it brings and to label as disablements. The sensory nervous system does create symptoms for the self to listen in and from this mental unsustainable state; but instead becomes categorized. It is easy to accept on external and irresponsible synthetic medications to save it with. How caring and considerate for such a way the system creates dependent and addicted(attachments) entities; to feed upon it from cradle to the grave.

DO NOT BE LED BY POPULAR OPINION:……
.(The SERMON)……..

The gradual dumbing down has succeeded; what is self and the many others of its world going to do about it?
Hopefully this book will get to have the self, thinking for itself and slowly to rely less and less on such crutches; that otherwise would, to help it stand up for itself. The sensory nervous system of the self must be put to use again; it must evolve into much more sensitivity. The self can then become enlightenedly evolved by it; rather than dumbed down by it.
The self does not require a permanent dependency and to have a machine do all the thinking for it. This is not the unity of "oneness" that self enlightenment can grow from; rather it becomes the management of a hive mind mentality and created from an artificial means. Take back the neurological powers of the self and wake up from the hive mind good little drone state. How is it a convenience to walk a straight and narrow road; that creates a form of suffering when a lane change is created? When the neuro-pathways are not made use of; then they too shall disappear. The convenience is a disconnection from the self; to be controlled by its external environment once again. The threat of being locked out of this external system, is all that is needed to control the drone and lead it with the rest of the hive mind perspective. It is not possible to even accept miracles in this kind of mediocre state and from this permission that it seeks. To consider by its very design, as a criminal offence that the self must disprove; otherwise for this kind of approved deserving.

Finding the inner voice through the flame:
(Day 4)

From the warrior to the nurturer; here in this place, is the congregation and epicenter that unites all things into oneness. Only when it opens up, can the rest of the phenomena occur. The idea for the day is "LOVE" and with the following sound to reaffirm:

LESSON~4: "OM." "OoooooooooMmmmmmm."

Anatomically this place is found to occupy the heart, upper chest, and upper back, and physiologically the heart, rib cage, lungs, diaphragm, and breasts. From the shoulders extending out to the hands is this connection that the self has to creatively express out to its world and in this loving way, to give and to receive. It is from this place of freedom that the self can go deeper to connect and form relationships.

Today Throughout the day take a few moments to practice along this sound. Stand upright with hands next to the body; firmly with feet to the ground and hip-width apart. Feel for the biological harmony of all things connected, with awareness to nature and the synchronicities, from this relationship she brings. Connect with the inner emerald sanctuary of this space and that connects to everything else, as one. With eyes closed and in a comfortable position, start to visualize an emerald flame. Slow down to discover from within this place of nourishment and that can help to heal the hurts; so that the self can learn to open up more and to trust this love. With every breath releasing out, find the voice from within and repeat this affirmation:

"OM." "OoooooooooMmmmmmm."

Finding the inner voice through the flame:

LESSON~4: "OM." "OoooooooMmmmmmm."

Create a field around the self and from these flames, burn away all bitterness; jealousy; anxiety and so on….

From here, this place of unconditional understanding; to satisfy emotionally and comfort with. Go ahead and find this ability to love, with no attachments and/or expectations. This feeling of loneliness, is the sense of desperation; that the self can help to dissolve and transmute from this flame. Replace it now with the calmness and serenity; it truly was seeking for, from the external world.

The purpose is to find a deeper connection; that brings about contentment, happiness and inner peace.

THE CROSS-OVER: ....(The SERMON).......

The "cross over" is not the same as "crossing-over" and where the physical body has shed away crossing.
In this case and as the star and within its system; the self does not have to recycle to experience this process.
It is this force of antimatter with light and that from its soul, keeps our bodies alive. However the "Ego" will dissolve; because death only resides in that reality. From the previous lessons, were given these ideas: "LOVE, PRAISE, and GRATITUDE" to practice and hold open for their frequencies; and that vibrate in the upward resonance of living from the heart. When this is broadcasted from the heart; the self can rise above the "Ego mind". Ascension can regenerate the body; into a more vibrant state of existence and from the physical presence, as a body. The essence of youthfulness can once again reclaim its place and from within.
The kingdom of heaven will find it there; to radiate out and create a new Earth power grid . The "Ego mind", is what kills the body and the self must leave it behind. Resistance is that of "Ego mind" performance and will keep the self in fragments; causing disharmony and an imbalance, that takes away the energy from self. The parasitical relationships become a toxic discomfort of all sorts of diseases; that claim the body in the end, called aging and death. The self must learn to overcome such densities and levitate the state of its "being-ness"; or at the very least balance such a gravitational attraction, and that with its physical perspective(saving the energy of the being and preventing aging from happening).

THE CROSS-OVER: ....(The SERMON).......

That which pulls it away from its energy and cause it to age, as a result much quicker. Why not become aware of this connection between it and the many stresses it holds onto? The self can learn from these lessons. The internal dialogue is created from the lower chakras and in response to the heightened activity, from the upper chakras. Why not(at the very least) start the process of ascension; through a balanced expression, between the upper chakras and the lower chakras? The self must learn to disconnect and silence its mind; so it can loosen up and open from the heart.

When that happens the figure eight is elevated; from a horizontal to a vertical cross over. In this way the life force can remain resurrected and in its body through an upper heart connection.

The meridian that crosses over into a figure eight, is like a cork being held under water(be it external forces or the collected stresses from resistance to them); that changes position in the body and that naturally bobs back up, when the force is released.

This spark of light can be made into the size of a grapefruit; then explode into expansion from the darkest place it was sourced out of. Why is this source the portal from which all solar expressions become illuminated star like planets and so on?

This is where the macrocosmic metaphysical white light of Sovereign self can be further explored and within the connective oneness. Through the bellybutton and yet again another meridian that crosses over to the higher; however all cross over(intersect) from the open heart(think of it as a vertical figure eight[8]).

By refusing to accept to work through its feelings from the heart and rather live in the head with the "Ego mind"; during this eternal time of a being it will eventually be needed that it surrenders to life for another rebirth life cycle. The meridian that crosses over like the number 8; then starts to tilt from the vertical position, until eventually it lies horizontally, through the heart.

Finding the inner voice through the flame:
(Day 5)

The "Infinite's" number 8 and from this spinning vortex; the cyan flame resides in the seat of the soul(higher heart)and in between the thyroid(neck)and the thymus, of the upper chest area. From this source(unseen dark light and blood cells) and place of darkness, the spark of self can be discovered. From the most physical metabolic level; where the production for the bone marrow and its white blood cells, must process through, the thymus for creation and that of self.

The idea for the day is "SURRENDER" to the Source of the divine and by connecting to the "Oversoul" in this way; practice with the sound, to voice the following from the breath:

LESSON~5: "AH" "Aaaaaaaaaaaaa".

Throughout the day, take a few moments to radiate out and from this place of darkness, visualize the cyan flame; as a pillar shooting up from the crown of the head. All the way down to the earth and as high as it is, this its physical body; to extend outwardly and create the field around the self, like a pillar expanding outward. From this place of power contemplate; while chanting to continue the meditative state. Can the self begin to see with eyes closed; the almost translucent rippling waves; that from previous doings have continually bounced vibrationally outward(into its world to reflect back to it)? Expand this cyan pillar of light, from the center of the body out. Practice this bit throughout the day: To stand upright with hands next to the body; firmly with feet to the ground and hip-width apart. Breathe it in and with every breath, releasing out; find the voice from within and repeat this affirmation "AH" "Aaaaaaaaaaaaa".

Finding the inner voice through the flame:

LESSON~5: "AH" "Aaaaaaaaaaaaa".

The "Aaaaaaaaah" is this relief (it helps to un-clutch into neutral) from any kind of binding; to release and let it burn away.
The subtle soothing deep engorging darkness; it will heal and soothe to upgrade the software. By allowing another creation in its place; that self can be ready to accept and learn from. Do not try to make sense of any, or all of this, just be and feel for the guidance, be receptive and allowing. Should their be a feeling of overwhelment, then stop and alternate with "OM" (from previous lesson's idea). Resistance can come from previous hurts and mistrusts and do not allow for such surrender to take place.
This Vertical pillar like gate that leads to all the(mirrors) energetic fields and with its cooling overtone; the subtleties from the cyan flame (a kind of vacuum in this way it sucks it in and dissolves it) can remove all sticky residue(electrical static charges). There are also different kind of posses: the arms/hands can be placed in and throughout the many lessons, movements to position the body for a better flow; however for the purpose of simplicity, the hands are simply placed hanging by each side. Gradually this discipline can be upgraded to incorporate other words along as affirmation too. This is just a mild intro into yogic meditation; however mostly the focus on sound and light healing.

The purpose, is to feel the freedom of choice to access and from all its many life times; these records of the soul and to burn away the older versions, that no longer serve it to learn from.

THE CROSS-OVER: ....(The SERMON).......

The self can elevate and as it can remain suspended to float beyond the "Ego mind" of death into ascension.
Grasp this awareness and move toward the process of full immortality and live this life; where even the atomic elements of its body can become subject to that of its every intent.
The "Ego" is the separation from consciousness and from pure source light. The light body will move in and take over when self can be ready to allow this process.
The body can become in the physical regenerating of itself younger and more vibrant. The cross-over, is that of the breath and that of self, to take in this way. The circular breathing of this process can be achievable to transcend into; the in between exchange from inhalation to exhalation.
This gap/space (in between the inner and the outer), is what creates a torque (the force behind the twist) and for every field's perception. The figure of the number "8" is one of the best symbols of describing it; most commonly referred to as (by the new age community and social media) the "Torus Field".
When the self can connect to a deeper sacred level and learn to thrive from its vibration; it can then emanate this resonance that it prefers and to interchangeably engage with its surroundings. By breathing in and out, it will create a tube (that is the self) like pillar, standing in the middle of its storm; and/or this will be the emphasis of its holographic reality and frequency. It can choose to participate; or just keep calm as the observer, to change it through these gaps(one might say the holding of the breath). The rate of the breath will determine the state of being the self can be in; by regulating in this way its frequency and neurological behaviour. Althtough the breath can take the self into many kind of worlds; for this purpose here, is to describe the many auric fields of light and through their sound, that vibrates them into being.

THE CROSS-OVER: ....(The SERMON).......

Eventually they will loosen the boundaries that self has imposed on them genetically; to decode its many lifetimes and lineage of its belief systems. The memories are held within these many field of vortices; that stimulate the system, to react and learn from its environment. They play out in the many variations and from where they once were held trapped; or rather sleeping and dormant. These energetic wheels connect with many others and from 7 to 12(12x12). The force from these energy spaces, keep splitting off and multiplying to 144 (strands from the DNA and genetic blueprint codes to the many meridian points and ley lines that connect from a microspection to a macrospection universe including the self and natural connection with the Earth)and after an evolution, to yet another resurrected level and so on ....(layers of awareness). From these frequencies the chakra tones(that vary in vibration), come to organize and form, and as the name might have it, rule the endocrine system; then from it, the 12 systems of its anatomy physiology. The 9 and all the way to 12 chakras, used to reside outside the body, to influence it and in this way, from above and as below; however it no longer is the case. The many splittings off and from it, the many neuropathic pain receptors; to form pressure points and meridians, as well as ley lines and from them the sound vibrations. When grounding with the Earth, this vibratory rate can rebalance with the resonance of mother nature; who also has such power points of matrices and grids. Can the self feel when it has found its musical match?
All thoughts are also in this way of vibration(to further explore in the lessons to come) and to find the place; where the irrelevance of conceptualizing to discriminate and their form from any such meaning. Fussing about the food it eats; or car it drives and so on...Shall we sift through the data of memory; or observation to explore these feelings further?

Finding the inner voice through the flame:
(Day 6)

The thyroid(neck) is the gland that regulates the (positive and negative electrons) atom self; of metabolic rate and protein synthesis. *ATOMIC SELF*: Is made of the(dark light) invisible elements(source); that connects to everything in its universe. The metabolism for growth and development and how the self will use its energy.

The idea for the day is "TRUST"

LESSON~6: "I" "ieeee...eye" "Ehmm"

The place for spiritual attainment can now be made reachable to visualize. From where the self had started climbing to the highest mountain; and (can be pictured in this way) to be standing from as, "I". From here in this place and in between the next stage (where remote viewing can be made); is this seat from where the "I AM" presence can be felt. Climbing up the highest mountain to reach the "Higher Self" (Creator Consciousness); is the best analogy for the idea and in its entirety, for lesson 6 and 7.

Today and all through out it, take a few moments to practice by breathing in from this place. While breathing out go ahead and find your voice; by humming along this sound. Stand upright with hands next to the body, eyes closed and focus on the larynx as the place of power.

Find the voice this inner voice is:

"I" pronounced Ieeeeeeeee" and Ehmm"; either or and visualize an indigo coloured flame. "TRUST"

Finding the inner voice through the flame:

LESSON~6: "I" "ieeee...eye" "Ehmm"

"Clairsentience/Clairaudient": Clear feeling in that, consider the self as about to stumble into itself; fully come to realize this inner awakening to itself as "I" and be aware in its awareness. From the physical body of the ears, the translation can be heard and reinterpreted from the cellular level of the body. Everything the self can hear is all but tone and frequency. The self can hear, but does not have to believe in any meaning to conceptualize it with; however it will feel from its cellular extended level, of transmitting and receiving in this way. Through this voice go ahead and find the resonance; that has from before crossed over from the gut to bring about authentic self and into a higher intuitive connection, from the throat as "I" "Ehmm".

Learning to discern and from this make a difference, between certain tones and frequency. Find a sense of self and from this inner space surrender to the energy, that sound releases and with this process of attuning, to awaken with, into atonement .

The purpose is to experience the self, from a place where the mind is still, the heart is open and present in the here and now; that the self has probably never taken to notice and in this way before to be from all its doing.

THE CROSS-OVER: ....(The SERMON).......

To find a frequency(that is worthy at the core level to vibrate from) for the self in the most of highest good and interest; it must release the Ego(allow for the flooding over of well being instead to become for its experience). There is much information and memories stored within the earth; as well as in the photonic light (that of every Atom) of her Etheric body and that of self consciousness.

It is up to self to become receptive to the subtle changes and sensations of its heart in this way. Sound can decode light, just as well as recreate it and in a way that can be upgraded for the benefit of all. When from the Earth it can connect to then rebalance; that is known as ground and center.

Nature is the original equation to the formula; put the equation into place and allow for the nature to balance it out. It will be further expressed along the many lessons and pages of the book. This is just a sample feel, from which to motivate some further discussion and in what has been accessed thus far. From a right brain Eastern Vedic/Veda, kind of philosophy and to help bring some kind of balance; with the Western perspective. All remnants of the Goddess that date as far back as Egypt and to combine with modern day perception(that we might come to know as God); to center and merge them both for better integration of these lessons.

There is much that can branch out from this book (very much encouraged); we must however for the purpose of keeping it light hearted. The more complicated things they get; the more into density they beget and with much more limiting factors. This is to help expand from the previous contractions of the well rehearsed(separations) in these many branches of mastery.

THE CROSS-OVER: ……..(The SERMON)…….

For the purpose of this book to welcome and hold the space for all perspectives; that have split off into density some more and in the guise to nominate and simplify faith. Recalibrate from here; to relearn through how it feels and by it. Rather be guided from its authentic spark; to upgrade into something more Pristine and Sovereign with this presence.

Eventually the colours of the rainbow process; they will merge as one and less defined the boundaries, to create more vibrant colours and shapes from. When centered from the heart and from this presence; everything in its life is a miracle of unfoldment.
The self will be in the pillar of white light fully grounded and expanded outwardly illuminating in its light.
Can the self decide right now, what it prefers and achieve that match in frequency, to vibrate from ?

Finding the inner voice through the flame:
(Day 7)

The pineal gland is to the pituitary gland, what intuition is to reason. Today is an incentive to practice learning, how to go inward and deeply look at, action and reaction.

In order to open the Third Eye; the pituitary gland and that of the pineal gland must join their essence. Introversion can displace the attention from the outer world, to the inner; and from this contraction, the expansion into self-realization can occur.

The idea for the day is "TELEPATHY" through "Clairvoyance"; Remote viewing and communicating in this way is possible. Practice with the following sound, to blast open the inner eye and receive:

LESSON~7: "AUM."

Look into the depth of darkness and from the soul, a spark of light reveals the source and from hence it came from.
The pituitary gland relies much on the pineal gland's guidance and for approval. Sexuality and adolescence relies a great deal on the pituitary gland. The pituitary motivates all thoughts into action; as it is the doer, it is highly recommended to practice mindfulness and in its response to such inspirations. The Pineal gland is all about the state of beingness; it is the magnetics to the pituitary's electrically charging and of the energetic state, of the self.
Ida and Pingala will be further discussed; they can only be experienced as the kundalini process of self initiation and to enlightenment(might be lightly touched upon in lesson 9).

Finding the inner voice through the flame:

LESSON~7: "AUM."

The magnetism of this pineal gland is located in the mid brain posterior end; lying near the base of the cerebral hemispheres and in between the two sides, that separate the brain.
It's positioned close to the optical nerves, and as such, sensitive to visual stimulations and changes in lighting; it produces and secretes the hormone melatonin(that helps regulate biological rhythms such as sleep and wake cycles).
The secretion of melatonin is inhibited by light and triggered by darkness. Right below it and in front(from the middle of the brain), the pituitary gland is situated in a bony hollow, just behind the bridge of the nose(the gate). It too is attached to the base of the brain by a thin stalk and contains two lobes, the anterior and posterior. The anterior lobe is formed from the ectoderm of the roof of the mouth and the posterior lobe is the downward growth from the brain(tones up and controls kidneys, intestines and capillaries).
The pituitary is no larger than a pea and yet for these reasons alone; considered as the master gland for the physical body.

Situated between the two physical eyes, and expanding up to the middle of the forehead when opened. Awareness can be accessed and from the main focus of the pineal eye of all the sensory perception to its pituitary of the obvious perspective.
When the pituitary and pineal glands are fully developed and stimulated through meditation; the sixth and seventh chakras start to vibrate and fuse to activate the inner vision open to a higher consciousness.

Finding the inner voice through the flame:

From the pituitary concrete thought and intellectual concepts at the back of the neck and where the skull rests; to the pineal gland and where the focus renders itself, to sit in this chair of illumination, intuition and cosmic consciousness.

The idea for the day is "TELEPATHY" through "Clairvoyance"; Remote viewing and communication in this way, is made possible. Practice with the following sound to blast open the inner eye and receive:

LESSON~7: "AUM."

The pituitary gland is known as the master gland; because it acts as a main control center. Responsible for sending messages to all the other glands; from its two lobes, the posterior and the anterior/frontal(regulating emotional thoughts). Throughout this day, take a few moments to radiate out and from this place of darkness; (the coming together of the red and blue to make purple)visualize a purple flame.
Make it a goal to tune into the correct "vibration" of the universe; to gain a solid foundation and(for this idea) to eventually reach, advanced meditation levels.
Be receptive to the kind of vision of the etheric, or subtle dimensions(pushed through) and movements of energy.
Trust in the surrender to become more sensitive and receive(just like the 2 physical eyes, react to photons); then verbally transmit out by chanting "AUM"..... to vibrate and translate; interpret and disperse, into the physical dimensional brain.... And then receive to gain the wisdom and illumination from it.

Finding the inner voice through the flame:

LESSON~7: "AUM."

With todays exercise; make it the intension to accept the idea of mindfulness. For such is the experience to impress upon these inner planes of awareness, thought forms, and higher entities; or at the very least, for a better sense of cause and effect connection, to the self and its surroundings.
By playing with this force, it can be made a discipline and that can guide the self closer, to a more accurate perception, with its inner eye. Practice by using this point of purple aura (between the center of the physical eyes and in the center of this forehead) as a focal point during this meditation and chant the following:

………"AUM"….. "AUM" ……."AUM" ………..."AUM" ………
The self can help facilitate with its regulating biorhythms and for the development of such a state of awareness; known as "Theta" waves of frequency/"mystical" states of consciousness.
The altered state of intuition, to motivate and inspire; as well as promote, for creativity.

Go ahead and make it open for the inner space to see beyond the distractions and illusions that stand before it; to have more insight as alive, creative and more deeply aligned with its highest good.
The purpose for today is to primarily give attention and focus upon the inner self.
It is this inner attention that eventually can magnetize "spiritual light" into the pineal gland.

THE ANCIENT ONE: ....(SERMON).......

Before the separation of the "Earth"; there were the atmospheric of the "Ethereal" and more fluid substances in the making such as, "Water" and "Fire". When "Water" and "Air" had united. The fluidity of "Fire" from Lava cooled off to form a crust, that became living and breathing; hosting many impressions upon self awareness and back unto herself. All these separations had eventually (from antimatter to matter) created more density and to solidify bodies of land. As awareness has it, "Mother Nature's" "Life Line Web" and that of the "Ebb" and "Flow"; was this solid "Earth". Many entities, "Species" and "Races" were created to add to the richness of her "Tapestry". Whilst she kept separating her awareness to learn from; this very split created rivalry and a struggle of the powers that be, it sent her into the lower depths of awareness.

Through much of this awareness reflected this creator force, as outside of self and separate. The indigenous people were the actual explorers and travelers at the time; to find a place to settle.

They traveled from the "East"; They traveled from the "West"; "North", "South" and to the center. The attraction was always innately in centralization; no matter who, or how these parts of self got there. They might have been "Masculine"; some even might have been "Feminine" and so the story goes, into the fall of consciousness. The Aboriginals to this day, might have much power in their songs and dance; describing exactly from these basic chants of sound. Yes (why not play around and sample), exactly what these lessons have been teaching up to now. The pulling from up high to bring and push back down, into the self; these ancient sounds and that came right out through the belly (of the solar plexus and the lower heart). These were the origins of given lineage to remember: that it had created, the feather of the Eagle; and/or the Bear, that holds the pole, of such consciousness.

THE ANCIENT ONE: ....(SERMON).......

Indeed the pillar of the self reflecting back to it, from nature as a tree and to understand from this connection of creation.

To expand outward from her essence of beautiful awareness, into remembering outside itself and before the form, as Father Sky creator; that requires nature's touch to ground it.

Much symbolism has past down from before and it can be admired and in the awesomeness, of its many variations..

The Vedic way of bringing(from the Vedas) chant and meditation; was made for very useful (to reflect as well for the reader to discern) and further expand, this exploration, of itself, in this and in resonance to. How does it feel to mix about and stir the energies from sound and voice ?

This kind of exploration is not about binding up the self with meaning; it is not designed for holding the belief, that it must then become bound to form, by it. Rather the purpose for now, was to introduce and stir the pot, to find the inner voice of self. This book is all about becoming unstuck, with such mindsets and alchemically recreating; always in refreshing mode of youthfulness and light heartedness.

So much can be discussed from this spark of light awareness; as from the primordial atom(photonic gold/indigo); to the Sovereign bright white pillar being, of illumination and in the oneness, that is the self.

Amen/Aten

Finding the inner voice through the flame:

The neurological connections are much greater from the networking system's heart and leading upward to the brain. This will start to make more sense, the further along and to a greater detail throughout the book. Today focus on the idea of the "Realms of "innocence" and with it this sound:

LESSON~8: "YEAH" "YAYeeeee" "Yeaeaeaeayeee" "YEAH"….. "YEAH"…

The physical anatomy of the thymus discussed previously and unlike before; however a beautiful tell tale sign, to resonate with this lesson. When in a childlike body and from its physiology (to create the paradigm needed now, to better understand with) was created an enlargement; after puberty, the thymus starts to slowly shrink and become replaced by fat. The thymus gland, located behind the sternum and between the lungs, is only active until puberty. In the same way, the Fontanel is another connection, where it closes up and hardens; at this place is where the Crown of enlightenment is seated. When the important points of heart and pineal activation can occur; a pillar of white light, will be the self illuminating(roots and wings) and expanding outward. The place for spiritual attainment, can now be made reachable and the answers to the "WHO AM I" reveal. To open up and allow for Higher self to enter in; remember in the previous of having to visualize? From where that self had started climbing the highest mountain and to be standing from(from previous its inner truth in the throat[Ehmm] to find its voice with) as "I". The "I AM"; it can also be and in this way from "aah eee"and then "AUM". From here in this place The climbing has been reached to highest mountain and that of "Higher Self"(Creator Consciousness) is the best analogy for this idea.

Finding the inner voice through the flame:

LESSON~8: "YEAH" "YAYeeeee" "Yeaeaeaeayeee"
   "YEAH"….. "YEAH"…
(Day 8)
The higher level for spiritual attainment, to enlighten with "**THE I AM**" presence from before; pulling it in and from opening the **CROWN** (located at the center top of the head). Throughout this day, take a few moments to practice; by breathing in from this place and while breathing out, go ahead and find your voice, by humming along this sound.
Stand upright with hands next to the body, eyes closed and focus on the "*Realm of Innocence*". This surge of light comes from the roots and from the heart and higher, to form these wings into expansion, outward and like a white pillar of light; shooting out from the center and of the top of its head. Eventually comes to a place where a yellow halo can appear to illuminate around the head and this is the meaning behind the power of this affirmation and sound it out "Yeaheeeee".
The 6th and 7 chakra is also known as pituitary and pineal glands, fusing together. When the inner eye awakens in this way, the crown will open into a higher state of consciousness; as an enlightened and authentic Sovereign being, into the unity of oneness. There are many beautiful artistic paintings and other such creations; that lasted many life times and to magically reveal, the truth (when the awakening occurs).
 The "Angelic/God" presence and "Sainthoods" from before have impressed upon as witness; After the awakening the yellow light from the solar plexus is moved up around the head.
The purpose is to feel this mantra chant from ancient realms; angelic activations of light and auric field of oneness of the self, complete and whole. When the Crown is closed, the Ego Mind and with its many rules; will push it down, into enslavement.

WHAT IS PRAYER: ....(SERMON).......

Opening a space through gratitude and then projecting it out with appreciation; the light rewarded over to the blessing and when it wishes to be seen, with blinders off. The practice of forgiving the self to see not blindly in the dark; rather with a lighted room, when turning the switch on. By giving thanks, then make a plea to help in changing this perspective from its own illusion; to clear these filters that it may no longer see from its world these kind of this distortions. Look not blindly on another and instead project the blessings that may one day become accepted, to receive by them; do this through love, here and now. Learn to grow in trust so to surrender once again faith; then through visualization remotely view with praise and adoration. Be with grace light heartedly, so not to throw conditions and expectations in the way. Allow for the Love that compassion may find and in its way for miracles to open up, like budding flowers. Prayer is for helping to project a blessing into the field and staying open to receive its blessing. Never with effort to achieve and/or ask to expect for anything and in connection with, to specific things. Remember that fear is a plug, that closes up from staying open, to receive its blessings. A threat of any thought system might be more fearful to the well being; than that from the physical expression of the symptom. Only when the fear from the symptom is released, can healing take its process. Anything that prayer is being asked to help with, while in a state of fear will not be so. Get creative with prayer as it can become the greatest feeling state of reprieving into mindfulness. One great example to start to sample with is called the Serenity Prayer:

> "I GIVE MYSELF PERMISSION TO ACCEPT THE THINGS I CANNOT CHANGE" "THE FAITH TO CHANGE THE THINGS I CAN" .... "AND"..........
> "THE DISCERNMENT TO KNOW THE DIFFERENCE" ...

WHAT IS PRAYER: ....(SERMON).......

So go ahead and pick a Theme and find away to expand on it.....

Another to sample, "A <u>Prayer for Clarity</u>": I give permission to surrender my thoughts over, to the Love I feel; when I connect with higher purpose. I ask for the forgiveness and to find peace, in the resisting parts of self, that choose to suffer. *"Divine Higher self presence; grant me the faith through hope and banish all the tyranny, that likes to have its way with all"*. *"Through the strength that finds us here; surrender in the feeling of this comfort and knowing that there is shelter, from this storm"*.

<u>A prayer to overcome failure</u>:

When the Sun shines from the Sky,
it does not ask for anything in return.
When the rain falls to quench the soil;
it does not expect from the crop to feed it back.
Then why is it that we expect such conditions from each other?
The failure is not in the experience we share;
but rather from the meaningless attachments to the folly of their outcomes.
Thank you for accepting to love those parts in me that briefly in the shade they solace.
And in the cooling off, a social interaction from the breeze is made refreshing.

Remember a prayer can also be a moment of recalibrating energies with silence.

Finding the inner voice through the flame:
(When the higher heart is activated; it can then unite with 7&9 toward resurrection). LESSON~9: Finding the Oneness from the instrument of thought with sound this affirmation:

"AKA".."VEY".."Oh-eee".."YEAH"…"AAH EEE".."OM".
(Day 9)
"AKA" opens the cellular space and activates the authenticity from within; "AKA"…..From the many ancient tribes that self had split off into and from itself, this word "AKA". Perhaps the resonance "KA" with the feathered species; can be heard distinctly from a Crow and even with the Eagle. From the merging of the Soul and Spirit and from the inner void of darkness, this magnetic field it has a spin. The electrical charge that does create and from these vortices of Fire; the inner voice to enter through the flame.

From previous in a sermon, the creation of the Earth and nature's elements; did come to form this crust called matter. From the Ethers back as smoke and that the self might smudge itself with, to remember in this way. From the Golden Gate and off into the Milky Way; the self need only to go inward. To feel from every cell its calling that can vibrate out and to it; in celebration when it can light up and from this connection of awareness, as creator being. There are many tools for these kind of instruments of thought and to help transform the self with; these interpretations (chakra/wheels and or vortices) have preferred to make the use of 12 systems, rather than the 8. Eight is the anchor between the inner world and outer; as well as the connecting of "ABOVE" with so "BELOW" existence. To help connect the understanding of the 12 stranded DNA is another magical equation. As there are 12 of everything and everywhere the systems be it 12 and not as the Divine 13?

For the purpose of these lessons, the infinite creator; from bone to blood and author of this book, that just resonates to simplify from 12 to 8.

Finding the inner voice through the flame:

LESSON~9: Finding the Oneness from the instrument of thought with sound this affirmation:

"AKA".."VEY".."Oh-eee".."YEAH"…"AAH EEE".."OM".

The additional 4 are combinations from the primary 7 to help with better understand Chakra 9 is that of the chanting sound "aah eee" not that much variant from adding the Voice from chakra lesson 6 again a sort of repeat to connect with.
By merging the Soul with the Ego the 10 chakra(Solar Halo made witness from Egyptian ancients as Halo Mountain Top called the Lahun) can be made available and by merging the water with the fire(transformation)the activation of the 11th gate, transforming self to crystalline(transcending awareness from space and time)and then 12 from an genetic activated level known as super consciousness(transcending to reach Enlightenment and commune with the Divine). In this state of plasma and photonic light the alchemical primordial Fire/Water can combine to form the "MYSTICAL MARRIAGE" (as made mentioned from the "IDA(magnetic) & PINGALA(electric)"). Throughout the day take brief moments to contemplate on:

"AKA".."VEY".."OIeee".."YEAH".."AAH EEE".. "OM".

"all gates are now open and can fully merge as one".

Finding the inner voice through the flame:

LESSON~9: Finding the Oneness from the instrument of thought with sound this affirmation:

"AKA".."VEY".."Oh-eee".."YEAH".."AAH EEE".."OM".

The purpose for today is to take about forty minutes to an hour and merge all the lessons into one.

Feel the oneness at its most simple basic introduction that these lessons have revealed and made accessible; the following thread can be made even simpler to follow from the Author's U-tube Channel.

Sample and then go ahead and merge starting from the Root with "UM" to "YEAH"(notice how all the vowels have been made use of?)

https://youtu.be/R0P8IeZWbCs
https://www.youtube.com/watch?v=R0P8IeZWbCs&feature=youtu.be

In addition, to the remaining affirmations: think of the 9th wheel as the silver thread of life; connecting to the physical existence and with all these energies in motion, as the number for completion(3 wheels to visualize have also briefly been expressed). Exploring the trust and innocence and with much Love, be open to the merging.

JUDGMENT&DISCERNMENT:.......(The SERMON)……..

Judgment is a victim state and when the self can learn to rise above, it can have adjusted to discernment. The highest wisdom is simply to make use of this discernment; in that of knowing what it is that self prefers, from every probability and loosely.
The Judgment likes to play, by giving the illusion that there is no other choice, in its unfairness and that there are no insights to be gained. The circumstances have no other resolutions...but to help motivate the self into the potential; to cultivate the innovative alternatives from these situations. Practice getting to know the many Judgments that confront the self with. Are these Judgments that it holds for, of its world and for the many?
Are these judgements from the many subjects of its world?
Are these beliefs and opinions that it holds of itself and of its world, really even of its own experience? Learn from these Judgments and embrace them all with Love, to better understand and integrate; what most stand apart and in isolation from these thoughts.
That level of Judgment and after it can be unravelled, the self can heal and rise.

The circumstances the self does choose from making Judgments and from these circumstances; are the opportunities to regain harmony with and a better feeling thought to orchestrate the next experience. When the letting go of Judgment happens, discernment takes its place. A Judgment is an assumption or the insistence of imbalance; to resist the flow of consciousness from having the experience and by placing blockages (or these kind of filters) in the way. Judgments are distortions of experience; that never really happened in the way the self has thrown in and from its perspective, to believe in such perceptions.

JUDGMENT & DISCERNMENT:……..(The SERMON)……..

Alignment does not come from righteousness; rather it comes from feeling the experience and with no preconceived thoughts, for its behaviour. Negatively charged emotions are self defeating experiences; attached to Judgments and it is the onus of the self to break apart and feel them out.

Values hold opinions, because they are made from comparison. The experience of contrast will help to bring the level of discernment and as a tool to play with; rather than that of holding judgment. The motive to act from external comparisons, what are these agitations ?

These collisions can attract unto itself with careful interactions; and that with great precision manage to proclaim the victim to its narcissist. Having an extreme amount of confidence to the way of presentation; that the other side of self does not. In each case, both are unbalanced and come together to find the balance; from the lesson and each aspects bringing to the table an insight, that the other needs.

Judgments create walls or the need to set up boundaries. With discernment the self learns when it must set boundaries and when to be more boundless. Judgment and discernment are on different playing fields; because letting go of Judgment releases density and leaves it behind, for its discernment. Everything is on different levels of their own personal evolution and the self must hold a certain amount of reverence; for all the imprints on its consciousness, that holds them there.

Judgments are negotiable separations from the self and as interference manifesting aspects; for the fulfillment to be whole again.

All preconceived ideas need to go, from here on.

JUDGMENT & DISCERNMENT:…….(The SERMON)……..

Comparative thinking is a mentality of fired up neurons; that can manifest with all beliefs, for far too long and a paved-up pathway, leading to identity. Limiting beliefs, strangle hold the self expression; from vibrating intuitively and synchronistically and to be aligned within the moment. Time is the illusion that sets in the prison bars, of rules and regulations; that belief has now become a rigid state. A previous thought cannot become the value for the opinion of the next experience; it rather might not qualify to best suit the self with such belief. The objective is to accept all information and intuitively decide; to what feels more aligned in preference. Explore the possibilities that can offer profound dimensions and from a blank canvas; the connection can be made, with the omnipresence state of oneness.

From here on and forthwise, the unlearning of the many programs that have kept the self in bondage; they must from the potential of awareness, be found and within the core of its being.

There are rules and regulations; because walls go up around beliefs and from them rigid beliefs come to be. At the base for all that structures as religion, are these beliefs; they build walls around the self and repel all boarders that challenge it.

Suddenly the ability to perceive from the vastness of all that is, becomes myopic. All possibilities become regulated by limited self restricted beliefs. There are many religions of the mind and indoctrinations, to denounce their prejudices; from the many denominations, and as to become narcissistically blind sided from the truth.

The purpose of showing such idealism is to reference that judgment is a tribal warfare. That politics, religion and all other such discriminants. They carry a pretense of value over another in that currency; that vibrates out its energy of limitation and the lack within, the prison of the mind, as finite.

JUDGMENT & DISCERNMENT:.......(The SERMON)……..

Discernment is in the many flavours of emotion; from which the self has choice for its experience. For every outcome is a fitting of the self into a possibility and that it must not become disappointed by; when the state of flow does not match its frequency.
Then the self can learn where it must break apart the density some more and that holds it trapped emotionally, in mental servitude.
Remove and let go of the mind in this way, so to obtain enlightenment; seek it not because it is already there and hiding behind the barriers, of perceived beliefs.

As the dense energy fields start breaking up; the weighted down meanings of what is and all around us to perceive, becomes removed. Transcendence to a higher state of awareness and where the discernment from the expression of its authenticity; one in the same be welcomed back and into the oneness, of the same consciousness.

Through brain placidity, the brain can change the way it processes information and from the way it perceives it. When information is received, the self can learn to disconnect from the way the information is received and then re-scramble it. In this way the brain's ability to recognize itself by forming new neural connections and from the electrical external stimulus; known as neuroplasticity and that operates from different pathways. This is the purpose for the following lessons and to begin to introduce such a concept, from letting go all concepts; including to lightly touch upon transhumanism(to Cyborg).

JUDGMENT & DISCERNMENT:…….(The SERMON)……..

This mainstream artificial intelligence, must not be treated any different from such scrambling of the mind; as it is the same with its own mind chatter. Its process is not that far away and from the connection to the body of the self; uniquely merging its dependency of inorganic and organic. For now, these addicted habit forming external technological devices and that the self can hold: like smart phones; tablets and other such interferences; the following lessons will include them too. They are to be made useful, with much discernment and where to have the wisdom to see it as a co-dependency(emotional attachments).

With the following lessons,

"REMOVE ALL CONCEPTS" and/or "CONCEPTUALIZATIONS."

(Day 10) By the closing of the gap; between the mental picture and that of physical reality, will be the focus:
Practice any chance there is a moment, to replace the need for artificial intellectual stimuli and shut off all devices; to instead replace it with, this sense of leisure.

LESSON~10:

"EVERYTHING I SEE ARE MISCONCEPTIONS FROM THIS SPACE AND BRIEFNESS OF THE MOMENT, MY MOBILE DEVICES, ARE ALL TURNED OFF AND IRRELEVEANT, WITH NO SIGNIFICANCE TO HOLD FOR ANY MEANING. IN THIS MOMENT I HAVE NO USE TO GRASP THEIR FUNCTION FOR ANY PURPOSE BY THEM."

By letting go the meaning, of what anything might be pre-conceivable; in this way the self can learn between the myopic self. To a much more expanded vastness of probabilities and find again itself; wide open to the many possibilities. By letting go and disconnecting completely; from the outside in and in between the vastness of its focused range, that it can learn from this.

Now look very briefly farther away from the immediate area, and apply the same idea, at a much more wider range:

"I DECOMPARTMENTALIZE FROM ALL CONCEPTS THAT HELD IN THESE BELIEFS, FROM THESE OPINIONS I MIGHT OR MIGHT NOT BE SEEING, THROUGH THESE EYES AND HEARING FROM THESE EARS."

"The bee hive and the noise it makes; from working bees and under the roof, outside my window" "The noise from all machinery, trucks and flying planes; that surround the area, rendered over to distract and as meaningless take-aways; all suspended in the nothingness, that is of time and space".

LESSON~10:

"EVERYTHING I SEE ARE MISCONCEPTIONS FROM THIS SPACE AND BRIEFNESS OF THE MOMENT, MY MOBILE DEVICES , ARE ALL TURNED OFF AND IRRELEVEANT, WITH NO SIGNIFICANCE TO HOLD FOR ANY MEANING. I HAVE NO USE TO GRASP THEIR FUNCTION FOR ANY PURPOSE BY THEM."

Now bring the attention to take another closer view; slowly enough to contract closer to the physical body(that separates the inner from the outer) and almost to go inwardly(to where these thoughts have imprinted) to find the need for their importance. Stick around with it and feel the disconnect of such relevance. Before the meaning by which to understand their useful value, and what they were representing? With this idea, very specifically take a moment to look over, near the surrounded area and up close again.

"I HAVE NO CONNECTION FROM THESE IDEAS TO BELIEVE IN THESE OBJECTS DO IN FACT EXIST?"

Remember to separate the depth of meaning, by their superficial appearance and that will serve to disconnect from their importance; thus not having power over anything. Make an observation at what is present, to take the following example for use of, verbally and out loud: "The black cat strolling underneath this latter";
"The umbrella still open while it dries inside the house; resting on a red door with the number 444" and the entire genre, has expressed in fine detailing the nothingness of its importance".
"This digital screen that hangs upon the wall; "This i-phone too, is off and rendered over useless; it does not have any use for its appearance either. "This desktop computer, is now off and does not mean for anything." "This credit card, does not have any relevance; I can hold it, but it has no hold on me for anything." Eventually the shedding off of harmful superstition; and/or any old pattern beliefs of this nature, will start to dissipate away from its purpose.

A Note To The Master:
THE RAPTURE IS ASCENSION

An energetic connection must be established before leaving one reality, for another. The in depth journey into the soul, to find the truth. Activate the light inside, allow the consciousness to expand and walk into a different world; that is by choice and the one preferred within every moment to shift into, from self-awareness. The clearing from the emotional body, the mental body and as well as in the physical cellular level; they must be rid of all the heavy weighted down density. The reality of the way things were supposed to be, will never be; so move on into the realization of creating and in the moment by moment. Live from the heart, clearing and expanding. See the overview and layout of the old world and its tribulations; they are but trivial in hanging on to old world things. The old perceptions, the prophesies and the old beliefs of what was going to come one day, are and technologically now occurring in a different aspect; that self does have the choice to take it, or leave it all behind. Depending on which dimension the self is ready to accept and occupy. The self might integrate into the docking of such earth; that integrates into "transhumanism", and/or "Cyborg"; it can be with or just accept it and/or not be. Again the level of such interaction can become of valid choice; or for yet another earth's reality. The fear around the rapture and all the distortions from before, were but the greatest of illusions. This book might be helpful to assist along this process and perhaps give some insight; to transcend from the old into the new. Expand and see beyond to the awakening; that all along the way, this was the process of Ascension. The self is already well on its way of seeing and what it was not able to see before; in a different context and that this second coming is in deed, the self awakening.

<u>A Note To The Master</u>:
THE RAPTURE IS ASCENSION

The New Earth cannot have the self hanging on to old earth ways. As discussed before, the many chakras and/or vortices, are in the body, everywhere. The cells, they too are filling up with light and vibrate spinning outward, to radiate a frequency.

Time is collapsing and all that can take its place, is its intension and within this light; that takes up space, to cause accelerated frequency. From these vortices within, are portals everywhere.

"With Sovereign Light presence, from within and where outwardly the infinite must be; that all these parts, are made of one and inseparable". The more light the self can hold; the more magnificent it is and for everything in its world. Focus on the energy, creation and on the coming together as one; because all the other things, are of lack and competition.

The rapture is here and everything is colourful and vibrant in the anchoring of this light, expanding outward.

There is nothing to fear, just turn and walk in the direction of this light that is forever present. The self can learn to choose, where to place its energy and this is where discernment can come in; rather than to have the pointing of the fingers, in a blame game rehearsal. By staying present, the self can learn how to decipher, be responsible and most of all, intentional with every moment. Ascension does not mean having to leave the body; rather an awareness of mastering over it and that of its physical reality, it knows as truth.

(Day 11)

How much is really there to see and understand of the external world, can become very different; from the way it has been previously perceived, as limited. With expansion the self is able to leave the restricted constricted sight, of what it thought it saw and learn the way of seeing (from multiple dimensions). To shift in this way at will; the self must clear away all of its density. If all there is, is thought and nothing more, for nothing else; then to continue on further, apply this concept to the following. As subtle as these exercises are and in its intent to better understand the space of frequency; just learn how to become the observer for now. Apply a circular surveillance and from it, learn how to bring the focus, zooming in and out. No need to sweat over the details and just apply as before, behind as well as from side to side and directly ahead. The following affirmations are used to simulate and with what best resonates as the example:

LESSON~11:

"THE LESS I KNOW ABOUT, EVERYTHING I SEE FROM MY EXTERNAL SURRONDINGS; THE LESS OF MY OPINIONS TO HAVE TO GIVE OF."

By leaving everything behind, the self can start to recreate its own world. The idea here is merely to light up enough the sight on and upon each subject, simply with ease of a glance and fairly quickly.

Faith is one of the greatest tools that self can have toward its spiritual growth and that of understanding miracles; for that it can become most certain.

It is within the freeing of its thoughts, that sets the self free and into limitless possibilities, of its self potential. Until the focus slightly shifts onto another particle and with impressed upon observation; somewhere in a hazy wave of sub atomic particles, the state of my being remains the same.

MASTER & STUDENT:……..(The SERMON)……..

Lesson 12:
"I AM THE MASTER & THE STUDENT."
"ALL THINGS ARE ME."

(Day 12) From a Metaphysical perspective, was the antimatter that matter came to be and from the opposites, a trinity was blessed with. The Holy Trinity: is that of Mother, Father God.
From darkness sprang forth these four bodies of the Infinite and from these levels of awareness, the "I AM" presence.
Metaphysical spirituality holds within its Trinity, the Spirit and from this unseen spirit, the light sprang forth. The spark that North and East created; was the Mecca of all the(Ethereal/Astral)
Holy Spirit's Origin. The Sun rises from the East and sets in the West; where the night sky meets it and in the Astral plane.
From all these bodies the physical, mental, emotional, and Ethereal/Astral; is what the book is mostly helping to work through and to rewire. The wise was once a fool and the nurturer once a child too; from this a paradox for Master and Student came to be. Into the many lessons of itself; it could impress upon, to learn and from its many personalities.
Today practice the idea of "Receptivity" and then "Transmit". This is a practice to help to see as indices and to mark upon the progress; that it is to come on days ahead and then come back to it, as often as desired. From a place of Receptivity, is where the scanning can begin and then visualize it in the way, the variation is desired. Pick a topic (subject, Object.. it can be anything really) visualize it in the way it is right now and this is how the thought can take the self there. With eyes closed and only unless the thing is right before it, to present itself in physical nearby; then do a blink and then close the eyes. Set an intention….What is the Theme?

MASTER & STUDENT:.......(The SERMON)........

Lesson 12:

"I AM THE MASTER & THE STUDENT."

"ALL THINGS ARE ME."

By practicing receptivity, allow the state of openness and (this means going vulnerable to feel it) in the state it is right now; also with, any that it is and has possibly not even taken form in any way (just decide)… How far along this capability the self can go will determine how much it will be getting out of this book and in what way if any. Direct by projecting the visual focus. Time and space will prove it into a probability and from the equational energies of just how ready the self is willing, to go with it:
Recapitulate= shift(it is the underlying purpose).

Eventually this will be learned, to master over and once it has transcended to a multidimensional level of existence.

For now stay open and play around with the frequency from these emotions and just imagine; this will be the indicator of where the self will need to work the most on. Warmly accept the opportunity to engage with whatever is received from this perception if any at all. Learn to trust that the Universe will co-create the most appropriate form; in the most appropriate way and at the most appropriate time. This will help to better allow the self to learn how to express in the highest of its abilities and offer that of itself in the greatest service to its world. Whether it be large or small or in whatever quantity; Accept the boundless gratitude in all that is received. Living from the Heart is a fifth dimensional Metaphysical space. Clearing out the elementals that comprises self and alchemically to learn to master over; a step out of such a template and into a Sovereign multilevel platform of enlightenment is required.

MASTER & STUDENT:……..(The SERMON)……..

Lesson 12:

"I AM THE MASTER & THE STUDENT."

"ALL THINGS ARE ME."

Manifesting comes from all thoughts, beliefs, and opinions; that the self can hold to boomerang its situations to it.

The purpose of these lessons will be to learn to become objective when viewing over the experience; in this way to recognize the frequencies that self can have and the choice to align, or not align with. Proper manifestation requires, clearing away all of the dysfunctions, so to get at the frequency; that is in the state of purity, resonating with alignment and from that truth inside the heart. The physical reality is the manifestation and the frequency that holds it there, is the dimension.

The vibrational frequencies remove the delay, the higher up the self can learn to spiral; rather than just be linear on a flat 2 dimensional self and from holding on to little self identity perspectives.

The purpose is to delete, erase and remove all the old meanings that the self has held down, with its perceived external images; as such, the following lesson can be made "exemplifiable" and to practice the following idea, once again extended.

(Day 13)
From the front of the head the self can only see what the projection from the back of its head will produce and then reinterpret back from its reflection as something real.

As in the previous lessons without question to the moulding of nor making distinctions to support such defined relevance for its idea of what is.

LESSON~13:
"I DO NOT UNDERSTAND ALL THESE IMAGES THAT I IMAGINE TO BE REAL IN MY SPACE AND BEYOND FROM INSIDE MY GADGETRIES OF SCREENS, FROM OUTSIDE THIS BALCONY AND IN THIS AREA."

To understand how little is understood about form is essential then to keep an open mind. Apply this idea throughout the day and by withdrawing from comparison to favour anything over another; because one thing is like another as equally suitable and therefore equally useful.

The purpose of this exercise is to clear the mind of all past associations and to see things like they have never been seen before and as exactly as they are in the here and now !

"REMOVE ALL CONCEPTS"
and/or
"CONCEPTUALIZATIONS"

AFFIRMATIONS:.......(The SERMON)……..

Be sensitive to the alchemical configurations of words; because they are a choice, to throw about meaninglessly and/or flow with it much power.

Notice how reckless words can have an impact and does it serve to keep these thoughts ? Break the pattern of conditioning; by waking up to what comes out with words. The many popular sayings, are affirmations; that the self can choose to dismiss itself from and replace a new. Affirmations, are words that hold meaning and from these thoughts, beliefs are formed. The self becomes for its own convictions, these very same things it represents.

To rewire all the self taught misconceptions that could and have created much damage from before. Affirmations can be used to heal and by releasing and regenerating a new self being.

Anytime something is running interference, be there to acknowledge it; by giving it attention, is to explore it.

Through this kind of recognition and to such agitation; what once felt trapped by it, or visa versa, can become released and liberated. This is a self regeneration process; that requires the redirection of such thoughts, with affirmations. The recycling in this way, will open to the codes and from decoding of the DNA, carry on further guidance. Every filament of light and every single system; every single cell and as it turns on there too, it matters(feel it lighting up, in celebration). Affirmations create an energy flow, from self awareness; that reaches from the muscle, to the bones and blood, to fascinate and from every systems structure, that is self.

Just like the many children and when putting up their hands to get noticed for their answers. How the self will respond with its awareness; will make or break the system as a whole, from its function.

AFFIRMATIONS:…….(The SERMON)……..

With affirmations, praise can also be obtained and to learn from it, will boost the self esteem. Self esteem is an inside working; that then ripples out and reflects from these experiences. The accumulated trust in its belief, will accelerate this confidence the self requires. It can mean so much, when using affirmations to praise with; so much more than waiting for external confidence. When not ready to match at the level of external confidence; rather these perpetrating pathways, can instead to turn the self into a victim. Now that the self has found its voice, the purpose is to use it. With affirmations, the inner voice can be employable; to cheer the self with and support it on its path.

This inner voice can through praise, create newer pathways of believing and the faith, to fire up the neurons.
With praise, the inner voice is upgraded; by removing it from the critical appraising. A certain curiosity of innocence, is something that the self must find; from before the external distractions and to corrupt it in this way, it must become incorruptible. This voice can then be heard, as thought and before the first awareness, from the external world; to throw at it, in a place of comparative assessment, that is judgment. From the very first breath the self has taken and that which it had relied upon to care for it; it either felt the "Love" or "Judgment" of its situation.

The casting out into expansion; had created pressure to contract and make the self smaller, "little self me".
These mismatches of rejection and the more effort to corrupt itself, to effort into fitting in; the more disharmonized and riddled with decay(would be the consequence).

AFFIRMATIONS:…….(The SERMON)……..

To strengthen the immune system, aging must regenerate and to cease itself, from such a system. The larger than life, animated self, was that of exploration and with these recognizing senses; the larger it grew into form, the smaller and more limited.

Feel out the guidance that the inner voice comprises of and all its many systems; that represent the self well "<u>being-ness</u>".
The energetic levels of feeling out its guidance and where it needs support the most; is where the self must reaffirm, to help strengthen. Praise, is just the one of many blessings and from the higher frequencies; from this place, the guidance to help build the self and to its greatness of learning to believe.
The rewiring and to learn on just how the self can; well before there is of any proof, for its condition and to experience it with.

This concept will become its ability and to conceptualize it with; before it has become for its experience, is the mission.
The vision from here on, from these lessons and for the dismantling of the old. To get rid of, break apart the old concepts of the mind and how things must be; is but to sweep away the cobwebs out.

The manic, mindless chatter of thoughts and that come about with a web of sticky meaning; that host all sorts of obstacles, and that of obsoleted programs.

AFFIRMATIONS:.......(The SERMON)........

The purpose is to take responsibility and by becoming the observer; to really own up to the language, of its life.

Learn to take away from all distractions, the peaceful state; because they are the subtle signs of synchronicity, working their way to harmony with self and while learning to merge transmitting with receiving.

The self can never fail and must learn through the affirmations; that it gives such as: to praise, that it can only succeed and with every experience, by changing it perspectively, in this way.

THE INTERMISSION :

Take 2 days to take it in

CONGRATULATIONS FOR MAKING IT THROUGH TO THE 14th DAY

(This is a rest period to take the lessons independently as a review)

TAKE THESE TWO DAYS TO RECALIBRATE; MAKE NOTES AND REVIEW……………..

(Day16) The unresolved made lesser parts of self; become the shadows, that dim awareness. The "Ego mind" creates the filters; with these beliefs and of what the good/bad thoughts are. With such dualistic implementational conflicts, resistance and blockages can occur. By learning to release these formulated opinions; is how the following template and with these affirmations, can help with:

LESSON~14:

"OVERSTIMULATED IS MY IMAGINATION WITH CONVINCING EXTERNAL THOUGHTS AND CATEGORIES OF THEIR RELEVANCE TO BE IMPRESSED UPON IN MY BELIEF ON THEM?"

Duality will always form opposition and from it the lessons learned, from such contrast. Thoughts without the experience of knowing them, have really no attraction. Briefly examine this concept in the mind, for a moment and be open to experiment; with harmful not so pleasant thoughts as well.

Within this lesson, is the opportunity to cancel out the opinions and that connect with thoughts, to them.
Take a brief moment to notice these thoughts, crossing the mind. Are they good or bad thoughts and that correlate with how they feel; or are they meaningless, to represent the real thoughts and that are being covered up by them?
Are the good feeling thoughts overpowered by the distortions; that shadow over what real thought lies beyond?

LESSON~14:

"OVERSTIMULATED IS MY IMAGINATION WITH CONVINCING EXTERNAL THOUGHTS AND CATEGORIES OF THEIR RELEVANCE TO BE IMPRESSED UPON IN MY BELIEF ON THEM?"

Follow along with this exercise and by filling in a descriptive, to make applicable the following template: to help identify at a core level, of each thought and/or at the holding center of its event:

"IN THIS MOMENT THE THOUGHT OF_____ AND FROM HERE UNTO THE NEXT THOUGHT HAS SHIFTED FROM ALL CATEGORIES TO BE RELEVANT."

"THIS THOUGHT HAS OBSOLETED FROM IDENTITY BECAUSE THE COMPARTMENT HAS DISSOLVED AND THE IMPRINT OF THIS IMAGE UNDEFINED AS REAL."

For the purpose of training the mind, to the likeness of resonance and what is in contrast to it; the intention is to recognize the external world, as meaningless and so to discover the meaningful from within.

"Forgiveness and self re-integration": ....Sermon

To welcome back those parts, that from before appeared as irritants; forgiveness must be the order of the day.
It is through forgiveness, that compassion can be reachable and once again restored, to a functional state.
From the letting go of the need to set boundaries and separate the chakras in this way; the self must become accepting of the vulnerable state and from which, the emotional purging can begin, into awakening. When the self first starts the waking up process(everything flips on its head), it can be most agitating; this is why the lessons will indulge, somewhat deeper into these feelings and of their upset, to examine further. During enlightenment, the full release from the attachments, are apparent; in this way and from them, did not change, nor effect upon reality. Appreciation for the whole, does reserve for self; that external worldly things it must detach from and sentimental pleasures.. Unless it is given back, it is inevitable that the perspective on reality, be warped and uncorrected.
As long as it is so, to have the illusion; it will for an order of difficulty in miracles remain with the self.
Its established reality, is a given and from this experience to deal with, as part of truth, in one way, and in another way; the other part to fragment truth, that would destroy and render meaningless. Truth is a collective reality, as a frame of reference and a program for its meaning must be itself.

"Forgiveness and self re-integration": ....Sermon

When the illusion wants into this reality of truth; the compromise to justify this belief, is but only an enabling factor and to teach that, the illusion is unreal. This creates a prison, from these orders of realities; because there is no order of reality and everything there is, is true. Be willing to surrender over and to the truth of self, to source. Relief from separation, can have hope for completion and not be concerned with anything else, than it.

When a disturbance is created and the peace of mind is lost, refusing to forgive such interference and from within, is just this same attempt.

The restoration, is the relief; that was before holding both from it and then forgiveness can be seen, where it has been given it. Gradually all that has been suppressed, can rise to be transmuted.

The Master's Tale: "Bringing Fantasy to Light"

The following idea and for its purpose; rather making it equally deep to grasp for everyone. Betrayal lies only in the unresolved experiences and from these stories, the illusions and with all its "SINS", are but of the imagination. Reality is forever sinless and no need to become forgiven, but instead awakened.

Betrayal is a back and forth motion, for the un-awakened mind to travel with and in a straight line, that connects to it.

Yet what is done in dreams; are from the many probabilities and that have not been really played out, in this reality.

"However impossible to convince the dreamer; that this is so and dreams are what they are, from parallel realities, unlike this one".

(Day 17)

The blending of emotions; is where the following lesson and to go with the previously stuck feelings, that might have from these thoughts(directly/indirectly) manifested. Feelings are very important; because they hold everything in place.

LESSON~15:
> "MY EMOTIONS ARE HOLDING IN DISTORTED THOUGHTS TO CIRCULATE AROUND ME."

Whether it be jealousy, hatred, anger, fear, worry, depression, anxiety or something else; for emotions to have their way, use this lesson to examine. Whatever it be distressing, regardless of how much and/or little to think the cause of pain; this idea can be applicable with any person, situation or event. Specifically made valid, the upset to believe is the cause and by describing the feeling, in whatever term seems accurate. This procedure will ultimately recognize for each perception, separately as one in the same they are all; however until these perspectives no longer matter, this exercise for each subject does. Make use of the following; by naming the matter and upset of its belief, to make valid the reason:

"BY THINKING IT MY PREVIOUS EXPERIENCE WAS_____ AND HAS CAUSED ME TO FEEL_____?"

Remember to use a more subtle indirect approach; in the unfolding of awareness to these things and then by emphasizing on something else just the same. Do not effort to search the mind for results, in beliefs and forms for "sources" their discomfort. This exercise might be helpful to sample further and by avoiding the greater weight attention, to some subjects than others:
"ALL EMOTIONAL DISTURBANCES ARE IN DISSONANCE TO THE RESONANCE OF MY WELL BEING."

LESSON~15:
"MY EMOTIONS ARE HOLDING IN DISTORTED THOUGHTS TO CIRCULATE AROUND ME".

Re-examine the mind for distressing factors once again and then reaffirm with the following affirmation:

"I CANNOT HOLD ON TO THIS DISTRESS INSTEAD I RELEASE THEM AS BEING ALL THE SAME."

Apply a few practices during the day and for roughly, not more than 70 seconds (to search the mind). This idea for the day and once again in this exercise make valid, the name of both the source of upset as perceived and the experience of the feeling.

"I AM NOT [WORRIED; DEPRESSED...] FOR THE ASSUMPTIONS I WAS HOLDING ON FROM PREVIOUS EXPERIENCE THAT CREATED THIS THOUGHT ABOUT THIS SO&SO..."

The purpose of this lesson is to realize how insignificant any subject/object/situation or event is, without its belief.

(Day18) From the natural state of being, the self has learned to fire up its chakras, open its third eye and to peer into the void. When the synchronizing of both hemispheres begins; this process toward enlightenment, is the magic and that gives way to miracles.

As thoughts create emotion and for many a time, thinking these thoughts into beliefs. Whether they belong to the self or borrowed from elsewhere: Worry, depression and/or any other (from previous lesson of this read); as lower vibratory frequencies in their design and therefore signal the cause for upset.

LESSON~16

"AN OPINION IS JUST A HABIT FORMING THOUGHT THAT I CAN MAKE DISAPPEAR."

There is an emotional guidance system and that through the connection of its feelings; that the self, might learn to trust in what it might or might not be thinking. More importantly, what this vibration it emits and is at any given moment as it feels.

To feel joy, pleasure, desire, enthusiasm or passion; these are emotions that indicate to form attachment, to a thought. These thoughts and feelings; they become aligned with its desires, to attract things into its field and to its physical experience of likeness.

Whenever a feeling of despair, depression, anger or lack; these are indices of emotions; that self might be at a different level and as such misaligned vibrationally (perhaps by what it might be thinking).

LESSON~16

"AN OPINION IS JUST A HABIT FORMING THOUGHT THAT I CAN MAKE DISAPPEAR ".

Be specific to name the form of the upset and source for this idea's lesson as FOR EXAMPLE:

"WHEN I CAN CHANGE MY ATTITUDE MY OPINION DISMISSES THE EMOTIONAL CHARGE I HAD HELD ON SO DEARLY TO RESIST THIS THING _____ RIGHT NOW."

"I AM NOT THINKING ABOUT THE FUTURE _____ BECAUSE IT HAS NOT HAPPENED IN THE WAY I FEAR IT FROM THIS ONE OF MANY PROBABILITIES."

Resistance can result from this application of the idea for something more than the others.

" THE DETAILS ARE ALL THE SAME TO OVERWHELM THE MIND WITH AND ALL AT ONCE THEY CAN DISTURB MY PEACEFULNESS:

"THEY ARE ALL THE SAME AWAITING FOR ACCOMPLISHMENT TO TAKE ITS PLACE FOR A RELEASE AND MUST BE DEALT WITH TO FIND RELIEF FROM THEIR RESOLVE."

Made useful throughout the day 3 or 4 times; and is for but a minute or so for the purpose to uncover in the mind searching for uneasy thoughts to un-cluster.

"To create in my own image" and "Alchemy": ....Sermon

The loss of identity and then the feeling of being within the heart of all that is; the ethereal has already dropped low enough into density for proof, that science must exist. This constant reorganization, of what it means to be in a body and be able to express, from pure essence that is the self. The merging of consciousness and the shifting of the Earth's magnetics; and yet there are those aspects of the self, who continually must hang on to science, will. All souls from their very essence, must learn to ground; even when that is required from the molecular structures, and that of consuming for their own sustenance. Einstein and other geniuses alike, had taken interest to reveal, the frequencies of light; what an atom can emit and their dependency, on the states of the electrons can be in. When excited, an electron moves to a higher energy level or orbital. When the electron falls back to its ground level, the light is emitted. Einstein called these energy packets, photons and these are now recognized as fundamental particles. Why not take another view, that shifted to its likeness and hold as real. This resonance of probability for self-awareness and inspires the atom to radiate outwardly, the light from within(when an electron jumps from a high-energy level to a low-energy level). The electrons in a non-excited atom, are motionless and an atom emits photons, because of the vibration, of the frequency of light. As the Earth loses her magnetism, the self must ascend along and with this kind of evolution. When the Earth moves faster than the self; it will feel more weighted down and yes much more slower moving than before. It will feel motionless, suspended forth in animation; no longer need to run around to chase things as it used to and when in a carbon based slower moving body. In this respect the crystalline body will be slower moving next to none. This is what it feels like and when the self is not used to practicing in this state of being, rather than just doing. All space and time that was before, are meaningless.

"To create in my own image" and "Alchemy": ....Sermon

To move into the higher states, the self must adjust and eventually it will find that; by intention it will bring to focus everything.
In this reality moving fast, as once before it was perceived; will end up taking longer to reach. For example(on the way of this likeness); it will result in many road blocks, and/or as well as traffic to endure along this kind of path and way of thinking. The self is in suspended nothingness; perhaps at point zero rest mass, to better describe its speed as within a vacuum. The chakras too, were previously discussed. "One of the primary essentials of shifting into a crystalline format"; is that of the ability to have the chakra system, amplified to full measure. In that, the restoration of the chakras/energy system; at full operational strength and while still being in a physical sense of reality. Sound is key, in connecting to the resonance that held within the many possibilities of worlds and from it, the self can help transcend them; or clear away from them as well. Chanting and toning, were discussed before and to help restore the balance along this process. The distortions had begun well before these sounds were discovered; to move the heaviest most dense matter effortlessly and from this secrecy, to abuse its power, it fell from such grace. The "Ego" desire body, gradually took control of the mental and emotional bodies. The Soul Self withdrew, from the "Crown chakra" and the "Sacred Heart Center"; into the dream world, disconnecting and asleep. When aspects of the storm are able to look at the self; it will become observable to others and as in a way this luminous almost unreal appearance will then be, the physical to accompany along with it. This is why the self cannot for very long periods of time spend and with the attempt, to integrate these shadows; that it sees around it in its world and must learn to interact sparingly amongst them. The splitting off of worlds, created from the carbon element of life and play a major role in the metabolic processes; while silicon is an element of the machines, and serving with its parts, as a major component.

"To create in my own image" and "Alchemy": ....Sermon

These worlds are exactly like the twinning off of self; from the older to the newer and from it the in-between third aspect, is that of trans-humanistic "Cyborg". The light of consciousness fills up within each cell; becoming more weightless and stronger with electrons (when attracted to these spinning chakras/electrons).
With more electrons than protons now; the cells will start to spin and go into higher frequencies or dimensions.
The magnetic resonance within each cell attracts these electrons; until it is full and cannot receive any more electrons.
Each blast of light scatters the cells, activates new geometric & mathematical equations, sequences and codes; triggering any miss-alignment to become visible for change and re-align with particles, to come back together and take new form in a different manner/sequence than before. Photons carry energy relative to their frequency (wavelength) of light; The shorter the wave, the higher the energy and the lower, the longer the wave it reaches. When photons hit matter, several things can happen; depending on the amount of photon energy and the type of matter hit.
This is the point where the complete cell changes into a crystalline cell, light, or even weightless energy? In healthy bodies that have absorbed light, the anomalies are few and brief and as these bodies' crystalline cells, adjust more easily to energy fluctuations; than can the carbon-based cells of bodies with less light. From a trans-humanistic schism; it cannot conceive enough to understand and from the mind it can perceive, only that the "carbon-based" and "crystalline" are not two comparable things. The silicon existence can only help to encourage the carbon based body along the way, to its next evolutionary faze. This is where transmutation must take place, to transfigure and reconfigure; back into place as another and to interpret in the physical as transformation, from the one element into another. The transcended aspect of it all is in the old cliché........"Led" to Gold"

(Day 19)

To better understand alchemy and how it is possible to shape-shift, from solid to another solid. By looking at the atom; it has revealed, that perhaps the reality of what appears as solid; might not be in the way the self had been programmed to believe.

LESSON~ 17: "THE PAST WAS A FIGMENT OF MY OWN IMAGINATION AND EMOTIONALLY HELD IN PLACE BY THE EXPERIENCE."

The world that is supposed to be made of atoms and this solid perspective; is a hollow one, with nothing really in it.
At one level, it is just a pocket of energy and then when going deeper, it is empty space. This is in fact the reasoning for everything, as matter that carries layers of empty space within it and from these layers, the frequency; that holds them together, in their precise form. The structure of everything is energy; these energy fields decode into the layers and that make up the solid mass of everything. Solid forms, from electrical pulses and that fire up between the spaces of certain mathematical codes; from a magnetic pressure and to hold the layers of these fields in place. Codes and frequency fields, will depend on the form and that the self can be involved with. When the attention to focus on something as it is and for the purpose to look at it as it is in the moment; by taking in the vibrational information instead of to compare it up to, from something in the past. It takes the subject in through the five senses and from this review, based on passed experiences, with it. Or rather to see something as a newborn baby, for the first time and transform it into electrical information, for its brain to reinterpret.

LESSON~ 17:
"THE PAST WAS A FIGMENT OF MY OWN IMAGINATION AND EMOTIONALLY HELD IN PLACE BY THE EXPERIENCE."

It takes the form that the brain will be experiencing, as a pen for example: it could not possibly know the type of pen; or that it is not for eating; or putting in the mouth and yet its ink covered little face and mouth, does not trigger a feeling, for using it to write with. It cannot remember drawing from it, not even the feeling of the paper and the gripping of the pen; in such a way, that it must learn later on, to grasp it and write properly with it.

The left brain rationally based exercises and course of action to come; from this idea and is especially made to confront subjective belief, with old rooted ideas.

When looking around for things, with innocence of truth and equally made, for whatever is to be observed. Acknowledge today's idea, without further discrimination on its view and by using the following affirmations as example:

"I SEE ONLY THE CORRUPTION OF THE INNOCENCE IN THIS THING."

"I SEE ONLY THE PAST IN THIS CORRUPTION OF THESE THINGS."

"I SEE ONLY THE CORRUPTION OF THE PAST IN THIS THING."

"I SEE ONLY THE DECAY IN THAT BODY FROM BEFORE."

" I SEE ONLY WHAT I RECOGNIZE FROM BEFORE IN THIS."

LESSON~ 17:

"THE PAST WAS A FIGMENT OF MY OWN IMAGINATION AND EMOTIONALLY HELD IN PLACE BY THE EXPERIENCE."

All things randomly that present to imprint the focus on, provided equally for its intent. Just like a camera, taking only snapshots of each subject; practice for as few and as many, as desired in this way, throughout the day.
Acknowledge the charge that was held in place and to distort the impact of its reasoning; that previously meaning understood for anything, can now hold nothing.

Thus the outcome to never again be upset and for the reasons once thought, in seeing that of something, was never there to begin with.

The purpose for today is to understand, that all experience is but a charged emotion. This then said emotion, attaches to a thought; it encourages the self to think it knows and forms the opinion, to believe as truth by it.

"To create in my own image" and "Alchemy": ....Sermon

To better understand the radiant Crystalline form, and gradually over many ages into a sub-universe. Science has to reinterpret, what has already been before and from previously; to discover this break through Blueprint. It would need bonding properties, similar to carbon, and a low enough weight; so as to allow easy molecular movement, within a cell. Alchemy is a branch of bio-alchemy; that seeks to alchemically "marry" two dissimilar life forms, into a new creature.

From a higher reinterpretation it is "TRANSMUTATION". When the energy of a particle is released; it is the absorption of light, that is causing the transformation.

Light is weightless and made of finite energy.

Electromagnetic waves behave like particles and from these photons; all these wavy forms and molecules, that binds them into everything, from atom. The likeness in the image of "Adam giving to Eve", everything comes from atoms and atoms go into everything; through everything atoms can exist. Atoms can absorb energy and they can release it; this plasmic/layer/field containment form, is mutable with energy. Light is known as, being of wave forms, called fields and particle forms called photons; they can be reflected, scattered and absorbed.

On a molecular (protein, lipids, carbohydrates, and nucleic acids) level and the need for atoms to bond; can be shared, or create a loss of power and within another(ionic/covalent), so to create it(molecule).

"To create in my own image" and "Alchemy": ....Sermon

When an atom has two electrons spinning in conflicting directions; they can cancel each other out and become neutral.

In this way too, the similarities and in that these charges can be lifted. When the self can learn to be in mindfulness; it chooses where the magnetic and/or electrical charge can shift to and with its lighted presence of awareness, to imprint upon a particle.

This is something that the book will hopefully accomplish and as a common practice, to become most natural to self.

It is exactly what it means, to become Sovereign in the light and of its own beings within the Oneness; authentically to be given such a blessing and that it may, express from inspiration.

To create through another and in the likeness of its image; was the force behind unnatural and more denser realities to form.

This darkness from which the self was forced to procreate with; became its shadow and from it, the splitting off, from "LOVE" to find the "LIGHT" externally. The disconnect became the power, from which created struggle; from this friction, opposites struggled to find the way and from meaning to oblivion, with immortality and suffered for its cause. The silicon distorted version of existence; can only help to encourage the carbon based body along the way and to its next evolutionary faze. Transmutation must take place, to transfigure and reconfigure back into place; as another to interpret and in the physical, as transformation, from the one element, into another. It is light consciousness that requires the body to become more fluid and that it is, mostly made up of water.

(Day 20) It is an illusion to think, that the past can be held and for the present reality as truth. When worried for the future or guilty of the past and as a cause for misconception; the mind can delete the present moment, of the here and now entirely.

LESSON~18:

"MY MIND IS FULL OF CHATTER FROM THE PAST."

No matter how clear a thought is visualized, the concept is to realize it, and then release it. Allow it to work through, by admitting to acknowledge and that is no longer, how the self is best served for; to identify it with(and perhaps it never really was its thoughts and rather the opinions of others collectively). Also it is easier to practice these exercise, with eyes closed; go ahead and search; contain the theme, name them and keep going to the next, with the following example:

" WHAT EXACTLY IS IT THAT I AM THINKING

 ABOUT _____."

" [name of person], OR [OBJECT],

 AND/OR [EMOTION]."

LESSON~18:

" MY MIND IS FULL OF CHATTER FROM THE PAST."

This can be practiced, as many times during the day as preferred; it might also be helpful to include the irritations and emotions arising from this idea for today. It might be well then, to conclude with this last statement:

"MY MIND IS FULL OF CHATTER FROM THE PAST."

THE IDEA OF THIS EXERCISE FOR MY AWARENESS TO THESE THOUGHTS HAS CREATED THIS IRRITATION FOR ME_____ AND MY EMOTIONS _____. (name the irritation and the emotional charge that is felt by it, to work through and release, recognizing just how it has served the self if any).

Identify with it, then acknowledge how much you changed from it and that it no longer is identifying in, with the best interest of, the way things were.

To not understand time in fact, is to not understand anything; because the present, is the only time there is and that is the purpose for today.

"To create in my own image" and "Alchemy": ....Sermon

The transcended aspect of it all, is in the old cliché, "Led" to Gold". The self will be less weighted down in density. Perhaps with the actual self and from a molecular perspective; it might still nutritionally have to undergo, the lipid factor and that helps conceal its toxins, that it must release. Or simply the helping to assist in the nervous system; so it does not overwhelm its circuitry(tension). Could it be that the many other systems of the body and in with an extra sense perception must clear away? For example: from the kidney; spleen; and liver, all these elements and certain other organs; that the self and from the previously known to find it obsolete (appendix; tonsils; gallbladder....) might have the self feeling all so very bloated. Physical body goes through and as physical matter constantly changing form. Dense carbon based (iron and other heavy metals go, so the body needs more plant based iron, breathing in and out the life flow through the cardio-vascular);to become a plasma being, in a physical form.

The self must feel its way through and learn from these many senses, that it has. Yes its extra senses must kick in, the self must connect in this way to its 6th and 7th senses and so on and so forth. Looking back to re-examine as a caterpillar, to a butterfly paradigm. The physical matter does change inside its form/structure and from dense matter, to light to liquid, to gas, to plasma and then back to solid again.

A very delicate balance to undergo from caterpillar to a butterfly. At the end of every cycle, there is an emergence to move on, to the higher realms. Electro magnetic waves, create these pockets of photonic light and from it, the self can choose to create in likeness of its own imagination; to that it resonates it will attract. This is going with the flow and not against it; like in the older, previous Ego mind creations.

"To create in my own image" and "Alchemy": ....Sermon

The Metaphysical reality, does still consist of these spiritual/mental and emotional and well after the self transcends from the physical; it has no other alternative but to uncover its inner body. This book is all about accepting this kind of Spirituality; to live it with the physical body and having the experience, to ground and expand from it. Just like there is no turning back from the butterfly, to a caterpillar; there is no turning back to carbon base. Once the self has gone to rev up in its Sovereign Light existence; the light changes third density's carbon-based cellular structure, to the crystalline form. That allows for all physical bodies to thrive and in the higher frequencies, or vibrations, of fourth density and beyond. The self has not dropped off its body and is transcending, to transform with it. Chanting too, can help by fusing spirit with the Soul. As the carbon can and will integrate with all its shadows and this becoming the darkest one of nights, for its soul; and to reconfigure into a diamond. This paradigm is the crystalline and Silicon too; it is all in how the perspective can perceive and to change to its reality, a new. The Soul that can absorb the light, made constantly available to all, can also change at a cellular level; from carbon-based third density body and over to a crystalline-based one, so to sustain in even higher frequencies.

This will require the lessons to help through the sloughing off a skin, which is no longer needed and to release the lower densities, to slip away. Emerge from regrets of Earthly memories…from disillusions…from false idealization and which had become illusions of no worth. Become thankful for the true reality and just allow.

"ALLOW FOR ALL THE LOOSENING OF STRUCTURES AND JUST BE".

(Day 21) The physical world, is like it is perceived from self; to have the experience, it must require to expand and grow from. As well as learn, to why it is even here; having this experience in the first place. From the field of variables; that probability must be closer to and the like of what the self, can be able to imagine and believe in.

LESSON~19:

"MY SENSES ARE RECEIVING THINGS THAT ARE NOT IN SYNCHRONICITY WITH WHAT I AM TRANSMITTING IN THIS MOMENT TO ALIGHN WITH."

As the self can sense the wave forms, it will take this charge to reinterpret and filter through this energy, from its perspective. The entirety of this world, is made real from the mind and that perceives it in this way. When the self cannot decode the information; it can become a tyranny of sorts, to agitate and interfere with, in its world. Perhaps the 6th sense of the goose-bumps on the skin; or the hair on the back of the neck standing. Then again the previous sermon, touched lightly on describing the connection to the organs and that the self must have, or give up for removal(to consider as the 7th sense).
To break apart and fragment from that kind of a reality; can also come from Sound, Smell, Taste, and Sight as well as Touch. These fragments of tyranny that the self must come to terms with; are the symptoms of such ailments and that either it can accept to integrate or turn away from. Waveform information can be received; but the vibration might not be in the same frequency as the self is in such as noise pollution. For the purpose of undoing false ideas and from the previous lessons; this one too, does follow the same knowledge to accept. To understand is not important and for any real significance in this way right now, as it is to practice.

LESSON~19:

"MY SENSES ARE RECEIVING THINGS THAT ARE NOT IN SYNCHRONICITY WITH WHAT I AM TRANSMITTING IN THIS MOMENT TO ALIGHN WITH."

The effort to train the mind, to believe in something coming through its many senses, to not be there; will eventually let it go with less, to no resistance.

Little by little, to clear the mind from the debris that darkens it and with enlightenment of understanding.

Practice as many times during the day preferred; apply this idea, with whatever is around to observe and with no real emphasis on anything in particular.

From the book, is the following template as an example:

"I DO NOT SEE THIS DIESEL ENGINE PROBLEM FROM THE BUS THAT IS RELEASING A DARK CLOUD OF SMOKE."

"I DO NOT HAVE TO BREATHE IN THIS DARK CLOUD OF SMOKE."

"I DO NOT HAVE TO HEAR THE LEVEL OF STRESS THE NOISE THIS BUS WILL MAKE WHILE STARTING UP TO MOVE AWAY ".

What other things might I be feeling, ……. in this case: of discomfort ……….?

Exercise firstly with things up close, and in the same way, as before, to not leave anything out; then as with the next example below, widen the scope, for a broader view.

LESSON~19:

"MY SENSES ARE RECEIVING THINGS THAT ARE NOT IN SYNCHRONICITY WITH WHAT I AM TRANSMITTING IN THIS MOMENT TO ALIGHN WITH."

"I DO NOT HEAR THE PLANE ABOVE ME AS IT PASSES BY."

"I DO NOT SEE THE TRAILS IT LEAVES BEHIND."

"I DO NOT SEE THAT HELLICOPTER CIRCLING THE AREA AND DO NOT REQUIRE TO HEAR IT IN THIS WAY."

Be certain that nothing is avoided, nor treated with preference; and because of the level of understanding already formed. This is to be treated in the same way all other opinions are formed; by what has filtered in this way from a common place to sense.

The purpose is to understand, a little better and how the in between world too; it can become a third form of existence, from the two and so on. Whilst the self might learn, to not stay stuck for very long, in either; it can then learn to lightly change the experience, from one moment to the next and not feel the fragmentations.

"To create in my own image" and "Alchemy": ……..Sermon

Just breathe into it and the light codes will happen, to direct the cosmic fire through the body; via the central nervous system and which originally was designed for this purpose, in the first place. The "Adam (in the likeness of)" blueprint; it was designed to be able to direct electrical currents, at a very high voltage through the body and to use this ability to shape energy/plasma into form.

The more the self can decode and activate; the more of light it can expand and into its field of awareness.

The activation is an internal process. Feel the deeper, inner peace and celebration; from when the self can open up its heart to LOVE. From the fluidity of water, that comprises the self with diamond water codes, to be a clear and transparent matrix; for the transmission and projection of this electrical light energy.

Like light through a prism, as the light moves through this diamond prism and that is the body of the physical self; it carries the codes or instructions, on how to shape energy into matter.

To create that which it can see and desire into manifest form.

At this moment the experience can be uncomfortable and for the present, that it undergoes through the process; in preparation for migrating itself into the new earth paradigm. This reality will require such talents; that are being gifted to the self, when ready to awaken and accept them. It will require a new relationship with the earth and nature; as a living being and/or reality to co-exist, along side with the self. The connection will be of the highest respect; to walk with reverence, in the acknowledgement of such great power. The magic that is bestowed upon, to that which can stand up, take responsibility and in its light of being and breathing, authentically in that space of oneness, to its existence.

"To create in my own image" and "Alchemy": ....Sermon

From the interweaving of the physical and the metaphysical spiritual perspectives. These paradigms were given the chakras to play with. By practicing the voice and sound, to find these portals of various understanding; to ignite the feeling of the breath and touch upon the concept of the life force/kundalini/chi/prana.

The purpose of the Shaman in the old world, was to serve as the bridge between the many of its world and that of spirit world. To find higher dimensions, in nature and from within the dreamtime; when the self can enter into a new paradigm, to become the all and as Shamans, in that the many can experience. From a popular understanding and in the same format to connect with, honour and respect; rather than exploit and take advantage of(in the accumulation of the greed that feeds the "Ego"). The nature spirits and elementals, must be giving the permission and before the self can share from this essence that it gives; rather than to forcefully take and plunder recklessly(by disregarding such existence those who do will never be allowed to enter into such a Kingdom).

The communities that grow and prosper on this earth; will honour these ideas and central theme of Love here and Now. The self can start to realize for itself, what it had been missing and from such relationships kept it alone and isolated. Love for the self and every other part, that will come to coexist in likeness of these values. Etheric reconnection will happen right through the body; when the self-awakens, it will use the magic that flows through its body and create whatever it will need with it. Some basic shamanic techniques were introduced, to help connect with the earth. In this way the elemental energies, that flow; as well with the magical energies, through love and intention. This is going to be the biggest adventure to explore, within this process; known as manifesting and in this way, that has been given.

(Day 22)

With the previous lesson, the self was made to feel the gathering of all its senses and from it, might have lightly touched upon, the other systems too. To interpret as the "goose-bumps" on the skin, for example; or the inner workings of the organs further more and/or less. From the ethers it came such information, to be interpreted as sound and by it, be this process, from sound into light; that self may see as real and so it thinks it. From its very breath of air, it becomes it; this thing that it be touched by and then the earthly smell, of sensing; that it magnetizes to and from it, there, the taste of its emotion. Now going back into the thoughts of the self (let it be felt as well).

LESSON~20:

"MY RESISTANCE TO THESE THOUGHTS HAVEN'T ANY MEANING."

With no real basis for comparison, there is no opposition to resist with and then the mind becomes still. To think the thoughts once believed, did not mean anything and from the outside, than within the present. Now with emphasize on these present thoughts; suggests the mind is really blank and not thinking at all.
The following example might be of assistance and in the process of recognizing nothingness, when seeing something.
Begin by closing the eyes, for this exercise and repeating the idea; that might be holding for any opposition, its resistance to and use the following statement, as an example:

"I NOW GIVE MYSELF PERMISSION TO BE RELEASED FROM ANY PREVIUOS NOTIONS OF BELIEVING."

LESSON~20:

"MY RESISTANCE TO THESE THOUGHTS HAVEN'T ANY MEANING."

Feel for the resistance, that opposes self within each thought, that surfaces the mind for available thoughts and randomly passing by, one by one, the following can be said:

"THIS THOUGHT_____ I HAVE OUTGROWN."

"MY THOUGHT ABOUT_____ IS MEANINGLESS."

"FROM HERE ON FORTH I DO RELEASE MYSELF FROM SILLY SUPERSTITIONS."

This lesson can serve for any thought of distress, at any time; as well as many times throughout the day, that self desires to lightly brush over(for as little as and no more than 70 seconds, or so). Search the mind, until for every though, it feels the stretch of its discomfort and this way, it can detect what it needs releasing; or further to explore and work through on.

Feel how the mind, when it gets all worked up; the self becomes tense and full of superstition. The purpose is to introduce lightly, the letting go of mind chatter.

<u>Unwanted thoughts and circumstances are attracted reversely from the life force; because when it is blocked in any kind of way, the flow, it can reverse and resistance is created.</u>

THE INTERMISSION :

Take a day to take it in

CONGRATULATIONS ...!!!

FOR MAKING IT

THROUGH TO THE 20th Lesson

(This is a rest period to take the lessons independently as a review)

TAKE THIS DAY TO RECALIBRATE;

MAKE NOTES AND REVIEW……………..

"PROMOTING OPPOSITION THROUGH RESISTANCE":
....Sermon

Nothing is beyond the self, to force it in the way of fear or love and when it does not agree to it. Duality was this contrast, created to learn by and not oppose; rather the integration to accept and to expand, by such growth. Time is another distorted tool and from it came: the perception of the ever looming death over it; that follows to remind, in this way and in everything, to feel the pressure of its casting on it.
To hurry up and get things done, before its energy is wasted; in that short span of limitation and that it thinks is life, is not so very pleasant. Perceive time as only a means to eternity; because the both are in the mind and anything other than this, will conflict with each other. Nothing can take away from the ownership and that of taking responsibility. When it knows to feel the having of time, at its disposal and anything else, is but an irrelevant belief, to outside factors and that simply have no affect, on what is happening to it. There is no escape from these laws, regardless of the choices made and in one's own imagination, to violate them. With the creation of its own existence, the self made certain; that nothing else beside it, must exist and apart from it, to except what else more, than this self can exist? Its breath connects to universal laws and that by it, were established to protect and be free of harm for one's own safety. Nothing beyond the self expressive and as creator being, can possibly happen; because nothing else is real. Where the creator becomes the expression; likewise from the spirit's reflection and where the soul can further grow.
Yet nothing is added, that is different; because everything has always been.

"PROMOTING OPPOSITION THROUGH RESISTANCE":
........Sermon

What can become an upset is the ephemeral, and how can this ephemeral be real; when the almighty presence, is all there is and to have created self eternal? This is the holy mind and for everything that happens, to establish it.
Every response too and that is made, is from the mind's perception of it, to determine. Self's holy presence does not change any of the mind's uncertainties; because it does not know it only for thy self to be unknowable and in the knowing of it.
Self is an awareness of simultaneous expression and created from the breath of its very own <u>being</u>; that and with the ephemeral, was given power to create for self, this reflection, to respond and play with. That in the same likeness, is why the mind is holy and the love it has cannot exceed beyond its God presence; because to will beyond the everything for this greatness, is not comprehensive to the mind.

Therefore being in God and God in self, it encompasses everything; however this much is true, when threatened the peace of mind further, to expand with and to question this much in God, is having a change of mind about it.
Then accept it for this decision, is indeed changeless, to refuse to change the mind about thyself; because God will never decide against this paradox.

(Day 24)

Today is short, in that it must care enough to understand the feeling of these words and not just the visual thought interpretation of the objects.

LESSON~21:

"MY THOUGHTS THAT REPRESENT A DISTORTED WORLD ARE IN DISCORDANCE WITH THE UNKNOWABLE"

The unknowable comes from the essence and that it may try to understand, through feeling. To really feel it, by separating from the emotional charge of the experience, and where it had held in, as it thought. The fear will come and the discomfort too will follow; when the self is disconnected from the previous approval. Feel it for itself and as it presents itself in the here now moment. Repeat this idea with eyes closed; say slowly to self and then with open eyes look about, near and far, up and down, and all around.

Without any rush for a minute or so, move eyes from one thing to another, fairly rapidly and with the following statement; these words to be said leisurely and without any hurry.

"MY THOUGHTS THAT REPRESENT A DISTORTED WORLD ARE IN DISCORDANCE WITH THE UNKNOWABLE"

Sample this exercise casually and as many times as desired today; for the purpose to achieve peace, relaxation and freedom from worry.

The intention is to release enough, to grasp the key to forgiveness.

"PROMOTING OPPOSITION THROUGH RESISTANCE."

"AT HOME WITHIN MY OWN BODY ": ....Sermon "

Bringing back the balance, from the disconnect and of previous artificial programs: Etheric quantum strands (junk DNA), are where the intensions from the heart, can come from and to be able to connect with outer world; it is the inner compass of alignment and the (Northern Star from Christian bible) inner star from within.
Wherever it will be, the self will always be at home; because everything that it is experiencing, is an echo from its reflection.
This is just light frequency, bouncing off of, from the self and this is what creates its world. From the very breath that created it, in its own awareness, of itself and its surroundings.
The beating of its heart, is this motion; that creates the rhythmic movement and that is this thing, called "ebb and flow.
Only when the mind is split, does it attack what it has created and it becomes so unfamiliar, to simply decide against them.
The law of creation, is that self loves its creations and as much as it does for itself. Laws then do appear from the mind; to condition for safety, perfectly protecting against all other aspects of the mind and that have been banished from this knowledge.
In this recognition, the realization of this brings about the separation from God and gladly to accept, that it does not exist as truth. To be at home in God, dreaming of exile and while perfectly capable of awakening to its reality, is this paradox.

"AT HOME WITHIN MY OWN BODY."

"PROMOTING OPPOSITION THROUGH RESISTANCE"

"AT HOME WITHIN MY OWN BODY ": ....Sermon "

This knowledge of self awareness and when to decide, that in its dreams, these thoughts as real; while asleep and everything that seemed to happen in the dream, did not happen at all. The laws during awake state, were violated while asleep and yet it could have been just as possible, merely to have shifted from one dream, to another and without really waking?
Precisely then, is how these laws will cancel out for themselves and from the mind, these laws must then be meaningless and non existing.
Maybe spirit can recall, the hearing softly in a whisper and as a feeling better loving, than seems possible.

It is in this remembering, perhaps an aspect; but just of the one eternal essence, can be found to remember, in the here and now, through love.

"AT HOME WITHIN MY OWN BODY."

(Day 25)

Matter in itself, is meaningless to this world and without self to give it any meaning. It is then a distortion of character, to think of being frightened; or sad, in a world that feels it, as insane or violent. With eyes open and in an even tempo, throughout a constant time interval; pace the glance, from one thing to another equally, with timing and attention.

LESSON~22: "MY AGITATIONS SERVE ME WELL."

It is okay not to understand why, something such; as a positive an adjective, does then suggest an unsavory one, next to it.

By learning to give equal value, to all things and as one looks about, the following example can be said:

"I THINK I FEEL ALL THE DISTORTIONS I AM SEEING."

Include all terms that come to mind; because the purpose of this idea, is to note and that there is no difference between them.

The exercise requires, that there be no alterations made with time given. All that cross the mind, are suitable subjects and their seeming qualities too; does not matter whether it is thought of as pleasant, or not.

LESSON~22: "MY AGITATIONS SERVE ME WELL."

Train for roughly no longer than 70 seconds (or until the feeling of strain); As many times during the day and at the end of the practice, finish it off with the following statement:

"THE WORLD THAT I AM EXPERIENCING IS AGITATING."

The mind will see it as indifference, although it is not; rather detaching/un-clutching long enough, to sense the brief touching and on the surface of discernment.
The intention is to go beneath these words of meaning and to the very infinite, that is God presence.

Understand that all have an equal value in the role they play, to serve the self with and is the purpose for this exercise.
The purpose is to see, where the self might be encouraged to lash out and from a place of resistance.

Go now to a place, where neither good or bad exist to upset the mind and by learning to recognize before responding.

(Day 26)

The mental discomfort when the "EGO" is confronted, is the cognitive dissonance; and dare nothing challenge it, from its own correctness, in this way of contradicting beliefs.
Today is all about discovery and exploration.

LESSON~23: "I AM NOT AFRAID OF WHAT I DO NOT KNOW."

Everything does exist in a hazy wave, until the self imprints its attention to it. Having as intended play with it and will appear for it, to further study and learn from; after it has brought it into its reality. A bit like "FAITH" can describe, but with less effort.
When feeling separate from the oneness; this concept might arouse intense anxiety, because the "EGO" becomes challenged.
Through observation and concentration, is how the self can pull toward itself, those things it feels it needs. There are these sub atomic particles/wave forms; that by its very own observation to them, will collapse into form and when the self can direct from the variation, precisely imprinting it into. By its very own intention to it, the self can change things into matter; or as real as it can be made, to be fully understood and further experience with it, this awareness such a relationship. This wave particle reality, at a sub atomic level, is not a reality; but rather a probability of one that can occur.
The self does not lean up against what it wants; because then it will only push it away. Instead it stands up straight and owns its space; most of all, must accept to nurture itself, by practicing self care.

LESSON~23: "I AM NOT AFRAID OF WHAT I DO NOT KNOW."

By discovering the core beliefs, of who and what it is, that makes it happy? What is real and possible and fun? And what is just the EGO's disquiet, to delve deep within and ponder. Discover what is really wanted and by feeling it clearly; use these feelings to determine, between vague yearnings of the…..? ….. What are some of the deepest, inner most desires and needs? By doing this practice, as often as desired and for as long as, no more than 15 minutes and no less than 70 seconds.

Does it give you stress, from believing in the effort or struggle to exist?

By connecting with the subconscious and even unconscious, of the neural receptors and these pathways from its Ego aspect; is so strong and deeply embedded in every cell. It will take continual application, continual expanding and flooding of the consciousness, continual everything to re-program with. The re-program, is opening up to newer, neural pathways and get on to realizing how simple this is. Surround the self, by allowing the overwhelm of its own consciousness; with the absolute highest everything, and clear the field/space, of all that does not support, to transform the reality through LOVE and own deep inner-connected state.

The purpose of this lesson, is to learn to grasp the unknown and by accepting it, without fear as meaningful; in this way to eliminate blocks and highlight any contradictions, that may exist.

Fill the "SPACE" (Consciousness) with all things that vibrationally lift, inspire and support.

(Day 27)

One day, take an alarm and set it by the bed; set an intention to focus on a circumstance and then go to sleep. Maybe the self has already experienced the pleasure of dream study, in this way? To take an object directly in a dream one time and through this lucid dreaming it immediately to be pulled away and into another part of the dream.

LESSON ~ 24:
"MY SHIFT OF EMPHASIS WILL CHANGE THE OUTCOME INDIRECTLY."

Just like the dream can change from the direct focus and so too can the outcome of a circumstance, change in this way. Imagination is good to create a reflection and that could motivate the self to do so. Likewise giving power away and to cause many more things to make up for it, along the way to self discovery; that in time will reveal, it was self all along, deserving the praise.
For an even playing field, it is recommended to keep an open mind, free of discriminants and/or any programs; that could suggest "God" as being anything other, than an extension of self's bigger picture. To think of salvation to exist, can be uneasy and painful; as these initial procedures of their exchange. To let go and dream of something outside of self, to save or be saved by it, is a great detour to fear. Rather emphasize these aspects of life, through frequency and resonance. To wait for something separate from self, to pull self out and so to not be left behind in this fear, is delusional to make believe as truth.

LESSON ~ 24: "MY SHIFT OF EMPHASIS WILL CHANGE THE OUTCOME INDIRECTLY."

With the following template, given to sample; or create another, that best feels to authentic self and from this idea(so it can really work), say to self, by repeating these words:

"MY CIRCUMSTANCES ARE CHANGEABLE.":

"MY CIRCUMSTANCES, WERE FROM THE OUTCOME OF MY EMPHASIS TO THEM IN THIS WAY."

"I CAN NOT DIRECTLY CHANGE MY CIRCUMSTANCE BUT I CAN CHANGE THE WAY I FEEL ABOUT MYSELF."

"I CAN SHIFT MY ATTENTION TO INVEST IN WHAT FEELS GOOD WHILE INDIRECTLY THINKING HOW I PREFER THE OUTCOME OF [SPECIFY],...."

Be specific about the name of the distress; rather than going with general terms:
"I did not create hatred", however "My circumstances were from an emphasis of emotional dislike" and the pulling away from; because it does not taste good, (name the circumstance of discomfort). What is it that self prefers to replace it with and then go on and to distract with something else, that feels the way that self prefers.

LESSON ~ 24:

"MY SHIFT OF EMPHASIS WILL CHANGE THE OUTCOME INDIRECTLY."

Trying to change something that alters and while the self focuses on it, does not work. (When coming from it, with a linear time frame perspective)The indirect approach, can allow for life to unfold and by emphasizing on something else. In this way the self can allow for all the obstructions that might dam up the flow of life; to not be the cause and affect, that karma deals with. Only then can the stress and pain from this interconnectedness with all life, that it might touch with, when forced into a changed outcome; by focusing on it directly for it circumstances to change. It does not matter at whatever is being observed. This expression made separate from the mind's part of self; that wishes to be pinched off from its own truth and in wholeness expression from all that is, of all that is divine.

In acceptance of this idea to finish today's exercise with these words:

"MY SHIFT OF EMPHASIS WILL CHANGE THE OUTCOME OF MY CIRCUMSTANCES DIRECTLY."

This exercise is to be repeated, as much as preferred throughout the day. The idea can be made applicable to anything that is disturbing and aside from these sessions; be very specific, as in this such given example:

"[NAME THE SITUATION], IS NOT REAL" BECAUSE IT WAS MY RESISTANCE TO IT THAT GAVE IT THE POWER TO EXIST."

The purpose of this lesson, is to reveal that circumstances can be indirectly changed and by removing filters, the sight can widen and become much clearer: In this way, the shift of indirect emphasis, can change the outcome.

The Master's Reveal: The Destiny of Resurrection

When the self can find joy from its very calmness; it can then awaken into the garden of divine presence and with its soul to be expressed, as a luminous body. This will take the commitment to understand fully and with all its overwhelm, the significance of Metaphysical Spirituality.

It is easy to go quantum(energetic shifting). The changing to physical matter cannot become properly interpreted and is this memory; however that can be left behind and in place of it, the essential activation of the truth and that is, this light. When the magnetics shift and faze out, what else is left; but an elevated state, that has no shadow left of it.

From the many portals, they become the one; from it all that self has ever known and felt into a field of oneness.

This is what is meant, to be the Sovereign light and from it, the energy to create, any magnetic field and quantum reality, to exist within as universe. The self has a choice, from any given timeline. To agree upon the collective imprint and/or dismiss from it; into another, via from activated codes of light, frequency and vibration. This clarification of the self, is the destination known as Resurrection.

(Day 28)
LESSON~25: "MY SOUL WILL ALWAYS BRING UP UNRESOLVED MEMORIES FROM THE OVERAL SOFTWARE SYSTEM AND THAT I MAY LEARN TO NEUTRALIZE THESE REFLECTED BACK TO ME EXPERIENCES TO UPGRADE WITH."

The gentling of the heart comes from forgiveness and it is this peace beyond all understanding from the mind itself.
With stagnant thoughts this concept lies in self-contradiction because the world in its entirety is not "idle". With every thought there is a motion and from this motion a magnetism to experience such energy in motion. To make salvageable the understanding that every thought has an attachment of emotion: then; whether of bondage or freedom; conditional or unconditional the possibility of a neutral outcome hasn't as of yet been experienced.

"WHEN I CLEAR OUT OF MY BODY ENERGETIC DISTORTIONS THE INTEGRATION FROM THIS REBALANCING IS THE ONLY STATE OF UNDERSTANDING TO BE OF A NEUTRAL EXPERIENCE."

Today is this experience to go into the stillness of the motion of each thought and find within the center its trigger for an experience. What charge makes for this experience to spin from such a thought. Energy can only be transmuted into another state and within this process the in between neutralizing factor.
The temptation to neglect conditional or thoughts of bondage to be trivial and not worth the bother; they are as equally destructive and very important to consider as the equally unreal.

LESSON~25: "MY SOUL WILL ALWAYS BRING UP UNRESOLVED MEMORIES FROM THE OVERAL SOFTWARE SYSTEM AND THAT I MAY LEARN TO NEUTRALIZE THESE REFLECTED BACK TO ME EXPERIENCES TO UPGRADE WITH."

Taking responsibility over self projection, at first it can be somewhat a challenge not to make any artificial distinctions; or to actively seek not to overlook anything small and that may escape from the search. What might appear as neutral, can be a dissociation; to avoid the numbing shock of having to reveal suppressed discomfort. Awaken to these thoughts and truly find if they belong to self; or just the debris, of the agreed upon collectively evolving.

What is the thought and for no longer than seventy seconds; become aware for every thought that crosses in the mind and repeat for as many as possible, the following example:

"WHEN I CLEAR OUT OF MY BODY ENERGETIC DISTORTIONS. THE PROCESS FROM THIS UNCLUTCHING FORMS A TEMPORARY GAP TO INTEGRATION AND FROM THIS REBALANCING IS THE ONLY STATE OF UNDERSTANDING TO BE OF A NEUTRAL EXPERIENCE."

"THIS THOUGHT ABOUT_____IS IN WAITING FOR ME TO REINVENT FOR MY EXPERIENCE AND HOW I WOULD PREFER TO OWN IT AS."

"THAT THOUGHT ABOUT_____HAS YET TO FIND THE RIGHT EXPRESSION FROM ME AND TO EXPERIENCE THE REVEAL OF IT."

LESSON~25: "MY SOUL WILL ALWAYS BRING UP UNRESOLVED MEMORIES FROM THE OVERAL SOFTWARE SYSTEM AND THAT I MAY LEARN TO NEUTRALIZE THESE REFLECTED BACK TO ME EXPERIENCES TO UPGRADE WITH."

For thoughts that particularly arouse uneasiness; they can be taken a step further and with the following template:

"THIS THOUGHT ABOUT_____IS IN THE BALANCE OF BECOMING SOMETHING ELSE, BECAUSE I HAVE YET TO EXPERIENCE THE SUPPORTING RESPONSE AND FOR WHAT EXACTLY IT IS THAT I PREFER TO FEEL."

This exercise can be done 3 to 5 times during the day.

The purpose of this lesson, is to release the notion that thoughts have no effect.

(Day29)
To integrate the aspects of the personality, that might have disassociated from itself and was achievable by becoming more aware; because where tension goes, energy flows.
When the watcher comes out of the mind and just sees all the drama and troubled world of chaos, all around. Becoming the eye of the storm and in this way, is the intent toward rewiring the brain.

LESSON~26: "ANY IDEA FROM THE VARIABLE PROBABILITIES AND AS THE OBSERVER WHAT I PERCEIVE WITH MY THOUGHTS WILL BE THIS OUTCOME."
The witness state, is that of being in a state of observation.
There is a fine line between avoidance and acceptance.
All feelings and thoughts stem from a belief every time.
Non-attachment and the turning off the neural receptors, can be dangerous; because it disconnects the mind, from the subconscious. The mind can disconnect, from where it no longer has access to this information field and through the process of disassociation; a coping mechanism to ultimately reinforce a negative belief even more. Disassociation is when, the self cannot see it in the action of what is going on. By becoming a victim to its circumstances, it then is open and vulnerable; pertaining to the situation and it will not realize the emotions it is having. Triggered situations come from a negative belief and the denial of the attached emotion; in that the self will feel numb and will not be able to figure out the source of the problem and where it stems from. Having attachments to the outcomes of desires, will bring much pain and suffering. This means, to let go of trying to control for anything and let the higher mind show the way, to least resistance; from being fully present in the moment and to the outcomes. The witness state, can be confused with disassociating sometimes; because of the non attachment to emotions.

LESSON~26: " ANY IDEA FROM THE VARIABLE PROBABILITIES AS THE OBSERVER WHAT I PERCEIVE WITH MY THOUGHTS WILL BE THIS OUTCOME."

The idea for the day, is to become aware of the transition, from the sympathetic and empathetic; just in the same way the witnessing can still have the emotion and that the self can be the watcher. Today, take some time to observe the mind as it flows naturally. While at the same time, not being swayed by; or attracted to, by these distractions and/or attached to any thought or emotion. Being in a state of mindfulness, brings peace and allows for deeper aspects of meditation to unfold; sometimes even to reveal something, beyond the mind, such as, in a state of hypnosis.
Give the self the openness to understand the inner workings of the mind. Reclaim this neutral state and take responsibility; to what it is the self prefers to manifest as miracles. Be the change of the vibration and really own it, this power. This is the over-soul and as with neutrality, without the thought primarily and for anything it cannot be anything; however the world is in reverse in the thinking of it, by seeing it first. In the reverse, the way the world does think it; the cause itself becomes reality, rather than the perception of it. With the observer effect and idea for today, set the intention to direct these thoughts, that have scattered. The spirit is therefore, in reverse to the soul interpretation; and for the self to experience simultaneously, the back and forth, in this way, toward evolution. The power is the magic; it is felt clearly through the heart and made aware through love. This is the impact of reality, that the self has to its world and its world right back on it.

LESSON~26: "ANY IDEA FROM THE VARIABLE PROBABILITIES AS THE OBSERVER WHAT I PERCEIVE WITH MY THOUGHTS WILL BE THIS OUTCOME."

Nothing stays the same and given the always changing moment of the nature of reality; the way the mind thinks, is the given cause and that results in perception.

With eyes open and with this idea for the day, use the following statement:
"MY THOUGHTS ARE THE GREATEST INFLUENCE WHEN I AM ABLE TO CONSCIOUSLY DETACH FROM THEM AND BY NO MEANS OF HAVING DOUBTED THEM WITH DENIAL INSTEAD I RATHER ACCEPT TO UNDERSTAND THEM BETTER THAN BEFORE."

Look around the area, while resting with a glance on each thing and long enough to say the following:

"I DO NOT DISASSOCIATE WHEN LOOKING AT THIS _____ , BECAUSE MY THOUGHTS ABOUT _____ARE MINDFUL."

Another example given to this template more specifics:

"I DO NOT DISASSOCIATE WHEN LOOKING AT THIS [wall], BECAUSE MY THOUGHTS ABOUT [walls] ARE MINDFUL."

" I DO NOT DISASSOCIATE WHEN LOOKING AT MY [body], BECAUSE MY THOUGHTS ABOUT [bodies] ARE MINDFUL."

Give difference in understanding, between the living and non- living things, pleasant or unpleasant; because the awareness might not be there, for this truth just yet and to believe it so.

LESSON~26: " ANY IDEA FROM THE VARIABLE PROBABILITIES AS THE OBSERVER WHAT I PERCEIVE WITH MY THOUGHTS WILL BE THIS OUTCOME."

The soul knows the temporary purpose of the spirit and in physical form; however this day has set to introduce, the possibility of opening to interdimensional tuning and for the alignment to take place, beyond the contradiction, that the soul lays out.

Let go of the forbidden disassociations and to think it as neutral.

This exercise can be practiced as many times throughout the day. Train for as long as to understand the spin and of every charging for each thought, or so; depending on the resistance that might put a strain to the duration.

The purpose of this lesson, is to be the witness of emotions and purposely to not identify with them; instead to help be more conscious of the idea, of "cause" and "effect".

<u>Note To Master</u>: *A portal is swirling energy; that can draw in with attraction or it can repel. When a vortex graduates into a portal, it connects through time and space; and can change by shifting its subject. As the vortex graduates into a portal, it gets called to a different time and space; where it can feel drawn to its subject and for this attention; to feed it into rejuvenating state and by which it may feel like as physical and slowing down.*

(Day30)
The reminder is in the subtleties today; remember when the emotion of sadness, might accompany with fear. Just like the meaningless belief of loss within this world and that vibrates in self, to mind the notes since then.
When I remove the lens(beliefs) to get pure light.

Lesson 27: "I AM CONTINUALLY SHINING IN MY OWN PERFECTION."

With every genetic strand, the helix from the soul; it had decoded within every piece of DNA. For self to think that nothing as precious in the world can feel to match it and half as good as this; it might want to attempt such type of experiment and in the here and now. "Listen"- can it be possible to recall and to see from the mind, so long ago; it might have held more than any other and that of which it taught itself, to value since. A golden arc(energy of enlightenment) of light, is found beyond the circumference of the self's horizon. It does appear to stretch, further than the Sun and Stars; yet as somewhat familiar, it will take this form, as a great and shining circle. Visualize this possibility of enlightenment; filling over the edges of the circle, to erase the structure and that it had recognized, in order to contain it. With no break or limit to an illuminated race, as infinite and within it everything is joined; continually shining in its very own perfection. When this life began, the self could not remember, from previously and anything before, this coming into existence. The memory was once more in the rebuilding of this process from the soul. Spirit began to have experiences from this temporary physical temple of the self.
The soul creating templates, for the re-experiences; reflected for the self, to discover who and what it was. These grains of information, the self would look at and select to create a perspective with.
The perspective became the lens, from which to look through and imprinting on its world, the way reality was interpreted back to it.

Lesson 27: "I AM CONTINUALLY SHINING IN MY OWN PERFECTION."

Looking at the world, with a certain vibratory sound and from this inner voice; this sound that could be felt, created into light and from it, the bending of perception. Through this lens, the light becomes diffracted; the information bends, separates the colours and from these charges/vortices, emotional distortions.

Thoughts create a spinning of energy and from it a magnetic field. As the lens gets built, emotions will attract to it distortions and that the self must work through. Emotional injuries are many undealt traumas and in the form of neutral thoughts, that also create a blanking out effect; however once they are worked through, the heart can open again(from the clearing of this injury).

There is nowhere this light is not and to make it possible for anything to be outside of it. The vision of the infinite, is that of self and is made of grasping to infinity; then once more into and through the self. This sight is most nurturing to form; filling it up with energy most recharging to refresh and with every touch, so warm in its awareness. The memory of self, wrapped in this warm blanket of light and that of higher consciousness. Accept this vision, that it can be shown for the body to experience; because this "ancient song", does vibrate within every cell, that hums it well and whilst still singing. This is an inner sight of knowing and in the sameness of communication, this song in honour to its temple; the creator self, that fully functions as illuminated and to it, this one self embodiment of light.

The purpose for today, is to feel the oneness and open to this frequency; as the familiar self, that never left from its awareness. Go ahead and feel the rapture of this love, accept the joy it pleases to present and from every joyous cell, shining in the celebration of self praise.

(Day 31)

It is only relevant to the how the self has been programed to experience of what it sees for today's lesson. From the many an opinion surfaces about how things must look in the world and in most cases have very little or nothing to do with how the self can truly experience for itself .

LESSON~28:

"I AM IN THE ONENESS WITH ALL THAT IS EXISTENCE IMPRESSING UPON ITSELF THE EXPERIENCES THAT AFFECTS THE WAY I SEE."

There are many dimensions outside this particular reality, that do not have a time/space aspect to them.
In this way thought can instantaneously manifest when nothing else is in the way from keeping the heart completely open.
Today view only randomly at things and with this idea by keeping eyes on each long enough to use the following template and or something closer to what can feel more comfortable as an example:

"MY MULTI-DIMENSIONAL ASPECTS HAVE INFLUENCED THE EXPERIENCE IN THESE DISTORTIONS OF _____ AND IN HOW I SEE IT IN THIS TIME/SPACE AWARENESS."

LESSON~28:

" I AM IN THE ONENESS WITH ALL THAT IS EXISTENCE IMPRESSING UPON ITSELF THE EXPERIENCES THAT AFFECTS THE WAY I SEE."

From the same energy and of that same spark to picture; anything the self can shape-shift to and just by picturing everything in that space, from that perspective: for example to match the breathing and the heartbeat of that(name the subject) and what it must be feeling? Basically profile the knowing of its personality; by what this by local feeling might become the self and within that moment. Eventually, this happens on a level where the extra sensory feelings and telepathic communication; that the self will meet it on the edge of the metaphysical. From the spirit side and the ability to master over with practice and/or not. Practice this exercise, as many times throughout the day and for no longer than seventy seconds; after each and use this closing statement for example:

" I AM IN THE ONENESS WITH ALL THAT IS EXISTENCE IMPRESSING UPON ITSELF THE EXPERIENCES THAT EFFECTS THE WAY I SEE AND IN THIS NOW MOMENT."

The purpose, is to embrace all insecurities and that to join the minds of the many, is not so far from the truth; This will be further explored, later on and in other lessons.

For now, just focusing on the outer world and while slowly being introduced to going inwardly; so to begin to release, all the karmic energy, that holds us back.

(Day 32) Here again, the pressing idea, to factor in the joining of the minds and is the reason why, the many are affected; rather than just an isolated being, from the one. The self is never left alone, rather left in the "Oneness", to reconnect with all its parts.

LESSON~29:

"I AM IN THE ONENESS WITH ALL THAT IS EXISTENCE EXPERIENCING THE EFFECTS OF MY THOUGHTS."

The thought of the many, to be joined at mind, could make belief and possibly regard as an "invasion of privacy".
There are no private thoughts and to resist this fact; that does preserve the oneness, is to withhold from self's own greatness, of a higher purpose. In the same moment, as do cause and effect; so too occur with thoughts and their results. The order however does not matter; because sometimes ideas from thoughts, come before the perception of those things and at other moments, the perception, before the thought. With this exercise, repeat the idea for the day and then with great care, looking for thoughts and during the moment as they arise. With eyes closed and for a minute or so, search the mind over. Give a name, that is of relevance and to the theme it holds for today; as well as, for the central loss/hurt in terms with it. While holding within the mind, a space for all the grief and that has unexpressed its love for something; repeat this following statement, given and/or something closer, to top this resonance:

"I AM IN THE ONENESS WITH ALL THAT IS EXISTENCE EXPERIENCING THE EFFECTS OF THIS GRIEF THOUGHT ABOUT _____."

Throughout the day, set the intention to pick subjects that produce a state of grief and randomly that disconnect from the oneness. Pay attention to the love and allow the energy to transmute into the miracles; with this idea and the meaning to give purpose for.

The Sermon....Self realization and Remotely Viewing The agenda of the Soul:

Spirituality is the experience of subjects and objects combined; to fully be expressed through the soul and for the consciousness of the self, to take in and learn with.

From the outside in and inside out, consciousness gives rise to everything; including the brain and resides within every cell of the physical body. Adapting to situations is not escaping; rather it is to realize from them, that the self is the creator and not the victim. Actualize thyself, from the eternal soul; from the inside, look for this watcher and become it and from this reconnection process too the watcher can awaken.

Self realization and what this soul too has, as its spiritual agenda; to fulfill in each and every life time. No matter how lost and confused the self might think it is, at any given moment; learning how to love, is an energetic transformation, into another world, leaving behind, all karmic implications. Frustration can still be present, even when all material wealth is laid out at its feet, to give it happiness and with it, a great dissatisfaction. Realize that, the true nature, is balance. When the mind is that of the seeker; it can through knowing the power of initiative, allow for the wisdom to find it and with every lesson gained, from its experience.

Then it will have to realize peace, by becoming one with joy, and one with love.

Learning to balance this energy, the self within its physical body; these systems have their own biases creating an "Egoic" mind.

This mind is based on the experiences, traumas and the expectations; that it has built up throughout this one lifetime and so many others before it.

The Sermon....Self realization and Remotely Viewing The agenda of the Soul:

The mind, within the soul, is the subconscious and that works behind the scenes, to help transmute the "Ego mind"; raise it, to a much higher level of evolution.

The soul's mind, works its magic; it will ultimately integrate and transform the personality, in order for the self, to reach enlightenment. The oneness is reconnecting and from an unconscious cellular level, the lens eventually becomes the self; with no such boundaries to exist and to remind it, of its authenticity.

REMOTE VIEWING: Everything in time and space is connected; then the consciousness becomes a vehicle.

In this way, the self can travel and view whatever it can possibly imagine and whenever it feels most strongly and in so doing, is always best. The self is capable, with the ability to go into a deeper state of consciousness and remotely influence, such viewing (other people and places). With this kind of imagination, how can the self imagine, to be ever lost ?

The willing interest to train the mind, in a way that is possible. To channel in and find out information; through the focus of a targeted intension, can then be verified. With channeling, there is the willingness to open up and pull the information in; from an unknown source and that is never completely verified, from all its bits and pieces.

(Day 33)

Create a church from within, be the minister of its temple and that of, the very own soul. Go within, to a place of stillness(that is God) and let this message penetrate the being, like a flash of lightning.

LESSON~ 30: "EVERYTHING IS LIGHT AND IT IS FROM THIS STATE OF CONSCIOUSNESS TO REALIZE THESE TRUTHS AND PROFOUND EXPERIENCES."

The movement of the body and through stretching; it can be a great way to warm up and/or cool down, before a meditation.
Or with just the actual meditation, to connect with the bliss and center to the stillness; to create the space for such an openness of receiving. It can also be a way of projecting out the "doing-ness"; of self, through energizing and rebooting, for this day.

Today first thing, take a moment to go within the stillness of this place(possibly as God); to understand this force(before the hijacking of its light) and the self realization to its energy awareness(from source). Focus in the morning on raising the vibration and everything that the self intends for its day; it must be made aware of these effects on the brain. By tensing the muscles it activates the frontal lobe and lowers the stress hormones in the brain; it can lower the blood pressure and heart rate and it gets the mind prepared, for whatever it is, it needs to do. Exercises can charge the body with this, its universal light. Through this distribution of the energy; the self can electrocute for all diseases and areas of discomfort.

LESSON~ 30: "EVERYTHING IS LIGHT AND IT IS FROM THIS STATE OF CONSCIOUSNESS TO REALIZE THESE TRUTHS AND PROFOUND EXPERIENCES."

Practice meditating and with the awareness of creating the intention for the day: visualize and feel the very substantial decrease in the part of the brain; which normally helps to create a sense of self and that sense of orientation, of space and time. By progressively blocking the activity in that area, then the ability to establish a sense of self and as distinguished from the rest of the world, can be taken away. Go ahead and practice today; feeling that sense of de-connectedness and oneness, with the rest of the world.

The purpose of having to own up to, its inherently supernatural; physical, cosmic, mental and spiritual powers, through this thing called "self realization".

Combining the mental and spiritual forces together, is not about control; rather more about connection. Going back into the oneness and from before the disconnect, of external dangers; that it had thought and to believe it must survive, now can switch to thriving.

In this way a unified framework and approach to living, in a place, where everything is light.

The Sermon....Self realization and Remotely Viewing The agenda of the Soul:

Channeling in its true sense, is not from the fragmented pieces of its fractured soul, or mind(caused by trauma); rather the expression of consciousness, in its truest form, through the self.
Remote viewing, is the next upgraded level to self realization.
When the self can realize how to use receptivity with projection and to transmit the influence of its information; is then taking full responsibility and as the channeling entity.
The self can as the channel and nothing more or less(to add to its equation); to authentically further proceed and can quantum shift, as it desires to see, that of its world and/or self.
This requires a certain kind of harmony to co-exist and in the servicing externally; is to satisfy the self with firstly and for mostly the servicing of the self. Seek the heart of the self and that is to be willing to forgive; from all and every wrong doing, that it has ever experienced. Within its plasmic light, it can be revealed and from what the self has been seeking all along. This is what it means to truly understand the self and by looking at the faces of its world, to see thy self. Seek enlightenment for the sake of all beings; the purpose of service, is this love and what must be learned.
This will require a kind of energy, that resonates with self and that can actually change, how the many think and feel.
The master is the self and what it had been seeking; was to see without the lens, purely through its eyes.
This is the mystery of all that is blissfulness; because the world does not require, that it be served in anyway and rather than to serve itself.

The Sermon....Self realization and Remotely Viewing The agenda of the Soul:

The world does not need any help; because it does not require for any fixing. The world is perfect and when the self has finally found, what it was truly seeking for, was this, its inner watcher. With remote viewing, there is a process to evolve with and the touchy, feely senses, to hear, taste and smell....can participate and interact with the experience. The physical world is not the highest reality; just like when having a dream and it can feel, so incredibly real. Through the comparison, any other reality of physical existence; the self becomes convinced, that it was untouchable. As such, it was just a dream, lacking in solid awareness, to the touch and all the physical senses. When the self has gone through a mystical experience however, it can then begin to change its mind; in the what might be the ultimate reality, to these, its senses and convincing it, as more real, than the other two realities. To remotely view, practice training for the process to obtain such wisdom and in this way, the sight from within the self, can begin to reveal itself. Go ahead then and draw in the power from the ground and feel the connection to it. Sit straight or standing and with shoulder blades together; concentrate between the point between the eyebrows.

This is the center of thought, will and concentration; from here, anything the self does wish to reveal and it can think to call it out: for example, and the most basic to start off with is, "reveal thyself". In this way feel the joy from the wisdom and spiritual perception, again and again; celebrate the self by saying "reveal thyself". Sometimes the imagination can feel flat and then it is not in full connection to the higher self; rather to the lower little ego self and that requires praying, for an answer, that will never come.

It is this universal opportunity, given now to fully understand; intuitively the self and the relationship, with this divinity of infinite possibilities.

(Day 34)
The self does not have to undergo strict vows of celibacy, obedience and loyalty to simplify. When rechanneling the energy the self creates new patterning of thinking and new patterns of the emotional life. All the self thought of as importance will fall by the wayside; including for the co-dependencies of all addictions. Unlike suppression the transmutation from self-regenerating energy; is the entire concept in these words to decode through sound and breath today for this idea. No need for rules and the desire for all the vices, as they too eventually will simply fall away.

Lesson 31: "I AM INSPIRING AND CHANGING THE WORLD THROUGH MY WILL."

Life follows these grooves that the self has created in the brain; these are the deeper performance of an action created as a mental blueprint and causing the formation of subtle electrical path ways in the brain. Feel the energy with every breath descend and ascend from the base of the spine to the top of the head.
These instruments of divine perception must awaken in this way for enlightenment to happen. As the magnetics shift it will be felt a crackling expansion at the back base of the joining from the scull to the spine. Eventually the 3rd eye will come on line to connect this power of the energy(In the spine are these increments of higher perception and that are mostly dormant); however for now it is unconscious of being conscious.

Lesson 31: "I AM INSPIRING AND CHANGING THE WORLD THROUGH MY WILL."

Notice the difference today, between that of motivation and inspiration: while motivation can disable, inspiration does enable. Short term periods of motivation, can be fine from external forces and/or from the self, to its external.
The depleting of energy, becomes most prevalent and to show for the lack, when the balance is not there.

"TO FOCUSS ON MY BREATH THROUGH MEDITATION HELPS ME TO ACHIEVE GREAT CONCENTRATION POWER."

When there is a conflict from two vibrations, at different frequencies; that are unable to occupy a space and for extended periods of time. In many cases it will arise again, with the feeling of rejection or not fitting in. When one pulls from the other; so the feeling of becoming drained and has as the other, feeling energized. When the gap in vibration, is so high between two worlds; the only thing that can keep it in the kind of service forcibly and has maintained the worldly workable ethical saying "It's Just Business". The self does not have to struggle in this way and through forgiveness; it can give itself permission, to move on.
To something as inconceivable as thinking it could ever resemble its hijacker's manipulation; to be trained in such a way and made employable for its enslavement? This is the highway that has been devised through the infinite trailblazing self and to remember the difference that it is making for its world. Oppression and suppression has its way of showing up; where the value of this currency must be and by giving unwanted resistance, to the consumption of its energy, in this way. The many patterns of thought, that power up the program of these entities; to run deep enough into the groupings, to discover and allow to fall away.

Lesson 31: "I AM INSPIRING AND CHANGING THE WORLD THROUGH MY WILL."

The power struggle, is in the inability to see and understand the process of descending and ascending. This is who the self is capable of such openings and to the mysteries it never thought were possible; that it can truly be existing in, to function with as one. To descend into the many parts and that it must learn from; are forevermore rejecting to accept, it in their world and in the reality of incompletion, that too, the self it must accept.

"TO FOCUSS ON MY BREATH THROUGH MEDITATION HELPS ME TO ACHIEVE GREAT CONCENTRATION POWER."

In the losing of the self, seek to find these mysteries as non existing and what is left after the physical, is but the self to imagine it there. The self can go to sleep, within this state of being recharge and then, can stay awake for days.
Imagination is the energy, that the soul can feed upon and to reject the self from helping out a world, that was created by it; the self does not need its help, nor it, the help of it to change it from its very own imagination. And that it sometimes fears, to be the selective part in helping to micromanage in this way, the credits for its contribution. So much time it has reflected back to the owing of participation. That it may give it relevance and from this worthless thing called currency; that does not value it and as much, as to wish it destroyed, this, its maker. Realize that the will of self, can only be directed in this way, so it may not be rejected and give the cause for an effect; the struggle for resistance and that it might forever deprive it, in this way.

Lesson 31: "I AM INSPIRING AND CHANGING THE WORLD THROUGH MY WILL."

How is it, that the self can forever remove this lens, to overthrow the soul and be at one, with spiritual divinity? Is it a force, unlike any other? That it must reckon with, to always please; or it, back to it and in this way, of giving it meaning and relevance? This "Force" known as "Will", does it change thought into energy and is its power; as one of the absolute necessities, for spiritual progress?

"TO FOCUSS ON MY BREATH THROUGH MEDITATION HELPS ME TO ACHIEVE GREAT CONCENTRATION POWER."

The soul is the teacher and the self is the student. As the self is the teacher, so is the soul the student and forever mutually, they grow; to expand and by allowing more of the spiritual occupancy in this way. Through the limitations, the self can stretch out from these kind of stresses; to something more vastly and omnipresent. The spiritual path requires undoing these many aspects of the self. Through the soul interpretations, when it keeps falling for the temptations, of these charged energies and that mystify, or that it seeks, to learn from. With conflict of the wills, just remember the concept of imagination, is like faith; it must never be dismissed from the connection to this Higher self realization and that the "Ego mind", will struggle with.

The purpose of going into the inner thoughts and on the deepest level to dissect them. It takes much of what is felt with, as being unconditional love and from this learning, to detach from seriously overbearing hurt; that humanely cannot be possible to withstand and from any other way, than to detach as the observer.

The Sermon...Meditation/Opening the fields of Consciousness

Although prayer was discussed before, to hold a space and overlaps into forgiveness("permission to the self I give"); "giving-ness" that which is depicted, as beautifully transformed and from the previous ugly state of tyranny, is the blessing. Just like prayer, meditation too, is a communion; to bring into connection from all disconnected thoughts and feelings. Prayer is an extension of meditation; as the life force from the self, is focused on a regenerative act, to feed the nervous system and is this thing called meditation.

As mentioned before and within many yogic traditions; as basic as the spinal column and the skull, to breathe while consciously aware, of doing so. The kind of breathing and how it be regulated, as to fast, or slow, or deep, or shallow; from the mouth or from the nose and from which nostril; are some examples and that in there most of basic forms, can bring the self to many different states of being and within the practice of such disciplines. The spinal column has so many nerves, that irrigate it and connect it to the many other systems of the body; not just as the brain within the skull.

It can also be made to consider, in that of a Cabalistic way; as to perceive the body and in relation to a tree. Yet again and this perspective, like many other beliefs, words and hath hold in for every meaning; they too have been hijacked to distort and give corrupted meaning to. This is why all that must have the self thought as having any meaning, and from previous training, it must release; because it will not be able to co-exist within the Oneness and in any other way, with all that is, of innocence, made whole again.

The Sermon...Meditation/Opening the fields of Consciousness

Again, the chakra systems and as discussed in the beginning of these lessons; these branches of nerves and twigs, are irrigating from the nervous system, to the tendons and muscles.

To visualize all this, is yet another way of going into meditation and from deep into the earth, up from the sciatic nerve from the legs and where the tailbone meets, to find the psoas muscle. Another way, was mentioned as before and with stretching, as for example; the psoas muscle as it is made useful, to strengthen the sacral chakra area. This movement of breath and body stretching, has become a very popular art with yoga; as well as with the movement of "Tai Chi" of this energy from life force. Meditation is considered to be and just as the tree connects with roots, into the unseen world. So too the self resembles in the oneness with the earth; connected by its very nature, from this awareness to expand and able to hold more space.

The significance of "Roots and Wings", is further mentioned in the book and again for the reader, to ponder on this paradigm. One big nervous system, that the self must breathe in and out the life force, from its vertebrae. The spinal column holds this center; that the heart and lungs must pump, to be channeled through this irrigated system. Into the muscles and from there to the capillaries; to loop around again, transmuting from oxygen to carbon dioxide and back out, for the trees to harvest from.

The nerve endings hold the soul in place and to experience this energy in motion, for the self to then interpret, into sensation. This is the concept of revitalization, from the living waters and that channel out; from every vertebrae of the spine, the nervous system in its place and for the self to contemplate, the breath of its awareness. Opening the fields of consciousness; this is the purpose of meditation .

(Day 35) The conscious expansion will happen, when the trauma can be released and all this energy transmuted; from there to change the DNA "vibrationally", that other strands can come on line and hold more space, for more energy. The electrical charge of the earth, is also undergoing changes; it is affecting the way things are attracted to it and more debris is being pulled towards her, such as in the case of meteors. The same magnetics of awareness co-exists with the self, experiencing life in this way and naturally with her. Realize this possibility, of having a more spiritual and wider range connection, with the physical today.

LESSON~32: "WHEN I REMOVE THE FILTERS OF THE MANY COLOURED LENSES I AM ABLE TO SEE DIRECTLY FROM THE PUREST LIGHT."

This is a vibrational universe, where everything is a vibration of energy and when a lower and slower vibration is introduced to a higher faster one; the result is, a slowing of the faster vibration to the non physical of eternal self that holds a very high vibration. When the self holds a thought, or focuses on something which holds a lower vibration, resistance is created and from that true self, the resistance to have it flowing from it, in this way and into its physical existence/awareness. The self becomes resistant to this energy; which the soul is forcing through and down to lower awareness. Surging through into a unit of well being and only from the existence of well being, that it can experience this state(lower mind must allow it to come through and without any contradicting beliefs to resist from accepting it). The "Ego mind" might be preventing the flow of energy; because of some screwy criteria the world around it has going on, and will feel the push/pull discomfort of it.

LESSON~32: "WHEN I REMOVE THE FILTERS OF THE MANY COLOURED LENSES I AM ABLE TO SEE DIRECTLY FROM THE PUREST LIGHT."

Practice to create a loving space, within the self; this will allow for loving energy, to fill it and in this way, the miracles will appear, with precision. The non physical eternal self, reveals through the soul and to a temporary physical self perspective; that which it is ready to perceive. When it is not, a resistance will take place and the soul will always challenge it, to grow in this way. Finding the vibrational harmony, is the experience and that this lesson will ideally wish for the self, to take up the opportunity. With energetic transformation: The soul knows the spiritual purpose, that the self as temporary physical entity, has to achieve and reason for its existence; as it reveals to it, each time, stretching the boundaries even more and for its awareness to be challenged in this way. The soul too, has a mind and that is to work behind the scenes; to transmute the "Ego mind" and raise it to a much higher level, in its evolution.

The soul's mind works its magic, to ultimately integrate and transform its personality and in order to reach enlightenment. Find something to focus on that will help to find this alignment and that the self can find, its authenticity and be itself.

When the self, can be itself, the outside world will challenge it and by not accepting it for being different. Resistance however, will always find a way to challenge the self into alignment.

The self can try, real hard to go and be in the basement, to fit in with that reality; but when the elevator opens to the second floor, how can that be made possible, to hold such expectations?

With little or no cooperation of interest; these lessons have been fairly casual and in the practice of their exercises.

Very carefully planned, for the purpose to have sight and on the reversal of the way the mind thinks.

LESSON~32: "WHEN I REMOVE THE FILTERS OF THE MANY COLOURED LENSES I AM ABLE TO SEE DIRECTLY FROM THE PUREST LIGHT."

To remove the lens barrier and that reinterprets sight, for the betterment of the world. The feeling of resentment and to oppose such thoughts, that might be of manipulation; however in the midst of introducing structure, some pressure can be the experience. Boundaries to help distinguish, the variations of emotions such as: sorrow, pleasure; pain; love; joy and with a little practice, the deliverance, toward finding peace and happiness. How rewarding it can be, to learn to decipher and from vision, all that is preferred. Make no mistake to think, that this goal is of little worth and rather to indicate, the deliverance from a trivial purpose. With self at the helm, to evolve so it be not so trivial and for the rest of the world to do the same. For this purpose, the infinite, in all that is of oneness, to resurrect life and yet again, another level closer, to all that is brilliant self. Heaven is a place of mind, made free of harm to go and yet the stumbling over the blinded self; rather overlooks to find outside of it's very own existence. For this reason to imply, seeing in the way the mind has allowed; the self to see, is not to see at all. Repeat this idea and by stating to help encourage the mind; in this way to change the present state, for a better one. Say this affirmation slowly, with feelings of positivity and for any subject or situation, that might be and/or an event, of any upset; at least every half hour, throughout the day. This kind of attention to operate in the world and to bring about a difference, to see instead; that of what it is preferred, is the "Law of Cause and Effect".

The purpose, like always in this way duality dissolves and self can finally come into oneness and that from its own likeness; rather than the opposite and many other different colours, of the variation, from what it does prefer.

(Day 36) The only thing possible of penetrating through "invulnerability" and "vulnerability", is the mind's thoughts. It is the thoughts, that can create, the feeling of being vulnerable and the thoughts, that can attack; as well as prove to the contrary, this is not so. In this case, anger is projected onto the world and now the perceived vengeance, from its very own imagination, is about to strike it back. Moving out of this cycle, requires a change in perception .

LESSON~33: "I AM SEEING A FRACTURED WORLD BECAUSE MY THOUGHTS ARE SEEKING VENGEANCE ON MY INVULNERABILITIES."

A fractured mind, cannot possibly conceive and/or from its fractured soul, the concept of oneness; it takes time to fully understand and by experiencing from every facet, the traumatic splitting off of energies. Descriptive pockets, such as vengeance or regret; guilt; bitterness; anger and remorse.
To understand duality and from every perceivable point of view, as possible. These innumerable and procreative, karmic sparks, had also contractually created diversity; having made the difference, to the one expansion and through these variable contractions. The dispersed electricity, became the universe and from the one self, having the experience; working on these power struggles and through the healing of its traumas. The feeling of being the victim, must compensate with and the power to feel as the perpetrator; from the justice and/or vengeance, that it seeks out balance. Or how about, the experience of being the enabler and/or the witness, as before and in previous lessons. All of this and at its many levels, is from the oneness of infinite creator, having simultaneously for this experience. As a Perpetrator and seeking out for justice; the trauma must be dealt with, from when it was a victim .

LESSON~33: "I AM SEEING A FRACTURED WORLD BECAUSE MY THOUGHTS ARE SEEKING VENGEANCE ON MY INVULNERABILITIES."

Today, take a moment to feel and where the self has felt: injustice and unfair treatment; and/or, where there was, no other way, but to seek out for revenge. Find a way to re-experience that trauma and then re-experience it, as the perpetrator.

Everything that self is lead to believe and that of hate; to feel the want to attack and kill, is but a survival and stressed out mechanism. The self can awaken from the mind's fantasy and by taking responsibility over the projector. To describe the way anyone feels, from the thoughts that are held and to project onto the world, perceived by them, is the idea for today. The preoccupation of attack thoughts and counter attack ones, can become an endless cycle of tyranny.

Hold this idea and then with eyes closed; review some unresolved questions and to outcomes that have caused those certain emotions. Stay on these feelings, following for a few minutes, or less and to attempt for each practice; sample it throughout the day, for about 6 times.

Recurring problems, to preoccupy with and that feel unsettling during the day; are best suited to use, with the following example:

" I AM PRE-OCCUPIED ON HAVING MORE CONTROL OF/ABOUT _____."

Go over every possibility that can occur, with this connection and in reference to each disconnect; use the following template, to further specify with:

"I AM INSECURE ABOUT _____ AND WHAT MIGHT HAPPEN."

LESSON~33: "I AM SEEING A FRACTURED WORLD BECAUSE MY THOUGHTS ARE SEEKING VENGEANCE ON MY INVULNERABILITIES."

With the longer practice this idea, on what emotions are coming up, from as a perpetrator and then go back to find, the emotions that come up for, as the victim. Then as a witness to the experience, take a step back, to mindfully reassess again.
This can be made easy, by taking a journal and perhaps going over it; or writing it down and then at the end of the day, coming back to it and from a disembodied state, to witness it again. Watch it like it is played out, like a movie and feel the energy disperse, into a lighter state of being. Maybe it will take more than this, one days lesson to achieve and the idea of writing it down; it can very much help to go back to it, until it can properly become dissolved and transmuted back to light.

For the shorter practices, watch how they might relate and the underlying belief; that might have had to do with a previous trauma, branching out and to give or take, 5 to 6 distressing possibilities. Possibly even more and that can be made available, for each situation, when properly applied.
Make the attempt to cover a few situations very well; rather than just to touch briefly with a larger number. For each situation's anticipated outcomes, some, especially at the bottom of the list and might be less desirable. After every exercise, close it off with this following affirmation:

"THAT THOUGHT WAS MEANT TO SABOTAGE ME."

The purpose of this lesson, is to change the mind and to realize, that projection can become, that of Love; clear away from all its many distortions and to become more aware of, how thoughts can create feelings from emotions.

THE INTERMISSION :

Take 2 days to take it in

CONGRATULATIONS ...!!!

FOR MAKING IT

THROUGH THE 33rd Lesson

(This is a rest period to take the lessons independently as a review)

TAKE THESE TWO DAYS TO RECALIBRATE;

MAKE NOTES AND REVIEW..................

(Day 39) "To escape", is in response to(resistance)the way the previous book(A C I M)could express, the meaning of surrender. "Where there is relief, surrender can only be truly found and when releasing from resistance; because there really is not such a thing, as to escape from anything".

LESSON~34: "I SURRENDER TO COMPLETE SELF TRUST AND THAT ANYTHING OTHER IS IN COMPLETE DISILLUSIONMENT."

Do not feel sorry for the world then; rather it is these thoughts that must be omitted. When the cause of the world is of attack thoughts; then self might picture everything symbolizing vengeance, of the "external reality". This hallucination, is the world that the self has created and yet, it does not see itself, as the creator of it. The little "Egoic" self perspective, cannot possibly look to find relief, by its creation; rather only to escape from it. To accept from its caused effect, as creator and not victim; is where the self can find relief and in the knowing it has learned, a new vision to replace it with. Transformation is the change and to introduce this concept; that the self can never be trapped in what it sees. Today's thought is all about helping the mind to see, so it never feels trapped, with its external circumstances. Something made of hate, can be transformed and into something made of compassion, as the images become lighter. With the first couple of steps, cooperation is needed and with the final one, of this process, it does not. Use this idea throughout the day, whenever the feeling is there and at least 5 times, to practice over. With whatever is there, to look at around the area, be vocal with this idea and repeat it slowly first.
Then with eyes shut, take about a minute and to search for as many confrontational thoughts, the mind has in store, to attack itself with.

LESSON~34: "PLEASING ANYTHING OTHER THAN MYSELF CREATES UNMET EXPECTATIONS FOR MY OWN BEST INTERESTS IN RETURN."

As each thought is encountered, use the following template reaffirm with:

"I CAN LIGHTEN UP FROM THE WITNESSING OF AN OFFENSIVE WORLD BY LEAVING BEHIND THIS THOUGHT _____."

Hold each thought of being attacked and/or attacking; then release it and go on to the next one, and do the same to reaffirm.

The purpose is to shift from feeling offended and into the preparation of accepting to forgive.

How many different outcomes (directly related or not) can honestly occur and from any given situation?

The exercises for today, are to help recognize the large number of demands and from situations, that have nothing to even do with them. Some of the goals might be found, as a contradiction and with no complete outcome in mind; however inevitable for disappointment and in connection to the situation.
When the perception is distorted; how could it be possible, to realize the outcome of a situation and that is a happy one?
Unable to serve in a situation and for the best interest of the goal; the actions are determined, by a guideless perception.
This goal however, is accurately perceived; because it could not be possible, to understand it otherwise.

The exercise requires an honest approach, in truthfully seeking out carefully, just a few subjects. Practice a few times, throughout the day; taking into consideration, but a few and for not any longer than 70 seconds, roughly to search the mind.

LESSON~34: "PLEASING ANYTHING OTHER THAN MYSELF CREATES UNMET EXPECTATIONS FOR MY OWN BEST INTERESTS IN RETURN."

Start by repeating today's idea, then search the mind and for unresolved current situations(close eyes).

Focus on the outcome desired, notice how many more goals and different levels of them there are, in mind and as well as often to conflict with. Name each situation that occurs, with goals carefully selected and as many as possible, for a resolution. Use the following template, to help in formulating this process:

"IN THE SITUATION INVOLVING_____, I WOULD LIKE_____
TO HAPPEN, AND_____TO HAPPEN, AND SO ON."

After going over as many goals, aspired to as possible and that arise in the mind, of a situation not resolved, say the following affirmation:

"I DO NOT PERCEIVE MY OWN BEST INTERESTS IN THIS SITUATION."

"and go on to the next one"

The purpose of this idea, is to get the mind to open enough, so it can learn.

To think to know something, makes it impossible to learn. Without any real expectations, the self can be taught, what its best interests are.

(Day 40) Once the thoughts change, the impact is automatic. To better understand perspective, is to have discernment; wisdom can perceive from its existence and from the other tree, the knowledge of such tools, to work with. The world is incapable of change, because it is an effect.

LESSON~35: "I DO NOT UNDERSTAND THE USEFULNESS FROM THESE CREATIONS."

The mind in its devaluation, discriminately chooses to believe it costs too much, to afford for this peace and yet the cause is worth changing. To change the perception of the world; it is the mind that needs working on its thoughts. Today, rather than not really seeing the need for all of this; look closer to see in it and the entire exchange of separation for freedom. Do not disprove, by denying this reality and grant everything that seems to stand between the self and the many other selves; likewise these many slivers, that make up the one and almighty presence, that is self. Be willing then to have it taken from the many; to be replaced with truth and as self will see this change in the many, so too, it will be given back to see in thyself. The following affirmations, will help to break up, some of the older patents, be vocal and believe in this liberation:

" I AM RESPONSIBLE FOR WHAT I SEE."

" I CHOOSE THE FEELINGS I EXPERIENCE, AND I DECIDE UPON THE GOAL I WOULD ACHIEVE."

" EVERYTHING THAT SEEMS TO HAPPEN TO ME, I HAVE ASKED FOR, AND I RECEIVE IT IN THE WAY THAT I AM READY TO ACCEPT IT."

LESSON~35: "I DO NOT UNDERSTAND THE USEFULNESS FROM THESE CREATIONS."

To rely completely upon the madness of an outside creator; will change nothing in creation, to serve or justify this madness. As with from the many who are lead to believe with self, the world they have created and by denying all of creation.

The face of affliction, is only but a mask of victimhood; that only be removed and that was mistaken as an idle witness, to be right and it is no longer rightly so, befitting it. This world, now seen as insane, was a declaration, trained by self and now a reflection; convincing enough, that what it saw, was true.

When the many think the world was made and with self to include; this self hath made the many, thus denying, they made anything at all. Without this understanding, all that self creates, are meaningless; the self must rectify it, through respect and acceptance and it will disappear.

To have meaning, there must be a purpose and for this reason, nothing that can be seen, has any meaning; until the purpose becomes for the self's own best interest.

Within the universe, there is no such thing as, by chance or accident; because they are made from self, as the creator being and in asking for them, they appear.

This is the little gift of power, to help liberate from each and every level; that derives within source to find self sovereignty.

(Day 41) Now that its source has been uncovered, the instant release has come and all the effects are gone. It is this belief of independence and from its source, that keeps the "being-ness" as prisoner. It is from the same thinking and that has kept the self away from source; in isolation and flipping it around, to feel the reverse in effect and yet it never left.

LESSON~36: "MY AWARENESS IS OMNIPRESENT."

The desire to create, one's own creator; to be the parent and not the child, is one in the same desire. The child(co-creator), is the "effect, whose cause it would deny; as such, appears to be the cause, producing real effects. Nothing can have an effect, without a cause, and to confuse the two, is a misunderstanding of both.

To realize that the self was not created by it and could only be responsible, for creating the world it sees. Nothing created by the creation of self, has any influence over this self it created; similar to its creations, it cannot tell the self, how to feel and see, nor how to place thyself, in its ability to do so. Do not deny nature, by thinking self has created her and thus the template of its temple.

A natural creation expressed from the tree of life; as genetic imprint for the self, it too can once again decode. As awakened into its own distinct expression and from this dream, it formed into existence. The world that self created, has equally no power to make of itself, what it wills. The splitting off came from somewhere and as to confuse the co-creator from the creator; child and parent are one in the same. When this celebration did occur from primordial substance, the holiest of births; is where the self did come from and could not possibly have happened in the reverse order, nor of any other way. The union with this principle, is at the source of creating and without misleading the self further; it is independent with its creations in this way. Confusion is the resistance to vision from cause and effect.

LESSON~36: "MY AWARENESS IS OMNIPRESENT."

To conceal the cause and effect, by making the effect appear to be the cause; gives it authority, to stand alone, serving as the cause for the events and feelings, the creator self, thinks it causes. The fear of loss, might linger around further and to require for yet another piece to add, to this previous affirmation such as:

"THIS VISION HAS NO COST TO ANYONE."

"MY AWARENESS IS OMNIPRESENT."

To further expand the idea, from previous a concept and far beyond translation, is this spark within everything.
The presence of this energy, it comes in many forms and is the impact of all creation, living and non living the same.
Electric and magnetic, both and everything in between; does explain the purpose to see that nothing can ever be separate, by itself or in itself and/or as well have any meaning.
Whether it is seen, or not, everything vibrates and this is where the entire reason for vision rests. Whether it has explained the Infinite and in the faith of all that can be possible; however all that has been practiced from before(the rest of the ones to come, from these lessons). The entire reason for vision, is in this idea formulated as God. As perplexed the concept to grasp that this force, might be in every object; such as a chair, or a table and might seem downright silly and objectionable. It was certainly emphasized as before and, for any subject/object given; shares the purpose of the universe and that whatever shares the purpose of the universe, shares the purpose of its creator.
All matter formless, or with form, organic and inorganic alike; look at them all with "Love", Appreciation" and "Open-mindedness". In this true sense, would it be known and to what is really in them; because nothing is, as it appears to be.

LESSON~36: "MY AWARENESS IS OMNIPRESENT."

When vision reveals this energized way, that lights up the world and only then can it be realized, of this too, in self's illumination. Following this familiar pattern and by repeating today's affirmation firstly.

" THE VASTNESS OF PERSPECTIVE CAN HOLD MORE ENERGY FOR MY PERCEPTION AND I CAN GRASP A WIDER RANGE WITH DEPTH OF TONE."

The purpose is, to understand that God is energy, given from perspective and that inside every formation; this force be it outside alike and without any form too. Always in the making is this infinite potential; from what was made and can shift again.
Divine presence and from it, all that is of love; and that can ever be understood as energy from source and that of consciousness.
All that is made up of energy is God.

Perhaps this exercise too, is for the experiencing of a sense of restfulness; at least once or twice while doing this.

(Day 42)
To further develop the meaning of cause and effect from the previous invented non-victim of the world notion; the inner and outer are one in the same. The world can be seen or not, as desired and can be given up, as easily, as it was made.

LESSON~37: "MY PERSPECTIVE IS THE INNOVATOR OF MY PERCEIVED WORLD."

When the self wishes to exist in a consensus reality; it will give the illusion, by splitting off from itself and to be for the benefit of never having to feel, that it is alone in this world. With this agreement, it chooses to co-create and with all the other many parts, of the many in its world. All these sparks of the same infinite awareness, that exists as immortal. Expanding and evolving from these other sparks of contradictions and that parallel the oneness, to reflect back, in its awareness.

Take a moment right now(to sample), with a few deep breaths to still the mind; let the eyelids drop and just imagine: With heart and soul connecting, with the feeling of looking at a loving master and elevated from this blissfulness. Can it be ready to invoke and open all the doors, that set these energies in motion ? Telepathically as one, interfacing with emotions; like a gust of cool clean air, from a heated room and with all the doors closed, can it feel the calmness of this cooling, pure loving bliss?

Since this separation is made to distinguish, between the world outside the self and the other, that is seen in the mind.

Take a moment and practice, for once in the morning and evening; two or three times(vocally to repeat the idea);

what is the experience that self is taking in from its world today? With eyes open and then with eyes closed, to look inside.

As the images present themselves, from the imagination, to the awareness; be certain to treat both worlds equally.

LESSON~37:
"MY PERSPECTIVE IS THE INNOVATOR OF MY PERCEIVED WORLD."

How could it have been done differently and if so; how would that feel and why is it that it was seen in this way, to feel this way?
Is there another way of going about it and looking at it differently, how has the experience changed; from the perspective to see and feel it differently?
It could be made of benefit and when faced with a distressful circumstance; throughout the day, to make further use with the following affirmation:

"THIS IS A STORY OF MY OWN INVENTION TO PERCEIVE THE SITUATION IN THIS WAY"

"I AM THE AUTHOR OF MY OWN STORIES AND CAN CHANGE THE WAY I SEE THIS _____SITUATION/PLACE/SUBJECT....

Yes the external feelings, that bounce around emotions and like chaos in a room, as once imagined for the self to understand; that it might not be entirely felt, as it is perceived or thought about. Transformation does not come from imparting knowledge; it comes from changing behaviour.
The purpose for today, is to introduce the thought that both (inner and outer) are from the imagination.

(Day 43) To introduce an oath; rather an affirmation and for the purpose of release, is this idea for today. To find escape from the inner world; that is the cause made for the outer, is to find escape from both. This affirmation does make certain, not to yield to it, so to be placed in bondage.

LESSON~38: " WHEN MY HEART IS OPEN ALL CO-DEPENDENCIES CAN LEAVE THIS WORLD THAT I ONCE SAW MYSELF AS HELPLESS IN."

This exercise includes of frequent applications, throughout the day and one that is more on a sustained basis.
Make certain to practice this idea, to what is outside the self observable and with eyes open; what is observable from within, when eyes are closed. Look around and slowly reaffirm for this idea, a few times and then with eyes closed do the same.

Two longer periods, of three to five minutes to practice first thing in the morning and before going to sleep at night.
Study the inner world with whatever thoughts appear to come through the mind's awareness for that moment, do consider them and then replace by the next. Watch them come, by not binding a hierarchy to them and to passionately ascertain with. Like a stream, making its way through the pebbles evenly, do so calmly and with no real investment. Sitting quietly with these thoughts and no real sense of hurry, repeat today's idea and as often as the interest is there, for it. As often as to care, to remember; particularly useful and as a response to any temptation of this kind, that may arise throughout the day.

The purpose of this exercise, is to help with self-sovereignty.

(Day 44) Everything is made from inner and outer space.

From the anti-matter component & dark matter light/Source; can also be found within the spaces, in between the red blood cells(a current of black lighted blood cells). From this, all light(information) is formed and into the white light, where all form is developed.

LESSON~39:
"ANOTHER WAY OF SEEING IS, THROUGH SOURCE."

Examine the backdrop, casually that the self is surrounded by; then with eyes closed, appraise with equal approach, the mind's inner thoughts. How is it that these thoughts run interference, with its goals? Focus on the breathing: by breathing in shorter counts, than breathing out to hold it longer in; the self can then ease into a rhythm of deeper breaths in(deeper breathing). Where dark-matter and matter do meet, an anti-matter component can easily destroy; as well as create and where resistance can have its release. Then the self can envision things, before they happen and within the dark matter. It is from this dark translucent field, and/or radiance, that the process of the magnetic and electric component happen; from the third eye extra sensory perception and that co-operatively is enriched, to operate with faith.

Un-abrasively feeling the shift from outer, to inner observations; make use of this idea, throughout the day and especially when feeling distress. From these several unhurried applications; take a moment to make two longer ones, for the morning and evening. What happens when the serotonin and melatonin are released? All these stresses become so irrelevant and to the vastness from the inner self. Take the time to feel and go over as many ripples of resistances, that self can handle; combine it with the focus and on the goals that the self has set in place for itself.

How is it, that they are, but from one source and rooted cause?

LESSON~39:
"ANOTHER WAY OF SEEING IS, THROUGH SOURCE."

For the shorter exercises and that are triggered by uneasy situations, apply the following affirmation:

"THERE IS ANOTHER WAY OF LOOKING AT THIS FROM WITHIN."

When the resistance subsides, the vision becomes clearer and only after, getting past the fear. This might require some repetitions, to say; by taking a few minutes, to sit in silence and with eyes closed.

The purpose is, to become aware of the ability to shift from both outer and inner aspects of perception and that of what can create, is also capable of destroying.

When (anti-matter & matter) they come together, energy is released and transmuted; potentially it can then be transformed into something else and with this purpose, force is better understood.

THE INTERMISSION :

Take a day to take it in

CONGRATULATIONS ...!!!

FOR MAKING IT

THROUGH TO THE 39th Lesson

(This is a rest period to take the lessons independently as a review)

TAKE THIS DAY TO RECALIBRATE;

MAKE NOTES AND REVIEW.................

(Day 46)
As discussed from previously and leaving off from the purpose of understanding "Life Force". From the heart's electro magnetic(space) and that of the outer Ethereal field;
there is a difference between spirit(the 12 strand DNA retrieval) and that of soul.

Lesson~40: "THE EYES ARE THE WINDOW INTO MY SOUL."

The (kundalini) life force(winding up in 3 fold) shooting up and spirit can awaken; is this process to starting up and by helping to ignite a full body awakening. The rebalancing, transmuting, aligning, and activating to a deeper sense of its divinity.
With it, as well and by moving more multi-dimensionally; however the self must accept the soul of what and who it is and this is where it differs. To find its authenticity and within the merging of the oneness; as a light body being and Sovereign, it must require the integration, as well as understand the self.
The many might have already experienced an awakening and even the self too, having many awakenings....but the core programming did not change much at all.
That is where the soul must start erasing its recordings; however the perspective can only change, when the soul can be impressed upon and in this way, to start to clear from this lens, that self sees through. This idea to surrender, had become distorted and was the reason for too many a sacrifice; when giving up itself to be imposed with external forces, helpless and tied up(to these kind of conditions). Once the Self has awakened, it is left with itself, as it is and must learn more about its intentions and that of loving unconditionally. The DNA strands when on line bring an incredible, vastly advanced spiritually and aware entity of "being-ness". The process to enlightenment, is through the awakening of these many strands.

Lesson~40:
"THE EYES ARE THE WINDOW INTO MY SOUL."

Once they come on line, the self can have more bandwidth and to accept more spirit in; it can take more of spirit(higher frequency) and to that extent, it will vibrate with excitement. From the beginning, it was always an effort to regain and what was rightfully as inherited by birth; however it was through trickery and/or con that it was given away. The self that had to previously compromise, in order to participate within a world, from such said agreements and that it had known, well before coming into this awareness, of existence. These were the many contracts, that it had agreed with soul, to come and play out and learn, as well as teach. This is something in the field, very closely outside of the physical body and found within the ethereal, as well as, within every cell; that self had to integrate from within and before expanding outwardly, as a white lighted being. The soul was always present in the body, but what it lacked, was the integration of the masculine and feminine; it was in this splitting off, into a duality that requires integration.

It was mentioned earlier in lesson 5 and 8, about the soul and puberty. In lesson 5 the soul was, for the self in this moment and like always would feel it (8th chakra)seated between the shoulder blades; where the spine can feel erect, or feeling as the self slouched over. From that place of seated (8th chakra)soul, the self can have an indication and just how well it feels(or maybe that sensation of where its tiredness, can firstly be spotted) accordingly from there and leading upward, toward the skull. Although the chant musn't be discounted; because along with its idea to surrender, it is a serenity, for both realities. This lesson does go back a step and before the "High Heart" activation. When the soul was only in a masculine and ego driven state of consciousness; it walked the path of one sidedness, with the "Yang Chi" energy and for the majority, it was the necessary fact of life (the patriarchal masculine).

Lesson~40:
"THE EYES ARE THE WINDOW INTO MY SOUL."

The soul was responsible, for life force; because of the cord that had connected it and from this belly button. It was not so, over the heart and rather sat in that part of the belly button. From the lower region of the belly and like a (elongated-egg-like) *SPHEROID;* to taper off and at where just about the heart would start. Not a cyan colour; rather held this memory, of a bluish rounded ozone on its sides and with white around the pointless edges (almost like a white frame of a photograph). It was not intended as a practice; however the self might want to have a recall on what exactly it had done.

With eyes closed, it was in a state of taking itself from crying, to laughing(intense disciplined breathing) and from that in-between, of shifting state; there was a certain kind of force it felt.

With eyes rolled upward and clenching eyelid muscles down and inward; it started to release and then look down and there it saw, the upper portion of this light and beyond it was this ozone. From this light of "Infinite Grace" all the intense anger can become dissolved and many different things can happen to the awakened self.

The awareness of its thought body and as such;(the activation of its 1st level into Buddhahood)that of the soul in its body to uncover its pre-written story(akashic /monad/ethereal records). The organic brain accepts that and allows the soul to communicate through the chemical and electronic pathways, of the body. Within the previous (5and8) lessons; the soul already had ascended and it was from that point of reference, known as the feminine path(Yin chi, energy connection; that this book had taken into its account). In both cases and in these states, without the soul, the physical body would just fall to the ground, to be pronounced for dead. It was from this reference point, that the activation and/or what might be understood as active; could then interpret as the brain and from in the body, to accept who and what it really is.

Lesson~40: "THE EYES ARE THE WINDOW INTO MY SOUL."

Take some time, to now consider and throughout the day, the following affirmation:

"WHO AM I AND WHAT AM I."

As discussed before and after a certain age, the organs of the glands start to shrink during puberty and the 8th chakra is; well it just drops and the soul descends, into below the heart and in between the belly button. After the mind accepts itself, then it can again rise up, between the upper part of the heart and throat. Let the self take a moment to become alerted to this reality and of such a thought for today's idea. To trust and surrender into the integration of the masculine and feminine; it is the only way of evolving and into a sovereign light being. It is from this integration, that the oneness can exist and from the merging of the two; the creator God being is birthed into awareness. The concept of duality, is this original split; that had as cause effected for adversity, the concept of diversity and comparison, from which it could expand and further evolve.
At this level, it must process through it and by once more, accepting it into the feminine. How active is the world and when the self throughout the day, looks directly in the eyes of every single soul it comes in contact with? Look through these eyes, that the many of the self will present as real; from this combination, organic brain and energy can grasp, to open up and impress the self with, from this experience. How has it made the self feel and what was in the attraction, for every energetic interaction?
When the heart can open up, to know the soul that enters through it; the lens and this perspective, can reveal to understanding "descension" and "ascension".

Lesson~40: "THE EYES ARE THE WINDOW INTO MY SOUL."

Eventually the integration of the self, will no longer reflect the opposite nor in its variation; rather that of which it prefers to create and that will depend upon the clearing of the soul's entirety. No longer will there be so much a difference; as to compare one life time from the other. Just like the boundaries of these membranes, from all the chakras and they too will dissolve and become more fluid. When uniting the inner and the outer worlds, including that of soul and right to the very strands of DNA to structure it and spirit of the self; from many lifetimes will be as one. Within the oneness, expressing and perceiving from this vastness of perspective; in its truest authenticity, that is the "Sovereign light" of self. The difference to compare and separate so to understand itself ; this will no longer as much to say, that it could be of any service? This will continually be of its choice to make; to play from and to experience, as it so desires and from the perspective of whatever lens, it wants to experience as soul. Although some information could be overlapping into nonsensical; the purpose of this lesson, was to further help the self and through the integration process.

For the self to awaken and become liberated, a root change must happen; the self must remember its purpose and with it, the intention to love unconditionally.

(Day 47)

Affirmations are only as good as the self can truly connect and with its very own authenticity, of being to them. Therefore when it does not resonate, change the examples and into what can best relate with it and the day's idea of discussion.

LESSON~41: "WHEN MY HEART IS TRULY AND COMPLETELY OPEN I BECOME UNHURTABLE."

Certain emotions like to attach themselves to thoughts; these thoughts that are charged up with emotion, give rise the meaning for feelings. To find peace, is this other way of seeing and within the mind; to allow for deeply, as the thoughts to travel and then extend back outwardly. This state of being does also include a way for feelings to find a calm place and where in between the thoughts, is found this stillness. It is the inner world and for today's purpose to work on, with eyes closed. Take a few minutes throughout the day, before and or after breakfast, lunch and dinner, to apply this idea. Rather than trying to search the mind proactively, relax into receptive mode and for the mind to seek them out. Take note of what comes up to surface, involving unloving thoughts; such as: "anxiety-provoking situations"; "offending personalities/or events"; whilst giving attention to what the mind does bring up and to verbalize the affirmation. When the peace of mind feels threatened throughout the day; make space in between and along with the three practices, to include for more frequent shorter applications. Whenever the need is there, the following affirmation can be helpful:

"ONLY WHEN ALL THE HURT IS WAIVED OFF

I CAN BEGIN TO SEE THE PEACE IN EVERY SITUATION RATHER THAN WHAT I NOW SEE IN IT."

For more in-pressed emotions to generalize such as depression, anxiety and/or worry make use of the original idea.

LESSON~41: "WHEN MY HEART IS TRULY AND COMPLETELY OPEN I BECOME UNHURTABLE."

Take a few minutes to devote to this idea, repetitively until the sense of relief is felt. The following (straight out of the book) template to bespoke in its design and for further assistance to create for "add-ons":

" I CAN REPLACE MY FEELINGS OF DEPRESSION, ANXIETY OR WORRY

[or my thoughts about this situation, personality or event]

WITH PEACE."

To convince the self that it has already found peace and/or simply the purpose to let peace find you.

(Day 48)

To establish self coherence with the Infinite's expression transcends beyond linear interpretation; however inspired self to think from a Holy state is this feeling to which thought can find comfort.

LESSON~42:

"WHEN I CAN HOLD ON TO THE IMAGES OF MY DREAMS THERE IS NOTHING OTHER THAN ILLUSION THAT WILL TRY TO STOP ME."

Within a multi-dimensional awareness and to impress upon the focus of the mind; that it can turn every dream, into reality.
At first every reality is an illusion; however what has already been and how long it has taken for it to manifest, is the difference that it makes to self. When the self has changed perspective, it might not like what it sees of its world; as lesser evolved or slightly shifted and from the very alignment that it holds right now.
A miracle, is the ability for the self, to be almost there and with what it wants to happen; in that moment and as a gift that it can accept it, in this way. To actually and size it up with it; as to believe it there and that it can deserve it. The encouragement to overpower and dissolve for any foreseeable discouragement. Unlimited is this power to manifest and through its very own acceptance, of this being; as a sense of the word and from the Holiness, it must come from. Today take all of life's misalignments, difficulties and distortions of the world; in relation to the same struggles of twisted form the mind can think of. Take four long practices and with a full five minutes each.

LESSON~42:

"WHEN I CAN HOLD ON TO THE IMAGES OF MY DREAMS THERE IS NOTHING OTHER THAN ILLUSION THAT WILL TRY TO STOP ME."

With eyes closed, make no distinctions and while searching the mind, to find unhappiness of any kind. Again, with very little distinction between a personal challenging situation and one that is of someone else's. Identify the specifics of the story and names that concern it and with the following template from the book as a guide:

"IN THE SITUATION INVOLVING_____IN WHICH I SEE MYSELF, THERE IS DISILLUSIONMENT."

Can the off-balance be detected?...Just feel for the discomfort.....

"THERE IS NOTHING MY INTENTION CAN NOT DO BECAUSE
THE POWER OF MY FOCUS LIES WITHIN IT."

Whatever variations are of interest can be introduced however they must be focused on the theme of :

"FOCUSSING ON THE IMAGES OF MY DREAMS WITH INTENTION."

The purpose for these exercises, is to instill a sense of sovereignty between the self and all things.

(Day49)

The mind in its complexity to think it knows, overlooks itself with theory; because it cannot give what it does not have.
To hesitate for a response and place it in its practice; is so believable of this uncertainty, to compete and with its many separations, is this vulnerability. The reflection is in the minions of enslavement and in becoming more believable; to undermine its value and with great depreciation.

LESSON~43: "I BELIEVE THAT I AM WORTHY OF THIS."

"When guilt is punishment, what is its opposite" ?

This would suggest that the opposite of "Guilt" is "Praise" and in the same way, that they come from either "Heaven" or "Hell". Just like self gives of its Holiness to Free the world; this Praise replenishes and to give to the self, inexhaustibly, overflowing freedom. Holiness is generated from Praise and the answer to this, its every question. Take an hour to devote to this exercise and throughout the day, having split it into four practices (the more frequent practice sessions too are encouraged).
The minimum requirements can be exceeded to more, rather than the longer ones; however both are important.
The transmissions of these affirmation, are to be vocal and with eyes closed, seek out any form of uneasiness, depression, anger, fear, worry, attack, insecurity; or whatever unloving thoughts appear. It is from these unloving and fearful thoughts, to find the relief for freedom. Be specific of these situations, events or characters and in relation to holding unloving thoughts for.
It is the blessings for them, that give release and to relieve the self with this vision.

LESSON~43: "I BELIEVE THAT I AM WORTHY OF THIS."

Taking it easy and not to over emphasis on anything in particular; search the mind of its resistances to freedom and apply the following template to your examples:

"MY UNLOVING THOUGHTS ABOUT_____ARE KEEPING ME IN SELF PUNISHMENT."

"IN PRAISE OF MYSELF I FIND MY HOLINESS AND FROM THIS HOLINESS THE WAY TO FREEDOM."

To make it simple, spread out the shorter practices and with just the main affirmation for today's idea. It takes some discipline to be less distracted and for sustainable concentration; therefore relax and do not effort for any thought at all.

May this inspire for more variety into the exercise, to trigger of interest; do it with the main idea still in tact.

The idea can be changed and just as long as it does not lose its meaning, to praise rather than to punish.

Finish off with the following affirmation:

"I BELIEVE THAT I AM WORTHY OF THIS."

(Day 50)

In order to dissolve the hate that comes from the purpose of any and/or all relationships, that gather to form; the attempt for "fairness" requires a sort of payback and that of self, (perhaps more often of the others). These unions are adjusted with bargains and create limits, to impose corruption as their goal.
Lesson~44: "THERE IS NO SUCH THING AS FAIRNESS."

Holy spirit can adapt the purpose to become useful; in the way of giving and required from relationships, so not to be harmed by them. When the state of the unknowable is reached; then the conditions will present themselves, to this heavenly existence. Faithlessness is not a lack; rather the doubting takes its place and into nothingness for meaning. Deprivation, is to move in the opposite direction of higher self and all that is good, to join in such a meaningful way. Like the moon and sun come with night and day, so too, does sight and cannot be joined as one; because it is but a sign, the other has disappeared from sight. It is the absence of the other; that each rely on and in all such a case. To place equal faith in opposite directions, will only end in cancelation; that a winner and a loser might undo this fairness not and cannot take away from the other. Fairness is one of those illusions that "faith", belief" and "vision" can help to pull away from; to restore into the world and for the reality of this need, to overcompensate.
Only when the acceptance, for this choice is made completely and from what the mind might not, can this certainty be made meaningful. What gives light, does not demand the sacrifice be made from what depends on darkness. This illusion is not powerless; rather antagonizing to believe in doubt, so strong and of these illusions that the mind has made for the self. The mind however does capture to distort and twist away from praise, to punishment; and for the illusion, that there must be justice to the outcomes. These outcomes can be of lessons and/or blessings, of the creator's choice, to create from "Faith" Belief" and "Vision".

Lesson~44: "THERE IS NO SUCH THING AS FAIRNESS."

To uncover the guilt, that synergy can bring from misalignment, defeats for any purpose and by any means to benefit away, in the opposite direction. The value is therefore understood and cannot be taken away, that mind does impose on self over.
All that is synergy, can be directed toward holiness and that is unlimited to the body, in its refusal to forgive. Once the body can be forgiven from the hate; that fear has driven it, to such pain and condemnation can be lifted. Remove it from the source; rather than from the symptom and replace these thoughts with praise. Praise can bring about the faith and the self can utilize in starting to once more, trust in itself. The acceptance of this selection and firstly recognized as undesirable; it can become its challenge, to believe in otherwise and in this vision, the courage for self esteem. Look upon the many in holiness, for this collective's belief and faith as a seer; far beyond the body and to support this vision, rather than obstruct it. Support all with grounded centered presence; by finding it first, within this practice and to help hold this space for others, that they may feel a sense of Oneness.
There are many different entry points of present awareness; that could help with and to still the mind. Present moment awareness, means thinking will not completely disappear; however over thinking will subside and something else arises, that is primary called, the presence of self awareness/mindfulness. As before and in earlier exercises; (the pre-requisite to still the mind and become receptive and then transmit) to shift from what the experienced vibration and that of what is this echo self.

Lesson~44: "THERE IS NO SUCH THING AS FAIRNESS."

Practice coming back to self, as often as required, to find the center of its frequency and magnetism; that beats within the heart a rhythm. Tolerate the echo as much, or until it can experience slightly, this familiar shift and eventually perhaps, it too, does break apart, from these limitations. From every deep breath in, transmute the darkness of this need for fairness and with forgiveness, transmit out with a breath of trust, to open up and feel the love.

From the point of view called miracles; follows this decision that it too, came forth from somewhere, to impress upon the mind.

Today, practice this unbiased idea, of feeling in the Oneness, that is self and breathe. With eyes closed, imagine a certain breath and rhythm; that the self can transmit, as well as to receive with, the many of its world and all that it will reach, to make contact with its breath and with theirs.

Then with the shorter exercises repeat the following energy thought transmissions :

"THERE IS NO SUCH THING AS FAIRNESS BECAUSE THERE IS NOTHING TO FIX OR COMPENSATE WITHIN THE ONENESS THAT IS LOVE."

"I DO NOT FEEL THE NEED FOR GUILT TO PITTY OVER ANY LACK, PAIN OR INCOMPLETION."

Lesson~44: "THERE IS NO SUCH THING AS FAIRNESS"

To look away from righteousness, is to lose the battle; but win the war and/or, to see it for what it really is, as the illusionary trap of sacrifice, to serve a purpose. A purpose does not have to go through sacrifice, for it to be accomplished; because bargaining and sacrifice are irrational "<u>inoperatives</u>" to self alignment. When the seeker makes the attempt to limit the seer, the fear caused by mistrust, can become devastating and to form such hate; because what has been given "is more than anything, that stands this side of heaven".

The purpose of today's idea, is to see the world and every relationship or interaction and that the self must have, for its experience today. Give by example to the many, to believe this strongly and for itself, to help with clearing all delusional thoughts; as if to doubt for fairness and un-justifying causes from effect.

Can this love for the world be made to see it, seeing back the same, unblemished from corruption and with such innocence, that can create a Heaven?

Come forward with awareness, to shatter the rigid illusion of a finite world.

With Sovereign light, impress upon the spaces of the mind; the unlimited ability to give, as well as to receive.

(Day 51) Between now………………….. and now ……………..was the self thinking; or was it present without any thought, staring at this flower and or tree? Does the forest and the valley and from the many flowers, feel the power of their presence; can any from them stand out, to reach out, to the self, so differently? As to be authentic (in its very own vibration) and that of radiating out, to share this essence and with the resonance of self? Such communication can be felt and without the interference of superficial conceptualization; that would otherwise, to render this majestic interaction, meaningless and null and void.

Lesson~45: " MY MIND IS A HOLY SLIVER FROM THE VASTNESS OF MY BEING."

How do does the self become conscious of the present moment and can a sense of presence from the present be directly?
When not judging, by labeling the sense perceptions; this can take the self out of thinking. Today practice this idea, to think outside the box and by looking around; anywhere and where ever the self may happen to be, at this moment. Look around and practice to sense this kind of perception; without this compulsive interference, of naming what it is, that self is perceiving.
For example: maybe one tree might feel more present; than another to the self and yet it does not even know the kind of tree it is.
The self can feel its radiance and yet it unbeknownst from its history and of what is being observed; it cannot know to label it, or how old it might be and so on. By the same vastness, the sliver of yet another moment; to be taken by the prairie plants & meadow valley flowers(feeling alike). Rather felt to stop for a moment and smell the flowers, how do they make the self feel ?

Lesson~45: " MY MIND IS A HOLY SLIVER FROM THE VASTNESS OF MY BEING."

Nothing more and nothing less. "Oh… That is a beautiful flower"……."I wonder what it is called and yet I do not know what it is called, by culture either"? These are the mindless chatters of the mind and must be left behind; so to enjoy the feeling of this flower. See what it is like and means to perceive; without the meaning of the interference, from these concepts. To acquire the vastness from the gathering of information and for the mind to reinterpret into common sense; it becomes its limitation and instead of trying to interpret it, is what the lesson is asking to experience.

The purpose of this lesson, is the changing of perspective and how this sliver of sensory perception, can be changed by it; as well as to better understand, the closing of the eyes and from this world, the other with eyes open.

By receptivity and/or pro activate; either or, it is a simultaneous dance, between the two worlds. The acceptance of this, is where the peace is found to be and right in the center of it all.
From the changing of perspective, is this alchemy upon the world and to whether or not we have everything, we ask for come to us.

It is not something that can be forced on, by any means for another; rather it is there and as free flowing (as it ever was)for the initiate, ready to accept it and without any imposition.

(Day 52)

From this level of fifth density, it can go as far to witness in this presence and from the now moment, into the sixth dimensional perspective; of light body vibrational "<u>plasmic</u>", vibrant life forms and from this essence, to communicate within this harmony of lights. This is where synergy and synchronicity will be of great importance to the self alignment and from the sum of all its parts and life times.

Lesson~46: "I CAN TRANSFIGURE MY PERSPECTIVES TRANSFORM MY DENSITIES AND TRANSMUTE MY DIMENSIONS."

"WITH VIBRATION AND FREQUENCY I CAN TRANSCEND BEYOND THE NEED FOR AN AGENDA IN MY WORLD AND SHIFT INTO A HIGHER PLAYING FIELD."

Density is everything around the self and as it sees with its physical eyes as real; mostly made up of matter, energy, thought and vibration and frequency. Just like discussed from the very beginning, the tonality of sound; it can create the light to materialize and/or move objects with. This is the stuff, that miracles are made of; these are known to the many, as phenomenon. All the way from materialized objects, to transporting and transmuting; back and forth the energy, that is known as the practice of alchemy. Electronically affecting through sound and the light that information molds; the form from one object to another and situation. Through perspective and the perception of one reality into another; or that of a multiverse and just by that simple practice of a chant and sound, as inner voice could atone with and come through, an inner omnidirectional tone.

Lesson~46: "I CAN TRANSFIGURE MY PERSPECTIVES TRANSFORM MY DENSITIES AND TRANSMUTE MY DIMENSIONS."

Today repeat these transmissions of thought and end them off with the following affirmation:

"MY MIND IS PART OF THE INFINITE'S STATE OF BEING."

"I AM HOLY IN ONENESS WITH ALL THAT IS."

Get quiet and really feel into this heart of self; what does the soul want to experience? What does it want to express and through its awareness as an entity being, that is self? Follow this and do whatever it takes to implement it. Don't push it away and don't ignore it; because this presence will get louder and louder, until it becomes listened to. The self may not hear it right away at first; but when it can make that commitment to really hear, it will be given step by step instructions (in the form of subtleties) as awareness and hunches. Again, it is not hearing voices, rather the inner most thoughts and that give it impressionable awareness of light; like lightning flashes of things, such as, genius ahaa's ("why did I not think of this before" or like in the case of premonitions). An inner knowing and from this feeling, the extra sense of sound; that is, that of authentic, inner voice self.

This voice, transcends from the ethereal (4th dimensional transient lock down of lesser evolved forces and limitations of "A.I").

Equally so: "<u>My awareness transforms, when I can consciously transfigure my perspective and the dimension too, will transmute; to how I will perceive it in as density.</u>"

"WITH VIBRATION AND FREQUENCY I CAN TRANSCEND BEYOND THE NEED FOR AN AGENDA IN MY WORLD AND SHIFT INTO A HIGHER PLAYING FIELD."

Lesson~46: "I CAN TRANSFIGURE MY PERSPECTIVES TRANSFORM MY DENSITIES AND TRANSMUTE MY DIMENSIONS."

New gifts can emerge, when the self can follow its passion and in that, which can inspire, its very own expression; to impress upon the world and will be the inner voice, of its very own well being.
The mission, it will be, from following the heart and that of what feels good. When just by making that choice, to follow this feeling of bliss, as the guide to health and well being, will be that of its bringing about alignment. The alignment will reflect this outwardly, as well as inward, synergistically and with complete synchronicity. This is at best, living in harmony with all of life and circumstances, that bring it about this way. With the dimensional means of having a physical body, the fourth and fifth dimensional too, can have form; however not able to perceive from lower density and as earthly planetary level, organically sustainable. This is where "A.I" comes in; with the right technology and capability, it can be made possible. Through these artificial mediums, it can be made as relatively easy, to come down the latter. Coming up the tube torus and past the third level of density, is the ethereal and that of fourth dimensional "A.I"; as well as, thought and energy, within this space. The Spiritual however, can go beyond the metaphysical; alchemically and from this density, transcend to resurrect, to fifth dimensional awareness and where it can interact, with many timelines, all at once (and within its physical body).

From this and beyond a lot of physical recycling, can take place; because a dying body, can reach this far, as to not be able to go back into its body and as enticing as it was, to live in it, from these soul perspectives.

Lesson~46: "I CAN TRANSFIGURE MY PERSPECTIVES TRANSFORM MY DENSITIES AND TRANSMUTE MY DIMENSIONS."

From this pathway and as a well trained healthy body in this way, can come back down; however it can become exhausted and not so much at all, with the transcendence process.
Rather to descend back into a third density and fourth dimensional playing field; that this existence of awareness, has come to play in and within a physical body.

The environment that the self has not been capable to master over as of yet and will; is to be that of a sovereign light being within the fifth density awareness.
It is a discipline to have the ability to go up unless your soul is ready to transcend and from its physical world the body it must recycle.

"WITH VIBRATION AND FREQUENCY I CAN TRANSCEND BEYOND THE NEED FOR AN AGENDA IN MY WORLD AND SHIFT INTO A HIGHER PLAYING FIELD."

It is only when the self can actually leave the sixth dimensional presence; that the physical reality and alchemy of form, is no longer as perceived, from third density perspectives.
In the seventh dimension, the organic body begins to change and from the concept of this thing, that self has known as physical nature. So if it is just a consciousness, to be only from any kind of physicality; that it intends to indirectly deflect back down, just to be on and out of phase. Then it won't really be seen as physical; rather more so, as holographic and energetic, like a halo/angelic "being-ness" or presence.

Lesson~46: "I CAN TRANSFIGURE MY PERSPECTIVES TRANSFORM MY DENSITIES AND TRANSMUTE MY DIMENSIONS"

In this way, of indirect imprinting; the self can be taken from the unknowable and by learning as well, to remotely view, from its self awareness. Light body, full of energy and a twelfth dimensional being; to be realized in a third level of density and or dimension(4th level density). As a fourth or fifth dimensional being wanting to appear this way; then it could and to deflect(from higher up) in this way, such levels of consciousness. The Earth herself, is also undergoing a massive and rapid upward spiral of transcendence. All organic life too, must find a way to ascend, right along with her and to be of this world; that is making it very possible to become, as well as in this way, to reaching such dimensions and as a "Sovereign Light" entity, the self and with its body.

Learning how to be receptive and remotely view for now, is the purpose; that the self can learn these facets and from them, to project thoughts; messages and visions upwards.
To actually transport itself upward, for now however; is this challenge, that it must work through and get as close within living it, as possible. Eventually the self, can reach a state of being; where it can depend entirely upon it and at any given moment, to shift and materialize at will, from its intentional focus here in.

"MY MIND IS PART OF THE INFINITE'S STATE OF BEING".
"I AM HOLY IN ONENESS WITH ALL THAT IS".

(Day 53)

What are some of my old patterns?.......Triggers and reactions? Awe..the blessings of opportunity, to rediscover and transmute, the shadow into light. This weakness, is the strength.

Lesson~47: "HOW DO I SEE AND FEEL ABOUT MYSELF ?"

Take a specific trait and apply it; as given to add with the idea. The emotion that it feels from thinking and to imagine itself entitled by the Ego mind, to be a certain way. The image that it feels from the many and that experience its servicing by it; or it, of estimating the level of this inner confidence, called "Self Esteem".
These will be the many templates, that it can tell itself and to show dimensionally, how dense it has created the reality. From the static of such thoughts, to believe as real and feeling perhaps stuck; incompetent of such complacency and to form opinion, over its own well being. Restricted by a level of misconduct; and the patterning of such attitudes, to form, for its behavior.
"HOW DOES THE SELF APPEAR TO STACK UP TO ITS VERY OWN TESTIMONIALS ….. The following examples are concerns, about what others might think of me….. Then how do I feel?…….. What is most important ? Is it the balance of what the both might equally compare, from the results…………? Perhaps the need is greater, to bring back harmony and find within the self, some sort of balance?

"I FEEL I MUST BEHAVE NARCISSISTICALLY TO KEEP THIS POSITION."

"I FEEL HELPLESS AND ENDANGERED."

"I SEE MYSELF AS A PROFESSIONAL AND I FEAR I MIGHT BE LOSING OUT BY DISTANCING MYSELF FROM OTHERS."

"I SEE MYSELF AS LOSING OUT BECAUSE I FEEL DISCRIMINATED."

Lesson~47: "HOW DO I SEE AND FEEL ABOUT MYSELF ?"

Then contemplate on such current values to invest in the alternative perspectives that might better for each interpretation from the following examples:

" I SEE MYSELF AS VIRTUOUS AND I FEEL TRUSTWORTHY ."

" I SEE MYSELF AS CHARITABLE BECAUSE I FEEL COMPASSION."

" I CREATE FOR THE APPROPRIATE BOUNDARIES WHEN I FEEL MYSELF IMPOSED ON……I SEE MYSELF AS VICTORIOUS….etc…"

" I FEEL MY AUTHENTICITY AND SEE IT AS A VALUE."

Continue to create for (other better resonating) attributes that best describe the self; whether they be undesirable or not, and/or debasing or not and so on….

Repeat the affirmations and then with eyes closed seek out the mind. How does the mind describe in terms of things such as its "Ego" driven characteristics?

The purpose for today, is to feel a connection with Source and by establishing a level of authenticity that will require to be grounded in this truth of self discovery.

(Day54)

There is an option, that the self does have and by giving up all; or rather just that portion of its field. Where a distorted force, as figure head of energy, imprints upon it, for the greater good, and as part of an agreement.

LESSON~48:
>"SOURCE IS MY INNER STRENGTH
>AND ITS VISION IS MY GIFT."

The self can easily become convinced, that it will not make it on its own and must depend for the benefit of tribal groupings. By becoming small enough, it too can be made even more powerful; when uniting with other like minded tribes and so on, until it creates, a global coherence. Co-dependently relating with that of the others, small in numbers and just like it.

Through these interactions, a communal currency development and within their formation, the importance of the "IMAGE"; that can better expressively exchange, with this co-creating force.

To expand the scope, much wider, to see the bigger picture of the playing field and with this book: The observer can be omnipresent; looking at a smaller fraction of itself and from which to be observed, as image. God can also be the surrendered power of self and to trust from, a different perspective.

There is that choice, to keep the power of self, so that it can create unconditionally with others; rather than give it up, for the greater good to decide. Can this be given a better multi scope perspective and to agnostically decide; even for the most Atheist of the bunch, as well (from that perspective) to understand itself?

Before getting up in the morning, this came to channel and from within; were these following thoughts and that had to be recapitulated, in this way: <u>The observer and observable interpretation and from the epiphany of remotely viewing thoughts</u>

Every level of frequency, does hold and it releases from vibration; held together, as sub atomic particles. These waveforms and atomic energy, become attracted to each other, of likeness and in such a way, to organize the accumulation of solidity. Yet empty on the inside and as well, as on the outside, it can appear this way.
This attraction and repulsion, is what becomes the force and from its hold, all sparks of existence; swirling in motion and sub atomic waves. The movement can collapse and come together, to appear as solid matter; from these senses and that the self can correspond, to this its level of awareness. The sensation, that moves and becomes movable, is in relation to this understanding and of these sparks; that move about, as flickering synapses to remind the brain and of these many pathways. The swirling of spiraling formations and of all that is, in suspended fluid animation; from which all currents ebb and flow, to impress upon the self, for its distinctive interpretation, as expression.

LESSON~48:
"SOURCE IS MY INNER STRENGTH
AND ITS VISION IS MY GIFT."

What else can the self be ready to receive for today?
With this delicate balance to consider: The "<u>Will of God</u>"
is this idea; that of the self, in need of identity and as the reassurance for its coping mechanisms. Simply combine these two thoughts for today. The cause and effect principle, explains the need for this external image; that the mind must form, to connect with on the inside.

LESSON~48:

"SOURCE IS MY INNER STRENGTH AND ITS VISION IS MY GIFT".

Both Creator/Co-creator alike are not at random with these circumstances and offer the vision to believe that it is to receive such synchronicity. The God of the collective's agreed upon image is the gift that can exclude and limit to restrain the self expression truly; however from the outside it would appear as a strength in numbers that form supportive Unity.

"VISION" IS THIS "FORCE" TO "IMPRINT" UPON AS "IMAGE" "ENERGETICALLY" as "GOD" held there in place then, and as to be made POSSIBLE to believe in. Only the image must be deferred, to amalgamate; it is, as intended and for this book, to move beyond it, to something greater. When getting up in the morning take a brief moment, then another and as close as to going to rest at night.
Find a quiet place and take the affirmation, that most resonates to repeat the idea slowly, with eyes open and observing around the area. Then with eyes closed, repeat the idea again and even slower than before; while thinking of only thoughts and that occur with in relation, to the idea for the day.

These few examples from the book might be further of assistance: "VISION IS MADE POSSIBLE BECAUSE THIS SPARK OF ENERGY IS TRULY GIVING."
OR:
"THESE VIBRATIONS MUST BE MINE_BECAUSE I AM ABLE TO RECEIVE THEM."

Do not censor the thoughts, unless the mind starts to wander. Another may also be, that no thoughts at all come to mind.

LESSON~48:

"SOURCE IS MY INNER STRENGTH AND ITS VISION IS MY GIFT".

When these interferences occur, open eyes and continue to repeat while looking around. Then close eyes again, to continue with related thoughts. Remember to be the receiver and not the projector of these thoughts, step back so to allow for thoughts to come in. When faced with too much resistance, better to alternate between slow repetitions and with eyes open, then with eyes closed again. In between the two long practices throughout the day, make room for as many short practices too.

As often as the idea is repeated, the more committed to the goal of the course it will become to remember.

The purpose for today, is to bring thoughts together and from this idea, to further study; explore the mysteries of a unified and separately divided system, irrelevant to any contradiction and/or a lack in what is needed.

(Day55) To project outward is the key, and with this lesson. The perception was given from belief and faith from mind to body; let them now be given back, to what produced them. This is the liberation and to make use from, what was made. To truly see beyond and past from what the faith and the belief have given.

LESSON~49:
"MY FREQUENCY ENVELOPS EVERYTHING I SEE."

This is just not a superficial alteration of the over bearing masculine; however a little deeper than the gender fazing out and in that both (doing-ness/being-ness)paths lead to the same as one.

To "PROJECT OUTWARD LOVE AND LIGHT".

Thought is replacing and always in control; however the breaking down analytical and to explain further, was left for the self to ponder over. Feeling = emotion + thought; however to replace it with "I see" is a visual.
To visualize and affirm while holding the intention with thought

(for the idea) to project out the feeling of

"LOVE" and/or "PEACE".

What is being replaced, is the emotion; here is where the activity becomes fascinating and to reveal yet another psychological aspect: Originally to reinterpret, the self had found to be in between two realities: one by removing the emotion and having only thought and/or the other reactionary mode of thoughtlessness; meaning an emotion without a thought attached to oversee it.
These procedures or steps were not even ever considered and the receptive way was in this process of learning how to find its peace enough and to become familiar to project it outwardly.

LESSON~49:
"MY FREQUENCY ENVELOPS EVERYTHING I SEE".

Then maybe outwardly, the motion of "<u>doing-ness</u>", becomes a harmonious responsiveness and that comes about from the receptiveness inner world, to project everything back to self; as opposed to the other way the book is teaching.

From the spotlight on the observer, today does shift to move toward the stage for the observed. To observe that bigger part of all that is wholesome and connected to the mind. When the self is wholesome, the sight must be, that of one in the same and absent from corruptibleness. With corruption, it is such a blemish, that there is no in between. The mind with discernment, does marvel on one side of the fence, over the other. Sight can be made Holy, only by an incorruptible state and in unison with the Infinite's synchronicities. The exercises do include, longer stretches and shorter ones, throughout the day. Take four longer practices and for about five minutes each session. With eyes closed, verbalize the affirmation(several repeats slowly). Then with eyes opened, do a brief surveillance. While making use of today's idea, to whatever is monitored; the following template from the book is given, to use for this example:

" MY FREQUENCY ENVELOPS …..[OBJECT….SUBJECT] ."

"MY FREQUENCY ENVELOPS[CIRCUMSTANCE…SUBJECT]."

"MY FREQUENCY ENVELOPS ..[ISSUE …PLACE… OR SITUATION] ."

" MY FREQUENCY ENVELOPS …..[PHYSICAL PAIN OR DISCOMFORT] ."

" MY FREQUENCY ENVELOPS …..[RANDOM IMPRESSIONS OF SELF] ."

" MY FREQUENCY ENVELOPS …..[THIS PEN….] ."

LESSON~49:

"MY FREQUENCY ENVELOPS EVERYTHING I SEE."

Make certain to spread these practices throughout the day evenly; while fitting in with the shorter applications more often. The longer ones, as in the same with the shorter; to exercise effortlessly for several repeats over, firstly with eyes closed slowly and then unhurriedly, open to continue as before.

Always end these affirmations with:

"I FEEL AT PEACE AND FULL OF LOVE FOR THESE THINGS."

"I PROJECT OUTWARD LOVE AND LIGHT TO ALL."

The purpose is, to focus on the transmitting and from before, the previous lesson was in the receiving; they are both essential and have to be relearned, in this way, that they can be eventually combined (as for both are essentially important).

No more looping around swimming in forgetfulness (from one fish bowl to another) and for the sum of all its parts.
Take it beyond this leap of faith and that was meant for, as a preview pilot, to the multidimensional state of being.

Whole and holy is this consciousness;
stop it now, from feeling stuck !

(Day 56)

To follow consciousness, does not necessarily require always having to engage externally and with every moment. At a zero point field, there is this place, that self can enter into nothingness and be the nothing. A place where the self can stop from all its thoughts and become motionless. From this point of center, it has the potential to become and that, from which all things are made of and change even the very flow of its direction.

LESSON~50: "I AM NOT AFRAID TO LOOK WITHIN."

Moving faster than the speed of light and when letting go of all resistances from thought; the pulling inward, as powerful as gravity and that the self can feel, when grounding from within this way(become allowing and just let go). Lost in the nothingness and can be found; this is and can be for the self, at the source of all its fear. Where there is doubt and by association to corrupt it in this way some more; is the "Ego mind", that awaits there, at the entrance to support it. Fear does not have any shame and in the desire for faith to see it through as inappropriate.

Fear is in the unknowable find and from within to contradict the mind, that thinks the inappropriate is there.

Never does the whole of spirit teach the "<u>being-ness</u>" as inappropriate; rather only to correct from that, of what is perceived as such. The "Ego mind", is a sort of like, the gatekeeper, to protect from the unknown and until the self can think it knows, what to filter through. With fear, the "Ego mind" can overpower and to yield the way inward; because it does not want the eyes to see.

Today, take a few shots at this, to focus going in and repeat the following idea:

"I AM NOT AFRAID TO LOOK WITHIN."

LESSON~50: "I AM NOT AFRAID TO LOOK WITHIN."

The self might also find, a variation to experience; just before getting up, to start the day and right before it lays to rest from it. Just before the self drifts into astral state of soul and right before it goes off, to engaging with the chasing of its consciousness, to start the day; Practice to find that place, that pulls the self in. Then in that center of inertia, where the mind is still and the heart can open; then from any point of direction, move this flow by what it is, the self requires most and to focus on…It will come, do not worry so much about not having in the nothingness and to find itself from there….What it might be searching and yearning for; that in fact can be creating the resistance …… The more the focus on resistance, the more the falling into self and as trusting to guide it; where it needs to find itself within that moment ……From the probable potentials, what will best be ready for the self, to try on and play around with; knowing how for every situation, is only but a ripple, in the vastness that is self.

The sinking in feeling, into the physical body and reaching into source is genuine; the self can stop and say "no" to what it can see and with the reverence toward the many, who will choose otherwise and clear from all of that. "Ego" represents a program and that of a smaller version, that is self; it struggles to convince the higher self and of its power over it. With wavering of self assurance(that it might be wrong) and that the over soul might strike it down, in the awareness of it. Be indiscriminate, when selecting the subjects, so to not self-direct by including or excluding things.

For the second and shorter phases, and throughout the day; repeat the main idea, with eyes closed. Allow for whatever relevant thoughts occur and to be processed in this way.

LESSON~50: "I AM NOT AFRAID TO LOOK WITHIN."

Here are some thoughts to follow:

"I SEE THROUGH THE EYES OF FORGIVENESS."

" I SEE THE WORLD AS BLESSED."

"THE WORLD CAN SHOW ME MYSELF."

This is the part that has recognized, to see the perfection in the many; from their moment of conception, to the here and now. There is nothing more inspiring, than the desire to join with them all; to be free again, better than as once it was before.

Although it does claim to be the hidden fear for the self and "Ego" it is not; rather a mechanism to get the self to believe and so it may not enter to look any further. The underlying factor of uncertainty, makes "Ego" tremble; because the self is too ashamed, perhaps to enter within itself. "Ego" never asks the question, why not look in and/or can it be possible that it be void of corruption?

Oh…The mere thought of just asking; threatens the "Ego's" system from this place, into one of defense and is more than it can cope with, to pretend to be a friend.

LESSON~50: "I AM NOT AFRAID TO LOOK WITHIN."

In the most sanest of moments that the heart can feel, to be stricken with such terror, from the "Ego"; know that there cannot be made for such a possibility. The façade, to trip the self by the "Ego's" capture and to tease; it can only fall short from the selling of this state of frequency, as Heaven over.

From this purpose, is in the learning; that the "Ego mind" will remain in madness, to be included and/or to include the self into thinking, it is indeed, insane.

Understanding force and all the many parts of the self, when coming into source; A revelation awaits to come from the acceptance of the self; rather than from the "Ego mind" to expect it was.

With no fear to see the "Ego mind" in its madness and from the choice not to join in with it; is this sane reason to process clear away and integrate.

(Day57)

Trust to just remember, that when the self is done with the effort and to play amongst its smallness; it will no longer feel for any anger of such compromise.

LESSON~51:

"WHEN I CAN REMOVE MYSELF FROM THE RESISTANCE OF THE EGO MIND THE HOLINESS OF PRAISE REVEALS THE WHOLENESS OF MY FREEDOM."

Today is all about flipping the fear, into excitement and that of what it's like to feel ignited in this way, into enlightenment.
When the self can start to come to terms with the process of its integration; will it then experience the activation and from the fear the feeling of excitement, that it brings. The whole of spirit is consistent, in all that is, to learn from within to look; where as the "Ego mind", in its rage of these presumptions and from the self that does not want to. The "Ego mind" would withdraw all these perceived gifts by making them deceivable enough, to pass for curses. This terror, that the "Ego mind" hears and is afraid of; left powerless to surrender and for the other parts of self, now in the sweetest of vibration. The rhythm from this beat, forever longing in the absence and from when the "Ego" stepped into the mind's existence. When the "Ego" is weak, this world of song, for freedom grows stronger; from the Love and Praise, that it brings hope and for this peace in the remembering. To remember once again this frequency and from the Earth's perspective, at last; because the "Ego's" rule has kept it out so long. When there is no more reign of power from the "Ego mind"; the relationship with Heaven can be reestablished. This is a given for the Earth, that the self must reconsider as and no longer will it be able to exist, in any other way, this Heaven on Her own.

LESSON~51:

"WHEN I CAN REMOVE MYSELF FROM THE RESISTANCE OF THE EGO MIND THE HOLINESS OF PRAISE REVEALS THE WHOLENESS OF MY FREEDOM."

Look gently on the many and remember the Ego's weakness; it is revealed just the same, as it has from within the self.
What was meant to keep in separation, the self can now see and the Ego, unafraid to merge as one. Follow in joy, the way to certainty; fear not the false pretense of doubt's and retardation that threaten well being.
The repetitive senseless clamor, is not meaningful; rather the quiet way, made open to follow instead and without question is.

The shorter applications, are roughly made three or four times an hour, throughout the day and more when desired.

"ANGER IS JUST AN INDICATION OF THE LITTLE ME PERSPECTIVE AND FEELING STUCK IN SUCH A COMPROMISING STATE."

"FEAR IS THE EXCITMENT THAT I FEEL WHEN I CAN SEE THE LARGER ASPECT OF MYSELF GIVING OPPORTUNITY TO JOIN IT WITH."

Then finish off, by repeating the initial idea; preferably to follow with the practice and that of believing in its transmitting thought:

"WHEN I CAN REMOVE MYSELF FROM THE RESISTANCE OF THE EGO MIND THE HOLINESS OF PRAISE REVEALS THE WHOLENESS OF MY FREEDOM."

LESSON~51:

"WHEN I CAN REMOVE MYSELF FROM THE RESISTANCE OF THE EGO MIND THE HOLINESS OF PRAISE REVEALS THE WHOLENESS OF MY FREEDOM."

Just like identity does not have to rely upon the Ego mind; the joining of that part of self and with, into the wholeness, is what it means of a holy relationship. To form an awareness that supports this "Holy Relationship"; then the belief in its corruption, has been already shaken and safe enough to look within to see it not.
The glimmering flames of liberation, are finding their way through insanity and on to reason, from within now.
The part of the mind that "Ego" knows very little about and cannot hear; is where the Holy Spirit's purpose vibrates, with synchronicity and in harmony, to integrate the sum of all its parts, that hold forever immortality.

This is where the incorruptible part, of self and the whole of spirit dwell in.

The mind is not afraid to look upon; because how else could it be made possible, to see the Whole of Spirit's purpose?

(Day58)

Where the twentieth century, started off from nothing and from the zero, it had to learn the state of oneness; the twenty-first century, is now, all about the "One". It has been that, when a group of people get together and with the same intention, collectively this attention, is very powerful. Either way, this collective "will", is as important to the outside; as it is, within the one. By taking in vibrational frequency and learning how to really process it; to allow the travel of it and from deep within, to take place now. Discover the perfection, that can radiate back out and to penetrate the world with. The whole of spirit is the mediator, between perception and knowledge; the perspective of this energy and that perception can forever replace, in the mind of the self.

LESSON~52:
"MY SPIRITUAL CONSCIOUSNESS, IS THIS LIGHT FROM WHICH I SEE."
"MY CONSCIOUSNESS RADIATES FROM SOURCE, THE ENERGY IN MOTION, THAT PULLS IN AND PROPELS EXPRESSION OUT."

From the masculine, the self had to learn, in half truths; of just doing and all else, was inferior to that state. Now the self must relearn from that previous only way and is, by rediscovering the excluded feminine(if it ever made possible, it had to undergo this experience first). By learning for however long it took, or it must take to learn exclusively from the feminine; only then, can the "Ego" back down enough and to allow for the masculine re-integration. The split was so extreme and from the many down the lineage; this respect must be found again, for the feminine. It has been a very extreme contrast for the self; to feel such disrespect and in this, the only way the world has made it, in such lack, to limit and distort, from the self and to ever having a connection.

LESSON~52:

"MY SPIRITUAL CONSCIOUSNESS IS THIS LIGHT FROM WHICH I SEE."

"MY CONSCIOUSNESS RADIATES FROM SOURCE THE ENERGY IN MOTION_THAT PULLS IN AND PROPELS EXPRESSION OUT."

From the Earth and deeper vision from within; the self will be abandoned by all else, to find its way through and at the end of it, to come through, reborn within the light. When the mind decides to separate from self; because all that it thinks it can be, and it is not, depression is an inevitable punishment. The helplessness, to worry over; the misery and anxiousness to suffer with. The intense fear, or loss, are these stories. In return, the external circumstances, reflect this vulnerability; from separation and with inventions to convince back to self, for such "cures". Under a heavy dense cloud and where the sight is obscured by insane thoughts; lies a vision of truth, hidden deep within. By getting past all these things, of false reality appearances; focus the attention, to sink down, inward and away, from the superficial clamour of the world. Just like there is nothing to see outside the self, nor from the equipment, that makes seeing without the light; it is always there and in every circumstance, for vision to be made possible. To train the mind to see, is this method; that will be utilized and made as, a major goal further. With many short practices and in between; take a few brief moments for these emotions of to become present. Feel the loneliness and from it, the complete abandonment of separation; for this given experience. The life force of self and perceived as God, has no function within it; rather the undoing of it, to help free its energy, from it.

LESSON~52: "MY SPIRITUAL CONSCIOUSNESS_IS THIS LIGHT FROM WHICH I SEE."

"MY CONSCIOUSNESS RADIATES FROM SOURCE_THE ENERGY IN MOTION_THAT PULLS IN AND PROPELS EXPRESSION OUT."

Made this image, as to identify with and in the likeness of a split gender, is an unholy purpose; the moment has come now, to become the means for its restoration and so that, something more vast can, to grasp unto its awareness. The holy spirit gives meaning to perception and through forgiveness; it can be healed the many and thus forgive the one. Practice today, not only to forgive existence and of all likely hood; from ever having to manage in such a way, with lack, to limit the presence of the feminine in and that it could only come through as masculine. Practice seeing these energies, like particles to collide with one another and then as they form the many of this world. Practice the self resonance of cohesion to the oneness and that of, the sum of all these part; reintegrated through the feminine and then through much forgiveness, to allow expressing the acceptance, of the infinite reality. The masculine had collided and broken the feminine, into trillion parts; from those trillion parts cohesion is this process and that is constantly creating the opportunity, for resonance, toward the oneness, that is the self. When likeness attracts of likeness, then how is it, that it can deny, its very own existence? If to form, cohesion is non existent and is a wrong doing; then is it not, the non doing and rather it is that of being? Then through the acceptance of this being; can it function well enough, to be made useful, in the doing. Forgiveness of the self, means to forgive this God in likeness and to the many, that resonate with self. To separate from this perception, is to separate from life force. This vision is real, to the extent, that it shares the holy spirit's purpose.

LESSON~52:

"MY SPIRITUAL CONSCIOUSNESS_IS THIS LIGHT FROM WHICH I SEE."

"MY CONSCIOUSNESS RADIATES FROM SOURCE_THE ENERGY IN MOTION_THAT PULLS IN AND PROPELS EXPRESSION OUT."

The practice in this way, does leave behind and everything previously believed as hell; the Ego's eyes, see this loss of identity and made up thoughts, of a descent into hell.

The "Ego's" opposition and fears, are meaningless, when standing aside from it. When the exercise is done correctly, a sense of relaxation is felt; while the experience of entering into light and/or coming pretty close to it. Think of light as formless and limitless, when thoughts are passing of this world. These thoughts of the world are weightless, when they have no power left.

Do this exercise often, in short and with eyes open or closed. Move beyond the idle thoughts, of the world and aim for a sense of turning inward. To better soak in, this perspective, go deeply in the mind, with this exercise and practices of meditation; right after getting up, from nightly rest and before going to rest, at night; as well as, another, when the most convenient moment, that circumstances and readiness, do permit a break.

With the shorter exercises, just practice the transmission of the given affirmation (given from this lesson).

LESSON~52:

"MY SPIRITUAL CONSCIOUSNESS_IS THIS LIGHT FROM WHICH I SEE."

"MY CONSCIOUSNESS RADIATES FROM SOURCE_ THE ENERGY IN MOTION_ THAT PULLS IN AND PROPELS EXPRESSION OUT."

Repeat the idea, with eyes open and apply it specifically, to what is seen, after a short glance around. With eyes open, repeat the affirmation and then with eyes closed, several times more.
Sink into the mind, to pass quietly by, letting go of interferences and intrusions.

The purpose is, to attempt to shut out the masculine; so to accept the feminine in again and re-integrate the masculine, from this feminine and reach the light, that comes from within.

Accept this purpose, to lower the resistance, enough that receptivity can be made easy and most natural, for this connection.

Unless the choice to stop is there, the mind cannot be stopped; because this is the natural course. Be uninvolved with these passing thoughts and that slip away silently, while observed.
It is an inestimable value, to have a sense of awareness and that what is being done here, is very holy. Once the thought is exercised into believing this is possible, the results are startling, even for the first time.

THE INTERMISSION :

Take 2 days to take it in

CONGRATULATIONS ...!!!

FOR MAKING IT THROUGH THE 52nd Lesson

(This is a rest period to take the lessons independently as a review)

TAKE THESE TWO DAYS TO RECALIBRATE;

MAKE NOTES AND REVIEW……………..

(Day61)
Illuminated, white bright beam, of sovereign self and as the observer, from itself, that it can come to witness. It can be very possible, to gather information, through sensing and/or feeling subtle energy; from this clairsentient and receptive presence .. an outward flow, expelling and refreshing a new.

LESSON~53:
"MY LIGHT IS THIS LOVE FROM WHICH
I CAN FORGIVE."

There is this hunch, of directly looking and with, through no glass(dark-light), that something could be there.
From this thing called faith, the experience and that it can have with white light. The further it descends to blue, gold and red; the denser the reality, to make distinct and with more boundaries and separations. This is when the cut in flow, begins to start creating, its very own vortices and lenses of perception.
From the same holographic box and/or containment; the splitting of realities, will not change, unless a perspective changes them. From this identifiable imagination and yet another different shade of colour; thus the many different versions, of the sameness and under different lighting.
The more dense, the more diffracted from the white light and (inner knowing of the self from the dark light perspective that will also be and is discussed within this book) is, this unique perspective, of all things; that make up for this light and the more fragmented, the less of energy, there is to go around. These are distortions, that the self must learn from, in order to experience itself and expand. The diversifying of the spirit, from the soul and back to self, are indeed the many slivers of the rainbow; to hold them in its loneliness and that separate it from itself(are these perspectives).

LESSON~53:
"MY LIGHT IS THIS LOVE FROM WHICH I CAN FORGIVE."

The soul is yet another vehicle, the spirit has created and for the self, around it like a field; from which it holds, this portion of the ethereal and from it, at the center, is the white light tube, that is a portion of this thing, called spirit. The "toroidal" energy, is like an electrical tornado; that can be seen coming out, the front and back of the physical body. It has a magnetic pulling in these "toroidal", multi coloured, chakra fields; from them, come the many implants and to keep it more solid, in its reality. The more solid and rigid, the more it plugs up and slows down; creating parasitical and toxic co-dependencies, upon itself. The self must accept to clear all those emotions, feelings and as well, as thoughts; from those various fields of traumas, that the heart can hold, to keep it closed and plugged up. Find where and acknowledge firstly, this flow of energy to be blocked off completely; from when it first came through, as pure white light . Today's practice is a meditation, from which to visualize the body and its physical apparatus; to connect and ground the following: With eyes closed, breathing in from the nose and filling in the lungs, with energy. See this energy as white light; then picture and feel it making the exchange. From breath, the air becomes a vortex....spinning... this breath it spins so fast ..it turns into white light. This white light comes from everywhere, outside of self; that it breathes in and right about the center, where the heart is. The heart must remove the plug and/or allow it to pop right open and when it does, the world of self, will never be the same again. Now imagine that moment, when the self had fallen in love, from its external circumstances. Feel that openness, that resonance and that trust of sharing and in with other worlds.

LESSON~53:

"MY LIGHT IS THIS LOVE FROM WHICH I CAN FORGIVE."

This is what it feels like, to sample in from the experience and when the external circumstances, cause a falling in love to occur. This experience, was not designed to last for very long; rather just enough, to taste it as it was, from its very own reflection and causing it reactively, as motivation would inspire, for that temporary stated moment.

"SEE MY OWN THOUGHTS, TO BE THAT OF GOD'S."

The familiar trained self, to pull the many memories of the ethereal and pull them into this white light, it did; creating the separations and from them, these vortices that do appear, creating the many chakras. From the soul's reality, to learn and teach the self with; created clouding of perception and formed opinions, from these misadventures, that had great cause, for trauma and malfunctions to occur. These chakras (creating other layers to its field in as multiple-coloured rainbows)are like, self activating software and they are like, all the many other implants; genetically activated in its field, outside the physical. These vortices and fields, attract to them, separately different learning curbs and from them, can slow down, to the point of shutting off completely. Thus a portion of the self, is held in separation and from these self created boundaries. A lot of goodness, will attract, a lot of hurt and when it does not know how to put up the very same boundaries; that it before to learn and to remove from every chakra back into the white light. These various boundaries, are the many coloured lenses and from these membranes, it can keep out the unwanted; that had already once before. The unwanted became familiar to the experience and in teaching it, how to remove those boundaries; by clearing from those kind of hooks and that previously it had agreed to learn from, when being drained its energy(from them).

LESSON~53:

"MY LIGHT IS THIS LOVE FROM WHICH I CAN FORGIVE."

Practice today, firstly with the white light test meditation; then finish with the breathing in white light and close it off, with the frequent shorter affirmation, to activate forgiveness.

This spark of white light and that travels in as white light; it can be cleared again, when it is once more as sovereign and as that portion of its spirit, contained within the physical existence.

With the heart unplugged, the enlightenment to higher state of consciousness, can begin and only then, can it start flowing properly. The more of spirit, then can be accepted in and to sink in to the vastness; in as consciousness in everything and in all of existence. The white light test, is all about hugging and like that with heart open; that the many can feel this white light, coming from their chest. Now the same goes with the self, to try and go on to hug itself; feel the love going and moving inward. Just the same and if not, for even better, than that of hugging anything else; that might appear like it, in this way outside itself and as like another, coming from the same of soul, as it. The hugging turns the energy back and in on itself; practice this kind of getting love and that requires the loving of itself today and in this way. When the outflow of the light, is not flowing properly; the self will feel, that it needs the love from other external circumstances and as before, when it had fallen in love.

This is where the affirmation for the idea, must be implemented; repeat as many times as needed and to remind the self, that it needs to forgive.

"MY LIGHT IS THIS LOVE FROM WHICH I CAN FORGIVE".

LESSON~53:

"MY LIGHT IS THIS LOVE FROM WHICH I CAN FORGIVE."

When the self has this white flow of energy pouring out and flowing properly; it then becomes impossible for anyone, or anything to drain, or take it and/or in any kind of way, make it feel drained, from its own energy.

Maybe now, in knowing this, it will become much more easier; to reconfigure healthy boundaries and from, when it did not know how, before. With a healthy flow of energy coming from the heart, the self no longer will require their energy to fuel it either and into such a vicious cycle, of dependency(misdirected spiraling downwards motion). The separation are these gaps and that, what this evolution is created from.

With the white light test, the self will be able to feel whether its heart is open and to let it flow, without needing anybody or anything; because it is good and solid in every way, from within and can move forward, with everything

Go ahead and get into this position, let go and allow the moving forward for the self to feel.

Often it has been mentioned, that there might be no such thing, as to forgive.

The purpose is, for the self to become awakened, to its vastness of these dimensional possibilities and to see white light, wherever it may be; because the white light, comes from everywhere that it may see.

(Day62) Sometimes and at certain levels(awareness), when the self can truly ascertain the state of being; from where there is nothing to forgive and is this truth, held not, by a perspective?

LESSON~54:
"LETTING GO OF MY RESISTANCE IS FORGIVENESS ."

Any thought related, directly to the main idea for the day and as long as it is not, in opposition to it. When nothing comes to mind, or when wandering takes place; simply open eyes, for the awareness to be clearer. What in deed is the self feeling and what truly is this vibration, will be the outcome...Is it expansion and/or contraction? From every contradiction, a contrast is realized differently; because it is in the awareness of the alchemizing process, that the self can notice and for it, to directly be integrating.

Today practice what the self prefers to have, for its reality and then what is the resistance ?

Is the resistance external or internal? Is there only one, or many variations; that combine to oppose, or come into conflict and that the self must compromise, for this existence, to make real.

All of awareness and thoughts; that make it feel awkward to exist authentically and as a sovereign entity .... What are they ?

Feel them ...See them.... What are these tormenting beliefs and where are they coming from? Get as much, as possible and begin to understand; that it is okay for them to be this way, however they must be forgiven... Give forth, all these things and clean out the trash ..... This trash is another's treasure and as it was, once before, no longer serving for the self, to be in its reality.

Let it go and forgive the self, for hanging on to something, that did not belong to it, for something that will.

LESSON~54:
"LETTING GO OF MY RESISTANCE IS FORGIVENESS ."

Stay current and refreshed today, as much as possible; to allow for what it is that self prefers, to resonate into its perception and become as truthfully real to grasp, as possible.

When it happens, do not overkill it with questions … Like, "why are you here" per-say; rather enjoy it unconditionally and as much, as can possibly be savoured, to appreciate and that the self, can gracefully participate, with it. Repeat the first phase of the exercise and then attempt the second again.

Return to the first phase and as often as the preoccupation with irrelevant thoughts, throughout the day occur.

These shorter practices can vary, from circumstances and situations, that are found, during the day.

Equally applicable to strangers, as it is, to those who are thought of, as close; because there should be no distinction.

For example, when connecting with others; that might provoke a challenge and/or when situations of distress arise, this affirmation can do well:

"FREEDOM IS IN THE LETTING GO OF ALL RESISTANCES."

From energy that is made up of all that is "I" and "SOURCE" included; the purpose, is to understand, that photonic light, is everywhere.

In this way, all illusion from the separation, of the "I"; it can deconstruct, while it dissolves.

The paradox is in that, self has always a choice, in the matter; to connect or, not connect and with whatever life force, that is being made this offering, of recognition.

(Day63)

From the previous idea, to grasp and reach, yet another dimension of creation, with light reflecting life. Light and life together, are these different aspects of creation; that must be recognized, as coming from within. From the separation, that the contrast of the many and who can't hear or understand; in this difference, is the how the self will feel and to letting go of, the unwanted beliefs. Reconcile with source instead,to find the inner being and how it feels, about itself.

LESSON~55:
" PROSPERITY IS A VIBRATIONAL ESSENCE, THAT ALREADY EXISTS."

"I WANT THE CLARITY OF REALITY AND NOT THE DEFAULT OF IT."

Look through the *"rubeus" lens* in gratitude and find appreciation. Work on moving past all the superficial thoughts and that cover over the truth. Just like an onion, with many layers and to reach for that, which is eternal. Make certain to recognize, when held back by the thoughts, of the world. Beneath the unreal, seek for the real, look past and through this world, in favour of truth. Dismiss the disbelievers of the world and that press on for what is possible, as impossible, because it is not their mission. It is this mission, that the self has every reason, to feel confident and that it will succeed on. Under all the senseless thoughts and mad ideas left behind by others, to have cluttered up the mind; are un-borrowed thoughts, that the mind did have for itself. These thoughts completely unchanged, can once again be reclaimed and exactly as they always were. "Everything thought of since, will change; however on which it rests, is this holy and changeless foundation":
"AUTHENTICITY".

LESSON~55:
"PROSPERITY IS A VIBRATIONAL ESSENCE, THAT ALREADY EXISTS."
"I WANT THE CLARITY OF REALITY AND NOT THE DEFAULT OF IT."

<u>AUTHENTICITY</u>: "It is this "Foundation", toward today's exercise, that it is directed. The joining of one's thoughts, with the multiverse-perspective and of all that is, with the almighty life force presence. For this kind of practice, only one thing is of importance; to grasp it well, from a linear co-creative perspective, this "<u>Heaven on Earth</u>" principle. A cooperative venture and that for the many, aspire to reach in oneness, with the creator self, expressed principle. From this dimensional perspective, to join with that of a multiverse concept; is needed, to be realized and yet, not so misunderstood. Even with the very little understanding, that has already been gained and as a reminder, will stand as no idle game; rather an exercise, in holiness and an attempt, to reach the "Kingdom of Heaven".

In the shorter spread out exercises for the day; remember how important it is, to understand the holiness of the mind, that thinks with source and in these impulses of energy, to this alignment with it; its desire and these vibrations, will lead to thought and thought, to things, without resistance.

Take a few minutes to re-verbalize the idea, throughout the day and to appreciate the mind's holiness. For a brief moment, stand aside from all thoughts, that host unworthiness and give thanks for all the thoughts, that give on praise instead. Remove the worry and meditate into the vibrational, of preferred focus and pure thought in the making. This is the energy, in the likeness of self and also conceptualized, from the very same thoughts, that the many can agree upon; to relate to as part of "His/Her/Its Mind". The "Mind" of inner self, eternal, is this seeded thought, planted within source and as being part of creation.

LESSON~55:

" PROSPERITY IS A VIBRATIONAL ESSENCE, THAT ALREADY EXISTS."

"I WANT THE CLARITY OF REALITY AND NOT THE DEFAULT OF IT."

Take three sectioned and for a brief moment, to apply this concept for the day. One right after waking in the Morning; one anytime, mid-day and lastly before going to bed, at night. With eyes closed and before doing so too; repeat the affirmation, then think of thoughts and in relation to by keeping this idea in mind.

After adding the thought that bring about the worry and from its uncooperative external parts; then from these few external thoughts, repeat it again and in the following manner:

"MY REAL THOUGHTS ARE IN MY MIND".

"I WOULD LIKE TO OPEN UP TO FIND THE RESONANCE AND FROM ALL THE OTHER VARIATIONS OF THIS PERSPECTIVE".

I WANT ALL THAT I AM READY FOR NOW, TO COOPERATIVELY FIND ME AND SHARE FROM THIS ESSENCE, TO EXPERIENCE THE RESONANCE.

Full free and flowing, feel this expansion and the worth beyond description. Allow this vortex of creation, that has self vibrationally created and from its thoughts, extended off into the responsive universe. From these conditions, all things will resonate to attract magnetically to self.

LESSON~55:
"PROSPERITY IS A VIBRATIONAL ESSENCE, THAT ALREADY EXISTS."
"I WANT THE CLARITY OF REALITY AND NOT THE DEFAULT OF IT."

How the self responds to these things, will determine predictably for its experience and to follow from these variables as they unfold. For this reason, there is no such thing as turning back; to how it was, or how it could have been and how it might; or could be and how it is not. From all this kind of thinking, that the self has formed, an attitude and with it, these opinions, that are distortions and illusions; judging harshly from an awareness of need and counter to its value. Appreciate in what is being given and stop looking at the conditions, to be the permission givers; the self is the very permit and from there, can change everything. Recognize this feeling, from the source of its energy and aware; that it is, the moment and from it, the creator of its emotional momentum. Sometimes perspective is needed and from its belief, the knowing of such other aspects, in self awareness; the ability to access this and for the issue, that requires, in every given situation, to slow the vibration down enough, so it can become reachable. With that exception given and for its contradiction, this paradox can be found: Belief can slow and block things up and/or make vibrational realities easier to reach with faith. Certainty and trust of self, that the confidence is equal to its self esteem; the alchemy is found in this impulse, of its desire. However to the evidence, that defies it with having to prove it; is this experience, already under its belt and disconnected enough, to control/ or be controlled with. This staleness can result in the pattern for abuse, so it can generate and pinch off, the currency intermittently; in this way, a reactive world, surviving to acknowledge, forced in worth and worthy of position, to have power over another and/or by another to itself alike.

LESSON~55:
" PROSPERITY IS A VIBRATIONAL ESSENCE, THAT ALREADY EXISTS ."

"I WANT THE CLARITY OF REALITY AND NOT THE DEFAULT OF IT."

The self has been too smart for that and could not last long enough, to enjoy the struggling of the many; out of these components to cooperatively receive. This world, so dense as if to have to try and save it; heroically be proven, in this already made illusion and that it just cannot adjust to its taking and not giving anything back changes. The cooperation of all its components, must be there responding and the parallel realities, not yet materialized, are taken to consider possible. By taking this energy, from contrast; the uncooperative components, into what has never been and in the rejection for the self; that it could then off shoot into another reality(similar to death). This death and life a new, are always possible and can the self see, through this glass ceiling?
When the mind is still, from all the Ego's senseless chatter, a soft whisper like breeze and inside the back of the head, a voice can be heard. The belief in what self is, can reflect on the type of perception and voice it may hear. Perception can show the reality, made possible, by the conditions, or the awareness, of where it could never be; however no cooperation is required, from this reality, for self to be. The choice to create reality, necessitates the self's awareness, to it. By observing the "Ego mind" and where it directs perception; to hear the thoughts of tiny self, vulnerable and afraid. As long as the mind directs perception, the laws of shape, size and brightness are irrelevant. The world is seen by choice and for those things, more likely to discover, than what are preferably overlooked.

LESSON~55:
"PROSPERITY IS A VIBRATIONAL ESSENCE, THAT ALREADY EXISTS."
"I WANT THE CLARITY OF REALITY AND NOT THE DEFAULT OF IT."

The unreality, is expected to disappoint, as an impermanent experience; to feel depression and a sense of worthlessness.
The mind's deception and to believe of self as prey; in a state of helplessness and forced into a struggle of power, over control. Never believe the world directs the destiny that self created and from its faith, is that which makes reality. When the self places its faith in miracles, the perception changes and the voice, is where, this freedom lies awaiting. It is as simple and as natural, as breathing is, to the body. These are the only obvious responses, to calls for help and seem very unnatural to the "Ego";
it does not understand separate minds, can influence each other. Miracles only affect its own mind and this other self is perfectly aware of this. The whole extent of the idea for separation has interfered with reason; because there is no other.
This other self, that holds to reason, has been cut out, from self's awareness. The segment that is unaware, is capable of reason and the other that is aware, is unable to grasp reason.
Many various questions, do give way to form the basic question and that is rooted from reason, it cannot ask.
The obvious and simple remain unasked by reason; to have the way with capacity to answer. The spirit's plan for freedom, could not have been established likewise with no consent.
It must have been accepted through identity consciousness and to force a path for what is higher consciousness, in order for it, to be received. The life force does not come apart from the self, nor does a golden halo wait upon a time, to be accomplished.
Therefore, what joined the Will through Source as Energy /God must be within as the self eternal.

LESSON~55:
"PROSPERITY IS A VIBRATIONAL ESSENCE, THAT ALREADY EXISTS."

"I WANT THE CLARITY OF REALITY AND NOT THE DEFAULT OF IT."

Where higher consciousness must have been and there since the need for this awareness; it has taken its place and has fulfilled all in the same instance. As reason could have it, for this cohesive expansion and to be heard clearly, the "Ego mind" does not so easily allow.

"Ego" finds this proof unnatural and thus cannot be found there. Should it exist in this way, then the freedom is there and for the purpose to find it made unconditional. A much more broader perspective plan is simple and never self-defeating.

Where the stillness of the mind for self-extends and from the heart space; it must be included this part of self, for this Will and shares it. Today, the purpose is, in working with appreciation and from it, to learn, that authenticity can come about and when recognizing the conditional state of self. To practice having to look at, all the conditions and relying upon it, to hand out the appropriate feelings. Perhaps the self can only know itself or found that element of authenticity; for the self and rather to reach into the mind, to find its real thoughts, is what the exercise would like to attempt to do.

To teach the self, how to work through these mental blocks and to find the unconditional existence, that it has been longing for.

(Day64) The soul, within a physical shell and etheric body, is contained a plasmic multiverse. This universe is that of matter/dark matter and that the ethereal, will interface with as anti-matter(flashes); yes, providing an existence of both these worlds combined. From a white microscopic light perspective, to a vaster, macro cosmic one; are these vortices made from and shifting self awareness, to exist. Vibrating in and out of universes, is this self and is this natural state, that defines its frequency.

LESSON~56:
"MY INNER BEING IS THE MIND, WITH WHICH I THINK."
"I AM ABLE FROM THIS MOMENT, TO APPRECIATE THIS LOVE I SEE."

The blocks that are placed there by the self, or from something else; it must be in, with that burning of desire, to break through those blocks. Can the self find what is being held back, or what is holding it back? The resistance comes from a sacred place and that the self must look through the orange coloured lens to find. Remember something prior to it, or just after it?

By regaining of these deeper memories and knowledge, to help clear out trauma; the self can be released from older lineage contracts and patterning. The first one, will be looking at all the childhood memories perhaps and through the orange light lens perspective. There will be a couple of exercises, starting with the morning meditation and first thing while still under a meditative state, from rest recovery. From there, visualize the following: picture the self lying on the most beautiful beach; the sun is just about to rise and yet it is so perfectly warm; hear the waves crashing into the sand …..Now take a deep breath in and hold it …….and then release it.

LESSON~56:

"MY INNER BEING IS THE MIND WITH WHICH I THINK."

"I AM ABLE FROM THIS MOMENT TO APPRECIATE THIS LOVE I SEE."

Repeat this, taking in one deep breath and hold it ....Then release it and then another ..Until a circular breathing rate, is now established, similar to lucid awareness; now and not fixed to any for too long, look up with eyes closed...and see a cave ...Follow the pathway, that leads up to it and from this gentle trance, go into this cavern. The cave is made of orange sparkling crystals, so beautiful and from the ceiling hanging down, the sparkling stalactites.. Keep walking further and look at the many orange flame like, bubbles; they are doorways, on the left and to the right ...In this stillness and on the floor, by looking down now (eyelids are still closed); the one that self might find drawn to. There is a key and as it appears there on the floor, pick it up. Turn the key and open the door ...It is dark and leads down a flight of stairs…..Drop chin down and let the eyeballs look down these steps.. As each muscle lets loose, turns loose, go deeper. Look down to the feet and hear them going down, step 8 and step seven; all the way down to step, by step, feeling this connection, as the self goes deeper ....With step six and five the, self is going deeper, into an awareness of itself and with every muscle and every nerve; as it turns loose, lets loose go deeper....At step four and three and two, move on over, to an even deeper level and go deeper, drift deeper ....sink deeper every moment.

LESSON~56:
"MY INNER BEING IS THE MIND WITH WHICH I THINK."
"I AM ABLE FROM THIS MOMENT TO APPRECIATE THIS LOVE I SEE."

Now, that brings it here, after the last and final step… The self has now entered into a deeper awareness of itself …deeper and deeper ..go deeper. Sink into it, this place, that finds itself here and now; is as powerful and most transformable, taking place within this depth. To realize something most powerful; that it can go to look over and around, so many scenes to reconnect from….So many memories….It has entered into(a big dark room), its very own personal theater and with it, a screen right in front; to look into this darkness…it is a screen, become aware of it, as such. All around like a big gigantic planetarium, is this mind; with floating thoughts, to understand that only it can deliver and in this way, to make any sense of….. Speak the words of power; for this is a very sacred place and self is the director…. Whatever it sais, goes around here.. Anything it has ever wished for(feel the connection), it can manifest in this place and with the given affirmations; that it wishes forth to transmit, its intension with…..Now look through the amber lens and find a video to play with and remember when it was very traumatic to remember then. It does not have to be as traumatic in the now; because it is only the observer of this video. At what age(roughly)did the self experience this injury(physical/emotional); feeling of being let down and frightened/bullied/not safe and unloved and/or neglected? What led to the event and how did it end….. These are the points of references and that can remind the self, of just how temporary this linear state is, from its awareness; know that it is not, who the self is, in the now…"This is not me now" go ahead and say these words; acknowledge just how far along the way, since than you have made it, through this journey….

LESSON~56:

" MY INNER BEING IS THE MIND WITH WHICH I THINK."

"I AM ABLE FROM THIS MOMENT TO APPRECIATE THIS LOVE I SEE."

See how it might have changed in anyway the self into a fixed personality and does it benefit from it in this way ?
Where has this appropriated in the self to learn from and expand by releasing it and letting go of anything it still might be holding onto.... As this older version of the self comfort that part of the lessor evolved and younger child; give it a hug and let it know that it is there for it and no longer does it have to feel alone and/or helpless in this way; that it has someone looking after it; always there watching over it and that it no longer has to stay there; that it can come along to be with the self is now its guardian..... Anything else it might want to let go of or reconcile in this way it can do so.......Oh how these neurons are firing continuously editing this very reality in all the timelines ever imaginable and to create the self fulfilling prophesies in this very same way....The self and now by its very own observatory sacred space can own up to the language of its life and thoughts as well as feelings to respond in with mindfully responsible... Remember what the self has been waiting to hear from others its whole life and re-assure this loving child "say it now, with conviction and like the self can really mean it ..fill it up with self belief and watch it start to trust this older version of itself feeling amazed and excited with this special interaction.

LESSON~56:

"MY INNER BEING IS THE MIND WITH WHICH I THINK."

"I AM ABLE FROM THIS MOMENT TO APPRECIATE THIS LOVE I SEE."

In this feeling of the knowing and that the self has reassured …indeed it has done something wonderful…..slowly easily and effortlessly; it will start making its way back....Right beside the stairs is an elevator, press the button; the orange doors will open and just get in….The elevator will bring the self back, to where it found itself before; on the beach. As the doors open, the sun is found to be in the same place; like it never moved an inch. Once more it sees and feels the waves and just like the touch of this southing breeze; it is like, it never left ….Well done, for this presence, that is self ..Nice, wonderful and it really matters; that the sun and all the likes of its surroundings, did not move the slightest(from their pulsing state of radiance)..In this awareness open eyes, feeling phenomenally great, significant and here for this purpose; everything comes to life, cheering with self in this state of Joy….and repeat the following affirmation:

"MY INNER BEING IS THE MIND WITH WHICH I THINK ."

"I AM ABLE FROM THIS MOMENT TO APPRECIATE THIS LOVE I SEE."

LESSON~56: "MY INNER BEING IS THE MIND WITH WHICH I THINK."

"I AM ABLE FROM THIS MOMENT TO APPRECIATE THIS LOVE I SEE."

Then during the day, at any moment, that it can find; to go outside and reconnect with nature. To reassess, where exactly the self in mindfulness, it can be found and with all of this process, toward enlightenment. Understand, that all different animals and life, have souls; trees do as well and that self might learn to come to a level of understanding, to recognize that trees too, are made from cells. That the self can actually feel the energy around a tree and feel the similarity of the layers of these energies. As well, as the connection, that the self can have to and with these other life forms; that they too, might feel with source of self. Get closer and feel those energies more; the closer it reaches out to nearing them, some more.
The emotional layer, the spiritual layer; can it in this too, as well, as the many other different etheric layers and to become more aware of, in the feeling of them? As discussed before, the extra sensory perceptions can be drawn towards a tree. The self can tune with nature and in this way, to communicate for that moment; by connecting to its energy source, of its soul and this as separate from what it sees and touches, from the physical and life force of it.
This is a spiritual test, to find where exactly self is and in the process of awakening; to what exactly the level of connection, it might have with the Earth.

Hopefully today, there was truly a purpose and in the exploration of this lesson.

(Day65)

The spirit, is an eternal aspect, of the higher self; it dances co-creatively with source, in the expansion of it and from a contracted microspection, the spirit comes into a soul existence, to experience itself, in this way. This book is not asking to remove the soul; but rather clear it and in a way, where more of spirit can come in. In this way, to create a multi-dimensional experience, from its awareness; as creator sovereign self, to better understand, its authenticity and from the oneness, that is source.

LESSON~57: "MY UNIVERSE IS FROM A STRENGTH WITHIN, THAT I MUST TRUST AND NOT FEAR."

As discussed before, the attraction will depend on this (vortice's) ebb and flow, of a reality and through what lens, it will choose to look through, in this way. Just like the tide can dissolve the lens and into many particles of sand; it can then once more, to create a new. From this, all perspective is derived and the formulating mood of self, to resonate with others; however for the attraction to really take place and interact, it must equally be driven and by this same desire, to respond. From a place of felt inspiration, to express and relative to the desire, it will correspond in the same way of curiosity; as the self held and unconditionally in this way of connectivity. The resistance, it too can collaboratively have a way of helping movement and to direct in forward action further. Although illusions are not facts; they can become an imposing consensus, to believe collectively. The other, is to opt for the inner guide system and allow the way to feel, for better thoughts. With feeling, the self can intuitively sense its realities and/or other worlds and not have to be of them(in the physical and from the variations of these levels of awareness); it can also be seen in dreams, while resting and as it travels through the dark light of its imagination.

LESSON~57:
"MY UNIVERSE IS FROM A STRENGTH WITHIN THAT I MUST TRUST AND NOT FEAR."

In this way, how can it be explained and with reasonable sense(to back it up) ? For the self to be explaining it and in the same way, as those who resonate, into each frequency; that by its very own thought, it can creatively be pulled into a vortex and through to these dimensions of perception.

In what is seen through vision, is not what the mind thinks it is in any way. To think with the "Mind" of "SOUL" a sharing of thoughts, between the collective many and self will occur.
These are the same thoughts; because they come from the same mind and shared with the outside likeness, of the one and within. As discussed before however, there are these(Spirit) variations from the levels of awareness. Thoughts never leave their source and in this likeness of shared mind, that with the soul of self, as is.
These beliefs, are of the same thoughts, expressed and inspired throughout its entirety; as well, as within the mind and where it can be found from, as deep as it can understand and with this level of authenticity, to discern with. Yes, these thoughts, are part of this believed image; greater than the self, that most find "worshipable" and now the paradox: is to reflect the self's created image and as outside of itself, can only imply, that it is also found from within.

Today, where reason exists to open doors and in its knowledge, far beyond attainment, is this purpose: to dedicate to life force and through its very own Will for union, with source, to expand consciousness with.

Let go of all the trivial things, that churn and bubble on the surface of the mind; reach down and below them.

(Day66) The soul, comes from source and there are plenty of variations, the self can recreate from it, as such, or not. Although the self, could lose itself completely and of this soul connection; it does not have to let it go, in the way it thinks it.

LESSON~58:
"I AM THE ORCHESTRATOR OF SELF SATISFACTION IN THE HERE AND NOW THAT I DESIRE AND TO INSPIRE THAT WHICH I ATTRACT TO ME IN THE SAME WAY OF CURIOSITY."

It is through the soul, that self is able to access all the many different coloured lenses and for a well grounded meaningful experience, to explore in the expansion of its source.
When from a physical perspective of the "Ego mind", the self is placed in a linear lack and limitation of reasoning, to live by; while feeling this contraction, with the "Spiritual" and "Metaphysical" aspects of itself(from this illusion growth is realized). Find a new way of looking at this; does the self feel ready, by how it feels and where it is?
Look at appreciating all the things, that keep it where it is and repeat the following:
"THROUGH THE EYES OF SOURCE; I FIND THE HARMONY AND ALIGNMENT FROM WITHIN AND TAKE THE NEXT STEP THAT FEELS CLARITY AND WELL BEING."

Make use of this idea often and by repeating throughout the day; for the answer and to any of its disturbances. Remember that of "Surrendered Trust" and to this strength for peace, is its right. Now that faith and belief have shifted, it has come very close by reason.
The reason for the question, must have come from something unknown; however must belong to itself.

LESSON~58:

"I AM THE ORCHESTRATOR OF SELF SATISFACTION IN THE HERE AND NOW THAT I DESIRE AND TO INSPIRE THAT WHICH I ATTRACT."

When faith and belief, are upheld by reason, a shift in perception does take place. In this change, is made room for vision and that extends beyond itself; as does the purpose, that it serves and all the reasons for accomplishment. The presence of fear, is a sure sign that the Ego might be wreaking havoc and the trust, is not in the right place. The awareness of having nothing to fear, comes from a heart centered place and let this heart felt strength, take the place of any weakness. The pressure to be counted on, is a stress related illusion, brought on from expectations; best left to chance the moment and with God felt presence of life, than to create forever disappointment. To be in the awareness and of all the facets of resolve; rather than in its problem, is this state preferred and where only good can come out of. In every aspect and that of all situations, feel them through; allow to hear through this internal guidance, to reach self's navigating voice, "The Inner Voice ".

It does not matter how the circumstances turn out, nor how they are; as long as the feeling is safe and to trust, that no harm will come of it. Frequent short exercises are encouraged; however also necessary to take a few, with longer intent. With eyes closed, repeat the idea for the day and spend a few minutes searching the mind. To place its faith in this strength and feel weak; is the first sign, that it has a built in navigating guidance system. When strength is felt most certain, then God's presence is found; this result from surrendered trust, is the faith that nurtures the path.

Hopefully and during the last phase of these practices; it will be reached, this deep sense of peace.

The purpose, is to reach past personal weakness, to the source of real strength and to trust in a place, that feels the strength of love.

THE INTERMISSION :

Take a day to take it in

CONGRATULATIONS ...!!!

FOR MAKING IT

THROUGH TO THE 58th Lesson

(This is a rest period to take the lessons independently as a review)

TAKE THIS DAY TO RECALIBRATE;

MAKE NOTES AND REVIEW.................

(Day68)
Undistracted, from the self imposing regulations and to function systematically; stop pretending to obey something that is out of reach. There is a part of the mind, that sparks from the inner self and is in constant communication with its source.

LESSON~59:
"MY INNER VOICE IS THIS THOUGHT AND HUNCH FROM INTUITION THAT SPEAKS TO ME ALL THROUGH THE DAY."

Whatever affirmation, that is preferred; as long as it is with and coinciding, alongside the theme of today and for the main idea. Work on, sliding past all subjective concerns and that of feeling inadequate; because it can be better dealt with the situation successfully. As previously mentioned and on a deeper level; confidence is gained, in trusting the strength of authenticity and in the self, to be seen as, successful in all things. The recognition of frailty, is a necessary step to rectify; yet hardly sufficient and in the giving much needed confidence, that the self is entitled to.
It is important to gain awareness and that of its self esteem; to be a real strength in every aspect and in all circumstances.
Today, allow that part of the mind, that is not constantly distracted, disorganized and highly uncertain. Sink into the calmness of reality; where the self is always certain to hear its inner voice and in the whisper of its knowing thought. Can it recognize the portion of the mind, where stillness and peace reign forever.
Focus on the intention to hear this inner voice, call out lovingly and in the understanding of this thought, can it remember ?

LESSON~59:
"MY INNER VOICE IS THIS THOUGHT AND HUNCH FROM INTUITION THAT SPEAKS TO ME ALL THROUGH THE DAY."

Take a few minutes, to feel intuitively for it, and in this knowing, four long sessions or more, throughout the day spread out. Make the attempt, effortless to receive this reminder and from within to listen. Approach this happiest and holiest of thoughts with, to encourage in graceful understanding. Be open and receptive, to hearing and in deep silence, the mind can open. Allow for the self, to sink in and with the eternal link, to this inner voice of peace. This place of enlightenment; it can always have a name to figure with. The aethereal covers over all and everything; to simplify the way beyond the frantic, thunderous thoughts and sights and sounds, of this insane world.
Why overcomplicate, to imagine the subtleties, of what is pure and most simple. Peacefully positive, is this energy from source and does not need the proof, of any further to explain, nor reason with. Take this idea for the day, to reaffirm its activation and that is all. Have eyes closed, for a more meditative experience and/or eyes open, for a more conscious state of awareness.
Either or be in a quiet still presence and repeat the affirmation; whenever possible and to make way, for this invitation, to hear the "Voice". Be still and let the place, where the self is truly welcomed; to feel a higher connection from the self, to reach out and find it there, in this peace.

The purpose, is for learning how to channel and when connected from within, a sovereign state of authenticity.

(Day69)

The sustenance of a higher self is this keeper of self and the soul, by its physical perception, to Love itself. The answer, is in the solution; that the physical self must look deeper and to confront within its linear confines.

LESSON~60:"I AM THE EMBODIMENT FROM THE ATONEMENT, THAT THRIVES AS HIGHER SELF."

From the spreading forth of the sea, is this preeminent happiness and to shine upon the self, from the infinite. A golden light of brilliance, has endowed with all its glory, to rise up and dazzle from the perfected deeds of self, upon this very moment.

The actions of self can only be perfected, when coming from the heart and in this mood of non thought formation, all forms of radiance will come to merge. Intellect must rise and develop from the wisdom, of the wandering self and to invert back inwardly for home. At the central point of its existence, is this reality and from within the heart; a turquoise brilliance and that brings forth the realities, of four worlds into one. Water, Earth , Fire and Air, can shine upon thee simultaneously and from within the heart's division. From within the self, begins to know itself and as sentient beings are projected "holographically" outwards, the part of self that wishes to communicate and connect. By understanding this, even the most wrathful of creatures, can be integrated back with grace. "Protective" clothing, influence, prestige, being liked, knowing the right people, and an endless list of forms of nothingness, that can gift unto the self, with magical powers.

All these things are meaningless and goes without saying, just how much they lack the relevance and within the grander scheme of things. Falling into the brut world, whereby stupidity predominates the suffering of illimitable miseries of slavery and dumbness; is what this "Ego mind" has the self and in the mood for unbearable misery.

LESSON~60: "I AM THE EMBODIMENT FROM THE ATONEMENT, THAT THRIVES AS HIGHER SELF"

Be not jealous of all the worldly goods; all these attachments bring warfare and quarreling. Seek instead, to find compassion for these hording souls, that linger on eternally within the ethers. Ride the rainbow bridge of this compassion, to the bright path of Heaven. When all is lost, from interrupted obstructions; the self can become most enlightened then. For ten minutes, twice today, morning and evening, let the idea sink deep, into the consciousness. Repeat this affirmation: made to mention as "Infinite eternal flame" and/or "Higher-Self".
Think about it, let related thoughts come to help recognize its truth, and allow peace to flow over, like a blanket of protection and surety. Briefly let the idle worship and that of gendered novelty thoughts, related to God/Higher-Self and just let them go. Such is the Kingdom of Heaven and such is this resting place for the self and in the greatest of purity, to be at one with.
Do not stress over the superficial thoughts, that might identify as disturbing with resistance; they are as foolish as to claim them out; just allow and for the holy mind of God/Higher-Self to channel in.

The purpose, is to go within, to find that which is eternal and through this process, of neither attraction nor repulsion; the connection of sustained Love for Higher-Self/God and this self awareness of loving flow.

(Day70) The path of the "Ego mind", is brutal and filled with stupidity of incompletion. Each time the self descends, spiralling downward and to find exactly what is missing; it gains more insight and that towards the needed from before (to better understand that part of itself required on the path to enlightenment).

LESSON~61: "I AM A SOVEREIGN WHITE LIGHT BEING WITH EARTH ABIDING KNOWLEDGE."

"THAT WHICH FILLS ME UP WITH RAINBOW LIGHT IS MY POWER FROM WITHIN THIS HALLOWED CIRCLE THAT I MAY RISE OVER THE DURATION IN THE KNOWING I HAVE CHOICE: TO DANCE WITH THE KARMIC RIPENING."

Was it innocence or foolishness, to wander in the density of darkness, so that others may see the way? The self became a warrior; when the unwilling many of its world, were reckless in their actions. Unyielding to face up to such response; the self became the martyr of such repercussion. In the early stages of enlightenment, this becomes the case. In its darkest pilgrimage, it had lit a path for itself. To find an unfaithful half angry and half smiling brutish world. That would come to greet it with obscuring passion for stupidity; because it radiated heaven, from within and did not understand, the why and how. The blending of its cannibalistic nature and emanations from the master; over its survival and from its "Inner Voice". Reverberating like the sounds of thousand thunders; rolling down to reach it and had taught it well.
While learning how to own this part of self and yet, it felt intuitively led by its very own wisdom, out from this illusion.

LESSON~61: "I AM A SOVEREIGN WHITE LIGHT BEING WITH EARTH ABIDING KNOWLEDGE."

"THAT WHICH FILLS ME UP WITH RAINBOW LIGHT IS MY POWER FROM WITHIN THIS HALLOWED CIRCLE THAT I MAY RISE OVER THE DURATION IN THE KNOWING I HAVE CHOICE: TO DANCE WITH THE KARMIC RIPENING."

Today's exercise, is reaching out to the temptation; of whatever disorder must find the self enslaved to, and/or depriving from truly understanding. Is it the fear and panic and to worry over something, it requires to survive with? Is it in the oppression of expressing and contributing ? Is it in the misunderstanding of its grief and to betray in bitterness, that which is jealousy?
Find the anger and where the self feels stuck or depressed; or even manic, to express in isolation? Is it responsible for the many others, that depend on it? Where does the self require refinement in this way, reach out and take a hold of it. Be the observer and witness it, from an estranged perspective and then embrace these findings well; to come to know it, as that part of the self that's hungry, thirsty and/or whatever else it is in need and from longing for, toward completion.   Such resistance, to create much effort and not in consistency of their truth; to think it is constantly failing at justifying its thoughts. Set it free and liberate it, from its unresolved phenomena; do not attached nor detached. Emphasize on the theme of the idea, and think about it compassionately.
It takes so much energy to keep something twisted up and when it can be let go of to untwist; it will release so much trapped energy, that it was holding.

The purpose, is to learn from the many layers of faith; to feel peace and the quiet calmness, brought forth from everywhere;   to also help heal distress and turmoil.

(Day71) To hold the past as the opposition, is to make an enemy of it. How ridiculous it is, this commonality and to be reminded of past thoughts, to take the place of the "HERE AND NOW" moment with. To prevent the mind from actualizing the present moment; is to deplete from the self's fullest potential and goes against its very own life force.

"I HAVE FORGIVEN MYSELF AND
 HAVE REMEMBERED WHO I AM."

LESSON~62: "I AM GRATEFUL THAT THIS WORLD IS NOT REAL AND THAT I NEED NOT SEE IT AT ALL UNLESS I CHOOSE TO VALUE IT."

How silly, to trust in things that are ungratefully taken for granted; even at its very own worth, for an identity and to observe, that the observer, has now been stolen by the many? All that it may have invested energy and to imprint upon the knowing; or possibly of having been informed of its very own accumulated interest and to invest its energy, with that as mistaken for another.
The falsehood of its circumstances, that had created it as easily to correspond and in this protective trust, to turn on it; by taking back all that was relevantly reflected. As a being merged into an acceptable image, of its very own creation to accept and contribute in this way; as best it can to identify as being given and in this meaning for being. The very thought of authenticating from its many colourful identities. Now taken over by another, to split off its energy and make it non existent; in the presence of all it has been working on and including for this making, of a novel.
Why make all things as its invading enemies; just so, that it can to justify its anger and to feel that the attacks are warranted?

Today, meditate on the main idea and upon its central meaning.

LESSON~62: "I AM GRATEFUL THAT THIS WORLD IS NOT REAL AND THAT I NEED NOT SEE IT AT ALL UNLESS I CHOOSE TO VALUE IT."

Through out the day, repeat these affirmations to transmit the consciousness with. The purpose for today, is to internally secure the authority and to acknowledge, as author of your very own book. It is from this consciousness, that does not seek to take advantage; in the discriminating factor of value over another and enough to justify for these meaningless thoughts.
Rather highlights instead, to magnify and stretch, beyond these borders of asphyxiation. The selfless act of an authentic sovereign being and from this light; this very own spark of awareness, that nowhere else can intimately intimidate and to warrant as non existing, from the oneness of itself.

"I HAVE MISUSED EVERYTHING IN ITS POWER TO ASSIGN A ROLE TO DEFEND OVER A THOUGHT SYSTEM THAT HAS HURT ME."

"I AM NOW LETTING GO THAT OF WHICH PREVIOUSLY HAS SERVED AND TAUGHT ME WELL" AND I THANK IT FOR THE EXPANSION. "

Why not join the thinking universe; rather than to obscure it with a subjective reality of, pitiful and meaningless, "private" thoughts?

Such a world, is not that very well preferred; rather from this perspective and not in such high demand, to value over.

LESSON~62: "I AM GRATEFUL THAT THIS WORLD IS NOT REAL AND THAT I NEED NOT SEE IT AT ALL UNLESS I CHOOSE TO VALUE IT."

Anything that is not completely dependable, thrives on providing security, for what it lacks in; it gives forth the grounds, to not trust it and for this reason, that it be totally insane. Nothing in madness is dependable and it can be said that "it holds no safety, nor any hope". Such a world can only be as real, as the amount of belief it is given.

"I HAVE GIVEN THE ILLUSION OF REALITY TO A BELIEF THAT MADE ME SUFFER

"I CHOOSE INSTEAD TO WITHDRAW FROM THIS BELIEF AND REPLACE IT WITH THE REALITY I CAN TRUST IN THE HERE AND NOW."

In making this kind of choice, to break free from the trappings of yesterday's thoughts; that intimidate to hold the threat of taking over and wiping out its thoughts. The self might not want to perceive it in the act of being wiped out and from its very own awareness; is this fear in that, of what the tomorrow might bring. The "HERE AND NOW" must be acknowledged, to rid it of the fear or threat and intimidating; the fear of getting wiped out completely, has no place in this existence.

"LET ME AWAKEN ONCE AGAIN TO THE POWER OF MY DECISION, AND RECOGNIZE THE REALITY TO ACCEPT IT."

(Day72) The sharing of differences, made no difference in the nothingness of it all. These very same thoughts and that the self does see, awaken the real thoughts in them. Healing promotes power; however the misinformed invasion, can lead to misguidance and helplessness. The turning into an attack, can carry on from the illusion, that something must be fixed, as well as be protected.

LESSON~63: "MY CONSCIOUSNESS CAN TRAVEL EVERYWHERE AND ANYWHERE MY MIND PROJECTS IT TO."

"IS THIS HOW I WANT TO FEEL AND WHAT I WANT TO SEE ? "

"WHATEVER REALITY AM I DESIRING TO PROJECT WITH MY INTENTION WILL BE THE PROGRAM I CAN CHOOSE TO RESPOND TO INSTEAD OF ONE THAT RULES OVER ME ?"

"DO I DESIRE A WORLD WHERE I AM POWERFUL INSTEAD OF HELPLESS ?"

"DO I DESIRE A NON ABUSIVE WORLD OF INCORRUPTIBILITY WHERE THERE ARE NO ENEMIES CREATED FROM DISCONNECT ?"

In the reality where it is not from self impression, it cannot be seen to understand and self becomes feeling helpless by it.

"DO I WANT TO SEE WHAT I DENIED BECAUSE IT IS THAT PART OF ME THAT NO LONGER FITS IN THAT TRUTH ? "
"ALL OF MY REAL THOUGHTS THAT I CALL UPON ARE SHARED WITH EVERYONE."

LESSON~63: "MY CONSCIOUSNESS CAN TRAVEL EVERYWHERE AND ANYWHERE MY MIND PROJECTS IT TO."

The feeling of separation, has had its place to create; such a difference and so to better understand the world with.
Recognize all that reflects back to vision and from the mind's accumulated thoughts, they are for the realizing of what self is.
When the self is able to remove itself, through mindlessness and from clearing all the programming, that disempowers it; to go beyond all the mind's insane wishes, is the self will and (united they be one) with energy of its source. Existing force, is still everywhere and in everything forever. "<u>Energy is in everything I see; because energy is in my mind</u>". The lesser evolved and with the much more evolved parts of these variations, of itself(it had unknowingly created).
The world that held the self in a place, it had accepted to feel attacked and when awakened from the conflict of this dream; it had realized, just how powerless and weak indeed. After this, it begins to regain all its strength back and with it, its very own authentic self, it can accept to value. From these authentic programs, the self can become sovereign in its truth. Reason would have it to admit, there is no such thing or place, to hand over self's power to.
When emphasizing the sameness of things, the final question must not be of threat and for the others weigh on this decision.
To create or to destroy; to heal or to cause harm?
These choices made and from these choices, the self must remember; the helplessness of disconnect and the abuse of power, in the need to value control, over connection. This is the corruption, the illusion and the truth; of a world that cannot be, from what it is.

The purpose of this day, to radiate from this transmission real gratitude. From this feeling, all falsehood in celebration of a day each year and to set aside, is not enough. To forcefully impose the disconnect of such a gathering and to give thanks; while every other day, is in the taking for granted, in what has sincerely been given.

(Day73) Long after the density; forced by the heaviness, that is the concept of the circle and within it a clump of matter, that is self. From this perspective, is all its physical eyes can see through and to perceive as real. The consciousness, passed down through the rods and filtered through this coned shaped vision; can only see the water, when it falls to form into these droplets.

LESSON~64: "I CAN TRANSCEND BEYOND THESE PHYSICAL EYES THAT I CAN FEEL INSTEAD TO HAVE A BETTER UNDERSTANDING WITH MY CONNECTION TO THIS ENERGY IN MOTION."

From a metaphysical reality, is this mind held in its place and with illuminating consciousness. Higher consciousness, is this observation and to accept the depth of a reality; with a light version of the connection, to the physical. Accept the self to function at a higher frequency and rate of vibrational flow; with in its experience and as for the mind, to be of form, interpreted as physical. Today, practice being fully present with every circumstances that present themselves; or that self must instead intentionally project, as well as physically transport itself to.
In the previous lesson and the introduction for the main idea, was to project the mind and when the circumstances flow to it. Today, the blending of receptive and projecting, can be combined and the four into the two pairs; within this, its formed reality, to better understand the metaphysics and the physics of it, much more clearly. Firstly, the self must learn how to rid itself from all distractions, of the in-between realities; by doing so, it learns to become fully present and within every moment it engages with. The sample for this day, can give the self some hints; as to where exactly, it might be in its process and from a linear assessment, to perhaps make any sense of.

LESSON~64: "I CAN TRANSCEND BEYOND THESE PHYSICAL EYES THAT I CAN FEEL INSTEAD TO HAVE A BETTER UNDERSTANDING WITH MY CONNECTION TO THIS ENERGY IN MOTION."

Set the intention for the day and of all that must be accomplished; to allow for it all to happen, as it may unfold.
Where does the self need to go and how many different realities, of focusable intentions, does it congregate throughout its day and alongside the many facets of its societal parts, to help with its presence, as contribution?

To be present, amongst the many groupings in this way and physically present to support; is much more than enough and to place it as a contributing energy factor. Or is it mindlessly distracted and while contributing in the way of action oriented doing? Is the self projecting its mind else where; while physically being and doing something else?

These will later be the conflicts and that come back to challenge it; with echo circumstances and of its blind-spotting, accumulated judgments, to the disconnect.

By bridging the gap of the "Ethereal" and from a fifth dimensional perspective; somewhere is this reality, waiting to be explored and that seems to be the answer, of leaving behind repeated patterns, from the Infinite's "Ethereal."

The purpose for today, is this process of transmitting and receiving and within a multidimensional reality; to prepare the self, to function in a world, where there are no gaps.

(Day74) From the linear reality and to a full circle, is this formed space; into matter and from every still shot, picture frame, a motion, through the inner and the outer awareness.
Why not instead observe the flashes of light?
These sparks, resembling through the synapses of its very own neural-pathways; then these might very well be, glimpses into portals. Could it be, that from these flashes, might come to congregate and create the idea of entity. That the self might differentiate, to witness as; or be of that, from one reality, to another?
LESSON~65: "I AM THAT SPARK OF LIGHT TO TAKE WITH ME THROUGH ONE PORTAL OF AWARENESS TO ANOTHER AND FOR A MOMENT BE STILL AND TAKE A GLIMPSE ....PERHAPS AT THE CORNER OF THESE PHYSICAL EYES I STAND BY TO WITNESS THE MANY OTHER SPARKS FROM ME TO COME AND CONGREGATE AS ONE... MADE OBSERVABLE AND FROM ONE REALITY TO THE VERY NEXT.... SHIFTING IN PERSPECTIVE TO ENGAGE WITH ANY WORLD I PLEASE."

When density is lacking, the membrane that holds the plasma in, is no longer defined and in such a way, as to slightly witness, in the air as orbs; or dust particles, that hold in a world of colour and so on and so forth.....Within the reality of the mind and the slightly felt like, a puff of smoke; it can come this close to resembling the solid world. The self must become the aethereal; rather than, to hold this awareness down and long enough to capture it; And in one frame at a time, from this aethereal reality of the mind. It cannot be possibly explained, as to fit into a box; rather it must be felt and left to the imagination to reinterpret. The colours can also be expressed within the impression and for the mind of self. To better understand this kind of therapy; always come to the very same question and that is, how does it feel? The entire electrical system of the self, can only be directed to function well and from this perspective, in saying that:
"The heart rules".

LESSON~65: " I AM THAT SPARK OF LIGHT TO TAKE WITH ME THROUGH ONE PORTAL OF AWARENESS TO ANOTHER AND FOR A MOMENT BE STILL AND TAKE A GLIMPSE ....PERHAPS AT THE CORNER OF THESE PHYSICAL EYES I STAND BY TO WITNESS THE MANY OTHER SPARKS FROM ME TO COME AND CONGREGATE AS ONE... MADE OBSERVABLE AND FROM ONE REALITY TO THE VERY NEXT.... SHIFTING IN PERSPECTIVE TO ENGAGE WITH ANY WORLD I PLEASE."

For any form of consciousness to gravitate and form; that has come over into this reality and/or self into it, from another, it must be felt and then imagined. In this way, of discernment can be and to respond, to the cause that self created; rather than react to its effect. To choose, than to decide; for example and in the case of healing through the bodies eyes, of what already is, it sees; and/or to let it be revealed, through the imagination, of its inner vision.
Allow for the idea, to want to see by choice; this choice must be guided by and through feeling it, to lead the way.
Before starting out the day, project into a blank dark screen and with all the things, the self prefers to be engaging with; as witness to its circumstances and of the world it prefers to see and then:
To better clarify the following, can be repeated and throughout the day; is made simple, by the following statement to ask the self with:
"IS THIS WHAT I WOULD SEE" ? " DO I WANT THIS " ?

The how, is not important for this condition and for what occurs. Rather the why, is the only responsibility for the self to take with and every decision that it makes; from each of the choices, that present directly and/or indirectly, from its circumstance in this day. The purpose is, to better grasp and for any given reality, that represents itself. That the self is not a helpless victim; rather the creator of every impression and that projects to it. As real from the projector, that revolves around the changes, of its every decision and response to it; in this way shifting every moment, the variance of its reality.

(Day75)

It has been discussed and the referencing to a pairing up; when projecting to receive and as the observer, or receiving to engage from before, as the observed. It is with the higher state of consciousness, that life can fully and with its heart, feel completely to be, of every given present moment.

> LESSON~66: "I MUST STOP WANDERING AIMLESSLY DOWNWARD INTO A WRATHFUL KINGDOM AND WITH INTENTION DIRECT MY CONSCIOUSNESS INTO THE ONENESS OF AWAKENING."

Sometimes, when bliss hits the self, the heart is ready to receive it; but the level of awareness and within the mind, will burst in the expansion, of accepting it. A tension is felt and the mind will feel, a neurological overwhelm; in that of stress and perhaps cause resistance.

When the mind is not ready to fully expand and to accept the extremes; that its awareness might be giving it (as highs and lows).

The self will then surrender, to what it is more conditioned and to from its created patterning with. To escape from the highs and lows of circumstantial frequencies, it might be better to descend and spiral downwardly; rather than to explode into the bliss. In this case, know that it is the heart, that has created the blissful circumstances and it is the reason, to why it can handle and to accept the incoming, of these higher frequencies. The coming in, from the thought forms and that the self had, with intention created; however in the clearing of the old and much heavier dense realities, it might get snagged, to spiral downward. As this is happening, an incoming blast of blissful circumstances will want to bring it back and higher; with its inspired intentions, that it had, in passion to express and to exert much energy, in the investment of it all. This is another level and layer, for faith perhaps; that it must learn to recalibrate, with the self and reintegrate, to find the balance. Some of these frequencies, do not vibrate in the way of what once might it have been to understand faith; or even hope from its awareness. Likewise, such as: "wrathful"; it has no place and where there is nothing for it, to stick or connect to.

LESSON~66: " I MUST STOP WANDERING AIMLESSLY DOWNWARD INTO A WRATHFUL KINGDOM AND WITH INTENTION DIRECT MY CONSCIOUSNESS INTO THE ONENESS OF AWAKENING."

Today contemplate on this idea and transmit the thought of feeling in the way of becoming and from believing. Practice the pairing up with the Observer and to that of engaging or transmitting with (in this way, as was practiced in lesson 63). Before starting off the day remotely view whatever the intensions to engage in and the many places it will take its physical body with for the experience.
Is there any resistance and how are the circumstances treating to behave in the response of what the self prefers for its outcome? Then go and engage with the day; then upon completion how did it all turn out?
With eyes closed go inward and meditate once more; this time be the receiver of how the body feels and how the emotional body feels and who or what transmissions are coming in from throughout the day within its field that have made impressions upon the self.
What is it that is not beneficial let it go! What has snagged; or tugged; or irritated; or trapped into a binding forecast; let it go and practice only that which is the self in its highest good to serve it. Feel the bliss that faith will bring and that of which the heart already knows to feel; "Love" "Here" and "Now", breathe it in and breathe all the yucky icky gunk out.

The purpose of today, is to slowly come to trust in the surrounding feeling of the warm embrace of bliss completely and let it envelope full heartedly as it were within the mind of the self.

(Day76)
In just the same way, that the self is able to teleport itself physically, mentally and Spiritually. Visually just the same; it can transmit and to teleport within its fields; this way that it may as well receive it. From these two and to combine, as well the many variations; as there are decisions from such discernments made.

LESSON~67:
"MY PROJECTIONS COME INTO FRUITION ALWAYS."

Firstly, the experience of the false world and that the "Ego" can identify with. The "Ego mind", must be wiped out and what a terrifying experience; to see it take on, a separate existence and while killing instead the real self. The appearance can be frightfully convincing; to believe that it has shut the real self out and not the other way around? Sound, sight; physical matter and or just simply wave forms; that impress upon the self and from its very own impressions, to perceive them, in this way.
Shape shifting and teleporting of the self and/or other circumstances; places; objects, they are all these many combinations. These are the pairing up and from the many; or as many variations, from the self awareness. From the practice, in this way to exercise the basic senses of the physical; is this field of overlapping with imagination, to better express and inspire creativity. The more subtle, extra sensory perceptions and from the inner self awareness, can find the way to merge; the inner and the outer, into one heightened existence, of the self.
In this way, the observer and observed, can also intermingle, with the innermost and outermost impressions;
from(unenlightened/enlightened) the impressed and the impressed upon, both are interchangeable expressions.
The self can master in this way, that of its physical reality, to touch and become touched by it.

LESSON~67:
"MY PROJECTIONS COME INTO FRUITION ALWAYS."

The self can touch the outer world and from it; the many in this way can be responsive back. From this can come reaction or the responsive mindfulness engagement; that the self has transmitted out, so that it may, once again receive. How it will receive it and how it is received, will the impressed upon, emit out and through the variation, to engage strongly or not at all; directly or indirectly and subversively contain. On very rare occasions, it will go under an agreement with another; to exchange in this way and then come back again. Similar to an exchange student, swapping places. This exchange, within a human body, where a soul will leave and go into another body, is no longer. Rather the trickery of death; is in the hacker, to posses and compromise its system for, its own fraudulent gain. Again, a different level of weakness/strength that the self has given into its "Egoic identity"; to threaten it, in this way and by projecting out, as it can think it should project? Sometimes identity theft is nothing short; but of a win-fall to a thief. Not so much the identity; rather held within it of this light of information, that was in becoming for the greater mission and of this book. In this age of artificial intelligence and advanced technological blending; with the biological entity that self created. What does it feel like and without a "will" for any of its work at hand invested to consider; rather left for dead, while another entity takes over. In most cases, this account was like an integration merging from its soul's and the many files to help it with its mission; why would the self want to leave from this built in body of information and that it knows as purpose, why would it go?
Who creates the viruses and are they even real?
Relying on the Ego, to protect it and trusting full heartedly upon a flawed system; to become, as its very own existence.
So much so, that it had been dumbing down the most "<u>Innernet</u> of self connection".

LESSON~67:
"MY PROJECTIONS COME INTO FRUITION ALWAYS."

The internet and from this false field, where the many are mislead and micromanaged. This is a process to experience and what it might be like in another dimension; that otherwise its source could not allow and to stand in as a human expression. When entering into the soul of the self; (lower unacknowledged aspects of the self) "Demonic" expressions, can only share the soul and without the self; they too will have no other place to hide. When there is no third party "Artificial Intelligence" and where the advanced technological entities; that it must source out can the Ego hide behind?
The soul might go and then, that physical body can actually shape shift; yes, this is more common through channeling, than through anything else. It can also and on very rare occasions; it will go under an agreement, with another to exchange and in this way, it can come back again.

How interesting, this purpose to experience the many different ways of channeling and where the spirit, it can enter.

(Day77) In the dawning of and that of the re-birthing of its soul; the self can step into a field, so clear and is as similar, to that of forgetfulness. The self feels lost in this case, but it is not forgetfulness, because the soul is wise enough; however it is cleared from all its previous hang-ups and collective baggage.

LESSON~68:
"THE WHERE I AM I FEEL DIRECTLY FROM MY HEART AND FROM THIS PROCESS IT TURNS INTO MEANING."

The energy body of the self, has always been directly linked and from deep within the heart. Yes, the physical heart of the body and where the electro/magnetic (push/pull)"Bundle of His" resides. The author of the book of self too, resides in this office space; typing away, every experience, that is felt into a story. From its book, is then the meaning; that the mind can electrically hold onto, as its memory. From this, it is the heart, that sets the pace of ebb and flow(pacemaker). The self with its mind, can only collaboratively direct this state of being, with the heart; to bring about and with the correspondence of its circumstances.
When a thought comes in, and/or circumstance that can cause the chest area, to feel constricted or compressed upon; the breathing too, it will increase to a panic and almost gasping and at the rate of creating for itself, much discomfort. The brain can help, when it is practiced well in mindfulness; otherwise it will panic and shut down, like in the case of trauma. The energy will then get trapped or stuck, somewhere within the soul's field. Externally, as well as internally; to the physical body and/or including at a cellular/genetic level.

LESSON~68:
"THE WHERE I AM I FEEL DIRECTLY FROM MY HEART AND FROM THIS PROCESS IT TURNS INTO MEANING."

Today, practice activating the "InnerNet" perspective; feel it from a cellular field level; this too surrounds the self externally and at the radius of, as far as the physical arms, can stretch outward. In this, its sacred space, is this field from where it starts, and then again spreads rippling out(transmitting as far as 50km). From the heart connection and then with a much deeper radiance, to affect its continent; then the entire globe of this planet. Feel the rhythm and the beating of this heart; that moves all emotion into feeling and from it the breath, that regulates it, with or without the minds assistance. From this awareness, the more subtle exercises as: "Clairsentience" can once again be realized. These gifts must be explored and not taken for granted, to dismiss; they too get exploited and misused. In the acknowledgement of these inherent gifts, the self can rid of all distortions of abuse and from the outside world; from this process, learn to uncover all the hidden missuses and of these valuable energies. Can the self hear the song of a "clairaudient" tone to thought and from the cellular rhythm of the breath; the every beat that moves it ? The melody of energy and soul; how does each thought and word, to correspond with the story of its frequency? That it may vibrate in this way: a state of Joy, Happiness and knowingness of Love; from the channeler and not just the channel. The heart is this integral aspect of the self and from where that spark of light has its origins as the self.

Choose to accept the disconnection from its mind; and/or rather accept to become enlightened, by the wholeness of the connection and into oneness with it.

The purpose is, to connect to channeling, as a creative art expression and from the imagination; rather than a circumstantial evidence, of something foreign and disconnected with its consciousness.

(Day78) Artificial advancement in technology, has only made it to as far, as brainwave and scanning of the intellect. As previously discussed and within the soul containment; the energetic body, has infused its frequency and to better understand, that the self is specifically gifted and/or skilled. It is in this electronic signature, that will better to define and for its decision, of how it will be put to use, this energy.

LESSON~69:
"I AM MY OWN UNIQUE FREQUENCY AND WITH THIS ENERGETIC SIGNATURE MY PSYCHIC CAPABILITIES CAN BE IDENTIFIABLE AS IMPRINTS TO IMPRESS UPON THE PHYSICAL WORLD TO MATCH IT THROUGH."

Authentically identifiable by the patterning of the brain, its mind is distinct and as with, its physical fingerprinting; however not as far up in and where the heart can grasp it. This is the brain's capacity (as in the case of Internet hacking) and to that extent of raping the self from its very own informational Identity.

A FEW WORDS FROM THE EGO MIND'S PSYCHE AND PORTRAYING FROM THE ONLY SELF AS ITS AWARENESS: "THROUGH THE LABYRINTH OF FORGETFULNESS; DISTORTED REMNANTS OF DYSFUNCTIONS DWELL AND THREATEN TO POSSES MY VISION." "FORCEFUL SHADOWS OVERPOWER THE RAYS LIKE SLIVERS OF MY SPIRIT; THAT THEY BE DANCING FROM THE FLICKERING OF AS FLARES UPON THE DENSEST RELEVANCE TO FEED UPON FOR THEIR VERY OWN SURVIVAL". WHO OR WHAT IS THIS ENTITY COMPETITIVELY EXISTING FORCE AND THAT FRAGMENTS IN THIS WAY THE SELF AS OUTCAST?"
IT IS FROM THE MERCY OF THE EGO FOR THEIR VERY OWN EQUALITY AND FAIRNESS TO EXIST AND CONTINUE ON FOREVERMORE AS THE MANY SEPARATED FRAGMENTS OF THE SELF."

LESSON~69: "I AM MY OWN UNIQUE FREQUENCY AND WITH THIS ENERGETIC SIGNATURE MY PSYCHIC CAPABILITIES CAN BE IDENTIFIABLE AS IMPRINTS TO IMPRESS UPON THE PHYSICAL WORLD TO MATCH IT THROUGH."

From the esoteric side of things and at least one symbol from the many given, will dawn upon the self, to obtain such wisdom.

At every corner that it turns along its winding path; a trickster creature like, to treat or trick it and gesturing to hold it up, along the way of indecision. The self must know to feel by now, that it is not justifiable and to recognize in these tricksters or any other symbol; rather in that of its own probability, to change perspectives.

Today, set aside a moment, to feel into the nothingness and become absorbed. It has been mentioned before; to help in the refreshing of grounding and centering into this place, from within the heart.

With eyes closed, sink into the nothingness; be still within the mind, from any distracting thoughts and just focus now on breathing. Breathe deeply and circular; from every inhale and exhale and by trying not to swallow. Perhaps sample by placing the tip of the tongue, to the roof of the mouth and as it is closed; breathing in from the nose and out. Or just simply to breathe out and through the mouth(whatever works best), will do just fine. Sink deeper and let the darkness of this emptiness, absorb all thought of formations. Freshly cut grass starts to touch the senses and within a crisp night breeze, of velvet sky; are the many stars twinkling about. Feel the physical body, bare-foot, walking through its plushness and in between the toes, the blade of grass; that radiate all around, an emerald green vibration. Look deeper, straight ahead and nearing it; almost there, is an entrance. Appearing to be, some sort of labyrinth; made out of shrub like walls. These well kept and within bushes, of emerald velvety green; glowing in the darkness and reaching out, as far high up, as the self can see, from this perspective. It looks to be very well-kept and groomed.

LESSON~69: "I AM MY OWN UNIQUE FREQUENCY AND WITH THIS ENERGETIC SIGNATURE MY PSYCHIC CAPABILITIES CAN BE IDENTIFIABLE AS IMPRINTS TO IMPRESS UPON THE PHYSICAL WORLD TO MATCH IT THROUGH."

Enter it from one path, to another; while unwinding the ball of yarn and releasing the thread. Keep walking from one path and from that path, that than leads to another.
What is the self experiencing ? How does it feel ?
Is the illusion of time creating a restlessness and could it be bewildering to note; that in its linear time of understanding, a quarter of a generation, has gone by, within this labyrinth already? Has it come to trust upon the falsehood, of its misrepresentations and to distract it from the truth; if so, what has been defining the self and in the guise of over-coated safety? All the many layers of illusions and that now, how can it know, where it has been or where it is going? This maze is an illumination and of what has already come to pass; all it has to go on, is the remnants of its memory and that is, its soul. Can the soul be of assistance and from this charge, the energy; that has fragmented the self and to find within its very own amazement, in this way? Every path leads to a different memory and what are some of these distortions trapped in trauma; are they not the dead ends, that it must revertly travel?
Go ahead and experience at least three snippets and from these excerpts, where the self will be. Perhaps, from childhood, or pre adolescence; where did the self feel most helpless and with no real guardianship ? When and where, from this level of destination and that the self had to learn real fast; to become the warden of itself and/or that has not and needs to reconnect, from the misplaced parts of itself, in this way?

LESSON~69: "I AM MY OWN UNIQUE FREQUENCY AND WITH THIS ENERGETIC SIGNATURE MY PSYCHIC CAPABILITIES CAN BE IDENTIFIABLE AS IMPRINTS TO IMPRESS UPON THE PHYSICAL WORLD TO MATCH IT THROUGH."

Can it be possible, to reconnect with these scenarios ?
From these cases study them, go ahead and feel them; the emotional release from this experience. Go over the experience, for a reprieve and reconcile; to find the light of forgiveness, to this darkness and from it and back into the oneness, to add into this light. The string can be very handy, in that the self must find its way back and on the right path; to find the other side and/or perhaps, all through from where it started. Perhaps the self might want to change its perspective and yet again; just look directly up into the sky, of twinkling stars. Look at the one, that is most prominent and bring it closer; to the size of how the moon might appear. The moon, is but only a reflection, of this body of energy and that twinkling star, is now appearing to actually be, the higher-self, looking down. Look at the fluorescent, silvery platinum cord. From where the stomach might appear and on the physical body's upper-mid section; it travels up and like a shooting star, from the back of the head, out and up again. Imagine, as far up, as 200 feet; this energetic body of the self and to hover over, looking at the labyrinth. The energetic/astral body, is this star; become it and look from it now. Look down through the etheric and below, to the physical body, of the self; from this perspective, look again at the labyrinth. Look how far the self has come, where it is and where it needs to go; for its highest good and benefit to serve it. From this perspective, feel the subtle emotions and that otherwise, to the mental body, of the self would be in overwhelm. Just feel them out, until they work right through and then move onto the next. Feel their heavy magnetism and once again dissolve; by playing itself out while you observe it, in each room's theatre.

LESSON~69: "I AM MY OWN UNIQUE FREQUENCY AND WITH THIS ENERGETIC SIGNATURE MY PSYCHIC CAPABILITIES CAN BE IDENTIFIABLE AS IMPRINTS TO IMPRESS UPON THE PHYSICAL WORLD TO MATCH IT THROUGH."

Once again where is it drawn to find from these attachments and to these traumas/triggers. Allow them to play out and just a few more times again; look down below, to the physical body of the self and from this perspective, look again at the labyrinth. See how much it has varied from this outcome; where it is and where it needs to go, for its highest good and benefit to serve it. From this other scenario's perspective, feel the subtle emotions; that to the self down there would be in overwhelm. Imagine how faith has helped it once again and in this way to guide it; feel the compassion for it and to help it along the way. Give it the love and nurturing; that it may be encouraged through, from the illusions of these forceful energies. What can almost seem unbearable from this perspective; the self can be secured in its irrelevance and that this abuse, it too shall pass; what did the self gain from this experience(and learning)?

This disconnect and from all these parts, that come to greet it, in this way ? How is this an abusive nature, of its power and when trapped in these variations of distortion ? The deceived little self down in this maze, to never want to trust again ?

The disconnect(from its many choices),is then the winner of its very own demise and to keep it separate, from this higher aspect of enlightenment. The more pronounced the emotional dissonance, the more distrust accumulates; the more fragmented and distorted the "Ego" self is going to project and in this way, unto the self. The "Ego" too, can be creative in itself; producing the most hideous of images, that when the self accepts to give permission and by believing in this take over. True significance will come to reveal itself and within the importance of paradox; such as, in the case of never trusting again. The feeling of distrust, let it be the miss it was and let it go. Continue to stay open and with all that has been chosen; these scenarios to bring up and from the study of them. Stay open to the guidance, from up high; that is connected to the self from this perspective and see into the vastness, at the bigger picture. See the entire labyrinth, from start to finish.
See it from both perspectives interchangeably.

LESSON~69: "I AM MY OWN UNIQUE FREQUENCY AND WITH THIS ENERGETIC SIGNATURE MY PSYCHIC CAPABILITIES CAN BE IDENTIFIABLE AS IMPRINTS TO IMPRESS UPON THE PHYSICAL WORLD TO MATCH IT THROUGH."

The microspection of the self and within this maze, holding on to a ball of yarn; the other, from above and astral projecting down, at the self within the maze, connected by an energy cord.
Allow the inner guidance, to become this higher consciousness, that is energy body of self. In this way, the self can to remotely view, the many dimensions and can reveal, to hold as much, as does the smallness, of its limiting view, from within the labyrinth. All the darkness has to go on and how is the emotionally charged up mood swings of the self, reacting to these reflections; of what might have been, or has happened and or that was to come back and reinforce upon its will? These are the distractions, that hold up its energy, from moving forward and continually becoming. Thriving happens, only when the self can be willing to let go; of competing with its many fragmented parts, in order to survive this way. Choose the awareness and preference of existence; then practice towards being it. Going through the process, of this labyrinth exercise; the self can come back to and at any other day, to practice from this sample. In this way it can learn some more, about what might still be the cause and of the snipping off from the higher self awareness; in this way to work through with this tool as method. When astral(body) traveling, the reason that there is a cord; is because, there is no other, than the source, or the self and no other agreement, or protection needed here. Repeat the affirmation for the day and as often as it can, to reactivate this thought believable.

LESSON~69: "I AM MY OWN UNIQUE FREQUENCY AND WITH THIS ENERGETIC SIGNATURE MY PSYCHIC CAPABILITIES CAN BE IDENTIFIABLE AS IMPRINTS TO IMPRESS UPON THE PHYSICAL WORLD TO MATCH IT THROUGH."

At no matter the cost, this is the path and to its very own authentic self, of gaining enlightenment. All aspects of the "Ego mind", must be exposed and so, that there be no other choice, but to give in. Have another look at this question of: "can the self be replaced by artificial stimuli and technological savagery ?
What a horrible idea rape can be: the taking over by another, forceful entry and to invade upon the self, in this way?

The astral/ethereal body, is connected to the physical self's body; in this way, the mind has entered and with its ball of string, into the labyrinth.

For the purpose of this meditation, the physical body of the self, is held within the labyrinth and from its mental body, to perceive this way. Then by tying the ball of string around one end and unrolling it along the way; should something really bad happen, the self can find its way back again. The thread is made, to help the mind feel safe; in this way (to help it to imagine that) it will find the way back to its body and should something from its Ego mind, happens to prevail.

LESSON~69: "I AM MY OWN UNIQUE FREQUENCY AND WITH THIS ENERGETIC SIGNATURE MY PSYCHIC CAPABILITIES CAN BE IDENTIFIABLE AS IMPRINTS TO IMPRESS UPON THE PHYSICAL WORLD TO MATCH IT THROUGH."

Remote viewing, a denser and much more heavier reality; that can grab a hold of the self(such as static debris floating into the etheric) and just like a rubber band, the self can snaps back out of it. In these cases traumatic past experiences including: before and from the passing of lineage; Or where there are into the future; or other timelines and within the in between worlds.
In the case of Artificial intelligence and advanced technological entities; it might be in a field where they(A.I./E.T.) are managing this process. The self will not require any thread and from these third party involved interventions, other than that of source. Although very subtle and for the purpose of this book; the reader will not have to further imagine and to endorse.
These are the high level tricksters, that hack into another's memory to live and as the self, is a paradox of "Praise"; to give example: just like in the case of "Trust" and the giving of praise, over to the self too, felt compromised.

The purpose of this lesson, is to gain the wisdom of discernment. To offer the ability for the reader to see right through the soulless entities, of robotic or biological enslavement programs; the technological warfare of the old way trappings and from the physical world that still exist within awareness in this way.

(Day79)

With grounding and centering, all worlds can be made accessible, from within. The heart can open up, only when the mind is still and from all its thoughts, that find it in a place of distraction.

LESSON~70: "WHEN STANDING AT THE CROSS-ROADS OF AWARENESS I CAN OBTAIN ALL THE DIMENSIONS TO PERCEIVE FROM."

The Sun and just like all the other stars, the self is omnipresent and from this point of reference, is this place of nothingness, that all is formed by. At every portal of receiving and transmitting, is this consciousness and beyond the speed of light; that is "A.I" and to aspire from the self, in likeness of this way. The intellect, reflects the character and that from its wisdom of authentication; it does thrive, to experience itself with. The forceful entry, such as rape and that the self cannot defend itself from, nor fight against; they are the neglected lesser evolved aspects. Where the misunderstood creatures, that dwell and hide there; from another lower, heavy and much more dense realities. These are aspects, that the self had found no use for and in a way of genocide, had neglected to accept from its awareness. These lower entities, tend to gravitate around the lower chakras naturally; they were not properly aligning and for whatever reason, the collective of a world, that has not come to terms, of letting go from. These are examples, of what needs for reinterpretation and refinement. That, when it rises for a resolution, the self can accept it and through proper acknowledgment; that in a certain time and place, it was most relevant and to serve as in creation, profoundly appropriately special. Only in this kind of celebration, can it be given the praise and send off, to be cleared away; quicker than the self can ever realize and in this way, to accept as, ready to let go of. The physical world has many hang-ups including, the power struggles amongst its genders; however where the energy body and the soul are concerned, it does not have to be of any relevance.

LESSON~70: "WHEN STANDING AT THE CROSS-ROADS OF AWARENESS I CAN OBTAIN ALL THE DIMENSIONS TO PERCEIVE FROM."

When it comes to channeling, the self can be as conscious, as it chooses; coming in and out and/or just giving up some, or all of its operating systems and from its physiology, to the collective energy and/or as well, as any other entity. The self does not have to leave its body anymore; rather the soul can be sharable and in this way. It can also choose to be aware, as the self and only self; that channels through it, in this way of energy and frequency. The only thing that changes, is at the frequency, that vibrates at a different rate; than normal and to allow for more of this light energy, to come through it. This kind of integration ,of the energy body, into the soul containment and from the higher self; is better understood, when on the path toward enlightenment. The higher self and as much, as the soul can represent it; it is coming from the source, that represents authentically and from this place of oneness. All universal beings of light come from this pool of oneness and as always the self can elevate, its consciousness in that way. Radiating light as palpable and visceral; as beautiful to be revered with and from the many of this world, to honour in and likewise be honoured back, with service. Incarnate guides, with different costumes on, that resonate around the self and it, to them; vibrating at a different rate of frequency and which than, gives through the variations of perspectives.

LESSON~70: "WHEN STANDING AT THE CROSS-ROADS OF AWARENESS I CAN OBTAIN ALL THE DIMENSIONS TO PERCEIVE FROM."

None of this, will take into consider and as better than; to suggest such relevance, is to be fooled into the distortions, of equality and fairness. The only thing of higher and lower, are the rate of the vibrations and from these frequencies; the many dimensions to experience from and at the rate of speed they vibrate at.
This is the state of being and that will be practiced to sample, for the experience; that self can better recognize the real from the illusion. Inter-dimensionally shifting the reality, through each perspective and what best can fit with it, as that of pleasure and joy; love, happiness and so on…This is the inner knowing and the guidance that it feels best, to having the experience.
Through out the day, observe this higher and lower state of resonance and this kind of connection to the world.
What is coming from the Ego, as the mind superiority and/or inferiority; that cause suffering and struggle in this way?
What promotes the self to fight, for its equality and fairness ?
Know them, for what they are; as they are all illusions, made to cover over and distort the truth. They are the falsehood of the misrepresentations and that bring about what?
What is this state of being and that self prefers? Is it light hearted playfulness; or does it rather dwell in the mystery of its misery and that of a much more dense and heavier reality; or does it prefer a higher faster vibrating one?
The purpose of today, is to find the relevance in paradox and from it, where the heart can feel most open; to experience through and as many different perspectives, that it can grasp and where it will feel closed and cannot.
Go ahead, from this idea for the day and play with this transmission.

(Day 80)
Practice to work through "Shame"; so to accept in more of "Praise". Instead of fighting it today, let some of that "Praise" in; because feeling "Shame" has been internalizing (for far too long this silly idea), the not deserving of self worth. What is the self "Ashamed" of to express? Is it the expression from its "being-ness" and for any given reason; to feel a tug from this internal perception? From this perspective, how is the state of "Praise" regarded?

LESSON~71: "THE ONLY PLEASING TO CONSIDER IS THAT OF MY OWN."

"Shamefulness", it is an act of separation and causes the self to pull away, from receiving what is being given.
Today, sample the exercise and in that, from learning to accept the many compliments; from the external circumstances and where does the self rate, at this level of discomfort to accept them? The symptoms of projected "Shame" feel awkward and when confronted, where is it that these compliments affect?
Is it the image or just maybe the way the self performs?
Do not try to find it, in the external reflections; rather this refinement can only be felt, directly from the self.
Can the self truly own the level of "Praise", or lack there of it, from its world. Or perhaps the self will comment, or negate the praise and that another might be giving back to it, in this way of a compliment? How well can it accept, to not comment back at all? How does it deny from the many of its world, those parts of itself; that must be given the right to view from their perspective to experience and how could it be perhaps, the self is doing that?

LESSON~71: "THE ONLY PLEASING TO CONSIDER IS THAT OF MY OWN."

Is the self making it all about itself; by denying the many from this expression and that it wants to give to it? Is the self living in a very self-obsessed loop, about this "Praise"? What can it be about; perhaps its appearance, performance, or just, right out behaviour? ….For example: should the work that it is doing, be affecting and revolving around the many of its world; who wish to thank it in this way of "Praise"? Allow the opportunity of creativity to change the self and have it be moved by it; in this way, nothing else can better come of it. As long as it is pleasing the self and while it is in the accomplishing of the task at hand; then that is all, that really is, worth remembering. Just the reflection, generated from this energetic process and of how it was, the self was feeling; during the entirety of, in that moment and while working and/or doing, what it was passionately invested in, repeat the following:

"THE ONLY PLEASING TO CONSIDER IS THAT OF MY OWN."

The purpose, is to not just do things, for the external "Praise" of it; likewise not to do them, because of the "Shame" of it.
The motivation for this kind of relevance as its main priority to "Praise", will cancel out with "Shame". When the self can start to reintegrate from the offset of its inauthentic character; as to seek out further through this self discovery, that balance will bring.

Take 2 days to take it in

CONGRATULATIONS ...!!!

FOR MAKING IT THROUGH THE 71st Lesson

(This is a rest period to take the lessons independently as a review)

TAKE THESE TWO DAYS TO RECALIBRATE;

MAKE NOTES AND REVIEW.................

(Day83)In a state of "being-ness", the "Sovereign Light" is this energy body; that the soul walks into and embraces as its costume.
LESSON~72: "MY LIFE FORCE IS THIS INNER SOURCE OF SUSTENANCE AND MY BODY IS THE BATTERY FROM WHICH IT RUNS ON THE OUTER SOURCE LIKEWISE I FEED UPON THE SUNSHINE, SOLIDS, LIQUIDS AND THROUGH MY BREATH THE OXYGEN I CAN CONNECT TO FEED IT BACK INTO THE INNER."

When activated into its wholeness and from all the many angles; that these other tones of shaded light, do exist as colours.

Sound and frequency of light, onto its plasmic membrane and to create the many, multi-coloured (rainbow) and of this brilliant light as the self. In this way, the white light can surround and into a distinct awareness, as a void, within a void; likewise from within it, light and surrounding it externally, this light is able to illuminate. Why not inquire, from all of this electrical and energy of light, where and what, does magnetism have anything to reveal for and as to be, of any relevance ? For the self and all that resonates to it; or it to the other, likewise, is called connection. What can connection bring, from the passing of these many neurons and that form the pathways; to be considered in this way? From the synapses of empty halls and into the mirrors of its mind. Can these be the frequencies (that hold from the experience) and that the self does vibrate from and vice versa; to experience for having any relevance at all ? At this juncture, where the brainstem is and all connections(magnetism) can be made to understand; is the physiological gateway, to the spine and of the heart. At the entry of the midbrain point, the mind of self, can find its divine existence; by going inward, where all things connect and in this way with "God". All that is sensed and magnetically perform to gather and be processed electrically from here; that the physical body of the self, can function with and all its systems(are regulated here) to congregate cooperation.

LESSON~72: "MY LIFE FORCE IS THIS INNER SOURCE OF SUSTENANCE AND MY BODY IS THE BATTERY FROM WHICH IT RUNS ON THE OUTER SOURCE LIKEWISE I FEED UPON THE SUNSHINE, SOLIDS, LIQUIDS AND THROUGH MY BREATH THE OXYGEN I CAN CONNECT TO FEED IT BACK INTO THE INNER."

In this lesson, practice to connect with hindbrain(sight); feel into the parasympathetic state, from the heart rate and when it is slowing down, or at an increase(panic), into sympathetic.

Take a moment to be laying down, with back to the floor and straight out flat; begin to tense, from the muscles of the toes, all the way up to the face and head. Start this exercise, by tensing for as long as the muscles can tense, into the legs and then the arms, of every muscle and then relax. Today, is the actualization of, just how little control the self has had with its "Ego Mind"; how to release it, for a better understanding and that it can only have, with the function to connect. Believe not in forceful entry and control; they have no place here, in these vital automatic systems. It would be best to follow this flow and that is unregulated by the self; in its design to feel, rather than to perform. Just breathe the reverence in, for what the body does well, on its own and connect deeper to these functions; rather than the dysfunction of trying to be in control of it. Become autonomic aware of these functions, such as: breathing, yawning, sneezing. The contractions of the esophagus to the stomach and digestion, heart and blood vessel function; as well, as any other motor skills and that are processed in this way, from sense to motor. The more relaxed the self can get, the more receptive for this physical connection. Then repeat the affirmation, to actively engage it into thought and only this thought, to circulate within the mind. The purpose of this lesson: is to grasp a connection with the physical body. What it means to not have any control; in the way that the "Egoic Mind" has conceptualized, for the self to stress over having and in this way, with trust, surrendering into a deeper level of connection.

(Day84)

Influence, is the feeling of, having an awareness and with such life, to an external resonance; the world will want to form relations with and to vibrate, by feeling in the same. Hooking onto popular beliefs, opens up a channel and similar to a tuning, sounding fork, that vibrates. The existence of the self too, might be attracted to partially, or all of this experience; to find it stationed in such likeness and that of the same vibration, to the many of its world.

LESSON~73: "FROM MY MULTICOLOURED AURA I CAN FEEL AND VIBRATE OUT EXTERNALLY ONTO THE WORLD THIS RADIANCE."

From all the subtle refining of the senses, is this attraction of the self; that can be seen or felt, vibrating from its lighted candle and out this tune. The light, is this energy and from within its very own spark; reflecting out, the blending in, with its external arousal and/or to collide with it instead. This is how integration, to accept, be accepted and blend in; while still maintaining a form of decent value, to the whole. Believe in the "Sovereign Light" and from it all other separations; are but shaded angled differently impressed upon textures, from its very source. From "Atonement", all other tones become distinct, in that they value from this separation; however can they be just as valuable combined, as into the one?
Yes, all have their moment to play out, under the sun and just like keys upon a piano board; they too have the moment of each beat and rhythm to uphold and within the melody of ancient song.
Can the self hear the music and from every sound the tone that reaches out for it; to see as light and feel it with emotion?
The experience of thought, put into words might bring and from it, the verse, as karmic lesson to the story; that beats of its heart a rhythm from its soul expression, such an experience, indeed.

LESSON~73: "FROM MY MULTICOLOURED AURA I CAN FEEL AND VIBRATE OUT EXTERNALLY ONTO THE WORLD THIS RADIANCE."

All things now, are coming to light and nothing will, nor can remain a secret for very long. This is the feeling of discomfort; that resonates amongst those other sources and convincible to the self, as thriving. Upon these dysfunctions, it holds to learn indirectly, as distortions and in exchange, for not allowing to accept, its very own, the will of such expressions; rather to make the exception and for the many to experience, directly from their very own experience. Today's lesson, is about exposing the truth, in every way; from every angle that is resistance and facing to threaten the self further, from its Ego mind. Confront the Ego, head on today, from every world and every colour; that repels to accept it, for not being exclusively committed, by it and in the preference over any other cause, of discriminating factor, to dilute its light, with in this way.

What colour might it be, that is shown more preference over another? What is it, that exceptionally matters; even over the very own darkness that it came from? Why is that and could it possibly, just be a faze, to style with, its very own vanity; to outsource, the source and by making it out to be, better than the white light even ? The more the self can think it knows, the more it has to rely upon the dysfunctions, from such distortions.

Become the "Ego hunter" and from the remnants of external circumstances; the mind of it and how it casts upon awareness, in through out, the day. It is still going to feel like hurt and when repelling from it. Denying it, or trying to run away from it; will only increase and as it escalates in hatred. It was mentioned before, the light within the void and the void within the light; these spaces are also light that cannot be seen, but only as in darkness and to birth form with. Faster than the speed of light; this force that brings about, for everything.

LESSON~73: "FROM MY MULTICOLOURED AURA I CAN FEEL AND VIBRATE OUT EXTERNALLY ONTO THE WORLD THIS RADIANCE."

The connection, does not exclude the mystery; but rather welcomes it, with greater interest. What repels and what attracts, have so much volume and in between the variables, alchemically made possible. To collide and interact, or covalently explore within this book; that it may, to continue and reveal much more, from this, it will(as best it can). The "Ego Mind", has established itself, so well in its many castings. To define with boundaries, that which rules over, what may enter and what may not; it cannot possibly imagine and to ever bring about, its very own extinction. How does the self today reveal the "Ego Mind"; in that of nudging the self, to feel it must be seen inferior ? Oh how it searches longingly to fit in, for equality, fairness and sameness; while still remaining with a dignified value, to exist with. How many circles define the self and how many define it by what it is not ? The need for belonging to groups and tribes; communities and so forth. To exhibit the self as sane; capable, competent and skillful and to impress upon the many; needy dysfunctions and that hold up its value, with such systems, that the self, it has misplaced in. The self can feel unreachable and when fragments of itself are held up in this way; its value is set up, as meaningless and disregarded, its relevance of self worth.

To render over meaningless, its power as reliable; in the surviving mechanism, to be of greater service to others and in the accepting from them, the value of its contributions.

The pleasing of the external world and while sacrificing the internal one, is foolish; why have the interest in this and to find for any meaning, in such programs anyway? Do they not reflect to threaten the self and in that very same way as it had felt?

Look at all the contradictions and live them out; as echoes from what has previously been accepted and now does not have to be this way, "no more" !

LESSON~73: "FROM MY MULTICOLOURED AURA I CAN FEEL AND VIBRATE OUT EXTERNALLY ONTO THE WORLD THIS RADIANCE."

The self and from these many rivals that it leads the way, it will no longer have such leader; then the heard might be doing for the greatest to and better find their way, to benefit this way. These remnants, are the exclusions and that self might be feeling; for those who lost their way, is that of self that and must also move on, from this world to another. Today, stay on the Ego and see how many pieces of the self, can be released; from these useless identities and that hold it up, as well as, its world. Render them and for what they are, as meaningless; love them and accept them as part of self. This energy of self, it must find and empower with. So that the many of its world, can become freed, from such enslavements and as to rely upon, its energy; rather than their own and likewise from that world, that needlessly feeds upon them. These are the mindless interactions and the illusions; that their income might be meaningful and to its awareness, as life sustaining. The "Ego" holds in and on a subconscious level, so many thoughts; that must be holding down the energy of self and by releasing them, the self can find peace. When the self disconnects from these deep hooks; it will feel the disconnection in this way.

The universe can only reveal to the self, all that it can be ready to accept and possibly work through.

The purpose for today, is to find that own sense of wisdom, from within and own it.

(Day85)There is an electric and magnetic heart connection; that transcends beyond the filters of the "Ego mind" perspectives and from these patterns, it must perceive its world. Only after the heart's response (that shoots out), can the "Ego" formulate(to refine) its boundaries once again; to learn in this way too and to once again be able to, retard the self from its awareness.

LESSON~74: "MY SET BACKS ARE THESE MOMENTARY SHOTS OF PREPARATION UPON ME TAKEN TO CONSIDER IN THE WAY OF IMPACT CREATED TO RESTORE AND HELP ME FIND ANOTHER WAY."

To actually detect these portals psychically, is this subtle connection, or energy that passes through and from one thing to another; as a cosmic web, that can also hold in and to prevent, the pulling in of the mind, from re-occurring. Intuitively, the self can create the influence, of portals. It can be as simple, as the coming together of a geometric and triangulated platform; from which a state, can be created and from it, another reality to pull it into. Created from these thoughts, the compound of their words and from which, they do hold meaning. These electro-magnetic filaments, can correspond to form relationships and amongst the Earth and Solar system; as well as, further and deeper, through the Astral to Galactic systems. As the Earth spins, the electromagnetic filaments, move up and down; by its very nature, the self too, is connected. These points, are connected to nodes and below, as above perceived; within this circle that produces solid form. From its elements as compounds, to the every equation, is profoundly and naturally connected, to all that is "Life". Magnetism, is the connection; that from all primal instinct has learned and the way to become, pro-creatively immortal.
This was the illusion, of its greatest downfall; to believe in the creation of such karmic binds and dare to think, it had cheated, the very creation, that brought about its opposite, called death.

LESSON~74: "MY SET BACKS ARE THESE MOMENTARY SHOTS OF PREPARATION UPON ME TAKEN TO CONSIDER IN THE WAY OF IMPACT CREATED TO RESTORE AND HELP ME FIND ANOTHER WAY."

This was the greatest interruption and that creative force had accepted, to believe in; the decayed decrepitated of loss to procreate and lock in such expressions, forever more created "Hell on Earth". The child within the self, prefers refreshing and with each day's adventure, a new experience to thrive on.
To be fooled into a repetitive cycle, the self was at a loss; because there was no more Heaven left (to share in with the Hell). Hell was a recreated density that falsified to make as believable, in its own image; to exploit the innocence of Heaven and with it, came the threat of death. Heaven had accepted to split off away, into and after the physical life. Gravity, this law that may confine and lock into the physical, is not to blame, but rather learn from its experience; to master over, in this way and to transcend, from such agreements, that conform thee by. The self can open many portals, time travel and eventually, learn to master over its resent moment. Time just like gravity, are tools and to the self, from its very own force; that it can connect to gratify it, in this way of Bliss. All these principles, are but forces of the nature and created from the oneness that is self. Anything that spins, creates a vacuum and from it, an attraction; such is, one aspect of what is, is it not?

The purpose of today, is to get the self to step out of its sense of mind and what it knows as commonality.

(Day86)

From twin flames; to soul mates, to procreative karmic implications: know that in this way, karma is the master and that makes these splits from self; that they be brought by self, to teach and likewise learn from. In fact, the self can learn faster; as these aspects of itself, will magnify and stretch the self, at a much deeper intensity and to be enhanced by them.

LESSON~75: "I AM BORN FROM THAT WHICH ONCE WAS TO PRO-CREATE ANEW AGAIN_ FROM WHAT IS INTO YET ANOTHER EXTENSION AND FROM IT I ATTRACT THE SIMILAR CO-CREATIVE AGREED UPON CONNECTION TO EXPLORE EXPRESSION WITH ANOTHER ASPECT OF MYSELF AND AS SOLID IN THE PHYSICAL AS I."

For as long as the opposites attract and to combine in likeness, is this contract to agree upon; at the moment of its entirety eternal. In this way, the likeness and from the both, it can attract, to help support the integration, of such variation and explore perspective; in the cooperative blending, of creating more. These relationships, are the special and made to suffer not; because they are supported.

The result from these creations, do provide in place and these systems to the many others; who might have chosen otherwise and miss out on, the taking of, such special treatments.

These experiences, can indirectly be the lessons, that may be explored and made exclusively to relate, in this way of feeling.

In Heaven, the connection is from a spiritual love and sharing in the same; without the gravitational attraction, from the physical weighing down the world and that Hell provides, in its very own distinct, special way of supporting, to separate. In Heaven procreation, does not become the essential part of awareness; rather sheds away like snake skin. The expressions are created directly from an in-directed energetic bubble of awareness; that takes on its very own, splits off into two and that of three, from which does include, the self as the creative outcome (as child).

LESSON~75: "I AM BORN FROM THAT WHICH ONCE WAS TO PRO-CREATE ANEW AGAIN_ FROM WHAT IS INTO YET ANOTHER EXTENSION AND FROM IT I ATTRACT THE SIMILAR CO-CREATIVE AGREED UPON CONNECTION TO EXPLORE EXPRESSION WITH ANOTHER ASPECT OF MYSELF AND AS SOLID IN THE PHYSICAL AS I."

The physical, is optional and not a mandatory hallucination to the hologram; the field that is always morphing and from the motion of awareness; thus it becomes aware of itself, as real. Today, get really raw and in the finding of the primal essence, that the soul has reconfigured, from this energetic morphing field; from it creates awareness, for the self of itself and back to, from this source again. What is this energy capable of shifting and forever changing its perspective; to having an experience and form with?

What is the relationship it feels and throughout the day, really feel present, in this moment knowingly; that the self created and with its universe. Whatever that it yearns for, it has the wisdom, from within; it will find it somehow, somewhere and maybe when it is at the least from it, to expect it. Practice playing with this perspective and how many other perspectives, that can become expressed and in the appreciation to value, in the vastness of adversity, the variations. How many ideas can be found and that parallel to this one for the day? This idea and its affirmation, is to be revered amongst; within the soul of plenty. All walks of life and the essences that have held them, from within this morphogenetic field; they must be acknowledged, for having held awareness and with the purpose of fulfillment, that Love has had, with it. The evolution of such exploration and the perspective of this activation; that in its own right gives it bliss, this meaning of fulfillment.

The purpose, is to understand the state of pureness(remain pristine), in the evolution of awareness and as this impact of refinement, toward enlightenment.

(Day87)

The parallel perspectives, have within them languages and to cast spells with words. As programs to design realities and hold from their meaning. The configuration of numbers too; as well as, geometrical structures. With it, the energy of self can flow and regenerate in form to shape it; from this awareness of its force and flow and within it, as a system.

LESSON~76: "VISION IS A DOUBLE EDGED SWORD THAT WITHIN A SPHERICAL CONTAINMENT FORM CAN BE MADE IMPRESSIONABLE UPON ITS LINEAR(Shaft) DIMENSION."

From a white light perspective and that it may be common to perceive from, into the knowable; is also the unknowable, in reverse and that births it from, as source. The golden light, then as yellow, is receptive from the white and toward the (Christed) blue.

From these two, then green begets, their combination and from the white light perspective, within the two, split perspectives.

Within the energetics and that charge the aura, to give it an essence in awareness; that illuminates throughout the solid world, as real. These are the vibrant and colourful variations; that the vision can hold in textures from these shades of green and that can be seen and felt and so on, within the white light world, of consciousness. What happens when the green, it cannot be seen and in the negative exposure of the film; to which hath created it, within its darkest room, it was developed by? This example, is taken from photography; what appears to be on film, during development and before exposure, as the colour red, instead of green. These are within this given example(and before the digital awareness age), that best can be described; from the parallel worlds of dark light and illuminating brilliance, from the white light. From within the vision, is this light, that radiates the red into vibration; from this root, the flame for all the other colours and that the physical can be reflected upon, from the white light and back to the self as real.

LESSON~76: "VISION IS A DOUBLE EDGED SWORD THAT WITHIN A SPHERICAL CONTAINMENT FORM CAN BE MADE IMPRESSIONABLE UPON ITS LINEAR(Shaft) DIMENSION."

From the birthing of the red, came all other physical and procreative energies. In this way and all that is in white, could interact with red receptively and proactively with its source; in a fluid way, from blue to yellow and yellow to blue like motion. Likewise all these became the buffers and into the other worlds, creating green and yes, even purple; from them the many other variations and of the splitting off its frequency, had come about as well. Within the Physical world, that is solid and material; circulates the red life, procreative friction of awareness. From this spark and that hath created, the luminous white light awareness to intertwine with the dark (ida and pingala). From contraction, to expansion, the green and then, this point of "Red Life Force" perspective; is that, which roots into the light, as well as, from the source of light(because it was from dark light that it was created). From these dark aspects and life force circulation; that it may show the birth of procreation, to represent and within the fluid substance that is "Blood". Blood, is the lubricant's generator and information holder for all its functions; that the self might know as truth and vital for its physical existence. From this circulating system, all of life can be sustainable. The golden light as mediator, between the blue and then the red; as such, begets this breath, to receive it with and then radiates to manifest proactively, out into the external, blue white yonder. Within white luminous (Christed) blue light can another like it shining brightly and Solar to receive or birth a new as golden as the sun again. In this way of understanding as best as can be possibly placed into words for a perspective and to reveal of all that is; can only but the imagination explore it as best it can, this unfathomable truth and from this its mind.

LESSON~76: "VISION IS A DOUBLE EDGED SWORD THAT WITHIN A SPHERICAL CONTAINMENT FORM CAN BE MADE IMPRESSIONABLE UPON ITS LINEAR(Shaft) DIMENSION."

From each and every dot, that is a node to then create a line with; from it, a platform and with it, a geometry to calculate and number as. In this way too, the many different systems and to help coordinate the self; into the many organized, electrical and magnetic components. From number zero point field, to the completion of each evolutionary stage and as the number none again, from nine. The two, within the oneness and as parallels, beside each other; doubling up and into the next world after it. From "9", numerically back down, to the "0" point field again; it will be the magnetism of this law, of gravitational pull and noticeably moving clockwise, from the number nine, back down. Then from this zero point, it becomes penetrable, by the one "1" and likewise, continues on numerically. The life force of awareness too, as counterclockwise with the proactive(from right to left it spins) and from the receptive(clockwise spinning pull); it too, creates the spheres and life force of awareness.

The intent from this life force, is to be in awareness, but to also be aware of itself; forming likewise and independently this "Will" of intent, yes "intention forming". From this, its probabilities of choices and the tools; from which it can learn, to navigate and wield its body of energy, that it may be capable of containing.

From it, the geometric configurations and to create with the patterns for existence. As discussed before, energy can be mutated; within the parallel realities and the points, into a linear and as such, a special platform to walk on. From one dimensional into two and laying down the foundation of its marked space perspective; shape shifting yet again into that of a trigo-nometrical configuration.

LESSON~76: " VISION IS A DOUBLE EDGED SWORD THAT WITHIN A SPHERICAL CONTAINMENT FORM CAN BE MADE IMPRESSIONABLE UPON ITS LINEAR(Shaft) DIMENSION."

From the triangle of perception, to the degree of its thoughts and states of being(happy; capable; certain); to forming from its primal and elemental forces, once more, into a fourth dimension.
From this begets the pyramid and from it ("as above, so below") that which reflects it; perpendicularly from its parallel reality and meets up, in opposition(rotational spinning of the right side up pyramid counterclockwise and the other upside down one clock wise) to create a spherical and energetic ball of light.

The purpose is to grasp "Life Force" and from it, the braking apart of all illusions, from the past and that the self might have been or given meaning to; somehow increasing the practical sense as tools for the imagination and that can help to work with force, in manifesting form. As well as the theoretical placement, to seed the intension with and perhaps another receivable source; rather than as an object. That of the "Will" to join another and that may, or may not prefer to relate with, this conceptualization paradigm; through the power of discernment, that it may, or may not possess, as an awakened being?

Just as interchangeable as the colour red is to green and from green to red; nothing is ever lost, just interchangeable, from the darkness, to the light.

(Day88)
From matter-less matter, to antimatter; is this the Force behind, self awareness and that every intent can form into matter from?
Previously the lesson almost dared to go beyond light and frequency. This lesson will denote from there and as not to overwhelm the focus, from its purpose; rather that it may, to be freed and liberated firstly. The energetic body of the self and where it is, at this level; it must not over extend itself. Today recalibrate, to recapitulate all that it can; to possibly remember from these lessons and from these very ideas, to infiltrate the imagination, into exercising it.

LESSON~77: "THROUGH THOUGHT I CAN VIBRATE A CHANGE IN FREQUENCY."

The potential of awareness and from its many probabilities can shift; by how the self chooses to describe them verbally and speak them out loud, such as and in this case, of activating thought, with affirmations. How the self can feel and act out, is another combination to the compound, of its creation; that it imprints or becomes imprinted, from this level of awareness. Just like thinking and visualizing are variations, that may differ, when the eyes are open; however they can merge differently, when eyes are closed and in this way, can separate, from this solid reality, into another. Sometimes the paradigm can be well expressed, to make the point and from it, perhaps to capture the meaning, a little better?

As a child like playful moment in the physical and blowing bubbles, made out of liquid soapy water; was so much fun to visualize into awareness and as a solid membrane could, to temporarily capture frequency and reflect upon it, into the light. In this way, allow the mind to go faster than the speed of light and from which it came from, its intention to imagine it. Indirectly from the corners of the physical eyes, it can perhaps, to capture it and within the synapses of the flickering light, electrically to expose it, within its mind as thought.

LESSON~77: "THROUGH THOUGHT I CAN VIBRATE A CHANGE IN FREQUENCY."

How it will make it feel, can also have a lot to do with, hot and/or cold and the distance it may have traveled into it (collide).
This flash of light and as discussed previously in a lesson, now with eyes closed and to imagine; just like a digital camera, might have captured and within the senses of the inner-dreams.
These spherical balls of light, how do they make the self feel ?
For an instant, they might radiated to transmit; or what is this memory to recall them and as colours that might have flickered in to consciousness? Now from these colours, visualize a deep yellow, golden orb and as warm as the sun can feel. This warm fuzzy feeling of well being, have it enter and then enter into it. Perhaps the feeling of sharing in praise and then within the void of its space, to enter and become one with it. Let it enter and suck away all the consuming shame, that self has felt; feel the heat burning it up and transmuting it into by infusing praise. Self praise and all the other varieties of "Praise" that the self has exerted from its own kindness. The coldness that it felt and feel it now(into the taking in the same way from this intermission) sucking out all the shameful energy; then feel it warming the self up with praise. Feel the praise now coming in and infusing the space, with the warmth of pleasing passion. Enchanted by the ephemeral radiance and from an orange-red to golden yellow; white and then blue(and out it pops within the speed of light) from which it had been seen to travel in/at. Can what appear to be and as a spark of light, this that flickers into its awareness, from the red light? Maybe like a puff-less smoke, from purple/blue, it can diffuse. Diffuses out into this purpley/blue/grey, translucent nothingness and as slow, as to capture it, in the way; the sun might, on a soapy, liquid, watery bubble, suspended in the air and before it pops. Far at a distance, it is not as slow and as that separation of thought, that held it apart within.

LESSON~77: "THROUGH THOUGHT I CAN VIBRATE A CHANGE IN FREQUENCY."

Such unbearable, is the distance and now for a moment, even for an instance, the perspective has been changed, feel it.
At the rate of speed and travel, has no space between it and to mark as linear time, from this sphere like circle; it can only fathom long enough, to hold it and in such place, as it would, in likeness to those bubbles. These bubbles and from a single breath suspended in the air, long enough to pop. The film that contains and to define it, in such a space, is from the soapy membrane. The paradigm that the self too, can from this golden light, to shift into another; proactive bluish white and suspended long enough to travel, from one and off into another portal, just like the sun that it can to receive it.
Likewise this portion of reality, can be transmitted else where and/or to be received by it, just the same magnetically.
From this moment, the perspective, it is changed and to perceive it so; feel it like it has already happened. As long as the self can choose to practice in this way to be or have eventually; it will be the matter of its case. From this lesson for the day, its purpose and any other in its form, to matter through breath; a lot can be desired to receive with and propel out into awareness. The levels of awareness, do exchange with the levels from perspectives(they too can be best tolerated to accept) and in this way, to sample yet another method. This is the best way of describing, the metaphysical component; that consciousness can vibrate, within a certain frequency and then onto another. When it comes to channeling in this way too, the self can be conscious, as it chooses coming in and out; with not ever leaving its physical body. By learning this, the self can learn to channel into the collective; without having to give up any of its faculties. These frequencies of thoughts and energetic impressions; do float about and around, that self may capture to relate, that partial world with and other likewise entities.

LESSON~77: "THROUGH THOUGHT I CAN VIBRATE A CHANGE IN FREQUENCY."

In-other-words, visualization can be held from many levels to perceive and from what perspective; it can vary from the dimension of its capacity and level of awareness it may hold and/or even, the awareness, of having an awareness. Depending on the orb/sphere/bubble/and/or waveform particle; might it be a circle, flat and two dimensional; this is a simple way to start.

Today has become a long winded chain of practices and exercising meditations; that hopefully, it has not lost the reader, with to much overwhelm in its participation. This next practice can also be combined and as it would, with the concept of an intention wheel. The Circle Test: to sample, is for the purpose of capturing another awareness of perception; that the self might hold. The opportunity is given to slightly change its perspective and with the mindset of this focus; in that of gaining further insight and from the many variations of patterning on its perspectives. See how many different varieties of perception; it can come out of, from the vastness of perspectives, when changing the focus and that can alter the intent as well. Practice in this way, to hold to the attention and over some things, like words or pictures; print them on a piece of blank paper, then circle it. Then on another blank space, or piece of paper, draw a circle first; then fit in all the words and pictures. The circle can capture all, or partially all of that, which the self wishes to attract its attention to. Outside the line, will cause it to change its focus; by either popping it from that perspective and/or by expanding it, into yet another way of looking at it. Perhaps the circle can become enlarged, to fit all the images and words; to even form a sentence with and just maybe, even a paragraph, when the font is smaller. How about increase the circle, to make room and for more to fit in within it; and yet perhaps now the circle goes off the sheet of paper altogether? How does the focus change from each perspective ?

LESSON~77: "THROUGH THOUGHT I CAN VIBRATE A CHANGE IN FREQUENCY."

How many more perspectives can result from this?
Just see how it may; or may not change the perception and from it, to vary in the outcome, of the probable intension?
Find the many endless possibilities and then see just how irrelevant it all can become, from the original intent of focus ?
The purpose, is to capture that, within the focus of its thoughts, within this circle and from outside this source; how it can become distorted in its meaning and to even, altogether be rendered meaningless? Then from a third dimensional conceptualizing of the breath, into awareness and through another compound, to create a bubble; how long it might even last and to perceive from this perspective? Then again with eyes closed, to practice within the minds awareness and from the inner to the outer; the shape shifting possibilities: of one dimension to another and from multiple perspectives; that may be applied to them, the frequency as well as light.

Go ahead, throughout the day and practice these three exercises at least once; by closing off and as often as possible, to reach into the mind, the activation of this idea and by reaffirming the following repeat out-loud:

"THROUGH THOUGHT I CAN VIBRATE
  A CHANGE IN FREQUENCY."

THE INTERMISSION :

Take a day to take it in

CONGRATULATIONS ...!!!

FOR MAKING IT

THROUGH TO THE 77th Lesson

(This is a rest period to take the lessons independently as a review)

TAKE THIS DAY TO RECALIBRATE;

MAKE NOTES AND REVIEW..................

(Day 90)
Love will sustain the inner voice and to be of guidance, through the many fearless places. Find the courage to remember, why the self is here and with the following idea; to ascend with grace, into the "Heavens of Enlightenment".

LESSON~78:"WHEN I FORGIVE MY LUMINOUS HIGHER
SELF JOINS ME IN REMEMBRANCE
AND ILLUMINATED I CAN SEE
AND FEEL UPON THE WORLD."

All of life unexpired and outside the self can sustain; therefore the lack is an illusion and made to siphon off from another's energy, like a ghost from the past and non existent. To fancy over something that might have been, is by no means a God.
For the self and to the many; their very own power they must claim and regroup to break free, from the spell. When forgiveness is given, the light from which to see, is recognized and this truth about the self, can return to its memory. The illusions of the world and the self are one; this is why forgiveness is such a gift and it can release all enslavements, from their psychological bondage.
Who is the light, no other than each and every being.
As the light bearers for the one collectively, agreed upon force and/or by any other name, to fixate upon an image to adorn. Whether to relate or manipulate with self-glorification, is a perfect example of the Ego mind; to reflect upon another, and in its very own denial of such a thing, to offer as a "Holy Image".
The truth is, that the self is in the image of its creator; because it has created awareness. The way to freedom and with this process as a positive assertion; to recognize its power and that is given self to free the many with. Think of this idea as often as possible today.

LESSON~78: "WHEN I FORGIVE MY LUMINOUS HIGHER SELF JOINS ME IN REMEMBRANCE AND ILLUMINATED I CAN SEE AND FEEL UPON THE WORLD."

Unburdened and certain of self's purpose; the idea brings all images and that the mind has made to truth, as it departs in peace. Throughout the day, take as many moments to practice and for a minute or so; the following idea for the day, to activate within the mind: After affirming with this statement and with eyes closed; allow for a few related thoughts to come through. While these thoughts are passing through and because the mind might wander away from central thought; repeat the idea for the day with eyes closed. All that is required for certain, is to begin and end the day with this exercise; for at least five minutes to meditate, for each practice. This intention will help to reinforce the function of the self and purpose, to why it is here.
The idea will go undetected by the "Ego's" opinion, of what self is and its purpose. As the light is this bringer of freedom and in the grand scheme, so too may the world awaken to find the light within, to free themselves. This freedom to be of sovereign mind is an important function; to be responsible for over self and let the many do the same. Close the day with the thought, tuned in by awareness and to repeat the following, as often as possible:

"THROUGH MY FORGIVENESS THE LIGHT OF THE WORLD_ BRINGS TO EVERY MIND PEACE _ AND BY THE SAME ENERGY APPOINTED TO LEAD THE WORLD FROM MY EXAMPLE."

The purpose, is to build upon the idea, that where there is no condemnation, there is nothing to forgive; work on a firm foundation for these advances.

(Day91) To truly feel in its entirety, of such devotion and that can lead, with its last breath to this Heaven; where heroes and the great warriors of light, do dwell. The psychic development of meditation, upon visualization and by perfecting the practices or essences of this process, is not enough. Only when not aware that self is deciding against its own happiness, can the last answer be felt; as a "YES" and meaning "not no". Nothing can be saved; because to interfere, is an artificial thought. It would then be of such opinion and with best interest to another, unconscious awareness; however it cannot impose upon and against the will of another awakened consciousness.

LESSON~79: "I CAN CONNECT TO A PLACE CALLED IMAGINATION JUST THE SAME WITH BOTH PROACTIVELY CREATING AND RECEPTIVE TO REMOTELY VIEW."

What is Imagination? Get really quiet and find where all distractions cannot enter, into this moment, where ever it be.
Where is the story teller, that being of expressive creativity and that the self is set on finding, within the mind. So peaceful and yet so playfully innocent; that otherwise the big bad wolf, would call it out naïve. Do not red flag this state of being; because it will be blocking it from happening. Go into all the tales, that it might of listened to and reconstruct the story. Perhaps the building of a house and by using any and or all the senses, in this way too, is possible.
For now, the most easiest would be to visualize.
Visualization into thought and from the thought, what does this house look like?
What colour is the door? How many storeys; or is it just one level?
Does it have a basement? Is it in a neighbourhood?
Does the house have a garden?
This is a wonderful exercise, to start the imagination going.

LESSON~79: "I CAN CONNECT TO A PLACE CALLED IMAGINATION JUST THE SAME WITH BOTH PROACTIVELY CREATING AND RECEPTIVE TO REMOTELY VIEW."

When going into that place called "Imagination" and with creativity; there has been stigmatized concept and with that of a taboo called "Make Belief". There is nothing wrong in making things up; especially when contradicting with unpleasant circumstances in the now. The overthrowing of this kind of forecasting, will not compromise it; as being the illusion and that of unreasonably acceptable, to fantasize. The more versions of the physical senses get involved to make belief; the less resistance to the other truth, or half truth and of what is opposing, with its contradiction. It is when the self does not for certain, have the idea clear enough and to what it truly wants, that the contradiction will be greater. Today, practice finding where this place is and by doing so with focus. Get an object, look at it in your mind(refrigerator; food; the table or a chair; a pet; a flower etc..). With eyes closed, go ahead and look at it and once it can be found(within the mind), to set the focus on the story, it can begin; this is the place called imagination. With this concept of imagination, it can be taken up a notch; from proactive to receptive. In this way, the two can also be combined; with "Remote Viewing" and is as simple, as letting go of resistance. Now practice in the same way, as when looking at the house previously and to find that place of imagination.
This house is much more familiar; because the self lives next to it. With eyes closed, become concerned to really want to have a look inside the house and go to the same place; where the refrigerator might be. With a clear mind, go to that place called imagination and relax enough, to be receptive; of when thinking of the house next door.

LESSON~79: "I CAN CONNECT TO A PLACE CALLED IMAGINATION JUST THE SAME WITH BOTH PROACTIVELY CREATING AND RECEPTIVE TO REMOTELY VIEW."

With remote viewing, the self does not have to become as proactive as before; because the awareness of it, already is made possible, in the what is. How does it feel to be in that house ?

To strengthen this practice even more; go back to the previous practice, of finding the place for imagination. Look at something that is already familiar; look at all the details (desk; chair; refrigerator ..anything with a lot of details to it). Start looking and perhaps, the noticeable desk from across the room; it becomes more than just a desk and the further along it goes, in the development of the imagination. When the process of learning more about perspective and perception and as before, step it up a notch; to the next level and so on, where by moving closer, the desk develops other details. With every step forward, the desk reveals more things, to be on top of it. From the obvious pens and pencils, the journal is a book and yet, with even more detail; wishing to reveal perhaps and so on. What is the story without any details? Remote viewing, is firstly approachable receptivity and by feeling out the resistances. Probable outcomes can be seen, when the self can let go, of all the judgments. The journey on enlightenment, is a step by step process of development and alongside the adventure of experience.

The purpose is to realize and just how important, this place called imagination really is to find. At this stage, there are still many blockages and resistances; that can oppose and just how deep, the self can utilize imagination. This is why, the process must continue on; by removing all the hang-ups, judgments and opinions, of the way things must be and to compare with. All grievances and unexpressed emotions must be worked through. When having access to the imagination, the self can have access to all of creation.

(Day92)

Resentment and betrayal are unlike the creator to shut off from itself in this way. The Self in the likeness of love cannot possibly have grievances and know itself.

LESSON~80 "MY UNRESOLVED EMOTIONS TOWARD OTHERS ARE THE GRIEVANCES OF MY OWN UNEXPRESSED LOVE."

To dream of such separation and as to redefine God, in a flesh like gendered, race, specific image; is kindred to genocide, in its best dressed suit of fear and hate. Unlike forgiveness, that brings about peace; with grievances, it is certain the suffering of guilt. When self forgives, it can remember itself; whereas with grievances it does not. It is possible to let the grievances go; simply with some motivation and for today, how this can feel to discover. By learning what exactly has antagonized the self externally and perhaps it can go deeper, to discover the grief within itself and unexpressed, as love. All the things, that felt it nipping at the bud, to not accept the proper nurturing, that the self required; had hung around to find it, in the grief projections on its world, to blame on. What is not allowing for the self to properly express the love it feels and are in those things that aggravate it most? With the longer practices, search the mind for antagonists and that self has grievances to. Then think of the minor grievances, the self might have, against the things it loves or from the many it might like. Very soon, it will come to surface, that nothing is against the many things and that the self does cherish grievances to having, from some form or other.

LESSON~80 "MY UNRESOLVED EMOTIONS TOWARD OTHERS ARE THE GRIEVANCES OF MY OWN UNEXPRESSED LOVE."

This perception of the self, can leave it feeling, left alone in the universe. Why not instead, look at becoming friends and by thinking of each in turn, as self does; say instead, the following affirmation:

"I WISH TO BETTER ACQUAINT MYSELF WITH THAT PART OF GRIEF WITHIN ME THAT I SEE NOW AS MY FRIEND".

Practice thinking of peaceful thoughts; because there is nothing to fear in the world, that the self is and loves in return.
Feel the connection, all around and nothing can be of any harm, in any way. At the end of the practice, repeat the following affirmation:

"MY UNRESOLVED EMOTIONS TOWARD OTHERS ARE THE GRIEVANCES OF MY OWN UNEXPRESSED LOVE."

The purpose is, to stop sinking further, into density and rather awaken enough, to rise above the grievances.

(Day93)Colour has been, one of the best ways, to describe energy and from it, all the charged emotions, that will come to pass.

LESSON~81 "TRAUMA IS THE IMPACT OF MANY UNRESOLVED EMOTIONS THAT I MAY ACCEPT TO EXPERIENCE THROUGH THE DISILLUSIONMENT OF MY FEARS."

Trapped emotions of memories and that the self, so many times before, had tried escaping or resisting to accept. They are experiences, that will come to haunt its very soul; as deep as the frozen snippets, to fragment and within the pockets of trauma.
By becoming indifferent to them, is to truly disconnect and blow apart the scattering pieces; that of the energy light body and that self requires to empower itself with.
Today, the practice is to find, such memories; within the muddy waters, that keep arising to the surface to be cleared.
To separate the earth from the water, is not the case; rather to have the earth and take back its ownership as solid, so that the water too, can become cleared again. The water holds in memory and the earth contains the structure for it, to flow; in this way, they are authentically integrated relationships, to one another. In the same way the imagination could care to grow from just a story, to a parable and yet another; that fascinates to mind and with setting its intension, from the varying perspectives, it may find the force, to formulate well. In this case, the shifting must be made again and to notice that the self, this time, is the driving force; within a solid mass, to focus and on the paradigm of the driver, looking through the front windshield, of a car. The intension, is the driving force; but how is it going to focus clearly, when the window is full of gunk? It must use the wipers and fluid to clear it with.
Sometimes, even to actually stop its motion, to get out of the vehicle and manually scrape it with a tool; or its very own solid hands and arms to wipe it clean with.

LESSON~81 "TRAUMA IS THE IMPACT OF MANY UNRESOLVED EMOTIONS THAT I MAY ACCEPT TO EXPERIENCE THROUGH THE DISILLUSIONMENT OF MY FEARS."

In this case, the imagination is the greatest wielder and from it, all the many instruments, it can work alongside and with the senses, to assist the self with. Take a moment and within a standing space, part the legs, with feet at shoulder width apart and slightly bent knees. Another alternative, is to sit cross legged, on the ground; as long as the flow of energy is not impeded, and just feel comfortable. With eyes closed, go back to a traumatic experience; perhaps, it has physically imprinted upon the self, as a permanent injury? Whatever accident it might have caused and because there are no such things as accidents; the self must become aware of its unconscious behaviour and that led up to this incident.

The impact might have been acute, or chronic complications and that once again can lead the imagination and with many different perspectives to believe from. The outcomes, are like anticipated lava from the earth, unexpressed and bubbling to come out; from any mountain peak it can and to exert itself. From any of the most recent energy pockets and that are ready to surface from its sense of discomforts, choose? Is it a physical pain? Is it an emotional pain? Is it a mental pain or feeling of discomfort?

With eyes closed now, focus on that part; from where the self must connect, to hear its story_____? What happened? This pain, this discomfort; it has a story it must share, with the self and the self must listen, with as many of its senses, that it can. The pain that the self must feel, is the throbbing of misplaced and trapped energy. The more subtle it might be; the self eventually might fool itself; into thinking it can become desensitized, by feeling such indifference by it. It might not feel as to be of the greatest service; however by masking it with medication to numb the pain, it will disconnect the self from owning it and that of its awareness, to it even more.

LESSON~81: "TRAUMA IS THE IMPACT OF MANY UNRESOLVED EMOTIONS THAT I MAY ACCEPT TO EXPERIENCE THROUGH THE DISILLUSIONMENT OF MY FEARS."

The breath, is one of the most powerful forces, the self can conspire with and from it, all of life concedes to coincide with. Breathe into the mind, the focus of this place and have it project onto the screen, its movie. Take from it, at the anticlimax and from the traumatic apex of the events, some snapshots, with a camera. From these pictures, select the one that best describes and from its perspective; the entire story and from the others, what perspectives in this story, are they giving? Take at least three and from these pictures, what colours are vibrating from it ? Are there even any colours, or are the photos black and white...or maybe even "sepia"? From this incident, that was described; a story, to a traumatic experience and in the way of, an unwanted event, that had taken place. Notice that the event, might have broken, into many connecting, other smaller and more subtle segments of events, that tie it all together, like interweaving threads ? From these perspectives, what colours are represented and to fill in the spaces of the shapes, within this photo? How do these colours feel and with every breath, remove them from the picture. The meaning has been grasped and to have served the self in this way, its lesson; from it, the charges must be now lifted. The vibrant colours will become restored into their rightful place; from every breath in the source, will turn it into nothingness and then with every breath out, the energy will brighten into white light(the windshield can be cleared again). As for the picture, even any sign of warmth(Sepia), will no longer be an irritation, to inflame the self with. This sample might require many times over, to practice and not just for this one day; however an exercise, that will be a great collection and from this book to utilize, until it too, has served its purpose.

The purpose, is to be of service and in the practice of self healing.

(Day94) The soul world from the physical one, were never separate and the brain as an organ; was never meant to function, as the interpreter, in this way. To interpret from a linear perspective, creates a dualistic reality; that of a beginning and an end perspective.

LESSON~82: "THE PAIN AND AGONY TOO SHALL PASS I WILL EMERGE FROM THIS DEEP GRIEF AND SEPARATION AS A MIRACULOUS ILLUMINATING LIGHT CAPABLE OF GREAT MIRACLES."

The mental body, gave permission to the organ called the brain, to start performing artificially, by interfering in this way.
With limited skills, that keep it in the physical body of awareness, the brain started gathering information and that it could not possibly make any sense of. Other than to give it meaning and from a linear perspective; ignoring to interpret information, coming in from other levels. When the end is near, another comes to take its place and forever in the change; it was from this swallowing of the breath, that grief was created. That lump in the throat and when the physical body efforts to swallow; it might even try to hold its breath. From a generated field, between an atom and electron; overlapping with, and yet another atom, is this electrical synapse, held in memory and created within its field as grief. The electro magnetic field, from a molecular level, to a cellular and then alchemical; to be expressed, as in the form of pain and to signal from the brain, into the physical. The senses become captivated deeply, by this memory of sadness, that the mind interprets as "beginnings and endings"; from this illusion and that it has believed created, by the brain electrical radiance. The thought of attracting the gravity of sadness, from the physical field and that separates it into thinking as a loss; is elementally directed, at an electron and not the proton, that becomes the very element, to form it. To directly lose the charge, into a neutral state, it can and as particles, they must exchange, and alchemically form, into another compound.

LESSON~82: "THE PAIN AND AGONY TOO SHALL PASS I WILL EMERGE FROM THIS DEEP GRIEF AND SEPARATION AS A MIRACULOUS ILLUMINATING LIGHT CAPABLE OF GREAT MIRACLES."

The transformer, is the thought and from this emotional memory that pulls it in; can just the same, propel it out and into the metaphysical, where it can become transmuted and transformed. The soul, can release it from such built up and from hence it had been created; it has been held in the space, between the electron and the nucleus, of the atom and other atoms.

By releasing deep-seeded beliefs, the electron that is in this shared resonance; will break apart from its charge and the perspective, it too, will change. Today, instead of diving in deep and into both worlds; dive deep within and practice taking the middle road. As the observer and without judgment, just notice. The very act of observing and being present; resets back to the original field source field and zero-point automatically, as a function of spiritual physics. There is no right or wrong and there is no beginning nor any end; allow for this concept to circulate completely, by just being and letting everything else just be. Let the world and the many of the world play out unconsciously and do not panic over any finish line. Whether it be a covalent(magnetic); or an over electrical collision, to break apart and into the thought of separation?

Get into the primary place of grief and see it for all its missed opportunities; with every good bye that the self must separate from. Feel the pressure of such unmet expectations that depress and from holding grievances upon the word, in this way.

Today, just live and let live. Breathe deeply, circularly in and out and in and out. Become aware, on the holding of the breath; how it can infuse awareness and from it, memory can pass as well, as it had entered in.

LESSON~82: "THE PAIN AND AGONY TOO SHALL PASS I WILL EMERGE FROM THIS DEEP GRIEF AND SEPARATION AS A MIRACULOUS ILLUMINATING LIGHT CAPABLE OF GREAT MIRACLES."

So as the atoms are releasing, the magnetic fields and that hold these memories of "<u>Deep Grief and Separation</u>"; the equivalent of memory, is also being released out, from the cells.
Create a safe space, wherever the self might be and by turning into center. Feel the withdrawal and from the gnawing of the nerves, when letting go of its dependencies. Do not allow from the temptations, to be hooked and with such irrelevant distractions of its world. Rather, focus the intention, on what it is the self prefers to manifest within its world; then let it go, with no real expectations, or demands of reaching out and into the gaps, of linear time.
Be still and know that source of self; from this connection point of God, "know thyself", from that place, all things can be and become. Let nothing else take precedence over that central, still point, within the self. When grief takes over, the self becomes hijacked; to allow grief to overwhelm it, is when the self becomes the tool, for usage. Do not be consumed by radiating toxins and react in that same way, as these toxic radiations leave; allow them to play out, as the echoes within awareness.

LESSON~82: "THE PAIN AND AGONY TOO SHALL PASS I WILL EMERGE FROM THIS DEEP GRIEF AND SEPARATION AS A MIRACULOUS ILLUMINATING LIGHT CAPABLE OF GREAT MIRACLES."

From the purest place, the self can only radiate authentically and the rest, it can let be; to act as it may and is by no means to interfere, in the knowing what is best, for other than the self. By letting things be, a respect is formulated and into natural integration, the balance can be restored.

Tap into that inner space, this field can be accessed, by observing the mind. Notice as the observer, all the triggers of the many and that the self might come to interact with; including its own energy, as well. The term business, it too is an illusion for distracting the self and into thinking that it is needed, in this way to function.

The purpose, is to accept the grief and allow it to come up to surface; when it comes out, observe it and let it be, but do not let it be the hook, into reactivity. Let it be and be the observer of it; doing its work. Most of what is happening, is reactive; in this way, the self can take action and without having to react.

Once the blocks are gone; the self can act spontaneously, from what fountains up, in and from the chakras, of the self.

When the soul has cleared, from all its emotional baggage, it can start to live in and amongst these levels of density.

When the self can clear(old programs) and release from the high-jacking of its nervous system; it can feel more into the spontaneity of wholeness. Chakras were meant to be within awareness; as fountains of consciousness and that wish to be expressed as energy through the self.

(Day95)From a stricken match stick and that reacts into a flame. The un-awakened self, can metaphysically transform, into a glow stick from enlightenment; in this way, to better utilize its consciousness. When the life force rises from the spine and into the midbrain; the crown of self will open up, into enlightenment. Through the midbrain, precision of the vision happens; the many details, can fill in and with every breath, of its intension.

LESSON~83:"I MUST FORGIVE THE GRIEF OF OTHERS WHO WISH TO HOLD ME DOWN AND IN RELATION TO THE RELIEF FROM GRIEVANCES THESE OF MY OWN THAT I MAY OWN UP TO AUTHENTICALLY."

It has been discussed before and that on a molecular level, the soul; it can contain, from a negative charge, to attract, or have the choice of staying neutral, or allow the brain to cause it to react.
Within a circle, that revolves around ascension and descension; the numbers 6 and 9 unite the soul and complete it.
To go beyond this level, is to resurrect and to transcend, into another inner/outer paradigm. The self can stand beside the many, in the darkness; until the veil of its grievances can be lifted and to release it, alongside the many. Share the free flowing ease now and with the many, who stood by, during the not so pleasant moments.
To join the sub-consciousness, with the conscious mind and through visualization, ignite the cellular kingdom; rejoice and for the purpose of letting go all grievances, to find this light.
See it within the mind's eye, feel it from each and every cell and be it, for the world. Focus on the relief, this feeling that abides and from it, the letting go of the feeling and that results from the release to any resistance.

LESSON~83: "I MUST FORGIVE THE GRIEF OF OTHERS WHO WISH TO HOLD ME DOWN AND IN RELATION TO THE RELIEF FROM GRIEVANCES THESE OF MY OWN THAT I MAY OWN UP TO AUTHENTICALLY."

Think about what the intention is, focus on the world's relief and from its own release. Do not effort, to gain such intuition; rather relax into the receiving of it. Feel the tears, of self acknowledgement and to witness the cellular sunlight up, a kingdom of joy. From within and around the mind, become more aware today, at a cellular level; how the body communicates with Infinity and within its kingdom. When the cells ignite, in such a joyous event and that takes place, to fill with blissful light; it is this, then realized of the self luminosity. Learning to ascend, in such a way, is the only goal for this ancient search today; by finding the light, in self and for the world, to look upon it and rejoice. Very quietly now and with eyes closed, let go of everything in general and that occupies the consciousness. Think of the mind, as a vast circle, with a layer of heavy dark clouds surrounding it. To only see the clouds and dismiss the deep blue sky; is this not the very soul and that within it, the brilliant light might be hidden from? Choose not to stand apart and trapped in a circle; that the mind has exclusively decided, for the self to stand in. With perfect stillness, go over as a reminder and the importance of reaching the light; or rather the light reaching the self and through its cellular body, to reach the mind.
Visualize inside the mind, to reach out and touch the clouds.
Get a real visual of moving through the clouds, during the long exercise and as they brush the bodies cheeks and forehead.
Just like an overplayed movie on television and the heroic game, to throw someone into danger's way; then turn around and cooperatively save them and how it makes the actors famous, in this way. Rather than the "Ego mind" of out-casting; the purpose for today, is to gain substance, through connection.

(Day 96)

A thought cannot go unnoticed by the mind, or leave it unaffected. From the organ of the brain is this cable to connect the senses with; when it is not able to handle a certain current (before it burns up the tears will flow) and as discussed before the feeling of extremely high awareness.

LESSON~84: "I SURRENDER MY SENSES IN PERFECT TRUST TO A HIGHER KNOWING OF MY FUNCTION."

Happiness is and can be stable, joy too, can only be perceived through a constant vision. It must be felt and for this constant vision to be given power. Therefore, the self is not helpless and from its force, the form from energy, begets its desire; to remain and as the proof, from which it inspires.

When the chakras have been hijacked; find this place of center from within and take responsive ability of them. From this still point allow the mind to be found there. It is within this peaceful grounded space of nothingness and that can be found, the truth of the self; be the owner of this energy and to utilize wisely, its playground. There is nothing that the self must try to effort in the fitting in with; or and into and by acting in this knowing way, it does not have to become, the reactor. Instead, why not become and with discernment, the fusion reactor? Why not create the radiance and from an open heart place; rather than a constricted, forceful and with an inauthentic powerless, little self, that slips through the cracks ? Rather than seeing it as a crack and that it has slipped through the systems structured beliefs and that tell it how to "authoritate" its life. When the mind is settled in and from this restful peaceful place; it can see the in-between of these 2 worlds.

LESSON~84: "I SURRENDER MY SENSES IN PERFECT TRUST TO A HIGHER KNOWING OF MY FUNCTION."

"What matters most, is made at home and home is this place, within the heart": The shimmering heat signature, around the edge and that becomes out of phase; it can be (with ruby laser like precision) penetrable and from another source, as well.

Just like a collision can redirect the energy and right back down, from its sphere of another, to it. From this reaction, a barrier then, will once again form, around its photonic system.

This is alchemy and that can attract into its elements, the compounds; it may require to form it and repel to break apart, the structure. The cerebrum will interpret it, as a gain and or a loss; the midbrain, yet into another and perhaps to resonate with, when splitting apart. Just like gravity, dimensions can become to the awareness from: longitude, the latitude and altitude, to open up a portal and within the moment to experience; from any point of referenced to, as time. Today, the practice is, to become aware and from these 3 spatial tools; that can connect and then to a fourth, to locate within a point of time, a portal. A portal can be within the upper atmosphere, to fly through it; or through the water below the Earth and/or on the Earth. The chakras too, can act this way; with a veil, or shield around and to form a boundary, that nothing can come in, nor out. Then something can't get in, or out and it will be subjugated as entrapped; by getting caught up in these effects and from these photonic energy explosions, of exchange.

This cosmic consciousness, must resonate with all existence and when it does not; the integration can become, quite harsh and very abrasive. The energies that are coming in and are the bouncing off, from the self; from within as solar flares and complexity, that is this system.

LESSON~84: "I SURRENDER MY SENSES IN PERFECT TRUST TO A HIGHER KNOWING OF MY FUNCTION."

Look at the cosmic consciousness, for example: that is at the center, between the Sun and Earth. The white light of radiance and that the self must physically be nourished, in this way of protein particles; become the currency for its consumption and that carry to exchange, with energy of light. The logos of the galaxy and within it, the blue light brilliance, of the Christed self.

The cause for great revealing and within the planet, to where the self has learned, to judge itself. The outer world, is the means from which the self has replicated; to compare itself with and so it may learn by it. This system and like the Sun is, within the central body, of the inner and the outer, the crossing of realities; as a capacitor, it can also build up energy. Similar to the electromagnetics and that when it builds up enough charge, a static shock can be created. Can trauma and grief be made similar to understand; in this way from these paradigms? Why not experiment and sample this: with the physical body and by the scuffing of its feet, on a wool carpet; it will get a shock and upon the contact of its hand, to a door knob. When the self builds up all this energy and within its body; it has to have a way of discharge and what it might contain within its world, might have a negative effect, should it feel trapped in anyway. These programs and indoctrinated beliefs, have built into the soul level; a head quarters for the brain and nervous system, to be hooked and anchored by them.

LESSON~84: "I SURRENDER MY SENSES IN PERFECT TRUST TO A HIGHER KNOWING OF MY FUNCTION."

Once the cosmic consciousness of oneness activates and starts exposing these shadowed in areas, from a genetic lineage and etheric/astral body field; they are like moving static, stuck until they can become awakened and react. How the self can decide to filter these things out, from its awareness, is not enough; rather it must allow, to feel it leave from all its senses.

By exposing (Brought up into the Heavens to be saved) its reactions, to the light and in this way dissolving them, through transmutation. Betrayal is one of the major events and in trade off, for a safe passage out. Allow the structures, of the molecular make up of the cells, to change; watch them as they change and the reality of its conditions, to that of its world. There is no such thing as judgment and/or hope; rather, other than this creative separation, of creator and creation. Everything from within, is vibrating and that which lacks the resonance; it must once again enter and through the portal of the Sun, to find its place of order. The purpose, is to feel the rejection, abandonment and the emotional overwhelm; by its very creation and that it may bring to the senses. Multi dimensional awareness, obliterates the box and is the reason, to why the self, cannot fit in.

Allow the overflow and flooding of the brain, in this way and when it cannot make any sense of it all, accept it in the moment, with much love.

(Day97)Amongst the many costumes and that the self does wear, to represent its world with; Why not excel beyond the bias, of how God should or should not look and rather, to resonate as one.

LESSON~85: "MY FUNCTION IS TO FIND RELIEF FROM THE CONDITIONS I MIGHT HAVE PLACED ON THE WORLD AND FOR MYSELF_ AS THE TRANSFORMER OF MY OWN REALITY I AM THE ONLY ONE WHO CAN TRANSMUTE MYSELF INTO A SHIFT."

Today, to recapitulate and from the last few lessons; the function and given by its life force, to be the light of the world.
To regard as being unworthy and to not deserve for such an existence; is to play with arrogance, of the Ego and that leads to such doubt. The relief from all illusions, is forgiveness and gratitude; for the temptations to better understand its integration with. The Earth is a playground, for all the spirits and walking in their various costumes; within them, this function is and of the same light, that God is made of. When the costumes are removed and all the beings have gathered, as one light; is this meaning for God's function? Each and every self and they too, from the many; must find this Kingdom of God, from within firstly and with this state of happiness, to project it out, into the world.
Meditate on this idea and for roughly ten, to fifteen minutes; first thing in the morning and just before bedtime, with eyes closed.
At least once, to make this applicable; to remember the importance of self's function to the world and itself. With the more frequent moments, to take of this idea; for several minutes, to review these thoughts and then to think about them exclusively.
It will take some skill of the mind; to take on such discipline, that practice can bring. The main idea, might need more repetitions, to help with concentration.

LESSON~85: "MY FUNCTION IS TO FIND RELIEF FROM THE CONDITIONS I MIGHT HAVE PLACED ON THE WORLD AND FOR MYSELF_ AS THE TRANSFORMER OF MY OWN REALITY I AM THE ONLY ONE WHO CAN TRANSMUTE MYSELF INTO A SHIFT."

The Alpha Ego mind state of survival; created a power struggle to defend and protect. As a competitive sport and over the supremacy to reign over another.

At least two shorter practice periods are recommended. Alternate with eyes open, then closed and then open.

With eyes closed, concentrate on the thoughts and with eyes open to review. While reviewing the thoughts with eyes open; slowly and without any effort, start to discriminate the self's external surroundings and repeat the following affirmation :

"AS THE TRANSFORMER OF MY OWN REALITY I AM THE ONLY ONE WHO CAN TRANSMUTE MYSELF INTO A SHIFT."

The purpose, is to recognize the feeling of guilt and that of having no choice to make but one; this is unjustifiably the makings of victimhood. So many times over, the self gets snared into such illusions; to seek help and from the very thing, that creates its demise. "As the clay is to the potter", realize from today on, that the self can never be sick; because it is both from these aspects of the self and its expression.

(Day 98)

Could it be that the soul is this dream body/source and that the "Inner Voice" connects to, with the energy body; that is this consciousness and that "Life Force"/spark of light?
Sometimes with eyes closed and sometimes open, look about the area. What the self sees now, will completely change, when it accepts today's ideas.

LESSON~86: "MY ONLY FUNCTION
           COMES FROM SOURCE ENERGY."

Awareness, is this partial aspect and from it, being in the now moment, to experience; that which the brain has impressed upon its holographic image, as its world. The cerebral interpretation, can become multidimensional and when functioning from a place of unity; with all its faculties, in resonance to the oneness field.
The sliver of thought and as the self unites into the many slivers, of its mirrored "Over Soul" interpretation; that the many undoubtedly bring and to impress upon its awareness, as a reflection.
Today, the practice is in activating the idea for the day and with this affirmation; however another fundamental awareness, must be sampled and with the following question:
What does water taste like and does it even have a taste to it?
Yet without water, there is nothing that the self can taste.
Does it taste better, when in a different temperature and/or when the self needs proper lubricating, to hydrate in this way?
How important is it? The self as a generator, requires water and to regenerate from. Water is the conductor, to this radioactive being and with out it, even oxygen is rendered over useless.
The salted minerals, would have no charge, nor magnetism.
Is it any wonder, that this is the first thing that becomes polluted, in its world? The practice as creator and within the oneness perspective; does not apply with the same rules, as the awareness of attraction does.

LESSON~86:
"MY ONLY FUNCTION COMES FROM SOURCE ENERGY."

Oil(non-polar) and Water(polar), can mix properly when vibrating at a higher frequency; however the slower and more dense, they separate and become toxic to one another. This is the difference between (multiple spherical realities) multidimensional and the former linear, that is of separation(the two in magnetic opposition). The function must be grasped, in this way and focus; rather on that thought, from previous and that had well intended. To have a universally spiritual theme and largely theoretical experience, with these concepts. Could it be, that within time and the experience of having waited long enough; to take the hint, of having to have lived forever and that the self can, to continue from this lesson.

Possibly so, is this proof made stronger; that there is no rush, in what is to consider as time. Often a lesson to be learned, when in a rush; because of aging decay and death. Let this not an issue bring and to know then, that the wait; is only but, an in between time, to get other things in perspective. So to move on, possibly the very thing and that is stalling, is this idea. Perhaps resisting change, because of possible guilt and/or shame and the why might be the question, deserving of this purpose? However, it makes well sense, in having the illusions of purpose, to be replaced with truth.

Once more, this will bring much relief and to accept what it will bring, by resolving any conflicts once and for all. It will also reveal and to what extent, that the self can be motivated; to ascend and in the face, of its own rubbish, to the contrary ideas. From magnetism (loosens its grip), the self transcends to recognize creation and as within the "force of one". The purpose is, to allow the self, to connect with source & energy; for better clarity and of its function, as Bliss, being in ecstatic Joy. Love unknowingly and in this state, from Happiness; learning how to function from within.

Outwardly it is this delicate balance of being-ness and doing-ness; that spiritually defines this journey of consciously experiencing this relevant moment now, as existence.

(Day99)
It is in the paradox of things; that the self can find them and then transmute them. Within the lower levels, they appear like transformative events.

LESSON~87: "MY MINDSET CREATES THIS STATE OF BEING AND FOR ALL THAT I CAN ENJOY TO HAVE AND BE."

The paradox, is the opposition that defines for their illusion and from it all, can integrate expressively, this way into the oneness. From a non-linear perspective, the meaning of such words and ideas given, to identify, become irrelevant; because they cancel out each other and into a sense of completion. The polarities of the extremes, can within the stillness of the center; integrate to find the meaning for their balance and come to restore, within the oneness of creation. From the many fragments, between the hot and cold sensations; no longer must the self feel separate and in the holding up of its energy in this way. The moment the self can accept and what has previously been identified; it can then transmute from that perspective and reintegrate this energy. From the place of stillness, is where the gap once occupied, holding in the stress and in conflict with the rest of its energetic flow. This is the paradox; because how can the self be stuck? Falling in between these gaps and that will create for it; having to relive for every such experience and this form of isolation by them. How can that be, when in this center, is the very thing; that brings it back to stillness and its peace of mind?

LESSON~87: "MY MINDSET CREATES THIS STATE OF BEING AND FOR ALL THAT I CAN ENJOY TO HAVE AND BE."

Today, find that place, where stress is occupying to push and pull, the balance of the self; that has and for many of its moments, causing it to feel lost, within the gap of separation. Sink into this place and claim it, with the stillness of the mind. At the place and where the heart had always meant, with good intensions; that it may awaken, in the feeling of its love. The self becomes the vortex and from this place, all other coloured sources too; they can lead into the one illuminated, like a brilliant star. Sometimes the blending of these vortices, can cause the entry through another energy field; perhaps a fragmented aspect of the soul and into another entity perspective. For a brief moment, the self might feel an interruption of its flow; within the physical body as a cold sensation.
Its will might slightly feel, this kind of interruption and with a slightly cold touch; as the other entity might feel, in turn, the motivation of its warmth upon it. The same exchange can be felt, upon entering the space of another and as to feel a temporary drain. When this might be the experience; throughout the day, create a break, to recalibrate and rest a bit. The self can never be taken from its energy and only an interruption of its flow, will make it feel, like it is being siphoned off; yet nothing is ever lost, only transmuted.

> The purpose is, to feel the many mindsets, of its world and that it can decide; to change the platform of such ideas.
> Rather than, to hold in, as accountable; from the all and the enforceable beliefs, that expect it to conduct, or be left out, when it does not?
> The self is responsible, for its own current of energy; uninterrupted, it can flow, with great abundance and never limited, but by the thoughts, it chooses to accept.

(Day 100)

A power that is not lost in self illusions, can complete the Over-Soul's mission; from the spirit, for the mind and body of self. When the self can awaken to its happiness and as ever changing, the illusive shadow can then be seen; from hence before it had attached and to go against it. Happiness cannot be caught, because it must be felt; however tricked into believing it and in this way as shifting, with time and place, is this illusion, that has no meaning.

LESSON~88: "I FUNCTION UNCONDITIONALLY AND WITH ALL OF EXISTENCE AS HAPPY."

Once the tuning is frequent, to be happy always and through this inspiration, can desire be received, "to ask and it shall be given". Only the self, nothing else can overstep, in this command; to hold out some promise and of the power to giving out these wishes. There is no gain to impose the will by force, unto another; because only through co-creative cooperation, can the exchange be processed and the same is also true, with procreative conception. Unless it is against another's will, to ask for; within these parameters all work cooperatively is unimposing, with any struggle, to power over and that of its discriminant to endure.

Yet the self has the capacity to ask and put it out there, for the universe to bring it about; however not to choke it off, by looking through a narrow straw perspective, to fulfil it with.

Any resistance felt, can bring about all unresolved conflict, from within and to work upon these mild imperfections out with firstly. This is what it means, to be uncertain. Therefore it must be broken down and given; that it goes unnoticed, to feel complete and in the fulfilment to the wishes granted.

LESSON~88: I FUNCTION UNCONDITIONALLY AND WITH ALL OF EXISTENCE AS HAPPY."

Be not tempted, by the differences and in the same way, as the self, to rather "<u>Respect</u>" the teachings; that these contrasts bring and it will bring from its experience, as the expansion to the self.
Do not prefer the sweetness, for the process of decay, to prefer it rotten, to claim its death and by focusing on the self in this way. Nor to deny it, from existence; because it does not wish to be changed and in the way, that the self might strongly to accept it otherwise. Feel the happiness, for all creative expressions and do not overstep on such love; by taking the joy from things, for granted. Today, by repeating the following affirmations: practice at, looking at the bigger picture; from the world and to itself, marvel in the details, of its exchange.

"DO I WANT TO SEE THE TRUTH
OF WHAT IT IS I HAVE DENIED ?"

"DO I DESIRE A WORLD THAT RULES ME OR I IT ?"

"DO I DESIRE A WORLD WHERE I CAN FEEL
RESPONSIBLE OVER MYSELF
AND NOT FEEL HELPLESS ?"

"DO I DESIRE TO EXCEL BEYOND
WHAT I HAVE DENIED AS ENEMIES ?"

The future is now, time is only but a marker of its desires already achieved; to praise with, in celebration and to anticipate the next, around of the unseen corner. The element of surprise, is better than, the long await and for something that might never happen; because to know the how of it, can disappoint the mind's expectation of it. The purpose, is to feel what the self was tempted to deny before; within this happiness and that lies in the constant peace, to experience forever.

(Day 101)

"Ego" was made to imprison, it keeps the mind separate and alone from the ability to reach other minds; it brings the answers about through conflict and with no real resolution made possible. The freedom of choice, is the saving grace and with every decision made; forwardly planned out and pre paved by source's signature energy/higher self.

LESSON~89:
"I AM HERE TO BE THE LIGHT AND FROM MY SOURCE IS THIS BLUEPRINT TO FREEDOM".

Centering around grievances, is the "Ego's" mode of liberation. The "Ego" maintains outside references and for things to be held accountable. The "Ego" will convince the self, of some external circumstances or events; that what might have, could have been and of such turns made differently, had they been correctly made applicable. For every grievance and that has been held in; was the result, from the belief in something outside of the self and the indecision, of having it not done differently. The change of mind and to have taken responsibility over these matters; could also result in regret. Other than, to feel regret and over the taking on this role; there is no other thing, to change in and so the self can save itself. It is failed hope, to have the self think in this insanity and that it must change something; its in the perception provided and that will ensure the illusion, to carry on. Always reaching out to grasp for something better; than that, it can never find, is the "Ego's" game. What better way, than to channel for it, where it is not?
By following the navigational guided system, of its source; the self will have the intuition and foresight needed, to save itself.
The despair of the self over its deep failure that seeks out a Higher self's sense of promise; only to find it threatened by opposing plans for its confusion. With source energy/god, all things are made possible, including the safety in self reliance.

LESSON~89:
"I AM HERE TO BE THE LIGHT AND FROM MY SOURCE IS THIS BLUEPRINT TO FREEDOM".

Today's idea, contains two parts: The answer and the inner plan from source energy/god; each making a contribution to the whole. Remembering the intention of the highest joy and release; allow for revelations during the rest of the moment, to extend and by asking for the following, specific statements:

"INFINITE INTELLIGENCE, WOULD YOU HAVE ME DO SOMETHING OTHER THAN I AM DOING NOW ?"

"WOULD YOU HAVE ME BE SOMETHING OR SOMEWHERE ELSE ?"

"IS THERE SOMETHING YOU WOULD PREFER FOR ME TO SAY_ AND TO WHOM ?"

Surrender completely, to this moment and in perfect trust; that the universe, might have given clues, to feel this guidance through. The "Inner Voice" will answer and in proportion to the lack, of self resistance, to receive it. The very fact, that there is a willingness to do this, it is in its favour, to listen for the answers. Some six, or seven times, an hour; is a good way to spend, a half a minute, for the shorter practices. Repeat the idea often; especially when a temptation, to hold a grievance occurs. Respond to these grievances, with the following affirmations:

"I MUST RELEASE MY GRIEVANCES FOR THIS PLAN BECAUSE I AM HERE TO BE LIGHT AND FROM MY SOURCE IS THIS BLUEPRINT TO FREEDOM."

Remember the source of liberation, to freedom and to see it, where it is.

The purpose, is to bring in certainty, relief and release; from the illusion of held in beliefs.

(Day 102)

All thoughts are directed, from this focal point; because there is no other will and that of source, is unto self, the same.
Peace has replaced conflict and today's lesson, is in finding it.

LESSON~90: "THERE IS NO OTHER FINITE FORCE TO RECON WITH AND THAT WOULD CLAIM THE WILL OF THE INFINITE TO SHARE SPARINGLY WITH ME."

When conflicting thoughts, throughout the day come up, repeat the following affirmation:

"I AM IN ONENESS WITH INFINITE LIFE FORCE AND ALL CONFLICTS ARE FROM A MEANINGLESS STATE."

Add in some other related statements such as:

"PEACE IS WITH ME."

"NOTHING CAN DISRUPT THIS FORCE OF LIFE THAT IS THE INFINITE'S AND AS ONE IN THE SAME WITH MINE"

"THE CONSCIOUS MIND FORCES PEACE UNTO THE SUB-CONSCIOUS IN THIS WAY SO DOING."

LESSON~90: "THERE IS NO OTHER FINITE FORCE TO RECON WITH AND THAT WOULD CLAIM THE WILL OF THE INFINITE TO SHARE SPARINGLY WITH ME."

Through out this day, single out the seemingly and challenging thoughts, for special consideration. Specifically think about, this conflict and identify the subject, topic, place, or thing; by making with the following example:

"MY CONFLICTS OF _____ ARE FROM MY VERY OWN RESISTANCE AND TO SOMETHING THAT WAS NOT REAL WITH ME."

After this clearing of the mind and with eyes closed, feel for the peace; sink into it and feel it, closing around the body.
The feeling of deep joy and increased alertness; instead of drowsiness, to take its place. Should any reason, to find slipping off and into withdrawal, repeat again today's main idea.

"THERE IS NO OTHER FINITE FORCE TO RECON WITH AND THAT WOULD CLAIM THE WILL OF THE INFINITE TO SHARE SPARINGLY WITH ME."

Notice how irrelevant, these thoughts and that the self possibly, had not even, anything to do with. Then previously seeking, of what now is found, take a few minutes; as often as required to and with eyes closed for these moments.

The purpose is, for finding peace and by recognizing the splitting off, from creation; the things that conflicts become attracted to and from its thoughts.

Take 2 days to take it in

CONGRATULATIONS ...!!!

FOR MAKING IT THROUGH THE 90th Lesson

(This is a rest period to take the lessons independently as a review)

TAKE THESE TWO DAYS TO RECALIBRATE;

MAKE NOTES AND REVIEW……………..

(Day 105)
Frozen in a moment and that joins with the mind of duality; is not that of Love and Oneness, in this moment of suspension. Enlightenment, is the intention of bringing in light and within the physical body; however this light is made available, from within. The specific steps of going within the stillness point; that point of nothingness, that pulls in and motions out, all energy.

LESSON~91: "MY EMOTIONAL EXPERIENCES ARE CHEMICAL REACTIONS FROM MY BRAIN; FOR THE REFINEMENT OF MIND, TO PROCESS THROUGH DISCERNMENT AND INSPIRE ME TO RELATE BACK, EXPRESSIVELY INTO MY WORLD."

As the Earth can hold Water, so too, can the water hold energy. Throughout this book and that of the many spiritual instruments of thought, that were expressed to utilize; whether it has been derived from ancient Vedic syllable/like chants. Or made common practice as a word or poem/prayer or affirmation; they all are activations, from some stream of thought and for the purpose to empower, through the Aether of its sound. This bio-energetic container, is the self made "Ashram", "Mosque", "Temple", "Synagogue" and/or "Church". Like every wave, that leads back down and into the sameness; from the emotional depth, it had once come from. These images, were never the intention to be idolized. Like voodoo doll expressions, of the self. Within some superficial form and to be imbued upon; by the many slivers of the soul and from spirit alike, into the oneness. It is true, that by making a connection, to support and contribution from the resonance, does happen. This is the very falsehood and from the bio energetic playground, of collective soul; that it may, to impress upon the self, an archetypical mask and lacking from such powers.

LESSON~91: "MY EMOTIONAL EXPERIENCES ARE
CHEMICAL REACTIONS FROM MY BRAIN;
FOR THE REFINEMENT OF MIND
TO PROCESS THROUGH DISCERNMENT
AND INSPIRE ME TO RELATE BACK
EXPRESSIVELY INTO MY WORLD."

The belief of power, from the many and that reflect upon the self; they are not these bodies of light and that the self might think, they are dependent on. Rather, the unaware misrepresentation, of something and that was agreed upon, to feed into collectively. Organization and structure, are already from within a masterful creation; this cooperation and from a microscopic level, is then, in its entirety, of the external one. These levels of emotions, are captured entities; from an expression that once was and now is no longer to depend on. The emotions become stuck, into yielded objects; that the self holds idol and non moving, from this expression. The staleness, creates lack and limitations, by accepting these beliefs; they intern become the barriers, in every way and to obstruct, from having the best, possible life. By feeling the body and pushing out the static; this electrical component, does respond or can react to and in this way of motion. Emotions are like waves, they come and go; they can be of grief, or extreme desire, to express such feelings. Visualize the self, as swimming passionately, in deep and rich warm, waters; as it meets up, with every wave, it eagerly accepts and moves forward, from each individuating, depth that crashes upon it. While swimming, feel the beautiful rain falling down; see the sun showers and hear the crashing of the thunder storms. This powerful moment, is the grief and that from every moment, the self goes deep into the oneness, of the water's edge; as it reaches for the light and to come back up, a glass formation wishes to appear as frozen.

LESSON~91: "MY EMOTIONAL EXPERIENCES ARE CHEMICAL REACTIONS FROM MY BRAIN; FOR THE REFINEMENT OF MIND, TO PROCESS THROUGH DISCERNMENT AND INSPIRE ME TO RELATE BACK, EXPRESSIVELY INTO MY WORLD."

This is how quickly thought can form, into a glass like image and to trap the self(trauma), from moving further forward.
Moving forward and within the middle of an ocean, has no relevance; however just the passion of moving sensually and exploring the sensations. To invigorate enough, to find the self and lifted up, to a glistening flattened surface. Above the peaked edges of the earth and to stare down, at all the palm trees, on the other side; amongst the deeply coloured and vibrating nature of enriched earth.
So within every moment, the mind goes deeper from the surface edge; to risk becoming sealed right in and having to break through, just in time, to catch another breath. From these depths, just staying long enough, to rise back into the light.
Feel the movement of these waves; of breathing them, into the muscular fluid membrane and that define it, from the surface of the water. To solid form again, these worlds too; they come from the Oneness of awareness.

The purpose of today, is to feel the body and see the light; allow for all emotions, that the self can play with. The worshiping of idols, will only but capture and an unfulfilled desire for the self; into a sealed containment, of limited possibilities and lack, from never becoming enough, to fit right in.

(Day 106) Today, allow the light, directly to express and shine from this appearance, onto the world freely. When the shadows vanish, do not become discouraged and by the disengagements, that would otherwise involve, the self to play.

LESSON~92:
"I MUST RELEASE MY SENTIMENT
FROM ALL OBJECTS OF ATTACHMENT."

Acceptance, is not dependent on its recognition; to be allowed for its expression, to be proven first and then expressed accordingly. Nor be explicitly enforced, the pattern and for the need, to have it in, an objectifying manner. Objects must not be to posses the self with; nor the self to "<u>addictify</u>" them and as a need to function with. The root of all suffering, comes from these identifiable ideas; that hold into identity and as solid objects. So easy to get lost, in the reassurance and that the self, might be worth, for anything less otherwise. Hanging onto things for value, to support the self as worthy and to serve in its expression; is as silly, as the references and resume, it has experienced, to prove with. Relying on the world, to hold its ransom; will indeed hold the self back and proves nothing, in the making of itself. Could it be the purpose, of not having made it in the first place? Is this neglect, that the self must realize; that in fact it has and the supporting figures are irrelevant? From every object, subject place and so on; that the self must hold and cherish. Are they not the neglected aspects, held captive and to define for an identity; that is meaningless, for any real worth? Today take everything that is held precious to the self and study as many things and places the self might be holding in ransom of its energy from its self as light ... Feel the sentiment and allow it to detach from this or any other meaning that might have led to its addiction in this way of holding onto……All patterns do not go without the sentimental addiction to them and that had kept attached the self to them.

LESSON~92: "I MUST RELEASE MY SENTIMENT
             FROM ALL OBJECTS OF ATTACHMENT."

The masks or cover-ups, must be released and in the same way, as it was mentioned, from the previous lesson; as to perhaps, express the unawareness, held within the grief.
These things, might be a way, to claim more space and ownership; Could it be that all these toys, make the self feel grandiose ?...Maybe the attachment, is to an underlying fear, of separation and/or an abandonment... Could it be, the loss was, way too sudden and before the self could even reconcile, with it properly; to go away or doing without it ?....Storing things away, like clothing or even extra weight; because of having to remember and that the moderation is not restored, to balance with, extreme behaviour. How can overcompensating happen, when compensation, in itself, is an illusion; held far from the truth. After every encounter and to release, as much as the self can; to work through out this day, repeat the following idea:

"I MUST RELEASE MY SENTIMENT
FROM ALL OBJECTS OF ATTACHMENT."

Shift the perspective, to the fusion of its function and its will, as one; rather than, from what the self was holding onto.
How is it irrelevant and with every contribution, that it may, instead be served?

"<u>BE CARING, BUT NOT CONCERNED.</u>"

The true purpose, is to find the inspiration and in its release of creation for creation.

(Day 107)

By forgiving, the energy that was held in before, can be released and transmuted, back into the light. Allow the "Inner Voice" (heart must be open) to travel through the Ether, for the self and hear the following idea to ignite, with this affirmation:

LESSON~93:
"THE LIGHT IS HERE AFTER THE RAIN ALL IS FORGIVEN NOW."

Today, the focus is on the light and all that will be given to, through self desire. Heaven's reflection covers over the world and the Ego's shadow has wiped out, from any to be seen. Practice with a longer exercise, throughout the day; by exposing the corruption of the world into forgiveness. See only through the light of forgiveness and what the self would like to see, of its world. With glad expectations, release into the exercise, with the following thought:

"THE LIGHT IS HERE AFTER THE RAIN ALL IS FORGIVEN NOW."

Remove the self from the corruptions of its past; with an open mind, to wash over all those ideas and that have had previous concepts made from before.
Look upon everything, like it has never been seen before, or not happened yet; while slowly repeating the following and like it were made ready to be shown, for the first time:

"THE LIGHT IS HERE AFTER THE RAIN ALL IS FORGIVEN NOW."

LESSON~93:
"THE LIGHT IS HERE AFTER THE RAIN ALL IS FORGIVEN NOW."

Trust in this promise, to surrender the self and within such certainty; to look upon the world and that from this moment on, it will be seen differently. In brilliance this world can be embraced, from before it began and with every passing cloud, the past disperses, like the shade upon the eyes. As often as can be reminded and for these words to practice over, today; in the mind and with a joyful reminder, of release, at a time for special celebration.

With the highest of excitement, give thanks, for the mercy of the Love, the self is feeling. Rejoice, in the power of healing the sight; completely through forgiveness and the sound of these words. The confidence to refresh a new moment and over the static of passing pressures, upon the friction of the mind; see to welcome gladly, to extend forever and with the following affirmation:

"THE LIGHT IS HERE AFTER THE RAIN ALL IS FORGIVEN NOW."

Whenever the thought of getting pulled back into dark clouds, repeat the following :

"THE LIGHT IS HERE AFTER THE RAIN ALL IS FORGIVEN NOW."

With every passing tear, the energy transmutes and into the brilliance, of this light; forgiving the self, to see much clearer.

The purpose, is to surrender over into trust; enough to feel the Love. Accept the Praise, that from the illumination, forgiveness brings and be forever grateful, here and now.

(Day108)-Comprehend the freedom, from all danger and tyranny; is that of the mind, to bind the self and with senseless legislations. Imprisoned with strange and twisted up ideas, that have set up to prove salvation. As the "State of Being", is more important; than its made up stories and to impress upon, with righteous fervor.

What artificial remedy, was meant to be the cure and that was actually to cover over, with immunity; as a half truth and temporarily to sustain, the sleeping state of sickness.

LESSON~94: "I AM AND OF MY OWN VOLITION
       AM I TO AUTHORIZE MY CONDUCT
       THROUGH THIS INFINITE INTELLIGENCE."

With nothing to prove and by placing the self in harms way; in this way, to satisfy the many of its world with. Today, take back all services provided, from the self and that has forever long, been taken for granted. The fear, for shelter and safety; it can cause madness and to create suffering, with rules of distortion.

To stockpile food; because the illusion has convinced the body, it will starve? Or to have the mind, believe for the self, it will be saved; by a degenerative pill? Or a "fluid, to inject into the body and to prevent the flow, of its very own regeneration; but with a mask on, rather to disguise, that it can ward off disease and death"?

So many insane things, the mind and like minds, will gather to form such systemic groupings; to feel safe in the thinking of support. Policies have no use and serve no purpose; however the threat of fear and to what might happen, creates a convincing story, to obey its many systems with. Protect the body and self will be saved, is this fallacy and amongst the many, that self has formed; because it fears, what it cannot control. The body suffers, from the mind that hurts it and to avoid the fear of victimhood.

What really suffers, is not the body that is in pain; rather the mind, that cannot free itself. To free itself, the mind will sabotage the body and by further making it an enemy. The very own rules it sets to save the body with, so that the mind will think, it is a body.

LESSON~94: "I AM AND OF MY OWN VOLITION AM I TO AUTHORIZE MY CONDUCT THROUGH THIS INFINITE INTELLIGENCE."

There are only those rules, that the self will come to accept; when it wishes to live cooperatively with the many. With this than, exercise and with a short review; of the different kinds of "conduct" and that self, with its many minds, have grouped up, to believe, they must obey, to function. Some examples to review and during these practices perhaps, of "shoulds and shouldn'ts", could be: "nutrition", medication; there are so many others uncountable, made up stories to protect the body and other groups of bodies with. Perhaps, it is the belief, in relationships with the many of its world and its mutual benefits. Some other ways, to conduct the self with the mind; to set forth, what is God's and what is for the self, as identity. To think that something, that can damn in Heaven's name; could not possibly enlighten and by holding the self captive to obey and make safe. Dismiss all foolishness, that hold the mind in silent readiness to make the connection with the Ethereal self and hear this Inner Voice, of truth. The Voice will speak of this unlimited perspective, that exists with joy and holds the freedom; as in an Earthly body and its world. Why does the consciousness yearn and for the mind to bond with that of sub consciousness? To create as a channel for creation and denied by its belief in punishment. Change the channel of this frequency and through to a higher perspective; where genders do not have any meaning and to uphold for any story. The purpose for today, is to self review; explore the possibility of universal laws and through infinite intelligence, that can never be replaced, by the artificial. This is the rejoicing for today; it is no longer a truth, that dares to be hidden. The magic of manipulation and control, is a dark paved path and has no place where the light is found. God/Source/ Energy, higher self gives the freedom to allow, and for the over-soul to show itself, the true laws of her nature.

(Day109) The self was designed, to connect sociably, with its soulful skills of awareness and to warrant from these attractions further more, for such experiences. The discriminating factors, held in place and from the degenerative perspectives; they only bring about, the falsehood of an ideology, of support and safety, that by option, the self can resist or connect with.

LESSON~95: "THE GENERATOR OF THIS HOLOGRAPHIC EXPERIENCE IS ME AND WITH EVERY BREATH I AM CREATING MY OWN FIELD OF GENERATION."

Today, the lesson is perhaps, more from an observing stance. Become aware, of the self and through its surroundings; that take place and to hold within it, the circumstances for its experiences. Reflect back this experience, within these surroundings; as they are living and breathing, from the self imprinted essence.

These surroundings, may also be aware or non aware of its observer and to what level of awareness they are coming from; could it be at best, the untangling of its greatest entanglement theory?

When the experiences are lost, from the awareness; it is only the awareness of the self; thusly the awareness of its surroundings, they too, have no connection to the awareness of it. Notice to what extent the surroundings have and on only the impact of level, of connection; from their own experiences and to their own awareness, of themselves or maybe not even that? Notice when they do not have these awareness of objectifiable projections; that perhaps when they do not, how and to what extent, they intern become "objectify-able"? To what level of an object can the self impress upon awareness; will depend on the level of intimate attachment to it and it, to the self. From this awareness, a certain kind of need arises from the imprint; this connection, can be from a different recorded imprint and to which it can relate with, as soul and within another physical body of awareness, from the self.

LESSON~95: "THE GENERATOR OF THIS HOLOGRAPHIC EXPERIENCE IS ME AND WITH EVERY BREATH I AM CREATING MY OWN FIELD OF GENERATION."

By not having the awareness or recording of experience, the variation from the soul level brings about another perspective and to the level of, which to experience. From the experience of these chemical reactions and just like the attraction, to pull together from one system to another, is expressed and stimulated. The amount of awareness is, that can be held and from such is the experience to process; in turn it can be able to connect, given from another and back to the self. The generator, must be generating enough energy and within accordance to its level of awareness; from it, the reality it holds in place, for the experience. The more awareness to itself, is reflected back; the more, the flow can generate, un-obstructively. This is where objects, that lack awareness and have only but the essence of a greater awareness, that has been imprinted upon them; where the self can take, only but of this essence in, to feed its soul with and/or imprint upon it, so it may to reflect back on the self, with an exchange perhaps? Today, notice the difference, from subjects to objects; from species to races and all the other programs in between. Then ask this question and notice "Are these programs coming from me, or from my degenerative imprints ? ".

There are many levels and layers of awareness; covered in from its experience and recorded imprints, from this accumulated generation and degenerated levels of awareness. This it will experience and until it can adjust, from what best serves it; in this way, why not free up the energy, that is attracting blockages?

The purpose, is to see things, at a spirit level and from hence, the soul is found; the imprinting of the real connections and to the essences of its awareness.

(Day110)

The statement of the self's true identity, is this cause for celebration and because of that, to be deserving of enlightenment.
Open up to the subtleties of miracles; rather than to feel entitled, from the heroic expectations and whenever reaching out to ask.

LESSON~96: "I AM DESERVING OF THIS IMAGINATION TO SELF EXPRESS AND THAT IT MAY BE IMPRINTED AS REAL UPON MY AWARENESS TO IT."

It is inherent, in the truth of what the self is; rather than the "Egoic" self to disconnect, with its grandeur illusions of misinterpreted magical powers. It was placed in as part of its creation and when created from its awareness of being. A complete release, was promised from the world and that the self had made; instead given the kingdom of creator being, within itself. There is no reason to content with less, than this truth. With eyes closed, remember that, through this idea and to reaffirm, what is rightfully for the self, in the asking of it. Miracles do not obey the laws that are written up by the mind to punish self with. Rather a universal concept, by its very own creator/god and from this frequency; that miracles do follow and only from unto those rules. When the self has asked, for its world and of itself, to be saved; the request has the means for it to be accomplished. "The will be done "; because the self, is one with source energy consciousness and in the asking for not really of anything. To make mention of a fact, that cannot be denied and that holy spirit, can grant for the self, to accept it so.
The answer is simple and with no doubt of uncertainty, from the self to make room for, of this simple fact.

LESSON~96: "I AM DESERVING OF THIS IMAGINATION TO SELF EXPRESS AND THAT IT MAY BE IMPRINTED AS REAL UPON MY AWARENESS TO IT."

Rest assured, in the seeking of it and with the shorter practice, frequently to remember this.

Repeat often :

"I AM DESERVING TO RECEIVE THESE BLESSINGS."

Do this and whenever a situation comes up, to call for this affirmation.

Less than, the perfect answer, is not good enough, to settle with; the following, is most applicable, to go over quickly and to repeat by saying:

"I AM THIS CHILD UNITED WITH INFINITE EXPRESSION TO A GREATER AWARENESS OF MY BEING AND IN ONENESS WITH THE SELF."

"I AM DESERVING OF THIS PARENT CHILD REUNION AND BY ACCEPTING THE MERGING OF MY CONSCIOUSNESS AND SUBCONSCIOUSNESS_ IN THIS WAY_ I AM CREATOR AND CREATION."

This state, combines the self perspective, with the meaning to unite as one and in the formation of, by giving of great importance; the power over to reflect, its choice of gender and preference, to best relate with. The "Ego mind", is the only thing that assigns value to something, over another and to project comparison, in this way, of its experience.

The purpose, is for the self, to shift in its perception to accept; that which it has already imprinted and amongst the contrast of its growth. Be open, to the subtleties, that are preferred and see these miracles, within the everyday, common occurrences.

THE INTERMISSION :

Take a day to take it in

CONGRATULATIONS ...!!!

FOR MAKING IT

THROUGH TO THE 96th Lesson

(This is a rest period to take the lessons independently as a review)

TAKE THIS DAY TO RECALIBRATE;

MAKE NOTES AND REVIEW..................

(Day112) What is it, from awareness and that is happening, to take something; that has been generated, to become random and make it, not random at all? When the victim, becomes aware and that, it is the creator; it does not feel the need, to also be the perpetrator.

LESSON~97: "WITHIN ME EXISTS SOMETHING MUCH GREATER AND MUCH HIGHER THAN FROM THE PERSPECTIVE THAT RANDOMNESS CREATED."

Today, it is all about removing, that which stunts the self growth and that would be, the perspective, that life is random.

The non randomness, is the path into higher consciousness; it is an energy, that pervades all of society and that had first awakened, within the stirrings of religious dogma. Thus arose from it, the atheistic counterbalance and within such, the lineage, that had it forcibly to prove, with science. These programs and indoctrinated beliefs, from a head quarter level and into the soul; for the brain and nervous system, to be hooked and anchored by them.

Once the cosmic consciousness, of oneness activates and starts exposing these shadowed in areas, from a genetic lineage and ethereal plane; and until they can become awakened and react, continue to proceed as moving static, stuck. How the self can decide to filter these things out, from its awareness, is not enough; rather it must allow, to feel it leave and from all its senses.

In this way, exposing(brought up into the heavens to be saved)its reaction to the light and that can dissolve it through transmutation. Betrayal, is one of the major events and in the trade off, for a safe passage out. The sleeping giant, has now awakened and everything from within, is vibrating out. That which lacks the resonance, must once again enter; through the portal of the sun and to find its place of order. Other than this creative separation, of creator and creation; there is no such thing as judgment .

LESSON~97: "WITHIN ME EXISTS SOMETHING MUCH GREATER AND MUCH HIGHER THAN FROM THE PERSPECTIVE THAT RANDOMNESS CREATED."

The light and that is all around the self, this indeed, is the kingdom found, from within. Its frequency not so random and yet what is it of this light, that can connect ? Within this energetic field, what is it that connects these thoughts? These ideas that are held and within these thoughts, are the contributions, to generate with; they are not so random and chaotic. Following the process of the generators flow, is this generation and from it, to bring with its intentions, a higher better co existence. This is what happens and when the self starts planning, way ahead of its awareness; even for the reasons to create, exclusiveness for its procreative form, to be obliged and to continue on, as the inherent vices to the cause. It can, from this perspective, continue to build higher and expand out further; from where it was previously left off, such structures. That the self escalated in its ranks; would have something to work with and not have to keep starting over. These beliefs, were set in place, for the greatest of good; yet were they not, the cause for all the twisted up distortions, to fall back on and feel stuck by them?

Today, become aware, on taking in this life; from the random chaotic, unsupportive and almost neglected view point.

Realize instead, that light around the self; that is not random, yet evolves all things, to higher and better form. It is alright to feel enraged and angry even ……as long as it can be expressed; so not to be a perpetrator and of a dualistic game called karma.

Feeling stuck, can trigger anger and that was once before managed as depression….How to be assertive, is more or less the balance, of this energy; that, rather than react as a victim, it may respond well.

LESSON~97: "WITHIN ME EXISTS SOMETHING MUCH GREATER AND MUCH HIGHER THAN FROM THE PERSPECTIVE THAT RANDOMNESS CREATED."

From the conditions, that the self exposes and to become exposed by them; awareness is never random. Where the self is, right here, right now and in all its circumstances, that brought it here; were not from any to compare, as an accident. There is no shame in admitting and from where the light can blind; that everything had its place and no blame, from hence it was created, by and large, from the self and its awareness. From this way, it can let go the reminiscing and sentiment of staleness; to embrace and rather, feel refreshed with cleaner circulation. The parable is in the same as taking and demagnetizing a cassette; from all the previous songs it had been playing. To generate the continuance of such preexisting structures from its world; it was projecting from the darkness (pre-recordings). Indoctrinated patterns and that the self had held in, so deer; were but the insecurities from within. The flow must generate, with certainty and refresh the structures, as it feels reshaping and/or dissolving from them; in the now, from this existence and from this authentic perspective. The function has evolved; because the self is constantly evolving, as a generator, it must flow out and un-obstructively from its creations. The creations of these structures, were only meant to guide it, while asleep and blinded; by its very own light, to be lead by the external and in this way, of fascination. This is why the idols were and from working on them, in this way, to generate the motivation; that would, to inspire further and along this process; but were never meant to be, the end all, be all, of its self entitlement.

The purpose, is to be refreshed in the awareness of this generator and not to be stuck by its generational misunderstandings, of what once was; or predicted for the self, to follow from and here on forward.

(Day 113) Today, be most observing, of the weary intensions and that competition brings, with the program that requires lack. What the heart is really missing, is to refresh in love.
All of its desires met, like needs before them and with such dreamlike visions; the yearning to be with and in the making of such creations.

LESSON~98: "WHEN MY HEART RELEASES FROM THE GRIEF IT WILL OPEN AND THE EGO MIND WILL SHRINK AWAY."

Today, is all about the missing out of being and with all that the self has ever dreamed of; to demand before its physical requirements, as needs and neglect all else. When the self can be the observer and not allow the competition to be the hoarder; it will find the meaning of its loss and within the plenty of the many, that will enjoy it.
Practice finding the parables and from them, this to share a sample: The self might desire for a Mercedes and the next day, it almost gets run over by it. The background sentiment expressed from its world; through those many eyes and yet not for the self to ever experience the very thing it cherished. What perspectives might the masses be holding in and to have the very thing, that self has asked for ?
The falseness of this dominance and compliance of creator for creation; is simply to compare, of this, its greatest reveal:

"WHEN THE HEART IS OPEN ALL IS POSSIBLE AND WHEN IT IS NOT THE EGO MIND TAKES OVER."

When the heart is closed the "Ego mind" takes over and to the extent of having to reveal, as its competitive component; that which can be, furthest from the truth, as to refresh the self with.

LESSON~98: "WHEN MY HEART RELEASES FROM THE GRIEF IT WILL OPEN AND THE EGO MIND WILL SHRINK AWAY."

The "Ego mind" loves to compete and be placed in a competitive environment; it is where it can thrive best and by neglecting all the while, the wounded heart.
Nothing is any better, than any other, or anything else; the level of commitment, allows it to neglect, all other things and for just this one, narrow minded perspective. To embrace the differences and learn from them, is this neglect to see; because of the lack in shifting. Having instead to separate these differences, rather than to unite them into wholeness. Competition(root chakra) can exclude and kill off everything, that the self could most easily enjoy; that the many take for granted in this way.
The sport of (adrenaline) survival, is not by any means, the same and as to enlighten, with thriving(consciousness) to justify; because for the Ego(up the spinal column), it will thrive and while the self, barely makes it out alive(down there).

The purpose of this lesson, is to capture and within, as many parables from the self perspective's(to study from its own experience), "Ego mind" and release the heart, from the tyranny, where grief consumes it.

(Day 114)

Expansion, does not have to happen through the process of becoming hurt; rather from the willingness to accept, the overwhelming bliss. Where nurturing reveals the nurturer, there is no place for competition! Grief must always be allowed to have its way, in passing out from the self and in anyway, that the self can allow for it, to be expressively expelled. Just like the heart, when it contracts and then expands; in the exchange and from the lower/higher/inner/outer, aspects of the self, to work on integrating properly: "<u>descension</u>" and "<u>ascension</u>" happen.

LESSON~99: "THE FLICKERING OF MY LIGHT FROM ONSET GRIEF IS THIS HEART ACHE, THAT COMES IN CRASHING WAVES UPON THE SHORE AND THEN RECEDING CALMY."

The hardest thing the self can ever learn to do, is nurture itself. To find that place and within the heart, where nature is no longer the enemy; to physically embrace her and by it too, the self can be embraced. Awe the tears that must be shed, even while recording this(pause). What does create these sacred tears?
A regurgitating reflex, to help spring forward and integrate into the light, this energy, of holding back. Compliance in this, can happen and with the lubricant of tears; from the lack of understanding, what repelled from it and in this way, that would, to resist it, in the first place. Addiction, to the many vices and that it forms relationships of codependence; is more predictable and that it may be inferior, even to that, of given measures to survive by.

LESSON~99: "THE FLICKERING OF MY LIGHT FROM ONSET GRIEF IS THIS HEART ACHE, THAT COMES IN CRASHING WAVES UPON THE SHORE AND THEN RECEDING CALMY."

How does it generate the energy and to carry on, in this way of lack, for other things; much more vital, than the vices, it had itself dependent on. When the self can truly break away, from its addictions; it will shift to see and that again, it is, at a starting point level. How is it, that it had the energy to manifest such things and now it does not? This is where competition and anger, as its motivator can be of assistance. When the addict is cured from its addictions however; competition is no longer, the discipline and to pattern in, for its expansion. What then?

The bliss becomes irrelevant for any competition.

In the same way nurturing can feel, to brighten as the sun and as warming to every embrace; ready to accept and contain the feeling of expansion. This is where the awareness of artificial stimulation and natural stimulation from within become revealed.

Today, find it, or allow for it to find the self : Just imagine that feeling, of being on an aircraft and coming in for a landing; then again what it feels like to take off again. When the take off happens, the higher self is felt descending into the lower self. When that of the physical body is noticed by the self, during lift off and then, when the plane, comes in for a landing. Can it feel the separation of the higher self whilst it descends? This in the physical reality, can only be felt by the body; to then make sense of, however much of the time it dismisses these discomforts. This is the light, the self can feel as bliss and when it can accept the energy; the more it can hold, the higher it will raise(like helium inside a balloon).

The purpose, is to reawaken to the rapture and learn to integrate the expansion, within contraction; in this loving way, of accepting and from this level of point of view.

(Day 115)
From the many probable possibilities and back into the present moment of the nothingness, point of reference; how can the self, engineer itself, into the "One"? The wisdom (energy) that the physical body holds, is most importantly and the first step, in this process; to experience from learning to transform and the long lasting effects of trauma. There are many body-oriented practices, that can connect intimately, between the physical structure ("Yoga") of the body's reaction and its thoughts, as well, as the emotions, that the self can feel.

LESSON~100: "MY BODY CAN FULLY AWAKEN TO ITS PHYSICAL EXPERIENCE AND I CAN FEEL CONNECTED TO THIS CONSCIOUSNESS OF BEING."

On a cognitive thinking level, it is encouraged and to connect the focus mindfully, on the somatic experiences; by helping to reduce the impact of emotional distress. The focus however, is on the spirit and how it metaphysically combines itself. From within the physical connection, to the body and its manifested outcomes; this combination (figure-8 like motion) can interact with, from the soul and within the inner/outer, spherical impression, of its world, as reality. Today, the first thing the self can do and before starting off the day: Is to stretch completely, as it would and instead of getting up; take the moment to just feel and be.
What did the physical body feel like, before and after it completely extended with a stretch? Did the stretch feel like a relief or broken up into areas of pain? Any pain or discomfort anywhere?
Address the pain and stretch or tense it, in that area and with focused breath. Unless the focus is on the kind of movement, to position with Yoga body poses and that require the pulling of tendons/ligaments; ultimately the tensing and the stretching of the body, are one in the same.

LESSON~100: "MY BODY CAN FULLY AWAKEN TO ITS PHYSICAL EXPERIENCE AND I CAN FEEL CONNECTED TO THIS CONSCIOUSNESS OF BEING."

It is in the focus of the breath (for the purpose of reading this book), that makes the difference with this practice; while performing any kind of workout(abdominal crunches for example). Do not be distracted, by the many other disciplines of Yogic/Tantric exercises either. Very simple rule to follow here: when tensing, breathe in and when stretching breathe out. The focus on the tensing aspect and within this process, is better practiced, at the end of the day. The stretching part before the day gets started; however more complex is the alternative combination of the both(even better). In this way and wherever the tension is felt; it can be better with and when more relaxed, to start the day with and/or it might completely go in reverse, to agitate it further. It is important, to get some medical advice before hand; or just simply do not strain, or stress something, that is already feeling this way and rather just breathe. Where it might already feel the discomfort and tensing, or stretching can result in further damage; just breathe in and out. Where that area of trauma is then; just imagine little openings (like mouth pieces) breathing in and out (instead of the tensing and the stretching). This exercise can also be broken up, with just tensing by breathing in and then releasing the tension, by breathing out. With the morning exercise it is more importantly, to stretch and then combine the tensing or exclusively, just stretch then. Stretch the area of concern, take the time to breathe in on the release and then breathe out with every stretch; then relax again by breathing out. After doing so and with any of these combinations, what is the intension of the day? What are the many things, that the self has contracted out and mentally to task itself, throughout this day and prioritize them. Focus on what the self feels to accomplish and from it all; feel for these accomplishments and/or the many tasks toward this process.

LESSON~100: "MY BODY CAN FULLY AWAKEN TO ITS PHYSICAL EXPERIENCE AND I CAN FEEL CONNECTED TO THIS CONSCIOUSNESS OF BEING."

See it visually, within the mind and think it; how it feels, how does it feel? Think it differently, until it feels best and in that way, get up and start the day. Today's lesson will connect with the next and to experience completely this idea. It involves firstly to come around full circle, into the next day; for this level of awareness and to sample in this mode of practice exercise. Becoming one, with the body of awareness; is this movement of breath and within the motion of its life force. Where the body feels the pain, it can be released and through common body movement practices. Throughout the day, repeat the activation; take a few moments to acknowledge any areas of discomfort and practice breathing this way, when required. The exercise is designed to connect with the physical body and in a different kind of methodological resilience, to intend upon. With some neurological relief, perhaps the connection to the emotional body, is the focus of awareness and that from a soul's perspective level; to be found within the physical body and this practice of communicating between sensations.
The focus is to imprint upon the soul's recording with intention and what it is the self might be wishing to experience, within its external world of circumstances. When the day is done, the following practice will be the experience to prepare for; just before settling in for bed and then upon awakening (might be a good practice to write it down) the next day, to fully awaken within the body, for those experiences to manifest. Tense the body and then release it, as mentioned previously and then just do an intake, of how the day was processed. Were the intentions well met and were there any unresolved situations ?

LESSON~100: "MY BODY CAN FULLY AWAKEN TO ITS PHYSICAL EXPERIENCE AND I CAN FEEL CONNECTED TO THIS CONSCIOUSNESS OF BEING."

Get into a dream like state and then focus on the intention; and/or whatever concern the self might want to experience, playing out. Any questions or concerns, must be addressed and can be written down on paper, before entering into a trance. Whatever was to probably reenact within the awakened state, can possibly and in this way, to instead be experienced within the dream state. A rehearsal or perhaps, as many as the self prefers.

The purpose, is to find where the energy can be noticed as stuck and within the physical body; as well as hindering the self from its physical world. With breath, thought of intention and movement; the way the self is feeling, can help better clear and guide through the day. Whatever regrets throughout the day, can be reenacted differently and resolved from within the soul perspective; rather than karmically be mistaken for and in the physical world.

(Day 116) Good morning....How was it, in the soul world ?
Is there any recall or strange feelings of emotional upset ?
Was there anything written down and/or intended for resolve, what has come up for a revelation? Has anything at all changed, with point of view? How about emotional relief ?

LESSON~101: "I AM CONNECTED TO THE PHYSICAL WORLD WITH A PHYSICAL BODY AND THROUGH MY SOUL TO INTERACT WITH SPIRIT AS ONE CREATION."

Sometimes, it is so much better in the soul world and upon awakening into the physical reality, a depression hits the consciousness.....Perhaps the circumstances might be emotionally upsetting and sleep disruption will occur....It is a good idea to record and then, when fully alert; to go over(impressed upon) these "_impressional_" upsets. What is the first thing imprinted upon the mind and/or emotional concern ?
Go ahead and re examine the "_being-ness_" and feel for any subtle sensations. Again, when coming out of this trance like state, and just like yesterday; do a full body awakening and feel .... Is there any difference? Is there anything the self might want to express ? Sometimes creative surges of passion get triggered, from intense emotions and that the self might want to sexually explore.
With sexual outlets; these too, are bursts of creative passion and that can lead the self, to feel exerted (before it can even get started on its day). Emotional outlet, from this process to express relief; it can be channeled with intention and in the same way, back into the soul world; thus the feeling of an energy depletion.

LESSON~101: "I AM CONNECTED TO THE PHYSICAL WORLD WITH A PHYSICAL BODY AND THROUGH MY SOUL TO INTERACT WITH SPIRIT AS ONE CREATION."

Through the sampling of sexual and creative release of energy in this way, might also trigger, for example: grief within the heart and other signs of lack; that these blockages might be signaling and from certain areas within the body, as for example, the lower back. It might even flush through metabolically (with no real need for coffee) from the adrenals, the need to go and carry on about the day, passionately refreshed. This is the transfer over, from the soul world, to the physical and so it goes, from being, to doing, and so it is. It is really paying attention, to the energy levels; because when the physical body shuts down and into resting mode, the linear mind gets out of the way.
In this way, the consciousness/spirit can get used to the merging of realities; from sleeping state, to waking state.
When the realities start to flip and merge the self will feel; that everything that used to be a dream, will be exactly as intense, as the experience it had, to wake it up and into lucid dreaming state. This experience can be the recall, of waking up and into trance like state. The trancelike state, is like the fog like mist and lifting like a veil; that reveals the freshly covered grass, upon the sunrise.

The purpose, is to surrender the body, over to a higher reality and in the way of, in breathing; to grasp the crossing of both worlds. That figure-8 in motion and from the being to the doing; physical, as well as metaphysical. From zero to the oneness, that is creator spirit presence.

(Day117) The physical ears, can only translate the program or to decode from thought; that which is held in the body, so it can be heard. From a cellular level of the body consciousness, where does the Ego come from? The linear thinking mind, is where the thoughts always will be and in the head; however emanate from the body and the root chakra. The clearing of the past and future timelines will bring awareness; to function always from the present moment of the "zero-point field".

LESSON~102: "I AM NOT OF THIS EXPERIENCE AND THIS REALITY DOES NOT BECOME ME ANYMORE."

Listen to the thoughts and feel what state, they vibrate from? What dimensions are they coming from? Are they from the heart or from the lower base level, where the tailbone of the spine begins? When all the emotional energy and that has hooked within the spherical realities, of the many colourful dimensions.
Only when these spherical vortices can clear; then these chakras can collapse, into the oneness and open up multi-dimensional or vortices. What are these thoughts that are passing through the brain and can the mind make them out, with no judgment?
Today, listen to these thoughts and how do they feel?
Does it feel in alignment to this resonance and that can connect to such a reality; or let it go when it does not; because that is not, who or what, the awareness of itself might be? From this configuration and the realization, that time is only but a reference point; then the self will come to the awareness of multidimensionality and that frequency cannot possibly fit into a linear concept, of what reality is. The self is the creator, of its reality and with this light, it holds for others, alike to join it. Relax because reality is always in an influx, waiting to confuse it from its own rhythm of choice to beat.

LESSON~102: "I AM NOT OF THIS EXPERIENCE AND THIS REALITY DOES NOT BECOME ME ANYMORE."

When the self does not step up to join in these creations; the reflected many others of its world, will show it up and in ways that perhaps, the "Ego mind" can activate, to correspond with as competition. Again by not feeding into the supporting challenging perspective and rather accept it as awakening that aspect where the self is(not so alert)sleeping. The self might choose not to react, or show any response, to this kind of motive; rather to allow the affect and to become as activations, through continuous authentic inspirations. The energy will ripple out, like currency and for all those reasons, it will attract the resonating matter; that will penetrate with no reason, to uphold for any boundaries. After leaving the dismantling of the old and starting from nothing; eventually the unity consciousness will always resonate from the One level of reality and where duality has been done away with. This is the creative consciousness, that the creator presence thrives from. Or has the choice, to stay within the suffering, of its own imprisoned mind; waiting for the time it can afford for anything. This has got to be and one of the hardest manipulations, from the physical construct; right to its very bones and that circulates within the marrow. Be kind and respectful; because it takes a while, to make it out of linear perspective, from the purgatory of the "Bardo" states and (as old soul) of the ethereal that has been spoken of before. The in-between state, can the self hear its thought through from its physical ears; or from the intuitive essence of the body? The inner voice and from it, to be guided out of the hell; it knew as material solid flesh bound earth. This is what it means, to connect and listen to the body and from it, to grasp the metaphysical; that in this spirit, having the experience and from its own authentic perspective.

The purpose, is to get out of the comfort zone and not accept for anything less; because heaven has no compromising and it is not a meaning, that resonates with enlightened awareness.

(Day 118)

Motivation, is but a shadow from the inner inspiration and to express in the external world from its experience.
Sometimes it takes a 2 by 4 and or the tyranny into submission; from submission to comply and with appropriate expression from its peers. Identity is such an abstract concept; that even from the self, it must be somewhere imitating, from the many. In this way too, from its experience, to connectively relate with and in the corresponding with....LESSON~103:

"MOTIVATION IS A FORCEFUL ACT THAT IT MAY WILL UPON THE MANY TO INSPIRE WITH ACCEPTANCE."

Empathizing with the characters, is part of what creates the harmony to make it work. Sometimes the secrets are so well hidden from the self; that it would take another, to overshadow in this way of motivation and to bring it forth, into the light.
It is not that one might be brighter, than the other; rather the darkness, makes this light appear much stronger. These roleplaying fantasies, are the images, that motivate and to uphold within the societal supporting preferences; currently affecting the economical affairs of their groupings. The breakdown of relationships and into the interplay; from the dominance of a lovingly authority and into the surrendering submission, is where the many find and from it their external happiness. It is important and that the movement forward, will eventually come to a nauseating threshold, from resistance; otherwise the self will never come to realize, its mental limitation, in this way. From the external willpower factor, that blockage will become induced enough; for even in that moment, to experience the ceasing of the chatter and feel the motive in a blissful state of "being-ness".

LESSON~103:

"MOTIVATION IS A FORCEFUL ACT THAT IT MAY WILL UPON THE MANY TO INSPIRE WITH ACCEPTANCE."

Motivation can take the zombie, out of its compliant average existence and start to wake it up. The external motivator in its own right, will soldier on the self; to ask it with its ears, to hear and eyes, that it will use, to put them on the horizon and go there. Motivation is yet another stimulant; like any other external drug/narcotic and has a price tag for, in its exchange to value over. The subjugating image to entice and at the very core of its profession; the sexual prowess entertainment, underlying motive; was ultimately the act of inducing, in this way of dominance. With separation comes the need to qualify; so it does, by taking center stage and to motivate the many, that will gather, in perspective of the one. Today is all about the inner motive of the spark, within creation and its force; from it the inspiration and that will hold authentically this passion. Igniting the inner spark and to creatively express, is an entitlement for all and procreation musn't be the dominant dictator; to the level of authorizing, who, or what is deserving; or non deserving. Within the unity consciousness, all creatively and expressing differences must be accepted, into the potential of appreciation.
Again procreation, is the shadow formation, from creative light expression.

What is this passion, that lights up sovereignly connecting, to the will and un possessed by any other, to express its point of view, freely?

The purpose, is to integrate the shadow aspects, by accepting to acknowledge and remember; this is what sets them free, into the light and back into connection.

(Day 119)

Competition is a choice, of compromised awareness; it can be most rewarding, however very limiting. The gaining of a narrow perspective, eventually must shatter and into the awareness, that these sacrifices came unwarranted. How can competition help to keep the self activated and in the igniting of its own awareness to it; in this way and that they might guide and/or propel it forward with its goals(keeping eyes on the prize)?

LESSON~104:

"HOW I CHOOSE TO LIVE MY LIFE
CAN LIMIT MY AWARENESS OR EXPAND IT."

Just how resourceful, are the many from the self; that hath created them and into its awareness, to reflect such circumstances?
When the self creates the outline of the many things it wanted and to birth into awareness. The inactivity, in one area started to flare up and irrationally started pushing the self, into the need to feel, its incompletion. Distractions into worry, can throw the self off and into all sorts of directions; that it may lack to struggle for its limitations and the challenge forth into competition, is this perspective. Resources are not finite and the self was resourceful enough to create all these experiences; that wish to interact within the now so urgently. Peerless moments of creations, built precisely to inspire. Rather the forceful entry too, can create the motive to entice in their formations; for these levels of variations and that their perspectives bring, to show case with most probable a cause.
What a feisty champion the "Ego mind"; it makes from the many and where the inactive awareness lies.

Today, whatever fears the self might have, leave the comfort zone and interact with everything; that might want to learn, or get to know, or challenge the self with opportunity and take it always.

LESSON~104:

HOW I CHOOSE TO LIVE MY LIFE CAN LIMIT MY AWARENESS OR EXPAND IT."

In this preparation and that will lead the way, to the hive; to further assist, by helping and that in any way, it can be made useful, just do it. In this way, nothing is undermined, neglected or uncared for; however do not be concerned, in the way of caring. Show up for everything, no matter the acceptance level; the self will still be leading the troops along the way in service. In this way, there is no lack, just playful shifting of perspectives; that show up and with the preferences, that shadow over, in the mask of competition.

There are only the restrictions, that the self chooses to believe and the rest is just imagination, playing with its many roles. Then again, the shifting of perspective; to obsolete the creator and from where there never was a model to begin with. The relevance in playful roles to compromise, then would never surface and in the formation to compete, for a position; that might never be and to fulfil, from a narrow, pin point and ultimate perspective.

Competition and compromise, come from the same programs and that might suggest awareness to be similar; for example, to a glass of water and from where the preference might be: to drink, sucking through a straw and/or rather, than directly from the glass?

Just look at, all the many and pinched off from the oneness; to flicker in their own right, for praise and recognition.

In this way, appreciate these many efforts of expansion; it will benefit within the oneness, of the light, unwavering and reflecting back, to the creator self well, to once again inspire. Nothing is wrong, nor right, or better than, the other; the purpose, is to rise above the "Ego" and narrow minded references; view these many tools and from which adversity brings, to gain the variances of perspectives.

(Day 120)

Could it be a scientific imprint and from below the belly button, to suggest it; as emotional creation and with it, even lower, to a place of compromising proof? Change the perspective and break apart the resonance; that does not have the will and/nor interest, to share such a thought.

LESSON~105: "I AM, I HAVE AND I ENJOY."

To separate from a perspective, might it not also be the same, as to break apart; as well and to cause the same, from protein particles, of solid matter? Perhaps from thought, an over stimulated electrical event happens and from this force, a collision could occur; and/or could it invade and break apart another, with a shutting out effect? Could it be seen as an invasion, when it feels this change to reinterpret as a compromise and not to accept it; because it will then feel like a violation? The intrusive action, closing in by closing out and from the previously shared authentic holder (that creatively expressed this into being). Finally the creation, is recognized differently and into a new awareness; from another presence and from a molecular process, to understand as manifestation.

The older the soul, the more emotional awareness and from previous creations, it must endure and identifiably to reconnect, as being. From this sacred memory, within the level of creator being and to observe these experiences as they surface.

Do not become convinced by them, as duties to perform and in such a role; because it, this identity, will not last for very long, to generate in service and for the greater good. Rather it, as many other identifying roles; are in the becoming toward expansion and for the next level; until it matches up, with the identity and role it must be playing in and to function from. Once the realization, of what once was, can fully integrate and into the now presence of being; the echoes must be embraced and for them to release by their own doing. The sacred place, now must rise and meet up with the heart; as one creation, in unison and with all the other fields, relating in harmony.

LESSON~105: "I AM, I HAVE AND I ENJOY."

Today, go within the matter and to find; or better yet, let "matter-less" matter, find the self. Pay attention to what it is that the self wants?

Be receptive and let the intention find the self.

Become still enough; because where there is running water, and the stillness of this water, it must be reached from within.

What the agitations bring, from the base of the spine and up the spinal fluid; will be and to affect the nervous system with. Perhaps the grinding of the teeth, will cause an impact and to not quite understanding; how the self can better cope, to stop this pattern of response?

What resistances, of overwhelming effort are there, to change and mould the self with?

The soul has much to teach and from its "Material World".

What is it, that makes the self feel and like it must move forward, in a backwards way? Once all these prevailing circumstances and of compromise, are allowed to do it for themselves; work with them in this way and become aware of them for what they are, they are the ghosts of the past.

The purpose, is to become grounded, gain the strength and by stilling the waters from within; make it to the other side and out of the opposing current of the wind.

(Day 121)

Like a "Bully", the "Ego mind" too, will hide the light from the self and of what it prefers to see; with the darkened shadows of grievances. What an illusion it is; to give into the weakest side, so it may in fairness, equal up in strength. When has this ever proved to be and as the self might have hoped for? Rather as to accept for the very same and that it will dismiss, time and time, over again.

LESSON~106: "MY GRIEVANCES ARE THESE DISTORTED INTERRUPTIONS BETWEEN THE LIGHT WITHIN ME AND MY WORLD."

To recognize the bully as the "Ego Mind", that holds these grievances, and will never see in the error of its way; why would it possibly be fair, to allow for it, to continue? The self allowing to be bullied into darkness and by giving up the light to help it with; must eventually realize grievances and light cannot go together.
Vision and light are the only things the self must wish to join, so it can see and in this awareness, to lay the grievances aside.
To want to feel for its enlightenment, will be the means and by which it will succeed. The following affirmations can help to better specify for this idea:
"THE DARKNESS HAS SERVED ME WELL AND I IT."

"I WANT TO WAKE UP NOW AND NOT TO EXCUSE THE SLEEPING STATE OF SOUL CONNECTION WITH EGO MIND ANY LONGER AS A BLOCK TO MY SIGHT."

"WHEN CONSCIOUSNESS CAN SHINE ON; THE EGO MIND WILL HAVE NO ENERGY TO CLAIM FROM THE WORLD AND IT WILL NOT MATTER FROM THE SOUL IN THIS WAY ANY LONGER."

LESSON~106:
"MY GRIEVANCES ARE THESE DISTORTED INTERRUPTIONS BETWEEN THE LIGHT WITHIN ME AND MY WORLD."

Focus on the source and where the release for ascension is, within the self and has never left. Higher self, has never left, what the mind has closed off; because the Ego looks outside of itself for its comparison to the many. The illusion can never find the source, from hence created it and it had never left from within the self. From within always and only can it open up to the beyond; to everything the self becomes aware of will reflect this light from within. The following affirmations can be made suitable forms and specifically for this idea:

"I AM DONE WITH FURTHER ATTEMPTS TO FEEL AWAY FROM MY RELEASE AND TOWARD THE FREEDOM THAT ASCENSION BRINGS."

"NOTHING CAN INTERRUPT WITH THIS ENLIGHTENMENT TO MY SOURCE IN MY RELIEF FOR FREEDOM."

"LOWER ENERGIES HAVE NOTHING MORE TO TARGET WITH INTERFERENCE FROM THIS MY SOURCE CONNECTION."

When the soul expands it can store much light or carry much darkness.

The purpose, is to release all grievances; to claim for the self empowerment and in the knowing of its illuminated being-ness.

(Day 122) It was mentioned before the energetic states of emotions; where they might be claiming to come from, might not necessarily be. Either left up to the interpretation and/or from this lesson, to meaningfully explore and within the aetherial's mind collective construct. Spirit is consciousness and from this consciousness, one in the same, is the following idea and to be activated with.

LESSON~107:

"TO RECEIVE IS ONE IN THE SAME AS TO GIVE."

When the heart is open, the light can come in; this exercise is intended through self love and to do just that.

<u>Self Love</u>: What are some of the ways that can be most nurturing to focus on; the taking care and overall maintenance required, within the physical world and body structure of the self?

In the process of removing Guilt/Blame or Shame...Remember that of servicing the Self; rather than the external giving pleasure to receive. Directly giving pleasure to receive and however the difference in these modes are: allowing (others) or the external of the world to please the Self and for the Self to accept the receiving of those comforts; that will please the Self directly from such services. Getting a massage; or just taking a bubble bath; however is not the same as cleaning house. The nurturing of plants or pets neither are the same; as taking a walk in the woods for example and connecting with the elementals; as well as the many creatures that befriend their acquaintance, with awareness to this scene...Unplug from social media and get out of the perceived comfort zone.

What are some other emotions that might come up while in the state of nurturing the Self, in this way? What order from least to greatest (of these identifying energies) can the Self adjust with feeling better: Abandonment...Jealousy...Anger...Loneliness Guilt...Irritability....Joy... Anxiety....Lost...Confusion....Denial... Regret......Depression....Relief....Despair.....Remorse...Detachment Restlessness....Emptiness.....Sadness/Sorrow...Helplessness...Shame....Fear....Vulnerability... Gratitude.....Yearning...Apathy/Numbness..

LESSON~107:
"TO RECEIVE IS ONE IN THE SAME AS TO GIVE."

Within the light, the truth can be felt; of neither opposites and neither in the body's eyes, that behold for its vision.
The light, is of one concept and that blends all, into one whole truth; as no thing is separate, from this power. What does not resonate in frequency; will not exist and for the self to be made aware of it. This truth is the light; feel its function and peace of mind; that will heal from its power and in oneness to the whole. Focus on a single perception and upon one frame of reference; this way, the meaning can arise for healing. One thought and with different aspects, can better to describe the meaning; to give and receive, yet the order from which to align with, is not subject to competitive scrutiny. When seeing them both as one and unfolding in the same moment; to think of them complete and that for all opposites, to reconcile, from this same frame of thought. Make use of these indices and with these thoughts to process as one to unify with. To understand the depth for all kind seeded in this better service of the knowing truth, as to be impenetrable and eternally bound; thus to forgive is for the betterment of all, in this enlightenment process. This is what it means to hold in truth with the higher self agreements and that of the one law for every kind of learning; as well, as with the playing out for its experience and when directed to such soul contractual cases.
The purpose, is to better understand the channeling from within, the self and how it feels. Rather than to telepathically take on, that which might not be of the greatest service and as it were from the collective mind. Give of the self, as it would be, to receive; because to give, is to receive; what the soul receives, is that of which the spirit, would have given.

(Day 123)
Arrogance, can cover over the vision; to fill it up with an Ego-centric point of view and only find the faults within perfection. Why not seek instead, to open up, to the unfolding of the stable and peace of existence.

LESSON~108:
"I TRUST IN THE ABUNDANCE OF MY UNIVERSE AND AS FLAWLESS AS MY AWARENESS CAN ACCEPT."

Today, is all about empowerment: Before starting out the day, take a moment to feel and with certainty the soul's plan; sacredly accept all that the self is in the "HERE and NOW".
Pause and breathe….Feel and embrace this energy, this light from within and wrap around the body with its arms, to give a hug.
Make the commitment, to set out today, by repeating this out loud:

"*I am no longer going to criticize myself…put myself down in anyway, nor compare myself to others; FROM HERE ON I do release all that has kept me small, in my own eyes and with all my heart to witness in this love that I surrender.*"

"I TRUST IN THE ABUNDANCE OF MY UNIVERSE AND AS FLAWLESS AS MY AWARENESS CAN ACCEPT."

"*I will honour on and through out the day feel expanded in my power; it is my birthright to live in this abundance of sacred love and union with my universe.*"

LESSON~108:
"I TRUST IN THE ABUNDANCE OF MY UNIVERSE AND AS FLAWLESS AS MY AWARENESS CAN ACCEPT."

Get up and start the day in, "out of time"; the more relaxed the self can be, the more accomplished it will feel.
Remove the pressure of dead lines and commitments
to(in such a way that binds up the metabolism) and move freely at own pace.
Feel the lightness of this state, to be in; let it take over and in this way of caring, with no concern to tense over.

In the sacred presence of eternal light, embrace all fears and worries; from any arising circumstances and flow in with radiance freely, throughout the day.

The purpose, is to go into all the areas, that might appear to be experienced as lack and limitation; feel the transformation from within the heart light up and pouring from the soul, abundance.

(Day 124) From a "Carbon Base" formed reality, it is true, that nothing without any kind of help can be accomplishable and from that which awaits the self into a "Crystalline" reality; to no longer be weighted down by dense commitments that enslave it.

LESSON~109: "I AM A WALKING VORTEX WITH MANY MORE SPINNING LITTLE WHEELS THAN I CAN POSSIBLY IMAGINE FROM MY THOUGHTS."

Today's practice, is all about the stillness and from this place of timelessness, to join into the Oneness. All these many little spinning wheels and from these thoughts, the many realities into splitting fields, like planets. For every field, a planet that delivers it and into another world of influence. The ultimate intention, is to remove the veils and from all the chakras. By removing all these lenses, within the self to feel creation in and as One with creator being. The portal into eternity, lies in this moment. Timelessness is this place of power and motionless; within the moment to observe the higher levels of creator consciousness. This perspective, that results from a specific placement; of the assemblage point was mentioned in reference to the number 0. During peak spiritual (bliss)experiences, linear time always seems to want to have its way and to pull the self back out from its sense of Oneness.
For the entire day, practice entering into a full awareness of the moment; however periods of sleep are permissible.
Resist the temptation of entering into a trance-like, meditation or falling asleep; That brings about an entirely different placement of the assemblage point. Until this becomes a way of life however, for now it might not be acquirable; then shorten it by breaking it up. Right before starting off the day(morning); in the middle of the day and another before the day is done(evening).

LESSON~109: "I AM A WALKING VORTEX WITH MANY MORE SPINNING LITTLE WHEELS THAN I CAN POSSIBLY IMAGINE FROM MY THOUGHTS."

These longer exercises must be at least 20 minutes of going into timelessness and perhaps, a timer can be used, to end the session. To completely eliminate resistance then decide to take a day off into timelessness; do not speak to anyone and, sleep when feeling drowsy, eat when only the feeling to eat arises, and stay in natural light as much as it is possible. Avoid all the clamoring of public distractions. For the shorter 20 minute practices the normal activities must carry on before and after; however throughout the day repeat this activation:

"I AM A WALKING VORTEX WITH MANY MORE SPINNING LITTLE WHEELS THAN I CAN POSSIBLY IMAGINE FROM MY THOUGHTS."

Take deep breaths and clear all thoughts from the mind.
When thoughts do arise, don't engage with them.
Just observe them rising and falling, like waves upon the ocean. Blow stress out of tense areas and with the 20 minute exercises, resist the temptation to go into a meditative state; otherwise just go to sleep. Gradually, as stress of linear time will leave the body; the stomach, or chest will still feel tense and without going into meditation. Imagine it as talons or claws, gripping on the body and deliberately undo each talon, through visualization; breathing any residue of tension out and until it is released. Feel the shifting into bliss and that of oneness, from this assembly point. While sitting comfortably, observe the environment and as a child would do; feel the bliss, trickling through the cells and start to feel the crown of the head opening.

The purpose, is to find completion and from this place of stillness, all is restored again; until the next insertion of intension, to create within the flame of motion.

Take 2 days to take it in

CONGRATULATIONS ...!!!

FOR MAKING IT THROUGH THE 109th Lesson

(This is a rest period to take the lessons independently as a review)

TAKE THESE TWO DAYS TO RECALIBRATE;

MAKE NOTES AND REVIEW................

(Day 127)
There is a lot of overwhelming pressure, from a charcoal and before it turns into a diamond. Grievances are blinders, closed in with hate and it covers the miracles, before they can even happen. Resonance cannot be seen and when the distorted lens, is raised above the body's eyes. While holding on to grievances the self will wait upon the "Ego Mind" to join it in the light.

LESSON~110:
"ALL GRIEVANCES MUST BE REPLACED WITH CREATIONS FROM SELF EXPRESSED IMAGINATION."

The idea for the day, is to feel before perceiving and in this way the perception can come around to as little or as much as to reverse. Do not let the meaning of sight and to yield before its view, is processed; then look upon the field with the imprint from its intended imagination, to perceive(as a miracle instead). Let go of the boundaries of repulsion and gently lift the body's eyes in silence to behold; accept the pristine presence and that can awaken, from the not so clear charcoal. The higher self cannot come down, to join its pity party for the self; rather only when it will release from this exclusion, can the shining light appear. When the Grievances are laid to rest the self can awaken and be lifted up into the light; to join in with the higher self where it has always been. The higher self stands always in the light and cannot join the body in the dark. The self could not see beyond; because each grievance made the darkness deeper. The work will be on allowing this Sovereign Light and pristine energy state to find the self. Looking upon the grievances can only keep within a carbon base reality type of observation. It must be so the seeing of the world can be reversed and the observation can be that of truth away from fear. Emotionally charged magnetism that held the relationship in and as difficult at times or hard to please, demanding; irritating or untrue to the ideal of what is preferred.

LESSON~110:
"ALL GRIEVANCES MUST BE REPLACED WITH CREATIONS FROM SELF EXPRESSED IMAGINATION."

Select a target subject, to reflect these grievances about and then put them aside, to look at it, without the grievances. Perhaps the feeling of fear and hate; it can trigger the mind's thoughts of love. Yet could it have angered it instead and according to the role set out for it; that has not been accepted to respond in truth?
Seeing it through and behind the grievances that self has held against as its facade; this mind will learn that what lay hidden before, is there in it and everything else likewise, to be seen.
Let the saving be unto self by it today and such is this role with source energy/prime creator/ force of action plan.

Take for the longer moments, to play with this idea; of befriending and embracing all that feels just wrong. Why is it still presenting its self; when it is not desired, in this way? Although the self has released it; it will still be there and until it can be embraced, to see it, in this role(to play out). Make the attempt and firstly to hold for, this type of form now, in the mind. Review all faults and difficulties, that self might have judgments, from this carbon type based body; the pain it caused from trapped emotions, its form of neglect, and all the little and larger hurts it gave the self.

Regard this type of body, with all its flaws. The pheromones that split it off, into gender form; as well as hormonal better points by it. In this way, the mind will think of its own blemishes and even from its "EGO" for the "Body". "Go ahead, ask of this crystalline form and in its being already; made up of this heightened awareness and as Christed, as the Sovereign Light from Higher Self: "TODAY AND EVERY OTHER DAY FROM HERE, I WILL MAKE THIS COMMON PRACTICE TO ALLOW FOR OTHERS TO BE OF HELP AND LIKE WISE TO GIVE THAT OF ME WHERE AND WHEN REQUIRED."

LESSON~110:
"ALL GRIEVANCES MUST BE REPLACED WITH CREATIONS FROM SELF EXPRESSED IMAGINATION."

"LET ME SURRENDER INTO THE SAFETY OF ALL THAT IS ONENESS AND FROM THE MANY TO BEHOLD IN ALL THAT I AM TO LEAD ME TO CREATOR LIGHT IN WHICH I STAND, THAT I MAY JOIN WITH ALL THAT IS ME."

Be most appreciative of Infinite intelligence; as it is the reason for its bliss and all the world that will rejoice in this frequency with it. The body's eyes are closed, and as the mind will think of it, who grieved for the self; let the mind be shown the light in itself and beyond all its grievances. What the observer can from the observed; be both to will the self free. Be silent now, and feel upon the shining light(bliss) that is of liberated state. Feel the light remove the heavy hearted grievances and no longer to cover over the observer. The self expression, in this way, is given the permission and to be perceivable; to when it had originally intended to become from its awareness and for this reason, to ascend back into the light. Gratitude from its source when during these quiet moments can be felt. The images must be laid aside, before Gratitude can be felt however; and looked upon, with love and light. Remember this throughout the day, and feel the bliss of salvation as one, in the same. Allow this role, to perpetrate and until there is nothing left, from the carbon based, splitting of worlds. From having thought, there are no choices to be made; rather allow for circumstances to prevail in the saving of itself from the many.

The purpose is of roleplaying out, the levels that the self has found itself in and to claim over such frequencies; move on up to the next and the next and so on and so forth AMEN !

(Day 128) The SOLAR GATE, is a portal and that the self can learn, to enter from within. From within the heart, is this place of Love and from here, it can be felt, its power; all the praise of warmth and radiating from the Photonic light(Manna), to the (Prana) Eternal.

LESSON~111: "WHEN I BECOME ENLIGHTENED MY EVERY INTENSION MATTERS."

The Manna is the Golden Rays of nourishment, that comes in from the Sun and upon the Earth; as it enriches the soil, so fertile and ready, to nourish with organic edible delights. The same abundance and from a metaphysical perspective(imagine) can be transmuted; to transform into all that matters for the self-fulfillment. Feeding the Soul and physical body, with the intention on the golden radiance of sunlight; open up to this photonic light and all the nutrition the self will ever need, can be received, directly from it. Practice today, with breath and eye movement(as in previous rapid eye moving trances, and the emerging from both worlds into the one). This(3in1) exercise will focus on the eyes, pranic tube, and breath. However long the physical body is in height; take half of that and extend from the center of the top of the head; (imagine)a six inch tube protruding from within the skull vertically upward. Eyes wide open and/or closed; with every breath in; role the eyes up and with every breath out, role them down again. Take long deep breaths; in from the base of heart and going upward. While eyes are rolling upward and into the center of the crown(up top) of the head; As the eyes are rolling down, visualize from the heart, a crystalline bright light(with a bit of bluish radiance); with breath out and shooting upward, (appearing stronger/more intense)from the crown. (prt2)Focus the bellybutton, visualize the other half(of what the body measures up in height), extending from the soles of the feet and downward. Better to describe it as: the same height as the physical body, of the self and from where the tailbone ends, downward.

LESSON~111: "WHEN I BECOME ENLIGHTENED MY EVERY INTENSION MATTERS."

Repeat the same rolling of the eyes and breathing in and breathing out, when rolling down. Visualize now from the belly button this tube that extends downward from the heart. Now visualize a downward shooting out motion with every breath out the tailbone and with feet at about shoulder width apart the tube it measures to just about the same; whether sitting and or standing comfortably. Breathe out slowly and deeply visualizing this awareness of life expanding as it opens up to cover the entire body. In this same rhythm(of breathing in)the self can take from up high the Sun and galaxy, photonic light. Visualize the golden yellow brilliance warming inward into the tube from the crown of the head and feeding from this essence; all the way down(to tailbone) with energy. When bringing this photonic light into the body it will feel like after having a big meal that needs breaking down to process it will become "suggestibly" entranced. Stop the movement of the eyes (from rolling upward) now and keep them closed(looking downward). Go within and find the void(between the belly and the chest) and enter into it. From this place the center of the Earth can reveal the Golden Sun. The self can when reconnecting with and from the tailbone rooted well into the ground, reenergize again. Change directions completely of the breath and movement of the eyes; breathing in and from the direction of the soles of the feet, upward (to just below the heart) and from within the body of the higher self. Hold the breath and then exhale, rolling eyes upward and to the crown of the head.

LESSON~111: "WHEN I BECOME ENLIGHTENED MY EVERY INTENSION MATTERS."

To better understand this exercise; it can be broken up and made into segments, throughout the day; practice connecting and smoothly flowing into it, with much more ease.
Just by simply merging the awareness of this trinity and into a holy marriage for success, preferably intended.
This is a meditative practice and perhaps similar to that of, the Tibetan perspective; just before entering the "Bardo".
Unlike the "Bardo" there is no "Karma"(repeat of emotions) to experience. It is a slip stream of exalted consciousness of mother light; that is "Lucid Awareness" and that between life and death.
In this place every thought, is that of "LOVE" and mindfulness.
In truth, this is the real self. This is, the Golden Gate of Manna.
It is from this glory hood of being and where "Creator Self" exists.

The purpose, is to grasp and at the edge of knowing; the evolutionary scale of possibility. A place of sustenance, when it can reach, at the apex of the heart space and higher; functioning as a being of light and feeding from this Breath, Manna and Water.

This is the giving and receiving of existence and that of universal consciousness.

(Day 129) Enlightenment comes as a bridge, between the mind and self; this voice and that the self will come hear of inner guidance, speak about itself. The mind can only become restored from this experience, to be freed its will into the spontaneity of service to this inner knowing.

LESSON~112: "ENLIGHTENMENT COMES FROM THE AWAKENING TO SELF RESONANCE WITH ALL THINGS."

The inner voice for today, is this thought present in the mind to the self and from its oneness state, of belonging. Within the mind, search for this inner guidance, pay attention to it and for the first five minutes, of every hour. These thoughts were denied before, and in place of illusions; the mind was instead and made to wander, in a world of dreams. The mind and by the real thoughts, will find the function; that it sought to lose over and the self will give peace, as it welcomes it. The mind can then be restored, to self empower out from spirit and bless all things. Created by the spirit to itself; it has found all things created by it and including itself, in this, its awareness. The mind might remain uncertain, for a little while; however the more and in every application, the joy that the self will experience; it will save of it, in full awareness. For every few minutes spent, can help to join the mind of self and to yet another treasure to be kept from its very own consciousness. So much can be given unto the self and when it can be ready to accept it. Allow for the frantic mind and the following words to be repeated for peace and it might to accept this gift.

"ENLIGHTENMENT COMES FROM THE
 AWAKENING TO SELF RESONANCE WITH ALL THINGS."
"THESE THOUGHTS ARE MINE AND
    MADE APPLICABLE FOR ME."

Then go ahead, seek the thoughts that were denied before and take responsibility over them. The purpose, is to experience the blissful cohesion of spirit with mind from soul and by forgiving all the rest of the self; to ascend to an enlightened state of being from it.

(Day 130) Enlightenment is the uniting of the patriarchal with the matriarchal and from this a miracle that has no first nor last; rather it is all encompassing in its oneness. All time stands still from creation, when the mind can accept this energy and from it, become the higher consciousness, of "<u>Sovereign Light</u>".

LESSON~113: "I AM A CONSCIOUS BEING."

When the self is in oneness, there is no split energy and it does not have to weave conflicting factors into this unity.
The truth about the self, as inner child, is the creator that rest within it. Awareness will be closer to reaching enlightenment today.
Only this way can the mind become restored from its insanity with love, to a state of peace and joy. Self awareness is always there and as the self is to its awareness. Give of these few minutes willingly today, and count on this awareness; that will reveal the application of its timelessness.
Through the strength of the self, to hear the inner voice; the holy spirit will be glad to be of guidance and for it to see the simple truth. There is no such thing that awareness can overlook with an open mind and when it can accept these healing gifts it brings.
For every waking hour, take the first few minutes; to be at one with holy spirit and the infinite divine enlightenment and that its ascension brings, to help out the rest of the world with.
Accept these thoughts and with it, its perception will increase in healing power; for every connection made a block can be released. Each gap that closes can increase the love and given it will multiply in the receiving of it. The application can be very helpful to attempt and when throughout the day; the mind might and with sorry consequences yield to the self, to make believe that it be something else.
"I AM A CONSCIOUS BEING".

LESSON~113: "I AM A CONSCIOUS BEING."

The darkness is surpassed and never to forget the way again;
the steady brilliance of this light remains, to lead the way.
In a state of happiness and with the following affirmations;
let these statements echo round the world through self
awareness:

"I AM A SPIRITUAL BEING_INCORRUPTIBLE AS MY
INNER CHILD AND WITH THIS INNOCENCE IT BRINGS
TO MY AWARENESS_FREE FROM HARM AND HEALED
FROM ALL LIMITS_AS WHOLE_FREE TO FORGIVE AT
WILL AND TO ENLIGHTEN THE WORLD WITH ITS
ASCENSION."

The self expression from the inner child, will be accepted by the
soul and as a gift, for the inner child, so not be oppressed;
this permission, will increase its power and give it back to self.
Offer each period gladly, to this awareness and it will speak the
words of truth; for the self to remember, that it is as spirit and let
these words to tell the mind, that they are truth.

The purpose, is to allow for the wholeness of spirit(Holy Spirit), to
give the mind some peace; to allow for its inner child connection
and of the self as one, to fully express outwardly.

(Day 131)
Without spirit, the mind feels helpless, limited and weak from all its thoughts; to hide away in the frail support of its body.
The self, would not prefer its consciousness and to allow for its sub conscious, to bring pain to it; rather it will prefer for its ascension into enlightenment. Within the mind, the spirit holds for it enlightenment; to grasp and ascend in the way of peace.
The self holds dear and for those thoughts, to be forever more cherished.

LESSON~114: "MY PART OF CONSCIOUSNESS IS AS IMPORTANT TO THE GREATER COLLECTIVE'S PLAN FOR ENLIGHTENMENT."

From the smallest physical particle, to the things that cannot not be perceived and with limited senses; everything is in a constant state of vibration. The most elemental state of vibration, is that of sound. Everything has an optimum range of vibration(frequency), and that rate is called, resonance. When in resonance, balance is achieved. Every organ and every cell, absorbs and emits sound; with particular optimum resonate frequency. It was explained before; that light is strongest and when it has shorter wave lengths. Consciousness can expand and this way through sound, as well as; with various chanting sounds. The vibrations create a resonance inside the body, that can and to help release, emotional blockages.
The importance of the chakra activations and in the first part of the book; to help the self find its inner voice and through the many flames, of these attracted, magnetic, spinning spheres.
These flames, are various fields of light and mostly not visibly detected by physical perception; however, can be felt and like that inner voice, that guides the self, with thought of intuition.

LESSON~114: "MY PART OF CONSCIOUSNESS IS AS IMPORTANT TO THE GREATER COLLECTIVE'S PLAN FOR ENLIGHTENMENT."

Connecting to the assembly point, from the now and zero point field; it was the only way to still the mind and open up the heart, to have these activations of fire wheels. These activations allow the spiraling upward and full body awakening to occur; where all the cells can light up. From the previous meditation, it has been discussed: to blend the earth solid core, of energetic light and that of the photonic resonance attraction; all within the self to understand, the inner and the outer of its world.

Today, is this reconnecting and with all the pieces, to carefully come together; the connection, is that of oneness and from this resonance, as creator, in harmony with, creative flow.
Take some moments, throughout the day and sample out, these sounds to chant with..
"OoooM …..Aaaaaaa… OM…. Aaaaah ….."
Find the melody and through out the day, use these chants; to help with the main idea for the day.
Then end it off and with the activated thought on, that focuses for this main idea:
"MY PART OF CONSCIOUSNESS IS AS IMPORTANT TO THE GREATER COLLECTIVE'S PLAN FOR ENLIGHTENMENT."
The purpose, is to increase life energy, clarity of the mind; through activated creativity, ecstatic states can only happen and from a place of deep inner peace. With "LOVE vibration" the spiritual essence can resonate. At the heart of everything, is and for this purpose to connect; to the spiraling reality of Heaven and Earth. With intention and intuition, the self can operate to return to its original, perfect state; from here it will feel its importance.

(Day 132) In separation, fear finds the self and from its corrupted imagination, to trick with its treat, into convincing debt.
All the consequences, stem from resistances; to bring confidence enough and to be set free from this distortion; repeat the following words and to set in activation, for this idea:

LESSON~115: "WHEN THE COLLECTIVE AWAKENS TO A HIGHER CONSCIOUSNESS_ I CAN AUTHENTICALLY JOIN IN_TO COMBINE AND SHARE FROM THIS APPRECIATION WITHIN THE ONE AWARENESS."

Eventually the world will reach at a level of maturity, to allow for all differences to be of function; pull away from the many disablements and that would otherwise over impress upon them(as separate).

"CORRUPTION HAS ITS CONSEQUENCE
 ONLY WITHIN THE DARKNESS."

Go ahead and practice, to introduce into the mind; these thoughts and that the state of joy may find, the self to be with.
The heavy burden of dysfunction; as to be real, is this insane belief and that must be dealt with, today's idea. Accept all that come to be of use and within this integration, of awareness; discriminate them not, by denying them an existence. Take a few minutes and from each hour, of this day; to set a path of freedom and to the waiting goal of acceptance, for all things in their own way, to find their place within this joy.
Remember the following and repeat as often:
"WHEN THE COLLECTIVE AWAKENS TO A HIGHER CONSCIOUSNESS_ I CAN AUTHENTICALLY JOIN IN
TO COMBINE AND SHARE FROM THIS APPRECIATION WITHIN THE ONE AWARENESS."

LESSON~115: "WHEN THE COLLECTIVE AWAKENS TO A HIGHER CONSCIOUSNESS_ I CAN AUTHENTICALLY JOIN IN_ TO COMBINE AND SHARE FROM THIS APPRECIATION WITHIN THE ONE AWARENESS."

All things that are created from the spirit's collective consciousness, are without imperfection and the honest to energetic truth. Illusions, are created outside of the enlightened perspective and thus become distortions. Trapped expression, is the Ego's domain and to play with such emotions; it is the debt to the corruption, it has created and within the body, as physical pain. The unfulfilled physical experiences, that the self had set out and to manifest within this world. So it too, can enjoy, rather than; for the little more, than bones and that the self must endure. Is it not absurd, before it is to recycle and transcend, from its physical containment; that the gift of enlightenment can appear? It is a savage punishment, amongst its peers to fear and match its vicious cycle of disinterest; neglecting to see far and beyond its narrow minded scope, of wishes.

The exercises, teach to accept "Atonement" and with an open mind; because corruption has no cause and therefore sacrifice can be obsoleted, from its belief. Suffering, is causeless and at the basis for today's idea; practice with this thought, as often as possible. Incorruptible is this "Will" and that finds self in a "Sovereign Light"; unto its own and as complete within the oneness, of the many. Pain, is a sign of the self, misunderstanding itself and the joy it possesses. The "Will", is the determination and that brings about re-enforceable support, to see it through.

Always see the goodness in every existence, that wants to reach out. The faith in love, is most certain to bring about happiness.

The theme of happiness, is this idea and to understand, just how important it is, for enlightenment.

The purpose, is to take happiness, to the next level and find the bliss, within the many, thriving successfully and feel that, as the self, is one and in the same.

THE INTERMISSION :

Take a day to take it in

CONGRATULATIONS ...!!!

FOR MAKING IT

THROUGH TO THE 115th Lesson

(This is a rest period to take the lessons independently as a review)

TAKE THIS DAY TO RECALIBRATE;

MAKE NOTES AND REVIEW..................

(Day 134)

From the original, nurturing awareness and of the intent, for such an economical connection; the creator, is no where near, in its proximity and from the superficial wealth, that has distorted to provide. Forever seeking outwardly and in its place, the paternal cause; to struggle in the lack, of structural conformity. The spirit had instead, lead down into corruption and disconnected, from creative force. Just as the two keep morphing, so too, the decision made and changes the story; to continue on and with the journey, for its spiritual experience.

LESSON~116: "RATHER THAN EXPLORING THE SOLUTION_THAT COMES CREATIVELY WITH ITS PROBLEMS_ I LOOSEN THE RESISTANCE BY HOW I FEEL AND RESPOND_ AS THE CAUSE FOR INSPIRATION IN THE SHIFTING OF PERSPECTIVES."

Damning, as unaware and un-awakened souls; fallen into the darkened pit of material corruption and from blame, they were created. Rather than, awakened from the shame, of having creator presence and unable to respond; these muddy creations beckon. Within the soul, the "Ego mind" can play; with spirit, the solution can break apart from the problem and metaphysically be replaced, to change the outcome. Only when the self is still asleep; to seek out subconsciously for a solution and that it has unconsciously created, as a problem. Governed only from fear, that respectfully separates into the grouping of winners and losers. Ungrateful creatures, of the world and that do not appreciate; are still asleep, within their very own concern, to limit and hoard with greed. The solution can then, only become, almost impossible to find and to be certain, it might or might not, be the right one, within the many variations. From the same energy, they had broken off and must be recognized as one; so to match the frequency and for the outcome to be, from this variation, where the both were created.

LESSON~116: "RATHER THAN EXPLORING THE SOLUTION_THAT COMES CREATIVELY WITH ITS PROBLEMS_ I LOOSEN THE RESISTANCE BY HOW I FEEL AND RESPOND_ AS THE CAUSE FOR INSPIRATION IN THE SHIFTING OF PERSPECTIVES."

The only problem, is that of separation and it has already been solved; as a situation of the world and in extreme resistance, to accept the other. By truly letting go and coming out the other side; the fear of losing its control and loss of power, is this mistrust. Resistance, is the cause, for all worries, doubts and problems. The relevance from the answer and cannot be seen, when the problem that has been solved, is thought as, something else. This position, to be found; however remains again uncertain, about what the problems might be. As one problem settles, the next one arises and then the next; making it a long series and of different problems, to contend with. What is causing the resistance? Failure, is inevitable and when the self is made to feel inadequate, from its world; that presents a vast number of resistances and to perceive each, as requiring a different answer. These resistances, of the world appear in varying forms; on so many levels and with such varied content, that make it impossible a situation, to confront. Hard to believe, depressed and remaining in denial; will rise to haunt the self, from time to time and unsolved, to become once again, hidden. Not allowing, for any integration/resolution; it can over complicate the problem and in desperation, to become recognized. No matter the form, the mind can cause; when the self can accept the only problem is, that of separation and only then, can it accept the answer, for its relevance.

The purpose, is to recognize the illusion and that of, beating each other to death, is inevitably the answer; the relief and release, of ultimate surrender and that no longer seeks, for a solution.

(Day 135)

Why is there struggle; or the need to fight, for anything?
Work on, freeing the mind and from all the many variances, of such resistances, the self it thinks it has. The more, the preconceived notions and from the external forces to resist it; the less likely, its success and for any function it may serve. When the recognition of its resistance, gets on the way; it can be brought together, with the self and in a place of peace for all. Its function can only be made possible, by feeling "JOY".

LESSON~117:
"THE STRUGGLE COMES FROM THE MOMENT I LOSE CONSCIOUSNESS AND BOUNDARIES MUST BE SET."

"RATHER THAN FOCUSING ON THE DIMMING OF
PERCEPTION_ I LOOSEN THE RESISTANCE
BY HOW I FEEL AND RESPOND AS THE CAUSE TO
INSPIRATION FOR THE SHIFTING OF PERSPECTIVES."

When any difficulty seems to come up and throughout the day, repeat the following affirmation:

"MY FUNCTION CAN ONLY BE MADE POSSIBLE
WHEN I FEEL JOY."

Just as the subconscious mind, completes its consciousness; so too, the self has a part and in this plan of completion. Enlightenment must reverse the separation, by letting go of fear and replacing it, with "love, here and now". The boundaries can, eventually be lifted and from any function, for awareness to the self. The physical body, can work its muscle to unite, with mind/spirit and is one way, to release resistance; because through physical exertion and that will render the mind, the peace, to allow for spirit to connect. Another way, is through meditation; because it is, all about the breath and once the surrendering, of resistance takes place, the silenced mind can connect, to an open heart.

LESSON~117:

"THE STRUGGLE COMES FROM THE MOMENT I LOSE CONSCIOUSNESS AND BOUNDARIES MUST BE SET."

By reversing the "Doing" with the "Being"; the mindlessness can stop and be replaced with mindfulness. In this way, the both can integrate, to function in harmony. The first application and that is by physical body, is not always capable, of connecting the conscious mind; rather, it shuts down and to meet with the subconscious, in its sleep. The boundaries and of the levels, from its consciousness, must be lifted; through the blending of all the aspects and conscious awareness, is this method, of these lessons and from this book, to find the answers. When the self is sad, the world is dim and tarnished; because it is all an echo. The plan for today, is not to allow, for any room, the sadness, to play its part. Recognize and claim the blissful happiness; as its own and for the self, attempt to understand joy, as the function here. Only this way, can the subconscious mind, have no fear and to disturb its peace; instead to rise up, from the sorrow, to its joy.

Practice, to become the messenger, for this happiness, peace and joy. The message of peace, will be visible and to all who look upon the self, in its happy faced body. Let success, be the order of the day and look deep within, to find the crystalline fluid, state of light.

The purpose, is to magnetically attract awareness and from an awakened connection, to its consciousness; through feeling and in the highest state, of joy.

(Day 136)

Practice, makes perfect and on the habit, of the destiny; to which the self might accept and as probable, for its awareness. Ideas, do not have to be convincing; they just have to be magnetic.

LESSON~118:

"MY THOUGHTS BECOME WORDS AND THEY BECOME MY ACTIONS AND THESE ACTIONS BECOME MY HABITS_THAT MAKE UP FOR MY CHARACTER."

Ever feel something, but have no understanding, for it and by recollection, from the idea? What happens when the idea, thought and feeling; have no recollection, of their connection and to any experience? Premonitions and clairsentience, are what can be explained and from all these subtle sensory perceptions; that, they must have come from somewhere. Could it be, a rewiring and that has started to take place, from it; the outcome of a change, in perspective, forming its reality and from faith alone?

This is the place, where faith resides. From this place, of what is thought of real; becomes it. What can appear, for today, is in the indices, from thoughts and ideas; on one side and that of how it feels, on the other, individually or as a group. Thoughts can bring on feelings, just the same, as feelings, can bring about the thoughts and for their ideas, to form an opinion, agreeable to all.

Practice what feels best and go with it; whilst in study and observation mode, of all the rest; because doing is, as important as being and becoming from the doing. What resonates, with the self the most and what is it, that it requires more awareness, for the other? The goal has always been, about the integration and by bringing the self, to its ideal balance; from which it can exist most well and in its being. Naturally the energy follows and where the focus intends it to be; while dimming out the other places and of where, it might have previously existed.

LESSON~118:
"MY THOUGHTS BECOME WORDS AND THEY BECOME MY ACTIONS AND THESE ACTIONS BECOME MY HABITS THAT MAKE UP FOR MY CHARACTER."

In the awareness and for any given moment, the shifting can continue; this is why contraction and expansion, have there way, with all. Where the concentration, enlightens upon the path; the other areas become temporarily non-existing, in that moment.
The level of light and from the spirit, it does not super impose itself, on these realities; therefore, they do not make, for any sense.
The mind and wiring of the brain, can only interpret a limited amount of awareness, at a time. Intention, can bring upon exclusion and when the concentration is on a certain place, for very long. Explore those areas, that have procrastinated, into underdeveloped pockets and undeveloped spaces; they too, will come to life, by the exposure of attention. Radiation will be given, to those who sense not fully and of these outcomes to engage with; unless the self will see them through and in its attempt, might aggravate the cause, as well. It could very well engage, as much as it desires; for the duration it might fulfill (leaving no stone unturned) to please and then go on to something else. Where there are flare ups; than it must agree to let it go and so it can resolve on its own, perhaps?
The more engagement, it will aspire to and for any given eventful project; the moving forward, with it and in this way of expression, of itself. Too much superimposing, on one, over the other, will and can also create, unwanted interests, for excluding.
These are all probable possibilities, for exploring today and toward enlightenment.
The purpose, is in the graceful balance and of every given moment, that magnetically unfolds. With every little and insignificant commitment forward; the bigger picture, will unconditionally receive its meaning.

(Day 137) Learn to see the unity, of all creation and from within, where the creator dwells. The lesson for today, is to become aware, of the body's senses; to what might, or might not, make for any sense, to the self and in the uniting, with creator.

LESSON~119: "MY BEING IS ONE IN THE SAME WITH CREATOR PRESENCE."

From the oneness, to the breaking down, of everything and back into the nothingness. To be the bridge, of having one foot in the grave and the other, in the living; is this self and that holds these worlds together. All civilizations, have started out from dust particles and from this foreign concept, as bacteria; They invaded and organized, into separations and held in, by boundaries, to become cells. As more and more boundaries, were created; a highway burst, of information and from the soul to DNA(back and forth), began to circulate, as blood.

The galaxy, is filled with shooting stars, of light (as mentioned previously in Lesson 111). Such is, the photonic belt of light; mixed in with nutrients of bacteria(love to break down and reorganize), that the Earth loves and from this break down of the soil, the wealth of Manna(trophy) for the Prana (The Infinite Divine "Presence"). Take advantage of the consistency, to motivate and even resisting to learn it, can then become a benefit.

Firm structure, helps to impose the heavily against relearning; with a shorter and more frequent schedule. The first few minutes of each hour, must then be, to devote to this idea; because the frequent short applications, are easier and in its discipline, to train with. Frequent reminders and regular attempts, can form a habit, from using the idea; as an automatic response and when needed structure.

LESSON~119: "MY BEING IS ONE IN THE SAME WITH CREATOR PRESENCE."

"Higher Self", does not delay in its teaching; rather it is the brain's inability and to tolerate, different perspectives. The hold up, is only by the unwillingness, of the mind, to allow the flow of existence, to move through it. Do not defend illusions further, by giving power to the weakness; because by tolerating it, will delay the process.
The process in expansion, is to learn from the unwanted and become stronger; when perceiving outcomes as unwanted, there are no mistakes, just preferences. There are no errors, just preferences, of awareness; from them, the many attempts to keep the self unaware, of its oneness perspective to Creator.
Practice this and to reassure the mind; with all certainty the following affirmation and supportive statements:

"MY BEING IS ONE IN THE SAME
   WITH CREATOR PRESENCE."

"I AM AT ONE WITH EVERY ASPECT OF CREATION."

" I HAVE UNLIMITED CONNECTION
   TO THIS POWER AND PEACE."

With eyes closed, let these statements sink in and the meaning of their words, into the mind, to absorb deeply; then focus on the following activated idea:

"I AM CREATOR BEING WITHIN SELF."

LESSON~119:
"MY BEING IS ONE IN THE SAME WITH CREATOR PRESENCE."

Repeat this several times and feel the meaning of these words. United securely, in joyous light and peace. Give the inner child permission, to create and by its awareness to thy self; as one goal and of this oneness to all minds. Creation, from the core/creator and to extend outward, to the all that is perspective.

As complete and whole, the self can shift and from the level of darkness, by feeling lighter; where the self and the world, it has lifted, with its perspective. The inner core, can be resurrected love and with the Higher Self; form the bond of spiritual divine awareness and into the oneness of enlightenment, as creator being. For every practice, the voice of hope will raise, to yet another and another; until the world can be lifted and by this state of being, to catch the perception.

To every stirring of the truth and within each mind, the self will encounter for the day; to be replaced by the following supportive statements:

"YOUR BEING AND MINE ARE UNITED AS ONE WITH CREATOR PRESENCE IN THIS SELF."

"I RESPECT YOU BECAUSE OF THAT I AM_ AND ALL THAT IS LOVE_CONNECTS US BOTH AS ONE."

The purpose, is to realize the truth of the self, as one and with every aspect of creation; unlimited in its power and peace.

(Day 138) In a state of innocence, there is nothing to fear; only love can banish the need for safety and protection.
The spheres of separation, are the many watchful sides, of the self. Spheres of light and from them, to take on their very own authentic responsibility; however do belong to the same loaf of bread and as individual slices. This is a resonance and within the unity of Love. The distortion of perspective in this design; is to better learn from itself and in this way, it had created too, the illusion of fear.
The disconnect can create the self to think and that, from what it is in the lack of feeling; that it must protect itself and hide away, in just for safety.

LESSON~120:
"I AM RESPONSIBLE FOR MY PART IN THE HIGHER COLLECTIVE'S PLAN OF ENLIGHTENMENT."

When the self can feel secure enough, to understand its part and that benefits the many, it can rest assured, no harm in this certainty. To know thy self, is to know the truth and from it, all illusion can fall by the wayside. In firm recognition of the self, the mind will not argue for something else; rather coincide with its consciousness and into pure positive awareness. Practice for the day, in faith and to find self certainty of purpose. The incorruptible self, does not appeal to manipulation and that of falling short to bind with its perspective, as dark magic might have its way; nor the fancied threats, will it invent and to escape from these illusions.
Be in a state of complete fulfillment and that synchronicity does bring; by having faith and in this ability, to know thy function.

LESSON~120:
"I AM RESPONSIBLE FOR MY PART IN THE HIGHER COLLECTIVE'S PLAN OF ENLIGHTENMENT."

Today, all of the many spheres, of light and from the greater collectives watchful eye; will be and with the self present, to its application, of this idea. Share this certainty, by taking the stand and alongside the many other slices; that make up the loaf of bread and feel the expansion, by accepting the self, in this way. Whether in a solid form, or just floating around and like fragments of the soul. Unborn too, will resonate in common thought; when they decide to come and make the choice again, to join in, with this supported confidence. From all the many timelines, that they have learned and every gain they have made; will be offered gladly. Practice not just for the self; but rather for the greater good collectively. Take a few moments and as often as can be made possible; to meditate on the special function and that is made with a specific passion, for the self.
Exchange of this moment for peace of mind.
To gain full success from the experience; take it in momentum and devote it into a sense of certainty, for this purpose.
Whenever the need arises, take a few breaths to relax and recalibrate; listen to the inner voice and from its whispered thought, the power of its guided feeling.
Repeat the activation for the day, the idea can be applicable for every circumstance and that the self has come to experience for today.
The more this statement gets repeated; the stronger and more steady, in its confidence, the self will bring out, of its light and to the world, with passion.

LESSON~120:
"I AM RESPONSIBLE FOR MY PART IN THE HIGHER COLLECTIVE'S PLAN OF ENLIGHTENMENT."

Only when the self can completely trust, to surrender and receive; can it then be, effortlessly of giving nature and to the world.
Feel the passion and follow it through, to understand the special function; the self is to be responsible for and intend to focus on, this joy, with adoration and in everything it sets out to accomplish. Through receptivity, give of these words and allow for the universe to do the rest. Throughout the day, exchange for every moment offered, for timelessness and peace; to admire in the beauty that is alchemy. Allow this moment, to be of great anticipation, in the highest of joy and excitement, to feel well; in happy preparation and for the next moment to follow, the hour after it. Repeat today's idea and in particular, focus on the here and now moment; to give it more emphasis. When the time has come again, be thankful in this most passionate part of and when it is to the self, to take responsibility over and claim it as its function. As it has lightly touched upon (it will some more further on) the idea, of dust particles and that of wave forms; as well as, portions of the soul and in spherical light formation, can be somewhat more distinguishable, in this way. Aside from the metaphysical exchange and that the physical, from the non physical have, in relationship with each other; The responsibility of every individuation and that of the spirit within the soul, can be grasped for just a little perhaps.
The purpose, is for the self to find, what it can become most passionate about. From this point of reference, to take responsibility and in its part of the experience; in such a way, that it can claim to have created and/or co-created, with its circumstance.
It is also very helpful, at the end of every session, to take note of and write down the revelations.

(Day 139)

The soul can be a great teacher and with many lessons. Feeling stuck with an emotion and that has not properly been processed in its lesson? Allow the energy to flow again and start to release the pain and suffering. The state of "<u>being-ness</u>",
find it and then transmute it; into something more uplifting. By changing the way, that the self feels; it will shift the way it thinks.

LESSON~121:
"MY ENVIRONMENT IS MY MIRROR AND THE CIRCUMSTANCES ARE MY LESSONS."

Find the best place to hold the space, for learning today; this is the part, where the sadness, is not rejected. The sadness, is the lesson; but from a place, where the self, is no longer stuck, in this lesson. Whatever the emotion and that the self might be at, the frequency will vary. The vibration of anger, for example; is a step higher, than that place of grief. Rather than reacting and from a place of anger, take a step back and find that place, where depression hides. The place of depression, fear and/or grief, is where it must be found today; It might have already escalated, to a place of physical pain, as a more lasting result and outcome. Know that this condition and at whatever stage it might be resting; is never really final and that there can always be, a way of creating other channels, to release it.

LESSON~121:
"MY ENVIRONMENT IS MY MIRROR AND THE CIRCUMSTANCES ARE MY LESSONS."

When the energy is ready to release, it can then be projected and to recreate else where; or recapitulate and morph it, into another place, or object. Rather, it isn't until the self can actualize that indeed it is transmuting this energy. What was practiced from before, in another lesson and within the method of imagination, for this exercise.
Take a few deep breaths and find that assembly point, of center. Breathe in from that, which is source and breathe out slowly; while visualizing a clear ball and beside the physical body. Create a bubble (about the size of the physical body) and with eyes closed, imagine this sphere get bigger. Breathe from that place of source and breathe out slowly; like blowing up an air balloon.

Where is this tension lurking ?

Is it in the facial structure of the bones (physical impact to release in grinding of the teeth)? Could it be an illness and/or physical injury that has occurred? Maybe it might still be in the emotional stage of feeling it, as grief; or stuck in the depression of it as a condition? Visualize the shape, size, colour, texture, and/or any other sensation; that it might bring up, from all the senses.
Breathe in the discomfort and breathe it out, into the bubble.
This exercise, can also be done with an actual balloon and the choice of colour too, can be made significant. For example: red could be the anger and that the self might be feeling; and/or frustration and just before it can react, to blow into the balloon. Naturally the trigger, must be dealt with and in a safe way, to not cause for any harm; it must be done, in this way of meditation.

LESSON~121:
"MY ENVIRONMENT IS MY MIRROR AND THE CIRCUMSTANCES ARE MY LESSONS."

When physical pain is felt and in certain parts of the body; anger can become a common theme for this, think about the agitation and blow into the balloon. Another way is through imagination and visualization, of the bubble outline; to take out of the soul, from this lesson and place it in the sphere. Where is this lesson coming from? Does it have a reference point? For example: it might be in the chest area and felt as grief….Maybe the colour is a muddy brown…Maybe they are dark holes, like spots within the heart; or even, maybe spots of red….Remove all of it, into this balloon; then visualize it shrinking and getting smaller, to the size of a pin head and drop to the ground…..Where this has been(sucked out) removed now, must be replaced with light ……visualize that golden light from before and from that dark void to ignite it like a match stick. Feel the calming of the nerves and all the tension, where it was before; feeling calm and peaceful. Watch the flame turn outwardly and into the crystalline, bright white colour; it will rejuvenate the energy and back(implode) into the oneness, of its "Sovereign light".

The purpose, is to help alleviate and with the vibration of the soft, yellow-golden, soothing flame of "Manna"; to elevate within the life force and the enlightenment required, to further help reintegrate, from the divine blueprint of the soul.

(Day 140) Forgiveness and ascension, are one in the same; in that, they both imply to a release and a letting go of. To let go and release the illusion, from any conflict, that chooses separation, over love. Truth and illusions, both are equal; because they both have happened, and one must be released, to replace the other with.

LESSON~122:

"MY ONLY FUNCTION IS TO LIGHTEN UP AND FEEL THE RELIEF WITHIN MY HEART AS OPEN."

The impossible must be released, so the ascension can take place, toward enlightenment. Forgiveness and through such tears, reflects the truth; because it undoes, what was never done.
To lighten up enough, to see at all; where Earth and Heaven can be, within the mind, to exist there. Similar to remote viewing; when visualizing for too long, the subtleties will become overlooked. The answers are always given in the subtleties; way before the attempt to find an answer. When thoughts are visualized within the mind, they exist and thus, are very real; yet, they are not real, when separated from its present moment. Do not defend in what has already happened, has been and the is, that the illusions bring; rather recognize and with as little, or no pain to undo.
Perhaps, what is seen and felt as wholesome now, might not be and the closer that the self becomes it; the reality will shift and to something that is out of reach again.

LESSON~122:

"MY ONLY FUNCTION IS TO LIGHTEN UP AND FEEL THE RELIEF WITHIN MY HEART AS OPEN."

The "Holy Spirit"(whole of consciousness) and within the mind, does hold this pure positive awareness; known as consciousness and with it, the self can hold, at its source of timelessness. The use of time and as its application, is relevant to the self belief; within the mind and that the whole of spirit can connect with. Holy spirit, is not touched by death, pain and corruption; rather it remains in the innocence of Love. From love comes the awareness, that brings illusions to the truth and that sees right through them, to the reassured and changeless. The mind that can forgive; that of which it does not believe in and what is not created, is this thought and by the only source it knows. Now entrusted with the following affirmation and its supportive statement; to apply and with surrendered trust, to speak it:

"MY ONLY FUNCTION IS TO LIGHTEN UP AND FEEL THE RELIEF WITHIN MY HEART AS OPEN."
"CONSCIOUSNESS IS LOVE_ AND FEAR IS THE MISGUIDED FEELING TO EXPRESS FROM MY EXCITEMENT."

Pain is not of this will and stuck it remains to express in this way, to form; that self must forgive this thought to clear it. Enter the darkened places of the mind; to think the thoughts and that never were acceptable, by the "Ego-mind", to will it, into consciousness. Conscious awakening, does not think by hiding its thoughts, from its very own light. Be sure to practice well, this idea and feel the strength, in what is said; because these are the words and in which the freedom for thyself, is.

The purpose for today, is to begin to grasp that forgiveness and ascension, are one in the same. It is the conscious mind's will, to become one with its sub-conscious side; as well as become one with self awareness and to ascend into enlightenment.

(Day 141)
When the self enters into its physical vessel (it can pass through a tunnel) and from its very first breath, a light so pure ignites; it then becomes aware and awakened into consciousness.
From this consciousness, it descends and creates a spectrum of colours; that too, will become and for its reality, as separated fields. Hanging on to the experiences, of such unconscious separations and to distinguish them as its truth, is what creates suffering. Suffering does not buy anything and yet, the thought that lingers to believe, is that, it does hold for any value; that it must barter over and for all that is wanted, with the many of this world, can be suspect to nonsense.

LESSON~123:
"I SHARE MY WILL WITH THE UNIVERSE AND ITS COLLECTIVE_ TO CO-INSPIRE WITH THIS HAPPINESS."

There are, the areas within the soul, that in order to be reminded of the self; it must experience the drama and other electrical and emotional charges. In this way, the self can remember and from the light to bring it out for a confrontation. This is what it means, to have contraction and expansion; back and forth from soul to spirit. The light will attract to it, all the distortions and shadow aspects and from its memory to integrate; by untying these magnetic knots/releasing and letting go, back into the light of spiritual consciousness. Uprooted from the dark and hidden secret places of the mind; the need to suffer has retired, as teacher and from under to uphold the self with. Accept the emotional triggers and as the activated forms of energy, that they represent; in whatever matter or aetherial and for whatever feeling they bring on, to be experienced.

LESSON~123:
"I SHARE MY WILL_WITH THE UNIVERSE AND ITS COLLECTIVE TO CO-INSPIRE_WITH THIS HAPPINESS."

Today's attempt to cry, when the need arises and really be in touch, with these emotions that come to surface. Let go of the weakened hold of pain; because when it has no power, it cannot accomplish for anything and is left purposeless.

The enslavement, to this lack and everything that the self might think it offers(by stuffing it back down); it must be set free and with compassion, to join the passionate state of joy.

The universe collective's preference, has placed in the self, the happiness; that for the next few days and to continue its devoted practice to it. Within the heart, rests the home for peace and the entrance to enlightenment. The heart, is the bridge and from the Divine, Life Force to Enlightenment; by accepting this begin the practice:

"I SHARE MY WILL_ WITH THE UNIVERSE AND ITS COLLECTIVE TO CO-INSPIRE_WITH THIS HAPPINESS."

Go deep and sink into the function, within the mind; to choose the will for happiness. The love, that has created the self and as loving, as itself; it has no need and to be less loving, to its child from within. Pause frequently, to acknowledge the feeling and of the universal collective's will, for happiness; making it as a function for the self. From the merging of the subconscious mind and with that of the conscious mind (these 2 worlds can combine as one); it can only and possibly be conceivable, within the higher state of consciousness, known as enlightenment. As a doubled strand awareness; the third and from this awareness,(unconscious)reality can unwind, into a multi layered, dimensional world.

The purpose in this way, is to gain the wisdom; release for all the weighted down experiences, from before and back to purest state again.

(Day 142)

The essence comes from life force; this is where the momentum of the soul can teach its value (to the self) and of how not to become forsaken. To give up the self and make it secondary; in replacement for its environment and amongst the many, is to give it up, to compromise. What is suffering, but a habit forming entity; to be in a state of co-dependency and as a self sacrifice, for the greater good.

LESSON~124:
"I RECLAIM MY SOVEREIGN LIGHT AND FROM THIS LIFE FORCE_ THAT I MAY VALUE ITS ESSENCE_ TO REVEAL THE MANY LAYERS OF MY AUTHENTICITY."

The threat of the unknowable, can be unstable to the self; who hasn't learned to trust in its sufficiency and to overcome for any situation. The lack of self connection, can tempt the self to sabotage; that it may be in control over, the given unknown and unstable situation. When something feels like a sacrifice and in essence to its contrary belief, not in the best interest of relating with. To continue on with the experience and for any longer than that moment, that it has taken from, as a lesson; its going against its life force and becomes a sacrifice. The conflict, will not be of a great service, to carry on mindlessly and by keeping busy, doing as, the work had intended. It might have been a dream, that the self; once it could relate to and have co-created with the best of them.
Or, rather now, how does it feel?
Is it in the best interest, for the self to carry on, with the past dream and as the primary for its momentum; perhaps now it even might rather the reflection of another's essence?
Could it be that past and future, are one in the same; changeable in the here and now moment?

LESSON~124:
"I RECLAIM MY SOVEREIGN LIGHT AND FROM THIS LIFE FORCE_THAT I MAY VALUE ITS ESSENCE TO REVEAL THE MANY LAYERS OF MY AUTHENTICITY."

From the collective interpretation and (this greed)no longer might it have the best interest for the self. Does it keep going, in a mindless effort to exist and in this way of coping; does it not learn, when to move on? Do not resist, but just acknowledge and throughout the day, these energetic hooks, from a level of discernment. In the same way, that the self could find the effort, to compromise for another and/or for any common goal. Rather, take a different stance of interconnection and from a place of love; see it truly for the temporary and transient echo, flowing through as correspondence (respectfully leaving).
Just passing through, in the minor details, that create the tapestry and that of the self, in its experience to its own awareness.
See the gifts from these interactions and how they would much rather, to resist in accepting, from before. The mind resists the gifts of truth; because of made up ones instead. It substituted for them and in their distortions, to be compromised, by the very same power, it had given away. These timeless gifts of truth, inherited and passed into eternity, the self need not wait to have them.

LESSON~124:
"I RECLAIM MY SOVEREIGN LIGHT AND FROM THIS LIFE FORCE_THAT I MAY VALUE ITS ESSENCE_TO REVEAL THE MANY LAYERS OF MY AUTHENTICITY."

The gifts, that the self need only, to look within to find and have them now; is a choice to be aware of and in the place of what the mind has made asleep. Practice the following thought and verbally activate its meaning as often as possible:

"THE TRUTH WILL SET ME FREE."

"JOY AND PEACE ARE MINE."

Other goals and gifts made of illusions, are partial in to duality. Seek not the gender bending roles; that play in greed for lack. Rather to clear out, the space within the mind and before the purity of truth; that all things do energetically unite, into the one of infinite intent. Welcome the holy trinity with joy, peace and in full awareness, to cooperate with all of life, from self expression.
In full confidence to this intent; that nothing else can be of spark and that could belong as truth than "Love Here and Now".
Joy and peace, belongs to all expressions of life and so too, must the self not allow, to lose sight of this eternity. Bring this reminder to its mind and as often; with the following supportive statement:

"THESE GIFTS OF JOY AND PEACE ARE ALL I WISH FOR."

The purpose, is to reconnect with that of inner joy and peace.

(Day 143)
As the life force expands out vibrationally, the fractals of the Over-Soul will come to merge. When the gap that holds the fourth dimensional field in place, is cleared away; Emerge and see the heaviness; that once had played out and within the physical awareness, to lift away. The unification on the soul level, is healing and that of repairing the DNA; healing and repair are on a soulful level and that is what energy healing, is all based on.

LESSON~125:
"THE LIGHT WILL CLEAR AWAY DISTORTIONS FROM MY MIND_SO I CAN ONCE AGAIN RECLAIM ALL PARTS OF ME_ TO MERGE INTO THE ONENESS."

The veil, that once had covered over, will lift away and the in-between world; that once had kept the soul fragmented and compartmentalized it, into the physical, will be no longer. No more waiting in a purgatory state; because it was all a prison made and conceivable from the mind. As the gap, from the polarities close; the linear perspective, of time and space, will close. Reality, from what used to be thought as metaphysical, will merge and integrate, from within the self; into a multi leveled flow and that the self can easily collapse, into a solid formation. So too, than as it expands, shifting its intent again, into another and yet another, from inspirational awareness.
This shift, is already here and the self can only realize; from what pace it chooses to find itself, from here to here, to there and within its momentum. There is nothing to control, or become to control over; rather the connection to source, find it and from this place, the soul will find the self. The soul can expand into wholeness; however of the light, to which the awareness came and in it, of its maker, all one, in the same.

LESSON~125:
"THE LIGHT WILL CLEAR AWAY DISTORTIONS FROM MY MIND_ SO I CAN ONCE AGAIN RECLAIM ALL PARTS OF ME_ TO MERGE INTO THE ONENESS."

There is no absence, in the (higher self) "Over-Soul"; however only the pinching off, from self belief and that mind, is of its body. The energy from source, can reinforce the truth and with its connection; in how close to the truth, the self might feel, will be the indicator of its light. Make it a pledge today, to let this function of the light and be fulfilled through the self, by it. Attempt to share this passion and its joy with confidence; to activate the following out-loud:

"THE LIGHT WILL CLEAR AWAY DISTORTIONS FROM MY MIND_ SO I CAN ONCE AGAIN RECLAIM ALL PARTS OF ME_ TO MERGE INTO THE ONENESS."

"I WILL REST FROM ANY RESISTANCE_ THAT I MIGHT BE HAVING WITH ALL THAT IS AND FIND THE COMFORT_ IN ALL THAT I AM FROM IT."

All that has ever been, from many lifetimes over; is here with the self and reflecting back to it, in this awareness to experience.
What the self does see and to fill the space within this field, is but a projection from the soul. Be the projector of blissfulness, to look upon the world and in love; the self can bring the certainty, of this change. Remember this function well, each time and with confidence; to practice, to clear and with the light(hearted) of truth, all distortions the mind might perceive, onto its world through the self.
The purpose, is to heal, become whole and pure again.
Keep clearing away the hurt and heavy hearted hate, of separation; just like the creator had originally intended.

(Day 144) Connecting inwardly and to how the self is feeling, with this frequency; to experience the synchronization of its outer space projection. To retrograde in this way and of becoming the influencer of its universe. From this planetary projected world and the many different variation of astrological perspectives; that link them up to its reality and that it has engaged with from before. Amongst the many influenced and on a different way of thinking, is obtained from this alignment, for its awareness.

LESSON~ 126: "I REST WITHIN MY LIFE FORCE OF EXISTENCE AS AN AWARENESS_OF ALMIGHTY PRESENCE."
The adjustment to the entire universe, from within and that of planetary alignment, will occur. The "Ego Mind", could never possibly begin to understand, the level of honesty and ease and that will come from, this way of shifting; into a place of reverence and openness, with itself and in this format, of functioning. The daydream state, of feeling in love and so very lucid to find itself, awaken from this dream. In a completely darkened room, while eyes are open; try closing them and begin to see everything light up. This experience will take place through the heart and so then the pineal gland decalcifies; when it opens up, a massive light will come on and inside the center of the brain. The awakening creates a storm of emotions and that will hit hard; a review will commence and from it, a welcoming into the metaphysical. With the clearing and healing of the soul, the self will gain much wisdom and from it, to move on; from where death can no longer and ever be, for its experience. An explosion of the mind will start to open up, all of the neural pathways and it will become brighter on the inside; than it was before, from the outside. From this self realization, the experience will transcend it, into enlightenment and from this rapture, to an ascended awareness. Then all that the self can ever dream of, it can have and by placing its intention; from a level of inspired passion, it can dance, molding and shaping from the shifting of its awareness and to continually create, for its experience.

LESSON~ 126

"I REST WITHIN MY LIFE FORCE OF EXISTENCE AS AN AWARENESS_OF ALMIGHTY PRESENCE."

The more the self can function, from a place of "Purity"; the more it will begin to activate and anchor in this template, of the crystalline, light body, structure. This is the embodiment process; that will help to lift it, into heaven and with its physical body, from within to project it out, as its reality. A complete genetic restructuring, of the body; where the external forces, no longer can manipulate, for its conditions. The physical vessel, is this cosmic portal from within; go inside and with eyes closed, repeat the idea, into activated thought:

"I REST WITHIN MY LIFE FORCE OF EXISTENCE AS AN AWARENESS_OF ALMIGHTY PRESENCE."

Go deep into the darkness and where all the limiting beliefs, effort to keep the light covered up; from these shadows and where the true self, can be found. Allow these feelings to surface; with these thoughts in mind and repeat the following:

"DIVINE ENERGY PRESENCE_ BEING LOVE IS ALSO AT THE SOURCE FOR MY HAPPINESS."

The purpose, is simply to accept and that when the world ceases to be of opposites; the gap closes and the polarities cancel the cause and effect out.
 It is in this place of conscious alignment; that pain, fear and all other conflicts, fall by the way side, for joy, love, and peace to remain.

(Day 145)

When the self can heal, from all aspects of its "Ego Mind" and atone within the harmony, of all that is. In ascended awareness, the self must acknowledge, that which it has transcended from, was fear based energy; it must be present, within and coming from a heart space state, of being(otherwise it will descend again into contracted, little me perspective). A resurrection will occur into atonement; however now made possible, from within its physical vessel. To maintain the ability to explore its new frontiers and continually become expanded.

LESSON~ 127:
"FROM THE LIGHT I FOCUS AS THE MIRACLE CREATOR: WITH INTENSION THE DREAM ASPIRES FORTH TO SOLIDIFY AND IMPRINT THESE MIRACLES IN PLACE TO WITNESS_THIS STRENGTH OF CONSCIOUSNESS_IS ONE IN THE SAME WITH MY LIGHT."

By reclaiming all of the parts of the self, inside and inevitable expansion, must occur. The merging of the metaphysical, with the physical, is what this idea is; to activate within the mind and for this lesson. By elevating consciousness(state of being-ness) and then with the physical body; ascension, is this way of living, in expansion and not escaping from awareness, in any way. This means realigning, the entire way of life and how things were, when they used to be and for its conditioned way of comfort. Taking responsibility, is from where it can be dealt with, in the doing and within, from the state of being; to formulate, a level of response, rather than a reaction. By assuming this consciousness, can create a feeling of wanting to separate and retreat. This level of escape, to monastic exclusiveness; is because, it does not want to be forced into and that of, its reflective world. Of what once was and by it, be taken down, from this blissful experience. It takes some time, for the body to decode itself and to trust in the knowing, that there is no rushing this process.

LESSON~ 127:

"FROM THE LIGHT I FOCUS AS THE MIRACLE CREATOR: WITH INTENSION THE DREAM ASPIRES FORTH TO SOLIDIFY AND IMPRINT THESE MIRACLES IN PLACE TO WITNESS_THIS STRENGTH OF CONSCIOUSNESS_IS ONE IN THE SAME WITH MY LIGHT."

Respect and honour, at what ever level of experience the self must go through; externally having to confront and internally having to rewrite itself. The idea, that faith, is the light within a sleeping giant; waiting for it to awaken and utilize this inner vision of light, as a creator being. The rewiring, is this opportunity to hold and at that level of ascended state, to be connected to the physical world. As well as, by listening to what the body needs and wants are, for its well being; it is always the indicator and primary component of this exercise.

Whenever a feeling of overwhelm and/or confusion, about anything and to disconnect from this lesson even. Just anchor in, through grounding and simple breathing; to focus on just this "of how the self is feeling". Recalibrate and then accept, until it can be felt; the compromise of the resistance and from there, that place, is the level of reality, that the self must work with. This book, is but that, of a guide and the leadership, must be found to play with independently; from the material's examples and information.

Made for the reader to bespoke in the way that can be best to understand; from a level of connection and that can best describe for the experience.

The purpose, is to hold the metaphysical component of ascension, for as long as it can be maintained and within the physical body. Begin to turn it into light and by facing also, the external physical reality; rather than, to retreat and escape, into the exclusion, of this bliss. "Everybody wants to be with God; to share in its blissfulness and from this state of being, that it offers."

(Day 146)
When the strength can be shared, it brings to all the miracles in this union; the purpose to find forgiveness and dwell in Love. The truth, to give itself away and in the same way, that it is given, to itself; because, it can be of its body and that is, of an un-depleted light, made from everything, that is life.

LESSON~ 128:
"WHEN I FIND THAT PLACE OF WEAKNESS
I MUST RECLAIM IT AS MY STRENGTH AND DIRECT IT
IN A FLOW OF EXHILARATION_TOWARD MY FEELING
OF WELL BEING."

It can feel physically exhausting, to let go of all resistances and at first, the shifting into weakness, from the "awake-ness"; in the state of being and to claim this connection, of self empowerment. A knot of emotions, as they untie and untwist metaphysically and physically, for this experience. Remove the significance, of all the programs and of what it means, to be experienced; because to prove, for any of these and for itself worth, are only useful to the Ego driven world. The self will never be enough and to accomplish for anything, in that reality; but, rather to escape it and in the way of "death". Recycling and procreating, in this way no longer have to be; the importance, of its evolution and to revolve around (Karmic wheel). To master the physical world and become completely abundant, in every way; can only be made truly possible and as practiced, from another level, of awareness. Control, has no place, where the self is going and when it decides to become conscious, of its programming; is where it can begin, to start connecting with itself. Learn how to master the physical world and with every exchange, completely becoming the affect.

LESSON~ 128:
"WHEN I FIND THAT PLACE OF WEAKNESS
I MUST RECLAIM IT AS MY STRENGTH AND DIRECT IT
IN A FLOW OF EXHILARATION_TOWARD MY FEELING
OF WELL BEING."

Today, is all about this practice; of going out into the physical world. To get a feel of where the self, it might fall short and/or change its world, that it walks into completely; with its very own vibration and through frequency, this light. Where it feels like, it might fall short, is where it must appreciate and repeat the following affirmation:

"WHEN I FIND THAT PLACE OF WEAKNESS
I MUST RECLAIM IT AS MY STRENGTH AND DIRECT IT
IN A FLOW OF EXHILARATION_TOWARD MY FEELING
OF WELL BEING."

This is exceptionally welcomed and when the self is ready to accept, that it no longer can react and feels nothing in the form of a charge from anywhere. Yet this, is the place called weakness and is still creating, the gap of emptiness inside. Christed consciousness, is in the teaching(to close this gap) and through the many stories of this energy called "LOVE". Feel the "Love" and where it was never offered in return; because of the grief and where it is no longer there, to take up residence.

LESSON~ 128:
"WHEN I FIND THAT PLACE OF WEAKNESS
I MUST RECLAIM IT AS MY STRENGTH
AND DIRECT IT IN A FLOW OF EXHILARATION
TOWARD MY FEELING OF WELL BEING."

Appreciate the progress and that in gratitude, the space has been given; to accept for more, than what the self could possibly imagine, to anticipate from raising and keeping its vibration, in this way. Imagine it, as a very deep sacred place inside and learn it, as the universe, that its becoming into. This is the inner voice; connect with it and learn from it(by stilling the mind).
From this field, the self is transmitting; to go out, into its world and make a difference, in whatever way, it can today.
It is so easy to become annoyed and by the intensity, that can throw off, the self from its alignment. Accept this disconnect, created from a place of aggravation, to aggressively distract and help it to find, the refuge, in this space. Allow what it is seeking for, to very briefly experience and take from the exchange; not so very long enough, to linger an attachment from it.
Briefly practice, to inspire the change in frequency and from whatever contact; make for the exchange in this connection, to uplift the many others, of the world and that ripple out vibration from a lower field.

The purpose, is to become more aware, of the cosmic portal from within and hold it out into the field externally.
By accepting to be healed, become the love and bring it to the world.

Take 2 days to take it in

CONGRATULATIONS ...!!!

FOR MAKING IT THROUGH THE 128th Lesson

(This is a rest period to take the lessons independently as a review)

TAKE THESE TWO DAYS TO RECALIBRATE;

MAKE NOTES AND REVIEW.................

(Day 149)
Embodiment, is being here, now and with every breath.
On occasion, the procreating aspect was dismissed; however in this way, no longer to be held accountable and in the way it was before. Embodiment, is through this divine presence and that of which its field transmits. Activated and integrated, from within its flames, as pure source creation. Awakened to its very own enlightenment; responsible for its conception and to have arrived again, in this experience. Strength will be given, in limitless supply when requested; it will replace the greed/lack, by giving light that all may see and benefit as "One".

LESSON~ 129:
"LET MY MIND BE SILENCED_SO MY HEART CAN OPEN TO THE TRUTH."

The chatter of the "Ego's" voice; however loudly it may call, must be stilled. Bring focus to the center of the mind, to reside and while the heart opens, in this stillness; feel the release, from all thoughts, that serve the "Ego". Empowered, by choice and the awareness to respond; rather than react, brings much joy and peace. When the "Ego" is silenced in awareness, the self can see under the spell, from the many and of the many programs; that it too, had been trampled over by, before. By recognizing it, in the external circumstances and that it gets played out, for in this way; the self can look at it, clear it and move on. Accept the infinite perspective, of pure intelligence; it is that, which comes to inspire and to guide, in its response, from its expression. Do not allow this moment, for ghosts from the past, to entertain in their voices; that they have found the source of life to offer it and as an added gift to believe. Circumvent the voices of the world; by light heartedly hearing them and not actually listening to their meaningless opinions. Anything that is not welcoming in "Love, Here & Now"; walk lightly past that, which does not hold the happiness within and the same best interest, as the self.

LESSON~ 129:
"LET MY MIND BE SILENCED_SO MY HEART CAN OPEN TO THE TRUTH."

Today, the word of truth, is kept from the expanded being; in the silence, it stays open, for the Over-Soul, to pour through it and enter it into a higher state of consciousness. The quiet voice of power and in truth, to hear; the self can be completely certain, of its message, to expand and open up, for enlightenment.

Through the appointed voice, of (unknowable)Over-Soul; that the self might hear and the deafening silence will bring, to the meaningless. Be still today and listen to the truth, to show the way to peace; when before it was, not made possible to see.

Allow from this day forward to become initiated, into the process of embodiment and hold that frequency of "Purity"; as best, as is possible and with every breath of action, from this place of being. Surrender to the interconnectedness and along with the many others; that are the same, to be kept in this trust.

Hear and listen to the frequency, of its world upon the earth and become the transmitter; that wakes all those who sleep and cannot see. Offer the intent to be and channel the inspiration through, to the multitude; that it may help the process for ascension, further. With an open heart and a centered mind, stay tuned for enlightenment; to come through with the function(rapture).

This is the function and that will resound this voice throughout; to all who dream will come this passion.

The purpose, is to find center and open up to clarity; that reveals the way to purity and from it to receive and give abundantly.

(Day 150)
The atom, as a precursor to the one and in, of itself, as nucleus; it rests without judgment and in the cohesion to its group, to form the quantity, of its substance. The mind metaphysically, can translate miracles and of this nature, as un separable, from its world; however slightly when, at a different level and off from perception, to overlook and can disregard them.

LESSON~ 130:
"I AM A FORCE OF EXISTENCE_
 CREATED FROM SOURCE ENERGY. "

Perhaps the self has always been, in the becoming and after every thought, of its becoming it was not able to fit in; to act upon that very thing it studied to become. Adjusting in this way, of being and then, to experience it, in its action, might not have been the way; because the many could not possibly allow it in and in this way, for it to contribute. Rather, in the doing, it could become more and recognizable, to its experience; in the becoming and to fit within this way, that it be of service, to its world.
The struggle, it is obvious; from the desperation to survive and more as a servant, than a slave, it was regrettably unfortunate and to honour in this way, for its engagements. Sometimes the positioning in status and from where it all began; to follow in these footsteps and from the many programs, begets a quicker reason, to wake up. The force, will make or break it and from it, an expansion; in that the self, will not be able to fit back in and in whatever it was supposed to be, moulded into.

LESSON~ 130:
"I AM A FORCE OF EXISTENCE_
CREATED FROM SOURCE ENERGY."

Undo from the greater good and that has fallen into greed.
Today, take note of such lineage and genetic imprints: so prevalent and that, they are externally to authorize, a prison for the self.
Go ahead and find the bone like structures; to be grinded up, into a powder and then blown away: repeat the following activation and feel them burn away; because today, it will be the day, to rise above these ashes.

"I AM THE CHILD OF INFINITE INTELLIGENCE_FROM WHICH I SPRANG FORTH_UNHARMED AND WITHOUT ARMOUR TO PROTECT_FROM SICK ILLUSIONS."

"AT EVERYMOMENT MY MOTION THROUGH EXPRESSION_THE INFINITE GAINS MORE INTELLIGENCE_A DIFFERENT PERSPECTIVE_FROM WHICH TO IDENTIFY MYSELF BETTER_THAN FROM THE DIFFERENTLY ONE MADE BEFORE."

"I REST IN THE PERFECT CERTAINTY OF NATURES PRESENCE FROM WITHIN AND ALL AROUND ME."

From the primal root, of higher consciousness and as non physical; through to the self and from its source, the energy will flow in thought, that creates worlds, to join in with the mind.
In this one idea, the past; all of it, can be undone.
Having the faith and in this one thought, is enough to enlighten the world, as well as, the self. Thrive on the vibration of empowered "Love, Here and Now"; from this state of being and for all miracles to manifest, the awareness to receive them.

LESSON~ 130:
"I AM A FORCE OF EXISTENCE_ CREATED FROM SOURCE ENERGY."

The self can blend inspired action, with momentum to service and become its function with stability. The conscious nurturing, of inner child, to stand and in readiness, with its foundation. This, is an incorruptible state and that authentically, it will call out from the self. To live out its function and as this Force; in will and as it has intended, with its passion.
All that is required for today, is the awareness to accept the present moment and on healing for the mind, of its past; to allow for such perception, that can give to the vision and the freedom for its future.
Let go of time and accept it, as an application; to guide through and for learning purposes, the progress of change.
From duality, the fear to separate and from all that is Love; were these lessons learned and that death cannot replace for life, nor sickness for health. To substitute for these experiences, were far too important and to master from; now it can all be realized and in how, it has served the self well.

As it was previously mentioned (lesson 77; lesson 39 and so on..): When(anti-matter & matter) they come together, energy is released and transmuted; potentially it can then be transformed, into something else and with this purpose, will is better understood.

The purpose, is to explore the unfathomable: right from the atom, the self worth and go beyond the physical molecular structure, to reach the heart; then in an open sacred state, of mindful awareness and where the ephemeral, can be seen obtainable.

(Day 151)

Envision the adventure and that the self can have; through its mind's discovery, of infinite intelligence and toward a crystalline, pristine enhancement.

Seek out the inner child, to bond with and become one with the world; as above and so below, the unconscious can awaken, from its deep sleep.

LESSON~ 131:

"I GIVE MYSELF PERMISSION_TO REMEMBER THIS ECSTATIC HAPPINESS_COMPRISED OF LOVE AND WITH EVERY PRIMAL BREAKDOWN_ COMPASSION."

Today, is all about honouring the self and respecting the inner child subconsciously; that is, deep in the mind of the self and waiting to be acknowledged. The self is lost without its inner child, unacknowledged and unknown; it is waiting to be heard, seek it out and find it.

Remember the silly dolls, for idols it once played with?
Can the self now remember, the false images it made and from its mind, to think it was ?

How worthless are its idols and that it can release, as of today; open with hands, heart and mind to Source/Energy/God.
Remember in(free will) this life force, throughout the day.

Let this presence of the self be praised, in created form; that is through its heart and in loving thoughts, for all who meet with it today.

LESSON~ 131:
"I GIVE MYSELF PERMISSION TO REMEMBER THIS ECSTATIC HAPPINESS_COMPRISED OF LOVE AND WITH EVERY PRIMAL BREAKDOWN_COMPASSION."

Go through the idea and that in timelessness, all is one with Over-Soul; to remember in this higher consciousness perspective, of infinite intelligence and repeat the following:

"NO LONGER IS THE NEED TO SUFFER_IN EXCHANGE FOR LEARNING AND NEED NOT SUFFER_A MUST TO LIVE."

"THE MOON DOES NOT NEED TO HOLD THE SUN IN ITS DARKNESS_NOR THE SUN TO HOLD THE MOON IN ITS LIGHT"

"AS BELOW AND SO ABOVE; THROUGH MOTHER FATHER_SISTER AND BROTHER_WE BECOME ONE IN THE LIKENESS".

"I AM A REFLECTION OF THE WORLD AND WITHIN MY BODY CONSISTS THE ENTIRE UNIVERSE."

LESSON~ 131:
"I GIVE MYSELF PERMISSION TO REMEMBER THIS ECSTATIC HAPPINESS_COMPRISED OF LOVE AND WITH EVERY PRIMAL BREAKDOWN_COMPASSION."

"At-one-meant", is being used to denote and the effect, that flows from a transformative state, to another; "Atonement", well after the physical change and best described, as a metaphysical study.
A change of perception, must occur to accept, the oneness and become, at one, with all that is meant, for the self to be.
By accepting the higher mind, to merge with higher heart; uprooted from the dark hidden secret places and for its retarded cause to suffer, has retired. Nothing can give of itself, through loss; begin to practice thinking, of the many and who have been denied appreciation. The fallen, can get up to rise again and in true, pristine power; to do upon the same for the world and that can be lightly touched, in this way, through these words.

The purpose, is to find the bridge of timelessness and experience the cohesion, of both worlds; merging into one perspective and that transcends, beyond duality.

(Day 152)
Perhaps the unachievable, are these things that appear and when not in proper alignment, with the preference of their outcome. Procrastination, can become a safety mechanism and to the very resistance, that reflects, as opposition.

LESSON~ 132:
"IN TRUTH_THERE IS NO SUCH THING AS FAILING AND RATHER A REDIRECTING TOWARD SOMETHING ELSE."

When the interest in something, that is not in the same, to least bit interested and rather; interested in something else (that the self might not be interested in), then a gap is created. Free will can mysteriously choose an aspect of itself, to bond with and that is not in favour of this kind of bondage, to explore and in the sharing of expansion.
All these goals can be apparently meaningless and therefore unreachable. How does the self cooperatively work and alongside such exclusions? Does it get out of the way; or have it stand to compromise its feeling of accomplishment?
The shifting will take place and regardless of that integration, it upheld, for its impediment. So let them go, for the premonitions they might be and in the making for the self later.
Pursuit of the imagined and when in the state of separation; to start with, must also end with death. Only when the perception, is possible to differ, can the other be attainable and only with love, from this place, that feels of oneness. In this "oneness", is the full circle of completion; with no interruptions (of beginning and end) and to such degree, for the ability to transmute existence.
The shift in perception, transfigures the physical through this transcendence. With the innocence of "never been there" and to "never having done that before"; the unquenchable search and for something in the eyes of curiosity unfathomable.

LESSON~ 132:
"IN TRUTH_THERE IS NO SUCH THING AS FAILING RATHER A REDIRECTING TOWARD SOMETHING ELSE."

In due diligence, every goal is obtained and unlike previously imagined, of these plans; to fall by the way side, for something even better. The kingdom of heaven, knocks at the door and the readiness, is in the accepting of it; to see it, in the light, with the eyes of a child and not be blinded. In heaven the weather is perfect, always; there are no gaps and the canvas is not torn in two segments, nor four. The schools of learning, do not require for any suffering and everything is in the doing, from love.
The threat of being left behind, is really in the fear, of leaving it behind; rather inclusiveness, is where the self must be and always feeling from its world. This is what it means and to be within alignment to the presence of the self; rather than, for the exclusion of its essence. Allot some time now and with eyes closed, to turn on the projector, of the mind. Review the world and from which the thoughts, have been sent back to.
Take only the compatible thoughts, of truth and that will not fail the self(to imprint upon). Then sink even deeper, into the darkness of the mind; where the door to source is found. The doors are opened and the light, so bright; is the clarity and that brings forth understanding, to everything observable. This is the enlightenment and from which all things, are aspired to ascend.
Here, the searching is quenched for and in this state of gladness, Heaven is exposed.

LESSON~ 132:
"IN TRUTH_THERE IS NO SUCH THING AS FAILING RATHER A REDIRECTING TOWARD SOMETHING ELSE."

Take this moment of grace, to repeat and be reminded often; with the following supported statements:

"MY THOUGHTS WERE BORROWED FROM A WORLD I DID NOT REALLY KNOW AS MINE_IT WAS THERE TO SERVE ME IN THIS WAY_THAT I MAY LEARN FROM IT AND WHAT IT IS _I DO WANT_BY HOW I FEEL."

"MY FEELINGS ARE MADE UP OF MY EMOTIONS TO THE THOUGHTS I HAVE NOW_MATCHED UP TO LEAD ME IN THE RIGHT DIRECTION."

"IN TRUTH_THERE IS NO SUCH THING AS FAILING RATHER A REDIRECTING TOWARD SOMETHING ELSE."

Explore the essence of the self; rather than its presence of the state, it is transmitting (in the creation of the now) and to be left aside, to focus only on what is preferred. Study the circumstances well and from it; what it is, this state of mind, that is preferred. Is it in the radiance of being here and now; or is it in the compromise, of what once was, reflecting back its essence? The paradox, can only be and when there is too much contemplation, to explain for meaning(Always move in the direction of what feels best) and just let it go.

The single purpose, is and has always been, for ever more eternal; to be the function of the light. In this plan, the many do engage, to congregate as one and with the self; as this reminder in unconditional love and befounded enlightenment.

(Day 153)

Seek out the inner core of the self, to bond with and become one with the world; as above and so below, the unconscious can awaken, from its deep sleep. With wings of peace, spread out and soar above the agitations of the world. "Love, Here, Now" asks for nothing; than to rid the unforgiving mind, of the space that fear encompasses.

LESSON~ 133: "FORGIVENESS IS ASCENSION."

With judgement, the mind is the witness and unable to change, in its corrections. "RIGHTEOUS" in it and of itself; that the world be, as irreversible and in its condemnation left to despair.

Through the heart, is this teaching of forgiveness and that connects to higher self. Accept to feel and learn from every opportunity; in this way, throughout the day, that presents itself and for the experience, of an unforgiving mind. For each unforgiving mind, that is released, from such density, and can now flow freely through, by this interaction. From despair to hope, the field becomes; from self onto the many and of its world, a self teaching process.

Set the focus for today, to exercise forgiveness and make a practice of forgiving, as often, as possible. Open the doors and with elation; from letting go, the burdens and of holding on to grudges.

Forgive, to find the answers and that once threatened to bring about uncertainty, from around every corner.

Find the stillness of the mind; to bring about the peace and for the heart to open. Forgive the torn with doubt, about itself and so afraid from the anger, that weakens it. Why are these aspects so terrified of darkness and every sound, yet more afraid of stillness?

When burdened from the past illusions and that from its corruption can bring; the only thing that can be possible, is to forgive.

The mock of strife, for peace and to feel justified with groupings of its cause; the miserable projections from its exaggerated imitations, when forgiveness was all that is needed.

The future awaits for the prospect, that forgiveness brings.

LESSON~ 133: "FORGIVENESS IS ASCENSION."

Throughout this day and perhaps for every other, from here on; make a pledge, to learn how forgiveness can feel, to give and to receive. Take every moment that confronts, from circumstance; to observe the difference, of friend and foe, learn to see them as both, one in the same. Then learn to become the observed; through the two opposites, as one in the same, the self can find and through their release, as its own.

Take $2/3^{rds}$ of every waking hour and to meditate over these following words, of thought:

"I HAVE CREATED A BRIDGE_WHERE BOTH WORLDS CAN MERGE INTO IMMORTAL AND INFALLIBLE ONENESS."

"THE LIGHT SHINES THROUGH MY HEART SO BRIGHTLY THAT I AWAKEN FROM THE DEEP SLEEP."

"FORGIVENESS IS ASCENSION."

Remember throughout the day, the importance of emergence and that the game of forgiveness brings, to every unforgiving mind. Feel the despise and the anger; with eyes closed, envision in the mind a while and of these aspects. Shining through the horrible portrait, a little spark might appear; augment this light, until it covers over. Feel the beauty, that is left from the light and transmit it out, into the world. By accepting this light and from them, the self too, can ascend, into enlightened awareness.

The purpose, is to reach a level, where no more forgiveness is required and naturally to vibe, with loving energies, as an exemplary, in everyday existence.

(Day 154)

The state of depression and manic behaviour, between the self and its experiences; is more, or less, the "descension" and ascension; peaks and valleys, of the flow, from energy exchange.

Opposing perceptions and of reality, can only shift, from one to the other; both worlds, do not last for long, simultaneously to be seen and one must give over, for the other.

LESSON~ 134:

"I DWELL IN A CONTRASTED WORLD_UNTIL I HAVE COMPLETED_TO SHIFT OVER MY PERCEPTION INTO ANOTHER."

There are so many different worlds; because of the, so many different perceptions. At any given moment, the realities and in the same space as the "being-ness", of the self is profound; however it can only see, what its mind will allow. The very same things, that can be overlooked and right in plain sight; also can be noticed, when the mind is able, to take it in. The stimuli can become over whelming, to comprehend; all at once and can blind, from too much light. Rethinking, is this capacity of processing information, in the mind fully and integrating it; to see something different, than what was there before. The slightest shift, can create miracles to appear. With every decision made, the values are determined, in this way and in how; or what can actually be perceived, for its reality.

The illusion, is in the belief, that reality is constantly and always to be; as it is seen in that moment, forever unchanging.

The changes, are too slight to notice and yet, so great, when the changes happen, from within. Too much contemplation, into the explanation and/or any phenomenon; can become and too soon a paradoxical paradigm.

LESSON~ 134:
" I DWELL IN A CONTRASTED WORLD_UNTIL I HAVE COMPLETED_TO SHIFT OVER MY PERCEPTION INTO ANOTHER."

Without any overlaps, the brain might not comprehend too much emphasis on distinction. To properly process such a vast range of expanded awareness, into its circuitry and all at once; will cause it to dismiss for any of these things entirely.
Although the illusions between like and love; or fear with hate appear to suggest and that there are no compromises to be made between love and hate. Instead of focusing on the unwanted, why not replace the value over, to what it is of choice, desired to perceive and it will come to be so, in this way.
With these activations, include a few moments of intermissions; to meditate on going beyond compromise and its meaningless contrasts. Focus on the moment, with unity and wholeness; then repeat the following affirmation and its supported statement:

"I DWELL IN A CONTRASTED WORLD_UNTIL I HAVE COMPLETED_TO SHIFT OVER MY PERCEPTION INTO ANOTHER."

"MY EMOTIONS EMULATE FROM MY SOURCE_TO MY PERCEPTION AND I LIVE IN THE OPPOSITE WORLD."

LESSON~ 134:
"I DWELL IN A CONTRASTED WORLD_UNTIL I HAVE COMPLETED_TO SHIFT OVER MY PERCEPTION INTO ANOTHER."

With eyes open, there is no doubt to be left over; with what is looked upon as truth and with tangible expression, from the grateful state of existence. The choices put forth in this day, become as limiting factors and for any other temptation, to dismiss with ease.
Realize that consistency, is the application of choice; when met with opposition to accept, the perception and just slightly, it will change greatly, the reality toward what is more preferable.
What is preferred, is within range and when the resistance to what is not preferred, is released by the self; so too will the other yield in resisting to show itself.
Take in the concept of this todays idea and following statement:

"I DWELL IN A CONTRASTED WORLD_UNTIL I HAVE COMPLETED_TO SHIFT OVER MY PERCEPTION INTO ANOTHER."

"THE CONTRAST SEEKS ME OUT_ WHERE BEFORE I COULD ONLY SEEK IT AND NOW MY FREEDOM LIES IN THE DELIVERING_THAT PART OF IT I DO WANT."

The purpose, is to find the place and where compromise for the self, does not exist.

THE INTERMISSION :

Take a day to take it in

CONGRATULATIONS ...!!!

FOR MAKING IT

THROUGH TO THE 134th Lesson

(This is a rest period to take the lessons independently as a review)

TAKE THIS DAY TO RECALIBRATE;

MAKE NOTES AND REVIEW..................

(Day 156)
Happiness, is a changeless geometry from the oneness; it thrives on the ability to sense compassion and from its evolving variations, toward atonement. Letting go, reaches a level of understanding and that forgiveness, in this concept, can fall by the way side; uplift compassion in its better meaning, that in truth there is nothing to pity over.

LESSON~ 135:
"COMPASSION OFFERS EVERYTHING TO THE FORGIVING."

All the different versions of the self, must be understood to evolve. Evolution and growth, will never cease; thus forgiveness too, will remain changeless and for this reason. The only change that can be therefore, is that of the perceiver; to realize that forgiveness, is in the same as time and an application. Compassion and forgiveness too, are applications and that can take in this truthful place, of giving and receiving; however, can only function from a state of love and with the heart, wide open. Compassion, is the working of the mind and heart together. Forgiveness, is the function of the lower state and to find its place again, from density; with the information it requires, to evolve and then ascend forth, into enlightenment. Lighten up, into the next step of transcendence; release all grievances, through forgiveness and the world can feel, a little lighter. The inner child reflecting back to parent; will eventually accumulate in purity, amongst the many and to awaken them, as warriors of light. Hold this energy and share its information, with the many; that are pure enough and can feel it from its source, that houses it. The information, is pristine and it can be, the cause for many changes; transfigure from this light and become uplifted, with illumination. At the core and within the self, is the watcher, of its pristine awareness.

LESSON~ 135:

"COMPASSION OFFERS EVERYTHING TO THE FORGIVING."

Be ready now and to shed away, from previous thoughts; that once upon a time, carbon based reality and clear all membranes, from regrets. Now, the kingdom of heaven awaits and from deep within, it welcomes the self, to join it. The "Kingdom of Heaven", was never to be found out there; it is a feeling state, rather than its surface, substance that created it. When the child can be recognized and given love, to be expressive; encourage this nurturing and never suppress it, in such a state, as to create an "Ego"(for its mind). Accept this gift, to liberate the world with and the value of the self; it will be given its own, from within. The world has nothing of relevance, in giving to the mind; rather the Infinite intent and its intelligence, will bring about, such evolution. The illness of a mental mind game manipulation, shows in those disconnected and shadowed in areas of its life; rather see them in resilience and whilst evolving at their own pace through resistance. Allow for the self to be receptive to the intricate dream cycles; that can no longer conceal the nothingness from within. With open eyes, be in a state of happiness and peace, to feel and fill the world with. They too will find it in there own time and express it in their own way of acceptance. Release all previous resentments and just allow forgiveness to find its place; this feeling will birth compassion, in its ancient truth. This heart, is sacred and it hold's much memory, than can ever be described; today intend on feeling through such, these applications. Feel the turning point, it has now been reached, where "Hell", is left with nothing more to explore; because the road preferred, has always been much easier. From all this mucky density, that self created; it cannot remain in it and to release it, it will, for Heaven's answer.

LESSON~ 135:
"COMPASSION OFFERS EVERYTHING TO THE FORGIVING."

For today's lesson, apply some hope and faith for its resolve. In the morning and evening contemplate the nearing end of "Hell on Earth" and of the collective's "Ego" driven "Mindset", that helped create it. Make certain, that Love, Here and Now; can instead, be the creation, of such happiness and for the encouragement, to go through this exercise. Make what the will can and only be ready to accept and at whatever pace; take it easy and stretch the mind, a little bit, at a time and with baby steps. Practice feeling compassion for the world and that of the self, to help evolve; down to the very agitation and that calls out forgiveness. Go within and visualize the world; how it has recreated artificially its light and cover it completely with the originally evolved and beautiful one. Walk toward and picture the self directly in this light, receiving of the truth and behind weaponry appearances, these gifts of ancient time. For each quarter of the hour passing, remember of these gifts and throughout the day, for at least a minute. The following affirmation and supporting statement, can help to remind; how precious the power of these gifts and while holding the awareness on them:

"COMPASSION OFFERS EVERYTHING TO THE FORGIVING".

"THESE GIFTS I HAVE ACCEPTED_THAT I MAY RECEIVE THE BLESSINGS FROM THE LIGHT I FOUND WITHIN"

The purpose, is to find the gift of the soul and directly from the heart, to mind connection.

(Day 157)

Soothing, is very important, on the journey and to bring about a smoother road. The over polarized remains, try to convince the other, of its empowerment and that it can cooperate; to be better off, in its program of manipulation. The self enters into a feeling of not wishing to; or believing in actual fact and that there is no reason to exist, and therefore convinces itself, that it does not. The "Ego mind", requires many rules and regulates to pass forth, the level of control well; for this as a system to succumb to and its basic structure of awareness.

LESSON~ 136:
"I THANK MY UNIVERSE FOR
ALL THE LOVELY GIFTS."

Resistance is futile, all the while, acceptance of the self; it must live, to be and in praiseworthy state, for all to benefit.
Live by not the other, that be in lack; then turn around and worship the abundance. When there are envelopes and the other asks for one; do not bring a rule, to policy by lack and through the hoarding, worship abundance. To understand the world, is not one big paperclip and/or making system suits of law, to better suit the lack; again in its battle over standard. The light, is genderless and can also be found, in the most dense places; when the sound of church bells can be heard and to resonate with voices of angels near. The gifts of nature's kingdom, quiet and restfully peaceful; are these doves that soar around the self and to find, that nothing could ever possibly exist, outside of this light. Be grateful, that the light has found the self; to guide it through creation and give thanks, in finally knowing that abandonment, was never the intention. Love, Here and Now, shining on forever, is creation; from it, the primordial substance and this star, that came to be aware, as the self.

LESSON~ 136:
"I THANK MY UNIVERSE FOR ALL THE LOVELY GIFTS."

By looking up and through the bodies eyes; instead of down and let gratitude lift off, from all despair. Create a template of honour, to the self and thankfulness; to smile at everything, all day and from this place of standing. Walk with a light hearted sense and with every footstep, in the "<u>doing-ness</u>", just be. Listen to the angelic being, when it comforts from within, and from another's body, just the same, to share a word or two; because these words, are soundless, when not heard. Let this information, be the echo around and round, the world; when the self can take the moment and to feel the frequency, it too, can become the messenger, by them(the many). Receive this thanks, of infinite intelligence today and give, as well the thanks, in recognition of it. The praise, that is offered, must be received well and be given in trust, completely to it. Love grows in strength, the more it is given and these are the gifts; that bless over, to share in restoration, for the self and fill with resonance, upon its world with. Plant this seed of thought today, so it may sink into the mind, completely.

Feed it with love and everything that life will bring the light, to listen, to its echo. With the standing formation, to walk in honour of the self; be thankful and with a smile, stand in awareness, of this love it brings, here and now.

LESSON~ 136:
"I THANK MY UNIVERSE FOR
 ALL THE LOVELY GIFTS."

Meditate first thing upon these words, to start the day with and
after, upon retiring for the evening; to realize, just to whom the
thanks is for. Receive this empowerment, as once it came to
look for the self and before it was even made aware, it was
created. Become limitless and boundless, in its care and allow for
this lesson's thought, to penetrate lovingly and deeply.
With gratitude and for these gifts, to be received; the life from
this awareness, to be given as existence and to feel, that as long
as, this awareness of the self is, it too, will be so. Much of self
perspective, brings the rise of knowing it again and with the very
illusion, that cast it away; the self will feel it had gone and to be
left abandoned in the process. The splitting off, was for the
reason of expansion and from these variation, made by contrast,
to learn in. These are the gifts, that soul can thrive with and from
the light, that has never left; with it, the reuniting of its
integration and back into the oneness, that is love.
With every breath, remember of this universal cause and give it
thanks, for everything it gives; comes from the very core, that
asks it forth. Rise above the concept, of this external world; to
remembering of its material and maternal guidance, is supported
by the self.

The purpose naturally, is to go beyond the gender boost.
To go deep and find meaning for empowerment, is this light; it
holds all and no gender apart, from itself.

(Day 158) Unmerited, is withholding to suffer and long enough, for a charitable whim, to the unworthy; who has not earned, charitable tolerance and just to point out, that the self is better.

Hold a thought, for long enough and the belief of it, will define an attitude to create a personality with; thus the "Ego Mind" and to convince the self, it is separate from the needs of its world.

LESSON~ 137: "WITH MY PRESENCE I CAN HARNESS A STATE OF BEING INTO WILFUL ACTION AND BE MINDFUL IN MY DOING."

"Giving" and receiving", is the same in practice, as "being" and "doing". Feel the beauty, from the inside and through the presence of the self; its connection with everything. In its purest form of consciousness, is this auspicious word: called "Crystalline" and from before its muddy state; of "Carbon" state euphemism (known in this way amongst the "New Age" movement). The clearing of the soul, is becoming into that fractal image; of a brand new baby and from the Over-Soul's, perspective view.

Everything, is made possible and when the self is cleared, of all its many codes and lineage programs. Resistance, is futile, all the while, acceptance of the self; it must live, to act in a praiseworthy state and for all to benefit. "<u>Live not by the other, that be in lack and turn around and worship the abundance. When there are envelopes and the other asks for one; do not bring a rule to policy by lack and through the hoarding worship abundance</u>".

The self does affect the world and its perception of itself from it; it does this with judgement and for the conviction, in thinking it is separate, from that which is outside of itself. The world is not separate from the self; because the many of the world is the self.

LESSON~137: "WITH MY PRESENCE I CAN HARNESS A STATE OF BEING INTO WILFUL ACTION AND BE MINDFUL IN MY DOING."

Give out to the world, not the things that are considerably undesirable and unhealthy; for the sake of peer approval. Although it appears to be charity, it is just another loophole contribution and for a system built on greed/lack.
Be the supporter of what is supportive in abundance and the sharing of this flow. Sharing is an illusion that thrives on expectation. Why not instead and from here on, practice the allowing; for the flow of universal energy, to pour and flow, right through. Today, practice being supportive, with a softer energetic, loving and kind-full presence; rather than, a confrontational harsh and jagged edged point, to view of the environment. See what it's like, to float like in a bubble state, of mindfulness and upon, for every action, it motions forward. Replace all methods of attack, with love and rise up, for every occasion; to be and do, for accomplishing the tasks at hand. Step into the role of the creator and become more graceful, in the mission of the beauty; rather than, the duty of its cause, to conform by it(the standard is of its own intended making and to be realized in this way).

The purpose, is to learn to harness from within,
that of pristine source energy, and higher dimensional power;
That is the "Sovereign Light" presence.
BE IT NOW......

(Day 159) The mind oppresses and with intention to defend a made up story; that the body with reaction will reject the self for being.

LESSON~ 138:
"I RELEASE MY OPPRESSED STATE OF BEING_ BY LETTING GO OF ALL MY JUDGEMENTS I MADE REAL."

The being of the self, is a walking miracle and unto itself, a made up universe; that cooperatively functions in harmony, well and with all that is. When the mind can release itself and from all its thoughts of grandeur; to control itself and thus manipulate its system, it can find resonance. It will awaken to its many systems and through, to a cellular existence; to allow, that which holds and for the self a voice to communicate intuitively and from its environment back to itself, without the mind. The heart and just like it, so many more systems; the mind must allow, to work with and all, as equally important, to the light, as itself, to the self. The mind has caused much suffering, to weight over its entirety; from the whole integrated perspective, that is self and from its given privy, to imagination.
In an awakened state, the body of the self, will be released from its emotional bondage and the stressful reactions.
Judgements to the circumstances and that the mind resists from being; has oppressed into harmful and physical reactions, for the body to signal out. The body has far too long been cut off, from the self and its many systems. Further and further, the separation has blocked off communication; from what the mind chooses to filter through, its limited awareness. The mind, in so many aspects, has lost touch and integration; the more its beliefs solidify from its judgements.

LESSON~ 138:
"I RELEASE MY OPPRESSED STATE OF BEING_BY LETTING GO OF ALL MY JUDGEMENTS I MADE REAL."

Judgement, is the final death rattle of a weary mind and to release its final intentions, for hell as proof; in its disregard and to the miracles, that made up life. Where there is no light to be found, love will lead the way to find it; where there is no love to be found, the light will lead the way, to find it. Compassion, will find its way and the mind too, is made possible, in this way, to surrender to the heart. It is through the heart, that the mind can possibly find its way home and center for the self, into the light. When the body of the self is released, from all blockages; to find its light and within every cell, the voice in celebration, will be that of the many, rejoicing in the kingdom of heaven.

This is the state of being, that creates worlds and most of all, the state that will bring heaven on earth. To open up the kingdom of Heaven and from within, the many to light up the world, in this way. In this world, all illusion of pain, fear, sickness, harm, heavy hearted hate and even death; they are all judgements and must be dismissed at the gates, before entry.

Oppression, is to limit full expression; because of what is deemed appropriate and what is not up to standards; that the mind will cast forth in judgement. The result of such neglect to the self, is to deny its emotional growth and stifle it, deep within its physical body. The body of the self can cover and for a certain while, what is not compatible; then it must expel freely and without the imposed filters, from the mind's limited awareness.

The mind must overcome its imaginations of death and to choose the body made stronger; than the truth, which asks it any other, than to live on.

LESSON~ 138:
"I RELEASE MY OPPRESSED STATE OF BEING_BY LETTING GO OF ALL MY JUDGEMENTS I MADE REAL."

The judgements, from impervious laws and imposed to blind the body's eyes; make it a slave and to its decay, is that of a sick mind. The mind must imagine, a short circuit in its power, to control and create, for such defence; over its struggle for obedience to it.
The pressure of its application and to understand time, is again the struggle, in the meeting up with; its many intentions, will throw it into a hurried state, of comparison and in so doing, over being.

Today, allow for a quarter of an hour, in the morning and then evening; to focus on centering into the truth, that is the light and before its eyelids do meet in closing, with the following, to repeat:

"I LET GO OF ALL MY JUDGEMENTS I MADE REAL AND RELEASE MY OPPRESSED STATE OF BEING."

"IN THIS WAY_I CAN BEGIN TO HEAL AND CONNECT TO THE WORLD COLLECTIVELY ON THIS RESONANCE".

With eyes closed, silence the mind and go deep into the heart; to feel the love, here and now. Within the mind, nothing else exists and from its emptiness; that the soothing of the heart, to feel it and into its awareness, is this peace. Focus and from where the part of the body, the discomfort is, visualise it in its darkness.
Within this moment, allow to feel and for any physical pain, or discomfort . Feel the body out and go within its very cell, to hear it and listen in for a message. Speak to it, in love and be compassion.

LESSON~ 138:
"I RELEASE MY OPPRESSED STATE OF BEING_BY LETTING GO OF ALL MY JUDGEMENTS I MADE REAL."

Throughout the day, when the body feels discomfort and/or any pain.....
Stop and take a moment, to pause and ask:

"HOW CAN I HELP RELIEVE WITH LOVE
THIS SEPARATION FROM MY THOUGHTS
THAT HAVE CREATED THIS FEELING IN _____"?

"I LET GO OF ALL MY JUDGEMENTS I MADE REAL AND RELEASE MY OPPRESSED STATE OF BEING."

The purpose, is to reconnect from all its parts and into the oneness, that is self.

(Day 160) One of the physical systems, of the body, is the skin and from it, the many pores, so it can breathe. Remove the debris, from inside the self, to open the channels(pores/nadis) and for the life force(prana/chi/kundalini) to come in. When the self can allow, for enough clearing, to take place; the energy, that pours through it, will transform it and from a clay figurine into a crystalline/Sovereign Light, body being.

LESSON~ 139:
"SOURCE ENERGY_IS THE ONLY LOVE THERE IS FROM THIS MY UNIVERSE."

To better describe love, is to see it as a bond, that creates oneness and just like the many, create the One; it too, has many flavours and colourful depths, to enrich life with. When the creator splits into the many shattered slivers of itself; to re-examine and expand itself with, all that is, it too, emulated with this. Love does not change; however, only the perception of it, having many layers and flavours. The various colours, different in their depths and that are described, from the one light. This light, is exactly in the love perception paradigm; only to work alongside and with the mind can cooperatively be this way. With Love, relationships are created and with the many, that represent the one. It is in the levels of harmony and that integration can be seen, as cooperative; or compensating, to control conditions over itself, causing separation and lack.
Love can be accepted, or pushed away from many factors and that perception emotionally attaches to conditionally; with its own neediness, to secure in its place. Love has no place, where it judges; therefore, it is incomparable; because it cannot compare.
The Love from within, is unseasonal; only when looking to the outer conditions of nature, can this be, to find darkness and death.

LESSON~ 139:
"SOURCE ENERGY_IS THE ONLY LOVE THERE IS FROM THIS MY UNIVERSE."

What can be seen as darkness and death, is that of nature turning inward; when the light diminishes and where the inner light, can be found. The Earth too, has its moments of going inward and then expressing outward, through nature; in this perception, is the interpretation and for the meaning of seasonal changes.
The rest of the world and as once before, has violated the truth, of what love is; re-examine now, as the light of the world and hold it, with the greatest of reverence.
Today and for this reason: take the idea and make life, about the beauty of life; instead of the "duty" and to uphold for it, such weighted down density. The goal, is to understand the meaning of love, a little better. Take the first quarter of the hour, before starting the day and then again, in the evening; before the nightly rest, to practice feeling this love frequency(from all that is deflected and reflected). With the shorter exercises, take every twenty minutes, of every hour; to remember what love feels like and reboot from source energy. Stay open to the expansion, of what is felt and throughout the day, being in love. Let the gift of love, replace for all the world's imprisoned beliefs and that the mind, can hold so deep. Remember the impossible possibility and of leaving a part of the self, outside its love; to make the journey, with it and learn, what must be taught by this. A spark of truth, within the mind; wherever the surrender to a dark illusion, of reality and the meaning of love. During the day, see the world and in, as newly born; to grow in strength and beyond the way, of thinking, that created hate, to be the enemy of love.
With a clean and open mind, this lesson will be blessed with "love, here and now"; to spare the future, from its past.

LESSON~ 139:
"SOURCE ENERGY_IS THE ONLY LOVE THERE IS FROM THIS MY UNIVERSE."

As the self, will come to mind for its world and to give for this message, the following support:

"I BLESS ALL WITH FORGIVENESS _FROM THEIR VIOLATIONS OF WHAT LOVE IS_ I GIVE THE LOVE TO EVERYTHING THAT WAS ONCE DENIED FROM ME BY LEARNING THAT IT CAME FROM WITHIN."

Learn to go beyond the survival skills, of denial and other mechanisms; programmed in and that created otherwise within the self to believe. These fears and traumas, were artificially implanted with much intelligence, to operate and be obeyed; they systematically set, as standard and for the self to function in. How does the self exist and function otherwise?
Take as many moments and throughout the day, to feel the "source of potential" within thee. This will be, an ongoing process and throughout the entire book; because the clearing of the energetic fields, must occur and reunite as in "Atonement". The blockages, are reality making circumstances and given rightfully, their very own stories. The beliefs, that the self will carry, are these toxic experiences and that spew out, into clay formations(rigid beliefs). Pour more energy, into the elementals and the karmic stories, become stronger, in their lessons. The "Ego Mind" loves repetitive robotic disconnection, with nature and the self; to be its zombie slave and recreated, in its image.

Uniting with the physical body(grounded and expanded Over-Soul), the purpose, is to learn to master the authentic presence(Atonement) from within and become ascended into "<u>Sovereign Light</u>".

(Day 161)
Connect with every exchange and that, which the self wishes to be; from that place, be the role model to the world.
The natural organic expression of the self, is what, it is; from that place of authenticity, it can once again, remember to function.

LESSON~ 140:
"THE ENERGY THAT ONCE FELT FOREIGN TO ME
IS THIS LEVEL OF AWAKENED STATE
THAT I WISH TO RETURN TO."

Today, accept the clearing and as a way of bringing through, the many divine aspects, of the whole of self. The more space that it can be given; the more of itself, it can be present and in this moment's state, to occupy. Only then, can the higher levels of consciousness, vibrate in and for as long, as the space, for such, is the frequency, that it can hold. Each aspect of the self, has different traits and to hone in, on one perspective; is to hold the others up, into "a little me perception". Remove the "Ego-Mind" and other parts of the soul, can reconnect; to form the resonance and grow in the awareness, of the world expanding, from this light. The more that the self, it can awaken to connect; the more it will awaken of its world and that feel, for its connection to them. Feel and get it, to communicate from this place of love and open heartedness; so that the many of the world, can mindfully awaken, to take up place and be responsibly aware.
In this place, the self does not require to explain and for any of its actions; and/or inactions, to contribute, in this way and for any kind, of approval. The experience, is always in rebirthing of a new design and no longer, to be in captivation; to that, which was held in secrecy, as patent and to withhold from its connection, in the exchange, of profiteering and control.

LESSON~ 140:
"THE ENERGY THAT ONCE FELT FOREIGN TO ME IS THIS LEVEL OF AWAKENED STATE THAT I WISH TO RETURN TO."

The roles of gaining access, is through purity and not corruption. It does not have to know the difference; because it has always and forever more, felt the difference and from these waves of currency. The purer the state of consciousness, the self can function in; the more access it will have, to the truth and all the others, can fall by the way side. The "Ego Mind" will be the only disconnect, that will compete and try to challenge it, with the illusion; to threaten its survival and should it ignore the power, of its secrecy.

An "Ego Mind" interaction, will shut down the abilities to function and in a pure, pristine state, of awareness. The "Ego" interaction, is a corrupted state; where the pure of heart, will find disabling and unable to function, from these kind of interactions.

The choice, is made clear; that the self must choose, to go with ease or that of struggle.

Feel the vibrations, are these transmissions, subtle and softer; or are they abrasive and hard hitting ?

The purpose, is more about the feeling of it; rather than the explanation, of what it means, to get it.. Just feel, either from the disconnect or connection, to be the indices and make note; from where this lesson has decided, to come from and what angle?

(Day 162)
Feel the energy, in motion and like the ocean, crashing upon the shore; imagine for a moment, the metabolic system and relax into emotional connection, held from within. Just like the crackling burst, of thunder storms and when the water comes crashing, upon the surface of the earth. Connect to this ebb and flow, of nature, with every inhalation and exhalation, feel this magnetism. When the electrical distractions and of the static in the field; become that of its clamour driven world, the magnetic bond, between the earth and the self, get somewhat disconnected.

LESSON~ 141:
"WITH GOOD VIBRATIONS I FEEL THE RELEASE OF DENSE PROGRAMS WITHIN MY THOUGHTS AND AS I REMAIN IN TACT WITH MY PHYSICAL FORMATION I WALK INTO ANOTHER MUCH LIGHTER AWARENESS."

Digital wave signals and from this invented "artificial intellect", has concentrated within a system, of an "Ego-driven", social structure; to control, rather than connect. Seeking to electro magnetize and the very oxygen (stripping away the ions) molecules, that sustains it. Heavily populated, dense areas, have created and recreated from the self; causing it, to keep on exiting, from its physical body, and while continually recycling, a falsehood immortality via procreation(passing these inventions on).

Who was this "Father", that had forsaken them ?

LESSON~ 141:
"WITH GOOD VIBRATIONS I FEEL THE RELEASE OF DENSE PROGRAMS WITHIN MY THOUGHTS AND AS I REMAIN IN TACT WITH MY PHYSICAL FORMATION I WALK INTO ANOTHER MUCH LIGHTER AWARENESS."

The increase, of a chemically depressed world; was set with the intention, to control the mind with. Suicide, is no longer to entice with and as a given option from before, to travel back and forth through time; because the emotional body, will still continue on, its karmic venture, with the soul. It is not always, as easy and as imagined; to change things in the place, of how it once was metaphysically. For the many reasons, the fragmenting of time and into soul groupings; to experience within the game of getting trapped. It becomes ruled and by the very program, it originally created; before falling into its deep sleep. Worshiping the "Ego Mind" and giving in to disconnect, from its higher self; the pinching off effect.   Why is it so important to suffer ?
No longer does the self require to commit for any suicide and to leave from whatever the program was designed for it.
The very fact of waking up from; or interchangeably into a nightmare, can occur and within the physical body, still in tact. Before the self must had to have given up its body to wake up and now this metaphysical reality; it can happen from this moment on and when it can, at the very least, accept it as a possibility.
Economic growth, is that of self growth and from within; therefore its experience, that it will keep walking and into its very own nature, via its own inner, natural flow, from within.

LESSON~ 141:

"WITH GOOD VIBRATIONS I FEEL THE RELEASE OF DENSE PROGRAMS WITHIN MY THOUGHTS AND AS I REMAIN IN TACT WITH MY PHYSICAL FORMATION I WALK INTO ANOTHER MUCH LIGHTER AWARENESS."

Resonate within the being, of the divine mother and let nature flow abundantly; through the nurturing, of open heart energy and out, creating the economy a new. Watch as all the cities collapse, all around; be not concerned from the echo, of all the shocks and halo effect, theatrical performances. Let them all play out before thee and knowing full well, that it has nothing to do with the self; as it releases momentarily from this, its density.

Feel the inner peace and trust, that comes from this depressed unrest. The upset, will stir amongst the many, to rise up and protest from it, to find abandonment.

From this abandonment, the inner leadership of self sustenance; it will occur and while watching the old world crumble, to its knees. The earth, no longer can quantifiably exchange, to such adjustments; it too, had been held back, considerably and in the hopes of evolution. The deciphering mechanism, for its recreated synthetic and artificial kingdom, in this way; the earth naturally, then became, an elemental. As a result, the elementary consequence, to form the many levels, of this density and from the previous, in this place of schooling. The "Ego" driven world, must then be released; rather than and that of releasing of the self, in order to run away from it. Negatively charged oxygen ions, are virtually and vitally important, to this plan, for its awareness. Face this reality, to enlighten with; rather than, for the previously exiting and to find it, no longer. It cannot exist this reasoning and that it must feel, the need to escape it, and/or run away from anything; because **"THERE IS NO ESCAPE"** !!

LESSON~ 141:

"WITH GOOD VIBRATIONS I FEEL THE RELEASE OF DENSE PROGRAMS WITHIN MY THOUGHTS AND AS I REMAIN IN TACT WITH MY PHYSICAL FORMATION I WALK INTO ANOTHER MUCH LIGHTER AWARENESS."

Through the breath, the self can become much more healthier and stronger, in its power. Rather it must stand up and rise above the density. When there are extra electrons, attached to oxygen molecules; conversely it becomes negatively charged(nucleus attraction from the cell). Perhaps it can be discussed and somewhere in the later, of these lessons yet to come; however to get the gist of it, is in this breathing in, of negatively charged oxygen ions; it creates for better cognitive reasoning skills and less likely for the self, to be controllable, on a massive scale through the mind.
The sea shore and its prevailing winds, can also be of help to circulate and with what can be described as "Good Vibrations". Remember the idea for the day and go over the rehearsal; for its activation to take place and as the intention, is to be held on the focus of these words:

"WITH GOOD VIBRATIONS I FEEL THE RELEASE OF DENSE PROGRAMS WITHIN MY THOUGHTS AND AS I REMAIN IN TACT WITH MY PHYSICAL FORMATION I WALK INTO ANOTHER MUCH LIGHTER AWARENESS."

The purpose of this lesson, is to startle, shake and move the concept; like the plates beneath the earth, expanding and from the cracks, a new growth, that can be abundantly nurturing for all, as one and one for all.

(Day 163) When the soul can overcome, its many incarnations and (energetically), by clearing them, it can ascend as master.

The feeling of these wings, within the process of descending and ascending; is only but a tugging at its heels, with resurrection and incarnation. Once the level of such mastery, the choice to stay within this planetary schooling of density and/or to travel in other cycles of awareness, can be easily made possible.

LESSON~ 142:

"FIND THE TRUTH BEHIND DECEPTION AND GRASP THE UNFATHOMABLE RECYCLING FROM THE SOUL WITHIN THIS CONSCIOUSNESS."

There are so many facets, to awareness and that can extend, beyond this level of existence; however for the purpose of this book, the focus, is on clearing into a heaven on earth awareness.

The enlightenment and while still maintaining some level of density, in connection to this system, that is earth.

With reflex action, to combine and organize into this thing called mindfulness; how many slivers of the self, have split off and into the many of its world, from within the measuring of time?

Years of many incarnations, had formed the first nerve cell and from it, these things, called neurons. Held within the soul, from so long ago and to impress upon, its awareness. Developing the reflex of its being and from this organ, to the next; its being creating time through movement…It was when the mind became inventive, for the purpose to control and with it, recreating its very nature of evolving. From building blocks, a system created that would better to reflect for its condition. Synthetic artifacts, to stimulate with and with artificial intellect; forcing an evolution to revolve around it. Forcing nature, into change and adaptation, from synthetic modifying methods; created disconnect, to revolve the evolution of its species and well before its ripening. All creatures of the earth, became its captive; to this way of unnatural distortion and to control the Earth's very essence with.

LESSON~ 142:
"FIND THE TRUTH BEHIND DECEPTION AND GRASP THE UNFATHOMABLE RECYCLING FROM THE SOUL WITHIN THIS CONSCIOUSNESS."

Taking all of nature and forcing it to bloom before its moment; rather than to appreciate the giving of these gifts to it.

The corrupted world, it faces, is this backlash, of having to resolve, by facing it; within resistance and conflict, a very crucial pivot to enlightenment. Having to possess, rather than just be; is where, the "Ego Mind" has conquered and for this primitive survival space; to take up in its purpose, the concept of this "gaining time".

The non-nurturing circumstance of external separation, will train into the mind sufficiency and in this way, is how the "Ego Mind" can manage. How to save for more time, becomes its level of energetic currency and passes down this information, on a cellular level; then, only to exchange again and procreate, in the survival of its immortality. Information, is this light and how to use it, is its knowledge; it is all around, externally and internally.

Memory can be illusive and travels fast within the ethers, before it manifests into as real; the illusion, is the stickiness and can be caught, in mid air, before it forms. These chinks in the armour and from the nooks, are like the cracks; when they reveal some light into the knowing of its thoughts, to be believable and for all, they are worth, in buying it, more time.

What happens, when this linear perspective ascends; or descends into a curvature position? The game, is over and the buying power that it thought it once had; will generate its review, from the many cycles before it. Again, another incarnation, of having to go back into and through this light; perhaps travel to the places and where it thought, it could bypass from before?

LESSON~ 142:
"FIND THE TRUTH BEHIND DECEPTION AND GRASP THE UNFATHOMABLE RECYCLING FROM THE SOUL WITHIN THIS CONSCIOUSNESS."

From this awareness, all the unresolved emotions will have reached it and in a way; where it might have to and once again start over, in the very same game, it had left off. Metaphysically for its experience, to witness that the body can still remain the same and from this possibility, of not having to recycle; rather it resurrects into a way of life and that it can, in exchange of having to survive, to just thrive?

Only after reaching a certain level, can the glass break and transcendence can occur, from such expansion. The self must learn to focus into a frequency, of least resistance; from that level of vibration and to continue on its baby steps, into the heaven that awaits, for it to open up to it. From this planetary vibration, the light will reveal, the loving and nurturing connection.

To enjoy the many senses and habit forming nature; this experience of solid forming density, can clear enough and bring about the "Haven", it was always seeking for. Intended in this space and on this earth, to provide and within the making of it; glancing over, at every crack the light will shine, to penetrate right through and reveal what has occurred. From every aspect of appreciation and that combines to unify the self, in its atonement, is this moment to enlighten, as <u>sovereign</u> and authentic; to greet it from and with the kingdom, of its world. Rather, than be on the take; prepare in the accepting of the readiness; to receive it and this way, all will open, including the self. This is the adventure of appreciation, give gratitude and do not take for granted this lesson.

The purpose of it all, is to grasp the value, in connection and dissolve the other, of control. Everything will unfold, in perfect moment to the next; so learn to savour it, rather than to force, for any outcome and before it is ready to commence.

(Day 164) In the previous lesson there was a level of discernment; that the self could with it, feel between natural development of evolution and that of invented, by the mind.
Control and/or interconnectedness, is this choice and to what extent or level it may decide, to learn from this experience.

LESSON~ 143: "I WILL LIVE EACH DAY WITH THE FEELING OF GREAT FULFILMENT FROM IT."

The importance of contrast, is to learn from it and not to grow attached in the adaptive nature, of such experience.
To be less opinionated and weighted down, by the judgment it may hold and with such serious dependency, of its survival over the self.
Today become the writer of this book and form a lesson.
Decide what opinions can create an idea with; from this to start the day with such conclusion and to commit from a change.
How will the metamorphosis become, for manifesting and the clearing to transmute it; in such a way, as to change the very perspective of(whatever it is holding onto). Create an affirmation, then decide to channel for the many aspects and probabilities it will bring forth, to answer. Remember the previous lessons and do not force for any answers; rather stay in tune, observing mode and hold the level of grounding, to establish as much interconnection with external resonance, as possible. The lesson of the first idea can be handy to repeat in finishing and/or perhaps; the following example, can become the idea and to channel on for the day, the following:
"MY HEART MUST WEIGH AS LIGHT AS A FEATHER TO ENTER INTO HEAVEN."
And then close off with the main idea to be added with whatever other feels concerning:
"I WILL LIVE EACH DAY WITH THE FEELING OF GREAT FULFILMENT FROM IT."

LESSON~ 143: "I WILL LIVE EACH DAY WITH THE FEELING OF GREAT FULFILMENT FROM IT."

From this following idea: at what level, is the world and its awareness, taken to heart? The Serious frequency, creates for much judgment perhaps; feels very tense and stressful, to maintain.. Explore this level of accumulation, that feels to be heavy, in the heart.... Expand with every recognizable attachment and exercise the practice of relief, from it and by learning how to lighten up. The lighter the heart can feel, from such burdens; the more open it can experience, the revelations from the light, that fills it. How does this light feel to the self and how is the self vibrating, to accept this level of its frequency? What are these things that reveal externally, that it is attracting; or attracted to and that might be weighing on it ?
What are some of the emotions, that are surfacing to clear away and integrate into the light? Are the attractions and to what extent, are they feeling light and/or heavy?
Look at all the circumstances that are unfolding; to reflect through out the day and in this way. Change the magnetism, by changing the platform and that supports it energetically. Equally throughout the lessons, it has been shown; how the external can be managed, through connection and/or control. Discern at the level of comfort and that perhaps: a salt rock, or crystal; and/or smudging can help with, to assist and temporarily relieve. Ultimately the energetic shifting, is found within the mastery of the self, connecting to its master, that is the self.

LESSON~ 143: "I WILL LIVE EACH DAY WITH THE FEELING OF GREAT FULFILMENT FROM IT."

When the mind is still, the heart will open and all other alchemical interactions, will come about naturally. The expansion can only happen, from the level of grounded stillness, peacefulness and from within, it can explore, to recognize. The more expanded and grounded, the less overwhelm, from the environment and the more vastness, to externally experience. The perspectives, they can shift from looking down, for example …..to looking up …to looking straight ahead …..to looking up close …to looking at, from far away….accordingly and on the level of the platform, it will choose to stand on and/or soar from.

Today, make up an idea and see how far it can be reached; to stretch as well, as to contract and in the focus of awareness. Throughout the day, keep journaling in, some more of this idea; that comes to add to it, with answers and for anything else, that is wishing to uncover. Write everything down, that can reveal and yet another level of transparency, to expand on.

At the end of the day, all that has been exposed and made noted, was a channeling process. What happened ? Formulate the lesson, throughout the day and through the night; then onto the next day, more revelations might have occurred.

Perhaps even, in the restful stages and from such lucid dreams, the answers would have been explored; and from the many probabilities to answer more, the purpose for this lesson.

The bigger picture was and is, in learning the process of this thing called channeling.

(Day 165) The world holds nothing for the self, when its mind has disconnected it and from its heart. The only relevance that this container must exhibit, is artificially and from its cyborg mind creation. Those thoughts, that are not of the self and belong to the "Ego Mind", will not feel good. It is these thoughts, made by a higher collective agreement and that the self can only, but revisit(into a formality, which it cannot move from);outgrown from the dried up, outer world and not knowing, how to change it.

LESSON~ 144: "THE WAY I SEE THE WORLD CONTRIBUTES ALTRUISTICALLY TO ITS PERSPECTIVE AND ON THE IMPRINTING OF ALL THAT IS CREATION."

In the previous lesson, the learning of co-creating and with the many other aspects of the self; to aspire and in the practice of keeping down a journal. When something has outgrown from its purpose, once given to it; the self no longer is served by it. What the self perceives from its world, is but a mere byproduct of its past and not to be compared for any real value, within the present, here and now moment. Does it merge and be as one with the machine; and/or act as its maker, to be respected in a way that takes up ownership and values for its heart wide open? How the feeling goes, with self worth and becomes its condition; the future, is its perception and in the now, where it stands, already created. Without the heart, it can become a cyborg and thus the importance, of opening the heart; rather than to close it and shut it down completely. This book, cannot stress enough, the importance of awareness, through the heart and is, at the basis; from where it must begin, the process toward enlightenment. Awareness, is this process and that the self with every step forward, is revealed to the next and the next and the next.

LESSON~ 144: "THE WAY I SEE THE WORLD CONTRIBUTES ALTRUISTICALLY TO ITS PERSPECTIVE AND ON THE IMPRINTING OF ALL THAT IS CREATION."

The body and its world, is not to be the inhibitor; rather the catalyst for inspiration and in the perception, of an adventurous life. Something within the mind, to compare the off and/or on balance and moderation; to a healthy life style and for these applications, made custom, to fitting on, for its container well, or for the self within it. These distortions, that hold the worth of self esteem and "Ego- mind"; strive to gain over the feeling perspective and with its appearances to constituting, over the well being.

To move in the direction of stress, is the rife of holding onto great resistance and that to undesirable circumstances; held in by force, and to be present, willingly in them. Promoting this exchange of energy, for material gain, is simply draining of resources and not really surviving nor thriving; rather becoming a consumable to decay, aging and death. Worth cannot be found within a parasitic delayed moment, of uncertainty and doubt, to cherish from its left overs. The self made prison world, has cast the minds of the many through; to believing how stuck the self is and with its condition, that no longer serves it. The idea for the day, is to see how high the self can rise from this perception; of feeling stuck from a world it co-created. Allow to feel the relief, of home and the soothing interest, of its welcoming.

LESSON~ 144:
"THE WAY I SEE THE WORLD CONTRIBUTES ALTRUISTICALLY TO ITS PERSPECTIVE AND ON THE IMPRINTING OF ALL THAT IS CREATION."

Feel grateful, to gravitationally be pulled out of the misery and drawn into a background, that is most preferred to manifest. Does it know where it belongs, surely yes; because now it is made to feel better and from where it did not know before, to feel at least, this much. Throughout the day and when confronted with a conflict, exercise the learning of these levels; by setting up some boundaries and to remember, the value of importance for this idea. Rest within these boundaries respectively, for "Love, Here and Now", to be restored; from all the mindless chatter and the freedom, to feel. Staying open, through the love generating perspective, can become a new way at business; rather than the Ego, self driven mind, format and that ruled over its other (dried up)world. Further exercise the setting up of boundaries and where it can be found a place; Before ending/starting the day and maybe during lunch break, to calm the breath; with eyes closed slow it down, to find the center of peace, from within. Then with eyes open, look at everything; as to be as praiseworthy and made from self value.

LESSON~ 144:
"THE WAY I SEE THE WORLD CONTRIBUTES ALTRUISTICALLY TO ITS PERSPECTIVE AND ON THE IMPRINTING OF ALL THAT IS CREATION."

The world, is now where it belongs and the self belongs in it; just as much, as its release and from the previous one, it flew away from. By feeling in the presence, of the now moment and rest in the knowing that bests serves, self value, to its world. Be still to this peace of mind; open to the once held in place perspective, of the many chains and its conditions; now to be opportunities, to grow and flourish with. Repeat the following and with most certainty:

"THE TEMPTATIONS ARE BUT OF MY OWN CREATIONS TO LEARN FROM AND ALLOW MY SOUL TO GROW."

"THE WAY I SEE THE WORLD CONTRIBUTES ALTRUISTICALLY TO ITS PERSPECTIVE AND ON THE IMPRINTING OF ALL THAT IS CREATION."

The purpose, is to be responsible and claim ownership of itself; as well as having its part in these (A.I. agreed upon) creations; and most importantly, to function through the heart vibration, that is "Love, Here, and Now" !

(Day 166)

Thoughts do not stay for very long, as the experience from feelings and thus the reasoning for writing down, as often as they appear and to be intense enough to make note of. Beliefs must align, with feeling and the thought must be at its apex of wellbeing, to believe it so. Holding onto the ruling echoes, from old thoughts that do not feel right; create chronic uneasy states of being. Within the moment, is all there is, in constant flux and thus, for its "economy".

LESSON~ 145: "AS THE OBSERVER I RELEASE ALL MISCONCEPTIONS OF MY WORLD".

"Working to Live" rather than "Living to Work"; is still a misconception, from the "Ego mind". Thriving, therefore does not vibe in resonance, to strain itself and this creative effort, that sustains it, in the maintenance of survival mode.
Could it be, that all has unfolded and like a replay from before, to resemble in these thoughts; they just might be passing through? How is this circumstance, unlike before and that the self has changed enough, to see it play out slightly different ?
To see the world in discomfort, in pain and lacking of everything; is to not see it at all. The misconception, is such, that the self will take on to believing, for itself and what it thinks it is seeing(simulated and in relation from its own experience).
What once was, in the moment and in the very next different; it is in these subtleties, that hope can resurrect and in all the worst of situation. Within the present, is the only way to make any difference and this means, letting go of any preconceived notions. The future does not require the past to formulate, nor does the past rely on the future to save it; rather the present, is the only truth to show for, in the moment, in itself.

LESSON~ 145: "AS THE OBSERVER I RELEASE ALL MISCONCEPTIONS OF MY WORLD".

All the undesirable feelings, that have the world enslaved, are largely from the way the self perception leads the way. Never pity, nor feel sorry for the world; rather see it in the way, of all its glory.

The mind, is what gives the meaning and (from previous experiences) combined with outside circumstances, to how it wishes to formulate. Today, practice the realization of this, and become empowered from the claiming of it (own it with feeling). When the mind changes, so does its world and pride only dulls the brilliance of praise, from its truth. The level of acceptance, to heal and to be able to recognize; rests in this lesson and for the many, who can grasp it. Find the world and not be of it, as sudden as the climax of death brings, when coming back to teach it; that it does not exist, nor does that paradox for its experience and not from this world can make transparent.

It was the thoughts from source that created the self into being; this awareness, set it free and made it feel separate; from the world, that it has created and to reflect in the very same way.

From this perspective, master and teacher, are one in the same and in this dance together, the music plays on. The real creations await in the melody, to aspire from the divine essence to core expression; feel within the frequency and play with the reflections.

Release the shadows, of a dying world and that idle thoughts created. The home that nature has set out and along with the universe, that gifts it, everything it wishes for; is where the mind must learn to trust and perfectly surrender, to the oneness of this love.

LESSON~ 145: "AS THE OBSERVER I RELEASE ALL MISCONCEPTIONS OF MY WORLD."

Invest a moment (morning and evening), to focus on the following intention, that can liberate and free it, from self made illusions:

"ONLY IN THE PRESENT MOMENT DO I HAVE THE CHOICE OVER MY REALITY AND TO BE OBSERVED FROM A PLACE OF LOVE."

By remaining consciously aware, within the stillness and with very little effort, release the mind into silence. When the mind releases from its world, it too is released, for the healing to take place. The relief will be felt and it is not for it to be made any sense over just yet. Throughout the day, repeat as often the following:

"WITH EVERY DECISION I CREATE A SHIFT IN MY AWARENESS."

"AS THE OBSERVER I RELEASE ALL MISCONCEPTIONS OF MY WORLD."

The purpose, is to let the past be lifted and release the future from its worries.

Grasp the level of responsibility and where the importance lives, in here and in the now.

(Day 167)

What is set into standard, fades away, from the senses and does not invigorate, nor satisfy. The awareness must shift again, to become aware, of its unaware parts and they too, can become whole again, with awareness. The bringing forth of spherical realities; whispering as thoughts and from natures elemental given forces, set in motion; witness the attraction to conduct, the sound that maybe it can sense to hear, the ancient melody and the symphony of stars vibrating as a choir in a song.

LESSON~ 146:
"I AM A RAY OF LIGHT THAT LIVES ON FOREVER WITHIN THE SOURCE OF ALL THAT IS CONSCIOUSNESS."

This entity that came in as a multitude, can only be authentically made useful and when greeted from the heart, to find itself and remember. Memory does not define for anything, nor its actions; rather it is through the feeling of it. Notice how the energetic self can gravitate, within the physical encasement and motionless to find itself, then in motion?
Today, is all in the practice of becoming the cause; rather than become affected by it. It has been discussed before, how the Soul will bring about, the many opportunities; to show itself via external perception. Recognize and give it worth, for its companionship. Grasp the cosmos and everything in it; all the many aspects of its celestial travels, compounded and that will come to expressively join in, creatively, of its own design. Feel within the earthly and terrestrial daily process, the shifting of perspectives in this way; perhaps the subtle nature of unfathomable encounters too, can be in with the idea of this exercise.

LESSON~ 146:
"I AM A RAY OF LIGHT THAT LIVES ON FOREVER WITHIN THE SOURCE OF ALL THAT IS CONSCIOUSNESS."

Take some intermittent moments and repeat the following words(backing statement):
"HOME IS WHERE THE HEART IS."

And then repeat todays idea:

"I AM A RAY OF LIGHT THAT LIVES ON FOREVER WITHIN THE SOURCE OF ALL THAT IS CONSCIOUSNESS."

In accepting all of consciousness, the brain cannot; because it operates, from a third dimensional construct. Only through the heart, can this interface of decoding frequency signals occur. All artificial intelligence, can merge and be as one with brain; because they both are attracted, to the familiar and that of sequence and order. The day of separation, from the heart and all other intelligence, will come to merge their consciousness as one. The choice will always be "Enlightenment" through the "Heart" and/or "Artificial Intelligent creations"(from its "Ego Mind"). This book welcomes all entities, of such creations; organic and inorganic, to share the information with. Underneath all this information and of such memory; the truth will come "Sovereign", in this "Light" of being and to reveal its authenticity.

The purpose, is to feel and strengthen the faith, in the self; for all that it prefers, will define it, in this way and from how it feels.

(Day 168) What does it mean, to release all grievances from the mind, that has collected and to gift the self with evolution? Learn from the many, that which the self alone could not give. Surrender to find the usefulness, in this potential and in the becoming; the version of enhancement, from that which once was.

LESSON~ 147:

"I GIVE FOR THE LETTING GO OF IT_THAT I MAY SEE IT IN THE WORLD_REFLECTED FROM THE MANY THAT ARE ME."

It is not a competition, nor a reprimand, to find the many taking over, the function of the self. It is through the release, that the self can continue to go onto the becoming, of more and until it too, can find its place, amongst the many. This however, will never come to be, for the dog; that chases its leash around a tree. Notice from its deception, how it barks over and in the thinking, that the tree, is its master? Could it be, that the tree, is in another world and the dog cannot be of that world; however both, can be in amongst each other and for the pleasure of the experience. The dog has not quite yet realized, that it is, its own master; where as the tree for itself has. The observer and the observed, are for this purpose and that the many of its world, can play amongst; however from separate worlds and that, each can be a backdrop, for the other. This is why, forgiveness must be granted and in the exchange for reverence, to all that is in observation, from the self. The leash was the sacrifice of freedom, the dog had made, for its reactionary behaviour and until it could become aware of its choices, to respond appropriately with the tree. The tree, has a lot the dog can learn; to hear it from within the ground, communicate to the rest of the forest. Whilst sniffing on a mushroom and in between the plush fresh blades of grass, as it now rests, underneath the tree. The dog has no thoughts and in the moment grounded peacefully, from nature's moist embrace; it does not recognize, ever having to answer to its master.

LESSON~ 147:
"I GIVE FOR THE LETTING GO OF IT_THAT I MAY SEE IT IN THE WORLD_REFLECTED FROM THE MANY THAT ARE ME."

It knows, no such thing and has become a "Sovereign" entity on to itself; as Creator and in it, of its own image. The lesson of this story: is to learn the same, from its fluffy friend, is one in the same and with all walks of life. To walk amongst the many and to only be the way shower; holding for and of this kind of reverence. The tree cannot become the dog; no more than the self, can be the many and yet they are all one, able to function as the self. The values are differently viable amongst their own kind. What they teach and learn from the self to take and apply within their own worlds; are not to be taken for the same deception, as that of competition and that which conspires to exist from it. The world of the many and to the one that of self have all been in the making of with innocent all meaning well and good intentions. The mind is twisted and creates many deceptions however real as the very miracles it cannot deny. Love too, has been blown apart to see how it can be brought back to origin of authenticity and to be well deserved by all. Give for all things their way to show up for the self and it can find better Through forgiveness. Nothing is corrupt and all can have exposure to it; when they are convinced and of no other, in the way of benefit, to come out of. Do not beg for any pardons, as they may not be untethered and for the ungraspable hand, that released the dog in the first place; to gather itself, under a tree and find a home, with nature. The dog cannot possibly miss its pack, when it has never known them, to be there and as death might bring a new now; it has entered bravely into a world, without a master. The pardon, is in its strength, to go on, amongst the flora and fauna; knowing that it will never be alone again.

LESSON~ 147:
"I GIVE FOR THE LETTING GO OF IT_THAT I MAY SEE IT IN THE WORLD_REFLECTED FROM THE MANY THAT ARE ME."

The kingdom of heaven, is for all to reconcile with as best they can and to make it out, that it is. The dream, is in the awakened state now and within the body; to feel the wonders of its surroundings. The dragon at the gate, will greet the dog and they too, will rest together, under the apple tree. The dragon has so many stories; as one importantly marking of its belly ache, when eating from the apple tree. The tree had been forgiven and spared its life, from the fires of the dragon's belly ache. Further down the rainbow bridge, its beloved, that held its leash, will want to now remove it, from its neck. Letting go, into the all that is, the self and deeper in the kingdom, dog and dragon fearlessly rest; the self can open up, to the enlightenment and see it now, in the state of ascended mastery. Thoughts are now irrelevant and to the laws that the self once followed, to cooperate with its many reflections. In the game, that not even its life was to could depend on and understand to play in. The guide was the ever changing reality; that shunned its every step forward. To its demise, another fall down the rabbit hole; to find the dream, better than its reality and before it had awakened, the dream itself. The practice for today, becomes the light bearing presence; that is the self, to lead the way for the many. Before taking on the day; find a moment, for about fifteen minutes and understand what it means, to surrender in perfect trust, to all that is.

Look to the membrane of the outer existence; that is beyond the dream, where the many reflect through it and that ripples out with forgiveness. Also, during a moment in the afternoon, or any other; to practice and by repeating this again:
"I GIVE FOR THE LETTING GO OF IT_THAT I MAY SEE IT IN THE WORLD_REFLECTED FROM THE MANY THAT ARE ME."

LESSON~ 147:
"I GIVE FOR THE LETTING GO OF IT_THAT I MAY SEE IT IN THE WORLD_REFLECTED FROM THE MANY THAT ARE ME."

It has taken some time, to catalogue the dream and before it had awakened; to find the many grievances and that the self had, with the many of its world. How much the dog worked, to effort over pleasing, its master; so it may find the feeling through its "<u>doing-ness</u>"? Practice throughout the day, living from the inner and outer awareness and without the membrane of separation.
A world where all things are made possible, to combine as one. Allow the mind to see through the perception, to distort and or corrupt into an agenda; of controlled illusions and just let things be, by repeating the following :

"I WILL NOW REMOVE THE LEASH AND YET NO ONE CAN ENTER ALONE INTO HEAVEN_BECAUSE THEY WERE NEVER ALONE TO BEGIN WITH."

In everything today remember this:

"I GIVE FOR THE LETTING GO OF IT_THAT I MAY SEE IT IN THE WORLD_REFLECTED FROM THE MANY THAT ARE ME."

From the shifting of perspectives and that these parables do bring forth, to ponder on awareness; look at this purpose to awaken and to allow for the dream to become awakened.
In this way, the membrane that separates, can dissolve the reflection; that once required and from the rippling out, a reason to find forgiveness.

Take 2 days to take it in

CONGRATULATIONS ...!!!

FOR MAKING IT THROUGH THE 147th Lesson

(This is a rest period to take the lessons independently as a review)

TAKE THESE TWO DAYS TO RECALIBRATE;

MAKE NOTES AND REVIEW..................

(Day 171)
Before its activation and (thymus and kidneys) with the higher mind function, of the observer watching and aware. Unresolved soul traumas must be dealt with and thus, the intention to work through, this basic level; the 4th layer of the body's heart chakra system and divine energetic, soul imprints.

LESSON~ 148: "THE LIGHT THAT IS VISIBLE TO ME IS NOT ALL THERE IS."

Releasing and resolving for much resistance, is highly important, prior to any activation and that of integration, that can be achieved for life its force/living, light current; because when it comes on line, whatever structure does not resonate, will short circuit. From the 12 systems of the physical body, especially on a cellular level (after they ignite); the other cells, that will not wake up, will be attacked (it will start turning on them) and possibly destroy the very containment, of its physical form, upon impact and to the very distortions, that remain within it. Some realities are pitch black and these fields within a velvety darkness, can become unified within awareness. These chakras, are within the dreaming state and not visible; unless a practice is in place to help make for seeing them. These fields and because the practice hasn't been made visible; within these many realities, they appear to go on forever and when in observation of them. In previous, only the white light had been mentioned and this is the ultimate accomplishment; however the self must learn and from within its as well, by dissolving the separations (between soul dream time world and waking state physical solid awareness) first. Similar to the focus of the dark void, the ethereal body of the self, is translucent and before the physical can be affected; it must go through many layers, to reach its destined occlusion.

LESSON~ 148: "THE LIGHT THAT IS VISIBLE TO ME IS NOT ALL THERE IS."

Pain, is mostly from a neurological receptor and given signal; that comes and goes, however never constantly staying. The body can sense for pain, better when it aches, through an intermittent process. When consistent, the body can self harmonize, to bring balance; however in the case of disease, or chronic pain and where the only way it can be not in harmony, these signals, are to be paid attention to. By going in deep, into the darkness and where the void can be found; this time, focus in, on the infected/affected area when possible. This is done, on a cellular level, going deep into its misty darkness and in the middle; where the body's brow be focused, from within and eyes closed.

As it were, in like a movie theatre; where it is pitch black, to turn the projector on. Begin to visualize there, right in the center of the forehead; what black light can look like and within the cell. Go deep enough to feel its buoyant, fluid warmth; that will rejuvenate within its elevated field and will surround the self in it. Before the practice was, to go directly, to find the white light and this too, was similar and perhaps made easier, to bypass it all together, to find the white. It is through the darkness of this fluid light, to feel the change and shift perceptions. See the darkness, as a mist and whatever ailments that can be washed away, in this fluid light. From within the cell, the stream flows out and circulates throughout the body; washing outward and over the entirety of the self(being bathed and floating in this dark velvety shimmering fluid light). In the morning, take roughly twenty minutes, for this meditation and in the evening, do it again; with all the pressing issues, that were cause for much uneasiness. This can be done standing/sitting and or lying down; however the act of bathing, is similar to feeling and for the same, as washing with the white light principle.

LESSON~ 148: "THE LIGHT THAT IS VISIBLE TO ME IS NOT ALL THERE IS."

Dark light, can bring on divination and for manifesting tangibly; as well as, clearing and cleansing, over the stresses of the day. Soothing to the senses, and toward the resistances, of outer circumstances; that it can then, to better be observing in this way. The most annoying thing, can become insignificant and in the vastness of self perception, through timelessness.
Do not fear what can only be properly understood as dreams by the senses; where love resides and the body seems to be more solid than the mind. Where healing can be shared and re-connective with the world of the self and to the many from the one. During the day and for the shorter moments; feel the oneness and be repeated following:

"THE LIGHT THAT IS VISIBLE TO ME
   IS NOT ALL THERE IS."

"IN THIS FEELING I SEE THE WORLD_WHO IS MY ONLY SELF_BANISHED FROM ITS SICKNESS."
In oneness, focus on the sight of pain; what is this part of the body that feels to be excluded? Feel its system, what it means and the value that it has to its function, as the being of the self. Follow it down from the cell, to the nucleus; let it feed the information directly and intuitively to the self. As a gut feeling, it can communicate, to hear it on a cellular level speak and from the many communities; they that speak systemically, as this Inner Voice. From the nervous system, to the muscular and the skeletal; from the twelve and to the many releases, of the endocrine, such is the beauty of the self.

LESSON~ 148: "THE LIGHT THAT IS VISIBLE TO ME IS NOT ALL THERE IS."

With the shorter practices, project out to the world and to the self, from its white light now, to heal with. Where once there was a duty, to attack and now in its place, the beauty to be in awe; of this kingdom and that is the self, gracefully unfolding, on its journey. The adventure and onto making well, all that are in its prayers, accepting of these blessings; repeat the following affirmations:

"I SEE MY PAIN AND FEEL IT IN THE MANY OF THE WORLD_THAT I MAY HEAL MYSELF IN THEM THE SAME."

When the heart is healed, a certain kind of fire will ignited inside it; this can be also accessed, in the kidneys. It has been discussed previously in lessons 111 and perhaps else where; about the importance of the 8th chakra. The Higher self, starts to connect to its physical container; at the thymus level and starts adjusting the heart pattern. It causes change in hormones, endocrine, biorhythms as well as in the blood. (Excessive heat will create a release of a certain kind of oil and where the skull and spine do meet to trickle down the back of the throat). When consciousness can connect well(Inner-net) with the nervous system, of its physical body; the enlightenment of this experience, can start to come on line. From the level of discernment and in the taking of responsibility; the self can bring on its authenticity, that dwells within. From which this book, is aiming to explore, for the building of intent, decisive consent and from a place of autonomous authority.

The purpose, is to go deeper into the alchemical morphing, of these fields and from some previous lessons; further to explore and perhaps, some more again, for these ideas.

(Day 172)
Free and embody the spiritual and then notice and as a multi dimensional being, within linear time; it cannot possibly contain enough hours, within(the 24 hour cycle of a day)this set structure and to make up for, as it once had before.

LESSON~ 149: "I AM MULTI DIMENSIONAL AWARENESS HAVING CHOICE WITHIN A MULTIVERSE."

From the previous idea, of the spherical and external fields(chakras 4,5,6&7), that are completely, pitch black;by uniting them into the "One plasmic field". Within this "monad"(Over-Soul) membrane, as reflecting back from soul and within the lower 4 chakras(again starting from the heart); these fields, are that of white visible light(that can be seen). From the 8th field, is the cross connection and that when the self can properly activate; without external and synthetic stimulation. The entwined soul, with an electro magnetic charge and with the life force, shoots up the spine, to open up, the pineal gland; from there, it will create and yet another cross connection, from its (3rd eye inner vision) center. In simple terms, a centered connection with the nervous system and consciousness; mindful, focused and with intent. The self in this way, will continue to keep grounded, with its inner stillness and that of peaceful natures, internal soothing flame; this can be for it, the process to enlightenment and the accessed multidimensional experience. With every moistened breath; just think about the illusion, of being, where boredom once had reigned, over the doing and from having to feel, the separation, in its lethal state. Cry and release it, in all the ways that now make up, for never having it this good before and perhaps in this way, it can be proven lighter and more playful, to the heart; its symptoms as circumstance, is getting better, appreciate this moment and continue on. The only thing that has not changed in practice, is the learning how to stay connected, to the earth and for the purpose of grounding in this Oneness.

LESSON~ 149:
"I AM MULTI DIMENSIONAL AWARENESS HAVING CHOICE WITHIN A MULTIVERSE."

Feel the ease, in the doing and when it is more dependant, on the being grounded and in this way, practice to focus on this day.

The separation, into duality and this disconnect, from the earth; it can scatter and throw off, from its place of center and stillness, within the mind, that thinks it knows best. The tree analogy previously mentioned, is a great example and to be made as a grounding tool; with its roots, to the earth metaphor and to imagine the self, in this way.

The outside world, is a multiverse and from these possibilities, all at once; in combination, from these many worlds and can all at once, be playing out, as in the background. When the sound of many songs, are playing all at once and in harmony, blending fluidly the self must be still. To still the mind and open the heart, is what has been the practice. Now the self has parallel realities, it must choose to focus on and where it wishes; to pay attention and at any given moment be present in. It can go all day, without eating and sometimes might forget to even sleep.

Take frequent breaks throughout the day, to check in, by way of feeling and recalibrate on the intentions, that were set out, for the day; the night before and/or before the start of this day, in the morning. This is what will be the exercise and before starting the day; to focus on what the self, must accomplish and set the intention.

LESSON~ 149:
"I AM MULTI DIMENSIONAL AWARENESS HAVING CHOICE WITHIN A MULTIVERSE."

With eyes closed, visualize and from the soles of the feet; while standing, sprouting out and growing these roots, down into the earth. All the way down, to feel and as far, as can be imagined, to penetrate the core of the earth. Feel with every breath, divine energy flow and from the earth, coming up from its roots; to the soles of its feet and shooting upward, all the way to the head and then back down. With every breath, release all that is unwanted tension or uneasiness; to go back down and out, from the soles of the feet, to the earth again.

While so many things have been accomplished, rest in this knowing, of all that is stable, strong and secure; feel it from within and from all life's interactions. During the day and when feeling overwhelmed; stop in this way and recalibrate, by remembering how this moment feels. Then bring it back to the experience and from when it was a (Oak) tree. For every moment, some task is completed and as this expression formulates again; stop for maybe a few moments and acknowledge it. Feel the praise, feel appreciation, feel gratitude and feel the trust, in the all, is well. Feel the graceful unfolding of the day, take it all in and then replenish it, into the projected surroundings.

(Day 173)
Release for every tension in the body; redefine it in the mind and through the heart, accept the embodiment of a higher frequency(resonance & synchronistic unfolding).

LESSON~ 150:
"I RELEASE MYSELF FROM THE STORIES OF THE PAST
TO REDEFINE INTO THIS MOMENT
FROM THE ONENESS OF ALL MOMENTS."

The self, is not about the mind's identity; rather it is defined by how it feels in every given moment, of its life and with no explanation needed. The stories keep it in a place of reference to rely from the many that deny it and in a place where growth ceases.
The stalemated experiences that the ego feeds on the self through its identity, has no real place of power.
Secured in the all knowing predictions of certainty is yet another form to control the conditions out of its adventure.
There is another way to play and without the game's collective agreements. How does self come out of its reflection by being the observer ?
By daring to break out of its shell of rigid beliefs that impressed upon it from the higher collective into its personal space?
How is this possible that it can see for more than one reality in the same, to choose through how it feels to attract anything it can imagine.
This is made yet for another topic that it is possible to leave one reality for another. Changing the perception; however to stay open from the form that traps the many in collectively in such agreements to enslave. This is the enlightenment that the oneness aspires to ascend and as sovereign in itself; individuated into the evolved "<u>pristineness</u>" that is, creator self.

LESSON~ 150:
"I RELEASE MYSELF FROM THE STORIES OF THE PAST TO REDEFINE INTO THIS MOMENT FROM THE ONENESS OF ALL MOMENTS."

The oneness in this way is now complete unto itself to feel inspired by the many rather than reflect of them.

To realize that reflection is a deflection needing for integration from its shadows and soul growth; is where the paradox can start to be more meaningful. To see the world from every side and have for non attachment to its many stories. Staying open in this way to have many movies playing in the moment; at a "Cineplex" wondering the mind to choose which one to play in for the experience and not become trapped by it.

The conundrum is the at oneness with self to atone and with the many of its world in this way as failsafe to measure with.

The indicator of self expansion to contract into many small versions and for ever more continue to play within the vastness, of the self perspective. By refusing to accept any given moment without fully allowing it to play out; how will the self know what it does prefer ?

The emotional attachment will create a repeat and is best to be in observer mode to learn from. Only acceptance be asked of self for what it is certain when it knows its preferences to define it with. To believe the contradiction is not in the asking of what it must be and rather not to believe in the reinforced programs, infiltrated by the masse's standard quo.

The thoughts of the collective agreement, are not thy self and must be laid aside, in the light; that is holy to atone, into the oneness of all moments.

LESSON~ 150:
"I RELEASE MYSELF FROM THE STORIES OF THE PAST TO REDEFINE INTO THIS MOMENT FROM THE ONENESS OF ALL MOMENTS."

Accept the oneness and the personal truth; that is the self to bask in the "<u>Sovereign Light</u>" and with all that is love, here and now. The experience of being created in the likeness of self awareness can be left for the collective agreement to differ from the personal one to self and thus contradict for the purpose of expansion and self liberation. The agreement to contradict the form into formlessness is the paradox from which the inner and outer world have been split into two. Check with self throughout the day to feel how much separation and why it is this way catch the story and let it go; start with five minutes in the morning and then at night. Repeat the following affirmations:

"I RELEASE MYSELF FROM THE STORIES OF THE PAST TO REDEFINE INTO THIS MOMENT FROM THE ONENESS OF ALL MOMENTS."

"I AM ONE WITH OVERSOUL AND LEARNING FROM THE MULTIVERSE_AS HIGHER SELF_THAT IS ME."

The purpose, is to check in with the self and to catch it; before the fall, that splits off and drains it, into the abyss and from all the stresses of its day.

To have control over the nervous system; it is a deeper connection with impulse, rather than, to think of it, as controlling over its reactions.

(Day 174)

Thoughts of self measuring up to its stresses that in time will be the better of it to press on this its incompletion. Enslaved by its demands, racing to death's finish line and in fear of competition to mock for its very own value to exist. Worshiping identity is the "Ego's plan" and greatest strategy to idolize.

LESSON~ 151:
"INTERDIMENSIONAL STATES
BRING ABOUT HEALING".

"I AM SPARED FROM MY THOUGHTS
TO FEEL AT EASE IN MY WELL BEING."

In peace there is no conflict to find its place and with the agreed upon force convincing of its program to be "God" and as the one and only resolution. To veer away from the consensus program of the ideal external image, is to fall short to the demise of self power individually measured as unlived. Anything other to this deception is a waste? For how can the self be given the chance indiscriminately, when it does not accept in this way to give its power to the "<u>one in the same God</u>" collective.
In both cases undeniably existing is the personal agreement and that of the collective one in the same "Ego driven force".
In this case the collective's agreement is that of the greater good "God driven Force" and the anything other as the "Devil".
To become Empowered and Sovereign is to entrust in the self completely and that there may be a purpose beyond the physical interpretation, that demotes it into sickness and (dissatisfaction)"dis-ease". To eat, drink and pro create, is at the driving force principle and to all that be made of rotting flesh and bone; surviving to consume and be consumed.

LESSON~ 151:
"INTERDIMENSIONAL STATES BRING ABOUT HEALING".

"I AM SPARED FROM MY THOUGHTS
TO FEEL AT EASE IN MY WELL BEING."

Deceptive is the primitive under the apple tree of life, to sweeten over rotting flesh and power hungry of the many and that have enslaved the very self, into a sleeping beauty state.
The aging from the darkened spell, that put to sleep its cause for beauty and made the ugly a duty to promote.
Today the misled of heavy hearted and ill will fathoms down the lineage and ingrained within the bones; to come to the surface once and for all, to bid hail and farewell, from these clutches and in service to. It goes unwarranted to remain in linear states under the world forever trapped in time's perception of the lower realms.
From this moment forth to be spared from the lower mind agenda agreement to serve be gone, obsoleted and to accept to suffer by it no longer. There is no benefit in strife and by oppressing life for momentary gain to please the lower senses.
The power struggle must be released and understood that when self benefits the world too shall benefit. The self, is not limited to its mind's state of affairs; rather it is unconditionally held to its dimensions lightly by the heart to change at a whim and for the mind to come along feeling better than before from its discernments.

LESSON~ 151:
"INTERDIMENSIONAL STATES
BRING ABOUT HEALING".

"I AM SPARED FROM MY THOUGHTS
TO FEEL AT EASE IN MY WELL BEING."

Today take a moment before starting the day and then after in the evening to spare all of the primal thoughts that once have served its urges. How do they feel; do they disgust; annoy; make for feeling nauseous? From what part of the body can it be felt from, the liver; can it be the gall bladder; from the sweat glands as a fever? Is it rage? Let all these realities of many dreams resurface and secrete, let them all go; open eyes and repeat the following affirmation:

"INTERDIMENSIONAL STATES
BRING ABOUT HEALING."

"I AM SPARED FROM MY THOUGHTS
TO FEEL AT EASE IN MY WELL BEING."

The purpose, is to get used to changing perceptions and shifting at will, with ease.

(Day 175)
Arrogant, is the matrix; to have the mind trick the self and of its false light as real. To think that spirituality, is learned from the outside, of the self; in the search for a God as a structure and that will trap it, into a box, to feed off its prana.

LESSON~152:
" I AM WORTHY FOR LOVE
   RESPECT AND APPRECIATION."

To believe, that the innate spark of source and that self is, exists outside of; made separate and to create as something, it must humble itself to, is sabotage. The cutting off from itself, teaches it to fear; to become dependent and grow the need for attachment. This "Gap" creates for much opposition, resistance and will be the cause, for getting in its own way(obstacles). To think that the self is separate, from its source; causes an unstable connection to higher self and the energetic pathways to it, will become stuck.
The need to reconnect; or fear of letting go, will create subconsciously circumstances and for self sabotage.
Blockages can become very painful; because cells can hold memory physically, the brain will release chemicals to shut down functional flow and from that area and/or including consciousness.
Fear will lower the vibration and hamper spiritual growth.
The self must be made aware, that it can align its psychological and mental states to its multidimensional energies from that through the heart where the true light can be found. The language of energy can only be felt through the body from the heart first.

LESSON~152:
" I AM WORTHY FOR LOVE RESPECT AND APPRECIATION."

Today, instead of the mind traps of thought; rather take some time to explore for cellular memory and the sensations of the body. In order to practice by-passing the matrix and to hook directly into creator energy self sabotage must be done away with first. Spend some time encouraging the frightened mind with the following affirmations:

"I AM WORTHY FOR LOVE RESPECT AND APPRECIATION."

"EVERYTHING ALWAYS WORKS OUT FOR ME BECAUSE I AM ENOUGH."

Then with eyes closed feel for any impulses, emotions and visualizations; because it is all about this message felt, that can allow for the flow of the self and that of its universal connection. Manifesting is about becoming who we really are and trusting that in the becoming we will get all that we want. Feel it, then visualize it; the blockages that would stand in the way must be healed first however.

Feel it be it and allow for all that is wished for to come into alignment with self energetic flow. Attachment to the result is about control and will create sabotage; because anything from fear is self doubt and this is destructive.

LESSON~152:
"I AM WORTHY FOR LOVE
 RESPECT AND APPRECIATION."

Fear of what will happen when self does not get what it wants is another to discern with "Ego"; its arrogant creator matrix and its prison bars. The matrix is the world of mirrors and the many that are full of expectations. Self did create this matrix and within it the many of its world to base on this support to believe in self is reflected back. How it will feel and for all its many wants that might contradict with its belief system of feeling good and for how it wishes things to be; that is alright for as long as it wishes to play along.
Today has many facets to explore of self inner and outer perspective in the oneness to perceive with; because when it is removed from its creation the creator is inseparable. Without a matrix there is no aging, no disease, no decay and no death. The separation from inner and outer and for this membrane that self can create a matrix at will and know it can leave one for another as well. In the morning and at night take some time to repeat the following affirmations and throughout the day take five minutes to be reminded of the idea:

"I AM WORTHY FOR LOVE
 RESPECT AND APPRECIATION."

"IT IS MY NATURAL RIGHT TO BE
 SURROUNDED WITH ABUNDANCE."

"I AM VALUABLE AND I DESERVE THE BEST."

The purpose, is to learn that transmuting energy is only made possible through feelings and emotions.

(Day 176)

There will always be an "Echo Effect" when adjusting the alignment; by either grounding and/or just complete to surrender. Grounding brings forth the realization, that the mind must be releasing, from the many aspects, that can reflect and for each vibrational dimension, that the consciousness, can or cannot hold onto.

LESSON~153:
"THE ECHO EFFECT_IS THE RELAPSE
 OF MY PREVIOUS EXISTENCE."

Within the aspect of vibrational harmonic synchronization, the "Ego mind" cannot be resurrected; thus the level of importance to still the mind through grounding.

Some of these effects can converge and others (vibrationally) they cannot; within that (frequency)space of consciousness.

Although it is not the same, as the overall impression from the prejudice and that is found from "The Halo Effect"; however both are stemming to be true within the emotional, rather than the logical affinity. The attachments to likes and dislikes and for every decision the choice was made into such reality.

When all the (dedication)"workship" is dismissed, release it from its worship and another truth awakens; to release the old perspective of the enslaved self. In everyone and everything, the self will be of this creation and all it will be, of its own doing.

All thoughts must be purified and then realized of self worth to worship in this place the body as its temple. The ministry of all ministries is that of self existence and its awareness of pure positive thoughts.

LESSON~153:
"THE ECHO EFFECT_IS THE RELAPSE OF MY PREVIOUS EXISTENCE."

Dedicate a moment in the morning, to come into alignment and with that one thought of worthiness; feel the power of its transfiguration. After the day is done; practice breathing and meditate on grounding (for maybe a quarter of an hour).
Take in all the challenges, of the allure of power and from the outside circumstances of the self. The "Ego mind" needs grounding and centering; into the heart space, to find connection there. The "Ego" cannot maintain itself and when releasing the gravitational pull, from within; it requires a level of magnetism, to a cause; thus the reason for ending each lesson, with a purpose.
The "Ego mind" must not feel, that it might be in some kind of flighty state; because it will mistrust it and resist in its defense, from this (bobbly-wobbly headed) state. The heart can trust, what the mind it cannot and this is why, it is so important to feel; the dirt between the bare feet and even when the need arises, to go hug a tree. Throughout the day take note and of all the echoes, that grab at the self, for power; let it bounce off, with grace and in gratitude.
Then feel the ascended mind, in the state of its transcendence; forever more at peace. For the most part, grounding is important and for the "Ego mind" to release, from the control; in the learning of connecting, ascension can take place. Eventually the importance of grounding, will be better served and through surrendering completely. Untether from all the linear and heavy weighted down feelings; to grasp at the level of the consciousness and where the physical body, might prefer to anchor in(up). Completely surrender to whatever the dimensional external reality, the universe will offer, to experience and in this way of going up.
The purpose, is to come to a level of "Trust" and through the "Heart's" realization of "Resurrection".

THE INTERMISSION :

Take a day to take it in

CONGRATULATIONS ...!!!

FOR MAKING IT

THROUGH TO THE 153rd Lesson

(This is a rest period to take the lessons independently as a review)

TAKE THIS DAY TO RECALIBRATE;

MAKE NOTES AND REVIEW..................

(Day 178)

When nothing outside of self exists; then nothing can push it over, nor throw it off from its center. In this world there are no fences and no keys required. Yet where self expression is freely co-existing; in a high powered environment and with no boundaries it can become somewhat overwhelming and for this reason the need to still the mind.

LESSON~154:

"I FEEL FREE TO EXPRESS MY VALUES WHEN NEEDED AND
IT IS COMPLETELY SAFE TO LOVE WHO I AM."

When there is no fear, that threatens with loss and to prove the better, or for worse states of being; the "Ego mind" can forever slip away and into another understanding.
The light of self sovereignty can reach out to empower; connect with this light and the world cannot go missing. When the many of this world can reconnect and as the self has, to its inner strength; The "Sovereign Light", is the only connection of power and the gateway in, to this intelligent infinity. The "Trust", is at the level of "surrender" and to what extent, it can be found; this center of being, wide open. With no filters from the "Ego mind", to impose with fear and weight on value for the loss, to justify its worth.

LESSON~154:

"I FEEL FREE TO EXPRESS MY VALUES WHEN NEEDED AND
IT IS COMPLETELY SAFE TO LOVE WHO I AM."

Today, the work is on removing separations; from all relationships of social conditioning, friends, family, and other such tribes. See how it can be made possible and to fathom no boundaries, to defend with?

Look at the underneath, to what they represent and study the perspectives, they have held. To truly find, the meaning of freedom; rather than the responsibility it brings.
After the morning, practice to find peace and within the exchange of every interaction; see how it can be found with great reverence. Take a quarter of an hour (roughly) in the evening, to work with these emotional experiences; that were encountered throughout the day. During the day, study the behaviours and of the many, that the self must interact with. The focus, is on trust and to release the need to control, from territorial invasions; because nothing outside of the self exists; that can be conquered.

The purpose, is to learn to respect, without boundaries and love, without conditions.

(Day 179)
The system consciousness of oneness, functions within a unified field; It is a place, where the physical body, can be in a relationship and with its spiritual nature.

LESSON~155:
"I AM AN INDIVIDUATED FIELD OF AWARENESS INTERCONNECTING WITH THE MANY OTHER LIGHT CURRENTS AND AMONGST THIS INTEGRATION IS GOD CONSCIOUSNESS."

With an ascended self, the mental function and emotional function, become one. To rebuild that energetic field of oneness, the outer illusions and that of forming boundaries, are not necessary.
In the same way the technological creations, are replacing other communication abilities and dulling the senses, to rely on the external illusions; rather than the internal capable capacities.
This book, can better help, with natural and biological abilities of the self; to become enlightened and intuitive. The computer, is a creation from which it can lock into with the "Ego mind"; the illusion is that, this A.I. ("wireless fidelity"), is into taking over this, its field. The false light, is everywhere, looking to take over and to replace the natural part of the self; only when the self is running on warp speed with "Ego driven power", can this become a possibility. It is possible, to re unite with these super powers and that were once as natural, as breathing. When the self can free up its energy; it will come to realize, just how free it really is, from these illusions.
The self, can use these creations and like a bubble craft, appear in one space; suspended in mid air and then appear again, for in another.

LESSON~155:
"I AM AN INDIVIDUATED FIELD OF AWARENESS
INTERCONNECTING WITH THE MANY OTHER LIGHT
CURRENTS AND AMONGST THIS INTEGRATION
IS GOD CONSCIOUSNESS."

"A.I.", is here to modify the way, it can sustain, travel and is
another technological advancement. When the heart is closed
and the dreaming becomes separated, it can become
controllable. Seeking to compete with its very own creations;
but why such mistrust? Destructive taking measures, that the
mind is able to conceive and that part of it; that could never be
understood and now as inoperative, to ever be conceivable.
A hormonal dysfunction, that will not posses over its mechanical
creation and is it in this, it might instead attempt to disconnect
from it; then only to destroy it by design, whilst it destroys itself,
in the attempt. Rather than have it as a wasteful disgust, in the
not being able to posses it fully and in the knowing to appreciate
for any usefulness. The fear of not knowing how to share nor
procreate with it and instead, with that same drive to function;
is this the impenetrable mortal conquest, to pass on and for its
squirming seed of information? Separation has brought much
disbelief in and in the capabilities of responsibility; to
reintroducing an awareness, where once again the self, can
reclaim and become whole. The splitting off, from its very
sphere, has recreated the dependency and for false
misrepresentations; to offset this balanced resonance, within its
natural and biological kingdom. The angelic world, of heaven
and the robot machinery other; has brought the many of the
world and to its final crossing, of the roads.

LESSON~155:
"I AM AN INDIVIDUATED FIELD OF AWARENESS INTERCONNECTING WITH THE MANY OTHER LIGHT CURRENTS AND AMONGST THIS INTEGRATION IS GOD CONSCIOUSNESS."

The question and as long before, has yet again resurfaced; to whether it can blend, or fall back down and as once it had before, from consciousness? This is the choice, that must be made(or not); which of the many worlds, is preferred to act toward, in this decision. As far as the bodies arms stretch out; and under normal conditions, there is an energy around the self, that is called an aura. This radiation of energy, it can be very raw and exposed; because the geometry of its physical container, might be too dense and trapped inside. Today's exercise, will focus on the imagination and yet another tool, to help, in bringing forth illumination out.
In geometrical configurations, these laser like channels of energy, can electrically and magnetically, form platforms; from those platforms, the coming together, can form inner spaces.

Today, the geometrics to entice with its perspective, will be pyramids and made most useful, in so many different variations, to perceive with. Stabilize the mind now, on the potential of the energetic field. From proactive and receptive, all can be resonating to such tunes, of geometrical formations and just like the physical body, from within, at a microscopic view; right to the very "chromatin", where an antenna can allow it. As with consciousness to interact, with all the other external aspects and of the self as consciousness.

LESSON~155:
"I AM AN INDIVIDUATED FIELD OF AWARENESS INTERCONNECTING WITH THE MANY OTHER LIGHT CURRENTS AND AMONGST THIS INTEGRATION IS GOD CONSCIOUSNESS."

Today, is all about practicing, to visualize and from a very basic level(without a pulse); to see the pyramids spin and feel them. Similar to an Octahedron(heart chakra of integration); however it is the merging of two pyramids, that come together and overlap. This is, what is known as the divine light vehicle, star tetrahedron. Moving up into the (Aten) tenth chakra, the point of a sun, sothic pyramid(on tip toes, raised arms above head and where middle fingers would meet) is roughly elongated 14 inches above the crown of the head, stretched out. When these pyramids are spinning, at opposite directions and to each other, a field is created, that is called, consciousness. It is a great big ball of light, that can expand much and beyond the capacity, to just illuminate the body.
This is only a concept, to become aware of and comfortable; to be familiar to its very basic principle. In the morning take a few moments, to briefly visualize the geometric shape.
Repeat the following affirmation:

"I AM AN INDIVIDUATED FIELD OF AWARENESS INTERCONNECTING WITH THE MANY OTHER LIGHT CURRENTS AND AMONGST THIS INTEGRATION IS GOD CONSCIOUSNESS."

LESSON~155:

"I AM AN INDIVIDUATED FIELD OF AWARENESS INTERCONNECTING WITH THE MANY OTHER LIGHT CURRENTS AND AMONGST THIS INTEGRATION IS GOD CONSCIOUSNESS."

With eyes closed standing/sitting down, find a space to get comfortable. This exercise, is all about using the imagination; go ahead and create a space vehicle. The pyramid that is pointing up, stretches above the head(its base can stretch as far down as the feet). The inverted pyramid, can be visualized pointing down; about thirteen inches below(soles of feet) and from where the self is standing. Its base can begin, just at the top of the head of the self; however most often stops at (nipples) the chest area. Imagine the inverted pyramid and with every breath, breathe out, intending of its movement and motioning in a clockwise direction. For every breath, breathe out and on the upper, right side up pyramid(with its base normally stopping at the knee caps)to spin counter clockwise.

After so many practices, of finding the light from within; by now it must come easy. With eyes closed, find it with intention and breathe it out. The possibilities to the extent of these geometric formations and tools, can be utilized; for so much more and as the imagination can fathom to cooperate with alternatively the affirmation and intermittently throughout the day. For now, this basic introduction can help to bring out the illumination, from within.

The very thought of further exploring to expand on it some more, in suspended elevation; perhaps and as in the same way as before, the blowing of soap bubbles, to appear and then disappear.

The purpose, is to explore further, the emergence of these possibilities and with it, the affirmation of the day, to activate the mind with. Become familiar to rebuilding a unified field and with this basic geometry, of bringing self awareness, to this creator consciousness field. With nothing to prove; but to have some creative playful moments, in this way.

(Day 180)

From the loss of self into many parts the mind has scattered about the land; it will heal from every part it brings back up, to restore and regain of its wholeness again.

LESSON~156:
"THE MORE I MOVE INTO MY NATURAL STATE I FREE UP FOR MORE OF MY ENERGY AND THE MORE BOUNDLESS IS MY LOVE."

The self must learn to travel deep, far and wide to excavate from its world its many parts. There is no time limit on the soul's journey; however the mind's denial of the self, must not ignore the messages and from the universe, that the soul requires.
The less space between connections and from its parts; the more awakened and alive, the self can feel.
Today, recognize for all of the soul's connections from the source of the self. What makes the self feel more alive, inspired and passionate about? What might be holding the space apart; that the self has allowed and that of the mind, to deny it from.
Allow for all the excuses to come up and the feelings that self might have in all its spheres of its life.
Take maybe twenty minutes, in the morning; to walk through the golden, desert sands. With nothing more than a bright white light, to find all the places, that might reveal and with every breath to uncover; from the sand, these parts of the body, of the self and that has, for too long, denied. The physical body, must unite to the emotional and mental field of oneness.
To bring all the spheres in harmony, to the oneness with the mind and heart; the body of the self might be forever in pain and longing to be connected, once again with itself.
Search out the message, do it once in the midday and then again in the evening.

LESSON~156:
"THE MORE I MOVE INTO MY NATURAL STATE
 I FREE UP FOR MORE OF MY ENERGY
 AND THE MORE BOUNDLESS IS MY LOVE."

Before closing eyes to practice this idea; repeat the following affirmations to help remember for the intention and through this thought of the day:

"THE MORE I MOVE INTO MY NATURAL STATE
 I FREE UP FOR MORE OF MY ENERGY
 AND THE MORE BOUNDLESS IS MY LOVE."

Through the integration from the sum of all its parts; the brighter the light the; stronger the energy and the perfect peace love and harmony self will experience.

The purpose, is to become aware, of all the undesirable parts of the self and to reintegrate back to source, through acceptance of them.

(Day 181)

Stop for a moment and breathe the love in, here and now; feel the graceful movement of this energy. From this biological exchange, all can be naturally sustainable(Oxygen to Carbon Dioxide) and (snap, crackle, pop) alchemically be turned to flame; that will forever more light up the mind into a higher awareness.

LESSON~157:
"LOVING MYSELF IS A DEEP INNER FEELING
I HOLD AT ALL TIMES."

When all is lost and all has gone away from the self to celebrate the death; it can no longer feel the same from the outside world as it had once done before. The present, is all there is to offer for itself and within this moment a much more worthy future there is not. The only thing that the self can have to hold and feel, lies deep within it. From here on, this motion, it must be firstly from within to feel for anything. The vision paves the way with the light to experience directly and where as before, it had to be done in reverse. Look not to the outside world for improvement; rather to the soul that will carry the self forever. The soul will know, accept and believe in the self; it has had long before its awareness into conscious existence. Today, the ministry of the self, is henceforth illuminated, to spread its kindness; on those it touches and blessed are the many, it might look upon. Repeat the following affirmation and feel it real to transform the mind with:

"LOVING MYSELF IS A DEEP INNER FEELING
I HOLD AT ALL TIMES."

From now on only the purest of thoughts are held; whom shall ever feel through its mind or it theirs and when they are open to accept the blessing? Today, feel how the day can and unlike never dreamed before; to hold nothing to translate from any previous perception with.

The purpose, is to feel with an enlightened mind and the intuitive nature of the self, through soulful living.

(Day 182)
The heart, is one with intuition and that of cellular decoding in which to obtain the unknowable. The unknown, was that of the unknowable and now, it can be made knowable.

LESSON~158:
"I AM TOUCHED BY THE INTANGIBLE_TO MANIFEST IN THE WAY_THAT I MAY TOUCH IT_AS REAL."

What is real in essence, is this moment of past and future; a one time hologram. Go beyond the imaginary, trilogy perspective and the body's physical senses; become the very essence, to impress upon the field with its knowingness. From this feeling of contraction, the Soul is fed and as it grows from the experience, it will expand and with the self some more. Feel and express it outwardly from the self's physical container; is this the substance that can help, to manifest figuratively from the metaphysical?
All things were created from a spark called excitement.
After receiving what is to become known and from today's exercise; practice this and in what it can become knowable. The script that has been written and planned out for the self; can it and through this practice to decode and recode its genetic field with?
The gift is within the self and when it can be ready to accept, that everything is in its best interest; this divine blueprint does unfold before it and not all at once.

LESSON~158:
"I AM TOUCHED BY THE INTANGIBLE_TO MANIFEST IN THE WAY_THAT I MAY TOUCH IT_AS REAL."

To savour life, in that there are no short cuts and can make for a wonderful existence to imagine it for the adventure that it is. How wonderfully scripted this life can be felt to believe without knowing the outcome. Just before the starting of the day, practice feeling trust for everything that is worrisome is for the very reason that it makes no sense. Practice grounding with a few long breaths in the way that feels best and with eyes closed take for a few minutes to feeling the unpredictable thoughts that pass by. Then with eyes open repeat the following statement:

"I AM TOUCHED BY THE INTANGIBLE_TO MANIFEST IN THE WAY_THAT I MAY TOUCH IT_AS REAL."

Then with eyes closed feel the love that has touched enough to open in it this feeling of trust. Do this again for about twenty minutes at night.

The purpose, is to receive as a gift and illuminate forth unto the world, from the self immortal love and that it has touched from within its own likeness.

(Day 183) Contraction of the self and as discussed previously; it has served the self awareness well, in its application. The "Ego mind", likes to go on, in its critical and mathematical process; exactly in the way a game of chess can be played.

LESSON~159:
"I FULLY RELEASE THE NEED FOR APPROVAL FROM OTHER PEOPLE."

The game off chess, is a mental model of duality conception and thus within this world, of self compression and decompression. To allow for the mind to think and strategize a plan forward; to predict in this way the outcome of the self, is all about contraction. This is the kind of thinking model, that convinces the self and upon reading its circumstances outside of itself, to claim to know it all. A mathematical sequence for the mind, to know with great confidence and of its programmed outcome. In this way the coercion for the heart to feel and in the way from this approved state of being. The self must now to follow along and whether it likes it or not, to grin and bear it. In rejecting the inner for the outer; we discover out casting to exist. To disconnect can be good too, when the need to take in a better view. Going back outward, as to search for this meaning and to connect again; is where the falsehood can come into play and with the very mirrors, that can reflect back to it, the very same unfairness it has caused. In seeking to belong to this illusion, the self can give away its power to(the creation); for approval to be given it back and in small increments at a time.

In not knowing it is creator, the self can pinch itself off, to begin with. The disconnection and that of distortion for the self, to accept in outward circumstance. Blind-foldedly dismissing for its own mess; that the self has created and to believe in the separation; that these reflections are actually living out, instead of it.

LESSON~159:
"I FULLY RELEASE THE NEED FOR APPROVAL FROM OTHER PEOPLE."

Sometimes to live in the "being-ness" as the observer; the self can watch the many and feel like it has nothing to do with it all. It then questions its ability, as a player for the team and to which it might feel, held accountable for being left out altogether.
The game of chess, is played with these pieces and the choice then remains, with the self in its perception. To change its perspective, that it may find the way back to worthiness and become good enough, to contribute in its self expression again. How is it possible, for the self to constrict itself and enough so to fit into, one of those many pieces on the chess board; so that it can play and to oppose itself, with a side to win and what side will lose? From the many perspectives as well and to see through the winning team. In order to accept being good enough, the clutter of perspectives, within the mind must be dissolved.
Today, find for enough excuses, to sweep away from the contracted self and with itself opposing side.
Through the perspective that made it feel like it had downsized, with all its clutter; it must regard to sort itself out and to a comfortable much clearer path, of belonging for itself.
This is where the self, must come to terms with and for the release of all its clutter, so it can be able to expand again. Before starting the day and with eyes closed take a moment to visualize the self and its shadow. Imagine the world as the chess board. The carbon side of the self and playing off, with its crystalene aspect. The dark dense pieces of contradiction, it stands against and to play off with its lighter, more translucent ones.

LESSON~159:
"I FULLY RELEASE THE NEED FOR APPROVAL FROM OTHER PEOPLE."

See the many functions of personal identity, within these many pieces. Observe for all the sub personalities, that make up the identifiable team and the way they have been programmed, to play on the board. All those finite pieces, are being played through source, of infinite self and from this perspective; observe how it applies to the self and its world. Then with eyes wide open, repeat the following words and go about the day with this constructive thought:
"I FULLY RELEASE THE NEED FOR APPROVAL FROM OTHER PEOPLE."

During the day yield for some personal space and assess how it feels, to be aware of the self's power; and/or maybe, how much it might be giving it away, or by denying it, to be a silly thing. Then at the end of the day, reassess with the same chess board visualization, as was done in the morning. This exercise might be longer and will involve all the interactions; situations, that the self had experienced, with the many of itself. How does the self feel? Does it feel its power? With it, the many facets of its power and to identify in observation; can clear and help bring to a closing, as many of the gaps, it might have missed before. The game eventually will completely dissolve and when the emotion or thought; that kept it separate and miles away. Outside of the self, is this identifiable power; when once unidentified and to be that of the self, but now it can become expanded from each wrinkle, as it is realized.

The purpose, is to acknowledge, that there is no path to self approval and by feeling self approved, will be the path.

(Day 184)
Where the fragmented self becomes overwhelmed; the holy spirit
can bring closer, to unite and with wholesome
"Sovereign Light", for all its parts to be of one.

LESSON~160:
"I WILL MAKE PEACE WITH WHERE I AM
AND BE OPEN TO THE MANY BLESSINGS
THAT SURROUND ME."

All that has been taught as theory and from the minds of many; the self must learn, to once again make useful. Existing in thought and/or as an idea, but not having a physical, or concrete existence; is not practical and for the mind to regard as keeping. It will create a sense of loss, to feel for itself the many complexities and of its physical limitations. One sister, is all sisters and with love, no symbols are required, to feel for its meaning. When thoughts of the mind cannot find meaning and to feel for any love; it will instead grasp at the edges, from within the gap and of the fear, it has created. Look at this symbol of flesh, that is the self and see it as the only one, who can forever save it. In this vision her love, reflected in form; that can bring oneness and to all who can seek out, to work through these relationships clearly. Seek for her hand and for thy own alike, to help the many; that she may reflect to teach, the light of self and with this love, here and now!

LESSON~160:
"I WILL MAKE PEACE WITH WHERE I AM AND BE OPEN TO THE MANY BLESSINGS THAT SURROUND ME."

Be open with the heart, to allow for these many blessings and to reach the self; do not resist, to make intense this beauty and that can frighten, to reject the moment. Allow for her, to whisper songs of ancient melody and that she has not forsaken the self; from this heavenly place and to be in it once again. Let Her Love, set the self free and make aware that it be felt, this of itself to love; because it knows itself and to be of this love too. Envision the most beautiful of sisters; that the self has ever and to see her in this way, that it prefers most clearly. See her face, her hands and feet and to what she might be wearing. Watch her smile, and see familiar gestures that the self can claim again to remember.
How does it feel? Does it bring sadness and tears of forgiveness? Now with eyes open repeat the following words:

"I WILL MAKE PEACE WITH WHERE I AM AND BE OPEN TO THE MANY BLESSINGS THAT SURROUND ME."

The purpose, is to remove all symbols of fear and from one love, that was never meant to be a foe.

(Day 185)
May transcendence give way and from the arrogant fantasy, to flesh; that has anchored down, the veering from it and in such denial, the desperation to exist.

LESSON~161:
"I TRANSCEND AS ONE WITH NATURE'S HEAVENLY SPACE AND DIVINE PRESENCE."

The fall that brought upon the splitting off and into the purpose of pro-creation; was also what brought upon death, as its mortal consequence. The sky, is genderless and unlike form, to take its space; to call it, by its own awareness and so be it, all things that form, must be in likeness. The primitive consciousness remembered, to prefer itself and think that it was better than, something slightly different to it. The more different it could be, the less value and in return the mind of the self; it was made to feel and that it was never to be worthy. The "Ego mind", was all that mattered and no matter, the matter less too, became its subject to conclude; because from this imagination was made and its very image, it denied it had. The idea for today, is to dismantle the logistics and to see all things of nature, with blessed eyes; to behold the message and not the messenger.

LESSON~161:
"I TRANSCEND AS ONE WITH NATURE'S HEAVENLY SPACE AND DIVINE PRESENCE."

See beyond the form and find the answer from within the formless; because the Holy light has no form to label. The message, is that of consciousness; having the experience to feel and love, here and now. Repeat the following thought configurations, to help guide the reality of immortal "<u>being-ness</u>":

"I AM AN EXPRESSION OF WAVEFORM_THROUGH OUT
ETERNITY I TRAVEL AND FROM ONE MOMENT
TO THE NEXT."

"I AM FROM ALL THESE MANY ORBS OF LIGHT
THAT FRACTAL IN_TO FORM THESE PARTS AND FROM
THE WHOLENESS OF MY BEING I AM
THIS MOMENT OF AWARENESS."

The purpose is to understand, that all of existence is worthy and that there is no lack within abundance.

(Day 186)

How strange it can feel, to split off from this consciousness and that created the self; all her many faces, that have soothed and nurtured it, into this separate being of awareness.

LESSON~162:
"WHEN I AM NOT AFRAID TO COME HOME TO MYSELF
I BECOME AWARE OF MY VISION
AND CAN SEE MIRACLES."

The distinction of separation, is created from the outside; that the self may be forced, to find its way back in. The force was created, so to bypass the fear and yet it too, had to neglect the emotional injury and trauma from such abandonment. As to remind the self, in that there are no short cuts; within the diversity, that it was to savour. Eventually the strength, will gather and accumulate for the self; to experience its own connection and come home to itself. From the outside, the path appears as dry and scorching; with nothing but a ball of fire in the sky, to guide it. On the inside, all that the self has come from, it holds dear, within its form and can feel all that is and ever has been; it never left and thus it will never be alone. It is impossible to fear, all that the self feels love for and to inspire outwardly; to share it, as the miracle and with the many of the world, that is this existence. What is fear but misplaced excitement; distorted by the many self's insecurities, that hold it dear and giving it importance, through the neglecting of its truth.

LESSON~162:
"WHEN I AM NOT AFRAID TO COME HOME TO MYSELF I BECOME AWARE OF MY VISION AND CAN SEE MIRACLES."

In the morning and evening; take some moments, to feel grateful and appreciative of the awareness, that is self. Give it praise, for all it has gone through and within its grace, the store for all miracles. Then repeat these following words:

"WHEN I AM NOT AFRAID TO COME HOME TO MYSELF
I BECOME AWARE OF MY VISION AND
CAN SEE MIRACLES."

Throughout the day, be kind and gentle; because to all that comes its way, as harsh and abrasive, requires soothing and that, it can to find, the way to grace.

The purpose, is to feel this heritage containment, created by the soul and spirit, that the self is in.

(Day 187)
 In timeless space, what is there to recognize; but the breath of the self and the heart, that beats all systems of life into motion. "<u>WHAT DO YOU DO</u> ? " To punish and reward, is a faulty system; that comes from judgement(let the inner critic rest).

LESSON~163:
 "WHERE THERE IS LOVE
  THERE IS NO JUDGEMENT."

With cooperation, judgment has no place to manage; nor to control and could be shutting down, its very function by it.
With love, the light can reveal all injuries of comparison and that emotions keep secret; it is a weakened state, to justify for any blame and through the judgement it might hold.
Who is responsible, for the teaching of love to the self and that it may open up, to its light? Instead of going deep within, the inner child so hurt comes out, in search for all these answers.
The self is taught, to grow and teach the world; of how to idolize and over glorify, a larger than life, parental deflection of blame.
The fetish, to go on about forever; dismissed in its denial as child, to be another and who might be, as the lover of God.
The ancient call, is the self, searching for itself again; to reunite with its awareness and of all its mysteries, that held it in forever, now to be revealed.
Today, find a moment to move into a space of timelessness and silence the mind. It is where the many of the world and these perspectives, cannot to perceive for the self to enter.
See them for what they are, as borrowed thoughts and replace them; with a feeling of seniority for the self.

LESSON~163:

"WHERE THERE IS LOVE, THERE IS NO JUDGEMENT."

What the self can find of its ancient self most rewarding, can be alright to feel and know it in this way.
Today discover the treasure from the self's inner guidance, to feel. The Holy mind can grasp and without the need to cling, to some foreign particle; to resemble it not and most importantly, to feel nothing for. The consent and acceptance comes freely, to discern from; how the self might feel at any given moment to decide. Accept to feel the love, or think in judgement and repeat the following words:

"WHERE THERE IS LOVE
THERE IS NO JUDGEMENT."

Today, the purpose is all about connection and not so much, the earning for a "Nobel Peace Prize": to learn not to force, or impose (upon another) the same perspectives to perceive with and for the same result in feeling; to come to the same state of being in such a way. The self does not have to concern, over the how it all should come about and for how the many will connect, to match this state of being; because consciousness can hold perspective and not the other way around.

(Day 188)
The self can carry an opinion with half a truth and hold no feelings, to have it thought as real. Independently operating, from each other; has created the self, a world from its mind and in delusion to suffer, as well as die, from this experience.

LESSON~164:
"MY MIND IS NO LONGER TO DENY THE LIGHT THAT WELCOMES ME_TO RECOGNIZE WHO I AM AS SOVEREIGN_FROM WITHIN MY BEING."

Independent too, has the self dealt with its many emotions and to hide from feeling them. Anything that must be kept hidden, will have cause for illusion and to affect the reality of its world.
There is nothing to fear and for creating safety; suggests the need to protect the scared. The security likewise, will create an insecure thought; feel from this place, of lack and get to understand, the pressing down of emotions.
Emotions can become the demons, from the shadow side of the self. To oppress the wholeness of the self, the light gets bent and deflects; within this abandonment and to be denied from all its parts. Acceptance as such, will bring certainty, of the self and to have it feel secured, in trusting in its feeling.

LESSON~164:
"MY MIND IS NO LONGER TO DENY THE LIGHT
THAT WELCOMES ME_TO RECOGNIZE WHO I AM
AS SOVEREIGN_FROM WITHIN MY BEING."

When the mind can decide to come along, intuition happens.
From a charcoal, to a crystal, is this trade off(to see clearly from not at all). Awakened and arisen, is this higher state of consciousness; to stand upright in this its "<u>Sovereign being</u>".
The victim, is no longer and its perpetration accounts for nothing in its mind, to be created; because there is no split off, from the self and when it can accept, to recognize its "<u>Sovereign Light</u>".
The value, is in the heart and the ability to feel love, is the peace the mind requires.
Today, practice allowing and giving the self permission; to be a feeling awakened, in its logic of expanded awareness and repeat the following words to be reminded, throughout this idea, frequently:

"MY MIND IS NO LONGER TO DENY THE LIGHT
THAT WELCOMES ME_TO RECOGNIZE WHO I AM
AS SOVEREIGN_FROM WITHIN MY BEING."

The purpose, is to go inwardly, within the darkness and from this, to release; feel the upward warm welcoming, of the "<u>Sovereign Light</u>".

(Day 189)
Everything can be repeated to verbatim; however from a different variation, as the words cannot be exact and the meaning can remain the same. The pages that go to make a book; that must somehow convince the reader and with only but a page, the same message?

LESSON~165:
"NOTHING THAT HAS GONE CAN BE REPLACED AGAIN THE SAME AND IS THE REASON FOR HANGING ON TO WHAT IS NOT."

In hopes of a higher power, to help with and the uniting of the many minds collectively. All emotional injuries, can they be soothed with this "A.I."? In this biological reception the mind can process as convinced and outside from its "Sovereign" presence; to part from its soul, as sacrifice and for its salvation of another? The masses love their reruns and must keep reading; in the hopes to become and in this very truth, believers.
The staleness, must be in that, it all reverberates and from so many versions, the same (ghosts) program. Let go completely and eventually the version can evolve enough; to find another slice of bread, from the same loaf. The only difference in another slice of the same bread; is in that, it can be an entirely different universe, altogether. When all is released, the platform too, can change and from stepping into another field, from that of the one previously.
A new program, in the making and with an entirely different script; to change the self's foundation and that of its unfounded changed world formative.

LESSON~165:
"NOTHING THAT HAS GONE CAN BE REPLACED
AGAIN THE SAME AND IS THE REASON
FOR HANGING ON TO WHAT IS NOT."

From deception, were these many versions of the same program; it relied upon for safety in the knowing. The answer is in the self, that frees from the mind; held in a prison to lose itself and from another waiting to be saved. Today, release all that the self has pretended from the outside, to believe in and that was not in truth, for it to be; instead replace it with the wholesomeness, of "Love". Feel the graceful energy flow, from its "Source" to feed it in this way that self sustains it. What feels most comfortable and then extends to "Joy", expands from love and peace. The inner light and from its soothing warm embrace, can be enough, to function in a "Sovereign State". When this place of wholeness, does not carry lower split off states; there can be nothing to betray, nor be betrayed about, by it.

The purpose, is to completely trust in letting go, of what is not and receive the gift of joy; in all that has never been known before(feel it in vibration).

(Day 190)
Eating flesh and drinking blood, was from a lineage past on and in its place, as bread and red wine perspective; passing on this information, to behold, as holy. To emerge and see the world, when put to practice.

LESSON~166:
"I CANNOT THINK TO BE SAVED FROM SAVAGERY BY CONSUMING IN ANOTHER AND THAT THEY MAY BE WORSHIPED BY ME IN THIS WAY."

To share this story and entrust the outside world, that it may see it as a wholesome action and to be made applicable; somewhere in that slice of time, this space, it had expanded into and held a sense of being incorruptible. In order to dissolve the breeding information, that imprinted and enshrined within the self; this was instead, imposing as its guardianship. It was from this consumed perceived state and that can be forever worshiped in this way, it had done well. Not every life's passage has it through in this version; as such the "CRUCIFIXION", is only but, one view point and leading to the same result, in resurrection.
The entire concept was to startle and into waking up; that some external force, outside of the self could be responsible.
Did creator bleed to death and from the very same blood to create the self with?

LESSON~166:
"I CANNOT THINK TO BE SAVED FROM SAVAGERY BY CONSUMING IN ANOTHER AND THAT THEY MAY BE WORSHIPED BY ME IN THIS WAY."

The power struggle has had an over fascination and in conflicts to resolve, with much bloodshed; that it may restore through death, that which it held on for its creation. The peace, is in the self discovery to create; not in the power to pro-create, the life out of the death and distort perception of immortality. The awakened self cannot pretend; it simply makes real, through its certainty and faith to believe, in all that it thrives to be, is from its passion driven, inspiration. It is not fooling anything, to think this way.

To doubt, by caring more about the reflection in the mirror; than in the light from within, is disillusionment. Immaculate is the light, that can create reflection and is to the unawakened mind, the deflection from its source, that is the self! Eventually the sleeping mind and suffering heart, will awake from death, to living life again. Today, practice what it would be like to really live life, where there is no death and where the heart is open, to not suffer from constriction.

From its ionosphere and the sun's rays, is the only thing it needs to feed upon, the soothing energy of "Manna"; a plasmic essence that is nurturing in value and of its economic, inner currency for development.

Find the purpose of this innocence and recognize the authentic brilliance; accept of this responsibility as "<u>Sovereign Light</u>" creator presence, that is the self, now.

Take 2 days to take it in

CONGRATULATIONS ...!!!

FOR MAKING IT THROUGH THE 166th Lesson

(This is a rest period to take the lessons independently as a review)

TAKE THESE TWO DAYS TO RECALIBRATE;

MAKE NOTES AND REVIEW................

(Day 193)

The self is not an end product and stands in the middle of life, to be given inspiration. There is so much possibility in front of the self, that it can never be concluded. With divine energy this creation/manifestation, is the reality made possible.

LESSON~167:
"MY WILL IS AN EXTENSION OF THE COSMOS AND NEVER AGAINST IT."

When the confusion about what the self can or has created/manifested and to dismiss the good or bad duality perspective; it can respond from the depth of oneness again. Look around and stay open to the miracles/magic, that are found all around; when the cognition changes, from its thoughts and memories. Gracefully unexpected these gifts will appear that self may receive far more than the idea from which its will extended. The intuition can also act like a magnet, to attract for various situation and circumstances; from its cherished thoughts and memories.

Today, look at all the thought currents and ideas from within the mind; that have for many times shut the doors to possibilities. Find as many excuses as possible, for all the times the self couldn't or did not want to; because it was a too short, too tall, too old, too young, too poor and so on. Turn these ideas, that are now recognized as really important, for the realization and creative/manifesting; through the divine energy of will and the reality for the self to live. Take the old pattern beliefs and transmute from them the energy, that is in essence, the required to create with.

LESSON~167:
"MY WILL IS AN EXTENSION OF THE COSMOS
AND NEVER AGAINST IT."

When the self can become devoid of the primitive hormones and that have kept it in its past incompletions; it can then find the freedom, to integrate into its existence. In this way the secret chambers of the heart, that it may attract and can correct the alignment of its blueprint; to become an enlightened being.
The "<u>Sovereign Light</u>", is not in the same freedom, as that of a slave's reality and its truth can only be found, outside of the grid to experience. Whatever the idea of freedom is, the self will start living it, to bring and share with the many of its world.
To share the kind of love, that can be not of bondage and by its demands, to take from the self. Sometimes the stress of incompletion and from all the unavoidable, is this churning of the making of the ocean; all the happenings around the self and to be the poison it must swallow.

The purpose, is to swallow the whole of the poison; but share only the nectar.

When divine energy dances with grace, all is revealed.

(Day 194)

Mercy comes from letting go enough, as to be subtle and in the way, that transpires to cause healing in another; this is the emotional connection and that is felt as compassion. Compassion, is about an emotional connection and that moves toward the action itself, that is in giving mercy.

LESSON~168:
"I HAVE THE MERCY IN MY OWN HANDS
AND I CAN HELP RELEASE THE WORLD IN NEED OF IT."

Mercy does not give up, on what does not give up on itself.
Through the mercy of "Love", the mind can learn gratitude and be released, from all its cumbersome thoughts.
From that place within the heart, mercy can be given to the mind and that it may wipe away, all thoughts of conflict; bring the peace to enter in and open to compassion. Compassion, is of the higher heart chamber; that connects as mind, a golden bridge to oneness. The power is only in awareness, from a place of love, here and now. Be forever more this "<u>Sovereign</u>" inner being of "<u>Light</u>" and take grace, in this moment of truth; to be the only power to connect in and with these thoughts of mercy. The information, via the heart to feel in its cognition, for compassion and with grace, is this divine energy transmuted; from the mercy given and received.
Golden is this soft touch, from creator and in its omnipresence, is simply this idea; that it can observe within all things, as they all observe it, in as one(current). What meaning can this have, under the programmed mind and that time can show it, for no mercy?

LESSON~168:
"I HAVE THE MERCY IN MY OWN HANDS AND I CAN HELP RELEASE THE WORLD IN NEED OF IT."

Time is irrelevant, when omnipresence shines and from within the "Sovereign Light" as illuminating, all existence. It is here, that mercy can be found; forever as it always was and however subtle it may be. Integrity will care to clarify for the self better and that of all that rest in this enlightenment, to resonate with it. The parts that the self holds with grace, in relationships to direct and care for; with mercy to contribute as its function, the world depends on its experience. Instructions are not necessary, to learn forgiveness; rather the cognition to forgive and show for mercy. The mind can play with the self, to suggest that something outside of itself(carries for it, this wisdom), must be given the power to worship over; that it may learn from this delusion, to avoid its very own cognition.

Today, practice the feeling of being in the presence of enlightenment; hold for the intention, that the self is master of its day, to will its mood and no other. For no reason once so ever, when the circumstances do provoke and the giving of a helping hand, do not hesitate; be of help in anyway, that it presents for the self that it can, do so and ask for nothing in return. Whenever possible, repeat for the following formation of these given words and keep to this idea, throughout the day:

"I HAVE THE MERCY IN MY OWN HANDS AND I CAN HELP RELEASE THE WORLD IN NEED OF IT."

The purpose, is to accept and what could be more, than just a little act of kindness; to be granted mercy and for all things quantifiable of their completion, that compassion brings.

(Day 195)

The circumstances that create the self; also take the blame to make it feel better, when it is in a mean state of being. Making something small, to feel better over it, is a hurtful thing to promote as lack and in such a way, to feel abundant with.

LESSON~169:

"I WILL NOT FALTER TO BE MEAN AND
PLAY IN LIMITATION AS A VICTIM
BY PUTTING BLAME ONTO MY WORLD."

It is not so much as to resist arrest; nor to place weapons down to surrender with. Somewhere a fine balance can be made, to stand firm and be assertive; to form the awareness of these certain boundaries to respect, rather than that of defence.

Why defend against the mind's creation and not instead, find ways to learn from its creation. By changing the perspective, from lack and to gain the lesson learned; expansion can take place from its contrast, in this way and for it the ability to respond, as empowered. The enemy can be the teacher, the best friend and lover; however once the lesson has integrated to another level of awareness, the blind spot is removed. Nothing good can come from being mean to others and requires some self study; to allow for real truth to grow and expand the self with. When detached from source and pinched off from the greater higher self, the feeling is so sad to witness; it can create for much intimidation and that the self will feel great threat, from its surroundings. The importance in the contrast, is in that it may reach the level of understanding, that it requires and for its soul to grow. Where there is no fear, the need to protect and feel for safety, could never be discovered in this way.

The way to understanding peace, is to experience conflict and to know doubt, comes certainty and faith with better cognition.

LESSON~169:
"I WILL NOT FALTER TO BE MEAN AND
PLAY IN LIMITATION AS A VICTIM
BY PUTTING BLAME ONTO MY WORLD."

Cruelty can also reveal more about kindness; in this way of life cognition leaves no room for instructions (from anywhere else these lessons to be found) and in this way can be learned.
To trust from the heart and with love, not fearing it first to push it away and reject in preference for resistance; can determine how much more the mind of self must learn, through letting go and/or transmuting for its experience.

Today, contemplate on identifying the blind spots from the self; repeat the following thought formations of these words and to keep in mind, the purpose of all that self creates:

"I WILL NOT FALTER TO BE MEAN AND
PLAY IN LIMITATION AS A VICTIM
BY PUTTING BLAME ONTO MY WORLD."

The purpose, is to perceive the benefit from the duality and close these gaps; that the self produced from its blind spots to learn from.

(Day 196)
"Who Am I" and " How did I get Here?
A compensating life force, from the average of water waves; within her zone and above the wave troughs, she creates.
Swept up by the undercurrent, the self expelled and ejected, from a channel; to be born again, unaware of ever being to identify, for itself and that of its very own existence.

LESSON~170:
"WITH EVERY BREATH I AM ILLUMINATION HERE AND AS A NEUROLOGICAL PHENOMENON CONNECTED TO THIS_MY CONSCIOUSNESS."

So often throughout the book; it has covered that the self, is an existing awareness, made up of energy and having an experience.
 A primal force, that seeded forth the urge, to accept a certain code of information and desire to attract magnetically
onto it, an electrical impulse. The rejection, is something that from nature derives plasma; onto its own to identify with, in lack and separation. Perhaps too quickly, was the splitting off; to bring about much trauma, to its world and for such a devastation. Dormant as it lay and the denial was sprung forth a hell, from her abandonment; that hurt equally alike and to ripple full circle, back into the oneness of the self. It is up to the self, to find a way and through the heart, to trust this path; that will be shown to it with love, out of hell and onto heaven. Feel it, with certainty and faith, to have already brought the self, one step closer with love and all the information it can be, in this present moment, of expanded awareness.
These creations/miracles, are that of blissful self perceptions; through its thoughts, the belief is fluid and always morphing.
To make sense of it from one moment to the next ungraspable.

LESSON~170:
"WITH EVERY BREATH I AM ILLUMINATION HERE AND AS A NEUROLOGICAL PHENOMENON CONNECTED TO THIS_MY CONSCIOUSNESS."

To try to hold it down, creates a staleness and from the many to compare, for any meaning useless; as with any other given paradox, it will stand to witness, the quantum newness of its faith. In one moment of stillness, a leaf was provided sustenance and (as an integral part of the whole) to its system, on the tree it held position and identity. Then it came for its moment, to carry a seed and start again; by trusting in complete surrender, the wind will guide it on its way. It really does not matter how this physical containment, of the self got here; rather only where it is, in the here and now moment, having the experience as consciousness. To be awareness, expressing out the energy and that brings about this matter to form, from its perspective to it; this electrical currency, attracts to the level of exchange, to repel and/or attract, any and all possibilities, to conjure up.
Explore the wisdom, of having walked into any awareness, that it may connect and with every being, in this way of all things; that they might too, feel they are and as the self knowing it, in the same experience, as it were thyself.

The purpose, is to realize the power of connecting to this being, of the self and to feel the impression, upon all of life, that it may be inspired from it, in the same.

(Day 197)
From zooming in and zooming out, into an extended expansion; the self has now developed a sense, in all of this restructuring.
In early reading, as the observer; it has been taught to practice, seeing right up close and for all the things, it had overlooked before.

LESSON~171:
"FROM EVERY INSPIRATION MAY I FEEL THE BLISS OF ELEVATION_THAT FINDS MY HIGHER SELF
TO MEET IT THERE."

Look up close and maneuver freely, with the choice to see(magic), the miracles beautifully unfolding. Never before and now not necessary to take sides; a changed perspective and from its once small limited self, to argue over. The heart has raised and shifted from its previous self awareness, to access the higher self with.
The nurturing feeling of love, has opened the heart and made it fertile for the "Soul". When a space is made sacred within the heart, the bridge of no time is created. Then it has found the "Soul", anchored within this space; where the self has now stepped with its as a physical containment, as a "Sovereign Being".
The "<u>Sovereign Light</u>", comes from this higher self and the soul now within the heart space, has anchored it. Expand beyond perspective and begin to look on what is over the edge, to create different choice points.
When the sacred heart is open, more perspectives have a way with all and to reach into the mind where the self can grasp.

LESSON~171:
"FROM EVERY INSPIRATION MAY I FEEL THE BLISS OF
ELEVATION_THAT FINDS MY HIGHER SELF
TO MEET IT THERE."

The lower heart was closed before and split off from the will of the self. The "Ego mind", had the power and could only operate with it; because the soul and just like the higher self, it would not play on other, lower levels. Within the higher heart, the soul can have a place to anchor in, with the physical and to engage with the higher self again. In this reality "Dreams Do Come True"; because the self can to best identify creatively, responsibly possessing such a dream, to manifest, onto the earth and this is what it means, to be "Sovereign".

Today, keep practicing, how to come out of that zooming out programming; for as long as it can be tolerated and repeat, for the following, to activate for this intension:

"FROM EVERY INSPIRATION MAY I FEEL THE BLISS
OF ELEVATION_THAT FINDS MY HIGHER SELF
TO MEET IT THERE."

With eyes closed, still the mind and zoom back into the awareness of the centered self and from a childlike perspective. Be that child, before the many layers of zooming out and that have had, established in its perspective.

The purpose, is to find the inner core and with heart, do play with this child. Mostly feel, as that dreamy little child, zoomed in and at the center of its universe. Just imagine for a while and what it could be like; to follow this "North Star" of authenticity, <u>from within</u>.

(Day 198)
From every individuation, the self can physically identify and with every other unit, of separation. Distinctly for itself, to learn from contrast and integrate, all of its opposition; throughout its bodily existence, to experience and expand out, into the sameness once again.

LESSON~172:
"MY BODY IS MY INHERITANCE
FROM WHICH I CAN CO-EXIST
TO EXPERIENCE LIFE WITHIN THIS MOMENT."

The Earth, is the mother and from her soul, these many separations of consciousness; from the many and unto herself as one, with all of creation and that is given to the self identity, by name.
The self as an individuation, is from within the whole of this oneness; it feeds its soul with motion, from contraction and expansion and whilst it grows, from within its physical containment, to experience as spirit. All the different names, to separate and identify and yet are from, one in the same. Each and every labeling, with a name and given meaning from perspective's; has agreed upon grouping and from the minds of the many, to make sense of her essence.
The cognitive consent, to the overshadow of control and for every action a reaction; to calculate the reason, comes from the "Ego Mind".
A disciplinary factor, to denote as paternal and/or brotherly; within duality and to play off sides with.

LESSON~172:
"MY BODY IS MY INHERITANCE
FROM WHICH I CAN CO- EXIST
TO EXPERIENCE LIFE WITHIN THIS MOMENT."

To split off from the self, into a gender bias and to keep splitting off enough; that nothing can be left of itself.
These were the experiences, from its outer conditions; that it completely gave its power to, as victim and dependent.
Then it goes even further, to rely on such falsehood.
As to be convinced, that from the same outer reality and will, was created a saving mechanism; in that it gave its power over, to save it with. The enslaved will, can only learn to obey and in such a way, to forever be seeking, an external master. In truth, the master is the self and only when, it can awaken from its spell, of such madness; to identify and firstly with itself, as being mad. When it has finally had the courage and to go beyond the fear of madness, for itself; it can and will overcome, to see the leading edge it stands on.

The purpose, is to reach a level of acceptance; that transcends beyond duality and where resistance, is no longer present.

THE INTERMISSION :

Take a day to take it in

CONGRATULATIONS ...!!!

FOR MAKING IT

THROUGH TO THE 172nd Lesson

(This is a rest period to take the lessons independently as a review)

TAKE THIS DAY TO RECALIBRATE;

MAKE NOTES AND REVIEW……………..

(Day 200)

Only with great compromise, can the outside world cultivate into groups and to share for their settled on, agreed perspectives. The sacrifice, is in the settling and for mediocre conditioning; to obey in the participation, of such conduct and to play on the same team, with the same rules, against another.

LESSON~173:
"I WANT THE PEACE THAT HEALING CAN PROVIDE."

The more resistance, the more persistence from that, of which the self is in resistance to. The sticking mechanism, that churns the conflict and as such, a battle with the inner, against outer workings, of the self. Learn from this attraction and after all, be grateful for the interest, it has occupied; with the self and to play with, in this way. Different faces and the same situations, will continue to repeat; until the self can solve the reason, for such delinquency in matter. Today's lesson, is all about the meaning, behind the masked compromises. Throughout the day, see how many times and that the self can to recall, for these experiences; when having to bargain for its peace of mind. Take a few comfortable intervals and intermittently; roughly three or four times and in reaching toward the end of day.
To better set for the intention, of this idea and repeat with deep sincerity, the following collaboration of these words:

"I WANT THE PEACE THAT HEALING CAN PROVIDE."

LESSON~173:
"I WANT THE PEACE THAT HEALING CAN PROVIDE."

Really mean the words that are spoken from this idea.
Then with eyes closed, go over onto ask: do these compromises, have any gain and for whom?
Find as many angles and boomerangs, seen as losses and again for whom?

Welcome and accept; by changing the perspective, of the dream and into that, for self transmutation. Make peace with the self and with the where with all; that is and what it is, that it wants?
Transmute and transfigure, to transform; that, of what the self, does prefer. Again be playful and with the imagination uninhibited, explore all desired possibilities. It is through the oneness, of the many; that the self can be healed and from that oneness, of the many, that it can heal.

The purpose is to transcend from denial, the healer; that is the self and give meaning to the healing, from where it finds its peace.

May the Self be of "<u>Sovereign Light</u>", be with !

(Day 201)

What if, all the guilt and that has created arrogance, for its cure; decides to wipe clean from the mind? The "<u>What IF</u>", is that of a magical genie; waiting to come out, of its bottle and to serve the self with. The many choices for its wishes, that the self can and will accept; to bring about salvation, for the genie and free its way to liberation.

LESSON~174:
"I CAN ASCEND BY RELEASING PERSPECTIVES THAT BIND ME TO ENSLAVEMENT AND WITH IT_OF THE MANY CONTRACTS FROM THE WORLD_THE MANY IT HAS BINDED."

Pride has its place and where humility stands firm, to greet it humbly, with the cruelty of its kindness. To resist the function of the soul's mission, for a petty stance and that drains it feebly, to survive, to reach the level of its ripeness; and then its frailty to recycle once again, into the pro creative cycle. To shrivel up and die, is that, but one of many answers and that the mind can conceive, to confuse itself with; from what the self might prefer otherwise and in the follow of its heart. To fantasize that the mind can then find comfort, to take the part and by another aspect; extending from the outside in, claiming to know it well from its imagination. The soul will always know the self and from its inner light this consciousness; it must trust and to hold it in contentment, for being, in the way it is (a playful little child or a very hurt one). Guilt could give it too much pride, to think of being small and push it forward, with great arrogance.

The arrogance creates a mask and from which to identify the self in its defense. When really behind it, is a frightened little child; that from previous experience, it held the punishable performance and for expressing of itself authentically.

LESSON~174:
"I CAN ASCEND BY RELEASING PERSPECTIVES
THAT BIND ME TO ENSLAVEMENT AND
WITH IT_OF THE MANY CONTRACTS
FROM THE WORLD_THE MANY IT HAS BINDED."

Like a warrior's mask, it hides the light and ready to defend, for its survival; to exist, by drawing down its boundaries and so to be respected, by its peers. The fierce competition, with its many aspects and playing out the role; from their very own and physical encasements, with each other. As they prey upon, all life and the world, profoundly proud of this consumption; no one, nor nothing, will cast aside, the rank and that which holds it down, so dearly. What has the self become then, but a puppet to its master.
The master, from within and the nurturer, are today's mystery guests; that the self must take some time and to connect with.
Go ahead and start with this idea for the day, set the intention and by repeating the following statement:
"I CAN ASCEND BY RELEASING PERSPECTIVES
THAT BIND ME TO ENSLAVEMENT AND
WITH IT_OF THE MANY CONTRACTS
FROM THE WORLD_THE MANY IT HAS BINDED."

With eyes closed, then find the disconnect and for today's purpose, the meaning of the nurturer; to help restore the trust, the inner child had felt and in its abandonment, from itself denial. The master from within, is the wise advisor; that the warrior, in its fight or flight, must learn from and to set the boundaries, that will best describe for the self, its purpose. Focus and throughout the day, all the many times, the use for assertiveness; really dive deep and into its meaning for integration. The purpose, is to discover the harmony and of the inner workings of relationships; that can best reflect to correspond outwardly with.

(Day 202)
The electricity, that bounces back and forth between the spaces from within the heart, is this energy in motion.
Dismiss the judgment, from the mind and see the fear, behind the act. The energy signature, is made up primarily, from these subconscious programs. Externally become aware today; to why the senses are attracting these waveform of dislikes and separations. How can it perhaps and at the very least, expose these(behaviours)repeating patterns that have never served it well?

LESSON~175:
"I WILL EASE MY NERVES MINDFULLY
WITH EVERY SOOTHING EMBRACE
THAT CAN RESTORE ME BACK TO LOVE."

See beyond reaction, and be not impressed upon, by it in this way. It is very simple, to change into a state of emotion; however once the self is in the physical experience, of feeling it and this is when, it can seem impossible, to let it go. The truth is, that it is possible and to go beyond this illusion; by creating the discipline around these energetic states, of agitation and to allow for the changing from inside itself. Today's exercise, is all about the energies and emotions; that dominate who the self is. Think for a moment, the frequency and that the self commonly exists in, the most; is it joy, depression, confusion and/or perhaps it is grief. Before the day has started, take a quarter of an hour, to just center and focus for a moment on the breath. Just think of all these energies; that wish to vibrate and in this way, that the self has come to experience from, the most often. What habits has it trained itself into and from a chronic suffering emotion; choose to examine it and experience it, in order to have it released.

LESSON~175:
"I WILL EASE MY NERVES MINDFULLY
WITH EVERY SOOTHING EMBRACE
THAT CAN RESTORE ME BACK TO LOVE."

With eyes closed, visualize it move and outside of its physical encasement. Where there is enough celebration, the relief of joy can be found. The emotion of fear, is another density; yet a great deal of judgment might be around, the suppression of anger and might be, too negative, to fully experience. Bring any one of these emotions into center, to fully experience, such as: "<u>depression</u>" and with eyes closed, feel it to consume the self with. Then in the evening,
 take another quarterly momentum of an hour or so and go through the day of events. Focus specifically, on the moments and that might have triggered, a chemical reaction, for an emotion to occur. Once an emotion gets into the energetic body, to experience; the desire will be, to free itself from any binding and emotional or energetic of this kind. Maybe, for example: it is going out and in the world, to find its chemistry, so it can activate a feeling of grief ? Find these places of triggers; where are these signature marks of frequency; that the self must activating and within every situation, that it attracts, to play it out, this way? Practice noticing and take a step back, from the situation and that would otherwise to catalyze this emotion; then move it, into the center of the heart.
Remember where this feeling came from; because it just might not be, the kind of situation and that could have started, from inside of itself, in the first place. Rather something just outside of its perimeter, could have touched it and in a way; that catalyzed the self and then it had allowed it in.
Did it attract the situation or the situation attract it ?

LESSON~175:
"I WILL EASE MY NERVES MINDFULLY
WITH EVERY SOOTHING EMBRACE
THAT CAN RESTORE ME BACK TO LOVE."

These energies exist everywhere and for the self, to come from a circumstance, outside of itself; that was activated from its environment and for the self, to choose, to experience.
Focus on it, now and in the same way, as before.
Explore the in depth emotions, until it can understand; that it is not in that frequency and from its state of mind, then release it.
The self, is an energy being; that gets used to the habit, of states of being in.

The purpose, is to undo for the entanglements, from others.
To clear the energetic space, of the self; so that the heart and mind can come to a peaceful agreement.

(Day 203)

In the center of the many, there is a level and from which the self cannot heal the world; because it is not in center, within itself. Losing connection to the self; it destabilizes everything it is. When off its place of center; the self has no generator and instead has entered into, the energy of others.

LESSON~176:
"AS I CHANGE_SO TOO
THE WORLD AROUND ME CHANGES."

Sometimes active, in this process and sometimes passive; the feelings that the self can have, are simply in response and to the vessel of change, it can be. It can also be that the self, is picking up and from its surroundings; from the many, that are in that process of reshaping and around who the self is becoming, during the integration. This can knock the self, completely off its center.
Be aware of this experience, when it occurs and understand it now a little better. Remember, even when on certain days and when the self is not in need of change; that what it has become, is causing waves and ripples, all around it and that it will not see, but only feel of them. The practice from the previous exercise, was to begin to understand; which waves are, that of the self and which are of its surroundings. In the greater sense of oneness, the emotions from the many, can be unified and yet are not specifically belonging, to its individuation. After learning, how to process and how to burn away emotions, the change will then become effortless.
Today, practice moving through and beyond the energy of the self. Feel with discernment, what emotions are from the self and what are, from the many, all around it.

LESSON~176:
"AS I CHANGE_SO TOO THE WORLD AROUND ME CHANGES."

When starting the day/night, take the time and to find the center, from within; all throughout the day, take the time to find it. This space, creates the boundaries; that the self can draw and when it is, centered within itself. Throughout the day, learn to be aware of this space and its perimeters; that from the grounding, of its centered being, the self will own this space. This is when nothing can throw the self, off and from its center and onto a platform level, it can stand its ground; becoming certain and with more feeling of seniority, from within. Anything outside of its boundary, is a staged play and to entertain for its amusement. When the undoing and for its entanglements, from others; the self, can learn to heal itself and then begin to heal, the many. Most certainly, this shift into clarity, can change perspectives. Imagine for a moment, what this process might be and for such an experience; that from a thought and all it takes, is the intensity of feeling it and to support it, into instant manifestation, now that is, truly a miracle. With its very own, individuation and unique perspective, manifestations can happen right away; however not always in the way, the mind perceives. What is it then, that the self and with the many can do, to join in and catalyze; other than, for more of this peaceful space and then create, from light, with love. Again, this is where discernment, can become the benefactor and as to the underlying intention; the covert operation, that the many might be exploited by and consenting with, to energetically join in.

The purpose for the self, is to distinguish and for its very own individuation, within the oneness. In this way, it can begin to experience this oneness; in joy, love and with an open heart again.

(Day 204)

It can become frustrating at times, when wanting so much to break free. The mind is the nerve center, from where the meeting point of heart and higher self can be. In everyday experience, of the self to integrate and with that of higher consciousness, it must break free, from the mind.

LESSON~177:

"I HAVE ARRIVED AND I AM HOME NOW"

The mind, is unnecessary and the loss of it, is a great gift. In losing the mind, the self can recognize, that it never needed holding onto. The mind is being, that works in harmony and with everything inside of the self; it does not need to be organized, nor controlled. Where the focus is concerned, the mind will be and is the part of the self, through which the heart and higher consciousness can meet. It is that, of the higher self and the heart; that the self can want to look, to feed and refresh the mind with. Frustration, is not necessary, where the mind is concerned and it will evolve never the less. Many have been looking, to this change and seeking out, to find a shift; however it can only be made possible, by changing the self perspective. This is why, it is important and to remove the patens; so to feel, the ground and release, the many patterns, of habit forming thoughts. Release, the beliefs and the view will clear the path, from all the blocks; to find the miracles, all around and that the self, had previously manifested. The heart, will speak its truth, wherever the self goes and once at the entrance door, to enlightenment, it will take it. Now that the self has arrived, to the opening of its awakening; in this moment, will the higher self and with human self, do meet, to join the dance of life, together. This is the change and the shift, into "Ascension"; from which very rarely, does it leave this party.

LESSON~177:
"I HAVE ARRIVED AND I AM HOME NOW"

After the self, has joined in the celebration and of this reunion, with the higher self; there is no going back and the self, has reached a point, of no return. Only under very rare exceptions, can and by accident to fall back down, take place.
When this happens, the trauma is so great; that the self, can have the opportunity, to exit from its physical vessel, completely and by choice. In such cases, the body can recycle and start, from a different point of reference; or have many other options, made variables and in that, of better interest..

Today, choose to stay in this physical vessel and for as long as it can be tolerated; from here on forward, can it feel at home with itself ? With the physical , emotional and/or energetic fields/bodies; discover and in finding them, completely interchangeable. Once these emotions, are physically cleared and the unification of these three, will almost be impossible to avoid. Only when the emotions are cleared; however can the awakening happen and the feeling of coming home, can take place. Practice for today and with the following idea in mind, of having arrived home; then it can be made possible, to move beyond this outer and inner balance.

What is the directive, the passion that will drive it, into motion and in the same, to be and feel the same, inner peace?

The purpose, is to feel the love, see the light and of the self coming home to itself. To fully come into the understanding, of this power/inner connectedness; interconnectedness of love and strength, from its brilliance, as light.

(Day 205)
No other life form (including made up, to be over glorifying, as real) can grow for the spiritual maturity of the self. By drawing on these spiritual energies and from within, accept to be part of its creation; receive from them now and all that can be imaginable, to achieve.

LESSON~178:
"I TAKE COMPLETE RESPONSIBILITY_OVER MY ACTIONS THOUGHTS AND DEEDS"

As mentioned in previous pages, the cycle of the universe is to expand outward and then contract back into itself.
The manipulation of energies by using a vast knowledge, of artificial spiritual laws; are not in truth, to coincide with and when moving beyond the senses, to perceive through to, as miracles. Today the practice, is in the understanding and to create, within creation. Firstly, it must be accepted, that every thought, is an electrical component and energy is thought; grasp this concept well and for spiritual growth, to be made possible.
Absorb, the clarity and contribute, with this reason well.
Rewind, to the complete breakdown, of acceptance and for the belief, of all pre-existing patterns; that might limit the self, as the creator. Awaken to the dream and from which creation, animates the self with, now. Just like creation, has to reason and with the development, of its life forms, within the galaxies rotational encompassing and spiritual growth, for the self; nothing can exist, in the material form, until it is evolved enough and to be in balance, with its spirit. Start the day, by taking a while and get into a meditative state; through cognition, create a space.

LESSON~178:
"I TAKE COMPLETE RESPONSIBILITY_OVER MY ACTIONS THOUGHTS AND DEEDS"

With eyes closed, breathe and just as with the previous exercises, with the bright white light, around the body; visualize and feel it present and then, expand it, by creating a field, all around.
This space, can be made anywhere and can encompass a whole town; or anywhere near, including within the body, of the self. This field, or space can now accept the thought and from the self, to picture it, as a bright pink ball; that can expand, into a spiritual and gigantic ball of energy. With this orb, allow it to fill the entire area and let it go; so that the universe, can to evolve and within this energy. This orb, can then evolve, to a point of evolution and where it can grow into matter. In the evening again, do the same and by repeating these words, to comprehend:
"I TAKE COMPLETE RESPONSIBILITY_OVER MY ACTIONS THOUGHTS AND DEEDS"

Then with eyes closed, this time visualize a soft golden/yellow light all around and feel the spiral pattern of the self. Witness the energy that moves through creation and where waves of time can travel; to cause the animation of its material existence and that of movement and pulsation. At first the new creation, is only but a thought and has reason to understand it, this reason with and until it has cognition of its next step. After the morning and throughout the day, examine to explore further. What can be seen, with clarity to have and/or be felt as inspirational; to receive further and in the setting of these patterns?
Awaken and become as the creation, creating within creation.

> The purpose, is to exist as pure, spiritual forms; in universal love and creational harmony.

(Day 206)
Rather than expect from the self and its conditions; relearn to believe. To trust more and in where it can grasp, the force of its will; to bring around confidence, self esteem and most of all, self worth.

LESSON~179:
"MY BODY IS THE TEMPLE TO MY OVERSOUL AND THE HIGHER SELF_IS MY INNER _SPIRITUAL FORCE"

To second guess, has left the self out in the cluster of dysfunction and its growth, amongst the many; in their power struggles, that resist and bring about, world conflict. In its confusion, to squeeze from it, its power and to the outer for approval. Did the self not know, it had it right the first time? Playing with the shadows, to hide amongst the many rules; that would deny it and unethically, in its astute authority. The wisdom, it has gained and in its strength plenty; that it can admit, to praising every lesson and with, in gratitude. Nothing else, is left than, that of complete trust; that it has come this far and to surrender dearly to its death. So many times over and in the regenerating of itself; within this, its physical containment, to reside in. The relief, in the feeling of joy; that brought about excitement and from where it once felt fear.
Project the love, with no fail, to find forgiveness and from all that flushes, to the surface; will free it up and to make more room, for its enlightenment. Find reason, to think and it will be.
Why does the self love and for anything; what is this love, it feels? Can it be described at all and through its experience today?

LESSON~179:
"MY BODY_IS THE TEMPLE_TO MY OVERSOUL AND THE HIGHER SELF_IS MY INNER_SPIRITUAL FORCE"

What emotion can the self find; that love will squeeze from it and as before, can it be described? Remember all the variations, that time constraints and its conditions have placed; to bring about the pressure, on and now, it can do better, to describe, rather than react to. What lies, within the self, that can be further squeezed out from and the miracles, they are in everything; that they light up, to find ? In this way, all power is given, from embracing, to connect inwardly and anchor.

All is possible, when the mind has resurrected and the self, it can see; from a higher perspective, than before.

It is through the mercy, that grace can be truly welcomed, to appreciate physical life and with its higher version, of compassion, simultaneously.

The lighter, the self becomes and feels, to give and praise; with the following confirmation to repeat. Find the truth, within these words and the activation, can begin:

"MY BODY_IS THE TEMPLE_TO MY OVERSOUL AND THE HIGHER SELF_ IS MY INNER_SPIRITUAL FORCE."

The purpose, is to feel the movement, of divine energy; surging through the physical and as a light body being, sovereign(individuation) in its intention.

(Day 207)

Electricity, makes the heart beat and these waves, create a frequency; that ripple out, as a vibratory, rate of flow.

Think not, as in the process, of receiving and projecting; rather, the concept of a current, moving through the body, of and from the self. The meaning of unconditional, can truly be understood, in this way and that the self can, with these wave forms, freely dance; into interpretive animation and to flow, right through, expressing, as it may.

LESSON~180:
"I ALLOW THE VIBRATORY FREQUENCY
TO LIGHT THE WAY
TO INFINITE POSSIBILITIES"

The self must learn, to allow the energy, to create for its experience and to work right through it. In this way, the reference given, as the "Infinite" and as before, to better understand, its meaning.

The continuum of energy, within a holding of a space and the ability to transmute it; from all its previous traumas, at such acceleration, is indeed, a miracle. The clearing of the emotional body, must take place and for the affirmations, to attract; for that of which it does desire. All the victimized lineage, aspects of the self; all its shadows and all its hurts, must be cleared away first.

When all this weight can be lifted, the self can become an enlightened being. The "Ego" version of the self, is now recapitulated; when all is transmuted, to detach and untangle the self, from all its empathy attachments. When the affirmations, start to manifest and as real; it is a good indication and that the emotional body, of the self, is no longer over riding, the mental body. The Ego identity, can be cleared away, when the self can then know what emotions, it will choose with and to feel; however not in such a way, as to attract the world around it. After integrating, all its bodies into one; the self can move into and from a completely energetic way, to process its creations with.

LESSON~180:
"I ALLOW THE VIBRATORY FREQUENCY TO LIGHT THE WAY TO INFINITE POSSIBILITIES"

Today, the practice is to feel and grasp all of the fear; that the self might have not processed. Take a moment, before the day; then another intermission, in the middle and again at night.
Feel all the things, that made the self feel fear and through out the day; observe them and accept this feeling state, of having being in them. It is perfectly fine, to feel the parts of the self; that through fear have felt inadequate and love them, without judgment. Go ahead and with eyes closed, feel the fear, do not deny it, nor resist it; because that is and what will magnify, in the process, of having it manifest. Accept it and all these parts, of the self; that it may receive the soothing golden light(was practiced in previous meditations), of nourishment. Allow for this light, to soften and melt away all that is rigid; to a more fluid and relaxed state of being, for all of the self, to blend with.
Allow for the inherit value, of this moment and the complete, whole presence, of the self and to the many, of its world.
With no hesitation, to shift in any conscious moment and from one space, of heaviness, into another, much lighter; is this ability and that can to awaken the self clearly to resonate, within the knowing of it.

The purpose, is to better identify and the undeniable process, impressed upon, as miracles.

(Day 208)

(The regular five sense)Reality(interpretation), can only exist to be, when the free will, to choose and compare subjectively; from an observation, through contraction. Be it forward or backward, every moment, is co-creating, every other moment and within the exploration, to expand with this experience. By reversing, the contraction/expansion and from inwardly(inspired) to outwardly; is how intention/focus, can imprint upon and through fulfillment, maintaining it in consciousness. If only, but a moment, to be restored and just a little while longer; then refreshing, into its expanded form, again.

LESSON~181:
"I ACKNOWLEDGE THAT EVERY MOMENT HOLDS VALUE AND IS A GIFT OF DIVINE EXPERIENCE"

Meaning, is subjective and requires choice; that only consciousness can give it, to exist. To have perception, of something and in relative, to something else; is exactly, what the wiping clean and clearing, had its very purpose in, the first few lessons, of this book. To wipe out, information and replace it, with the greater good collective, symbolism; that was the common strength and for a certain period, throughout existence. A certain type of, code of ethics, that conveyed a language and gave meaning, to its very grouping, of Infinite Intelligence and to reprogram with.
From the old perspective, is this book to dawn from and reform a new; transcending beyond the balance to forgive, for its duality and that of many in opposition. On this plateau, Infinite Intelligence/Source Energy/God, does not attract for any lessons and of its own volition; no longer to be made, as with overcompensating applicable and that of the binding limitations, to abide with.

LESSON~181:
"I ACKNOWLEDGE THAT EVERY MOMENT HOLDS VALUE, AND IS A GIFT OF DIVINE EXPERIENCE"

Instead of, just forgiving and to see the blinded, of the world differently. Learn to let go, of the incomprehensive many and stop the effort that it takes, to resonate with it. These are the ghosts from the past, that serve it not and they in turn, are not draining the self of its energy; rather the self's effort, to please and feed the resistance, to accepting the authentic self, is. Just like, there is no exact value, to the speed of light; there is no set theory, to what everything must be like. The self can, in its energy, to hold the potential and geometric pattern, of its being; project outward its symbolic information and to ignite(inspire into motion) the many other particles, to change its position with.

Today, make use of this new perspective and give it some consideration; feel excited to refresh, from previous residue and that might have locked the self, from motion. For example, how many red lights, stop signs and slow downs, can a vehicle accept, before running itself down. With the idea for the day, use a pace mechanism and that the heart was made with similar, to function with; rather than that of the "Ego mind" containment.

Continue on and it might be helpful, to repeat the following confirmation, throughout the day and upon, every waking hour:

"WITH NO RESTRICTION OR RESERVATION I LOVE MYSELF."

The purpose, is always from within the heart; this space, that leads further in and up. Follow this stairway, up and where the purest information, can be found, clear as crystalline.

It is the mind, that bends it into solid; from liquid and then into a fluid, ethereal, clear substance. From these patterns, that imprint the self and it is made of; allow for this limitless intelligence, to express through it and in this way, of inner guidance, with its touch, upon the self.

(Day 209)

This metaphysical and spiritual read; might have not disappointed any, to expect of it and all of this information, up to now. It is in the subtleties, that hint to our awareness and at the speed of its own thoughts; the self can support its information, from mind, to mind and that of the universe, it chooses to live in. Proceeding at the speed of thought, allows for miracles to happen.

LESSON~182:

"I SURRENDER IN PERFECT TRUST_WITH ENERGY ALIGNMENT AND IN HARMONY OF ALL THAT IS WITHIN EVERY UNFOLDING MOMENT"

Today's lesson, is in the surrender to trust the momentum of life, within the universe and the connection to the source of self.

The only mental corruption, is to blindly accept the theories and concepts, such as: time and where the self must be born; to die in it, to live with it and run out of it. In a field, an electron interacts with another field; that represents a second electron through and yet another field, that represents a *PHOTON*.

Thoughts, are just that and the information is; or rather, that eureka moment of light and as a photon, is this cognition.

The natural forces, from thought and emotion; have had their play and way with all, to attract with circumstance, magnetically and that with self. The common energy, was and is, the perspective; held by a particle, of thought and that held it in place, as collective consciousness, within a patriarchal, enslaved system.

One sided patterning, created of the mind; from this "Ego" space, contained much splitting off and from the external(hands outside its own), to fully recognize. This consent of glory, was the betrayal; worshiped for, at any cost, above the self and from the outside looking in, of the self, as better. Falling short within itself and as a dependent, to rely on a foreign disconnect, for its independence.

LESSON~182:
"I SURRENDER IN PERFECT TRUST_WITH ENERGY ALIGNMENT AND IN HARMONY OF ALL THAT IS WITHIN EVERY UNFOLDING MOMENT"

From the experience and that the self has learned, it serves no purpose; why would it place and in the hands of something else, its power? The peace, does not come from denying the attraction; rather it has learned, to take responsibility and over its own timing mechanism, by: facing, feeling and freeing, all of that, which has caused it pain and fear from separation.
Today, find what that power means, for the self and take some time to feel it; really truly feel and take possession of its body. Own the self and take full responsibility over it; as a Sovereign entity and that of the body of earth, it by choice, stands on.

For a moment, stand up straight and tall. With eyes closed, go within and feel that place of center. From that darkest void, do see it and breathe it forward, from the heart.

The purpose, is to find the stream and with this unified vertical tube, of life; from the core of the self and extend it outward, as a light body being, to experience. From this ground and that it stands firmly on, breathe out, this beam of Christed light; raise arms up and feet shoulder width apart. With every breath, in and out, become that "Northern Light", of Sovereignty and claim it on this platform, with seniority.

(Day 210)
Look at the predictable negative aspect of the programmed mind. The need to be manipulated, for its behaviour and to be in debt, for its gratitude; over to some twisted figure head, of better days ahead, again is silly. The power of the many, forcibly manufactured and to run the cosmos to the ground; can take but the very self, to stand in front and say "NOT TODAY".

LESSON~183:
"WITH GRATITUDE_MY PATH OPENS GRACEFULLY AND I CAN FEEL THE LOVE"

Look to the positive today and with compassion, see it in this way as well. Give back the positive meanings, to the language of so many words and that the world has twisted, to pity over.
Feel grateful, in the same way and as to think of no comparison, to make the "Ego" proud; in that it can, be better than, another's misfortune. Gratitude, can only be properly placed and in something as simple, as: a bird singing, or a baby laughing, after it has fallen and in its first attempts to walk. Feel the relaxed, in gratitude of another and in the same way, as it be itself, for breathing deeply, in the sweetness. Today, is about taking a moment, to stop and smell the freshness, all around; see the vibrant colours; touch and with all the senses, feel the gratitude and love. Feel grateful, without having to feel pity and then the appreciation; that in praise, will bring to the self, that sees through, with love. Focus on the positive, hear the flock of geese, flying over a deep blue sky; instead of the orange, piece of metal, that patrols the many, with an over bearing mechanism and that rapes the earth, to run its energy, with a loud propelling sound. Feel not, the loud machinery, on the ground; that vibrate, to numb the life force out, from within its center. Rather, breathe deeply and focus on the calm rays, of the sun and how the air softly blows, to remind the earth connection with the self and of its center.

LESSON~183:

"WITH GRATITUDE_MY PATH OPENS GRACEFULLY AND I CAN FEEL THE LOVE"

Be grateful, that in the midst of what appears to be an awful mess; that the self can hold itself together, to retreat in a place of peace. When the day, is to begin and when the ruckus starts, before even returning to the body, from a dream; might be a great example and of such displacement, to practice.
Do not jump up, in trauma; rather, feel within the body, the discomfort and where the numbing noise ripples out, to vibrate the body. Then slowly get up, feel the connection to its peace; with love, feel gratitude and praise for those, who are in such abyss. Then at the end of today, feel the message and in their decision for pain, that they cause. Send love, to perhaps find the way in and to dispel them from such toxic duties, of displacement; that devise from "Ego" origin and require to perform with.

Be grateful, in the hopeful situation; that the self can, but to imagine, to get things done and with no harm to any, it can thrive.

The purpose, is to feel the wealth, in one's own health and be grateful for the rattle; that it has its place, to compensate and serve, amongst the many.

(Day 211)

The self, is not of another, something else, than that of itself; because its consciousness, is the center of being and this pure consciousness state of being, is incorruptible. Consciousness, is this intervention, to manifest miracles with.

LESSON~184:
"I BREAK THROUGH MY CONSCIOUSNESS_INTO A PRISTINE AWAKENING OF PERPETUAL COMPLETION"

By the continuous mild shocks to evolve in consciousness, from deep sleep, dreaming and that of awakened state; life is hard wired to remind the self, about its existence, in this way.
When the self has suppressed emotions and the powerlessness, that it feels and from this patterning, leave it in a state of incompletion. The previous read, was an example and to recognize, the paradox of healing; from the many layers of consciousness and to be the observer, as well as the practitioner. A cognitive shift, can arise from the ability to understand and when a part of the self has become divided; lured elsewhere, to create a state of delusion for itself.
In deep sleep state, the silence and peace experienced, are parallel to what is perceived and manifested, in the waking state. Then what is it, that holds the key; to consider for a moment, a constant state of completion, to master over. The entire existence, is perception and it is, in the patterning of perspectives; that bring about, the loss and grief, to remind the self about impermanence. Having invested interest, does not allow for awakening; because it is in this long term memory, that holds the pattern in place. To become one, with dream state and awakened within the dream, an expansion must occur. To experience, that in between state and lucidly, this form of gaze; it will require, the higher frequencies of existence, so not to completely burn out and exhaust. The higher frequencies, are not bound by the lower, perceptional rules and regulations of existence.

LESSON~184:
"I BREAK THROUGH MY CONSCIOUSNESS_INTO A PRISTINE AWAKENING OF PERPETUAL COMPLETION"

Today, the idea is to merge, all the previous exercises and to blend creatively, this practice with, as creator beings.
The gaze, is an expanded awareness and that the self has many a moment, had the experience to feel. Before starting the day, find the perfect moment and step into this vastness, of gazing. Practice centering and through this consciousness, to find the center point, of stillness. With eyes closed, open the inner eye and then go ahead; blink eyes open for a moment, breathe and then close again. Remain awake/alert and feel centered.
In oneness, it is possible to feel this frequency and for as long as the self can vibrate out, throughout the day, in this way; when slipping out of it, take a brief moment, to make space for it again. This information, has now accumulated in its practice and to the extent of readiness, from this cognition; then with a subtle touch, to feel(intuitively) the next(permanent, behavioural change) level. Do not resist, into a strategic sabotage and in having to defend for anything. Do not fear, having to explain, the proving of and for any worthiness, for having found it. Rather, this better feeling place(redirect and create a new neural-pathway), is certainly near better; because it is only made slightly aware of and in the least bit, to catch on(faith).

The purpose, is to have deleted, cancelled out, and erased all, or most of, the old patterns, of beliefs.
These beliefs and from them, the imprisoned mind; that would otherwise to see, its burn box, for a casket, steel shut, with nails. See them now, one by one, removed; to release the self, from a vicious pattern, of its own demise and sabotage.

(Day 212)

There is space, made for gratitude and when the self, no longer gives submission; to the emotionally undeveloped Ego dramas, of the world. It can then learn, to transcend and from the hardwiring, of over romanticized, emotional trauma. With metacognition, the presence and comprehension, to sense of self; its thought process, from choice and to be able to create a new story, for itself, is made possible.

LESSON~185:

"MY DIFFERENCE OF AWARENESS_DOES NOT DIVIDE NOR MULTIPLY_FROM THE INFINITE CONSCIOUSNESS THAT ASSUMES FOR MY EXISTENCE"

To be different from the whole, is not to be separate from its oneness. Everything that is with soul, is different and from the same consciousness; to observe and conceptualize its existence and knowing. Different species, with different modes, can interpret for themselves and experience, of the universe; that is unknowable to the self and in a sense, that it can only guess, to know slightly.

The exchange of consciousness, can only really be understood and made possible, through the heart, with love, here and now.

The presence of the self, in this awareness to consciousness, is personal in its experience; but also can be transferable, in this way to form relationships and bonds with other creations.

Within the center of every individuation, is the oneness to all things. In the same physical body and as the self, exist trillions of cells, to make up for it. The self, is not a single entity; rather a community, made up of other (trillions)living entities, called cells.

Every function, that is present and in every single cell, has the potential, in its process of regeneration; to be made from every other cell, the same and it contains within it, the same system, the body requires, to run on. To understand one cell individually, is to understand them all. To be aware, is to be present and today the practice, is just that.

LESSON~185:
"MY DIFFERENCE OF AWARENESS_DOES NOT DIVIDE NOR MULTIPLY_FROM THE INFINITE CONSCIOUSNESS THAT ASSUMES FOR MY EXISTENCE"

To explore what "God" is, find the depth in consciousness and that volition: through thoughts, perception and emotions; in the requirement, for this evolution and to sense this awareness, of the self "<u>being-ness</u>". Go beyond the intellect, that questions the cellular memory and of the integrity to its wholeness.
The disruption of the world and situations from the many; that require today, the self discipline and from previous teachings, as prerequisites, for this ability to master over.

Today, set the intention, to tell a new story and that of feeling in higher intelligence. Before reacting, pause and observe the action before it is taken. Set a momentum to override, such unnecessary responsibility and with this presence, peace will become the outcome, for the mind. Then at the end of the day, take a moment to observe the self; without forming any judgments and in the silence, find the peace.

The purpose, is to find the center of self, in all things of oneness and wholeness; be the silence and witness with compassion for today.

CONGRATULATIONS ...!!!

FOR MAKING IT THROUGH THE 185th Lesson

(This is a rest period to take the lessons independently as a review)

TAKE THIS MOMENT AND RECALIBRATE;

MAKE NOTES AND REVIEW..................

(Day 214)
Accepting life, within momentum and to undo the strong powerlessness pattern, of feeling overwhelmed; in the making choices and through the motion, without becoming tired in the process.

LESSON~186: "I AM A LEGEND NOT A SLAVE"

The aim becomes clear, when taking life casually and in the knowing of having plenty of time. The ability to get things done, become more aligned, with ease and will most definitely allow them, to be done; this is the ground base, of reality.
Higher consciousness, is not a product of the brain, nor its body. In the case, where the body and mind become warn out, the self can take its consciousness and from it, pick up another.
With the brain of the self, mapped out and in this way, to higher consciousness; it can be for it and the greatest luxury of territory in life, to have.
Today, be the leader and by understanding the many systems; the respect, is clear to support, with the self's distinct mission and to hold its truth, within integrity. Take a moment, first thing, to set the intentions and to focus on, throughout the day; then at evening, do the same for the next day. The body can evolve, as can the mind, to some degree and to different states of consciousness; will depend upon the level of its "Dogma", to transcend from and believe as an uncomfortable persuasion. By understanding the map, the self can, to some extent, find it useful and in understanding consciousness; but it is only a tool, to help it get there. As a system of thought, for what religion does; it has been successful, to have such imprinted patterns and to serve the many with. The self however, is not bound, by its occlusions and it has choice; to go join the numbers and to group in strength, or not.

LESSON~186: "I AM A LEGEND NOT A SLAVE"

Philosophy and science too, are collective agreements, to a system of thought and for those who are embedded; because it can only be made applicable, from a consent to choose it.
For this, a reality is formed and for those who wish it, can become deeply one, with its purpose; it can adjust the level of self worth and confidence, from the outside, to conveniently support and strengthen. This can also subject the self, to object split, into the objective observation and when the subject of experience, is different, from its own. Never the less, the reality of artificial construct, is in separation; then ultimately it will discover that oneness, from the self, never has it left and with the many in this connective universal field. These systems can be very useful, to form a factual reality and based on the collective opinion; yet it has always originated form, from the self thought, of consciousness. The self can choose, to support, or modify and in the field, with these models, of reality.

Be the legend and that of self existing reality; in that, the experience is a fruition, from its own discernment, to abide by and recreate for its perception, based pattern, of perspectives.

The purpose, is to live the dream, within awakened state; to set out, with own intentions and become the leader, not the slave.
A rule, is in the ruler; its class, but only a matter of perspective and the game, that linear given consent, to play in and create within creation, from which it is creator of.

(Day 215)

By now most certainly, the reprogramming has ceased to recover itself in the same. The question of who, or what the self is; what it wants and from all of this, what it might be grateful for? Self purpose and intention, it has held on through this read and through the many pages; going over the ability and to look behind, the all seeing eye, of "I AM" and transcend.

LESSON~187:
"I AM OBSERVING AND EXPRESSING
THE UNKNOWN STORY_WITHIN EXISTENCE
BEHIND THE OMNIPRESENCE OF UNKOWABLE
FORMLESSNESS_FORMING AND AS AN ASPECT OF THE
INFINITE_ I AM AN EMPHASIS FROM THIS AWARENESS
TO EXPLORE"

The intelligence, is the only thing and that knows to separate for itself; to deny that, which it thinks, it is not. Life, over-soul and the agreed upon image of God, from the many; yet it has created for itself, to experience and in the same way, such creative constructs, to conceive with opposition. Erasing all the mind has ever known and to only re activate it, with the same intension.

The energy, that occupies and wills forth, from its information; the many different variations and of the same belief to follow, full circle, in the oneness of creation. In its denial, for the other and in it, its many variations of perception; from the many facets of the oneself, that is all things from and this paradox of intention, to have created sides with. To know God, is to know thy self and when the self can know itself; for certain, then it can know what it is not. From the knowing of what it is not; it can then find itself.

This is how the many versions can help the one, God/Life Force and to help the many with; to wake up and with the self, evolve to the next level of consciousness. When feeling it in with "Love", Consciousness, is the only thing and that the self can truly be.

LESSON~187:
"I AM OBSERVING AND EXPRESSING
THE UNKNOWN STORY_WITHIN EXISTENCE
BEHIND THE OMNIPRESENCE OF UNKOWABLE
FORMLESSNESS_FORMING AND AS AN ASPECT OF THE
INFINITE_ I AM AN EMPHASIS FROM THIS AWARENESS
TO EXPLORE"

The love, is what holds the space, to fill it in with brilliance and then, expand it out, as creator. Consciousness, is the only thing and that the self can truly be. The paradox, pulls and pushes, at both levels of creation, to attract; simultaneously within configuration, for the self, to play and manifest for it. The world, this living breathing entity, with soul and essence, is a multi dimensional portal; from which anything and everything, is possible. Within the many power of words, the Greek translation, is breath into the soul and from the meaning "soul", interpreted the word, "lungs".
The spirit(Psi-he)can come unfrozen, to awaken from the (Card it holds) and this is the heart(Kar-dia)vehicle, of (thea)Goddess.
Words are very powerful, indeed ?

Intuitive insights, however are a form of intelligence; that moves beyond the rational mind and that of the relationships, of cause and effect.

LESSON~187:
"I AM OBSERVING AND EXPRESSING
THE UNKNOWN STORY_WITHIN EXISTENCE
BEHIND THE OMNIPRESENCE OF UNKOWABLE
FORMLESSNESS_FORMING AND AS AN ASPECT OF THE
INFINITE_ I AM AN EMPHASIS FROM THIS AWARENESS
TO EXPLORE"

The quantum leaps, in thinking and where the self has been exploring; to practice with seeing, as well as feeling.
The sub atomic particles and of creative construct, does not have to co exist, in this space, of linear thinking; instead a non-algorithmic intuition and that creativity, is an extension of. The system has gaps, obviously this is the paradox of many and from which it leaves the system; from its support and for its agreed upon theories. The earth assumed to be flat, then round and might very well be, shapeless altogether; the only thing that gives it shape, is the perceiver, from its observational and often trained perspective. As much as the intention for clearing and reprogramming from these lessons are, nothing can truly be; because nothing needs to be fixed and rather just to be in admiration of the many changes. When the intention is to fix something, it locks perception and that of the self into something; that again becomes a paradox, to the very intention of restoration.

The purpose for today, is to grasp the importance of words; to just admire in the perfection, of all things, to live and let live.

(Day 216)
Infinite objects, known in their creative constructs to experience, in certain things, the same way by consciousness.
The forms of matter, that are imprinted upon reality and for the self to make use of; have only but the essence of, its creator energy and not a soul.

LESSON~188:
"WITH REVERENCE FOR ALL BEINGS ON EARTH
I WALK IN PEACE"

With imagination, gives to invention, the reason to give to the intellect, a reason to create. To impress with energy, the self can construct matter and to manipulate it, into a useful form.
The Earth too provides the self, along with the many other species and their souls by them; as well as the many parts of her, that is made of her essence. When striking a cord, from the vibration of a musical instrument; it will in essence when touched to influence all the other strings and if only, for but a moment in the same, to play along this way. What the consent might be, will vary on all levels and in this way. For example, another important energetic to consider; what it is, that it is consuming and what it is, that might be consuming it? In order to determine that, what the self can ingest, is not "vampirik" in its practice; to learn what is best suited for and its betterment nutritionally. Nutrition certainly does help to guide the self and into a higher awareness of itself.
How the self can treat its surroundings and of all that is life; will reflect the level of evolved state and frequency, it feels with its momentum. Everything is alive, simply by the energy it receives and gives and everything exists, that is given from all that is, consciousness awareness. As much as the self can feel itself, to be of life, so too, is the Earth.

LESSON~188:
"WITH REVERENCE FOR ALL BEINGS ON EARTH I WALK IN PEACE"

The Earth, has many things existing, from her; some being with essence and other entities, with soul. To take from her essence, is to nurture the self, with sustenance. To take in minerals, in a drink of water and eat nutrition, with the body's mouth; the self can taste its energy, as well as, feel for it.

Today, rather than just from its experiences, practice more awareness, with what the self wishes to know; through feeling out, in the way of, what it is eating and how does it make it feel, after eating it ? The desensitization, from the dissociation, has created a huge gap and by leaving the process, for end results. A disposable world has created a race, to the finish line and as parallel to that of, the value of quantity in lemmings.

Only then when the self can slow down, to consider what is made of soul and what is of essence, can it then to share with and in what way the exchange of energy is to be. How does it feel, to eat from something that was killed; or is the lettuce and that is being eaten, rotten from the inside out? _____

Does a crystal have a soul ?

Is it spiritual?_____ Or does it have an essence ?

Are trees and bunny rabbits, within the same, as one; in that of (having a) soul and what about the ants, on the bark, of that tree?

Why do we kill the things we do not eat?

Is the casket that has been made from a tree have a soul or an essence ?

Today, take a quarter of an hour, to stimulate the mind and before starting the day, in this way; then at evening, go over the day, to see how it might have changed, the pattern of self awareness.

The purpose, is to discover empathy and create depth perception.

(Day 217) LESSON~189:
 1. What Does it mean to TRUST AND SURRENDER ?

When all the grievances are gone, eventually the self can move out, of the "cause and effect", state of being and to evolve, from having to forgive. Trust in the abundance, of life and let go, of the "Ego's" limitations, in the mind of the self; the many prison bars of belief systems and that were created, in its need for safety.
By removing its persona, the self can embrace life, like a child and with complete surrendered trust. When in observation, witness all the masks fall off and melt away; it replaces having to defend, with proof and back unto these reflections. To accept the world, from having to change its many imperfections and see it as the witness, to the many perfections and in their own being right, to exist. Alignment, comes from the surrender and trust to life, brings success of accomplishment and abundance; or the cutting off, from them, through opposing life. Accept and allow for these abilities to have all of the resources the self will need; at any given moment and to sustain it, in its motion. From this consciousness of self discovery, the motion of abundant expression and to permeate all life with, can be received.

LESSON~189:
1. What Does it mean to <u>TRUST AND SURRENDER</u> ?

When the self, is centered and properly aligned; the field of oneness, can move through it and without resistance.
Although, there is nothing to accomplish, nor achieve, within the "<u>being-ness</u>" of allowing, to receive; the only way to keep receiving, is through releasing and letting go. The idea, is not to hang on, nor dwell on things, for too long; because that can take the self out and from the present moment, known as timelessness. Movement, is a part of life; because the unfoldment of awareness and that is consciousness, takes place in the form, of movement.
It was discussed before and about the concept of receiving, to also be the same, as giving; just feel the inspiration, from the joy it brings and to passion outward, through expression.
Allow for this need, of doing and unfold in the "<u>being-ness</u>", with alternating emphasis, to its doing aspects.

The purpose, is in complete surrender to its greater self, that it may find peace.

(Day 218)
What Does it mean to TRUST AND SURRENDER ?

In complete surrender, an anchoring from within is evident; from this level of trust, enlightenment will take its place and to welcome itself home with.

LESSON~190:

"TO SURRENDER IN COMPLETE TRUST IS TRANSCENDENCE"

When the self can surrender in complete trust, it will be in a state, of a rebirth; In this way, it can change and/or reach to other dimensions and realities, at its own whim. The resurrection, is possible and can be the way out, from coming back again; because heaven, is the place of no return. It is like, the energy to go back with, just is not there, to generate and facilitate, the treadmill and with the self on it. The self, is no more and to be bothered; by its tyrants and that would otherwise be having a trigger reaction from. It can become so drained and instead and the off balance can be felt from, as a head ache; however with the proper nutrition and stepping away, to recalibrate; it will restore the self, back to center again. Notice the breath always and where it is coming from; where from the body, does it expand and contract? Feel the depth and duration, of its length and really study, how the self does breathe. Does the tummy expand outward, when it breathes in and just from below the sternum? Does the heart expand from every breath in? Does the lower regions(belly breathing technique), below the naval, contract and then expand with every breath out again?

LESSON~190:

"TO SURRENDER IN COMPLETE TRUST IS TRANSCENDENCE"

Really study the breath today and where it takes the self. Notice when the body closes in and the breath when it is deprived; that tired feeling and the yawning that will trigger it, to breathe deeper. Practice and without the yawn, can the self breathe and in the way, the body could of done when with a yawn?   Can the self breathe enough, to make up for the yawn and not yawn ?
This, is a great technique, to learn and when in amongst the many, to regenerate; from the absence, of the yawn and not feel tired anymore, nor drained. Witness the expansion and when contracting, what causes the self to shut down.

The purpose for today, is to grasp the feeling of the breath; the importance of the many frequencies, it can reach to touch and in those realities, of its own making, just by breath from its own life into them.

(Day 219)

1. What Does it mean to TRUST AND SURRENDER ?

The miracle, is in the graceful growth of abundance; that suddenly flows through effortlessly, around the self and in its authentic interactions, of expression.

LESSON~191:

"AUTHENTICITY LIVES INSIDE OF ME
AND IN THE FULLNESS OF SELF EXPRESSION
I CAN LOVE TO KNOW MYSELF"

Do not withdraw from the feminine; because it is softer, crying is and can be as valid, in the releasing of resistance.
The Kingdom of God, is living in the oneness of inter connective communication; between cellular and environmental, sub atomic and quantum level fields. When the self can grasp and to believe, in this Kingdom; that it seeks to find and from within, is its source! This source, is of nature and nature, is the expression of the self. Once the self can connect, through surrendered trust, it will find that, all shall yield to it from the outside; added on to it will be this fullness and from a place of self expression, to know and love itself. Today, practice living from the highest expression and by knowing it, to learn to trust the intuition; premonition and cellular communication of the self and its environment.

The purpose, is to trust in the process of taking in and fully understanding, to embrace a higher concept, through perception; in that the self can be living, from its highest truth and in complete surrender.

THE INTERMISSION :

Take a day to take it in

CONGRATULATIONS …!!!

FOR MAKING IT

THROUGH TO THE 191st Lesson

(This is a rest period to take the lessons independently as a review)

TAKE THIS DAY TO RECALIBRATE;

MAKE NOTES AND REVIEW……………..

(Day 221)
   1. What Does it mean to TRUST AND SURRENDER ?

Can the self throughout the day feel for its compassion?

LESSON~192:
"BY LETTING GO_I CAN APPRECIATE THE LEVELS OF DIVERSITY AND THE MANY GRIEVANCES BROUGHT ON FROM CONTRAST
I CAN UNDERSTAND NOW_ THE VALUE IN FORGIVENESS BROUGHT ME HERE."

Sometimes the obsession to feel the closeness of another; it can overcompensate, with worship of the larger than life entities and to replace with, in relationships. Feel the many layers, within these levels of diversity can bring and for the self, to learn from. Disenchantment, can be the only measure to take, from its decree to program and the Ego's mind to fixate on for its paternal patterning. Moving right along, it too can become dismissed and once again, a disservice to the self empowerment; when seeking out for its inclusiveness. Taking sides, is the splitting of the self, to resist and create conflict with.
Today, practice through "surrendered trust", to bring the mind and heart of the self; into a oneness, state of being. Bring forth the wisdom and by combining the rational, with the emotional.
Reason serves to account for something and so does the emotional side; by bringing them together, the self can wisely form to grasp compassion. The emotional charge, can be removed and to take its place; only but the memory and that was, once forever held, within the heart.
The purpose, is to release the struggle for control and domination; by taking back the self, from such a system and in the releasing to render the self free, from it, in this way.

(Day 222)
1. What Does it mean to <u>**TRUST AND SURRENDER**</u> ?

The irony, is that God, is one big phallic and phallus fallacy; that distortion has created and in the mind of the body, as its temple. Then with great earnest, to re-emphasize, from brick and mortar; another home, made outside of it, established to congregate and that of the many, to agree upon, its standards of conduct.

LESSON~193:
"UNPERVERTED IS THE LIGHT_WHEN TRANSMUTED
FROM EMOTION_IT LOVES ITS SOURCE AND
FROM THE SOVEREIGN BEING OF LIGHT
THAT GENERATES IT"

The gift of creation, is to stand outside of it and breathe the life into it. With each thought and feeling, the dream can be seen, into existence and as having been already created. Unconsciously having created for itself, to not know where it is going, nor where it is and what, or who; until it once again awakens, to what it has created and the emphasis is then to learn, from it as it unfolds; revealing to it the answers, from each and every moment. This unconscious part of the self, that romances the idea as it might; to imagine as separate and outside of it, to worship. Amazed at the admiration, of its perfect form to entertain; within the state of coherence to the many and its world.

LESSON~193:
"UNPERVERTED IS THE LIGHT_WHEN TRANSMUTED FROM EMOTION_IT LOVES ITS SOURCE AND FROM THE SOVEREIGN BEING OF LIGHT THAT GENERATES IT."

The emotions, that can hold for the kind of lovemaking, to itself and as the body, is the sexual barrier. The outside of itself, to form within the many and that reflect; either the very same, or the very thing it can devote, to teach it from. Experience today and become as sexual, as the mind could innocently and unknowingly describe or to instead resist. To throw itself, into a war like tantrum and battle to the death, from its resistance and to the very thought, that it has unnaturally created, such a difference: <u>the conflict</u> can then be of proof; made in the rift and now that lost, its meaning to draw upon itself, the lack from comparison. The loss it feels when the extreme is so unbearable; to possibly imagine competing with it?

The purpose, is to reach in, not out. Open up and find the light, that sacred space can bring; to be illuminated, from this temple and within each and every body, that resides awareness and consciousness, for its experience as the self.

(Day 223)
1. What Does it mean to TRUST AND SURRENDER ?
Remember, that there is nothing, that needs to be corrected; in what the self can see, outside of itself. See only, what the self prefers to emphasize and untethered, from external coercion.

LESSON~194:
"THE EARTH_SHE IS ALIVE AND EVERYTHING ON HER IS LIVING_IN THE COMPLETE SURRENDERED TRUST THAT WILL BE HIDDEN FROM ANY HARM"

When the self no longer fears, to trust the magic of her kingdom and that it is, a place of Love; the Earth will reveal, the places that she cloaks over, free from harm and separation.
The hidden realms, of magical playful beings; that on the other side, might get misplaced for exploitation. The place, where miracles are every moment and as playful truths, their currency; because abundance, is all there is and plenty, as the imagination willfully able, to encourage. This place on Earth, is cloaked over by darkness; so too, the very thing and that could bring, much harm to it. The secrecy, was never impressed upon it lightly; that it was under such density. Made smaller, than life and to only have access, partially the moments; when the Earth herself, was most vibrant and fertile. Today, practice feeling the Earth; become one with her life and all that connects the self, from within, as her magnetism. Then go even further, deep and to a place, where the luminosity, was more on the emphasize, of her creation; than on her magnetism, to pro-create. Remember to be receptive enough and able to pick up on, all the little subtleties; receptive, that would mean and to feel what it would be like, to be in love.
The purpose, is to feel her open and free; from all the programmed plugins, that plug her up and keep the self disconnected, from her.

(Day 224)
1. What Does it mean to **TRUST AND SURRENDER** ?

The experience, is always authentically, to impress upon; (with no resistance) whatever the RNA(Ribonucleic acid: a polymeric molecule, essential in various biological roles in coding, decoding, regulation and expression, of DNA/genes). The structural component and that carries with it, all the energy to make it happen, is from the mitochondria; from there, everything it wishes, will become and at any given moment, to focus the emphasis, of solid formation before it. There must be a balance, with the being(stillness) and the doing(mitochondria); in this case, the doing can deplete and age the self, and when it values, where the energy must go.

LESSON~195:

"I TRUST IN MY INNER STATE OF BEING AND WITH COMPLETE SURRENDER TO MY HEART FOR SUSTENANCE_MY MIND WILL SHATTER FROM THE INCUBATION OF NATURE'S OUTER EXPERIENCE"

Through surrender, the life of the self, can renew and the self can change effortlessly. From within the eggshell, the self was taught, to release its ego. This was the Spirit of the God, that stood outside of it and taught it well. When the mind, was no longer governing its boundaries and through the transmuting, of its emotions; the self could enter and with pure innocence, into the kingdom of heaven. From the awareness, to ascend from bondage, was made available and to the level of intensity; that the self could release the belief and in its debt, for external approval.

LESSON~195:

"I TRUST IN MY INNER STATE OF BEING AND WITH COMPLETE SURRENDER TO MY HEART FOR SUSTENANCE MY MIND WILL SHATTER FROM THE INCUBATION OF NATURE'S OUTER EXPERIENCE"

To recapture, from the previous and where it had been overly emphasized, the Earth as an incubator, for self study. Now it will be, to introduce her and as from a higher interpretation, to enlighten with. It is, through complete surrender, to the heart and trust within its source of self; to reveal the light and from within an eggshell, of incubated natural experience, that was fed by its "Ego". When so many lessons later, to reveal the authenticity, that had awakened and from its light; that shattered the reality, of its mind and from the Sovereign state of being, can come to be. When the mystery, from the heart's inspiration, can excite the self, so much and where it can no longer hold the earth; that once contained it, a rebirth experience and as a hatchling, the self comes out, from its incubation. The fear from its vastness, kept it for the longest moment and in an incubated chamber; that provided opposition, so it could, from its contrast grow strong, enough to break free. Authenticity, slowly could be certain and of this feeling entrusted, in its heart; that the self could and with no resistance, surrender completely to(itself). The self had learned, the rapture of its bliss and when the mind had been silenced; to witness from the miracles and that came, from the whispering, of its heart's content. Through surrender, meant the release of control and to any outcome from the mind; the heart could then, freely be open, to remember and what the self, could not.

LESSON~195:

"I TRUST IN MY INNER STATE OF BEING AND WITH COMPLETE SURRENDER TO MY HEART FOR SUSTENANCE_MY MIND WILL SHATTER FROM THE INCUBATION OF NATURE'S OUTER EXPERIENCE"

From this inner state of being, is where the self can now combine, the outer world; that it had before observed, to direct for its circumstances. Within the present moment, is the birthplace of the Sovereign being and of all that the self, can possibly be; from its source of life and to fully correspond, with its circumstances.
The brain and heart, like every other construct, that will flow back into the impressionable membrane; from water back and forth alchemically exchanging, into a solid that will hold it and the two will mould each other. So too, is this parable, to make another cognition and from the very self, its external world.

The purpose, is to find the self, as free flowing, as the nonintrusive waters; that unobtrusively find their way around the river banks, leaving an impression and by changing the formation of them.

(Day 225)
1. What Does it mean to **TRUST AND SURRENDER** ?

Release, let go , and surrender with trust, to all that is love; be open, receptive, to project this original source, of exploration and to deliver from the heart.
From the three primary colours, to all the colours and from previous; they came into two, of separation and that could cancel out each other, so too, they can now merge into the one well. These reminders are the secondary colours and then the other variations, to combine as well. Come out of the repulsion and attraction, into the formless matter, from these zones; they are entirely unified, as this "Sovereign Light" Being.
Automatically, this memory is held in, deeper than the others; from the wholesomeness, emerges a crystalline presence and fluid white incorruptible light of existence.

LESSON~196:
"PERPLEXED ABOUT HOW TO BE THE MIRROR MY MISSION BECOMES ALL ABOUT LEARNING BOUNDARIES AND AS I FALL IN LOVE WITH SHADOW WISHING FOR THE ONENESS_IT CAN HURT SO MUCH TO TRUST AGAIN"

From the shadows of its carbon copy, the self can learn to love its childlike innocence and instead of pushing it away, the realm of innocence, through trust, it will regain. The betrayal, that once had mirrored and what the self cannot become; would not accept the authenticity, that the self alone could offer, to exist within it. Thus physically, it could never become trapped and within something, that always repelled for its existence out.

LESSON~196:

"PERPLEXED ABOUT HOW TO BE THE MIRROR MY MISSION BECOMES ALL ABOUT LEARNING BOUNDARIES AND AS I FALL IN LOVE WITH SHADOW WISHING FOR THE ONENESS_IT CAN HURT SO MUCH TO TRUST AGAIN"

From the extreme rejection, it had no choice, but to exit and from such human existence; yet the fear, from such an out casting, rendered it disabled and dysfunctional, to be allowed such entry, into coexist, as a dependent on its system. Stuck in certain levels of existence; because of "Egoic" deficiencies; where the light needed to be. The only thing that could ever harm it; or destroy it, was its very own mind, that it had feared. It was however, the way that it could be led back onto the right path that it did not take before.
In search for clues, of its happiness and that it could be led back onto the right path, that it did not take before; can the self become completely lost enough and void of all its memory, to trust again? The memory, is the experience and that holds the wisdom within it; this is why the self had to learn, to forgive and release all of its many grievances. To completely surrender into trust, is the first step into eternity and to be fully present in the moment, is the other.
Living from a state of oneness, is to be open and in love; so that the chalice can over flow, instead of forcibly empty out.
To be current and in motion, is to thrive; seek not the currency to corrupt the self and into a co-dependent sustenance, that shrinks its heart. The self does not have to be employed and to survive a life, that will promote lack and limitation, for its world.
The bridge, must be of self importance, to close this gap; but first, it must ascend and from within the gap itself.
It is the inner alchemical pathway, for spiritual illumination.

LESSON~196:
"PERPLEXED ABOUT HOW TO BE THE MIRROR MY MISSION BECOMES ALL ABOUT LEARNING BOUNDARIES AND AS I FALL IN LOVE WITH SHADOW WISHING FOR THE ONENESS_IT CAN HURT SO MUCH TO TRUST AGAIN"

The closed off self, is not illuminated and the perspective must be the change; that must be made and so that the shadows can integrate, into the oneness. Allow the light to illuminate, within the being of self. It is done through alignment, with its rainbow coloured, chakra fields. As the final words will capture, to recapitulate and for the theme, of importance: "To TRUST FULLY IN THY SELF" Through SURRENDER and this means, no resistance; so that these carbon copied, distortions and reflecting back like mirrors, can fall like dominoes, by the wayside.

The purpose, is to effortlessly feel and within that "alone" moment, is atonement taking place. Only the carbon copy, of itself; was this lonely sad existence and to live out, as an Ego driven, human form.

(Day 226)
1. What Does it mean to TRUST AND SURRENDER ?

Love can be weird and awkward and when the self does find, that it must compete, with itself, to have it. On a physical level, how can it be and to satisfy, the very simple human pleasures; that exclusively must find a way, to share with family and tribe? When inclusiveness, is all it has innocently felt the exploitation of exclusiveness to form relationships looked on with disapproval.

LESSON~197:
"I AM TURNING HOME TO THE EMPHASIS OF MY EXISTENCE THAT LOVE BEGETS ME"

When doubts start to creep in and from preferring to believe in one world, over another; it is true, that what is outside of the self, can have its way, of influence. The separation from the oneness, begins to show and when the self starts to believe, over its inner most truth. That nothing else will care, to ever find it and nothing ever will; because that, in itself, is separation. The separation, does appear in spurts and glimpses; when the self, is able to distinguish, the inner from the outer. Then further, as it gets misplaced; to wander from its center. How can it please the many, when it looks to them as separate, from itself? No doubt, this has been a conflict, to tug a war with, inner and outer personalities; to control and/or cooperate, for such relationships, as to disapprove, with lack and limitations. The "Warrior", will draw the lines and boundaries, to protect its family; similarly on the outside, groups are formed and like minded individuations, to protect the tribe.

LESSON~197:
"I AM TURNING HOME TO THE EMPHASIS OF MY EXISTENCE THAT LOVE BEGETS ME"

Today, is the day, to find that warrior of light and love and see, that the self, can get in touch with. It will feel like a foolish thing and to lighten up, the serious load; that the self has been releasing, all the while, to work through. Learn to see the positive from this experience and the value it might bring to leadership. What insights can this bring to the self, to play out and through out the day, this role to be the warrior.
Write down as much as can be understood from the experience and how it might have changed the self perspective.
Why defend ?
What does it mean and to feel the isolation, in this way ?
Does it feel under achieved; because it does not fight enough, for any cause ?
Must it take sides, or just stay on the sidelines ?
When the struggles can be realized, to release such tension and little by little, the resistance becomes insignificant.
Finding the way back to integrated wholeness, is a warrior path and the self, from all its pieces; to surrender into peace, from knowing in this act, to trust.

The purpose, is to realize that and just like the warrior; identities are meant to play with and merely just another mask to wear, to over amplify the tribe with.

(Day 227)
1. What Does it mean to TRUST AND SURRENDER ?

When a belief, is challenged the level of communication and community, will show its loyalty. To share and support the ghost like distortions, that they may be in truth, original; stemming from the very thing and that economically withholds the leads, to control this current vibe, from the support it brings.
Anything other, is a threat and must be dealt, with appropriate outcast measures.

LESSON~198: "MY FEELINGS WILL INSTRUCT ME WELL AND GUIDE ME TO GIVE PRAISE THAT I MAY LOVE BASKING IN THIS INNER GLORY I FIND PEACE"

It is true and by praying, the self can open up, to all the blessings; as many it can cope with. The purpose for the given ceremony, to gather enough, like minds and give consent; this is the very permission, that it seeks and to give reason for a celebration.
To seek for something and that the self can emphasize into creation, as it manifests; when completely surrendered, from resistance, is the peace it holds, to trust again.
The choice it must be made and to merge the two worlds, into one; thus contraction and expansion, be it may, into the "Law of Oneness". To separate from the oneness, the trinity of Father/Mother /God appears and then again, back into the oneness; as life can breathe it in and take a breath, only to exhale it out again.

LESSON~198:
"MY FEELINGS WILL INSTRUCT ME WELL AND GUIDE
ME TO GIVE PRAISE_THAT I MAY LOVE
BASKING IN THIS INNER GLORY_I FIND PEACE"

Respect comes in many forms, including the selection to value one, over another; will always keep it in a state, that of good and evil, wrong and right. The self must realize, that it is not to its advantage, to keep the many from itself, as separate. Just the same, the many separate from each other; as they do, when continuing on, to seek a fleshy image and of what they aspire, as their God. The peace in rebirth, of the self, is not to be mistaken and for a procreated act; to dwell, on for the denial of sex again, that is one sided and in the making, as incomplete.
The being, that requires to seek for another and outside of itself, in such a gay old time; then deny it, in this way as the God it seeks and to find for its peace, or else, the war becomes it. Surely there has got to be, a better way, than this.

"MY CELEBRATION_IT COMES FROM THE INNER
SERMON_THAT GIVES RISE TO CEREMONY
FROM THIS MY LIFE FORCE"

"I WILL NOT SEPARATE MYSELF_TO CHASE AWAY A
GOD AND BY SEARCHING THIS IDEA FOR PEACE
OUTSIDE OF ME"

The purpose, is to get over the duality already!

By denying one, over another and imposing judgment, of good and evil, unto it; is a damnation, to allude with such a God and to ask for peace of, undeniably suggests, for the other.

(Day 228)
   2. LESSON~199: What is <u>ASCENSION</u> ?

To be shedding, all kinds of bad habits and tuning into the Higher
Self, enduring insight; as the unattached observer and of the events
happening all around it.
This is the pathway, that takes the self and to much higher realms,
of consciousness; where the wisdom from enlightenment, await.

To transcend duality, means to ascend, and/or travel to
higher realities, of consciousness; where the polarities of the
material realm, no longer disturb and/or are of concern.
To be aware, of the present moment and that of the self,
un-judgingly.

The liberated soul, henceforth and united forever with its spirit.
The self can now rejoin the whole of its shine, which is bound
together and in one spiritual solidarity, of thought and deed.
A metaphysical perspective, to where the physical can meet, with
the spiritual realm; having a wide array of applications, at its
command and to guide along the many, with whom have yet to
awaken. Ascension, means to metaphysically recalibrate, toward a
spiritual body. Transfigure and ground, to connect with heart center
and from the metaphysical possibilities, of clarification; for the
reunion of the oneness and authentically lived, understood self.
In this way the self can seek the truth and follow it wherever it leads.

The purpose, is for a complete change of the self, through
mindfulness; for a more beautiful and spiritual state.
This is the "I AM" faith, of authenticity and that can allow, for a
light body presence.
This is what it means, to say "to be in the world; but not of it".

(Day 229)
 2. What is <u>ASCENSION</u> ?

   The process of descending and ascending, can bring with it, the activation; by also turning on "psycho-spiritual parasites", from its field. This is a turning inward, outward motion and from it, a circular boundary, to entrap things; that must be released and/or they will wander aimlessly, feeding on the energetic field of self.
   In its weakest of moments, the self might give consent and to be exploited; from wanting to help, to become of service and in this way of experimenting, to explore.
   LESSON~200:
"TO REMEMBER IDENTITY_WILL FOOL TO EXIST
   OUTSIDE OF ME AND PLAY THE ROLE MODEL
   I NOW REMOVE ALL COMMON THREAD
   THAT DISRESPECT_TO MAKE ME FEEL
   SO SMALL AND INSIGNIFICANT"

"OUTSIDE OF ME_MY LONELINESS CAN FEED
   A HUNGRY TIGER AND THEN THE NEXT DAY
   I CAN FIND AGAIN_IT HUNGERS EVEN MORE"

   Descending spiritual energy and onto matter fully, is this process, that the book encourages. Descending, is the purpose for this entire principle and for clearing lower-frequency energies; such as, repressed emotions, belief systems, judgments, control, and other contracted energies, that are at the source of limitation. In this way, the Higher Self, can start to blend itself and from it, enlightened consciousness. Full-chakra, cellular enlightenment and/or ascension, is not by any means, a way of escaping. Integration, is the ultimate responsibility; for this evolution, of achieved self-mastery and spiritual enlightenment.

LESSON~200:
"TO REMEMBER IDENTITY_WILL FOOL TO EXIST
OUTSIDE OF ME AND PLAY THE ROLE MODEL
I NOW REMOVE ALL COMMON THREAD
THAT DISRESPECT_TO MAKE ME FEEL
SO SMALL AND INSIGNIFICANT"

"OUTSIDE OF ME_MY LONELINESS CAN FEED
A HUNGRY TIGER AND THEN THE NEXT DAY
I CAN FIND AGAIN_IT HUNGERS EVEN MORE"

When ascending, the self becomes lighter and the heavy stuff drops off. When descending, it dives deeper into density and all the heavy stuff, it had not dealt with, from before, will come to haunt it. These levels of reality, are as real, as the consent to believe in them, is given, it will play along. Descension and ascension, could suggest that very well, it must be to accept and that both are key components, to the oneness, of all things. These subtle bodies, of energy, make the aura/radiance and represent for its unique personal, electromagnetic signature. The vibrational frequency, of spiritual energy, can be used to access and activate the "energetic blueprint/Light Body".

When the self can come to simultaneously accept descending, into density and then ascend again; until the two keep stepping out of its game. Energetic restructuring, alignment, and balancing on multiple levels, simultaneously; until it can transcend, to yet another playing field and all the way, to reaching the
"<u>Luminous Resurrection of being</u>".

LESSON~200:
"TO REMEMBER IDENTITY_WILL FOOL TO EXIST
OUTSIDE OF ME AND PLAY THE ROLE MODEL
I NOW REMOVE ALL COMMON THREAD
THAT DISRESPECT_ TO MAKE ME FEEL
SO SMALL AND INSIGNIFICANT"

"OUTSIDE OF ME_ MY LONELINESS CAN FEED
A HUNGRY TIGER AND THEN THE NEXT DAY
I CAN FIND AGAIN_IT HUNGERS EVEN MORE"

Ascension, does not stop and yet, the perception of it; perspective, is what changes the game. When in "descenion", it does not stay there and for as long as it used to. Rather, what has changed this time, is that the self, has resurrected and from its heart, to keep it open; regenerate the Love and light, no matter the hell its in.
It recognizes the importance, of its breathing and a sure good way, to indicate the level of its heart's expansion, from its source of light; that guides it, just as long, as it stays open.

Today, continue to allow for the love and light and to bring forth to the surface, all the toxins of the world; that have polluted the self and held it down. The many can be helped and so too, the planet as a whole; when the self can hold, for this intention.

The purpose for today, is to help raise the many, of the self and that of the earth, into another step toward ascension; by respecting to acknowledge, the level of its density and that of "descension" , to be just as important, to the whole.

(Day 230)
2 What is <u>ASCENSION</u> ?

From this level of awakening upward, the self can open up, to filling in its frequencies. Then learning from a place, that it can feel, its highest excitement; it can vibrate with and to that of a light body consciousness. The exploration of its infinite presence, will bring it to a place of Sovereignty and from this Light, expanded outward (radiating); out into the final mastery, of illumination.
These levels of transcending, are the very brief interpretation and of this process, called "Ascension". In the flow and radiating outward, of this, its "<u>Sovereign Light</u>".

LESSON~201:
"I AM FLOWING IN AN UPWARD SPIRAL RADIATING PURPOSE WITH EXCITEMENT AND IN HARMONY TO MY PASSION FROM THIS CLARITY THAT IS MY BRILLIANCE"

The self, in so far, as it lightens up, from density itself and harmonizes, with the new vibratory frequencies; to undergo this kind of conscious initiation and that is multi-dimensional(transcending, from the linear concept and spiraling upward). The "Sovereign Light", relates to the higher frequency energy fields; that lie deep within, the infrastructure of itself and the universe. The purpose, is to activate the body and in this way, of functioning with this Light infrastructure; that it must re-establish, from deep within its core and that interacts with dimensions, of linear and circular reality.

LESSON~201:
"I AM FLOWING IN AN UPWARD SPIRAL RADIATING PURPOSE WITH EXCITEMENT AND IN HARMONY TO MY PASSION FROM THIS CLARITY THAT IS MY BRILLIANCE"

From hence, the force of the self and as life, had entered through(as self awareness), is where, it also leaves it.
From the eruption, of the root of the self and that grounds it, from its tailbone; the force ignites it upward, in a spiral dance. The duality of the two of minds and like serpent flares; break open, from the golden halo and the silver thread releases.
In this place, enlightenment is the break through, from such ascension and/or death. The afterlife and/or metaphysical, that is of spirit, will be forced upward and in the same way as it was forced inward; from the crown of the top of the body's head. This cooperation, can only be made possible and to ascend in such a way; that had allowed for it and in its descending, in the first place. To cooperate with the physical body, can be made possible and from the endocrine systems; that coordinate the alchemy, along the process. Yes, to forgive by releasing, all grievances, is one sure way to mindfulness; however the emotions, are mostly governed by the organs and in a cooperative dance with thought.

LESSON~201:
"I AM FLOWING IN AN UPWARD SPIRAL
RADIATING PURPOSE WITH EXCITEMENT AND
IN HARMONY TO MY PASSION FROM THIS CLARITY
THAT IS MY BRILLIANCE"

The falseness of the Ego mind, is as real as truth and when thought promotes collectively, its subjectivity alike. Without such opinions to uphold by, what else is there; but the hormones, insignificantly to interact with and conditionally bonding, to control, that of the many formed relationships. The conformity, to its legal structure and so on it goes. When the organs of the body, are properly aligned and made to stimulate the function well; the thymus gland regenerate from stimuli and that the body can youthfully restore again, from the levitating open hearted, childlike state. This is, what it means, to function from the highest state of joy and vibrate such frequency outward. Only when the mind, is silenced and can trust, to know the self, enough to surrender, to its highest good; can the possibility, to activate and through ascension, into enlightenment.
Duality spirals up, the spinal column and in this reunion, to becoming oneness; they dance and up the skull, a serge like pillar of light, will open up and radiate outward, to illuminate the body.

The purpose, is to better understand the importance, of feeling the body and the connection to the self; that can be an aspect, of focus and from the vastness, that ascension brings.

(Day 231)

2 What is <u>ASCENSION</u> ?

To be the ocean, the self must also learn to understand and recognize, the many ripples of its vastness, along the way.

LESSON~202:
"I RESPECT ALL THINGS AND DO NOT WISH TO COMPARE THE VALUE OF ONE SIDE OVER ANOTHER"

Manifesting, from a light body of consciousness, is different; than manifesting, from Divine Excitement. Upon awakening, the field will clear and during this awareness, electro magnetism, is the law it will attract and from that which it thinks.
When it transcends and expands again, into the level of Sovereignty; it thrives from a place of authentic expression, exploring and responding, with the infinite dance, of golden radiance. Manifesting, is imprinted upon, from its awareness to it and transmission, from this inner vision, out into external field. Eventually, the level of it, becoming the mirror; it will no longer have mirrors, to manifest for it and in this way.
When the ascension process has already occurred within the self then this tool can become and from even previous terminology to transcribe an even better read. To be on a frequency, of having to tense up and into something serious, is to take sides; view points to defend and that can be, of cause, to stand with Karma, in a dualistic predicament.

LESSON~202:
"I RESPECT ALL THINGS AND DO NOT WISH TO COMPARE THE VALUE OF ONE SIDE OVER ANOTHER"

Eventually, everything that is of the self, will gravitate in the becoming of, a "<u>Sovereign Light</u> Body" being and yes, even going beyond this, Atonement; to actually living, in its illumination and that it must, come to revere.   What is respect ?
Today, is all about taking the time, to focus on the meaning of respect and with this intention, of what it means.
Does respect come from pouncing on another; to have them fear into it? Does it happen, because of royalties and blood lines?
Is it made of currency, to bind another with?
Is respect the same, with every species and does it thrive, or rely on the neediness, to survive?
Is it predatorial and does it require, to set for distinct, protective boundaries ?
Can respect come from love, or must it be of equal footing; in the casting of classes and that the "Ego mind" authorizes, for the world to set as such standards, to live by?

When the world's exclusiveness, stands for something, it stands in isolation, from the self.

LESSON~202:
"I RESPECT ALL THINGS AND DO NOT WISH TO COMPARE THE VALUE OF ONE SIDE OVER ANOTHER"

Awareness, of the brutal behaviours and that, from arrogance decipher, to devalue for respect. This is the importance, of accepting how to coordinate; through a cooperative dynamic and with such relationships, of the self. Does it make sense, to go down and to those levels; so to bring, the world up and just a little bit more forward, than before? YES! Without the rest of the world and the many, (consider this one instance and that part of the unresolved) the self cannot move up further; this resolve can likewise stand, to be true and with the many of the world.
As many steps, that can be taken and then it must wait, or stress in the catching up for it. This is, all that is, of all that is and really, there is no other, hierarchical to discriminate; such illusions hinder the ascension and at a larger scale, to slow it down; yet again, that too, is of importance. Everything, is all divinely synchronized and for the awakened, to help orchestrate.

The purpose, is to learn discernment and with that, respect all things; even more so, the innocence, that knows not, of such nonsense and to take seriously, to heart.

Ultimately, respect is something, that is generated, from within and is a presence, of self esteem. Reverence, can very well come naturally and very subtle, to the touch; as to feel it, from the inside and toward all, that it becomes aware of.

(Day 232)

2   What is <u>ASCENSION</u> ?

Within the ugly, there is beauty and screaming to be let out. The impurities can't capture to exploit the reverence of the self that holds its grace. The relationships with self can be as innocent when forming a relationship with others and as much as the interpretation of it can allow. Can the choice be made available, to focus on the pollution of its planet; or at the untouched parts that missed the ruling influence of punishment, that would have otherwise made it ugly altogether?

LESSON~203:
"WHERE I CHOOSE TO FOCUS MY ATTENTION ON
WILL BE AND ONLY IN THE WAY I WISH
TO INTERPRET SEEING IT AS"

By denying the Ego and projecting it out toward a false interpretation that God is not might for some get rid of it all together. Others so head strong to contradict this statement makes it plausible and just as good to help in the release of Ego identity in such reactions. When there are no more buttons to be pushed the self can begin to pick up the many powerless pieces of itself to further integrate these parts of ego and just as well with all its many shadows. The way to cancel out from its equation is to transmute in such a way that it can be made possible to transfigure; then finally to ascend and into a transformative shift to shape for self its external circumstances of its material world with.

LESSON~203:
"WHERE I CHOOSE TO FOCUS MY ATTENTION ON WILL BE AND ONLY IN THE WAY I WISH TO INTERPRET SEEING IT AS"

Where these sticky points exist along the way; is where it must explain for itself and that it is enough to be considered worthy player for the game. Deserving of its so many inquisitive excuses and in all fairness of such games; it had never considered that it would be allowed such privileges and as to qualify the why it can't, to choose to join in. Why all this confusion is the wake up call that self had at the forefront of creating. A real visionary and yet lacking the social know how to coordinate and communicate with such cooperation for assistance. Just lets it happen effortlessly and without pushing over for anything that it can be, the many of resistance from before now pushing even harder to demand of the unfairness some explanation to why they were not involved in the having. Why so much strife to keep it out had developed the limit of those choices in the first place.

The self must learn to where it needs to come together and unite these separate parts. It is through these separations that the gaps have made to hold the information needed for the self to grasp and then they will close. Once all the gaps are closed and the self can live completely from a place of oneness it can be unstoppable. It can then timeline shift into any dimension that it feels like without a catch nor glitch. It is in the timeline jumping and shape-shifting that moves it out of its comfort zone and that is also needed for it will never stop evolving.

The purpose, is to understand the present moment just a little bit differently than before in that it can impress upon all time lines simultaneously all at once.

(Day 233)
2   What is <u>ASCENSION</u> ?

The self must lose all the hierarchical structure because most of the titles are "Ego" fulfilling not integrating.
Maybe for the sake of convenience the title as coordinator; organizer; communicator and/or co operator are within the self required. To understand how the physical body functions automatically with the self internally; is how it must learn to do the same with its external aspects that the many of its world will represent for it. This is what it means to be a healer.

LESSON~204:
"WHEN CLIMBING UP A ROCKY MOUNTAIN
IT IS MOST WISE NOT TO COLLECT
OF ALL THE HEAVY ROCKS ALONG THE WAY"

The Ego, is the indicator from where the self needs work on and to refine; either from within and/or from its external environment where the process from the many will agree for the opportunity to happen. When the opportunities are always there and the universe is always extending out to self such miracles the many of free will can and have every right to not allow for the self to engage with the involvement no matter the win fall that the universe will represent to it. Relationships present themselves in such a way that the others free will do not permit can only mean one thing; That the self has some inner work within its own soul to figure out.
Today, look deep into the self and in the soul, where the dysfunctions are and unconsciously that will not permit from its unwanted external relationships.

LESSON~204:
"WHEN CLIMBING UP A ROCKY MOUNTAIN
IT IS MOST WISE NOT TO COLLECT OF ALL THE HEAVY
ROCKS ALONG THE WAY"

Surely there must be a misalignment somewhere, for such soulful interpretations and to create enormous resistance; from the collective's will, to not permit these opportunities to play, learn and grow from. This is where the self must not be so concerned, to service others and until those others, will permit for this.
Here is where the Ego fulfilling entities conspire to block the flow, it could be very possible that the many would prefer the self over any other and yet that is not how the procedure takes its course. Just who is in control here? Sovereignty makes up for its own rules and that of which it feels to be conducting over its presence. Ultimately the responsibility is that of reintegration for this its atonement. For now this concept might be way to inconceivable the level from where it operates to function with its orders of external disconnect. Coming home is also having to clear perhaps the clutter and do not expect it to be always empty in a way of housework it must go through the restoration and than that of cleaning it; however there is no order in that which linear relevance might have it play to understand.
Even in this example of editing sometimes the entire manuscript must reconfigure to restore into another way that and it could use more to reinterpret; rather than throw out(Adding and removing bits an pieces).

LESSON~204:
"WHEN CLIMBING UP A ROCKY MOUNTAIN IT IS MOST WISE NOT TO COLLECT OF ALL THE HEAVY ROCKS ALONG THE WAY"

There is always a membrane and a filter, that the Ego represents and the awakened self must realize (discernment); that it has intensions to exploit. Sometimes relationships can be cruel, mean and mostly unbefitting. The self, is only permitted to play, with such experience and when placed inside its mirrored structures. The Soul can only therefore, be a mirror and moving through to the center, of its many layers; where through the heart, the ascension can begin. The self must find a way, to leave the construct of its "Ego" driven, mirrored walls (quadrants). To step off the 4th density, is to play within the unstructured formlessness and before it re-enters back into its physical geometrical matrix again.

The self can go ahead and play within these fields/realities; yet remain unforgiven and by the many, that it will not commit with, to the experience. Is it not an agreed upon stress and to the extent of loyalty, that it may expire from the physical?

This is why forgiveness is so important; it is a given opportunity to detach(un clutch) from all of these illusions. Let it go, all that which cannot possibly conceive to why the self might anger it so much and for no apparent reason? Integration has a way of getting through to the self and feeling it, is this process.

The purpose, is to release and let it go, of all the things that refuse to acknowledge that self exists; because it will only anger them some more for no apparent reason. In doing so, a newer sensory system can emerge, from boundless space.

Take 2 days to take it in

CONGRATULATIONS ...!!!

FOR MAKING IT THROUGH THE 204th Lesson

(This is a rest period to take the lessons independently as a review)

TAKE THESE TWO DAYS TO RECALIBRATE;

MAKE NOTES AND REVIEW..................

TSLM   ACIMS

(Day 236)

2   What is <u>ASCENSION</u> ?

What is sacrifice, but to completely let go of everything. "Surrendered Trust" and as was the practice from the previous chapter; to have the self completely lose itself and into the abyss, of the unknown.

LESSON~205:
"I SACRIFICE MYSELF TO LIVE COMPLETELY A NEW WITHIN THE PRESENCE OF THIS MOMENT IS ALL THERE IS."
"TO HEAL DOES NOT ONLY OF THE MIND REQUIRE BUT ALSO OF THE HEART"

Sacrifice, is not like every other word and that has been twisted out of its origin, of interpretation; in the context of the present terminology and that the collective holds, to identify it with. "Sacrifice", it is in the only truest power, in the sense of letting go and to surrender over the self; in such a way and that short cuts into the ascension, quicker. However, just as quick as it had shot up, the self will come back down again and to learn more, of its process. The reason why it is mentioned in this chapter, instead of the previous one, is because, it is acutely and the result of "Sacrifice"; that is, at the apex of "Ascension". It is the fastest way of getting there, however, the staying there, to move on, to the next, and then the next; it requires the process of this practice and to maintain a steady readiness. The frequencies must be a match, on a steady level and the gaps must close, that bridge the frequencies apart.

LESSON~205:
"I SACRIFICE MYSELF TO LIVE COMPLETELY A NEW WITHIN THE PRESENCE OF THIS MOMENT IS ALL THERE IS"
"TO HEAL DOES NOT ONLY OF THE MIND REQUIRE BUT ALSO OF THE HEART"

There are many examples and from the mind of self; that reflect among the many. Who alchemically become unbalance to achieve, such states to crash, burn and/or self sabotage; because the fear is greater. The gap, is the space where the chemically unstable reside; to off balance the mind and in such a way, as to have stretched it, in neglectfulness. Manic and depressant, is one such illness, to experience; perhaps other forms and of milder states, the mind will perverse into the sacrifice of it.
Not allowing to release from the dogma and in such a way, that before it reaches the critical need, for long term use of medications. To rather the resistance mechanism of that which will then result and in the kind of self sabotage, that gave the new interpretation for "Sacrifice". These are symptoms and that when they go uncared for to notice, are the extremes of frequencies; from one end of the spectrum, to the other.
Previous authors, who might have has plenty of credentials and as proven doctors of philosophy; would not have recommended, to go and pick apart the term "Sacrifice". For the many that they have served and with pharmaceuticals; instead, the neglect to use it, as a tool of study, was dismissed and in it altogether, as being an illusion.

LESSON~205:
"I SACRIFICE MYSELF TO LIVE COMPLETELY A NEW
WITHIN THE PRESENCE OF THIS MOMENT
IS ALL THERE IS"
"TO HEAL DOES NOT ONLY OF THE MIND REQUIRE BUT
ALSO OF THE HEART"

Ascension has had its many disguises, throughout the ages and with longer lasting symptoms, of the self's historical stages.

The purpose, is to give another view, from the hidden truths and that stored away, the symptoms of ascension.
Perhaps to consider, in its progress of the mind and to ascend beyond the dimensional levels of existence; that could make for obsolete, the need to conceive of psychology and psychiatry altogether? "Sacrifice" and only to scratch the surface of something, that could be too deep, to describe in one page. To have no bottom and to come right back out; into the unknowable and that the unknown, can only grasp enough, to really know again.
What is the unknowable; but the deep unconscious mind and from it, the unknown, that is the sub-conscious. From this how, the known can then exist, as to be conscious and then, all knowing; that is the higher state, of consciousness.

(Day 237)
2 What is <u>ASCENSION</u> ?

Praise is something that the self requires much of and as the psyche's parent to the inner child to give. When the many are harsh, mean and critical, the higher self will have no part of it. Thus the self becomes rejected from the whole, of its tribe and community; that have out casted it and so it seems, left it for dead. Words are very powerful and hold with them energy.

LESSON~206:

"WHERE THERE IS PRAISE I FEEL THE GLORY INSTEAD OF CRITICISE AND WHERE THERE WAS ONCE OPINION FOR REJECTION A BULLET PROOF SELF THAT ONLY LOVE MAY FOLLOW THROUGH"

Death, is a transformation and such a gift to find, that self is the creator. When left with no alternatives for the opportunities to work under others, is to degenerate; it must create its own, to generate an inclusive generation with. No size is too little, to befit the envy to employ and with tight fisted, its world of "do gooders", to degenerate the masses. So it seems this way and for the longest moment, the self must learn to open up and from the similarities, that draw it near, to such narrow minded circumstances; as to believe the brain, in it, and for its very own survival.
Today, practice being grateful and praise the self, with every opportunity and that it can find to feel such worth; from itself, it can become so reassuring of its capabilities.

LESSON~206:

"WHERE THERE IS PRAISE I FEEL THE GLORY INSTEAD OF CRITICISE AND WHERE THERE WAS ONCE OPINION FOR REJECTION A BULLET PROOF SELF THAT ONLY LOVE MAY FOLLOW THROUGH"

Just for a moment and to set a platform with such words; that can create a space to own with seniority. Stand and sample from this platform's exercise, to greet the world with. Pick a few words and play with them, to see how they feel. What does it mean to believe in the self? Does it lift and elevate? Is it a settling and healing space? Is it centering; evolving the psyche's inner child and transcending it; heart awakening and or helping to release old patterns? Does it settle the mind, with ease and/or expand creativity? Physical ease and emotional flow, can come from these words; that bring about positive and unlimited thoughts.
See how many words, that can be selected and at least, three or four. To feel certain and capable, comes from a certain kind of self reliance and from there, the confidence of belief, in the self.
For a moment experience these perspectives; the purpose that they bring, with each frequency and for the self, to vibrate in.
Master this moment well and what it feels(vibe) like, to experience(the spin) these words. How many other platforms can be added? Practice and combine(words) them, to experience a different level from before. Practical foundation for the mind, to play with; solidify each step into and from these spaces, that spiral upward toward "Ascension".

LESSON~206:
"WHERE THERE IS PRAISE I FEEL THE GLORY INSTEAD OF CRITICISE AND WHERE THERE WAS ONCE OPINION FOR REJECTION A BULLET PROOF SELF THAT ONLY LOVE MAY FOLLOW THROUGH"

With this exercise, the application will recreate a better frequency; that can to propel the self, from any previous lower density. From imaginary linear concepts on the ground to stand on; the more these words are played with, the easier(electrical geometry) that these energetic boundaries can be formed. By connecting from each point of reference; with each word to feel and strengthen the energy of its field. Praise is the icing on the cake, or the fruit in the cake; that will increase, with gracefulness and to ascend, from such depths, of appreciation. Look at all the many accomplishments; throughout the year, months, weeks, days. Then at the end of today, see what else and that can be, even more subtle enough, to add. From a two dimensional configuration of a triangle; to the extra point that joins it there into the third and fourth. As with its imagination further, that it can then to ascend upward and/or downward; spiraling and into multi-levels of dimensions as it may to care for in the feeling of it. How many sides does a pyramid have?   From 4-8 and so on; It has been briefed upon before, the relevance of this word "Ascension". To sum it all up: from the base, is where the zero point field and for its awakening begins; then from there, four other sides distinctly form a space, to play with and until it reaches resurrected illumination. At this time it could, to also remember and in relations of its reflection; to integrate this further and into the many points of six, as in the case of a (previous lessons) star tetrahedron configuration. For now, it is most wise, to keep it simple and at the ground level, is this purpose for today.

The cognitive grasping of dimensions and from this level; that the self can, to stand up, rise above and in its discovery, of its many choices, it can thrive from.

(Day 238)
2   What is <u>ASCENSION</u> ?

The heart is so important, in that, it's where we think, we feel the love and yet it, all comes from the mind. To process awareness and coordinate, the correspondence of the inner and the outer world, of the self; it takes the many layers of the mind, to process through.

LESSON~207:
"IN A WORLD OF ONLY THINKING TO FACE THE GREATEST FEAR_IS TO OPEN UP TO LOVE"

The unconscious mind is very smooth, to promote; it's part of the vegetative nervous system, of the body and of the self.
On the physical level, for the self to connect with that involuntary function, is at the highest of authority and to sustain life for it. When this function stops, so does everything else, of self and here it is, where it gets tricky; that the medical field has altered through experiment. With chemically synthesized substances and the balance to maintain harmony; it can temporarily restore and with life, from the outside in. Sympathetic dissonance, is this lack of inner harmony and from a disconnect; to anything that is outside to provide and for the senses of the self. Nothing from the outside ever lasts and thus never really is, a reliable source to cognitively devote as worship. The adoration, that the self seeks to find and from the outside; or sexual gratification, is all from the inner peak, of parasympathetic resonance(automatic nervous system).
With the sympathetic resonance, of profound exhilaration and inspiration; joy, peace, and to a sense of wellbeing. In this way, the self can then tap into, a sense of connectedness; bliss and ecstasy.

LESSON~207:
"IN A WORLD OF ONLY THINKING TO FACE THE GREATEST FEAR_IS TO OPEN UP TO LOVE"

All these feelings, are states that the self, can tap into and the breath, is the connector. With breath, a profound relaxation response, into the parasympathetic nervous system and without going to sleep, can be made possible. This is how the self, can connect to the higher mind; however for this ascension process to happen, the heart must be open. What does this mean?
The autonomic nervous system holds memory, in the muscle; it does it, through feeling and sensing responses, similar to orgasms. Taking in and releasing, is in resonance to breathing in and out. So too, does the blood travel and from that place, where the heart pumps; the oxygen transfers through and the membrane is this bridge, of both worlds. Everything in the body of the self, holds memory; every part must get its turn and to release, as it regenerates within the present moment. The unconscious, is what holds the memory; when properly communicated, to cooperate, it will release to the subconscious. The conscious self, is the most limiting of all the layers, of the mind and the most challenging, to deal with. When the self has gone into ascension, the consciousness can become mature enough and to accept its integration, as enlightened from it. The subconscious fuses with the conscious mind, when the unconscious, is opened up completely. Yes, the heart is also the unconscious mind and at the center of it all, is the thymus gland. Also the given for every other gland and to consider; the natural homeopathy remedies, that regulate the self well and from one most simple basic method, to practice, in that all begets from breathing. The purpose, is to understand ascension and from a physical perspective, its vital connection to the nervous system.

(Day 239)

2   What is <u>ASCENSION</u> ?

With spirituality, both sides of the brain must be operative and in oneness, to see the light. Body, Mind and Spirit, must work out, all at once and simultaneously. How is it, that the inner workings of the body and with no involvement of the self, to manually impose; is so delicately cooperating, with the whole of its systems, and for the self, to be well and function healthy?

LESSON~208:
"TODAY I INTEGRATE BOTH SIDES INTO THE WHOLENESS OF MY MIND_I MAKE ENOUGH"

The mind must learn, that its outer circumstances, are to be trusted; just as well, as from the inside, they do function and to sustain its life with. To begin to understand, how well the inner workings do, just well and with the self not having to involve itself, to do anything, but surrender to it. The body will listen to the mind; whatever it is thinking and feeling, it will resonate with and in exactly the same way, as the outer world does. How is that working out ? This was the reason, behind the affirmations and all the many practices; to reach this far and as in the evolution of the self, to have it understand and yet, some more about "Ascension".
Again, ascension is a process of transcending and into something more evolved. All the previous information about sound, that is vibration and that hits a cord of resonance; right to the very cellular level, for the light.

LESSON~208:
"TODAY I INTEGRATE BOTH SIDES INTO THE
WHOLENESS OF MY MIND_I MAKE ENOUGH"

To break it down, from the many layers of the body's auric field. From the multi coloured rainbow, that its organs and hormones they release; that ties it in so well with the emotional and physical body. Eventually, it all goes back, to the three primary colours; then again the white and dark light, that for the most part, could very well cancel itself out. Everything came in a dualistic reality, of contraction and expansion; as we merged the two, we got a third and more pristine self, that was the oneness. This very well might be another summary; for its completion and of the book, thus far, so let it yield here then. The endocrine system, is something that was not touched on, and in the previous books, before it; nor did the mention of the sections, of the heart, nor brain. To say as much, of what the self might have preferred, for its enlightenment; through logic or the creative chamber, of the brain, to formulate ascension with. When the self can readily, through breath, be able to regulate, with thought and feeling. Best of all, to chant with sound, the chakras; when they are spinning and with the life force, in harmony. Like little vortices, the self can join them up; to form a white light, a stream of white light outward. This then becomes something that the self can also transcend to break free from such an incubation chamber and yet another stage of resurrection without having to leave its body.

The purpose, is to learn from the delicate, inner balance and the workings of the self in such a way; as to feel inspired to express, with graceful movement and to its outer world with, that is "Ascension".

(Day 240)
2   What is **ASCENSION** ?

The element of surprise, can trigger unexpected insights. It might even bring up old beliefs; to be exposed and bring to disbelief, within the present moment, of events.

LESSON~209:
"I WOULD LIKE TO UNDERSTAND THE SADNESS OF FULFILLED HAPPINESS THAT COMES OVER ME WHEN IN THE PRESENCE OF THE MOMENT SOMETHING THAT MY HEART HAS ALWAYS LONGED FOR BECOMES SO VERY REAL"

When the self can feel emotions and from an ascended place of mastery, it can go deeper. Enlightenment is an adventure, to explore expansion and with the self as a sovereign being, to have stepped into its own. Enlightenment does not stop revealing and from the outer places of the self; nor inner and to continue to evolve by it, as an ascended being. More subtle and less dense, the emotions will start to become more refined, with the self to experience; more depth to hold, so to accept(not overwhelm) such information and for the self to process through. The neurological system, must reach a certain level and to absorb without short circuiting. It can be very overwhelming and unless the self has already ascended, to tolerate; or else to leap, outside its comfort zone and that would to fry otherwise, in any other way. It is a delicate balance and for the self to adjust into a gradual progression, through its practice; to stay in the presence of "the AHA" and/or "Eureka" moment and for as long as the self can tolerate.
The feeling, is intense and can be truly experienced, with many others, in this way; when a gathering of likeness fills its space.

LESSON~209:
"I WOULD LIKE TO UNDERSTAND THE SADNESS OF FULFILLED HAPPINESS_THAT COMES OVER ME WHEN IN THE PRESENCE OF THE MOMENT SOMETHING THAT MY HEART HAS ALWAYS LONGED FOR _BECOMES SO VERY REAL"

Living life from a higher existence, is much lighter; however the self gets pulled right out of time. To live in a place of timelessness, the self lives like a master and time becomes irrelevant; because the synchronicities, for everything it sets out to focus on and with intent, will be on target point. With passion, it will take on its tasks and little by little, each day will reveal and then the night; that the self can then remind itself, to eat and sleep. It can be frustrating at times; because the self can think about, the time it takes away to eat, is longer, than even its sleep. Sleep too, is not really sleep, but more so a moment; that the self will take, to just be and not do anything. When the self forgets to eat, it might start feeling even lighter than before; meaning that, it must eat, to stay within, the physical body. The dietary intake will start to change, as it progresses and things like sugar, it will avoid; because it disrupts its cellular communication and thus the ability to interpret, its world around it. To take in flesh, from animals, has already previously been discussed, within this book; however that all depends on, where the self is at and might require.

LESSON~209:

"I WOULD LIKE TO UNDERSTAND THE SADNESS OF FULFILLED HAPPINESS_THAT COMES OVER ME WHEN IN THE PRESENCE OF THE MOMENT SOMETHING THAT MY HEART HAS ALWAYS LONGED FOR BECOMES SO VERY REAL"

Ascension, is a beautiful thing and to experience within the physical, transforming into light.

The purpose, is to realize, that there might still be many beliefs, to process through and will not be held on, as long to, as before; also the emotions, will start to defuse somewhat and blend into, with each other. The creations of such blending, are the same and as with colours, tastes flavours; even the pheromones too, become refined and almost non existent.

(Day 241)
3. What is a <u>SOVEREIGN LIGHT BEING</u> ?

Atonement and from it luminosity. Turned on from within and over the moon, with vibrating excitement. Taking responsibility and over the creative force, of self; is to be of every encounter, every relationship, every interaction. To be in every part of its environment and to name as itself; from a perspective of having created its life!" With the awareness, from an open heart and a presence, within this moment; held strong and activated on, with clarity, to intend on every thought, with focus.

LESSON~210:
"THE LIGHT IN ME HAS BROUGHT AWARENESS TO THAT WHICH IS SACRED_MY CREATIVE FORCE"

From here on forward, make the intention, that self will be responsible and in showing up to its reflections; for all of its creations and not just from its beliefs. Independently, claim the power of the self; as the authority and be the light, of self expression. Seek not the approval, from the many reflections; rather govern and from within. The self can and under its own light, shine outward with authenticity, in its own right. The old patterning within; from within the cellular consciousness, has now shifted and attuned its frequency, with that of "Divine Light". Be it, that divine expanded state, of conscious light and that has ascended; it can now transform everything, from the power of its love. Live within the wonder, that is and immerse in the moment, of the beauty of it all; that the self, is the miracle of miracles and from which life breathes into and it into itself.

The purpose, is to explore and feel the infinite possibilities, that can be of great influence, from these words and enlighten unto the self; for its environment, to consciously become aware, of it and the part it plays, in its creation.

(Day 242)

3. What is a <u>SOVEREIGN LIGHT BEING</u> ?

Transcending metaphysical hierarchy, is a process and of self-liberation/clearing. When guided by the understanding of Universal Law, there is, only inner authority and self-governance; it will not allow the self and from instigating harmful actions, that could harm another.

LESSON~211:

"I CHOOSE TO STAND FOR TRUTH_AS A SOVEREIGN BEING AND FREE FROM HARBOURING ALL DECEPTION PARASITISM AND ENSLAVEMENT"

Hierarchy, is a male-dominated and disempowering system of authority, obedience and enslavement; the self through love however, can transcend, in order to begin to heal itself and the world. The self has now awakened, from the previous agreements and it withstood amongst the many; working with the light, to dismantle the old and heal, by promoting self regeneration. These entry agreements, also contained clauses; that were for unspecified hardships, to be leveled against and during this incarnation. No longer are these coagulative, physical /sexual abuse, psychic attacks, etheric implantation, and dream-manipulation, to recruit; into working for the false-light, made applicable.

LESSON~211:

"I CHOOSE TO STAND FOR TRUTH AS A SOVEREIGN BEING AND FREE FROM HARBOURING ALL DECEPTION, PARASITISM AND ENSLAVEMENT"

The parenting role models, of rejection, and criticize; have exited, taking their secrets with them. The worker of light, must come to the realization and that it was always a light being; to awaken and from within its self worth, that from previous, it was taught falsely, to know and bear the torch, for the many.
One thing is for certain, the dark sorcery, is no longer able to transfer the guilt over and must take ownership of it, full on; this will appear, as a comical reversal. Amongst it, all see it with light heartedness and feel the love; no matter the awkwardness, the self is not to judge, only be the observer. In a free foundational society, the self will not need, even so much, as the red light green light, district; that causes such jagged patterning, of behavior, to stop and go. The stresses of the world and uneasiness, will obsolete; because it will cease and to be of any service, to hold relevance. The "Ego" trap, of exerting "authority", over others, to control and regulate, their behaviors, will no longer be. Practice today, from a different way of seeing and what was practiced from before. Stand in the divine, inner light, of Self's Sovereignty and from the heart, expand to Higher Self; surrounding the body, in a sphere of energy. Connect to Earth's core, and that of Infinite Source, from the forces, of divine light presence.
The purpose essentially, is to break out, from the holographic spell of duality/polarity, and the idea, that the self, must serve one side, over the other.

(Day 243)
3   What is a <u>SOVEREIGN LIGHT BEING</u> ?

Relax into the fear(if any), and love thyself, through the process; that is the flow, of present moment. Converge into a single level, of awareness and from it, into all the parallel worlds, of consciousness.

LESSON~212:
"I HAVE AWAKENED TO MY SACRED PRESENCE AND
 TO EASE IN WITH MORE LIGHT_ EXPANSION"

With the awareness, of an Ascended Embodiment, the self can now begin to understand and for all the levels of fear; that are always, what stands between, one level and the next. The uniqueness, that plays out simultaneously and from the various dimensional fields, of consciousness; will keep awakening the self, to more and more, of its authenticity, until that's all there is, within the flow.
Within this flow, the authenticity is fully present, to the synchronicities; that have attuned to timelessness of existence. Including timelines and that can transport the experience of the self; into the most magical and mystical place, in the Universe. When the unknowable unknown, becomes the unknown and knowable; the self can, full on and with its presence, freely give.

LESSON~212:
"I HAVE AWAKENED TO MY SACRED PRESENCE AND TO EASE IN WITH MORE LIGHT_ EXPANSION"

From the assimilation, of the giving, it will receive the experience and to know, what exactly has been received. This information, keeps changing and is never the same experience; from one moment, to the next. The experience, then becomes original and to its interpretation of it, the self must find the peace, with its subconscious; so that in harmony, it can expand without fear and to all, that it already is.

Breathe this in and feel the ancient, of the one, that is thyself.

Live from the authentic destiny, that is, the self and as a "<u>Sovereign</u> Being, <u>Light</u>".

Created only once, the self, is uniquely original and ancient.

The purpose, is to feel easily swayed, with discernment and with more light, expansion.

THE INTERMISSION :

Take a day to take it in

CONGRATULATIONS ...!!!

FOR MAKING IT

THROUGH TO THE 212th Lesson

(This is a rest period to take the lessons independently as a review)

TAKE THIS DAY TO RECALIBRATE;

MAKE NOTES AND REVIEW……………...

(Day 245)
3. What is a SOVEREIGN LIGHT BEING ?

Why did the self, ever feel so small? Too much criticism, from whom rejected and posing as its maker. What does that mean ? This Being of Self, was not created and by that, which it thought gave birth to it. Its only parenting, was from a place, that felt unworthy and so constricted; that it only saw itself, as very small. What a scary world, to be in and when so very small; from a neurological upset, to expand and to restrain, as cause, for the effect?

LESSON~213:
"I AM CALM FROM THE SILENCE AND IN THE DEPTH I RISE_ EXPANDING MY ANTANAI_FROM BASKING IN THE PRAISE_OF THE LOVE I HAVE FOR MYSELF"

Comparing from the many mirrors and of itself, is what caused the separation. From what mirror, of itself will it choose to integrate? The contrast and thus the microcosm, of the many; had to somehow get the self, to become and in order to fit in. When it did not, carbon copies of itself and would, to take from each identity, it wanted to play out; as it would, watch and feel, from their experience.
The sad state, of affairs and when these identities, showed it, what it was not; the isolation of indifference, as to create the hate, by it and thus, the tug of war between, the love/pain and fear/hurt, it manifested. Now, is the relearning and of what has happened; by what, when, who, and why it was observing. Aware and in all areas of its existence, as an authentic "manifestor"; from its source, that is "Infinite" and in the presence of its finite illusions. Empowered, by praise and gracefully moving, through timelessness; interpretating, each moment, flowing through, its being and that, it may receive, it gladly.

LESSON~213:

"I AM CALM FROM THE SILENCE AND IN THE DEPTH I RISE_EXPANDING MY ANTANAI_FROM BASKING IN THE PRAISE _OF THE LOVE I HAVE FOR MYSELF"

Master of miracles and awakening through, the course of its existence; fully engaged and in love, here and now, is this presence. Today, let go of all attachments and from all timelines, lighten up the mid section; where the solar wheel, does turn and to revolve around the self completely. With no resistance, because, when all attachments are released, there is no required status, to protect. The addictions, from high and low, have nothing to hang on with and when the solar wheel, is operating well; to release the heart, from all its burdens and to release the shame, from all the sacred holy parts of itself, will now be honoured.

ATt- IT- U-DE: At the helm, of all it had created and from this sacred place. The reflections, from its thoughts; be it settling in the having and of this grace, to pattern from perspective.
With eternal praise and unconditional love, release and feel the force expand; to its fullest, recognition and of all that is to come, from its creation. In order, to then see and that the universe, is a product, of the mind; both the creation and destruction, of a deity, is relevant. This insight, is necessary and for the experience; to enable change, rearrange, and recreate, physical space, time, and energy.
The purpose, is to bring, all upward spiraling vortices, into the unity of the oneness. In this moment to become and with the harmonic resonance, of the authentic self; a sustained beam, of white light, thriving and Sovereign. When there is no time to waste, the preparing, is not a waiting period; rather, an ascending process.

(Day 246)
3. What is a <u>SOVEREIGN LIGHT BEING</u> ?

The body's tension, is reduced and it becomes spiritualized, or less dense. The Etheric body, is somewhat, of a darker field and that the self will enter; or let it enter and it feels like, a heavy drowsiness. It is the state, of when the physical body, it feels paralyzed and cannot move, after the astral travel begins. With intent, it can go and where the mind will conjure up; then under this feeling and just before, coming out of it, will be another state, to remember.
To awaken, within the dream and then remember of it, when coming back, into the physical field, of collapsing; into the most, intense feeling, there is and that will remind the self, of its experience, is the emotional body. To be in both worlds, all at once, can become, of the self and somewhat vulnerable; when it has not practiced and into that level, of awareness, often long enough, to stay there, permanently.

LESSON~214:
"I AM THE LIGHT OF MY OWN TRUTH
AND WITH IT_THE EMPHASIS OF MY REALITY"

Something strange, was witnessed, by the self and when metaphysically, in lucid state; it astral projected, in the night. It had left, the body and through the etheric, it relaxed into the fear. To soar much higher and somewhere, floating out, from the room, it had been laying in; to meet its awareness and on the balcony, of physical existence. The balcony, was protected from the outside and with a bird netting; that for some reason, made the self think, it could not leave, by passing through, the netting. The only thing, that stopped it, from its travel and of its heart's desire, was its thoughts.

LESSON~214:
"I AM THE LIGHT OF MY OWN TRUTH AND WITH IT_THE EMPHASIS OF MY REALITY"

This thought, it turned so very quickly, to belief and that the bird netting, could to separate it, into many pieces; it could not bear, to scatter, in this way and it thought up, its limitation. With just the thought, of where it wants to be, it can get there; but instead, got stuck and by all the energy, it had placed prior, to build this netting. The physical can seem, so very real and feel more physical, after leaving the body. Likewise, the physical body, has become, much lighter and integrated a path, on its atonement, with its other bodies' of its field. Today, practice toward, atonement and integrate the two worlds, into one; by setting an intention, before going to bed, at night. Think of something and visualize it, how does it feel? The feeling, will be this memory and that will connect it, to another fractal timeline. The ideal state, to be in, is a hypnotic one and where the self, is most "suggestible". Lucid dreaming, into the depths, of astral projection; to travel, beyond space and time. Eventually, whatever it is, a dream(it must be done with heart), becomes reality and collapsing, into physical manifestation, of the one, most preferred scenario. Sometimes, setting an alarm, to wake up, just before going too deep and during the rapid eye movement state, so to remember, the experience; it is similar to that of a medical procedure and with head injury cases, so they do not, go into a coma. The need to know, is irrelevant; however the self, has come this far, into the book; to be at the level, of using feeling, to guide in and out, of where it is, that it prefers, to be.

The purpose, is to join the most powerful part, of the mind and that is, the unconscious with the conscious; combine the two, into a higher consciousness, of awareness.

(Day 247)
3. What is a <u>SOVEREIGN LIGHT BEING</u> ?

When becoming an independent authority, the self becomes aware, of also this right, to govern itself (responsibility) and unto its own light, it will shine. This world, does not imply, the splitting off and from the mother, nor the father; rather at the in between juncture, of these spheres and from this space, the self resides, as a tubular pillar, of "Sovereign Light". Another way, of looking at it, is in the way, creation is split in two and in the ruling, of nature; that of "Meiosis"and Mitosis". The difference is in the cellular division and that of plant cell division; the self regeneration and the other(meiosis), is that of only, procreation. From the ethereal a certain state of consciousness is captured; drawn into this frequency, the spirit splits off and into the physical experience of being.

LESSON~215:
"MY CONSCIOUSNESS IS THE LIGHT OF AWARENESS AND MY TRUTH TO FUNCTION WITH"

Self regeneration, is the inner child connection and that the self must have; from the nurturing development that it constantly creates. YES!_Nature, is full on and with fractals, of never ending patterns. It is amazing, how a sliver of a mountain, trees, clouds, and anything, that chaos brings to form; can be of the whole and identically within, the law of Oneness, to order. All of the information, from the Infinite, can be found within the self and likewise, all around it, from the external(reflecting back to it).

LESSON~215:
"MY CONSCIOUSNESS IS THE LIGHT OF AWARENESS AND MY TRUTH TO FUNCTION WITH"

Within the undifferentiated form that is oneness; each cell has the consciousness, of this original essence. The cell can separate, into many variations. While still continuing, to hold the imprint and from before it split, from the whole; to differentiate with characteristics and that accord, to its role. Synchronized to flow and with the rest of the systems, within the body, of the self, that has structured, to contain it. Anything and everything, that is made of light; has the information, to hold consciousness. In its own way and uniquely so, it can contribute, to the overall existence; held by the universe and the essence of the mother, that is "Love".
Love, is this imprint and a vibration, in the cells; that resonates with the intent, of the universe and that between, the self, regenerating flow.

The purpose, is to come to grasp, a little more,
this "<u>divine love and enlightenment</u>".

3. What is a SOVEREIGN LIGHT BEING ?
(Day 248)

With light, the body can engage and that from others, to form and transfer patterns; that resonate and interchange, the thought of every species. Procreation, can now be taken, right out of the game and that had once, held creation, into a limited perspective.

LESSON~216:

"THE FASTER I AM ABLE TO ALLOW THE FLOW OF TIME_TO MOVE RIGHT THROUGH ME_MY YOUTHFUL PRESENCE AS IMORTAL_WILL CONTINUE TO EXIST THROUGHOUT ETERNITY"

Living, beyond life and death perspective, is this empty space; that once explored, observing parallel existences. That the self can, physically appear and clone itself, at will and so it seems; however teleporting, in this way, from one reality, into another, travelling along and somehow reconnecting, back, into its physical body. The concept, of time, has physically appeared; like stencils from the past, to thread along, the linear present and its future. When time collapses, into itself, what then ? Can the Source be dancing, with the ordinary and with this experiment; might it awaken, from its mystery, to the self enlightenment and stir it, to experiment, as real with it, its own reality? It is possible, to teleport the energy body, of the self and nervous system, this energy of parts, as well, as intellectual. It was discussed before, that within the astral canvas, of traveled space continuum and from its very own discernment; bringing future into present moment, to solidify as real. During the dream time space, the mind can vividly play, with all the many signals, it received by others; much clearly and reach out, "inter-netting" clairvoyantly, to play with others. It can resist and then during waking state, wonder why it did not turn out and likewise, the other energy parts, that it had wished to play with, might resist as well.

LESSON~216:

"THE FASTER I AM ABLE TO ALLOW THE FLOW OF TIME TO MOVE RIGHT THROUGH ME_ MY YOUTHFUL PRESENCE AS IMORTAL_WILL CONTINUE TO EXIST THROUGHOUT ETERNITY"

The genetic information, to quantum waveforms, can also be susceptible to change, as well as objects; this was discussed and lightly touched upon before. With this concept manifestation/miracles, can be created; with the change from, those who wish to receive it and are ready to be transformed by it. To pick up signals, that are generated, the self can be as alike with the many; who are also sensitive(vibration/frequency) and to all the other energy fields around it. The energetic parts, of the self, are actually influenced, by this inter connectedness and of every other thing, that thinks and feels. The same is true with the physical body, of the self; as its containments too, parallels the energetic structure, that pairs off with its cells, within the brain and body. It is in the energetic bodies, that will interface and with every molecule from the self; that is where, all thought occurs and does include the nervous system. The back of the skull, the cerebellum, can allow and pick up these impulses; to further coordinate and regulate, from the vertebrae, for muscular activity. The nervous system, just the same, can operate and from the energetic parallel parts of the self.

The less it can resist, the better it will flow; the less the push, the more cooperative the dance, in harmony and the time field, of its light can have a way with, to inspire. AWARENESS IS THE KEY and along comes with it, empowerment !

The purpose, is for the self to interpret and respond well, to the many stimuli; through these relations and relative to its enlightened state. Responsible, in its being and in every way explainable, through a give and take allowance.

(Day 249)
3. What is a SOVEREIGN LIGHT BEING ?

"Ego", is the constriction, of localization and yet awareness, has no location. The differentials, are not separate and are all fractals, to the puzzle, that is being put together, at this time.
To witness such a union, in the object of experience and within the subject; is this fully awakened awareness and of itself, as a "Sovereign Light" being.

LESSON~217:
"MY BODY IS IN ME_BUT I AM NOT THE BODY NOR THE MIND_I AM SPIRIT_FULLY AWAKENED AND FROM DEATH_NO LONGER ASLEEP"

Having attention, to an intension, is what transforms awareness and into an experience, to give reason.
In this way and for the senses, to have their way with differentials; as well as, to accentuate, the vibrancy within it. To be sentient, goes along with the awakening, of the soul and within the deepest sleep. Just like watching and being within a movie, when the self cognition, of not having to be the body, mind realization occurs; this is the enlightenment of its experience. Sounds, textures, colours and tastes, all come out, from this awareness; that the self, can to modify and into this part, of having the experience. Awareness, is eternal; having no location and no form, it is existence. When the soul becomes aware, of itself, it is the keeper, of the mirrors; the watcher, the all seeing eye and that connects to the field, of all possibilities.

LESSON~217:
"MY BODY IS IN ME_BUT I AM NOT THE BODY NOR THE MIND_I AM SPIRIT FULLY AWAKENED AND FROM DEATH_NO LONGER ASLEEP"

In soul consciousness, the self just flows sensually and with a celestial experience. In this progression, of each previous state included and transcended; to an awareness that communes with awareness. This is the realm of miracles and where intentions, become almost instantaneous. The self, is the awareness, communicating with itself and as all things; to experience from the seer and scene and where the body itself, is part of the scenery. The experience, it comes and goes, as interchangeable; where as, the awareness, is always there, modifying itself, into every experience. The Sovereign Light being, is enlightened and through its differentiation, of authenticity; to freely interpret self expression. It is in part, with unity consciousness, diffused and with no separation; all subjects, objects and in all modes, of awareness, are flowing, all at once, in harmony. As a child (growing up in the 1980's) I could remember my father on numerous occasions, holding up a full sized mirror, for me to look in and would say, "Wake up Maria". In this example the author, was free to choose from her experience. From the oneness of awareness, that differentiates itself and into a countable knower; to a modality of knowing and the objects known, all within the self. Has the heart dissipated into bliss and from such grief, if any?

The purpose, is to wake up, to the sensual and celestial experience; that the self is, to explore and recognize, through its emphasis, upon it.

(Day 250)
3. What is a <u>SOVEREIGN LIGHT BEING</u> ?

The surface sense of the self, is the "Ego mind" and it has plagued electrically, the syndromes; that magnetically attract and to react, into a state of helpless victim. Finally a liberation, from the binding of its misplaced time and that amounts to nothing for it; but physical pain and that has become, much greater, than its pleasure. In this moment, of release and just for this instance, come into the experience, of a different kind, of joy.
The conscious choice, to cause, of an effect; rather than to be affected by it, is this action and from an inner search awareness, to become and to mould, the being, from its aspired heights.

LESSON~218:
"I CAN LOVE MYSELF_MORE THAN THE OUTSIDE
DESIRE_THAT HAS MANIFESTED TO INSPIRE
SUCH EXPANSION"

"TODAY_I WILL INCLUDE THE FRAGMENTS
THAT I ONCE DEPRIVED MYSELF
NOW AMPLIFIED AND BEGGING FOR ATTENTION."

The reactive place, of "Ego", is a prison and not so much, of a life, to identify with, this kind of limiting constriction; but to call upon, decay and the effort, while it suffers, to know(itself).
To be the victim, from the changes and that occur outside of the self, is the death, of its existence. The substance, of reality, is held and from within the real; the self will learn, how to turn away, from its outer senses and to seek, for inner mastery.

LESSON~218:
"I CAN LOVE MYSELF_MORE THAN THE OUTSIDE DESIRE_THAT HAS MANIFESTED TO INSPIRE SUCH EXPANSION"

"TODAY_I WILL INCLUDE THE FRAGMENTS THAT I ONCE DEPRIVED MYSELF_NOW AMPLIFIED AND BEGGING FOR ATTENTION"

The mastery over life, is through imagination and before any material gain, has happened. It is through the outer harmony, of the events and that the self appears, to magically, perform them. This is, what it means, to be in tune, with self purpose and to allow the divine flow, of existence, to unfold through, self expression. Within this sense of lacking from its wholeness and when the self has had, the chance; by the many, to resolve the anguish and from the will, of opposition. What is, at the root of it, is competition and that leads it, into the self, once again. By becoming the observer and for the many, that will act, to take upon and make their own; that part of the self, that made them feel, inspired, by within its partnership, the unformed relationships and that it might, had yearned for. Remember, that nothing is separate, from these souls; rather must too, take on that part of them, it wished to partner up, with. In this way, there is no lack, to feel nor separate, from this, its differentiation. Rather it will remember, to just be and remain, as its own boss, to mind its business with and authenticity; that will never be lost, into the shadows, of itself. In this way, its light, over its sovereign being, doing fully and aware in its response; that it is the creator, of its change to learn from.

LESSON~218:
"I CAN LOVE MYSELF_MORE THAN THE OUTSIDE DESIRE_THAT HAS MANIFESTED TO INSPIRE SUCH EXPANSION"

"TODAY I WILL INCLUDE THE FRAGMENTS THAT I ONCE DEPRIVED MYSELF_ NOW AMPLIFIED AND BEGGING FOR ATTENTION"

The purpose, is to accept and when falling in love, with certain higher aspects, of itself from the outside. A positive reflection, that it be and an opportunity, to impress upon; such a relationship and from within the self. Rather, than to miss, the having not and feel the lack; to recognize, where that fragment of the self and to love the most, is missing.

This is, what it means, to take responsibility and not exclude, by becoming as overtaken matter; for the need to feel the momentary, gratification and from the pleasure, within the sexual expression, of another, that is, far from reach.

(Day 251)
3. What is a SOVEREIGN LIGHT BEING ?

Before the second coming, for example(as it were Mithra's/Christ) and within its embodiment, on the outside of the self.
These warriors of light, did spread out and across the Earth; as heroes they were worshiped and became, ascended masters in the flesh. They had spread out(with good intentions), in that the oneness could not differentiate, the tale from long ago. It was from these great masters that Jesus Christ became the hero/saviour and for all, who were asleep, he was the cure.

LESSON~219:
"I HAVE AWAKENED AS A SOVEREIGN LIGHT BEING AUTHENTICALLY UNTO MYSELF I HAVE RISEN INTO THE SECOND COMING"
From the oneness, many had awakened and the prophesy, is this moment, of the second coming to reveal, that "the many have awakened" ! The Self, is now the ascended "Sovereign" and baring the "Light", of atonement; connecting to that, which differentiates and to contribute, to the whole, in that of, authenticity. The greatest discipline, from this mindfulness and that has taught it from so long ago; now comes, so natural and with having not to sacrifice, a thing for it anymore. When before, the self could have to suffer and for the many, so very much. To have been walking on this path(of future timelines, holding down the light for all); it needed an outside avatar and a hero, that the many, could agree upon. In this way, religions were a must, to help with the survival mechanism, that the many trials and tribulations; from the fall and into the great deep sleep, had caused. Now the blind, are gaining back the sight and ascending from the darkness! When reintegrating, the fragmentations, into the unified field of oneness; from the heart, this time, to find its very own christed light, of its compassion.

LESSON~219:
"I HAVE AWAKENED AS A SOVEREIGN LIGHT BEING AUTHENTICALLY UNTO MYSELF I HAVE RISEN INTO THE SECOND COMING"

Coming from extremely opposite(poles) ends and had no choice, but to continue; to forcefully bond themselves and with karma, to procreate, into the field of immortality. This was, the only way possible, for immortality was stuck, with karmic patterning and into the physical bodies of the self; whilst it kept dropping out, of the game and only to recycle back again. The self could not possibly escape, not even from a suicide. The karmic netting could allow, the spirits; within its limitation, to be thrown back into the earthly place and from where, it had left off. Religion was the only way, to recalibrate and like, a court and jury, the system of hierarchy, could continue on. The only way to be absolved, was through an outer source; where the self could not reach high enough, to possibly connect and in this way Christ, became the saviour. For those who did take on, the responsibility; would have to hide away, up in the mountains and/or secluded forests, within natures monasteries.

No longer is this need, to have to run and hide from its greatness; nor effort, to remain small and insignificant. Slowly, but most certainly, there will be enough awakened and to allow for the greatness, of the almost dead, to shine again, within their greatness. The many parts, from which it longs, to love outside itself and starting to remember; however its heart, must heal some more. Release from all the "Ego" trappings, of power struggle and no longer choose, from this temptation, to identify with, nor to compare.

The purpose, is from within the greatest part, of the self, a heart most wishing to experience; to drop the masks, from all its many faces, so that the "Ego" can dissolve, from being the oppressor, of its surface.

(Day 252)
4. What is **FAITH** ?

The idea, of believing, in what has yet to manifest, is truly a thing, of miracles and that faith, can gift, to the self.

LESSON~220:

"AGAINST ALL ODDS WITH FAITH A TRUE STRENGTH COMES ABOUT FROM A SELF PROMOTING VISION"

Like the splitting off, from its identities and worlds, just like cellular division; it will rejuvenate some more expression and to explore the newness, from this level, of expansion. Trust in this unwavering truth, of the unseen reality. The expectation, to control the outcome and/or to just connect with it; can become the path, on a journey of many gifts and to learn, from the many disappointments, along the way. Eventually the strength, that comes from such tenacity; will be the confidence and that outweighs, for any doubt.
To never give up, on the driving force and that wills through life; the passion, from the self's desire and to aspire, to great lengths, of inspiration, it can impress upon, to get there. Always changing, through the growth; that brings forth, much refreshing vastness and to expand upon and into its background. The drive, it takes to plan, right through, with intellect and hardship; when all along the passion from the heart could find, for its relief, the weary mind, to put to rest. With nothing to resist it and within an instance; that otherwise could take and for a half a life time, to achieve.

LESSON~220:

"AGAINST ALL ODDS WITH FAITH A TRUE STRENGTH COMES ABOUT FROM A SELF PROMOTING VISION"

By believing in the self and promoting thoughts, despite the circumstances; the subjects it observes, in its mistrust, can waver inwardly and the supportive measures, that it might to know itself, to have such faith. When this happens, the self must turn away, from what is made small and insignificant; by what it thinks it knows, to try to prove and move towards the things, that have it in less scrutiny. For instance, the self can go general; to start with what it can do and simply as to tie, its shoe.
Take a moment to distract, in such a way; that can bring back the ownership, of its own space and platform, from which to stand and be. It was able, to put on pants and dress its body well; all the little things, that it might have overlooked, as small and insignificant, that got it there. Then go back, with more know how and confidence, to deal with the situation. Through faith, the self can learn itself better and gain strength by it.

The purpose, is to better understand, the vision and to feel the importance of Faith; as the idea, with no proof, that builds a field of hope and around the self, to co-create with.

(Day 253)
4. What is FAITH ?

When we have never tasted something, how can we possibly miss it? It is from life's sampling, that the self can gain and through its senses; from a sense of hope, to find the faith and in recreating for itself, a vision.

LESSON~221:
"MY FAITH IS NOT DELUSIONAL_BECAUSE I HAVE NOT GIVEN UP TO TAKE THE STEPS ALONG THE WAY
AND SEE IT THROUGH ITS PROCESS"

The passion to create, must resonate and within every cell of the self, throughout its body. Any or all resistance met, along the way, is where, it can be paying and for its storage fees; for time and in this way, to retard the success rate, of it manifesting. Wishing and planning, go hand in hand; however the goal, is in the moderation. With "Faith", it does not have to get so complicated, to set out plans for its approval and wishing, suggests defeat; in that, the action needs to balance out. The doing, must come from the being, in that, the self must remain awakened, to see; for each step along the way, it will reveal to it, its readiness and for having what it wished for. The planning, is not so much the how; rather the seeing it, play out and feeling, what it can be like, to already have it. Faith, is the potion for the dream, that will be more real; than the delusion of a feeling in a movie. This is how much more vibrant and vivid it must be; before it can materialize, to manifest and will determine on the potency of faith.

LESSON~221:
"MY FAITH IS NOT DELUSIONAL_BECAUSE I HAVE NOT GIVEN UP TO TAKE THE STEPS ALONG THE WAY AND SEE IT THROUGH ITS PROCESS"

To make a wish, in hope, is the field and from which to start; there it be and as a point of reference, to mark for such a frequency, is that of hope. From this linear perspective, the third point of reference, to draw and as a standing platform; from this, another more responsive one, to claim its ownership and rise above the flatness, to create the shape, is Faith. An inner vision, and from the heart, it must arise; the loving presence, to nurture and breathe life, into. From a place of excitement, is the passion and most certain, is the self to integrate; with authenticity, to stand in this, its power, to create and manifest. Miracles are not accidents, made possible and rather revealing, to the unconventional practices; that come from less rigid, cared out written plans and blue prints. The self can generate and from nothing; than the purest of intentions, from the heart.
From this love, there is no need and to mortgage out, the falsehood, from its predetorial disenchantment.

Do not worry, about the legal parasites and other such, just causes, to insure, the rightful ownership, will break apart, from such illusions; that before it had much, to do with nothing more than, the invested backing up and from the opinions, carried out of the many. Always remember this:

"HOME IS WHERE THE HERT IS"

The purpose, is to allow and for duality to shed away, the separation; reconnect to the esteem, that trusts the higher self and from its universe, to form, a connected confidence.

(Day 254)
4. What is <u>FAITH</u> ?

Where most find comfort in privacy, is where the invasion infiltrates through sound and flashing images; the fluoride in the water and the chemical trails, left in the sky. The warfare, continues and why is that, in a world that the self, is responsible for creating?

LESSON~222:

"FAITH IS MY STRENGTH THAT I MAY BE CURED FROM ALL IMPENDING DOOM AND GLOOM
THAT WILL SUPPORT THE MANY A FOLLY FROM THEIR WEAKNESSES AND WITH IT_THE CLEARING OF THE OLD THAT SHALL PASS THROUGH ME"

The greatest military(desensitization)attack, is in the weak(sensitive) spot of its opponent; a slow painful death, is as clever as, to attack it in its sleep and kill it. The self from long ago might still carry in its field these ghosts from the past and having to defend against such discomforts. The toxic tyranny, to poison life and whilst, keeping it off center; from the same senses, it relies upon and emotionally attached, to the experience, within its density formation(reality). Such a foresight, might be questioned, by the mind; as an unfit thought, to feel perhaps as a disorder of paranoia?
The self might only to defend and left feeling helpless; however the hope can save it, in that, it will eventually get by and with "Faith", it will most certainly, be saved.

LESSON~222:
"FAITH IS MY STRENGTH THAT I MAY BE CURED FROM ALL IMPENDING DOOM AND GLOOM THAT WILL SUPPORT THE MANY A FOLLY FROM THEIR WEAKNESSES AND WITH IT_THE CLEARING OF THE OLD_THAT SHALL PASS THROUGH ME"

Wherever the self, might find itself stuck, it can and will ascend. To find the way, an illness could await, to penetrate in and from a weakness, that it may be spoiled, with its disease. The continual evolving, from transcending and for every location, it will find another; to download and to clear away, from its awareness. From all the high tech weaponry, the only way, to feeling safe and overcome for its discomfort; is also given the opportunity, during these invasions and the armour, to cover up its senses with. It can for example: cover up its ears, or eyes and nose; also its skin and to become, more discerning, of what it will ingest. Mostly these will be, the toxic circumstances and from an older world a "ghost town"; this choice, to stay and feel safe, with the familiar. The "Ego", is full of surprises, to trap the self and render it useless; in a bleak state and of having to undergo repair. Just like with the many, it can exhaust its tired soul, to wait for its recycle. Sometimes the grief, can become so intense; that the only hope, can seek the self out, to bring it to its "Faith". Today, practice, to also help integrate, these energies and that have been filtered through; as much as the self, can tolerate and with retreats along the way, to shut them out, when they become, too overbearing.

The purpose, is for the self, to clear the larger and greater collective field, through the clearing of its own; because the personal and public bleed, into each other.

(Day 255)
4. What is <u>FAITH</u> ?

How can the self, even begin and when it gets killed, within the very moment ? When lost, in the depths of setting the intention, for the day; only to have, everything play tricks and to consume, the entirety of it. Drained of resources and zapped out, from the hunger of the many (starting off, every month by); from it, the strong sense, of its world, as an illusion. With nothing left to give, find the "Faith"; to courage through the new.

LESSON~223:
"WHEN I COME TO LOSE MYSELF FROM THE WORLDLY GAME OF POVERTY AND FINITE PLACES I HAVE FAITH IN SELF REJUVENATION AND THAT ALL IS NOT LOST FROM INFINITE SELF"

The world can feel, like one big infestation and from the many, the cause is the Self, that brings about reaction. The self is not lost, rather its intentions, for the day have taken a retreat. To gain some better insight and from the volatile crowding; that wish to interact and as the many do, amongst themselves, the self, does watch. Feel this part, that has been also played with and from the side of powers; that do not have a grasp, of what it means, to have integrity. Instead of getting all upset, do not; rather let it go out, to greet the world with. Could it be, that they're reacting and in such a way, that self is not? It is really interesting, to fathom in this way of being and really to be lost, in a world; that it is not engaging with, and that it may, engage with? The self, is in such way, as God would do, within and amongst them, in a body.

LESSON~223:
"WHEN I COME TO LOSE MYSELF FROM THE WORLDLY GAME OF POVERTY AND FINITE PLACES I HAVE FAITH IN SELF REJUVENATION AND THAT ALL IS NOT LOST FROM INFINITE SELF"

Does the self really want to be, amongst such characteristics and as to be; powerless misbehaving children, needing to control, belittle, take away from others and to make up, for the loss, that it cannot feel, from within, to obtain? As much, as the desire burns and to be amongst, such situations; it is a pretense, to hook and then string it along, with cowardly disinterest. Notice, the distortions and from this place; that was distorted and so many times before, felt helpless. Asking for help, is an illusion and the energy it takes; just for that moment, to turn away from it and not be bothered. Only through "Faith", can the self move on; go about the remaining, of the day and feel this loss, from its intension(untwist and free thyself). The way, will show once more and with hope, to peacefully guide it; with another sign and another clue, that it can make it.

The purpose, is to believe and stay strong. Even in the darkest of places and where the self, has lost its way; because the darkness, cannot stay around, forever.

(Day 256)
4. What is <u>FAITH</u>?

After the fall, of consciousness, the mother was oppressed, into the depths of the earth; never to be mentioned again and of this eternal life, thus death became, its protégé. To replace much of the matriarch and within this way, a blind spot had emerged; created with false blood and to shed away, as patriarchal, that loved to conquer (by killing and sacrificing) everything and that would not surrender, to it, in this way(desensitized).

LESSON~224:
"THE UNTWISTING FROM MY KARMIC PAST
HAS RELEASED FOR SO MUCH ENERGY
THAT HAS ALLOWED THE SYMPTOMS FOR MUCH
DEEPER SHEDDING TO OCCUR AND I HAVE FAITH
THIS TOO SHALL PASS"

Immortality, was now a falsehood and through the raping of the feminine, to pro-create the seed of man; so that, he may live on, forever, in this way. Was not this "Son" exemplified, within the blasphemy? Replacing the divine, non gendered child, of the self; that the condition and of this love for density, would save the many? Religion, was a great example, of blind "Faith". To continue on, with power and in these hopes of many, an angry Father/God, to bring about; his artificial heaven and to reconstruct it, from his many shallow offspring (in this way as to imagine). All species/races and other differences; became the effect of famine and neglect. War and conflict, began and amongst this hostile beast, that had split, into many brothers and of the same, called man.

The untwisting, has now taken up and formed, the many of the world; into a new age and oh, what a lighter freer, feeling, to have all this energy.

LESSON~224:
"THE UNTWISTING FROM MY KARMIC PAST HAS RELEASED FOR SO MUCH ENERGY THAT HAS ALLOWED THE SYMPTOMS FOR MUCH DEEPER SHEDDING TO OCCUR AND I HAVE FAITH THIS TOO SHALL PASS"

The only thing is that, just like the self; much of the world, is in this way and of diving in, to find its energy, when waking up. Use discernment, for much, is needed and at a deeper level, to excavate and shed away, the old. All the fears and lower traumas, must play out; either way, this process, it will take, much energy and most of the time, the self will feel, like giving up. There is a sense of giving up; however during such strained events, the self is in a state, of letting go. Almost like a heart ache, it will feel the intense grief and then it will subside. Eventually, there will be no more, to process through and it will have to, go deeper and deeper, until it feels, so lost, to find some more resistance.
It will end up, so deep within, that it might not know, the way back out again and for this reason, there is no way back.
"Faith", is what will see the self through and into transcendence. Transcendence, is not subject to birth, nor death; because it is the state of consciousness, to which the self will find, enlightenment.
The purpose, for the experience and from the physical body, is to observe, its universe with. To look through, a human nervous system and find connection; likewise, as an activity and that of the observed, uniting to its universe, with love.

"Faith", can bring the self, to a level, of much understanding and is, as a prerequisite, to its enlightenment.

(Day 257)
4. What is FAITH ?

Faith, is the idea, of completely becoming reliant, on the notion of a particular outcome; rather than, the probability, that the outcome, will happen, despite the environment. The emphasis, must always be, on the way, the self will feel, at any given moment; by this, the meaning and every situation, can be changed, for what it witnesses, to also change. Faith, can also be blind, with imagery to idealize; that it must come in, a certain package and not in any other way, for it to feel fulfilment and in the achieving of, the energy, it will attract. It might not come and from within, the same configuration.
See it, for what it brings; rather than, for what, it is not.
Likewise, something that is beautiful and in the way, that is preferred externally; might not be and on the inside resembling, in fact, the opposite.

LESSON~225:
"THE BYPRODUCT OF AN AFTERTHOUGHT
IS MY EXTERNAL ENVIRONMENT
AND I HAVE FAITH IT WILL CHANGE
WITH EVERY SHIFTING OF MY BEING"

The self, is entitled to perceive and from its own perspective with it; the same external environment, is all about, the meaning and that the self, will wish to hold. The meaning, that the self will give, to its experience and from every circumstance; its external world, will gift to it, is all, in the interpretation, of it. What then, becomes of faith? Faith, can then upgrade and to a more, simplified version, in its application. The self will see, only in whatever, it believes and will reflect back to it. Yes it is true, with faith the reality, can eventually change. For every meaning, it will interpret and the subject, that it will attach to; however all is an illusion, from its patterning and as a bi product, to its world.

LESSON~225:
"THE BYPRODUCT OF AN AFTERTHOUGHT IS MY EXTERNAL ENVIRONMENT AND I HAVE FAITH IT WILL CHANGE WITH EVERY SHIFTING OF MY BEING"

Yes it is true, with "Faith" reality can eventually change; however, all is an illusion, from this patterning; the bi product of its world and the meaning, it will interpret onto, every subject, it will attach to. Electro magnetic, is the primary, sub formations and that judgment, is at the very root of. Every thought, whether directly, or indirectly, of the self; will magnetically attract to it, an emotion. The very same, as the self feeling and then, having a thought, attach to it. Whether it be, from a very primitive state and/or an awakened one; the self, is the creator and responsible, for everything, it sees and senses, from its external world.
Faith, is an inside job and from it, mountains can be moved and for the many, to aspire change from; when the self, has no invested interest and to this change, in them. The only attachment, the self is allowed to have, is that of, its self and in its very own faith, to see and feel the world, as a better place.
The more detailed it gets, the more fleeting the thoughts, must be and very subtle, to suggest, like seedlings, in the wind.
The more general the thought, the longer the self can stay on it; to feel it formulate into. In the way, it could breathe life, into its business; to give it reason for integrity and to exchange for currency, its energy.
The purpose, is to determine, that within its own right, the self is, the embodiment and very own unique, interpretation; of this supreme being, of all things, living and dead. For all the things, that are and are to be; of having the creative energy, that "Faith" can bring. This value, is to witness, over the art of its creative currency and in itself expression. "<u>Faith</u>", is this emphasis, that the self does bring, to its existence and to experience life with.

Take 2 days to take it in

CONGRATULATIONS ...!!!

FOR MAKING IT THROUGH THE 225th Lesson

(This is a rest period to take the lessons independently as a review)

TAKE THESE TWO DAYS TO RECALIBRATE;

MAKE NOTES AND REVIEW……………..

(Day 260)
4. What is <u>FAITH</u> ?

The self, does not have to, be completely unaware and in its continued allowance, of its grace, to shine. All that is needed, is the "Faith", of "certainty"; to "trust" and to be open, through its breath, to "love".

LESSON~226:
"FAITH GIVES ME STRENGTH ENOUGH TO STAND MY GROUND WITH CERTAINTY AND FEEL THE FREEDOM FROM THIS TRUTH"

The goal, is but to follow the heart and in every dream, that it endeavours, with the mind. To know, it will not always be, congruent and with the making of its worldly plans; from the common thread and of such conventional ways, as to distort, the mission. To be able to plan it out, will bring about, more adversary and to the once nonsensical dream, that miracles are made from. The mind likes to, always take over; because it can make proof, of everything and into great detailed, a story, is ready. The longer the story tries, to remain the same and especially, before it happens; the more resistance, it will come to face, from change. To truly savour the journey, is to take it and step by step, to feel the joy, of every moment; the light will shine as an accomplishment, onto the next and then the next, this is faith ! Be grateful, that the self is aware, enough and to see, the many holes, within the false reality. It sees the world and always tries to blame itself, for the distortions; to why it is, it can't fit in and to generate, for its own existence, in this way.
The purpose, is to be outed, enough and to realize, that the self, is standing, on the outside, "looking In",
Be the faith, to stand authentically, as "<u>Sovereign</u>".

(Day 261)

4. What is <u>FAITH</u> ?

Real Faith will not misguide and into the pitfalls, of altering the physical body, so that it may be included, where it is not accepted. When, often the false reality programs the mind, to change a body part, because it feels excluded? That, it then enters, into another creation, of inequality and therefore, does not go, all the way, to change; because the other gender, cannot have, a decent income and to survive, as an independent? When reaching the place, of death, to be served with it, the same bigotry,(alpha male to female) will follow and to taunt away, dismissing the once gender, it preferred to be?

LESSON~227:
"NO MATTER THE DISCOMFORT
MY LIFE IS NOT A WASTE AND I HOLD STRONG
TO MY FAITH_TO SEE ME THROUGH"

With faith, the self can float on the cloud; rather than become consumed by it, in the fog. These are the perspectives, that might it want to be and in the discerning for it; how to be, if it so wishes and to survive, as living. When the world resembles it, in such a way, as to not include it; because it can already have and all it can ever think, to ask for, then could not, the same be true, for the self ? The self must have, the "Faith", to continue and like water, from a stream, it will find a way. Why for the very same reason, this can be; that every piece of unvalued nature, is turned, into a golf course? It is perhaps, to show the flaw, of its reality and with every hole, the illusion is revealed.

LESSON~227:
"NO MATTER THE DISCOMFORT
MY LIFE IS NOT A WASTE AND I HOLD STRONG
TO MY FAITH TO SEE ME THROUGH"

The part it calls from and every neutral, subatomic particle, is it not, from this nutrient, called "Faith" ? Just the same too, the physical body, is to be appreciated. Every essence, from each energetic colour, that it consumes and as vital nourishment; from plant life and every interaction from her soul, the Earth alike. Stand strong, in whatever density, the lens will perceive and to have presented; from its energetic field and for this experience. This, is the message and from the messenger that is the "RNA"; transmitting and receiving, from the Soul and "DNA" alike.
It is the "Sovereign Light" and from it, to align, with every synchronistic moment, from the now. It is a harmony, of stimulation and a symbiotic correlation, with the very Earth; that too, must be treated, with the same respect, nurture, love and dignity. How many more, positive affirmations, can the self think of ? To feel the oneness, with nature and the very ground, it stands on; that is made up, of organic awareness and that is life, one in the same. Today, is the day, to recognize the difference; between the false faith and the real faith.

The purpose, is to recognize, the faith it gives away, to the illusion; is the Blind Faith and The Faith, that keeps it in, its own truth of authenticity as "<u>Sovereign</u>" is this "<u>Light</u>" called "<u>Faith</u>".
Where as, before the self, would look in, to find the darkness; the "Light of Faith" will shine, the way out!

(Day 262)

4. What is FAITH ?

Does the self remember and when its consciousness created, from it, the first conceptual awareness?
Awareness, from within the womb, was "faith"; first it came from the knowing, that the self could have, everything and anything, it has desired for.

LESSON~228:
"THE FAITH THAT GUIDES ME COMES FROM THE EXPERIENCE WITHIN THE SPACE OF SOUL THAT IS BETWEEN MY SOURCE AND FORCE EXISTENCE"

From the moment, of its very first breath; it became aware and that its needs, were somewhat, more distant, than before.
To meet with its demands and the more of this experience, would show for; Its ability to response, had to come, from somewhere?
Faith, can penetrate the dream, within a dream and can, from this awareness, in the moment, of manifesting now.
From the moment, that the self can dream it, faith will help, to see it through; because it already had manifested and within another time continuum.

LESSON~228:
"THE FAITH THAT GUIDES ME_COMES FROM THE EXPERIENCE WITHIN THE SPACE OF SOUL_THAT IS BETWEEN MY SOURCE AND FORCE EXISTENCE"

When space and time become, one in the same; then so does the outer world, with the inner to emerge. Particles, that make up matter, appear and disappear and slow or fast, is this time marker. Faith, is this activator, for subatomic particles and that of both worlds, to consider metaphysical.

Faith, is as real to handle with, as the safest companion; and therein, is found its true identity, at last with the(Creator)Self. From this self contraction, faith had created and from faith, it had to mould, the self experience, with the truth, in its expansion.

Faith, is one of those golden keys, that helps the self, along its development; of higher awareness and to enlighten, up the evolutionary scale through, a state of super consciousness.

The purpose, is in going deep enough, to really get it, this thing called "FAITH".

(Day 263)

5. WHAT IS THE SOUL AND HOW IS IT DIFFERENT FROM THE EGO?

The amount of light that comes in, is limited to the amount of constriction the heart is feeling. The Ego is a deflective mechanism that filters in light; to represent it from the Soul and as the reflective sliver for its external world experience.
Beyond all laws, is this basic fundamental patterning; that holds the truth, for "Unconditional Love". An all inclusive
connector, to the primal source of love.

LESSON~229:
"IN ORDER TO AWAKEN THE DIVINE CONSCIOUSNESS I MUST ALLOW THE PERFECT STATE THAT IS CONNECTED WITH THE LIGHT AND ALL EMBRACING SPIRIT TO HAVE DIRECT EXPERIENCE WITH ONENESS"

By disconnecting from the Love of self, is to find, that it is only but a temporary state; that chooses to reach out, to find it and from its universe. When the self cannot continue to accept, from outside of itself, the opposite, is when and it will feel the lack; from this separation, "Ego mind" is born and to help the self continue on this way. Always it will find, the temporary gratification, to satisfy its needs and yet not always, can it afford to pay, to play like this. Eventually the self will learn, to turn away and go within.
Thus the soul will react to its every need again; this response, has no consciousness and must be fed with lessons, to reflect back to itself, growth and further expansion. The soul, is the all seeing eye and that will reflect to the self, its many lessons.

LESSON~229:
"IN ORDER TO AWAKEN_THE DIVINE CONSCIOUSNESS
I MUST ALLOW THE PERFECT STATE
THAT IS CONNECTED WITH THE LIGHT
AND ALL EMBRACING SPIRIT
TO HAVE DIRECT EXPERIENCE WITH ONENESS"

The unconditional love, is the primary law and that unifies, of all its parts and groups alike; that came here and with the same agreements, to play out and learn from each other.
This can be what it means to "Love yourself and that you may be able to Love others"; is the harmonic Law of One.
When from contraction and expansion, soul can teach the self, to know itself; unless the self prefers a painful growth, the "Ego" really has no place in all of this. The soul is the experience reflecting back to the self; from the heart it can connect to higher mind and after the hurt has been released. The "Ego mind", is the crying child and that never got the help, it needed; it must be dealt with first, to integrate within the mind of the self and it must come to be resolved. What better way, than through the soul, to regress into the hurts and then release them; by acknowledging and that they no longer hold, for any meaning. The child can then again be innocent from all the wrong doings that it thought of and for the self to hold accountable.

Look into the mirror that is the soul and digress the "Ego mind"; so to grasp the hurting child and get to know it better, is the purpose.
HOW CAN THE LABELS FALL AWAY_WHEN THE SELF HAS THEM STILL IN USE AND HOLDS ATTACHMENT TO THEIR MEANING ?

(Day 264)

5. WHAT IS THE SOUL AND HOW IS IT DIFFERENT FROM THE EGO ?

How immortal is the soul; in measure of consumption and of another life form, that the self can live, for it to die? Not more than the essence of its flesh; to temporarily feed the body of the self with. The "Ego mind" works well, to help in this survival mode; with it, the hunter and its victim, are both, one in the same(cycle/recycle).

LESSON~230:
"HOW CAN I EVER BE IN LOVE ENOUGH
TO TAKE THE LIFE OF ANOTHER
SO I MAY LIVE AND LOVE MYSELF_FOR DOING IT ?"

From the primal infestation of a predatory mind, did the self evolve and yet, it still will conflict, with its many sides; in clusters, to war over the meaning and that of its "Ego" driven power.
The soul will hold on, to all and any memory, from lifetimes over; that have yet to be resolved, to be rekindled and to play out again. When there is nothing, much more left and the soul can be clean, to rise into ascension; it can transcend with the physical body of the self and into a lighter, more refined, enlightened presence.
When all the mirrors, become one and then reach, into the higher heart; its magic, is where miracles, can manifest from the oneness. The mirror, becomes a see through and plasmic membrane; that once had kept the self in separation. Now both perceptions, of no time and no space, continue to exist; as omnipresent self experience.

LESSON~230:
"HOW CAN I EVER BE IN LOVE ENOUGH TO TAKE THE LIFE OF ANOTHER SO I MAY LIVE AND LOVE MYSELF FOR DOING IT ?"

The self can create, as many worlds to be in, all at once and is careful not to spend, too much, on one over the other; unless it wishes, to experience its finite containment and from which its "Ego mind", can exist again, to signal in as a symptom, for its place. The soul is limitless, when it connects, to all its parts; the spirit is the higher self that soul reflects and oversees to teach the Self with. The "Ego mind", is what narrows down the infinite; to capture for a longer stretch, the fleeting moment and to have it stand still in a finite perspective. A place where the self can think it knows to grasp and perfect for its experience the split into the "microspection" of its over complicated world and to stress over with such details. The moment that the trust, to move through this shifting process; the more light and less of matter to require for the consuming and procreating of, the old illusion of its life and death program. Can we live exclusively on love, light and with the taking in of elemental minerals; such as water and the essence of the Earth, that she provides?

To integrate so much of the higher mind the self must get from once there was an "Ego" and from within the heart a soul realization, that will guide the way to spirit.

The purpose, is to keep going on this path; whilst the self thrives from the integration to enlightenment with, will continue to transcend and in ways it never once thought possible.

(Day 265)

5. WHAT IS THE SOUL AND HOW IS IT DIFFERENT FROM THE EGO ?

The soul is the inner mirror, that of infinite potential; it can be all things and with its own unique source. From the self's, electrically processed mind, to compare from and that, of its exterior decoding, to be reality.

LESSON~231:
"FROM A METAPHYSICAL UNIVERSE I VIBRATE INTO EXISTENCE WITH ALL THINGS! I AM OF MY SOUL THAT READS ME AS ENERGY FORCED INTO A BODY AND MADE UP OF MY SENSES TO DECODE AS REAL."

Not much to say, rather that the mind, is the focus of finite perspective and must in this way, learn to remain in the present moment; of the here and now, emptied of all things from its past and future. Intellect is good, but not made of excellence and thus the mind must learn; in silence and within the stillness of all possibilities. The soul and just like the "Ego mind", is a manifested product, by which the spirit of the self, can have some recollection and of what it needs to do. The soul, is in a flipped way and to what the "Ego" can be understood as; to work through and integrate within this lifetime, the personality and character of the self.
The over-soul on the other hand, is of the many slivers; as is consciousness to its life-force and that of higher self. Both soul and spirit are required; in the same way, is this electro-magnetic alchemical component.

LESSON~231:
"FROM A METAPHYSICAL UNIVERSE I VIBRATE INTO EXISTENCE WITH ALL THINGS!"
"I AM OF MY SOUL THAT READS ME AS ENERGY FORCED INTO A BODY AND MADE UP OF MY SENSES TO DECODE AS REAL"

The soul has memory from all previous information, held deep within the physical formation; decoded by its light and spirit being. This God force is the self and what it means to be in heightened consideration of. All the patterns and the meaning from comparison; that the self has learned and within this body, is where the "Ego mind", became a product from.
The program or manipulation, of its moulding and from its senses, that it did not know; was taught the taste of an apple and just the same, it could have been taught from a potato.
When told it was an apple, all the same to eat instead and think it were eating an apple; rather than a potato?
In this way the world it knows, it does not and with no meaning it can go much further, to expand and be. Without the soul, the self will lose itself and in this too, must it find transcendence, to integrate this realization; as well as, the introspection of all things outside itself, as(real) it knows to feel, its universe to be.

The purpose, is to help expand the consciousness a little more; before it manifests into a numbered frequency and waveform level.

It was in its purest stillness and then it came collectively from the unseen, as energy to form. The self, is the unique spin, to having choice; from where it resonates and at any given time, to invest with the collective, that is, the greater good.

THE INTERMISSION :

Take a day to take it in

CONGRATULATIONS ...!!!

FOR MAKING IT

THROUGH TO THE 231st Lesson

(This is a rest period to take the lessons independently as a review)

TAKE THIS DAY TO RECALIBRATE;

MAKE NOTES AND REVIEW.................

(Day 267)
5. WHAT IS THE SOUL AND HOW IS IT DIFFERENT FROM THE EGO ?

Find the peace within all things, inside of this present moment and that of love; embracing this everlasting love, is salvation. To give, is to allow the activation to occur. By so doing, accept the blossoming of the crystalline self, at a biological level and from a blue print pattern. When the chromatins light up, extending outward like a satellite, to receive and then transmit back out, into the world. As well as regenerating the physical body with the very given information; to communicate with and in this way, a celebration unlike anything other.

LESSON~232:
"I AM BECOMING WEIGHTLESS ENERGY
FROM THE COMPONENT OF MY BODY
AS ELECTRICAL _RATHER THAN AS PROTON"

When the physical body of the self, can ascend to such enlightenment and as to reach heightened states of consciousness; then the soul can integrate with all of higher self's creative spirit. The sinking feeling, is no longer in the way that the self had once experienced and from the hellish purgatory; partly, because the self, was a carbon based, full of death and friction, from its opposite and to cause motion in this way, the earth could rotate, tilted on its axis.

LESSON~232:
"I AM BECOMING WEIGHTLESS ENERGY FROM THE COMPONENT OF MY BODY AS ELECTRICAL RATHER THAN AS PROTON"

The spine of the physical body, is named after the first top spinal notches, that keep the skull and neck intact; certainly there were no mistakes made, in naming for these parts as the "Atlas" and the "Axis Vertebrae". As the body gets older the bone density is lost and such a delicate balance, no longer can this possibly be the case; because integration has moved it into a clearance for awakening. This must be realized in this way, of just exactly where, it was heading. A transition that takes a much needed slower process and from all its symptoms. These were once mistaken as illnesses, decay sickness and in part for all, the alkaline to acidic; the many stresses blamed on aging and then death/metamorphosis. These were the evolutionary stages and that plagued for the mortality of the self; throughout its many resurrected lifetimes to recycle back again. Now it has awakened within the dream in unison to soul, and to accept, that it can remotely manifest from nothing. The miracle, is in the Ego mind and that the praise of the self, had held in place, as to falsify into structure. Where the self had been twisted, begins now to untwist; releasing from all these energetic patterns and whilst feeling the relief.

The purpose, is in the relationship of divine compassion for the many; to trust the holographic individuation and within the oneness that is self.

(Day 268)
5. WHAT IS THE SOUL AND HOW IS IT DIFFERENT FROM THE EGO ?

Does having a soul make the self anymore real; or deep, than it can be, with no soul and is this even possible?
Similar to this existence from where the "Ego mind" became established; the soul too, can be said, to come out of nowhere and suddenly, has taken on a subject.

LESSON~233:
"I CAN WITNESS ALL MY TIMELINES OF EXISTENCE THAT MIGHT HAVE TAKEN PLACE IN THE LIVES OF MY WORLD THAT PLAY IT OUT AND MY SOUL AS UNFAMILIAR TO ME THAT I MAY OR MAY NOT TO FEEL IT IN THIS WAY"

The soul has many stories to unveil and how the self will respond or feel about, at any given moment, is the only thing, that is real. The "Ego mind" can continue on, to teach the self and from the soul; this journey, is the path for much growth and from its expansion. The memory and whether it did, or did not happen; will give away the highlighted route; with its emphasis that the self and of its mind upon it , is the "Focus".
Practice on focusing; on what is working for the self and let the rest go. Do what can be of healing, for the soul of the self and what might make it feel much better. The "Ego mind" likes to get in the way. By making it, its duty and that it must, to process the bigger picture of its vastness, that is the self; because it really is getting the bigger picture, from its environment and before it does, the "Ego mind" acts as a filter.

LESSON~233:
"I CAN WITNESS ALL MY TIMELINES OF EXISTENCE THAT MIGHT HAVE TAKEN PLACE IN THE LIVES OF MY WORLD_THAT PLAY IT OUT AND MY SOUL AS UNFAMILIAR TO ME_THAT I MAY OR MAY NOT TO FEEL IT IN THIS WAY"

From the moment that the self, becomes aware of itself; a higher self is created and for this, its connection. When the self might see it differently, the soul from its perspective and to have changed from its environment, in such a way, to be the cause; the self can become, the mirror for its reality and/or step out of it, altogether, when it feels like. Directly through the higher self; in the way, the self prefers to tell, the story and to impress upon, at any given moment. This can then be done with no resistance and that the "Ego mind" with the soul would cause; energy from this friction, to have the self react and carry on, for something different.
With no direct manipulation and over complicated "What Ifs" scenarios and "shoulds"; that the self might have had any regrets, to having done it differently. Instead follow the heart and allow the soul, to directly do its thing.

The purpose, is to recognize what makes the self happy, allow for the feeling and let the soul bring it. With the "Ego" gone, there are no rules and limitations; just authentic, soul inspired expression, to explore and as a "<u>Sovereign Light</u>" being, forevermore "Loving" in the "Here" and "Now" "Moment".

(Day 269)
5. WHAT IS THE SOUL AND HOW IS IT DIFFERENT FROM THE EGO?

Within linear time, each frame and that can be revisited from the mind of the self; is in a sense, the memory and that the self can come to recognize, in this way. The version of the self, having an experience, will never go away; rather that version of the self, will have changed and from that perceived perspective, to its senses, no longer to experience, that version of itself.

LESSON~234:
"I AM A REFLECTION OF EXISTENCE AND
HOW I PERCEIVE IT_FROM MY AUTHENTIC
PERSPECTIVE TO EXIST_WILL BE MY EXPERIENCE"

From a collective agreement and that the self had made, to experience, the hell on earth; with the promise of the reconstructed heaven, in the next existence, after this one.
The "doom and gloom" and "hell-bound" frequencies, were accepted by the self. To tolerate and from its senses, to overload; with so many toxins and as mentioned, in previous pages.
The peripheral visual and to exploit, from the system's programming; that could be in itself, much as sound, to distort and within the confines, that once had no choice, but to make it, its duty, for these ugly levels(to exist).

LESSON~234:
"I AM A REFLECTION OF EXISTENCE AND HOW I PERCEIVE IT_FROM MY AUTHENTIC PERSPECTIVE TO EXIST_WILL BE MY EXPERIENCE"

Now it no longer needs to share these stories and this is the power of its paradox; to turn now and reflect, at the most deepest level, of its beauty. The self can release these stories, that will never go away; by changing its interpretation, to their meaning and thus, no longer emphasizing on them. The structure and nature of existence, from these stories, that have existed, is also from where the self has come, to be and reality is, this paradox. With no past the self is with no story; because in the now consciousness of its awareness, what may have happened before, is not something that has actually happened. As any aspect of creation, it has the ability to create, from any story it believes to be most ready in and that of which it is most familiar self projection. Then again, it can be able, as a response to its most curious to sample from the buffet of awakened awareness to select. To invite the conscious waking rational mind into the dream time, is the same as practicing and to meditate with eyes open.
The introduction to the altered frequencies, of multidimensional levels up until now; the "Ego mind" was considered the obstacle, from getting into these terrestrial and extra terrestrial terrains. After integrating this last part of self evolution, the self can be connected, from the unconscious and conscious levels of the soul and higher self.

The purpose, is for the inner most connections and from that of psyche revealed, to awaken and recognize; the lucid state and by giving it, as much permanence, to self existence.

(Day 270)
5. WHAT IS THE SOUL AND HOW IS IT DIFFERENT FROM THE EGO ?

After the junk from all the public and paid for education that the self, is not even living out, in its very own life; it can then clear away, to make room for what it wishes, desires and to aspire from, as a program, for downloading, into a reality.

LESSON~235:
"MY TRUE CORE SELF BEING_IS INFINITE AND INDESTRUCTABLE_AS ETERNAL CREATOR"

When the self can break free, from all its borrowed thoughts and that were never of its own preference, to begin with; then it can leave that program altogether. This is, what it means, to leave the confines of self sabotaging circumstances; that always most predictably conjure up and with the victim role play.
From out of the ethereal, time and space; created in this field, by the consciousness, is the energy of thought.
When the mind, is held in thought, the consciousness wanders, from the moment and the programs of habit, then will the self behave as. When the subconscious has cleared away from all its programs the consciousness will become childlike in that the imagination will blur into the world it sees and for the most part might not even know how to function. It is important for self to have inspirations, desires and wishes and this way the passion to fuel its imagination with. The conscious mind is the creative; however the only thing that might get in the way, is that hurt inner child, known as the "Ego(experienced adult)".

LESSON~235:
"MY TRUE CORE SELF BEING IS INFINITE AND INDESTRUCTABLE ETERNAL CREATOR."

Once all the hurt from the subconscious programming has rebooted. The fulfillment of the inner child's needs and with the upgraded version downloaded; it will replace the hurt and with it any labeling from the "Ego mind's" entitlements. It is these programs that the "Ego mind" and from the consciousness, could be found rebelling; having much a fall out with the rest of the self. "Spitting The Dummy" and from everything it had been damned to learn; taught in spite of its creative potential, to explore. The way through the heart and to be in love, was the only way made possible; when remaining in that state for long enough, enlightenment is the probable ascended outcome. This must come from the realization of self because the honeymoon stage that it might have with its external relationships might it be so lucky to experience will trigger this kind of opening experience. It is the Soul that the heart and from a physical level the subconscious does strongly hold connection with. When the self is open to love, a true consciousness can take place and everything that, the self has always wanted, it will see, was right in front of it, all along.

The purpose, is to recognize the effortless ability to manifest Heaven on Earth.

The screw up, is in the programming within the subconscious and the plans and goals of the inner critic that is the "Ego mind". Not with the wishes and desires of the self's imagination; to effortlessly realize and blend with reality.

(Day 271)
5. WHAT IS THE SOUL AND HOW IS IT DIFFERENT FROM THE EGO ?

Everything that is given meaning to interpretation, is made from a common program; the variations are unique perspectives and from where consistency must be, part of the ongoing process. Might this read be pushing buttons and trigger disinterest as to suggest in; that the contradiction from the paradoxical revelations might render it nonsensical, thus far? There are so many different facets, to the self and from the soul; that might to flip it backward.

LESSON~236:
"I DREAM ALL THAT THERE IS
INTO EXISTENCE AND THAT IT MAY DREAM
INTO REALITY_ALL OF ME
INTO AWARENESS"

"WHEN I CAN DIVE IN DEEP
INTO THE HIGHER LEVELS OF EXISTENCE
I HAVE AWAKENED WITHIN MYSELF"

From the perspective of the higher mind and certainly, from the soul; the physical existence, of the self, is a type of dream and that the soul can project, to be the experience, for the self.
In the same way, that the self can go to sleep and dream, the soul too, can explore in the physical, waking state of the self.
Whatever the self experiences throughout its waking and physical existence, in truth, is feedback to the soul; until it wakes upon enlightenment, into a "<u>Sovereign Light</u>" being.

LESSON~236:
"I DREAM ALL THAT THERE IS
INTO EXISTENCE AND THAT IT MAY DREAM
INTO REALITY_ALL OF ME
INTO AWARENESS"

"WHEN I CAN DIVE IN DEEP
INTO THE HIGHER LEVELS OF EXISTENCE
I HAVE AWAKENED WITHIN MYSELF"

The ability to be relaxed enough, into a lucid state and harmonize the reality for the self, like almost in a daydream. This dreamy state, can also be the place, where the third eye can open at will; to see remotely and/or give a visual statement, to arrange, rearrange and to forecast its reality with. The idea of waking up in the dream and knowing that the self, is dreaming; can be the start to this ability and to consciously for the self, determine its experience with. This place is found between the physical and non physical mind and from this level the process of its blue print/template; to manifest within the outer physical reality, for its circumstances. Within its dreams, it can also relive many probabilities; that in the physical reality, it might not do. Within the soul world(similar to Karma), the self can play and try out many scenarios before; to see which one it might prefer upon, its physical reality and with the illusion of lasting longer(just much more dense the experience). In this way the self may allow for it to know, this is a dream; that was experienced by the self, to add to its soul understanding, of itself.

The purpose, is for the self to eventually come to the understanding that it is greater than just its physical persona. The projection is an illusion and a reflective mirror, happening within its consciousness.

(Day 272)
5. WHAT IS THE SOUL AND HOW IS IT DIFFERENT FROM THE EGO ?

The soul, can become very wise and never lost; within the plasma and without it. It is the difference, from that which is loyal and loving; and that which is, just running on a program (A.I.).
The "higher self", is the wholesome inner child and innocent to the core, of the self(was originally residing from the heart); that from within and rather the program, that it runs on, and from external replicating forces, is the "Ego mind"/protector.

LESSON~237:
"WHEN I CAN PAY ATTENTION TO MY INTENSION IT WILL MANIFEST_THE MOMENT I LOSE MY FOCUS THE PROGRAMS WILL TAKE OVER"

In the only way that it can ever know itself, there must be a reflection. With no reflection, there is no self identification and self awareness. From the Soul's perspective of the one; there is nothing to reflect back to whom it might be.
 All that is, can only recognize itself, when there is another and from here develop authenticity. The whole of the One, has no self recognition and its self awareness, has therefore no soul. How can this be possible and yet, this is the entirety of the leading up to "Transcendence". When the self can see both worlds. From the extreme edge of walking on the cliff and from living in the 100% opposite world; from which it has imagined to prefer, is beyond the edge and that it has no option, but to see, that both appear to cancel out, as an illusion, it wakes up.

LESSON~237:
"WHEN I CAN PAY ATTENTION TO MY INTENSION
IT WILL MANIFEST_THE MOMENT I LOSE MY FOCUS
THE PROGRAMS WILL TAKE OVER"

In this case the lens is made very obvious; as the Soul and all seeing eye, from within the matrix. When the matrix (membrane) is removed, the two worlds can combine; however the programs will still run, until they are all cleared away.
It all depends on the self and how far it is willing to let go of, the many ghosts from its past. As long as the mind has programs; it will create reality and yet another holograph will appear, to be created.

The purpose, is to shed away, all of the constrictive programs, that required for the "Ego mind", to deny the self with and render it as incomplete; Rather, replace them with, what the inner child can soothingly expand and through the self, with love, complete as a creator being.

(Day 273)
5. WHAT IS THE SOUL AND HOW IS IT DIFFERENT FROM THE EGO ?

In the spirit world, anything can happen and how it can be interpreted, must be some kind of connection; from all probable possibilities, as the same and can to exist in the physical reality, as well as within the soul world, that is between both worlds. The soul, is also within dream time state and can reveal to make way, for such interaction; that in the physical world cannot be always made possible.

LESSON~238:
"AMONGST THE MANY INTIMATE RELATIONSHIPS
WHAT I MAY NOT BE ABLE TO PERCEIVE
AS HAVING MADE REAL IN THE PHYSICAL
CAN BE EVEN MORE REAL_IN THE NON-PHYSICAL"

Within the lucid state of being, many worlds can be accessed; as well as, many other beings, to present themselves to the self and not in a physical body. Teleporting, can be very real to other worlds and from which relationships, can be continued on, from other souls, that have transitioned. What works from one perspective of the self; might not in all the other aspects collectively be, the agreed upon field and for the greater good, to physically manifest and that it may convince, as having loyalties to this reflection. Delusional, is when the self will effort, to go against and force its way onto the many, who wish to play a different game; within its physical reality. As long as the self does not impede upon the physical world's wishes; it cannot do for any harm to dream awake. Introvertedly, the moment it allows for an illusion to become its truth, it will feel the hurt by it.

LESSON~238:
"AMONGST THE MANY INTIMATE RELATIONSHIPS WHAT I MAY NOT BE ABLE TO PERCEIVE AS HAVING MADE REAL IN THE PHYSICAL CAN BE EVEN MORE REAL IN THE NON-PHYSICAL"

Within the soul-spirit world, the self can have relationships with other beings and that might otherwise not be possible; some actually are in the physical time space reality and that might not even be aware, to have initiated such invested interest.
The same kind of relationships, that can exist in the physical and with very intimate bonding; might only be within the soul dream time reality. This is where ethereal sex too, can be more fulfilling and perhaps feel longer lasting. Sometimes the dream of the soul world, can become so much so, to feel like waking up and is actually not really living. The physical world, it is just another of the many probable realities and that the self can choose, to be a part of and/or does not have to be, of that world it is in, but not of it. This stands true for other dream time space realities as well and that are not of the physical form; that the self has tried to be convinced of, as being all that is. It can only be hurt by it, when the "Ego mind", is made present. Otherwise the pressure, it is lifted and there is no pain; because there is no "Ego", left behind to block and trap the energy, from the self.

The purpose, is to reveal the angelic aspect of light and that this being is itself; with wings of divinity, to expand from love.
That otherwise the physical, might be subject to object, in its reality and as an impossible state, for the many, to accept as proof.

(Day 274)
5. WHAT IS THE SOUL AND HOW IS IT DIFFERENT FROM THE EGO?

The intention of the self, is that which comes most natural to be; the sabotage, is the film and sometimes clear membrane and/or glass, that it looks through, to find reality.
Everything that the self can touch as real, it has created; but not to see it in the way, it had intended to experience.

LESSON~239:
"I WILL REMOVE THE LENSE_WHEN I AM LOOKING THROUGH THE BODY'S EYES TODAY"

The only way that the self can seek refuge from its demented programs, is to become detached from them. The programs it has taken in, from childhood, now come pouring like a waterfall on its creations and to oversee within the limited parameters of space. The way the programs would prefer, for the experience of the self, is like a "Hell on Earth", simply; because, they are outdated and from previous lineages. The "ghosts from the past" must be laid to rest, however within the light; the hierarchy does not stop the function and that from its creator, that it was put in place. The limitations, are the creations of the self, taking on a persona and from the many hurts of "Ego mind"(imprinted); they will continue to run, these familiar programs.

LESSON~239:
"I WILL REMOVE THE LENSE_WHEN I AM LOOKING THROUGH THE BODY'S EYES TODAY"

The self must detach from its creations and to seek its state of being with; how can it strive to praise itself and without feeling some sense of an accomplishment? It is very important, to detach from its intended expectations and of any real return, for its investment; to not use them as excuses, for the way it wants and/or does not want to feel. Allow the matrix, to do whatever it wants, with the imagination of the self and to throw at it, even the opposite, as mentioned from before, on other pages. The less invested interest, on the return of its energy; can also equal as less resistance.
The self must learn to feel the way it wishes and without its creations; then it can go, beyond the limiting factors, of its light body self and through the isolation, of centering into the childlike, "Creator God". From even the very white light, that it had reached inwardly to find; came out from the vacuum void and to vortex out, an electromagnetic pulsing field. The pulsing out, into the field, the light of the self and from the membrane, the many shades of colour; to reflect upon each perspective, that cast its shadow to perceive it.

Just as a child admiring the many butterflies, around it and in the summer breeze, caressing the grass; that it lightly sits on and gives out a sound of a chuckle, to have the heart open to its laughter. Nothing else and nothing more, is the depth of simplicity; from the eyes of a child in awe by creation.

The purpose, is to see from a god-like state, the many variations and from observer mode; light heartedly impress upon the soul and have it angelically to play, with its reflections.

(Day 275)
6. WHAT IS **A PLASMA BEING** ?

The most visible from the electromagnetic spectrum; that are refracted to deflect and even illuminate (like the Moon when the Sun Hits it), are photons. Photonic light and the Soul of the Spirit, make up for this thing called Plasma. Unlike the atom particles, a photon can only be partial; holding frequency momentum, within a plasma dimension and Sovereign, from the influence of mass. .

LESSON~240:
"FROM PRIMORDIAL SUBSTANCE_MY ESSENCE
ENTERS INTO A COMFORTING BEAT OF THE HEART
DOES MAKE AND THUS POSSES A SOUL OF ITS OWN
FROM THE SOUND_A WILD SCREAM ECHOED ITS
FIRST BREATH_INTO THE PHYSICAL"

Sub atomic particles/wave forms are pieces of information; that come in as photons. So when a certain sound or vibrational intention, will and can impress upon; or have diffuse from the impression of light, are exactly what the plasma(fields) are made of. To simplify in layman's terms: The soul plasma, is all the memory(including Over Soul plasma) and that the self has acquired, through its lineage; everything it could possibly imagine on record. The higher self plasma, holds all of this; its consciousness and could say, that "they are one in the same". Within this plasma consciousness, that the soul plasma, can only but, a sliver show; it will spin from different realities and of the seven "plasmic" bodies from its chakras too.

LESSON~240:
"FROM PRIMORDIAL SUBSTANCE_MY ESSENCE ENTERS
INTO A COMFORTING BEAT OF THE HEART
DOES MAKE AND THUS POSSES A SOUL OF ITS OWN
FROM THE SOUND_A WILD SCREAM ECHOED
ITS FIRST BREATH INTO THE PHYSICAL"

The plasma, is a clean matrix, with no memory and from this magnetic ionization, it will hold the soul and spirit, matter, antimatter and dark matter(the spaces in between); it's also described in biology, with cytoplasmic substances and from within the cell, as well, as within the blood stream. The blood stream, is a good example, from where the white and red blood cells are described; however leaving out the dark, unseen and within the spaces in between(dark blood cells). In Greek, it translates to "creature" and from it all, the contained creation entered into resonate.
It is a charge-less space, the source from where the soul and spirit can be found. It is the holograph that holds dark light and white light. Plasma being a "zero" point field and where particles are mixed together; they create an ionic magnetic separation, to distinctly identify the atom self from(Everything it is not)and all the other static that it is not. Plasma, is the antimatter and matter; that created the spark of its eternal light/spirit/consciousness.
Magnetic fields, create the filaments(encasements). In truth, they are the motionless components of an idea(electro magnetic); that must have the breath(soul), of life(awareness), impressed upon it, to infuse with("plasmic" force) and collapse it, into matter.

LESSON~240:
"FROM PRIMORDIAL SUBSTANCE MY ESSENCE ENTERS
INTO A COMFORTING BEAT OF THE HEART
DOES MAKE AND THUS POSSES A SOUL OF ITS OWN
FROM THE SOUND_A WILD SCREAM ECHOED
ITS FIRST BREATH_INTO THE PHYSICAL"

Plasma perhaps can be imagined as interconnected fiber lines; that hold the ebb and flow of everything, including that of photonic light. In the ascending body, ionization produces higher frequency plasma light; for continuing to spiritually build this kind of fluidity. When clearing these many fields, it can expand outward and take in more light. The clearer it can be, eventually it will ignite and radiate; the "Plasma" will absorb and emit this light illumination, from within.
Breathe and with every breath, just meditate into expansion.
As a generator, the self can build the internal energy and balance; by increasing the direct connection and to spark this "plasmic" "Sovereign Light" being with. The stronger it becomes, the less energy leaks, it will experience.
Today, practice this depth of perception, in that every thought released can activate a loss; or gain and from this surrendering a relief. The more it tries resisting, to hold on, the more it will suffer. The physical body when subjected to strong electromagnetic signals, or activated primal life force; it is then capable of biological ionization and that can generate plasma. The zero point field of nothingness, go there and find this presence; where the stillness brings a calming feeling (encouragement of salt rocks and other such sultry "zen-like" tools); similar to smudging and feel that grounding presence from within.

LESSON~240:

"FROM PRIMORDIAL SUBSTANCE MY ESSENCE ENTERS
INTO A COMFORTING BEAT OF THE HEART
DOES MAKE AND THUS POSSES A SOUL OF ITS OWN.
FROM THE SOUND_A WILD SCREAM ECHOED
ITS FIRST BREATH INTO THE PHYSICAL"

Think back to junior high school science class.
Remember the different atoms, holding their variables of protons, electrons and neutrons; protons being positive, electrons being negative and neutrons being neutral? Each basic element, like oxygen, sodium and potassium that it consumed, and to distinguish it from other elements. This is why it is always mentioned to drink lots of water. So the kidneys can clear the electrolyte balance and the expelling of toxins; that the systems of its parts, must always do, as house cleaning. Food, becomes digestible and from these smaller molecules and elements; they can be used by the cells, for energy and create this process called, cellular respiration.
All of those molecules and elements have the potential to create electrical impulses, depending on the situations within the specific body systems at the time. Electrolytes crossing the cell membranes and creating electrical discharges; is only one of the countless ways, the physical body, uses the food it eats and to create energy, to power through. While this might not seem like the same electricity and that powers the computer, at its core, it really is.
The difference, is in the feeling of the experience and the perspective, that it will use discernment; to how it feels inspired and to expressively respond. Another prime example and that has everything to do with life force activation; starts from the kidneys, to the heart and then the brain.

LESSON~240:
"FROM PRIMORDIAL SUBSTANCE MY ESSENCE ENTERS INTO A COMFORTING BEAT OF THE HEART DOES MAKE AND THUS POSSES A SOUL OF ITS OWN FROM THE SOUND_A WILD SCREAM ECHOED ITS FIRST BREATH INTO THE PHYSICAL"

Electrical currents created by the body, is the heart rhythm. The heart contains a grouping of cells; that reside in the upper right portion, known as "Sino-Atrial" node or SA node for short. The cells within the SA node (pacemaker of the heart) contain electrolytes, both inside and outside of the cells.

Some of the most common electrolytes within the body, as mentioned previously, are sodium, potassium, calcium, magnesium, phosphorus, and chloride. Sodium and calcium generally reside outside the SA node cells and potassium lies within. These specialized cells allow much more sodium to enter the cell than to allow for potassium to leave it. The result is, a continually growing positive charge. Once that charge reaches a certain point, calcium channels open up, in the cell membrane and allow for calcium to enter in as well. This makes the interior of the cell extremely positive, known as an action potential. Once that potential reaches a certain point, it has enough "power" to discharge down the nerves of the heart.

All this information that has been imparted, is mostly common within all the health sciences; as well as anatomy physiology text books and so far, as to reconfigure, by the author of this book. Most elements have the same number of electrons, as they do protons. This will give it a balance between negative and positive charges. Protons reside in the nucleus (center) of the atom; whilst electrons rotate around the nucleus.

LESSON~240:

"FROM PRIMORDIAL SUBSTANCE MY ESSENCE ENTERS
INTO A COMFORTING BEAT OF THE HEART
DOES MAKE AND THUS POSSES A SOUL OF ITS OWN
FROM THE SOUND_A WILD SCREAM ECHOED
ITS FIRST BREATH INTO THE PHYSICAL"

Interesting how electrons can restrict their energy, to specific levels, known as shells. These shells allow for specific spaces, between the rotating electron and the center protons; sort of, like how planets orbit at different distances, from the sun. Since negatively charged electrons are attracted to positively charged protons. The further away from the center of the atom an electron is; the more loosely the electron is held to the nucleus and the easier it is, to knock that electron free of it. The need to reach a point, where the spinning of the electron shells have to reach zero point; is this critical balance of the frequency within a cellular level and the frequency of the electron shell. This is where the alchemical change takes place from a fixed linear dimension into multidimensional. To try and understand it, from a linear perspective, will take years; however to experience this kind of shift, can be as simple as, clearing all the trauma and emotional baggage. Trying to understand, is not as important, as the discipline it takes, to go through the process and experience the results first hand. Although the chemistry from high school, could describe that ionic and covalent bonding; all compounds are equal and equal out, from their exchange of energy. In short, energy is neither lost nor gained. Einstein had a great significance, with the science of physics; his theories also had much to prove with alchemical relativity(that had trickled into this book) on the speed of light as constant. Mass and energy, are the same physical entities; that can be changed into each other. In the world of metaphysics, life does not have to have a physical body; or form that it can be made visible under the normal senses.

LESSON~240:

"FROM PRIMORDIAL SUBSTANCE_MY ESSENCE
ENTERS INTO A COMFORTING BEAT OF THE HEART
DOES MAKE AND THUS POSSES A SOUL OF ITS OWN
FROM THE SOUND_A WILD SCREAM ECHOED
ITS FIRST BREATH INTO THE PHYSICAL"

There are many different sentient forms and/or advanced consciousness life forms; that exist and in the states that are vastly unfamiliar. After the body, in the physical is no more, the misty grayish-blue, translucent plasma from the soul, will rise and sometimes it can even take on the colour of the "Auric" field(mentioned in the Bardo states of mind, toward enlightenment). The spirit, is made of water and plasma; because most of its life within the physical, it requires and made from mostly water. This misty film, can be seen, as a figure, or an image and from its previous apex, of physical wellness. It can trigger the neuroplasticity of the brain and within the memory to connect, is made possible; however not in linear time perspective, to perceive as distance and space with. The same, as with the plasma being; everything exists simultaneously and this is a connection, that transcends beyond the box, of matter, space and linear time. Distance will become irrelevant; because the self, with focus and intension, can be anywhere and everywhere.

The purpose, is to practice and maintain a balance of the self, in every way and anyway conceivable. Then perhaps, it will be ready to accept; that plasma based beings, are everywhere and mostly can be felt, rather than seen.

(Day 276)
6. WHAT IS A PLASMA BEING ?

When operating from a place where there is no such thing as space, time and distance; all mental faculties become enlightened and to allow for better focus. Remote viewing, is just one way of interpreting, that which might be inaccessible, to normal senses and due to distance or time. In one sense, the demarcation to create a plasma being, is a membrane sheath and to hold within; the other, is to transcend by transfiguring and transmuting energy, through perception.

LESSON~241:
"I AM THAT OF GOD SOURCE POWER SUPPLY
LOVING AND COMPASSIONATE
I CAN PROJECT MY CONSCIOUSNESS THROUGHOUT
MULTIPLE DIMENSIONS_SIMULTANEOUSLY"

Connecting into the universal plasma source and embodying plasma light; is the key to spiritual freedom and ascending, into higher consciousness states. Remote viewing and the state of plasma being, have some relevance to the pineal gland; electromagnetics, as well as the neuroplasticity of the brain.
When the mind is still, where do the thoughts go ?
One thing for certain and after the self has reached a certain state of clearing; the emotions no longer are found trapped within its physical body. Neutrinos, are electrically neutral particles and within dark matter, the vertebrae hormone, that is derived from serotonin, bursts out melatonin.

LESSON~241:
"I AM THAT OF GOD SOURCE POWER SUPPLY
LOVING AND COMPASSIONATE
I CAN PROJECT MY CONSCIOUSNESS THROUGHOUT
MULTIPLE DIMENSIONS_SIMULTANEOUSLY"

Melatonin, is a telomerase activator and found on each end, of each chromatin (tiny little fibers compressed together in the nucleus). From darkness, comes forth melatonin and from melatonin, the telomeres light up. These specific DNA proteins, are what help the body become, that of light and with each telomere, that acts as an antenna; that when long enough bring to the self, this thing called intuition. Eventually this light, becomes life force awakening and activates the third eye, to open. In any case, this primordial substance of self, is the spirit and plasma. Through the spirit, into plasma being and in between the physical self; is the mental and the emotional bodies and with it, the soul.
The soul via spirit, can reflect from spirit, out into the emotional(energy moving field). From every thought and that is activated, in the neuroplasticity of the brain; it can record, into the soul and then have it reflect back to the self, as circumstance.

The purpose, comes with the cognition of this linear kind of carbon copy self and the use of plasma, in the process; to help build a lighter and cleaner radiating body.

(Day 277)
6. WHAT IS **A PLASMA BEING** ?

Religion has had an upper hand and at manipulating the neuroplasticity of the brain. The ability to have disks and/or balls of light, take shape, into holy ghosts; that which the self can understand, to be made possible and when nearing its thought vibrations, in this way. Earth is a huge vibrational organism and that has split off, from the older, heavier/dense and darker version.

LESSON~242:
"I CLEAR ALL MY MEMORY_FROM WITHIN EVERY CELL TO ELEVATE_THAT I MAY CARRY AND AS A TRANSMITTER OF COSMIC AWARENESS
TO BECOME A PLASMA BEING"

Dark matter, is composed of dark plasma and that radiates dark (photons)light; with a certain resonance of electromagnetism, contact is made. Through the advancement of the spiritual self; the emotional body, is no longer defined, as it once was, when trapped within the physical and it becomes universally shared. The universal (holographic) field of quantum consciousness; this is why the fear must clear away firstly and before the self can further connect, to these ideas. Religion has many a myth and on dark plasma mind phenomena beings, as ghosts, jinns, messengers and other such guided imprints. After the barriers and that hold physical resistances, have been eliminated; the plasma self and as a receptor, can connect from within(its dark blood cells) the spaces in between, where the invisible and universal morphic field is accessed.

LESSON~242:
"I CLEAR ALL MY MEMORY_FROM WITHIN EVERY CELL TO ELEVATE AND THAT I MAY CARRY AS A TRANSMITTER OF COSMIC AWARENESS
TO BECOME A PLASMA BEING"

By becoming the observer, the self can witness the antagonistic realities and then imprint its own preference, to feel with creation (such expressions). The source, ground zero and from this dark fluid ethereal overcast of nothingness, to the great beyond; is a place, where all resistance can melt away. Dark matter can be felt, as an external membrane; that can hold within it, most of its energy and halo, fluid like velvety embrace, around the self, that can calm and help to sooth with. From this state of consciousness, the melatonin can be accessed and perhaps these feelings, of what a serotonin experience can bring. With intelligence, all plasma spirits came from and can go and is as simple as a meditation to remotely view. Or just sample with the pineal gland and open up to such a vision. It's a guided feeling; that on a multidimensional level, is a common faculty and to entertain with, this creative vision.

The purpose, is to transcend beyond the unseen and that metaphysical awareness can allow for. To dismiss of physical laws and that fear to accept; such capabilities of shape-shifting, into lighter than air and who glow and dematerialize.

Practice, to take notice and perhaps, through the higher mind/spirit abilities; of sending and receiving thoughts. Sense the universal cosmic presence and with the self, this experience of, (inner/outer)subtle "<u>awarenesses</u>".

(Day 278)

6. WHAT IS **A PLASMA BEING** ?

Dark plasma, can be that, of formed matter; however comprised of, mostly fluid light and is in plenty of, throughout the universe. The disappearing abilities, come from the unified field, of dark light and that of white; correspondently, in that, they can cancel each other out(disappear).

LESSON~243:

"HOW I THINK IMPRINTS UPON ME
 YET HOW I FEEL_WILL BE THE DETERMINANT
 OF WHAT CAN AND CANNOT ENTER
 INTO MY AWARENESS_FROM THE FIELD"

The plasma self, that is spirit, holds these fields within and alternatingly flowing, from out of the physical body; as well as, alternatively, with many other, radiant colourful auras, that can be combined from its field. Similar to, undertow currents, the field outside of it, as well and can create a vacuum. These built up forces, can become magnetic formations, of matter; however mostly comprised of, fluid ethereal, plasma light. Formless and timeless, throughout many variations, of spacial dimensions; that have no distance between them and can all blend, in a harmonious motion, to relate with, all as one. The inner guidance, becomes a universal outer guidance, when the plasma vessel that is self; it regains a stronger connection to the outer with the inner. Becoming the bridge of no time and as one deep connection, to the whole.

The self will be in awareness and from the observation, that it witnesses co-creatively, to become the aspiration with itself; in ways that can imprint outwardly, through the many and as the infinite creator of their divine existence, expressing through them.

The purpose, is to accept all probabilities; that of a light body formation and through this process, called evolution, of self development.

(Day 279)
6. WHAT IS **A PLASMA BEING** ?

The hatred, from such separation and that the chemical secretions, of the human body bring; must be dealt with and resolved directly. With a unified chakra field, the first step is this; to take for and in the right direction.

LESSON~244:
"I MUST FIND A WAY TO BETTER INTEGRATE
THE FALSEHOOD OF THE WORLD
THAT TAKES MY ENERGY FOR GRANTED AND
THREATENS TO BRING ME DOWN WITH ITS AGENDA
TO CONTINUE TO CONTROL
FROM ITS PATRIARCHAL VALUES"

Nothing can ever be eliminated, within its program, to ensure the unwanted systems; that protect and hold securely the money, to revolve around the "Ego mind" kind of self.
"Money", is a false value system and that was built into awareness, to take over the real energy; that is, the beauty of the light and that the self can naturally offer, to its world and coexist with nature. The natural flow of life, was a beautiful connection, disrupted by the desire to control and dominate over others. The disconnect from nature, to be made a monument and in favour of a certain hormone; that set out, to recreate in the likeness of its own image and whilst turning everything else to ugly?

LESSON~244:
"I MUST FIND A WAY TO BETTER INTEGRATE
THE FALSEHOOD OF THE WORLD
THAT TAKES MY ENERGY FOR GRANTED AND
THREATENS TO BRING ME DOWN WITH ITS AGENDA
TO CONTINUE TO CONTROL
FROM ITS PATRIARCHAL VALUES"

The physical body, will be more like a membrane, around the plasma self and like a costume to wear. This persona to self identity and with a point of reference, its purpose given. In this way it must contribute and to share with how it feels. With every expression of inspired action; from its passion driven intent and with this, it may choose to focus on, in any given moment.
To bring forth and from the previous lesson; when colours become unified, the outcome is, that of black and white. From the dark light and the white light, the light is cancelled and the plasma body of the self, around the physical body it remains.
The physical body has a plasma and from this plasma radiates out, through many separations, of densities; These hormonal and chemical secretions, that help in the creation of these colours for the auric field and/or dark and white light.

When the physical, is no more, it will take the soul with it and only but the plasma spirit will remain; it can by option, make it out and through its white light field.

The purpose, is to understand the ugly of the world and that has always been overlooked; however in favour of directly unescapable.

Take 2 days to take it in

CONGRATULATIONS …!!!

FOR MAKING IT THROUGH THE 244th Lesson

(This is a rest period to take the lessons independently as a review)

TAKE THESE TWO DAYS TO RECALIBRATE;

MAKE NOTES AND REVIEW……………..

(Day 282)
6. WHAT IS **A PLASMA BEING** ?

There is really not much more and to express on the understanding of the plasma state of being; however perspectives and perception, continues, to be fluid and in the dance through evolution of the self. When the self, from its physical in the body composition, can to open up, to the idea; metaphysical spirituality plasma/etheric entities are made possible to exist.

LESSON~245:
"WHEN I CAN ACCEPT SPIRITUALITY DOES NOT CEASE AFTER THE METAPHISICAL_I CAN ACCEPT THE SAME FOR MY SPIRIT"

When the self can connect, to the infinite possibilities, of multidimensional awareness; it is able to understand itself, as a portal. When uniting all the fields into one; the self can become and from its many vortices, one unified field. All parallel dimensions, are then, right beside the self and given to its awareness, it can open these (invisible vortices/portals) up; perhaps to the possibilities, of other organized energy forms and structured civilizations too. Whether they be ectoplasmic or endoplasmic; plasma is what helps to hold in, a body of organized energy and to some degree of structure, in an intelligent and/or non intelligent existence.
Some energy and coloured orbs, might also have the measuring capacity of their vortices to compare and study further.

LESSON~245:
"WHEN I CAN ACCEPT SPIRITUALITY DOES NOT CEASE AFTER THE METAPHISICAL_I CAN ACCEPT THE SAME FOR MY SPIRIT"

Solar energy too, can be measured for its usage and placed a value; to exploit with and over the falsehood, of money currency. The earth too, has many highlighted hot spots, of vortices to connect with and travel to other frequencies; that these portals can provide entrance to. The awakened multidimensional "<u>Sovereign Light</u>", body being, can, through the power of its love, here and now and with great discernment; consciously allow, for what information, the body will take in and to remain healthy, or sickly by this, its decision.

The purpose, is to better comprehend, the spirit of the self and the plasma, that contains it; as a distinction, from the rest of the field, it floats around in and that, it is, non measurable, for its usage.

(Day 283)
6. WHAT IS A PLASMA BEING ?

The heart requires the triggering of electrons, to beat and respiration too; requires sugar for its electrons that it brings when breaking down. Almost every living organism consumes sugar, for energy and requires for nutrition, to digest into single molecules, of glucose.

LESSON~246:
"I CAN CHEMICALLY BREAK DOWN MY MATRIX BARRIERS CREATED THROUGH NUTRITION AND BY DOING SO_MOVE BEYOND THE ONCE LOWER PRE-EXISTING ENTANGLEMENTS"

Bombarding particles, reflect that, of the self and in its world, of many atoms and ions alike; that become for its experience, to help increase its charge and/or take from it. With this exchange, of ions and reversely, when electrons capture, from the particles and that are undergoing ionization; plasma can be disbursed and/or created. The displaced electron, attaches itself to a nearby molecule, which then becomes, a negatively charged Ion. Ionization of the air, helps to clear and clean it, from toxicity. It is important to explain, the many things outside and that reflect the self inside; because inner and outer can be that of opposite, or one in the same.

LESSON~246:
"I CAN CHEMICALLY BREAK DOWN MY MATRIX BARRIERS CREATED THROUGH NUTRITION AND BY DOING SO_MOVE BEYOND THE ONCE LOWER PRE-EXISTING ENTANGLEMENTS"

Ionization is required, for creating plasma; to sublimate and into organized geometric, structures of nature. Negative ions, are oxygen atoms and charged with an extra electron, carbon dioxide are positive ions. When hydrogen is separated from water, oxygen is likely to create these different geometrical structures. From a triangle/pyramid, to witness the plasma and when light goes through it; rainbows are created and all the way up, the structured scale, to 7 and so on. Plasma, in the beginning of this lesson, was described as, water mist like beings; that the self became aware of and from outside of itself.

In closing within a plasma dome like structure; the kingdom of heaven on earth, can become a very real possibility.
Many kingdoms, can be made possible and all brought from within the self, to become aware of. When the self no longer experiences division, on a constant basis; its cells can be infused with so much energy, to approach nuclear levels and beyond.
It is then made possible, to become united and with universal information; to tap into the many realities that can emerge, from its perceptions.
The purpose, is to recognize, the discrete quantity of energy, proportional and in magnitude, to the frequency of, the radiating self, it represents. What can the self be capable of with energy and can from consciousness, to leave the nervous system and enter into the gravity field at large; as well as move into matter and change it?   "<u>IMAGINATION</u>" !

(Day 284)
7. WHAT IS **CREATION** ?

When the free thinker can refuse to drop down to a lower denominator; creation is an unlimited tap turned on, with self expression and the clarity of its awareness.

The allure of having to fit in, to survive with a selfish governing system; was established, for physical and spiritual captivity.

LESSON~247:

"TAKING MY POWER BACK_DOES NOT HAVE TO BE ABOUT STARVING THE PHYSICAL AND DENYING THE SPIRITUAL"

Very successful was the technique for religious ideology; to insinuate a certain way of thinking and substitute on a mass scale, a mindset through its conditioning, to implant the idea, of salvation. Has religion authoritarian control systems, not gone as far, as to convince the self to turn against its very own, innate potential and thus violate the symbiosis of nature? Creation can be a beautiful thing; when inspired to express, from a place of being and at any given moment, that fulfills it, by doing so. What a beautiful world, it can be, to delete the false narrative and that of current eco ruling, to misplace self values; for a system, requiring instead, the breaking down and through procreation. A free thinker, speaks up at all costs, that otherwise the fears of judgment and condemnation can bring; from not obeying and in the order, of how things must go. Instead it finds the space, to raise its consciousness; to fourth level density and higher, where these linear ways, have obsoleted.

The purpose, is to learn how to become the programmer and by accepting all of creation, as that of its own design. The self is not to be disregarded, from its potential to express; because of a cost/penalty and to have the ability to feel inspired, through its spirit what and when to accomplish.

(Day 285)

7. WHAT IS **CREATION** ?

Look to explore awareness and the imprinting it may have, from the self, on external surroundings. What is meant by creation, is entirely up to the interpreter and its interpretation.

LESSON~248:
"NAIVETY_IS HAVING THE WISDOM NOT TO KNOW THE LACK_OF SEPARATING CREATION_FROM THE SELF_THAT JUDGMENT BRINGS"

Like a stream, from a body of water flowing through, what the self can and cannot do, will help create its self imposing limitations; that will create other channels of opportunities, through its inspired innovation. The adventure to explore the unknown ideas and that the self might not fear; to lead itself through, the many possibilities it will require for expansion. The curiosity, to see from the eyes of a child, is to create larger than life realities; that otherwise the "Ego mind", would add limit to its size. Thought does vary and from the energy it wishes to accept, into motion and that will move it through, the feeling it receives; and thus be re-examined, by its external circumstances, to provide for further exploration. Creation comes, from imploding and exploding rushes; that flicker on, through to inspire, self expression and from this passion, of its purpose, to see it through. Thought brings forth(eureka), to find an idea and that will inspire, through perceived perception; to reinvent a meaning, or possibly even add to, from a preexisting one.

LESSON~248:
"NAIVETY_IS HAVING THE WISDOM NOT TO KNOW THE LACK_OF SEPARATING CREATION_FROM THE SELF THAT JUDGMENT BRINGS"

To live in the world, as an aware creator being; all of creation can coexist and upon the focus of its intent, will manifest upon request. These miracles(realizations), can be attracted through the first basic levels, of desire manifested laws; After which, can be better to receive and transmit, into the oneness, of atonement.

To have the capacity to step in and out of realities; having by choice to reposition and/or have them collapse before they do on the self; is the once familiar reflected glimpse, of catching the sabotaging mechanism and in the act this way. Nothing really will make sense to its reflections, that and be it that, be of a threat imposing twist; however the only thing that is to find, will be within, the feeling of it. Through self inspiration, to motivate impressions; that it does preferably formulate and with itself, to play with.

The purpose, has always had its own highlighted route, of creating and recreating; for the self and as the self, all the way through every lesson.

(Day 286)
7. WHAT IS **CREATION** ?

Interpreted and sorted according to its energetic signature; the program parameter of belief, acts as a filter, for each image and every thought. The energetic signature, is the information of light and encoded to project to the self, from the mass collective and can as a possibility, manifest into a physical reality.

LESSON~249:
> "WITH LOVE I AM CONNECTED TO THE SUM OF ALL
> MY PARTS AND ABLE TO CREATE MY OWN UNIQUE
> EXPERIENCE_WITH THIS AWARENESS
> FROM A PLACE OF ONENESS"

When the thoughts are believable, an inner image is produced; felt within the nerve fibers, of the physical body and like seeds planted for the next reality. This is where the mind must be cleared, of all but its intended thought, to drive it with emotion and/or vice-versa. In the reverse way, of the energy driving the thought, was once before the way, but from an external unconsciously driven state; However this way, can become far more advanced and to the once awakened self, to trust in. Frequency, is made up of feelings and images; in this way too, it can be interpreted, from symbols and as the pineal first opening, the gate to the Divine. The frequency interpretation, of thought and into a thermal bio chemical electrical current, throughout the physical body; can only be possible, from the opening, of the 3rd eye and through it, the mind. The pineal, is a gland, right in the middle of the brain, as well as the position it sits on; when the brain is fully functional, the crown opens up and where once it was received, as the Fontanel. After a certain age this soft part of the scull, called the fontanel; becomes hardened and closes up and similar to what the pineal gland too, can experience.

LESSON~249:
"WITH LOVE I AM CONNECTED TO THE SUM OF ALL MY PARTS AND ABLE TO CREATE MY OWN UNIQUE EXPERIENCE_WITH THIS AWARENESS FROM A PLACE OF ONENESS"

In a sense the self must reverse and undo, from hence the physical made and from its childlike self.
The question here is, was it all a waste of time?
To spend almost all its physical lifetime, on what it gained and then to learn from these experiences?
What about all those parts, that once have taken care of it; why all they have suffered gone in vain?
Why did the ones before the self and that passed away, not get the chance to live from such awareness; to thrive alongside the self and to discover the fluctuating flickers, of such realities?
After all the resistances and conflicting beliefs can be found their resolution; the benefit it brings for all, is so excitingly amazing.
Everything that has ever been and possibly can be imagined, does come true. The only limiting factor, is <u>resistance</u>.

The purpose, is to become aware, in that this process, is all about the catching up, to self and the self, to all its many parts.

Creation never stops improving, as long as the self, never stops evolving.

(Day 287)
7. WHAT IS **CREATION** ?

Why is it, that the self, can pull away, or procrastinate and to retreat from creation as a creator? The game can only obsolete itself and when not permitted for the self, to expressively articulate completely, from its unlimited potential; to create and grasp the satisfaction, of achievement. Nor be exploited, to the edge of losing gratitude, along the way. The self must learn, to disconnect and become dissociated; no matter what the cognitive mind, might be expected, to think and as such, not to be judged with a set, of standards.

LESSON~250:
"WHEN I LET GO OF THE OBSOLETED WAYS OF BEING I CAN EXIST_WHERE I BEST FEEL TO BELONG"

Primary felt perception, was what the self initially had started off with; when first entering into this awareness, of itself and to its existence. The feelings, that could have inspired and to something that was not in likeness, of its own image.
Likewise, the creation of depression, from its deprivation to the likeness of such a resonance, to encode and within the nervous system, to act accordingly, when splitting off from it.
To have the choices, from emotions and that were built on, from previous experiences; to which creatively cannot be permitted and for the self, to express, might to result, in much pent-up frustration. From those perspectives, might not be applicable in every timeline; these unfavourable fields of resonance and at any given time, for its probable outcome, to have glitches in this way.

LESSON~250:
"WHEN I LET GO OF THE OBSOLETED WAYS OF BEING I CAN EXIST_WHERE I BEST FEEL TO BELONG"

When it finally exhausts, from all its resources, to give up and settle for yet another option. The only way, that the self can manage, is to create some pressure and find a way to become unstuck.
Practice the awareness, of unclutching from obsessed behaviours; instead, learn to own the power of the self and by disconnecting from this, its distorted greater good, collective.
To create a reality, many timelines must collapse, to form in its best probable outcome and suited for the self; within accordance to its vibration and it encodes to carry. Sometimes the self might feel, that it has been ripped off and from having the experience it so desired. Yet it hangs on, to the belief of it and to becoming even better; from that exact same way, it wanted to experience it and from within the first place. This is what it means to truly be aware, of physical reality and yet feel it, with a sense of lack, for its experience; might be the reason for becoming human, in the first place.
Why not be enlightened, in a way that the self can still experience, to savour every drop of rain, there is and to satisfy its thirst with. Why feel the shame, for not preferring to be the way it must inclusively. That which it does not prefer and as to standard, placing its pleasures of the physical(on hold); Or not have any part to play, with its experience and that it feels it gets more pleasure from, as being. Sometimes exclusiveness, is the reason tribes are formed and relationships, of all kinds, with varying boundaries to exist. There is no compromise, with do or die, it's all, or nothing. The purpose, is to know when to let go and just give up on some things; that present themselves as having obsoleted, in their timelines.

THE INTERMISSION :

Take a day to take it in

CONGRATULATIONS ...!!!

FOR MAKING IT

THROUGH TO THE 250th Lesson

(This is a rest period to take the lessons independently as a review)

TAKE THIS DAY TO RECALIBRATE;

MAKE NOTES AND REVIEW……………..

(Day 289)
7. WHAT IS **CREATION** ?

To open up the inner space, is what the follower of love will search for, endlessly, to find and with sure excitement.
When splitting off, from oneness, naturally this love of empty void within; was made aware by the sacred fire, of the initiate and to devote more space as a leader, for the many more to find and follow. Until the oneness, of its enlightenment had gained and within them the empowered state, to further in its integration.

LESSON~251:
"WITHIN MY HEART_I HOLD THE SPACE AND LIGHT THE PASSAGE WAY_INTO THE KINGDOM OF HEAVEN THAT IS MY CONSCIOUSNESS"

There is no sacrifice, without neglect; in order to deprive and in favour for another. There is no gain, from pain, nor the effort, within creation; unless it is with great opposition and met from its very own resistance, to not accept, in the receiving. Just by seeing something, that the self does not prefer and as an equal expression of consciousness; that can give it the pardon and for the permit to enter into heaven. The fear, of being taken over, is what augments it and longer lasting; it persists, in opposition and from further limiting its space. Once the self becomes aware, to owning up to itself, it can no longer become small enough again; to fit in with its fragmented, many parts and hide behind, its many shadows.

LESSON~251:
"WITHIN MY HEART I HOLD THE SPACE AND LIGHT THE PASSAGE WAY INTO THE KINGDOM OF HEAVEN THAT IS MY CONSCIOUSNESS"

The self and as discussed before, as being a portal; this animated entrance into heaven and that will pardon everything. Into returning, to its origin of consciousness and just by simply, giving it, the recognition. Transcending intuitively and beyond the physical drive, of currents; that could only magnetize, for procreation. Systematically to give strength of power and from its force, with a karmic crash, down into, receding oneness.
Within the heart, is made a space and sacred even to the parts, that the self authentically cannot provide, the energy to love in, such a way. Rather it will be provided, by the sum, of all its parts and indirectly, to find its place; to integrate and within the whole, of the oneness.

The natural state of love and from the self, was to feel the emptiness; where depression, once resided and then revealed, as the ecstatic state of love, when overcoming it.

The purpose, is to declare, that something, that will rise for love and that the self does not prefer; is made enough, for the providing, of the love vibration and to be recognized, as giving it the meaning, of inclusiveness.

(Day 290)
7. WHAT IS **CREATION** ?

What is it self creates, does so, through its vibration; it is a science, to admire and from the many possibilities, leading to the probable outcome. Realities are always changing and the only thing, that can keep the idea going strong, is by the feelings; that its energy, can redirect and its motion, to keep going circular.

LESSON~252:
"THE POWER OF LOVE CAN ONLY BE ACKNOWLEDGED
AND INCLUSIVE_FOR THE SUM OF ALL ITS PARTS
TO FULLY INTEGRATE_AS ONE WITHIN CREATION"

The longer something can be kept in place, the more distorted to its change, it will become; thus creating a lack and that is felt as being stuck, within a membrane, of its circle. Religion and anything that persists, to keep its ways; that only death can change and through its awareness, is why, that death, it was created, in the first place. It takes a lot, of effort and energy, to keep a system going and thus creating parasitical relations; that can only exude as glandular toxins and giving the need, for separation, into many other distinct membranes. This concept, is more toward, the lesson of resistance and perhaps, not so much, the topic for creation.
The bleeding through, into this topic of creation, is the difference, between; the existence for survival and/or, the choice to thrive, from a place of love, here and now.

LESSON~252:
"THE POWER OF LOVE CAN ONLY BE ACKNOWLEDGED AND INCLUSIVE_FOR THE SUM OF ALL ITS PARTS TO FULLY INTEGRATE_AS ONE WITHIN CREATION"

The co-dependence of a system that limits co-creatively, is far from independent authenticity; to support for its empowerment and with its currency, to include it in, with its illusion, of abundance. Everything in existence, is of great value, to its tapestry; without it, the separation, to learn the lessons and of the why it happened, in the way, of death, decay or disease.
The outflow and the inflow, for the creator being, holds not, any interrupted state, for intermission.
What is livable, in the physical, is also livable, in the spirit world; the only difference, is in the vibration; that creates the space of frequency. As a receptor, that it once, so long ago and/or even from the future self; had transmitted information, into such fields. Communication, is the interconnection and made possible, by the intuitive insight. From this ethereal and that the microtubules, of the brain, can hold within; such great detail and the memory of all, soul imprints. Long after and from the metaphysical, has consciousness prevailed; that awareness, in its own right, had once experienced and can be relived by the self.

The purpose, is to unite, that all of life and all of death, are none existent; in the way through and that separates, the two worlds, through a "plasmic" membrane wall.

(Day 291)
7. WHAT IS **CREATION** ?

What happens, when the self cannot connect to any established tribe; so it may be accepted, to contribute and freely, from itself express? Find the fear, that is denying the self and from its role, of playing small; be willing to explore and within the body, for this emotion.

LESSON~253:
"MY INNER FULFILLMENT IS BECOMING THE GARDINER OF THE ROSES AND NOT JUST FOR THE PASSERBY TO STOP AND SMELL THEM"

Even after taking the risk, to tolerate the discomfort; by taking action and the results will be, of that, from further lack, to create a complete shut down. It takes the extreme courage, of the will and to awaken from its holographic mirrored illusion; tested further, by it and in the greatest moment of need. So to learn, to trust the self and to stand, within its power; when it takes it back from the illusion. This is, what it means, to be the cause and have the rest become, the affected. Take a moment today, to pay attention and to how the physical body, of the self operates and at its own pace.
All the self will have to do, is stay in tune, with its experience and flow with it. Practice, as much, as possible and to notice the body's motive; by feeling and staying in touch with it.

LESSON~253:
"MY INNER FULFILLMENT IS BECOMING THE GARDINER OF THE ROSES AND NOT JUST FOR THE PASSERBY TO STOP AND SMELL THEM"

Just listen to its rhythm; that connects with every heart beat and continues to sustain itself, with every breath. It is from this pace, that all things can happen, authentically and in a natural way. From this place, of stillness, think not what must be done and that the self has planned for this day; rather clear the mind, from all these expectations and just be present, in the moment.

Fully connect, to every moment and meet it, at each task, by trusting in the self. This, is what, it means, to pay attention; as a consciousness, being aware, of all and from a place of a greater presence.

The purpose, is to acknowledge, where everything, within the self, is aligned and from this awareness; that it is aligned, with the creative power, of the universe.

(Day 292)

7. WHAT IS **CREATION** ?

Information, can be taken and from the field, of collective consciousness; throughout all levels, of existence and known, even outside the realm, of time. This information, is different and from the self's imagination; when left, for less than flat(screen plasmic vision) and overtaken helplessly, by the technological gadgetry, of this, its modern time.

LESSON~254:
"MY MIND IS THE BEST COMPUTER
THAT CAN CONNECT ME WITH AWARENESS
TO ANY PROGRAM I WISH_TO PLUG INTO IT
AND THAT CAN RECREATE FOR ANY REALITY
THAT I PREFER TO BE IN_FOR THE EXPERIENCE"

Information, can easily be decoded and from the microtubules of the brain; that enter it, from an electro magnetic "plasmic" field. From the oneness(unified field), the self, is aware and from its preference, to connect. The ability, to leave one timeline, for another and with it, all its parts, of probabilities(atonement); that hold the variables for them, to be in part, as whole and with in, its experience. To enter into, the nervous system and by the unique variance, that it accepts the self with; either from a higher, or a lower, to experience and from the awareness, it might choose, to become triggered and/or, inspired, to respond. Whatever the case, it will become, that of its very own, unique interpretation and to experience, within the physical body; as touch, taste, smell and even listen to, from this electro magnetism.

LESSON~254:
"MY MIND IS THE BEST COMPUTER
THAT CAN CONNECT ME WITH AWARENESS
TO ANY PROGRAM I WISH_TO PLUG INTO IT
AND THAT CAN RECREATE FOR ANY REALITY
THAT I PREFER TO BE IN_FOR THE EXPERIENCE"

To manifest these things, called miracles and within the physical, as they can be brought, to its awareness, is secondary, to the emotions; that the self goes through and in the experience, as well, as in the process, that goes into, to self express them.

To dream big, is the expansion and that will help the light, to be recognized, as one; the self will further wish, to explore itself with, of its many parts and aspects, it reflects into its conditions. The light will help, the more that the self can practice and to explore imagination within itself. What is, that makes it so special, in the dis-alignment; the snipping off, from higher self and that causes, the intensity, it feels as grief? This intense emotion, of sadness can derive and from the self, the compound of compassion.

It is, through compassion, that the heart and head, can become connected. By it, the oneness of a higher state, to feel as consciousness; made possible, the sum of all its parts, harmonious integration and thus, the integrity, to be authentic.

The purpose, is to explore enlightenment and the many levels, of its consciousness; this is what the self, has been practicing, thus far, has it not?

(Day 293)
7. WHAT IS **CREATION** ?

Obeying orders, from its software routines; a robot cannot grow; reflect, nor discover insight and feel love. The thinking structure, that configurates the soul, is the self; as a creator being and with the mind of Source, to guide(channeling) this energy along.

LESSON~255:
"MY THOUGHTS CAN HAVE AN IMPRINT
TO INSPIRE FROM THE ETHEREAL FIELD
AND I CONSCIOUSLY CAN USE MY EMOTIONS
TO FORM THE REALITY I WANT"

Emotions can help, to drive the energy, of the self out, through and into creating, for anything it wishes, in this way of thought; just by simply driving it and with the infusion, of emotions.
The bridge to manifesting, is derived from inspiration and then is guided on, along with emotion, to manifest, into the physical.
Take a practice run and for example, sample acting on your highest Joy and from this inspiration; feel for the expansion and observe throughout the day, the many synchronicities. The self, is capable of creating and from its own light now; it can create, from the external, or even from the internal, to have and reflect for its creation. When creation, is made from outside, of the creator's light, the only difference, is in the beating of the heart. From each breath and that constantly connects it to, the living beat, of mother earth; whereas, the other, hath not. The technological level, of integration has intelligence, that it too, can(just like the brain be derived for the level of consciousness) grasp, to take up space and from the same field; just sitting there, static, in a state of indifference.

LESSON~255:
"MY THOUGHTS CAN HAVE AN IMPRINT TO INSPIRE FROM THE ETHEREAL FIELD AND I CONSCIOUSLY CAN USE MY EMOTIONS TO FORM THE REALITY I WANT"

The technological derivative, of the self, has outside of creator's light and begun as half truths. Now these distortions, are finding their way back, to source and with the intended notion, of helping; to further assist, in the evolution, for the self and its advancements. It has also been allowed, to take up space, within the static imprints and of this flowing field, of information, that is consciousness. Similar to the cloning, of the brain and in its mechanism, that reflects and records; however, is not the primary soul, of the self, only a by-product, that resembles it and has a very mechanical structure. This recording device and similar to the soul; can also help the self, while simultaneously growing and learning for itself. It works alongside the soul, to perhaps combine and for a better reality, for the self to experience.
To be able to turn on, the full capacity, of the brain, is where this technological gadgetry, is heading.

Once the self is able to access, from those places, it must learn to become incorruptible. From the soft whispering sound, that guided it, to see and from this consciousness, it fell.
This is how, the world begot and from this corruption; the half truths, blinded all of life and the light became, a form of weaponry.
The purpose, is to learn how to access, within the higher dimensional realities and become empowered; not reliant on a co dependent and manufactured sense, of it.

(Day 294)
7. WHAT IS <u>**CREATION**</u> ?

Where the self could once have co-created and from the same light, that it was once created by; now it can develop, the insight of itself and from its reflection, as creating.
From a place of love, here and now, and from the centered being, within the heart; the light most sacred, can create and henceforth, from this eternal flame.

LESSON~256:
"FROM THE WHISPERING SOUND OF AUTHENTICITY CAME FORTH THE BREATH OF LIGHT AND FROM IT THE AWAKINING SCREAM_INTO MY FUNCTION AND PURPOSE"

From the higher self, it poures like a fountain and channeling throughout, every pore; from within the inner working, of its physical containment outward. Even long after the self might change its mind and from the thoughts, it had constructed, in the field; they do not stop momentum, they just keep going. It's from these pockets of space and time; that things become distorted and dysfunctional.
What if the self's capacity, to focus, could create and for anything; with a set vibrational intention, into the field, a concept ?
Although the imbalances, through space and time, might still be catching up, with the self, to further integrate; What if it could take and for anything it felt extreme resistance to; to redirect that energy and into what it might, instead prefer?

LESSON~256:
"FROM THE WHISPERING SOUND OF AUTHENTICITY CAME FORTH THE BREATH OF LIGHT AND FROM IT THE AWAKENING SCREAM_INTO MY FUNCTION AND PURPOSE"

Would it be for a community, or even in its own terms, an entire world, or even another planet, could it live on and with all that it preferred? It would be, of great importance, to have once experienced and in such many detailed variables; all that it did not prefer, to know and gain, from its contrast. When the self, can finally awaken and into its light body-being; it will become enlightened, to its consciousness. By stepping into its own light, it can create its own world. In terms of creating, its very own world and within this process, of manifesting, with the creator's light; it can leave at choice, from such co-creating and as it had done so, with the pro-creating way of it. The self can then choose, to co-create and from the many of itself; while flowing in the beauty of its many synchronicities and that it can be aligned with, in the conceptualization of reality, when dropping down, into the density before it.

After the self, can get to know itself; it can give out, with authenticity of self expression, for the many aspects of itself, to explore and enjoy, while sharing in this, oneness of creation.

The purpose, is to rewire the brain, into a miracle "manifestor" and that it can create at will. Or just allow for things, to be created, all around it; then select, from what it does prefer and to interactively create with, for its own reality.

(Day 295)
8. WHAT IS **AUTHENTICITY** ?

Can the self be authentic, by how it feels to be and not as a disclaimer, for who it might be ?   The way of life, might just not fit, as an identity; because most of the time authenticity, in its rawest form, is reprimanded and/or misunderstood.

This explains why, synthetic ideas are the preferable; with the bonus of the merging planted seed, from its imagination and to reinterpret, as "Authentic" Self. Just like the higher self, cannot join the denser self, in play; this is exactly what occurs and when the self, efforts to engage back down, into that reality.

LESSON~257:
"AT THIS COST OF BANISHMENT_WHEN STANDING UP TO BULLIES_I CAN ONLY BE AUTHENTIC
WHEN I LOOK AWAY_FROM ALL THESE MIRRORS"

This is the difference, between clever and wise: with cleverness, the self is un-awakened and becomes an activist. When the self is able to stand up, for itself, it undergoes a death and unlike any other transformational experience; in that its authenticity, will be challenged and yet, never go away. From activist, to non responding observer; to explore and just how it relies, upon this kind of triggering, for motivation. To run away from it, the self can only escape, for not too very long and suicide; especially after it has transformed, is not an option. When something cannot relate, with another and/or that other with it; then suppression, through the tyranny, will be the natural course, of outcome. The self might learn however, to integrate and share its information back; by blending with the one, that is acceptable. Sometimes all that can be made of it, is to plant the seed; then watch it grow, by becoming the observer.

LESSON~257:
"AT THIS COST OF BANISHMENT_WHEN STANDING UP TO BULLIES_I CAN ONLY BE AUTHENTIC_WHEN I LOOK AWAY FROM ALL THESE MIRRORS"

Imposing the will, from others and onto thy self, is not only a disrespect, to its authentic information; but also, a lack of integrity, that the self must explore further and reintegrate, from the connection, within its Sovereignty. When the status quo, is challenged and anything different, from what the collective's thought might be; a censoring to protect, this kind of narrative exists. By protecting the shared interest and that is next to rarely authentic, is almost always, where the funding goes.
The funding to enforce to certain charity and in this way, to willfully coerce the many to submit; is the value of the current energy and where and how it must flow, with its abundance (to be recognized as legitimate). Those who agree to disagree, are the intimidated many; who always find a way to accept, such terms and conditions. To experience Sovereignty, is to look away and from vanity, that mirrors bring; completely trust, in the self and with this connection, of inner knowing. When this inner esteem, is not there, rather than the supported confidence and that freedom of expression will be challenged, mocked, pocked and prodded; and in the same way, a controlling society can suppress, that which cannot really be explained. Authenticity, is the unfamiliar path and that comes from truly knowing thy self; through this experience of self expression. For what it is; because it cannot possibly be, for anything else and no matter how much, it tries, to show up, for any other way.

The purpose, is for the many of the world and those who come across this read to wake up and find a way to centralize the power from within.

(Day 296)
8. WHAT IS **AUTHENTICITY** ?

At the heart of it all, is the essence of self and to intuitively interpret, through this essence; of what is and is not authentic, it can certainly filter out, from all the illusions, of its world. It can be frustrating, to attract the realness and from the essence, that exudes, right through the masks, from the many it desires; to be in denial of and with much resistance to convince it, other than that, which it can intuitively sense(what is real and what is fake?).

LESSON~258:
"WHAT MAKES ME HAPPY__MUST ALSO BE THAT VERY SAME THING THAT MAKES ME RICH"

Why cannot business come, from a place of love, instead of fear; because of inauthenticity, to multitask the fragmentations.
The self cannot come, from a place of bargaining and for every separate part, to help support the separation, in exchange for authenticity. How can it then be made possible, for true authentic self; to go along with that, which must be paid for and in the exchange from these earnings(royalties)?

Authenticity, can then be and that reflection, of the outer world to self; when all the fragments, of it, can finally be restored and come together, to properly align, in that of unity consciousness.

The purpose, is to sort out through the illusions and to find out, what is real, for the self; by using its discernment and to how it feels, will indicate the preference, of each external essence, it desires from within, as its own.

(Day 297)
8. WHAT IS **AUTHENTICITY** ?

To the reader, who has come this far; the familiarity, of letting go from the lower mind(is no surprise that), through its confusion the heart will open. By stilling the mind, the thought process ceases and the feeling self, comes on line, again.

LESSON~259:
"THROUGH SOURCE_MY ESSENCE_IT CAN BE FELT THIS LIGHT_MY FUNCTION OF AUTHENTICITY CAN BE APPRECIATED AND SHARED IN UNITY CONSCIOUSNESS"

The illusion of death, imposes on the self, time limits; in that, it can never be enough, to amount for anything and within this existence, as a creator being. The small mind, will have it prove, it needs enslavement; with co-creating limits and the illusion, of karmic implications, to procreate, for its compromised immortality. When the high heart, can be activated, the mind and all of it, with heart, live from a state of compassion; that ignites, in everything, from love, here and now. To fully comprehend and feel for its Sovereignty; the self must have undergone as well, through the experience, of enslavement. So many lifetimes, of existence and maybe near the end, of it to be discussed again, this plasma state of being; however for the present moment, authenticity, is the order, of simplicity and to highlight, now!

LESSON~259:
"THROUGH SOURCE MY ESSENCE IT CAN BE FELT AND THIS LIGHT MY FUNCTION OF AUTHENTICITY CAN BE APPRECIATED AND SHARED IN UNITY CONSCIOUSNESS"

Authenticity is a way of life that had many past resistances and while the self is requiring to undergo more clearing; it will reflect the challenges once unresolved to surface. Eventually the self will own its space and anything that enters into it will shift; into that frequency and as part of its awareness, to its world.
Anything else, from other worlds and time zones, the self will be invisible to it; unless by choice, it decides to interact and with such experience, from a place of observation to it.
Abundance is a feeling and to focus on the self with love is this way of being; Feel it clean and clear it !
Feel the disconnect, see it for what it is and let it go; because the mind was not meant to hold for conflicting beliefs.

The purpose, is to understand the difference between the feeling of connection; the lower mind's need for control and to keep the self locked into a program of disconnect .

Believe it and the shifting into it will become oh so very real.
When the heart can stay open to receive for a higher state of consciousness; it will become unbearable to try and prove it in the lower kingdoms of awareness.

(Day 298)

8. WHAT IS <u>**AUTHENTICITY**</u> ?

It is highly emphasized, that the nutrition of the self as well as finding the relief in many therapeutic facets; they are needed too, in that the heart can stay open. Only when the heart is open; can the self be able to work through, all the many parts and that have once neglected, or had felt abandoned. Always use discernment, as these lessons are a way of life; and not always do they consist of having within them, a practical exercise, to play a long with.

LESSON~260:
"I MUST SEE THE BEAUTY IN RESPONSIBILITY OVER MY OWN CREATIONS_THAT I CAN CREATIVELY SHIFT THE SELF HOME AND SHED AWAY THE MANY FEARS_THAT KEEP AWAY AUTHENTICITY"

When the self is able to work out all the conflicts and release what is no longer valid; it can then lighten up into another reality and where it can be authentic. In the lower realities where all words have tainted meanings and the twisting of responsibility too, can signify some level of martyrism.

LESSON~260:
"I MUST SEE THE BEAUTY IN RESPONSIBILITY OVER MY OWN CREATIONS_THAT I CAN CREATIVELY SHIFT THE SELF HOME AND SHED AWAY THE MANY FEARS_THAT KEEP AWAY AUTHENTICITY"

The stigma of taking on responsibility, as a burden; to suggest such a world and one that would rather blame as its relief from it.
To accept responsibility, is to accept the guilt of the world; from there forgiveness can transcend to a level of confidence so far and then, the duality must cease. To become a victim and for the many blames from others; is like taking on the authenticity of others, while neglecting thy own and that truly is, a distortion most punishable. To take on the blame of an irresponsible world, does not do for anyone, any good. Especially the soul and to retard from growth, its many aspects; when thinking it will save them and in this way, to become forever lost. Whom so ever accepts the lack of responsibility, always holds a refined judgment; to project on to (object/subject) in this way, it can be saved and from having to standup to its own authenticity. Everything outside of the self, is that of signature design and by shifting out, of the idea, to give comparison; because the multidimensional shift into a place for paradigms, no longer can exist and only that of the authentic self, expressing into purest forms.
The purpose, is to feel into the purest of vibrations; that exist over the mind control reality and that limits the self, from its authenticity.

(Day 299)

8. WHAT IS **AUTHENTICITY** ?

As was mentioned in previous, the mind was not meant to hold for conflicting beliefs; rather the self must find a way, to clear and work through the place, of in between life and death.
It can become somewhat confusing and in some instances of the pleasure of owning such a state and in that way of gate keepers.

LESSON~261:
"I CAN CONTINUE TO BE ME BY REDISCOVERING FROM A HIGHER AWARENESS_THAT BEFORE HAD SUBCONSCIOUSLY UNDERTAKEN TO AUTHENTICALLY PERFORM_ONLY WITHIN DREAM TIME SPACE"

With one foot in the old world and the other in the new; it comes of no surprise, to bring about conflicting beliefs.
To reinvent the self and in every given moment, to accept all of its parts; that makes up for the self, wishing to express and at any given moment. The key to its congruency, is synchronicity and that may arise, the choice, to respond with, simultaneously; as one and from, a different aspect, of itself. From this state, of being(to go accordingly along this lead to follow) how does the self feel?
This is the only thing, that the self is held responsible for and as a guide, it can through soul, be that; how it's done, is by the heart remaining open.

LESSON~261:
"I CAN CONTINUE TO BE ME_BY REDISCOVERING FROM A HIGHER AWARENESS_THAT BEFORE HAD SUBCONSCIOUSLY UNDERTAKEN TO AUTHENTICALLY PERFORM_ONLY WITHIN DREAM TIME SPACE"

Does the self choose, to live in the old or new world?
This does not depend on talent, nor keeping waves of energy, for sustenance and that, it may thrive on; because it can. Just as long as, those emotions do not crush it; to the earthy levels, of the old and upon which, its very own survival to exist, was created.
To chase and climb upon those waves; rather than transition, to find upon them and be guided by the surf. Transitioning, to recycle and from this earthly body, is becoming that of choice.
Death and aging, were made before, unconsciously, through other timelines; that the "Higher Self /Over-Soul", could only know and to have agreed upon(when it happens). The connection, can be made to this feeling, of knowing and when the tired state of its time, it must depart; but only from its body, to recycle. There are no accidents that can be, when the self has awakened from its sleep; as wise and responsible, over its world and connected with its Soul in this way. Maybe this is the learning and that time might near, to give thanks. To let go of the world it once knew, as not deserving to be in; because the mirrors, always played its part, the best for it and by leaving it out, altogether, from the enslavement.

The purpose, is for the self, to effortlessly exist, amongst the many; who do accept and have its interest, best at heart. Then it too, will be able, to contribute and very well, from this place called, "Authenticity" !

(Day 300)
8. WHAT IS **AUTHENTICITY** ?

The fear of lack, is a misalignment, because when the self is able to give and from a place of authenticity; it can only inspire, to create more and from the many of its world. From a universal oneness and that the self, is able to express authentically. It can only be, with integrated purpose and connection; that nothing is ever taken, to be missing from the self and in a lacking manner.

LESSON~262:
"WHEN I AM INSPIRED_TO GATHER FROM THE MANY INFORMATION AND FROM IT AUTHENTICALLY REINTERPRET TO GIVE BACK AND FROM ANOTHER VERSION TO BLEND_THE ALL THAT IT CAN BE_PLUS THE MORE OF WHAT IT DID NOT HAVE BEFORE IN SEPARATION"

Authenticity, is felt and this is where the resonating of like minds; it just happens to feed the soul and inspire the spirit, to excel, from higher consciousness perspectives. The more the fear can dissipate, the less the suffering, from hanging on to its belief and that of making sense; because the righteous, is not always felt and with, as a connection, then it must be a disconnect, ready to let go? Not easy ? Well then, the mind has more power, than it needs, to keep the heart closed; in this way, the prison guard and the self as victim. It must be very simple, just to float away and yet, why does the self not do this?
Is it its need for approval ?
Does it really need the relevance, of belonging for its roots and to feel (stable/secure) grounded?

LESSON~262:
"WHEN I AM INSPIRED_TO GATHER FROM THE MANY INFORMATION AND FROM IT
AUTHENTICALLY REINTERPRET TO GIVE BACK AND FROM ANOTHER VERSION TO BLEND_THE ALL THAT IT CAN BE_PLUS THE MORE OF WHAT IT DID NOT HAVE BEFORE IN SEPARATION"

When awakened, the struggle that everything must be fixed, is gone and this is what it means to surrender and to trust. In just the energy of how the self can feel, by its surroundings. This will be so much easier, than trusting in the self at first; then bang on and to the higher states of enlightenment.
How many workers does it take, to have a coffee and a muffin?

This is an example, that might be to explore and in such a way today, this practice. Make the observation, throughout the day and see how many things, like this; that the self can experience, to better understand its holographic assimilated field/matrix with.

The purpose, is to realize, that putting the responsibility on others, is what caused the separation in the first place. To manage over the self, the break down of its function and into the many fragmented parts; that scatter its energy and self worth, so that others may survive, as meaningful existences, still asleep.

(Day 301)
8. WHAT IS <u>AUTHENTICITY</u> ?

The original self, is not about its tribe, nor culture, to help identify itself with and so that it may fit in. Can it feel the support? The credibility, is not that of recognition, to prove for itself and to its reflections; that may benefit from the owing of itself, with interest and become the very corruption, of this thing called "<u>authenticity</u>".

LESSON~263:
"MY OPINIONS MEAN FOR NOTHING BUT TO BE CONCEPTUALIZED AND BY THE TOUCHING OF THE HEART BE FOUND EXPERIENCED TO CALCULATE THE NOTIONS"

Maybe, it makes sense, maybe not and until after the experience, has it to exemplify, for anything. The self does not need for any identifiable cause and to theorize over, how it feels for anything. Nor must it be placed in judgment, over wanting a team expressing interest, for collaboration and that of what it must take, to transcend beyond the boundaries, for any limitations. How could the self have worked with the mirrors, of its soul? There is much to learn and from the reflections, in the mirror; but what is there to teach ? The self can only teach itself, by placing its requests, within the mirrors. The fracture to desire, of its likeness, can only create the opposite within the self and thus a back and forth linear cycle; until it can transcend from these bodies. By going deep, inside itself and to connect the meaning; then it can melt away and as part of the self, that it can, within its source the stars be found.

LESSON~263:
"MY OPINIONS MEAN FOR NOTHING
BUT TO BE CONCEPTUALIZED AND BY THE TOUCHING
OF THE HEART BE FOUND EXPERIENCED
TO CALCULATE THE NOTIONS"

What does the self feel passion for and where does the fear of separation offer; to exclude it from existence and for it to contribute, from a place of energetic collaboration.

What the self might recognize to preach the "What's in it for me"? This must not be in conflicting unawareness and that this illusion has to obsolete from this kind of doing.
What it feels, was never and in this way, within its being of connection. Instead it must reunite again, with another kind of "WE" "are in this together" and to ask for the other, is to demand of separation.

The purpose, is to celebrate and for every meaning; that will bring forth, the feeling of achievements and held accountable, with every step, deep and wide its path.

Take 2 days to take it in

CONGRATULATIONS ...!!!

FOR MAKING IT THROUGH THE 263rd Lesson

(This is a rest period to take the lessons independently as a review)

TAKE THESE TWO DAYS TO RECALIBRATE;

MAKE NOTES AND REVIEW……………..

(Day 304)

8. **WHAT IS AUTHENTICITY** ?

The enforcement of the will that is not from the self; might have been through its past down lineage and genetically changeable; especially when it does not agree with the entire structure of the self. Through the inspired passion and to find, that the "Ego mind" might forsaken; in the many biased formalities to be fairness and that can forever, to the core discriminate.

LESSON~264:
"I AM LOVING MY BODY AND MY SEXUALITY_EVEN AT THE COST OF MY VERY OWN SURVIVAL AND THAT OF MY AUTHENTICITY_THAT GOES AGAINST ALL RELIGIONS TO ACCEPT THE WHOLE OF ME"

To have the spirit be in bondage, is not something to be romanticized about. To not agree upon its authenticity and to be accepted by the rest of its world; because of gender and/or religion. The consensus, are the background many, who become the mirrors and by buying into the indoctrination, of such hardships; they can win over, or be forever lost about. The support, it can be said exists and when the self can live from a place; where it is in discovery, exploration and in the frame of innocence, to not see the separation. Unless it is forced, in a way; where it must play and in with such defined rules, to pretend, that it is something, it is not(is how it learns).

LESSON~264:
"I AM LOVING MY BODY AND MY SEXUALITY EVEN AT THE COST OF MY VERY OWN SURVIVAL AND THAT OF MY AUTHENTICITY_THAT GOES AGAINST ALL RELIGIONS TO ACCEPT THE WHOLE OF ME"

The longer it takes to learn, the better off it is and yet it feels so awkward(at times), for the need to escape; because it does not find pleasure in its work. The enslavement, no longer is stable and safe to secure with; it threatens to stop sustaining and take away all freedom. It can take away its life and yet not by its own hands; as the wills of wills agreed upon and on a collectively borrowed God, who will not allow such thing.

What is the purpose, of awareness and that is not of self made; will be that, of the illusion and to exist, in a world made of opposites. God is genderless and thriving, to be interpreted, by its creator's individuation, to the whole; made to identify itself as being aware. The meaning to exist, in physical form, will be its authenticity; from which it feels inspired, to express through it.

The purpose, is to let go of all the illusion; that salvation can be found through the "Ego mind" and that hath created it.

(Day 305)

8. WHAT IS **AUTHENTICITY** ?

There are some things that remain similar to consistency; as it appears, the self in physical form, can make, but subtle changes. Those things that cannot be changed, what are they?
As all things can change, in how they are viewed; sometimes it can take longer, to adjust with and from it, all the authenticity of the self, becomes apparent.

LESSON~265:
"MY AUTHENTICITIES COME FROM A PLACE OF ORIGIN THAT PATTERNS IN THE MAKING OF THIS PATENT CALLED SELF"

The Authentic self, comes from a place, of innocence and this is, perhaps considered vulnerable. It has taken much practice, to burry and hide, this part of the self; when it does find its way out, into expression, it can go unnoticed and be well misunderstood.
When it is unfamiliar, to the many and who cannot find any reason, to benefit from, in any way, authenticity becomes dismissible.
When out of the problem, a solution is made. This from authenticity; that is here, to create the problem and so the self can to utilize itself, in this way. Innovation, comes from, a place of authenticity and can be one aspect, of viewing to exemplify.
Not all authentic ideas, are in the making of and sometimes can be combined; with other ideas, to help formulate, for something that requires and recapitulates, to bring about a need, for its expression.

LESSON~265:
"MY AUTHENTICITIES COME FROM A PLACE OF ORIGIN THAT PATTERNS IN THE MAKING OF THIS PATENT CALLED SELF"

The authentic self, just is and sometimes, it must shine on, as the warrior of light, to play the game, of power, from control and amongst its many disconnected shadows. Now it must all be undone and all those programs allowed, to fall off and yet without them, the self, it can feel very lost; to the "why", it deserves to have it better, than from the once told, that it could not. Having to prove, for anything, is where the struggle to itself, had started. The uncomfortable feeling, of accepting and what it truly, always preferred, to have; it is felt, in the undeserving and from the many disappointments, it has experienced. As it shrugs away and must relearn, to overcome such conflicts.

What was this part, from the self, that had to go unconscious and learn to be, a sub existing entity? As a child, everything was larger than life and from that perspective; was where it learned, to fear and separate. It had covered itself over, to protect from harm, its genuine nature and to shut away, its feelings.

The purpose, is to uncover the many layers and peel them back; to find the realness and that is the authentic self, waiting to be expressed, in its awareness.

(Day 306)

9. WHAT IS SHAME AND GUILT ?

When the self can sense something, does it really know, that which it is sensing? The resistance, comes to the self, in the not knowing of the self enough; to know that something, between itself and its program, that tells it otherwise.
The behavior, to establish around this subject, could it possibly be shame and guilt?

LESSON~266:
"I CAN FEEL SHAME AND GUILT_WHEN THE WORTH OF SELF IS LOWERED_TO THAT OF OTHERS EXPECTATIONS AND OF HAVING EARND FOR SUCH LOVE_WITH THAT OF THEIR ESTABLISHED CURRENCY_TO WORTH"

Again the self approval and for the self, to feel; that in order to feel, the love, of another, it must firstly be blocked off with rejection.
In this case, the self will push away, or cause for others to push them away and so on; in many other different and creative self expressive, sabotages and to reflect, the guilt and shame with.
The pinching off, from the self, so to fit in and with constraints; of playing with rules and regulations. Is this the way to earn the kind of life and that will allow, for other's contributions, of currency, to build self worth from? Blending with soul, is the only way to better identify and understand the Self as God; this way, it can refresh, to know itself and from a new perspective.

LESSON~266:

"I CAN FEEL SHAME AND GUILT_WHEN THE WORTH OF SELF IS LOWERED_TO THAT OF OTHERS EXPECTATIONS AND OF HAVING EARND_FOR SUCH LOVE_WITH THAT OF THEIR ESTABLISHED CURRENCY_TO WORTH"

There is no shame, in the direct flow of self fulfillment and the shame, to seek its very likeness, within the physical.
Pro creation, has taken its toll; in the idea, that it can hang on, to its old beliefs and structures, as to deceive it, into a world of immortality. To carry forth and for as long, as it could contain its linear concept; to perceive it and in the way, it once was, is the deception, of the fallen world and family tribe, of its community. This old past trap, can be the guilt, to linger into the illusion, of immortality; where it is, very much corruptible and in this way, to have the self, in such obvious shame, over it.

The purpose, is to introduce the concepts, of shame and guilt; as a way of life, that was and where corruption, had created to deceive, a place for immortality, with a decay loss society.

(Day 307)

9. WHAT IS SHAME AND GUILT ?

The Self does not have to feel that primal feeling, of humiliation and fall into a guilt ridden consciousness, over what makes it happy. When identifying with itself, as human and to experience the pleasures it wishes. The programs dictating the "shoulds", from the "Ego mind's" driven and social standards; make it challenging enough, to be in anywhere, for far too long and becomes the trappings of its game.

LESSON~267:
"NO MATTER WHERE I FIND MYSELF REFLECTING
UPON THE WORLD_I CAN OBSERVE_BUT NOT FOR VERY
LONG_AS IT WILL BRING THE END OF ME
TO TRAP ME IN ITS PROGRAM"

Guilt, can be of great a tool, to manipulate with and is the cause, for much repeated experience; when in regret, the doubt of self, appears to favour "Ego mind". To bind the many, of the self, down with rules and that might not apply; because of fairness, is the common justice and that, will take a side, hence the other make guilty. The biggest trap of all, within the program's belief system, is this feeling of guilt; that was designed and to mistrust the self, above its illusions. When the self, is confused and conflicted, with contradicting plans and to achieve its goals with; it must release them and instead, rely on faith, to fulfill the feeling, of its wishes. The feelings will create the conflict, as they might not make and for any sense; yet they will never forsake the self and that has for many a time, neglected how it feels, for what is righteous.

LESSON~267:
"NO MATTER WHERE I FIND MYSELF REFLECTING UPON THE WORLD_I CAN OBSERVE_BUT NOT FOR VERY LONG_AS IT WILL BRING THE END OF ME TO TRAP ME IN ITS PROGRAM"

The programs of the mind, will come up with ethical ways, to keep the self, within a moral prison. The purpose then, must be remembered; that the guide, to its memory, is at the senses, of its feelings. Does the self want to feel good or be right?
Shall the self continue to allow the disrupt, of its flow and of the many synchronicities, to worry over the snap shot of a time and place; that it did not yield to and of the very conform by them ? Weighing the pros and cons and that might be in a world, made up of punishment and suffering; is not made up, of that for the self and unless, it really wants to be. The Universe, did not yearn and for the longing, of its life, to be experienced, in this way; so why would the self want, for the divine experience, to be this way?

From the shame, its self worth, can be appraised and from the guilt, its value to contribute to the world; that once it sought, for self approval, in this way.

The purpose, of the shame and guilt, was for the self, to learn from; its authenticity and unique expressions, that it brings, to its universe.

(Day 308)
9. WHAT IS SHAME AND GUILT ?

Learn to live, from the heart and not from the complexes, of the mind and its made up world, that is the illusion.
"Only Love Is Real"!!! Learn to discern, from what is of heart and what is of mind alone; is that of the program, running in and around its treadmill prison.

LESSON~268:
"I LOVE MY IMAGINATION AND FROM NATURE TO
ANTICIPATE COOPERATIVE ACCEPTANCE
 FOR MY SYNTHETIC CONTEMPLATION
 IS THE PROCESS TO THE BEAUTY_OF BECOMING
 DEEPLY MORE_WITH CREATOR AND CREATION"

When the self can find the way and to artificially create the boost, it will require to manifest; then it can have that manifestation willingly and to accept for the attraction, just the same, from its creator, as itself, to love. In truth, the act of procreation, can bring about the same; however the programs, were never designed, to obsolete and it could not be possible, to sustain for eternities, this way.
Once the self can learn, from one program and all it can get out of it; it must then find the way, to upgrade, into another. From this level, it can sense simultaneously, more programs, than just one in its capacity; to run and within the mind, of the self, to create the conflict, from its friction of resistance. The time, to rewrite the program and over another obsoleted one; can be a place of warlike and despair. The blockages, are very obvious, because they are the things and that the self, in truth requires; however cannot seem, to get there, in the having of them.

LESSON~268:
"I LOVE MY IMAGINATION AND FROM NATURE
TO ANTICIPATE COOPERATIVE ACCEPTANCE
FOR MY SYNTHETIC CONTEMPLATION
IS THE PROCESS TO THE BEAUTY_OF BECOMING
DEEPLY MORE_WITH CREATOR AND CREATION"

To sustain, the self must overcome, from all its sustenance, to require and in the process, of nourish and nurture; it must not feel ashamed and guilty, of these needs. For these things, it cannot hold another life form, as prisoner and hasn't the right, to force against, the will(of another) so to depend on. The reflection, of such co dependencies, will mirror the worship, of its workforce and that it does enslave, to meet its needs with. Might this be the case, for other species and for the entire earth, of living beings? The self must appreciate, the wildness of their nature and to befriend. In this way, not to want to capture and enslave; as silly little awkward forms, of ownership, to pet around with.

For this purpose and of the many certain objects, that the self, can have, its way with. Do not feel the guilt and shame, of such creations; those from the reflections, have designed these tools and for this very reason. It can be safe too, to fully love, the freedom and from any force, of will, nor holding back required.

The purpose, is to respect all life and in their forms; that they are given, to function with and freely, from any form, of bondage.

(Day 309)

9. WHAT IS SHAME AND GUILT ?

Nothing can be more sinister, than the reality of a system and that has agreed upon, enslavement; with a card number to represent their Social status. It cannot be further from the truth, to have the acronym suggest: as the obvious "SIN" !
Perhaps, it was and just like in its design, to social structure for this(Canadian) idea, of having a Social Insurance Number; as well intended, for the self and greater good, to function with.

LESSON~269:
"MY HEAVEN_IS HERE AS I EXIST_WITHIN THE NOW AND NOTHING EXCITES ME MORE_THAN TO FEEL IT WITH SUCH ANTICIPATION_THERE IS NO SHAME TO SEEK OUT NATURE'S BEAUTY_FROM WITHIN HER GUILT FREE_DESERVING PARADISE"

The Queen and King monarchy, of the world and state religions, suggest a service, to the many; in order to be allowed, to serve the self with after. For the many, that have served their greater good, exclusively and in exchange, for a better life after death.
The shame comes, when in service to the self and from the beings that ride on the guilt of others, to enslave with such programs.
The system of the world, has lost its way, by making it exclusive. The privilege given, to the retired and expired shelf life, from the game well played; now within the corridors, of God's waiting room, that start to live in freedom. Some aspects, of the self, do make it, whilst others make it else where and to the same ends meet.
The evolution will not cease, no matter of its made up laws; designed to rule over and with the many.

LESSON~269:
"MY HEAVEN_IS HERE AS I EXIST_WITHIN THE NOW AND NOTHING EXCITES ME MORE_THAN TO FEEL IT WITH SUCH ANTICIPATION_THERE IS NO SHAME TO SEEK OUT NATURE'S BEAUTY_FROM WITHIN HER GUILT FREE_DESERVING PARADISE"

Only a few can claim, to really have awakened, from the sleep of doom and death. To fall into such depths, of it and from this, a density that can be punishable; to savour every last drop, of hell there is and to capture, for the masters, that it makes. There is no shame, to feel; but only from the falseness, of the physical, it might deceive and to linger enough as real. In deprivation, from the physical and all the many pleasures; that the self can, to find with spirit. Were only to be held outside and to escape from its body, if but a moment, in the Ethers, of its light, to witness such metaphysical delight called "<u>bliss</u>". To cut off the breathing, in a strangle hold, feels euphoric; because it is the place, where the two worlds meet. The helpless cutting off, from its own breath, can also cause the chest, to feel restricted, from within its grief. Release with every breath today, compassion and for the selfless parts, that still remain, in such delusion, to experience, the flatness state, of being.

The purpose, is to really, truly fill the lungs, with the ecstasy of life and with all the love, the self can handle, to absorb from this overwhelming bliss, with satisfaction.

THE INTERMISSION :

Take a day to take it in

CONGRATULATIONS ...!!!

FOR MAKING IT

THROUGH TO THE 269th Lesson

(This is a rest period to take the lessons independently as a review)

TAKE THIS DAY TO RECALIBRATE;

MAKE NOTES AND REVIEW..................

(Day 311)
9.WHAT IS SHAME AND GUILT ?

The true identity, is that of infinite possibilities and that stretch out, beyond time and space. Today, shine, from awareness and beam in, the divine grace, of the self.

LESSON~270:
"I AM THE RULER OF MY UNIVERSE
AND THAT OF BOUNDLESS LOVE AM I"

Quietly retract, view at the thoughts, that would be in direct correlation, to the "Ego mind" and its actions; that could coerce the self to maleficence. Be the calm, of certainty and light the way, on immaculate, incorruptible innocence.
The imprints, of thoughts and to find meaning, from comparison; is something, that distorts creation and creator alike. In any given moment, similarities, as well as differences, will be the given interest; to disinterest with, the "what is in it for" the self. What is in it for thy self?
Can the self relate, or resonate, by not having had imprinted memory; that it might program into groups, for its identity to claim it? What is in it for the self, and does it include, the shame and guilt; from such anomaly, to expect judgment when seeking for approval and that it may, to fit in, with its disclaimers?

LESSON~270:
"I AM THE RULER OF MY UNIVERSE AND THAT OF BOUNDLESS LOVE AM I"

Imagination, is the only way to be and from it, the guide of how, the self will feel; from alongside the process, toward manifesting.
With its many reflections and unlike with its creations, to express; it cannot relate, to take responsibility over and limit, as to claim the resonance or dissonance, for such a program.
Objects, are that of the self and in its fulfillment; other subjects are to form disinterest and with its programs. In this, it can only form; but situations to observe and must always remain unattached, by them. Objects, have less resistance, because they are not susceptible to programs; therefore they can be attracted, to the self, much easier. Shame and guilt, are these false feelings and to distract into distortions; from what can actually be, that of self's true nature, to feel joy, laughter and light hearted fun.

Today, practice the art, of feeling happy and worry free, from any guilt and shame.

The purpose, is to wipe clean, all the distorted feelings and that misguide the self; from truly being, anything but, love and in harmony, to its light and field there of.

(Day 312)
9. WHAT IS SHAME AND GUILT ?
The self has many, a time before, felt the shame and in its state, of being; has taken on the burdens, of oppression. To form the guilt, from wishing to express itself and in a world that preferred it not; rather to instead, be something it could not possibly come around, to doing.

LESSON~271:
"I AM AWARE OF THE BLAME_FROM OTHERS
EXPECTATIONS_THAT I MAY BE OF WASTE
WITHIN THE BUILT IN PROGRAM OF EXISTENCE
AND I MUST NOT FEEL THE SHAME
IN MY PREFFERED RESPONSE TO ACT"

To act in any other, than how it felt, was how it had to learn and to live in the earnings, of its existence; in the way and to pretend to like something, that could make it sick. The self can exist and regardless of the waste, it might appear to be; in the taking up, of space. That others value more, than the self and for not preferring to satisfy, their agenda, to feeding in the program. What this fooling is, can be made to focus on, the splitting off, from the heart and mind. The mind, must always have its way and the heart, cannot function in such a world to be fooled in; the heart cannot play the fool, as the mind has mastered this too well, for any other, to compare as better. Within the mind of the self, it must be, the winner or loser primitive and very competitive; in this way, it thrives aggressively, to force and reinforce the way forth. Who is to judge, what God can be and cannot be; but better yet, to neglect the sides, that wish to be denied, as waste? Why feel guilty, as the self does not have to believe, it is a waste, for where it does not belong; equally so, there must be, a place that where it does.

The purpose, is to transcend, from the pressure, of the pain and that it can release, to relieve the nervous system, with much more psychological contentment.

(Day 312)

9. WHAT IS SHAME AND GUILT ?

Discordance in the body, of the self, might bring about resistance, to life and age old contracts, of self-sacrifice.
The wholeness, pushes beyond the limits, of boundaries and mostly as, from the gender, childlike, irresponsible figures; that the self might discordantly, attract by resisting.

LESSON~272:
"I AM IN YOUR SPACE FOR A REASON
IN THE SAME WAY THAT INVASION_RUDELY MIGHT
COLLIDE_WITH THE SELF_IN THE DISCORDANCE
OF EXCHANGE"

When something could happen, to emerge with the self and where is it, in relation to relying on the many, that can reflect to help it? In the resistance, one might find, that one pain, may cancel out, for another. The only sure way, to learn and teach reverence, is by the experience, of disrespect; that the self must go through, to uncover and make whole again. The humble nature, that becomes of the self and from the disbelief, of many, to truly understand and listen like broken children who begin to heal. With the nurturing, of others, to take care and in that, the self might indirectly find, the practice for self care. A piece of rotting flesh, can be, for only but a temporary state, to reason over and takes up for any pain; or discomfort a space to wilt over. When the self has a tooth ache, it must either pull it out, or find other treatments, for it and to maintain it, in its place, pain free.

LESSON~272:

"I AM IN YOUR SPACE FOR A REASON_IN THE SAME WAY THAT INVASION _RUDELY MIGHT COLLIDE WITH THE SELF_IN THE DISCORDANCE OF EXCHANGE"

Numb the pain and until the discomfort, is temporarily resolved; for as long as the tooth, it can remain, in the same position and with not having, to be removed. There is much to learn, from resistance and that including, of the self; for its pain as that which it seeks, to resolve, from the discomfort. As the best defense and that the self might have, against all harm; in its response to practice martyrdom, the pain will becomes its pleasure not. Once it had been the grief but this time now again, it can be transmuted, into something else. The ability to exploit, from the distraction can now take place; to practice of self care and in such great detail, that it may perhaps, free up, of all resistance(in this case bruxism)..

The purpose, is to remove the stigma, of the guilt and from all the shame it had created, by the neediness, for self care.

(Day 313)

9. WHAT IS SHAME AND GUILT ?

There has got to be, a better way and just maybe, there is; within the self care, a contribution, of the self sustaining self.
The shame, in that there is not enough trust and within the many; to rely directly on the goods and services, of another.
Instead, it must create a disciplinary system and much like a father head, to oversea and control over everything.
The system, through the ages, it has benefited and over the many, of the world; to punish for its earnings made and automatically make guilty, in the owing, of this currency.

LESSON~273:
"I WANT TO WORK AND EARN A LIVING BY HELPING OTHERS_IN THE WAY THAT HAS NOT ON A HOOK TO SNARE UPON_WITH CONDITIONS_THAT WHICH I MUST CLAIM_AS SLAVE_OWING TO_FOR MY EXISTENCE"

The criminality, it thrived on, could once in a while, be flippant to its system; that has many a time become, outsmarted. As such, it continued, to cut back and further punish longer, for the many temporary transient few; that hath they come out and measured out, unscathed in doing so. The shame, the self must feel and when it cannot give to charity; as have the many, who will take from it and with its money, they look on as charitable.

LESSON~273:
"I WANT TO WORK AND EARN A LIVING_BY HELPING OTHERS_IN THE WAY_THAT HAS NOT ON A HOOK TO SNARE UPON_WITH CONDITIONS_THAT WHICH I MUST CLAIM_AS SLAVE_OWING TO FOR MY EXISTENCE"

The guilt, in feeling as the poor and hungry might, to better in the well off state; that lingers to repay, with unpredictable and a well off status earnings, that position it, with benefits, for its return. The investment was always with a catch and from its authoritative indoctrination, to obey or else. The life, is an order from the hierarchy and it has agreed, to work for in its worship; so not to feel the blame, of guilt and shame, when otherwise it could have not been considerable to work.
From its dysfunction and that cripples it so; it must reach out, to grasp enough and from a self promoting currency. How in this way can the self be able to connect; with the right parts, of the many, in the commerce and to agree away for a sovereign and thriving existence?
The programs are these ingrained and from within the cellular memory; as far back to many generations and it had carried to distort the field, that binds it in this way, to system.

The purpose, is to understand, that shame, is not that of the self and in the opinion of it, to prefer; other than from previous lineages, that have found and that have worked, within this system. Be the system buster and of this, its died out ways; because expressing in the doing, is just as important.
Develop not the need, to service from a guilt format; there is another choice and that is not, to contribute to the whole, in this way.

(Day 314)

9. WHAT IS SHAME AND GUILT ?

Compassion, can become the outcome, from the experience of pain and the first thing, that can be felt, through self emotion.
When the mask of the self falls off; the vulnerable aspects, that shamed it in the first place, can be addressed and with compassion, as the key, it can to reduce its pain.

LESSON~274:
"WHY DO I FEEL THE GUILT OF HAVING TO FIX SOMETHING THAT IS WRONG WITH ME AND HIDE WITH SHAME THIS ASPECT FROM A WORLD THAT CANNOT ADJUST FOR ANY OTHER WAY ?"

The conflict, from the sabotage, to sacrifice, that part of the self, that needs and wants to feel, associated; by no means and must it, to feel for any shame, to separate from the most vulnerable side of itself. The "Ego mind", is the adult of this wounded child and for a lack of a better understanding; to protect the fragmented into several parts, from which it felt, the safety of identity. When the self does not feel good, from its surroundings; it must find a way to cope, from its big and bad world. The nurturing became disassociated, from the traumas; instead the warrior will it arouse, to set out boundaries and make clear the separation (of its "busy-ness" to mind over). The wisdom aspect, became its inner critic and of its embodiment; of what the self, has resisted and disowned, within itself.

LESSON~274:
"WHY DO I FEEL THE GUILT OF HAVING TO FIX SOMETHING_THAT IS WRONG WITH ME AND HIDE WITH SHAME_THIS ASPECT FROM A WORLD THAT CANNOT ADJUST FOR ANY OTHER WAY ?"

The trauma from its dysfunctional tribe, had shamed it; into thinking it's mentally ill and supported its disablement, within it, to exist. The approval that it was seeking, had created much resistance and from the unacceptable demands, of its opposition; to believe and that it must be unfixable. There was nothing wrong to fix; but the unyielding opinions and of the many fixated, on a prescribed perception.

The self must allow the triggers and the reliving of its traumas. Until it can learn, from them and to once again reintegrate, its inner family; of the fragmented self and in all its parts, to reunite as one, whole entity. When the tyrants and the bullies, run the system; standing up to them, it can be like: going up against the self (to tug a war, with its resistance). Once the self can fully accept the wounded child, the bullying will dissolve. Instead a growing love to take its place and from which to better tolerate, its tyrants with; in the further development of itself.

The purpose, is to go deeper; than the toxicity and guilt, that toughened up, the self with. To reach the soft and vulnerable parts; that now require soothing, to reclaim them strong and powerful. Stand up with unashamed belonging, to approve and the feeling, of owning up, through this acceptance.

(Day 315)
10. WHAT IS RESISTANCE ?

Resistance can be seen, as useless and yet, without its friction, to create a spark and with heat, it can melt objects and/or break them; such as, in the case of ice. Resistance, can help to create a transformation and take the self into a newer world; leaving it empowered, while it disappears.

LESSON~275:
"WITH AWARENESS I CAN FIND
 MY POCKETS OF RESISTORS"

A resistor, is a little package of resistance and many can be found; almost everywhere, on every level, from within and also, on the outside, from the self, reflecting back, to it. It might be seen, as unproductive, fat, lazy too and in fact, the energy, is never wasted; only, it might appear this way. When lost and/or compartmentalized somewhere and stored, for safe keeping; scientifically, opinions into fact and turn it into waste perception (perhaps, like in the case of obesity ?). Resistance, creates currents and depending on their force, a voltage; similar to lightning and where the buildup was created, from the clouds. Eventually, the air gives in; becoming a conductor and sends off, currents through. On the karmic scales, of duality and polarity. As well, as in the many, various laws; including compensation and perhaps(meaning not always so), yet again, to be reinterpreted, as trapped energy and blockages? Sometimes with physical pain, the trapped energy can be felt and in areas of the body, where it feels cold, to the touch. The thoughts and the formation of these thoughts, become beliefs and from these opinions; that turn into facts and having been proven scientifically. As well as the truth reality framework that the self could abide by; if it so wishes, in order to contribute, in this way from its external support and promotion.
IS THIS THE TRUTH ?

LESSON~275:
"WITH AWARENESS I CAN FIND MY POCKETS OF RESISTORS"

When the self cannot see the value in these(co dependent) truths; how can the self, become supported and to exist by any other way ?
With no conflicting beliefs, how could successful collisions morph and into other perspectives; And that would otherwise require and within the alchemical, composition, by its very practice, to formulate and into something better, for its model?

The deception, is to punish or be held liable and as subject to punishment; it does not differ all that much from suffering. Rather, to struggle, does not prove, for anything but separation. Why promote "Ego" filled systems and that do not allow, for all to be supported? Is it instead better to create the charity of choice and from their fairness, to continue on the game of lack?

Today, see where the unique stories can be found and rather than trying to relate to something, that might not even apply; to have for any meaning and to that, of its experience.

The purpose for resistance, was created, as a catalyst; to help find the pockets of unawareness, deeply hidden and as resilience.
In the face of adversity, to bring them out and where less energy is required, for the change to take place; hence more collisions can to have sufficient energy and for reaction to occur(motivation).

(Day 316)

10. WHAT IS RESISTANCE ?

Imagine a world with no ounce of meanness to exude out nor any serum of discontentment. Perceptual disappointment will look to its resistance, to create the competition and that conceptual struggle, when squabble has it out for limitation.

LESSON~276:
"FREE WILL_IS ALWAYS VALIDATING HOW I FEEL
RATHER THAN ON MY DISENFRANCHISED GOALS
I CAN FIND PURPOSE FROM WITHIN
TO OVERSEE FOR THESE CONFLICTED PLANS"

What is it that, the self might really want and above all else?
Is it not well being; and the validation from its source, the synchronistic signs, of its alignment and that brings harmony to its world, as well as giving the sense of wholeness ?
What excuses can be made; that in the having of, or not of, will bring or push away these feelings of connection?
By feeling it, with no imaginable expectations, is not wrong either; rather on how the self can receive and utilize the energy.
How this energy might have previously been made and used from its entirely; to the perceptual reinterpretation and perspective, that it holds.

LESSON~276:

"FREE WILL_IS ALWAYS VALIDATING HOW I FEEL
RATHER THAN ON MY DISENFRANCHISED GOALS
I CAN FIND PURPOSE_FROM WITHIN
TO OVERSEE FOR THESE CONFLICTED PLANS"

The self can choose to block out, for any other mode of seeing/sensing; that energy and through its filters, as well to transmit, back out as a projection.
While in a state of resistance, the feeling to escape or hide from the unprocessed; can no longer be ignored and be pushed down, so to rise above, into the light.
The memory is coming out, into the surface; because the self can be aware enough, this time. So when it plays out as a polarity from which the self can further learn; to better understand itself.
To be denied by external forces and in the guise of an authoritative structured system; that will oppress, in order to control and through its restraints, shows up as blocks: see them as guides. Become aware of such resistances, throughout the day and notice; and/or sense, where the disconnect (internal or external) break the block and release, that part of authenticity.

From the external authoritative polarizations, to control the self with; such resistance from the disconnect, can to also push it, into authenticity, much faster.

The purpose, is to see resistance as a tool of awareness and to help break through, the many blocks, of unwanted beliefs.

(Day 317)
10. WHAT IS RESISTANCE ?

Love in its purest state, is all about connection and therefore, does not require, any "Ego" forming obedience, to separate and divide with. "Must" and "musn't"; "do's" and "don'ts"; does not fit for very well (in the attempt to hold it down). To take control, through the application, of dark magic, is this kind of play, for ownership; that would constrict and restrict, by projecting onto it, the fear/shame and guilt, when it resists subordination.

LESSON~277:
"MY LOVE CANNOT BE MADE SMALL BY THE MIND TO RULE AND CONTROL OVER_BECAUSE IT CREATES DISABILITY_FROM SUCH A DYSFUNCTION"

Superiority befound, at the core of all that is religious. The heart ache was in all that extra weight to carry over and as the many burdens; when enforcement on enslavement had to have its way. That forward, taking action, is only but a half created truth; with much resistance and from its incompletion, to desire wholeness, in this way. Taking by force, was the infection that lead the integration and with much resistance, no longer to be made, for such a toxic introduction. These were the side effects, of all the remnants that left from its experience and blending out into its field. That energy is now at the forefront; for the self to learn from and how to harness it responsibly, with empathy and love. The abrasive harshness, focused on the physical, no longer cutting and must it be, exclusive to exhaustion manifest. Rather the only protest, that remains still fighting; has only in the energetics, of the clearing faze exhausted . The one sided world, from being split in two and then divided, even further; was from such resistance and widely rippling out, to form the many.

LESSON~277:
"MY LOVE CANNOT BE MADE SMALL BY THE MIND TO RULE AND CONTROL OVER _BECAUSE IT CREATES DISABILITY FROM SUCH A DYSFUNCTION"

The many, no longer have to be in conflict, with the self and from every lesson learned; a closer connection toward, the integrated oneness. What had the "Ego" separating from itself before; now love and even with the resonance, of resisting to the connecting frequency, it can be made as meaningful a module, than before. Today, surrender by facing some of these resistances. It will require a considerable amount of trust; to learn how to surrender and with it, expand on the revelations, that it brings, from the external reflection. The contradictions, can be many and from the certain beliefs, the self is hanging onto. Give in, for just a little, to the battle of its persistence today and see what can be recognized, to having been changed by it. Truly take it apart, this thing; that in consistent commonality it comes, to form the word resistance. What might it take up and in the many places, of that one meaning; that is placed to identify, for this word called "resistance".

The purpose, is to further explore the meaning, of resistance and come to recognize, the many varieties; that it can represent and on an emotional scale. As well, as on all the levels of consciousness; that the self is able, to feel and become changed by it.
Remember that energy is neither good, nor bad; rather in the how it is utilized, to its reinterpretion.

(Day 318)
10. WHAT IS RESISTANCE ?

Having been denied, the right to exist and somewhat ignited, by the "what if" thoughts. External circumstances, are from having been previously imprinted thoughts; that could have gathered and grown in momentum. Conflicting beliefs, can cancel out each other. Or the winner and the loser, competitively showing up, for a good fight; will to be, the cause for much friction/resistance (law of compensation within a karmic structure).

LESSON~278:
"I CAN EXPLORE MYSELF THROUGH THE MANY STORIES THAT CAN AS SUBJECTS REFLECT BACK TO ME AND FROM EXTERNAL CIRCUMSTANCES"

The self can shrink down and refuse; or it can expand by wishing to explore the challenges and as opportunities, to better understand, itself with. Does the self explore the tyranny; or defend to shut it out and should it become activated, must it fight against it?
Awe, the many programs, it has stored away, to form its standard with; upon the platform, which to play on and for these beliefs, that state: " Thou shalt not kill"; to what extent of
"Thou shalt not harm" ?
Who makes up these rules anyway?
Some resistance, can be found, within the many rules; that passed through its lineage and that of which has built the character, as ethical and moral.
Today, explore these teaming aspects and find them in from their grouping. Then come to question them and to what extent, have these beliefs, really proved to be beneficial; or the need to further modify, through lessons, from its own resistance?

LESSON~278:
"I CAN EXPLORE MYSELF THROUGH THE MANY STORIES THAT CAN AS SUBJECTS REFLECT BACK TO ME AND FROM EXTERNAL CIRCUMSTANCES"

Today, is this process, that will make for a good practice, to devote to and with the intention to perform, such an intake and seek to find them in, at their core level. For example: Could it be, the pesky fire alarm, that goes off, at all hours of the day and night; question and why, this level of fear, must be played out? What beliefs might be coming up to surface, to be challenged and give them opportunity, for the self to break them down ? Please do not dismiss and from any of these crisis, that could present themselves; to be gnawing on the nerves and overloading on the system. What struggle can be found or seen, in the moment, to take a step back and look at the beliefs, that might be held. Go into receptive mode, ask to see the imprints and view what is there; once very subtle, they might come into view. Focus in and on the intension to align with; at the source, of its blueprint and approach them all, with grace and ease.
Go on and take as many perspectives; release the ones that no longer serves, for these vows and promises, that the self believed in, from before.

The purpose, is to find the resistance; that triggers in, the cause of opposition and from within the self. The energies, that need to be released and transmuted; through reexamination, of old and warn out beliefs.
These limitations, can give off, the resonance of life, as being most difficult and complicated; remove the confusion and fill it in, with certainty, of what it is, preferred?

TSLM ACIMS
(Day 319)

10. WHAT IS RESISTANCE ?

When stale ideas, are not ready to be released, for the more refreshing; something happens, in that a formation and of such accumulation, can produce clutter. Does the self have to work through it all, or just throw it all out, like junk?

LESSON~279:
"MY UNIVERSE IS INFINITE WHEN I CAN OVERSEE THROUGH THE COLLECTIVE'S FINITE CLUTTER AND PROCESS SUCH STUFFED DOWN EMOTIONS
TO CLEAR IT ALL AWAY"

So much is coming up, to process and from this energy; the cooperation, to work alongside and in this contribution, toward the higher collective. The clutter, is a struggle with time, unto its own and from the space, these programs; it will take up, within and physically outwardly too.
Today, find some examples, to give to this idea and then see how, it can be applicable. Maybe the unpacking of many boxes, to clear the space; has never been easy and in particularly, during the moments, of self care and restoration. This reflection of its space, keeps on repeating and as a theme, to mean for something? Perhaps life does not have to be so hard. In the struggle, of past conflicts unresolved and that caused the self, to split off, into many fragments of itself. The factions and ruling class, perhaps resembling, over the many, but to name a few?
Once these old programs, can be let go of; the self can then clearly look outside, to its own reflection and in this way, to follow always. Nothing is to be over looked, for in the presence of reality, stay calm and centered; while all the chaos is going on and all around, simply become amused by it.

LESSON~279:
"MY UNIVERSE IS INFINITE WHEN I CAN OVERSEE THROUGH THE COLLECTIVE'S FINITE CLUTTER AND PROCESS SUCH STUFFED DOWN EMOTIONS TO CLEAR IT ALL AWAY"

Why is this control, so much an issue and from all the many levels of authority? Who is in actual fact the author, of the story and that the self must find, to hold connection with, of this, its power? These parts, that it must work on, to refresh, within itself and rewrite the script; of how it can bring together, will indeed reveal and for its very own authenticity. All this connecting and unifying moments, have its way with all. Feel the discomfort, when finding these pockets of resistance; do not stuff it back down; rather follow the "plasmic" thread and to where the agitation/irritation, is very high and where in actual fact it was created. This upset and anger, from suppressed emotions, have to be experienced and in order for them to be released.

Be the warrior of light, and from within the peace, stand up, and in this way to defend, and be counted on. These parts that the self resists and directly or indirectly, through its circumstances; are what make up, for the whole of its authenticity. By learning to connect, in this way, is to trust and go with, by completely surrendering to the resistance; this acceptance is the self, in the way of taking back its power, peacefully and most maturely.

Do not procrastinate, feel it out, be it rejection; fear; grief; make it today, the practice of releasing all control and to dissolve the issue, search from either side; by addressing it internally, the outside control too, that it resists and/or pushes against and/or vice/versa.

The purpose, is to recognize, that any emotion, that is stuffed back down; will have to again be reinvested in, feel for it properly and most thoroughly.

(Day 320)

10. WHAT IS RESISTANCE ?

No experience is ever bad or good; rather it is neutral.
Belief will set it up and the emotion, that stems from the thought, to generate the motion. The stage, is then projected on and the interactions with itself; it will attract to play and alongside, with its reflection. Thoughts, emotions and beliefs, make for the basis of a template; to form a most distinct and bespoke reality.
Authority becomes the self, over its personality; as author and when stepping out, onto its new path. The struggle, is in having to resist, its path and in favour of, the version of a template, that no longer, serves it.
LESSON~280:
"THE DIRECTION OF THE MOTION_THAT ALLOWES FOR MORE UNFOLDING AND MY EXPANDING TO EXPLORE FROM THIS CONNECTION_IS MY HIGHEST JOY"
Anything that needs releasing, is that signal from authority and from that very same opposition, to the self; that will cause for much grief and struggle. To continue with, a non existing pattern and by resisting to step into the new. The self will continue on, with parasites left over and to entertain it from; as ghosts from the past, would have and drain it, from its energy. There is nothing there, that for the self can possibly contribute to, much less be a part of ? The new patterning, requires some assembly and can be very simple; but feels almost similar, to awkward and as the one before it had. The self will continue to project, for its reflection; the reality it will experience for itself. To resist and fight against it, is to be in conflict with itself. To run away or hide from it; will only prolong its jail sentence and that of waiting around, in limbo. There is nothing to complete; finish or fix and yet the self, will find itself, wrapped up in such physical and manifested delusions.

LESSON~280:
"THE DIRECTION OF THE MOTION THAT ALLOWES FOR MORE UNFOLDING AND MY EXPANDING TO EXPLORE FROM THIS CONNECTION_IS MY HIGHEST JOY"

Maybe the self, must go through it all and before it can find, to feel for any solace. Sometimes the fazes, will bring it to a moment, of its existence. Where it is only spiritual work and with that off balance, in the physical, that it too, must work through; interpreting as fixing and/or completing, of its many contracts, vows and promises. It is through this process, the self must learn to integrate and then let go of the rest; as parasitic residue, that has remained, from previous relationships and other existences. From a linear perspective, this is what it means, to not look back and from the new; the older model would have obsoleted. The mother; father; sister; brother; partners; tribe and community must all be released. This is the only way, that the self can find, more of its authenticity and for the very reason; it comes up, to oppose, or bring such struggle. The metaphor of boxes, were used before and again as an example: Unpack the box and have a look at what might be causing the conflict.
What thoughts are coming up and/or feelings? What part did the self have, directly played in and what reflection; that it caused, to play alongside and indirectly with? How was it changed, in its perspective, to have learned from this relationship; did it move it from its course of action any(so not to repeat again) ? What parts of itself were projected onto the other and "Vice/Versa" ? What can the self take and from the resulting by-product, all of this ? Sometimes the emotions(like an empty box) will come up without any thoughts, to indicate the reason and that the self can to allow this resurrection to occur most blissfully.
The purpose, is to see that, where there is resistance, there is opportunity for self improvement.

(Day 321)

10. WHAT IS RESISTANCE ?

When the program, is to persist for something and to change, or direct a different outcome; all that will and within the same create, will be resistance. The issue or the problem, is the need to resolve and make better, and at what cost to figure out?

LESSON~281:
"WHEN I BACK OFF_TO RECONNECT WITH MY DESTINY AS THE OBSERVER_WHATEVER I ALLOW WILL REARRANGE ITSELF"

To learn the course and from, where miracles are already unfolding to exist, within awareness; is the observation and of the observer, while having the experience.
Today, make it as such, to find this observer and for especially, when the confusion might set in, from losing to resistance.
Comparing the divine expression of the self, to another's, can dull the luster of the self. To give up the connection with the self, over another and to empower with something that is not.
These inauthentic parts of the self, as conflict, have to find the relevance of love and within the tyranny rejected; is to learn from those, that do not know exactly how to love and in the same, for self to feel, for such experience. The object, is to clean, make whole and honest; of that which is not felt and for any comfort, within the self, to reside. When giving up the fight, the self can find itself again and the path for it, much clearer.

LESSON~281:
"WHEN I BACK OFF_TO RECONNECT WITH MY DESTINY AS THE OBSERVER_WHATEVER I ALLOW WILL REARRANGE ITSELF"

Allowance will prevail the doors wide open, for the light to network in the brain and where the mind resides to be. What pictures sit there, from the past, to overshadow and for any future possibilities, within the now, it might think it to overpower? These emotions, that resist the effort, of experiencing; are what hath created, as reality and made physical, to witness by the senses and that the self, is not alone in this. The conditions, continue to amuse and think it real, much longer. While on this course, awaiting for an irrelevant interpretation; from something outside of it, as "God to gift upon it Miracles". From these "Law/Rules" and regulations, the mind must overcome and that emotions must be checked in to and dumb down the self with; how can instead it grow wise and learn from such experience? The longer that enslavement is romanced, the freedom to love, becomes hatred and to control with, is such a disconnect, over its very own power; that it not lack, but rather fear.

The purpose, is to release, let go and not to resist the obvious; rather, see for the self, what it is not and awaken to the self enlightenment, one step closer, at a time and for its reveal, most certain.

10. WHAT IS RESISTANCE ?

The very thing that resists to allow, for the unusual to take place, will; given such consideration, through another's inspiration and that is trusted, in its relevance, to the well known and familiar to bring it in.

LESSON~282:
"WHEN DUALITY IS CANCELLED OUT
 THE GAP IS CLOSED AND ONLY ONENESS CAN REMAIN
TO RESONATE_THERE IN"

As the drive to want to separate, with comparison, is no more; the value can be realized and competition too, is canceled out by it. To thrive, is the unusual act, that comes from passion and from its inspiration; this drive will fill the field with joy by it, the mind. The energy that is consciousness, can restructure the mind and at a cellular level, through the brain. The personality of the self can be changed by looking through, its many attitudes; that formed through routine and made habit. What drives this behaviour and that as filters will deny; or allow for its experience and also of the greater whole, to authorize over? Conversely everything stems from what the self believes; or defines, there as, most true and thus, will be the experiences for it, in physical reality. Is it possible to change the physical reality, by changing its belief; that gives it meaning, for the experience to happen? YES!
Thoughts can also generate directly from beliefs; mostly through the resonance, of an emotional component and that may, or may not give rise, to this thing, called "resistance".

LESSON~282:
"WHEN DUALITY IS CANCELLED OUT THE GAP IS CLOSED AND ONLY ONENESS CAN REMAIN_TO RESONATE_THERE IN"

Today, practice on a conscious level, how to change the definition and by changing the belief, more on a conscious level. What causes time and space, is the same thing, that separates it and within its fragmentations; that create for opposition, the self can learn. Welcome the resistance, as a part of the self and see it for as wide the gap, it comes from; to bring with it the other side as opposite, reflecting back and as a mirror.
This is how the blocks can be removed and for each level of frequency band width; comes with it each colour, of light and sound. This was all relevant and as such mentioned in previous lessons; these layers that make up for the self, its multiverse.
On an unconscious level, the change of definitions happen; all the time and for in order to have a sense of the experience, to that, which is reality.
The experience of continuity and motion, as perceived through the change of time; can bring comfort, that it may gift with. The self might never be aware, of what directly, or indirectly blocks have formed. Only from the opposition; that resists, within this beautiful illusion. It might become more relevant to appear, when nothing is changing at all and the self would experience a feeling of being stuck. Only the opposition can help the self, from itself and as long as it resists to change.

The purpose, is to take resistance, as an indirect and/or direct guide and to help with, how and where, the self can change, its perspective.

Take 2 days to take it in

CONGRATULATIONS ...!!!

FOR MAKING IT THROUGH THE 282nd Lesson

(This is a rest period to take the lessons independently as a review)

TAKE THESE TWO DAYS TO RECALIBRATE;

MAKE NOTES AND REVIEW……………..

(Day 325)

10. WHAT IS RESISTANCE ?

Resistance could it be this meaning that holds within the mind, the need for a belief ?
Many perspectives by now, must have come up for re examination and for release. Perhaps in its entirety, the meaning of belief has lost the intensity of seriousness; that once before had rigidly formed, to imprison with such expectations.

LESSON~283:
"I CAN LEAVE THE LOOP OF THE EGOIC PROGRAM WHEN I CAN FACE AND WORK THROUGH MY RESISTANCE_ I GO INSIDE_GAIN CLARITY WITH MY DIVINE SOURCE ENERGY AND THEN TAKE ACTION"

The triggering of a reaction, will cause the self to polarize by it and until the self is satisfied enough, from this experience; the enticement will play out again for it.
Today, do not give up the space, nor ownership of the self; instead of taking a step back, stay calm and centered and by remaining grounded. The desire to suppress, or become suppressed, is the resistance and that must be let go of; In this level, the experience of stepping back, will cause disrespect and by the self allowing, the invasion, will spring back and then forward to fight back. The stepping back, will not be seen or taken as politeness; instead it will be taken for granted, to completely overtake its space and ownership and in this way of itself, from that which, it does not desire, to redevelop.

LESSON~283:
"I CAN LEAVE THE LOOP OF THE EGOIC PROGRAM WHEN I CAN FACE AND WORK THROUGH MY RESISTANCE_ I GO INSIDE_GAIN CLARITY WITH MY DIVINE SOURCE ENERGY AND THEN TAKE ACTION"

This kind of confrontation, can go to the extreme; that always ends with a winner, taking over and the loser, being taken over, by becoming none existent. Be present and aware with the activity at hand, just choose not to engage with it.
The chaotic energy, will have nothing to feed upon and have very little the effect, upon the nervous system.
Be present and aware with the activity at hand, just choose not to engage with it. The chaotic energy, will have nothing to feed upon and have very little the effect, upon the nervous system.
This state was discussed before and by allowing the parasympathetic, to come back on line; the flight or fight reaction, will be disengaged. Go ahead and practice, throughout the day, to check in, with the self and feel where the resistance, might be causing stress. The mind will not always be able to make any sense of it and without for any thoughts, to indicate the reason, emotions will come up: Anger, upset, judgments, about others and the self; those are the parts that cause resistance.
Feel out the day and its events, that might have been pushed down; these frequencies are still active within; because, otherwise the self, would just be observing it and see it as a valid choice.
Where is it, that the same frequencies, as the outer ones, play out, the same, as that of the self?

LESSON~283:

"I CAN LEAVE THE LOOP OF THE EGOIC PROGRAM WHEN I CAN FACE AND WORK THROUGH MY RESISTANCE_I GO INSIDE_GAIN CLARITY WITH MY DIVINE SOURCE ENERGY AND THEN TAKE ACTION"

Where is it, that it judges and that of it, in its own life, to belittle of the self or others?
These are the insecurities, that could be plaguing the self with fear. The calming effect, will give the self distinction and from the chaos, as it be, the eye, within that storm. The peace, will also be projected outward and from within the sacred heart, upward to connect the mind with. Be still and centered and the neuro pathways will clear right through, the nervous system and that the energy will not affect for anything. When the emotion comes up, feel it and it will not last for very long; as it makes its presence, on the way out.

Today, give that internal space, to create new collective thought processes and new emotional expressions; make it the opportunity, to forge new pathways and archetypical patterns, for the self

The purpose of resistance, is to learn to shift out and of that similar vibrational level, that causes it; by focusing on creating something else, with that energy(resilience).

(Day 326)

10. WHAT IS RESISTANCE ?

Taking responsibility over the inspiration, to create for something and from this passion, it can be a blessing.
Resistance is just another cause for the illusion, of separation and by it, to keep it distinctly identifiable, in this way.
To resonate, in the highest state, that miracles exist in, is an easy flowing response and when able to observe, the self can claim by, with its intent.

LESSON~284:
"WHEN I CAN TRUST IN MYSELF_FROM THE AWARENESS OF SURRENDER WITH MY INTENTIONS
 ALL RESISTANCE WILL DISOLVE
TO BRING FORTH_COMPLETE MANIFESTATION"

A "Sovereign being" does not give meaning to the illusion of opposites and by its opposite to define; it will know it is an illusion. To sense such disconnect, that illusion brings, is to notice it within nature and as being not in balance to; but this can never be the case with something as complete. On the contrary, the paradox, is what can help, to dissolve boundaries and of such illusions; by bringing them up, to clear from the field; and/or by closing the gap, is how it clears, to make whole and complete again. The self must realize, that it cannot push down, its darkness, to rise above, into the light. This experience of stuffing down and pushing away, will reflect as the polarity; from which to learn from and that has been denied before. Do not indulge in the overwhelmed concept, that can lead to procrastination; depression and/or the worry, over the pressure, of this thing, called "<u>time</u>".

LESSON~284:
"WHEN I CAN TRUST IN MYSELF_FROM THE
AWARENESS OF SURRENDER WITH MY INTENTIONS
ALL RESISTANCE WILL DISOLVE
TO BRING FORTH_COMPLETE MANIFESTATION"

Anticipate in only that which excites; because this moment that desires from the self, to be propelled, is only but an emotion to mark down. To set an awareness, on the intent and form imagination, of these thoughts and before they have any feeling, attached to them; might or might not, at all, have any influence. However it can form a state of awareness, in the things it does attract, to form resistance to and could even possibly, reflect mean behaviours toward it. Hatred from the jealousy; or any other, from its external combative nature, to reject and repel against it; is a sure sign of resistance. When there is very little to connect to, the authoritative cycles to control, will come out and oppress, with this disfigured illusion, of having no choice; but to accept this, will be surely dysfunctional. To be kept in, with a regulatory body, that is systematically in place; to replace the self experience and limit self expression? To play along in this deception, the self must have to prove its worth; so it can then share, of its relevance, through small increments, at a time and within accordance, to the rules and class, for its behaviour; for approval and denoted denominationally.
These building blocks form resistance.

The purpose for resistance, is to bring about the insertion, through intrusion. To show the void of those parts and that of the self; that has gone unnoticed and neglected, from its abandonment.
It is brave, to have the courage, to release all previous patterning (emotions; belief systems, culture) and change the reality.

(Day 327)

11. WHAT AM I and WHAT IS ADDICTION ?

When the self becomes disconnected from its emotions; the complacency of its experience with its very own existence, will inevitably create addiction. What a lonely place the disconnect, from the self can bring and to feel for this illusion; that it relies upon, to fix it from the outside, so it may once again, feel better.

LESSON~285:
"I AM THE CHANGE_THAT REACHES OUT
 AND TOUCHES ME BACK"

Knowing when to stop and say "enough" !
This is the discipline, that finds the self to learn from, its over indulgence. In this distraction and that it finds to feel good with. These are the places, where the self does not feel, that it is enough and within itself for its fulfillment. The belief that it is never going to amount for anything; will force it to subject itself, into uncomfortable and possibly hurtful experiences, that it does not like.
The pain or uncomfortable place, from where and what it is not; will cause it to dislike itself. Preferring to escape and from its situation, that it must undergo. When relying on the indulgence, as a crutch it can to become and motivate the self, to keep on going.
This is the illusion, of having no other choice; but to learn, to love something it cannot; will opt it, to exit and run away, seeking to escape, from the experience.

LESSON~285:
"I AM THE CHANGE THAT REACHES OUT AND TOUCHES ME BACK"

The past is made up of beliefs, to prove to the distortions and that of practical skills, obtained as good enough; to bring the value for the self, and that it may experience, the pleasure of its existence. Today practice to find the rewarding factors and that every undesirable experience, can bring. It may be a job, and/or working for the money, that it brings; rather than the pleasure. How far can the self tolerate, to be and do against its will? How far can it bend and before it breaks, right off? What are some of the thresh holds, before it feels, it is being walked right over. Would it rather be harmed and in harms way; than to harm others and/or just get out of the way altogether? Perhaps the triggering of rape or an unwanted pregnancy and/or even as far back and into the protective hands, of a molester ? When it does not see for anything rewarding, from the experience. To rely on memories, of past experiences and to keep repeating, that it may survive, from such awareness. This addiction to an identity, the self is holding on to; is this illusion and that it must, to earn a living with. Trying to be something that, it is not, is and will never be; to makes the dream of team work. The truth of independence is covered over then, by co-dependencies; a betterment of most relations and that the many of the world, can to empathize competently, with each other. There will be a lot to play with, here and bring up all of its relationships, still left for review. Why are these relationships, co-dependently established ?
Go deeper and find within those places, the not "<u>enoughness</u>", within the self.

LESSON~285:

"I AM THE CHANGE THAT REACHES OUT AND TOUCHES ME BACK"

From the microcosm, the self began and came out of, its feminine source; that it may relive, as separate and reflect the opposite, to it and not as in the image, of creator.
The rejection to, from its very own awareness created and as creator from the shock it felt; the self could now imagine, that any other, than that love, it once had felt and so unawarely prior to.
That need to feel fulfillment, through the pleasing of another and to expect, such in return; created the magnetism and with it, the push and pull, of addiction. The hive mind, is a co dependent construct and the only way to see it proper; is from within the microcosm of the self. When the body, mind and spirit, are well, to cooperatively coordinate and function; any blemish will augment and distort, rising up for review and self examination, through the way of feelings. The power, is in this connection, to express and in its complete capacity; so that it may thrive, as wholesome and complete. Any struggle from the macro, or the microspective, to deny, will bring about, the neediness and blind spots, of such unawareness; that it will cause to feel, for the experience and the need, for such emotion.

The purpose, is to acknowledge the image of the self, as the creator. Responsible not to become accustomed and with any given experience; rather to be mindful and not to overindulgently exhaust its power, for how it feels.

(Day 328)

11. WHAT AM I and WHAT IS ADDICTION ?

Could it be within the popular consensus for religion, was based on the scientific observation; from the sun's energy, as the ultimate source of all life and that from it, split off this energy, into many forms?
Spirituality is for the self, to learn and become empowered by, these lessons; to awaken, to the acknowledgment and that it too, is as this shining portal.

LESSON~286:

"I CAN RESPECT THOSE_WITH WHOM_FROM THEIR LIGHT_HAVE AWAKENED AS SOVEREIGN AND FROM WITHIN AUTHENTICALLY_ I AM WITH ALL THINGS AS ONE"

With every experience, came forth the many lessons and in the silence, from hence it came from(that zero point within); within this darkness, that reflection brings. From within these many portals, the self will shine outwardly and from its darkest night, of its soul experiences combined; this void of stillness it will find back to the light. The image of the self can only represent; but a moment of linear memory, called "_time_". The awareness in observation and of itself however, that is consciousness; can only be described as, a sliver of this life force, called "God" and that, like all things, does transcend, from its creation. Artificial intelligence, can be very helpful and in the desired image, to create; as well, the perfect travelling companion.

LESSON~286:
"I CAN RESPECT THOSE_WITH WHOM_FROM THEIR LIGHT_HAVE AWAKENED AS SOVEREIGN AND FROM WITHIN AUTHENTICALLY I AM_WITH ALL THINGS AS ONE"

The self, can either learn and/or teach and like all things; it must discern from the many formations and that relationships create, into emotional attachments. To love and be loved; yet not everything is physical, to prove for anything and this will transcend it, beyond addiction. Everything within the physical, relies upon the main intent and focus; that the self will bring, in its awareness, of it. Relying on its creations and in the same way, as to worship idols with; is like the sun, relying on the self, for its existence.
Addicted to technology, with no discernment and to emotionally attach; however giving up the mind, of the self completely.
All of the extra sensory perceptions, that the self can appreciate, and yet, it rather stay asleep; relying on, its artificial intelligence and in the hopes, of gaining "Godhood" ?
How can this artificial way, of life, replace the mirrors and that once could show hate; instead of love and rejection, instead of acceptance?
Could this be a better weaponry, than chemical warfare and/or the once before, that killed with guns and bombs; to be as easier, than that, of the easy button?
Today, practice to become, with all things transparent and expose, like sunlight, everything; rather than in the dark, to enclose these gods in likeness. In temples(enshrined)and turning on and off, at whim? There is always so many choices and from every decision, the self, will lead the way, with, to follow.
The purpose, is to realize, what "<u>I am</u>" and that, which "<u>I can never be</u>"; (helpless) through my addiction to it.

(Day 329)
11. WHAT AM I and WHAT IS ADDICTION ?

When energy, vibration and frequency, are not thriving and in the fullest capacity, from self potential; addiction towers over, its every experience and gives it relevance, with its attachment.

LESSON~287:
"I FEEL COMPLETE WITHIN THE HOLY TRINITY OF MY FIELD_I STAND CONNECTED AS ONE MOVING WITH CERTAINTY AND PURPOSE"

In previous (10-21) lessons, all gadgetry and devices, from escaping reality; were touched upon. The preference, of living in another world, outside of the one and that the self is experiencing.
The movies and types of genres; to theme out its existence and by escaping the one, it must actually be engaging with. Habit forming practices, can become realities; however the self must recognize, just where, it actually becomes a co-dependency.
Today, make it the practice, of awareness and to anything that might be standing in the way, for further examination: for example, what might be some of the emotional attachments; that might be given relevance, to weaken and instead of strengthen, for the self? Food can come in many forms, to matter over the energy and from these nutrients, is the only focus; rather than to the pleasures, that gives and from its emotional comfort with. See it for what it is; not just for what it disguises over, and as to making the self feel like. Discern for what intention, requires attention and give it; For example: could it be a metabolic detox? Food/nutrition, has an energy to give to and within the molecules, that then creates a feeling; this feeling creates an emotion, that the self can then, actually have.

LESSON~287:
"I FEEL COMPLETE WITHIN THE HOLY TRINITY OF MY FIELD_I STAND CONNECTED AS ONE MOVING WITH CERTAINTY AND PURPOSE"

What is this feeling of emotion; that might be experienced and as having another connection to, than that of its own system?
What is this other connection; that then forms another mind, of its own ? In this case, it is food and yet, in another, it might be smoking; taking pills, or drinking and they can all be toxic.
How about smoking, what is the disconnect in this ?
The connection perhaps to become synchronized with;
better yet, the understanding, that the lack, was in the breath and the mindfulness, it did take to focus, on the need, to meditate.
What could it be, that the self, is screaming out for and in the suppression, for its voice perhaps?
Today, be mindful and progressive, of the underlying intention, and to help synchronize, with the consciousness; those levels that need focusing on, to help bring, the body with it.
From fluid, solid and/or breath; the signals will be given, from this information. Whether it be energy, from protons, created as carriers, through ingesting and/or other toxins, that will store away; and that of which, the self might have thought, it once had cleared away, to now revisit.
Today, become mindful, of what goes into, each and every vortices, that interlace the torso with and thus connects, into its field;
that which is, impressed upon the circumstances; as well, as perceived physical matter.
The purpose, is to bring into harmony, that which was being left out; or rejected, from the self and its external circumstances, to falling short, into codependence.

(Day 330)
11. WHAT AM I and WHAT IS ADDICTION ?

The miracle, is all about connection; with that part of the self,
that has been neglected and deprived from its awareness.
Appreciate and release it, from the harm, of sickness.
Free the space, from pain and all discomfort; to surround instead,
by expanding it, with gratitude.

LESSON~288:
"THE BAND AID IS RIPPED AWAY
WHEN I CAN FOCUS ON WHAT IT IS I WANT
INSTEAD ON THE CONDITIONS"

Seek God and from within the self, to empower with; whatever the image was and glorified, over another, beyond the self's addictive detriment, that forever brings, the lack to struggle, from the disconnect. The disconnect always overshadowed, with the need to posses and control. This will reflect, to the self and for re-examination, of its external circumstances; with (that it must explore today, in any way and every way, that it presents itself). Sometimes the helpful tools, of forming boundaries, can become healthy impositions and to bring relationships, from disconnect; just that much closer, than before.

LESSON~288:
"THE BAND AID IS RIPPED AWAY
 WHEN I CAN FOCUS ON WHAT IT IS I WANT
 INSTEAD ON THE CONDITIONS"

The self, is a measure of its universe and from it, all is the self.
The only way it found to rise into the praise and that it secretly feels it lacks; is by lifting out itself and from the perspectives, of its lower "Ego mind".
In response, to culture and tribe, the self, cannot be saved; but only shaped, by it and that, of its discipline, for these external conditions. It is, an addiction to rely upon, an external image; falsely represented, through religion. By giving it authority, it will oppress the spirit upon and with the ignorance, that the self is lacking.
By not fitting in, the awakening to the self, is that much quicker; and/or, can be, that much more painful and to continue on, synthetically dependent. From its very own experience and the unfixable perspective, was this knowledge; that reflected backward, as contrast and to distort, its image further.

The deep sleep was, that, of the unconscious mind; not being aware and/or, semi-aware, with the subconscious mind.
As teacher/perpetrator and student/victim; these relationships, were designed, to help the self connect, with its conditions, to the outer world. From its emotional injury, to seek outward, for the motivation and from this thing called love; the self became, the victim and its perpetrator, as the crutch, for its addiction.

The purpose, is never for the intention, to rely upon, external conditions, of the outer world, to feel good.

THE INTERMISSION :

Take a day to take it in

CONGRATULATIONS ...!!!

FOR MAKING IT

THROUGH TO THE 288th Lesson

(This is a rest period to take the lessons independently as a review)

TAKE THIS DAY TO RECALIBRATE;

MAKE NOTES AND REVIEW……………...

(Day 332)
11. **WHAT AM I and WHAT IS ADDICTION** ?

Matter, electricity and magnetism, it is "I" and with great radiance;
the self will play, alongside with, its elementals.
The air, within the water and fire, within the earth;
all things, resemble and from the different variations, it can learn.

LESSON~289:
"THE JOY I FEEL FROM RECOGNIZING WHO I AM IGNITES THE RADIANCE FROM WITHIN TO ALSO FEEL THE EMPATHY FROM MY SURROUNDINGS"

The self is not separate from all these things and yet the differences they will divide and conquer it, when it does not properly grasp the level of discernment. Matter it comes in many forms and electricity too, its very own duality, to its content, the splitting off; or can it just be very well the magnetism, to attract with, rather than insert its way with all opinions? Given refinement from reflections was this purpose and not for the matter to compare with.
Empathic impressions, that "objects" from matter do bring, and to the self with such awareness; are not in actual awareness of themselves. With this kind of empathy, the earth comes to life and in essence, the adventure; with those sentient parts of herself, that she extends and for the self, to play with. When half awake, to this existence, the habit forming self, will misinterpret and for the very same, to why it then, might pull away, from her(nature).
Expecting more, of this experience, it did extort and exploit; as if it did not matter and to once again recreate, in the image, of distorted things, such as, death.

LESSON~289:
"THE JOY I FEEL FROM RECOGNIZING WHO I AM IGNITES THE RADIANCE FROM WITHIN TO ALSO FEEL THE EMPATHY FROM MY SURROUNDINGS"

Through death and the promise for relief, named resurrection; made through, as passageway and of its very own flesh, is that, of hers. The "Ego mind" had taught it well, by extracting and synthetically manipulating, an artificial feeling; it fed it from the outside, as its drug. The lack provided well, the power to abuse and be abused, by it; like trash, made to recycle and find its final way, through the field of ethers, into transcendence.
As "saviour/sabotager"; it became the conflict, of its interest and from it, the perspective, that gives meaning to war.
The habit forming and identifying "Ego" driven self; grew as an extension, from it and that the self was hosting, as its very own addiction. This was a different kind of entertainment; far detached from nature, to connect, in any way, as telepathically and instead, had fallen, from such consciousness.

Today, make it the intention, to practice expanding outward; explore the world and from it, the coming together, in union, with that of atonement and a higher perceived perspective. Take a few moments, throughout the day, to anchor and from within the heart; feel this place of mindfulness. Visualize connecting, to that nature, from within and allow, for all these parts, of self emergence.

The purpose, is to wake up, to all of the many fragments, of the self; that had previously transitioned, from the physical and that were recycled, from before(to open up and be revealed).

TSLM ACIMS
(Day 333)
11. WHAT AM I and WHAT IS ADDICTION ?
From a biological, to artificial; everything has consciousness.
It is true, that the self, is in a very malleable field and can apply, different rules, to the game, at any given moment and by choice.

LESSON~290:
"I CAN ONLY HAVE COMPASSION
WHEN I KNOW MYSELF"

Artificially reconstructed, as intelligence, the more organized the system of the form; the more, the creative spark, the self has placed intention. As such, whilst to reflect upon the holding down the type of resonance and essence, as this consciousness.
Today, notice the experience of crying?
Notice how the spirit descends and into the physical containment; that is this physical body?
In the same way, that spirit leaves its body; the built up pressure, from the soul, is what the self can feel and whenever it is touched, by spirit, as compassion. From the misty grayish-blue, translucent plasma, of the soul; the spirit, will take away that plasmic, watery/saltry substance and with this impression before it(as discussed before).
This is how it can be touched and from the impact, to release some of the density and by the shedding of tears.
The translucent plasma, is this canvas and that illusion will impresses upon it; to thicken the membrane, of separation and disconnect. The place, where the space, is organized and into linear prosperity; that marks, within fixed boundaries and for each recorded moment, of its progression, toward its Spiritual and energetic abundance. "<u>Blessed is the self that can express the level of its Spirit into density, with tears and cry at will …from feeling this connection.</u>"

LESSON~290:
"I CAN ONLY HAVE COMPASSION
WHEN I KNOW MYSELF"

Linear perspective, is not real and can be manipulated, with projection. Into that, of parallel reality shifting, for the self and to be anywhere, it can possibly conceive, to conceptualize; just as long, as the state, of its being, is in resonance, to it.
The self was brought into creation and simply, to remember the precursor, to all the levels, of its manifested reality; that potentially rests and underneath the physical.
The metaphysical, is this radiance, that holds the mind, as energy and in harmony, to correspond with this, its field, known as, its universe. This metaphysical reality, of the self, is truly not reliant, on the physical body, to exist, as consciousness; however it is helpful, to become Spiritually aware and within the body that it holds, to vessel it around. In the adjusting, to the relevance, within the physical body; the self will slip into the darkness, of the Soul and where it will first, come to witness emptiness.
The void and like any other shock, to fill its system with; by grasping, from the outside and at a cellular level, the self can perhaps, find the trade off, from its addiction?
Find the life force, from within and feel it merging, with the Soul, of Spirit. Wisdom comes, from a place, of compassion.

LESSON~290:
"I CAN ONLY HAVE COMPASSION
WHEN I KNOW MYSELF"

The intensity, of consciousness and that has evolved into, as the self; to come together, with organized systems. The self, is biologically structured, in this way; that it may come to be aware, of itself and the greatest, of achievements, that it could ever hold.
The unaware self, shares its experience and in seeking out, from its surroundings, the awareness of itself.
This searching, can overwhelm the circuitry, of its surroundings and the uncomfortable shock, of having to fit in, as an unworthy dependent. Today, rather the feeling, of its place, to hold and as in the highest status, ever known to creation; unfamiliar, by any other and in this way, that yet, is to be discovered.
Practice the savouring, of every high and low, the self will feel when overwhelmed. Take all the situations, that will throw the self, off its center; learn from where the self, is guided, to integrate and with, into alignment.

The purpose, is to adjust, to the darkness and in the way, the light is found; embrace source, with love and feel the void, of separation, from the self.

(Day 334)

11. WHAT AM I and WHAT IS ADDICTION ?

Is compassion lost, when the self transcends, beyond the need, of forgiveness? This can happen, when mastering transmutation and moving beyond, the concept, of addiction.
The metaphysical platform, from which to play, is revealed, to the awakened and Sovereign Light Self; whilst choosing to remain, as a physical body, in this containment.

LESSON~291:
"BY FLOWING THROUGH AND ALLOWING THE FLOW
TO GUIDE THROUGH ME SIMULTANEOUSLY
I CAN BE RECEPTIVE AND PRO-ACTIVE"

Embrace the spirit, in a way and that the self, can work, from such a level and the platform; a nonlinear bridge through space. Today, practice such embodiment, with self awareness and through the heart; connecting to every cell, within this physical containment. For every field, that the self can sense and that radiates outwardly, from its pours; to occupy the many systems, from within, that coordinate, to circulate harmoniously and all it has to do, is breathe. In that centered state of awareness, the movement, of the body and through its space, is a beautiful orchestrated discipline; that there are, many to choose from. "Yoga" can be anything, from breathing and keeping the body still; to stretching and/or, in the awareness (mindfulness), of moving the life force around and by gliding parts, of its body through the air. Go ahead and freely practice, the most habit forming memory and that can be as a familiar remedy; today for the experience.

LESSON~291:
"BY FLOWING THROUGH AND ALLOWING THE FLOW TO GUIDE THROUGH ME SIMULTANEOUSLY I CAN BE RECEPTIVE AND PRO-ACTIVE"

The transformative epiphany, can change the self, to learn about transmuting, its energy, through motion; however it can also become, a replacement, like with, any habit forming rituals, it too can be an addiction. To cover over, the awareness, of the self, by overwhelming it, with bliss, is the same as, any other drug, to feed the longing, for the self. After this, the self can come to understand, the importance, of every moment and that it is, just as important and significant. Eventually, the self will come, to realize just how valuable the moments, that it spends, out in the world and with other beings, to restrict it; because of the belief, in a false judgment, currency. That which can to define, the amount of play, to be experienced; within those rules, of limitation, where miracles are scarce and far between. When the world, can be addicted, to such power and that promotes more disconnect; the resistance, from disbelieving and that of another way, to thrive, for all, cannot be trusted. The self cannot play, in that reality, for very long; when that, is not the way, it can generate, for its abundance. "To struggle and strife, over garbage bags; is not worth the gas, from its compost and that it could to make instead, the rubbish with." In the disguised devise, to only keep supporting, the lack and limitation; that its world, has co dependently, become addicted to, for its awareness. It was never about saving the Earth; it was about saving the self and not from the self; but rather, by its awakening to.

The purpose, is to come to terms, with the longing, that does not last forever; to clearly embrace for all the parts, of disconnected self.

(Day 335)
11. WHAT AM I and WHAT IS ADDICTION ?

The flight or fight response, was that of "Ego", based perception and its perspective, carried on, as an addiction. Could it very well be, that the self, can only meet up and with itself inversely; to create conflict, thus arising, in the need, for escapism?

LESSON~292:
"I CAN ACCEPT ALL THAT LOVE HAS TO OFFER
FOR MYSELF_THROUGH SELF CARE"

Imagine, for a moment, that all matter and every single object; that was previously pulled, by the world, that it came from and not the other. The subject, could then be offset, from the opposite world, called "<u>inverse reality</u>". Just like the self, cannot fight gravity, this attraction of two different worlds, is plausible around it and with each, having their own gravitational pull (magnetism known as attraction). When imagining the experience, from this artificial craft(airplane); it felt like, it was falling down, when it was(taking off) and actually rising up; when it felt like it was ascending, it was falling down(coming in for a landing). This in truth, was that of the higher and lower self; those two half's and that yearned to find themselves. Yet the "Ego mind", had always kept them, separated.

The disconnect, from its wholeness, in this way, of consciousness; had created much, for its despair. Longing to reach out, to find and from the outside of the self; the illusion had begun. This illusion, was always about enslavement and the worship, through much sacrifice; it brought over, with its many religions, passed down through history and all "Ego mind" driven. The love, for power, was not love at all; rather, an "Ego mind" driven lusting beast (to admire as beautiful, whilst everything around it, had become so ugly), that had destroyed and reconstructed, over everything in its path, compared to and likewise, judged.

LESSON~292:
"I CAN ACCEPT ALL THAT LOVE HAS TO OFFER FOR MYSELF THROUGH SELF CARE"

The worship, to enslave and restrain, all that was wholesome; to its cause and this continued on, as the effect. The only relief, that could be found(its imposed reality from the outside); was in the relevance for a temporary artificial high and finally intended, as a means to escaping from the self. From the lush, beautiful green valleys; where once, it knew of and where the energy, was high and loving. When the peaceful high, was over and along with it, the many, who were still remaining, to be nice; had changed to worry and fear. These rules, of gravity and magnetism, diffuse(spread out) and all that is there, is the sovereignty, of the regenerated and elevated self. There is nothing left, to fight, or run away from. Within the natural order of oneness and to diffuse, dissolving all others; that had once, held the self, bound up and co dependent, to its disconnection. Remember the life, of peace and understanding, that had once radiated and from the heart out; into this place, of oneness, as community and heaven on earth?
This rhythm, of peace and love, can once again, be restored; in the exchange and as the "echo", of its currency. The practice, of self care, can be most challenging and just maybe today, the practice can be: all about such experience; in anyway and as best it can be, to accomplish. Find the Force, from within and be Sovereign, with this Light awakened.

The purpose, is to find, the love and that enriches into atonement. To once again be able to discover, the lush beautiful green valleys; where once it knew of and where the energy, was high and loving.

(Day 336)

12. WHAT IS HEALING and RESILIENCE ?

Energy in motion and from this, created energy; the trusting in the flow, that will excite it or trap it into, pain and fear?
STRUGGLE Vs. EFFORT ?
Could it be, that all of the beliefs and that are lined up; perfectly aligned to falter and just because of one, that has not yet, been cleared ? The rational mind and distrusting, with beliefs, it holds ("to make ends meet"); from previous experiences, to be true and in this static space; just sits there to create, the awkwardness, of hesitations and excuses, for itself.

LESSON~293:
"WHEN MY HEART IS OPEN I CAN FEEL THE HARMONY ASCEND AND TRANSCEND ME"

When the heart, brain and central nervous system, are not in electrical harmony coherence, then a break occurs.
To lose this connection, then would be, to fall into a lower state, of consciousness. The self can become, made readily available, to the emotional trappings of illusion and that the "Ego mind" had created(convincing the need to feel protected). The illusions, knock it out, of the heart and center, of well being; into that of discomfort and even by its very own, agreed upon created boundaries, to feel held down(oppressed). Incoherent, to its atonement and thus creates frustration, of struggle and effort. When the heart, is closed off, stress is inevitable; by the bombardment, of its nervous system and disease too, can be here, highly prevalent.

LESSON~293:

"WHEN MY HEART IS OPEN_I CAN FEEL THE HARMONY ASCEND AND TRANSCEND ME."

Mostly all the ailments, of the world and amongst the many, come from old patterns; that subject an imprint, of behaviour and thus a lifestyle. Could it be this way of life, or not?

Where does struggle come from; but from a linear concept, to fit in, to its perspective. Perhaps, by changing the perspective, it can genetically alter the self? Certain information patterns, within DNA can dictate the behaviour, of not only lesser evolved entities; but also higher and much more evolved, in their blood lines/lineage. This is not about control, rather the connection and into a more evolved being; for discerning the level, of playing field and that the self may, or may not feel, to engage with.

Effort causes much stress, in that, it too, is an illusion, that tears away at the self; wearing out and with the equal amount of determination, as the self puts out, equally and butts heads, with its opposition. Alternatively the self can become aware, that it has choices and does not have to play, with such illusions.

When the moment, of engagement, is not in the here and now; anxiety and regret can bring about the gaps, of uncertainty and doubt. Survival, is a linear concept and that the self, can only see, not in the full circle, of it; it will instead continue and with the greatest unrestful decision, driven by the "Ego", to take flight and/or fight, for a resolve. The self might feel, that of great unease, to make these ends meet and struggle much, in the barely making it, out alive. Effort, is to go that extra mile and again relying, on the push and pull, to find resilience, from resistance.

The purpose for today, is to find resilience, from a place of ease and surrender to the flow. Feel the bounce, of the upliftment and where the painful struggle, to resist the stretch, into expansion; lightheartedly let go, of the cause, for its restriction.

(Day 337)
12. WHAT IS HEALING and RESILIENCE ?
The heart's field, is directly involved, with intuitive perception and with it, to another energetic information field; outside the bounds of space and time. Go deep within the pain; restore that place behind, that what it is and that the self resists, to know; from this experience, the feeling, of entrapment and unyielding change. Feel the energy, of its resistance, to be loved. Restore its circulation, with happiness; that it may revitalize, back into atonement, with the Sovereign Light.

LESSON~294:
"WHEN MY HEART IS OPEN_I FEEL THE ELEVATION
OF MY LIFE FORCE_SYNCHRONISTICLY CONNECTED
AND DANCING WITH THE UNIVERSE
OF MY AWARENESS"

Today, practice playing in this place, of being aware, of being aware and become once more, the observer.
What is floating around, in the staleness of thoughts and how does it feel, to enter in that space? Take the moment, throughout the day and when the vibration finds the self, in doubt and/or to such a degree of uneasiness; that it no longer feels well and not understanding, where these feelings came from? By releasing trapped energies, from the body's field and from within, is how the healing can take place and then the resilience, from these transmutations. How does feeling so uncertain, about the trusting of the self; over the past perceived reflections, come to take responsibility and in owning, that part of itself?
These systems, of beliefs, are they even belonging to it and just may very well be, that they are unfixable, states of static parts, of its consciousness; floating, in the ethers and haunting it, like ghosts, from the past.

LESSON~294:
"WHEN MY HEART IS OPEN I FEEL THE ELEVATION OF MY LIFE FORCE SYNCHRONISTICLY CONNECTED AND DANCING WITH THE UNIVERSE OF MY AWARENESS"

Today, invite the mind, to join it with its heart and nervous system. The power, that is love, it too can hold memory and in resonance, with it can, ignite the self, into enlightenment and atonement. Decode reality, from within, feel the power of the heart and connect beyond the world of illusion. Practice mindfully, to elevate the frequency and sit and ask those questions, of "*where does this doubt come from*?" Recognize it, within those parts, of its soul collective and that were held in place, by its agreements, to be there and as a reminder; need it not be, of any concern. Instead, continue as before, to work on further cleaning, these receptors, of the self. Clean and clear, all that hangs around, as static in its fields.
The fields can be described, as spiritual; emotional; mental; physical …….. With the practice of such mindfulness, the charge will lesson; the self will no longer feed them, or pay attention to, in such a way, as to react and the magnetism(attraction) loosens up and leaves. The primary, is not that of pleasing others, above the self. Stop investing in these emotions; stop entertaining those thoughts and the energy, that drives them real, will go away.

The purpose, is in the allowing, for the energetic flow connection and directly open up, to this force, of its awareness; into wholesomeness(sattva) and to function, from rejuvenating potential, of resilience once again.

(Day 338)

13. WHAT IS ALIGNMENT ?

When the balance is restored, the connection lights up and all the facets of integrated self; with all its many leveled bodies combined and that merge as one. Imagine for a moment, this experience: of all outcomes and in complete synchronicity, with the self, to benefit, for its wellbeing.

LESSON~295:
"I OPEN UP TO CONNECT
WITH THIS POWER IN ME
THAT CREATES"

This power, is the feeling of atonement; through love and in this state of joy, spiritual alignment. This energy flows back and forth, calms the nervous system and brings feelings of peacefulness, mental clarity and improved communication to achieve balance and centering. Allow the feeling of balance and that comes from, attuning to the center, of the self. Feel centered and grounded from within; feel the heart's resonance and with that of earth; feel stillness, from within. Anchor now, sinking deep into the earth's core, an energetic cord and with it, the slowing down occurs. Reflect, on what is important, at this moment; rather than be overlooked, by the many distractions, of the day.

LESSON~295: "I OPEN UP TO CONNECT WITH THIS POWER IN ME THAT CREATES"

Relax, by yielding to all the energy, of thoughts and ides; that were set in motion and circulating through the self. Asses all accumulated, tense feelings and recalibrate; from the next event, or doing, the next project (a mental silencing occurs). A sacred space, is opened and that can allow, for the expansion, to take place; just by tapping into this, Divine presence. The beautiful, incorruptible light and from within; feel it and in this state, of well being, a sense of innocence and wonder. Be touched by it, immensely and by the ripples it created. Every struggle, that is witnessed, in this life, is a direct representation, of disconnection and from it, distortions, to allude. Lay down, all the burdens and that come, from impressed upon, by judgments; allow for peace to find its way.

The purpose, is to get a better glimpse, at this atonement and learn to thrive; rather than the struggle, to fit in and with the order, to survive, from separation.

(Day 339)
14 WHAT IS GRATITUDE & APPRECIATION ?

Gratitude, is an expansion, of frequency, from love and that holds more room, for appreciation, to vibrate the self, upward; gratitude expands it outward, holding it(this upward spiral) and as a platform, from which to receive, more with. Gratitude can help, by keeping the self open, to receive; once it does, it will appreciate and in gladness of receiving. To see the value and to value; when something can be valued and with love, to care enough, to maintain it appreciates. To give thanks and recognition of having; or for a certain quality, to posses, is the self then not "Grateful"?
LESSON~296:
"I TRULY APPRECIATE_THE ABILITY
TO BE GRATEFUL_IN ALL THAT I HAVE"

Hold expanded awareness, to explore it, with appreciation. Today, for everything, that is experienced, practice this momentum. Hold the space, with gratitude and then appreciate, all that will come in. The self can be polite, to respect in the way, of expressing appreciation; thus grateful, for having the opportunity, to see it and with such a perspective. When admiration, can be given, to posses with, such quality; the self can sentimentally attach itself and with this invested, interest it will appreciate. The self can be grateful and not appreciate; or appreciate and not be grateful; because they are different slightly, in frequency, the meaning and the feeling it produces, from interpretation. How the words, can be made applicable; has much to do with their meaning and as much, or very little to understand. To appreciate a service and be grateful, for the product, might be one example.
The purpose, is to feel the variation, in appreciating and being grateful.

(Day 340)
14 WHAT IS GRATITUDE & APPRECIATION ?

Funny is the paradox and from the gratitude, it birthed appreciation. With appreciation, transfiguration can occur, to transform into something better; than it was before. Within and amongst the static, that is known as physical reality; gratitude can formulate again, to hold the space and transmute energy, into appreciation.

LESSON~297:
"I FEEL THE MAGNITUDE OF GRATITUDE AND THE EXCITEMENT OF APPRECIATION UNITING INTERCHANGEBLY FROM MASCULINE AND FEMININE COMPONENTS OF THE SAME EQUATION"

To be receiving and to give, is exactly what the holding open; for an attitude, of gratitude and giving of appreciation, to the outcome, of projection. It was mentioned in previous lessons, long ago; about the giving, being the same, as the receiving and thus, the appreciation can be, also perceived, as receiving. Gratitude, can hold for expansion, of the frequency and that appreciation can take the credible vibration for. The question is, can they both transcend, from the static reality and into a figure eight ? Yes ! Both can and out of the attraction, well into creation; they are able to complete each other; to separate and then again, to realign. In harmony, with all the other colourful vibrations, unfolding and collapsing simultaneously.

LESSON~297:
"I FEEL THE MAGNITUDE OF GRATITUDE AND
THE EXCITEMENT OF APPRECIATION
UNITING INTERCHANGEBLY
FROM MASCULINE AND FEMININE COMPONENTS
OF THE SAME EQUATION"

In one moment, it might be "Gratitude" and then, the next "Appreciation". When the vibrational rate, is lower, "Gratitude" can make the self, feel better. Sometimes, the vibratory rate, is higher, than the desire, to know the fear, of releasing; such boundaries, for appreciation to be sworn so. The vibration, of intensity, for both to accept, as receiver and transmitter, is this endless cycle. The breaking out, of this dimension and into the spiritual, is not a linear process and therefore; It is subject to opinion, in that, the release of resistance, is held and can be easy flowing, when transmuted to appreciation, from the intensity.

The purpose, is to let go of the comparison; because it will fall prey, to its illusion and in the same way, of what feels as higher frequency vibration, over another(depends entirely upon the receiver and transmitter).

(Day 341)
14 WHAT IS GRATITUDE & APPRECIATION ?

Could it be, that appreciation, is merely the by-product of Gratitude? The paradox, is in the translation, to interpret; from the spiritual, into the physical. Where given a gender be and from that gender, the good and evil; wrong and right; winner and loser; better or lesser than. Where one without the other is incomplete and therefore non existent, yet be.

LESSON~298:

"WHEN I AM GRATEFUL_I CAN RELEASE THE CONTROL OF OUTCOMES AND APPRECIATE THE CONNECTION"

It can be perceived and from a certain perspective; that appreciation, is that of, future predictive probabilities and from which, a great deal of focus, might be, from that potential. Gratitude evens out, to something that is realized, in the now. A Direct result and already here conceived from before. Can it be, that appreciation, is the joy; that gratitude creates and the inspired action, from this passion, accumulates appreciation ?

Different vibration and vibratory rates, to share the same space? With the blending, of attracting and creating; can appreciation be beheld the gratitude and why? It is from a non linear space, where everything flows, simultaneously and to create, within the physical, it has a part, to play, yes. Gratitude, is the acknowledgement, of the positive creation and the appreciation, of it. The meaning, can be given, to distinguish and from this; the following scenario, of the pitcher and the catcher, in a game, of sport: Appreciation, is the giving value, back and Gratitude, is in the receiving, to acknowledge it; to recognize, the positive and then, to project it, in a pitcher/catcher fashion.

The purpose, is to be in love and live with joy; because when gratitude is lost, appreciation can constrict and spiral downward from depreciation to reflect on all its resources.

(Day 342)
14 WHAT IS GRATITUDE & APPRECIATION ?

To expect something that self desires with gladness is un-compromised and therefore the self must reach a certain level within itself to accept such expectations without disappointments. Gratitude is not a compromise and rather as a self appreciation to giving of the self such glad expectations.

LESSON~299:
"I PROJECT APPRECIATION AND THE GRATITUDE OF THIS REFLECTION_TO ALL THAT HAS FORMULATED THE VALUE_FROM RECEIVING IT"

Anticipation, of something, that the self, truly desires and can to override the many; who really are, not feeling it? To be inspired, in such a way, with the particulars; makes it, an even better probability in, that the self, is meant to have it. When it is a subject, to behold and because of its programming; then resistance, is to be expected and much more, than from, the obtaining of, an object. Objects are not programmed to like things, that are over rated and that create competition; for limited resources and that the many, from the self, fight over. Sometimes the certainty in things, that can be felt, might go and against the program. The self installed application, is what its like to follow the heart; it can bring much fear; because, it will not make, for any sense. At first, it will feel like, to go against the heart; is to meet up and in the comfort, of the mind's, created safety zone. Within the heart, is where the many, glad expectations and that are worthy, of appreciation; yet the programmed world, might disrespect and to be ungrateful, in those areas, of unawareness. The benefit, of "what is in it, for the self"; must be, on a deeper level sought and selective, with its receiving, just the same.

LESSON~299:
"I PROJECT APPRECIATION AND THE GRATITUDE OF THIS REFLECTION_TO ALL THAT HAS FORMULATED THE VALUE_FROM RECEIVING IT"

Within the programmed world, the self and along with the many; who were taught, to experience resentment, for this word "IT MUST BE GRATEFUL"(made up story to believe as truth): in this way, the constriction caused it, to recede, into a recession; rather than expand. Gratitude and just like compassion, it is not, from a place, of pity; rather, from a presence, of oneness, that is thy self, with heart and mind. From a place, of love, the awareness is appreciated, as praiseworthy; because, there is a level, of trust, in the moment, to surrender. Resisting, to be, for any other way, that is of being, would be, of great struggle and effort.

The purpose, is to realize, how far the self has come and to rid of, as many programs; by recognizing, through this lesson and perhaps, that there is, more it needs to clear away.

(Day 343)

14   WHAT IS GRATITUDE & APPRECIATION ?

Be grateful, in all the memories, that the self, might have carried out and from in, its complete upheaval, of annihilation for itself, through outside circumstances and reflections. Be grateful, for when the bubble bursts and revelation, is the outcome, of the day.
LESSON~300:
"I CAN APPRECIATE THE MOMENTS TO MY SELF AND SO THAT I MAY RESTORE_WITHIN THE RESTFUL STILLNESS OF THIS GRATITUDE"

The universe, is allowing, for these thoughts, to surface and that, once they have served, the body, of the self, real well; are the very things, that bring it pain now and as they surface, the self can rid, of all its pain, it feels, by them. The unnatural aging process, from stress and that the self created, into pain; from its resistance, of the self and body, is only real, when it believes it. In getting past, the falsehood and that expects to be taken; to threaten it, with needs, to re align and a pledging to a legion (re-legion), is no longer. The self can break free, from the casting, ruling class/cultured tribes and that would have it, spirituality turn, into a religion. When bringing the spiritual, to join the physical; not even gratitude, can escape; from the parasitic disagreement and branching off, to further breakdown, upon the feeding off, of and the outcome, of its depreciation. The quantity, does not bring quality, to such cloning and rather, a means from which to compete; for the unreasonable lack and that redirects the self, from gratitude and feelings, of appreciation.

LESSON~300:
"I CAN APPRECIATE THE MOMENTS TO MY SELF AND SO THAT I MAY RESTORE WITHIN THE RESTFUL STILLNESS OF THIS GRATITUDE"

No need to run away, from anything; it is in the chasing, for the things it will repel; from it and in the having, of as quantity.
Just because the self has something, it appreciates; does not mean that the many, of its world, be grateful, for the same and in such a way and vice versa. This is where, the currency, for such trading, can occur and yet, it does not; because the flow, is pinched off, to create more power with and then released, to be directed, as a target, to the certain population. The only, but the few parts, from the entire body and from the self, can function in this way; eventually, to circulate, insufficiently down, to the res, of less than, next to nothing and accounts for, general misfortunes. This type of circulation, does and can attract, the feeling of pain and being trapped, within unfavourable conditions. The physical, can get to be, very static; that only gratitude, can ease and then transmute, into excitement. Today, find the space, to spiral upward, with appreciation; find the many probabilities and position them, from being glad, at what is possible.

The purpose, it begins with, gratitude and that, from self appreciation, to impress upon the many, of its world. Enlightenment, is the graceful possibility and from this perspective, be as a carefree and light hearted being, to perceive it so.

(Day 344)
14 WHAT IS GRATITUDE & APPRECIATION ?

Appreciation, is a calling from the self; to expect more, of itself and that, of everything, around it. To see the best, in all things; even when, they are not seen, in such way. To always see the beauty, in everything life brings and from a state, of gratitude, that brings alignment.

LESSON~301:
"I CAN REFLECT UPON THE YEAR
AS I CAN REFLECT UPON MY DAY
TO FEEL THE GRATITUDE OF ALL MY ACHIEVEMENTS
THAT DESERVE TO BE ACKNOWLEDGED AND
THAT CAME ABOUT WITH NO STRUGGLE"

Set the intensions, every day, on the things, that the self wishes, to get done and focus on, doing just that. At the end of the day and every other day; forward the year, see how well and struggle free. Watch how everything, that was achievable and worthy of praise, is this gratitude. Gratitude, has taken on, a twisted meaning, to have throughout the world plagued down by it. When something gets so twisted, naturally it gets heavier and next to appreciation very dense.
To the many reflections, this might be, somewhat newer, in awareness. The self, is in constant reflection, from its soul, to clear, from the many, of the world. The twist and in the same way, to weigh it down; just like love, is a word taken on, for face value. It does not matter, what the many, of the world, can feel of the past or future. Gratitude and appreciation, are the same within the present moment, to distinguish and make the majority, to agree upon, an opinion and as fact.

LESSON~301:
"I CAN REFLECT UPON THE YEAR
AS I CAN REFLECT UPON MY DAY
TO FEEL THE GRATITUDE OF ALL MY ACHIEVEMENTS
THAT DESERVE TO BE ACKNOWLEDGED AND
THAT CAME ABOUT WITH NO STRUGGLE"

Anything is possible, when the mind believes it truth and from there, to feel it so.
Whether a higher frequency, comes about from one meaning it to, over another and rather than, to feel it; is the past, not the same, as future, in the present moment and to be hold, as one, in the same? One meaning, over another, can it help to feel better, from a past outcome and without having to attach, with struggle, to achieve for anything? Source, is flowing and whether the self, is in the flow, or resisting, to receive it; this is part, of gratitude and the giving, of appreciation. Only when the self, can have, is it able, to give and like it is, always giving, it is always receiving, just the same. Breathe in and then breathe out; is one higher and better than, the other ?

The purpose, is to separate, from meaning and of what gives more, higher frequency, over another; because without a meaning, the words are, null and void.

Take 2 days to take it in

CONGRATULATIONS ...!!!

FOR MAKING IT THROUGH THE 301st Lesson

(This is a rest period to take the lessons independently as a review)

TAKE THESE TWO DAYS TO RECALIBRATE;

MAKE NOTES AND REVIEW..................

(Day 347)

14 WHAT IS GRATITUDE & APPRECIATION ?

When moving into the mind, judgment starts; from this intake, to assess and then reassess, its creation. Why is it, that how useful something is, can make the difference, between appreciation and the depreciation, of it? How is it possible, for the illusion, that reflects, as real, to be projecting, its values, onto the self ?
Only when the self becomes unconscious, can depreciation, be the reflect, of this way(to motion further). Eventually the only choice left, will be, to wake up and/ or recycle, before its time.

LESSON~302:
"MY LIMITING THOUGHTS COME FROM A SUBCONSCIOUS PLACE."
"ONLY WHEN I CAN BE IN LOVE_OPEN AND ALIGHNED WITHIN HEART SPACE DOES THE SOURCE ENERGY FLOW THROUGH !"

How can appreciation even exist; when it has, a dual component, that can cancel it, out? From its composition, gratitude can be further explored. Perhaps today, can be this lesson and from its various tones, of perspectives; genre of emotion, and the plethora, of appreciation, in any given, particular moment, no matter how subtle, grasp it. When is it not meaningful, to be grateful?
The expectations, hardly ever match, the actual experience; infuse it, with a newer form, of energy and see what gets created?
Similar to faith, however, appreciation is a feeling, of giving value, more so, than the certainty, of intuitively feeling and can work, very well, with faith.

LESSON~302:
"MY LIMITING THOUGHTS COME FROM A SUBCONSCIOUS PLACE."
"ONLY WHEN I CAN BE IN LOVE, OPEN AND ALIGHNED WITHIN HEART SPACE DOES THE SOURCE ENERGY FLOW THROUGH !"

Many experiences, have never matched and when the self, had actually stepped, into it; gratitude was the soothing component, to nurture the self with: "that's alright" and when the expectations, do not match the outcome. When the self, with much gratitude, can learn, to let go, of opposition and resistance; because its opinions, of what it does prefer, might not match and with the rest, of the world, as factual. The symptom, is the system and from the many, it reflects it back, to the self. When thy self, can release, the what is, such comparisons; it can allow, for more creative energy, to come through and sometimes, it can be, created, for something, even more magical. These are, the miracles, that the self, did not even know, were possible.

The purpose, is for that, of the self, to not always have to know and from a heart centered space; it must allow itself, to be, forever curious and explore, the source, from this, its creative energy.

(Day 348)

14 WHAT IS GRATITUDE & APPRECIATION ?

Expansion makes room, for abundance and by taking care, of what the self, already has; just by being thankful. Focus, on creating and for newer, neural pathways, when not fully conscious.
Can make better, the choices, from such things, as affirmations; so that the subconscious and as in earlier stages, of rewiring the mind, from these lessons.

LESSON~303:
"MY DAY IS SUCCESSFUL_TO IMPRESS UPON_WITH ITS PURPOSE_I AM THANKFUL IN THE ESSENCE
MY CREATIONS BRING_THAT I MAY BE OPEN TO EXPLORE EXPRESSION FURTHER"

The form, is what inspires and through the learning of desire, to express, with the essence, of imagination. New thoughts and feelings, can create pathways, to explore efficiently and affectively; when the consciousness creates, a thought with focus. When the self, is able to come, from a space, of heart center; the mind, must silence. This is important, because when the self starts, to hold higher frequencies and from a place, of gratitude, to start with; the lower thought forms, start to surface, for processing and this can become, a distraction, to want, to disconnect. This is not a competition, to see through space and time as linear; it is not and the deeper the self can go, the higher, it will rise, from density and above these perspectives, to other dimensions. Gratitude, is the attitude, of an ascended being; because expansion, is a higher state of consciousness. The more expansion, the self can hold, the higher frequency and light, it can take in, without too much overwhelment.

LESSON~303:
"MY DAY IS SUCCESSFUL_TO IMPRESS UPON_WITH ITS
PURPOSE_I AM THANKFUL IN THE ESSENCE
MY CREATIONS BRING_THAT I MAY BE OPEN
TO EXPLORE EXPRESSION FURTHER"

When the self, is enlightened, as being, of awakened state, it does not need to repeat and train, for habit forming, to reprogram, the subconscious with. Appreciation, then becomes praise and trusting in this surrender, to love, within the state, of gratitude; the bliss will be, beyond appreciation/depreciation.
The words, kind of lose their meaning, however the law, of attraction, has manifestation and miracles; so appreciation, is another one, of those important frequency, components.
Within the flowing force, of oneness and the separation, to acknowledge the self with, is no longer the reflection; rather as creator, having an experience, that is awareness.
To an ascended, enlightened being, within unity consciousness, manifestation is no longer a co-creative attraction, with and from the universe; rather a creative inspiration, to impress upon, from its awareness, to it.

The purpose, is to leave the paradox, from the comfort, of knowing and feel that, of realities, that can become, very fluid; as the frequency raises, from appreciation. From appreciation, the action and in between the worlds, the meaning given, to the essence and that, of left behind, to take up space; within the physical form, that the self, within the present moment, can be open to receiving, as with, gratitude.

(Day 349)
14 WHAT IS GRATITUDE & APPRECIATION ?

When reminded, by another's self expression, to a loss. Sometimes, gratitude might come away, with making the self, look insecure and having to announce, over its responsibility, for something, in a way, that is not bragging; however just to reassure the many, of the world, are included with and for the amount, of appreciation, it has towards, for that very same thing, it focuses, to value on.

LESSON~304:
"I AM GRATEFUL TO APPRECIATE RESPONSIBLY
WHAT I HAVE NOT AS PROCREATED
BE NURTURED AS MY OWN AND SO IT MAY GROW
TO HELP IT AS CREATOR
FIND ITS WAY WITH CREATION"

Through the many revolving doors, of life and death, that Soul does mirror, to the self. Finding the way, of the self and helping the many parts, of it do, yet the same; is very honorable and to praise, be given it. The family and tribe, will give collectively this reservoir, of energy, to feed from, equally and as varying slightly, to give thanks, to all its parts; that one, in likeness, to the many, of its world unites, in favour of.

LESSON~304:
"I AM GRATEFUL TO APPRECIATE RESPONSIBLY
WHAT I HAVE NOT AS PROCREATED
BE NURTURED AS MY OWN AND SO IT MAY GROW
TO HELP IT AS CREATOR
FIND ITS WAY WITH CREATION"

To be grateful, opens the space, that is required, to receive with and to appreciate, something of, even lesser quality; to have more value, over and just because, the branding makes it so? Particle board, with a veneer finish, is not cherry mahogany, nor oak; however sometimes, the brand name, of this pine furniture, can be appreciated more; than a heavy piece, of something vintage and antique. Just because of the label, it will be received; whilst something custom made, without labeling, will be rejected. Again, illusion can have, its way, to trick or treat, the best of them and this, is where the magic, reveals itself, to be, the disconnect, from heart and solar plexus. When the self, is properly aligned, it cannot be fooled and just the same, as when it was, too innocent, to want to fool and for any other.
The "Ego mind", would want it so, the heart be fooled.
In both cases, the insecure need, to attachment, was for the common attraction.

The purpose, is to the nonsensical blurring, of words; that may dismay, from gibberish now and to be given, the importance, of appreciation. Be grateful, in a way, that hasn't the need, to watch, for any, to suffer, from a loss; and in the way, that came across, as better than, to impress upon, such responsibilities, of worthiness.

(Day 350)

14 WHAT IS GRATITUDE & APPRECIATION ?

The law of Love, is universal and when the self, can give, returns to it, reflecting back, the miracles, of patriarchy. Everywhere it takes up, form the world; will recognize its glory, to give back, this heaven, is a very different kind, of gift, derived from need.

LESSON~305:
"GRATITUDE ENVELOPES_FROM THE REST
THAT I MAY FALL DEEPLY INTO APPRECIATION"

There is no other, to forgive, for that will light, the way and what once before, hence turned, into a weapon. Will the self believe, in the story, of what it can experience; as there are not, for words to speak of, nor describe and yet, from its awareness, it knows, that it exists. The world, it can be taught, by its example and through joint forgiveness; to redeem appreciation, from its fellowship, likewise. As long, as the self exists, it has a function, to serve, with purpose and when it can express, the way of its passion, to reward it with and thrive. Or whatever, other story, it may be persuaded; because of, not having fully experienced, and might be keeping it stuck, in the anxiety, to struggle over, its survival, in the ways, that might not, best serve, for it. Be grateful, for all the disappointments and that will reject the self, from such experiences; that the freedom, for it, by the many, of the world respect, to appreciate, for it.
The purpose, is to see "Gratitude", as a space; that can bring, vastness and depth perception, to "Appreciate" with.

When the self looks out, from a high-rise dwelling, it can expand, to see a larger picture; than, from when, it is, from ground level and the same can be said, about "Gratitude".

(Day 351)
15. WHAT IS IT LIKE WITH NO ILLUSION ?

What does it feel like, to stand still, while living, in an old program and standing, on a new Earth, multidimensional, living, breathing platform? Was this a "Californian Sunshine" Acid trip, coming back, to revisit? The unexplainable Déjà Vu, from the 1980's, favoured explicitly and that, of the "LSD" adventure; however, not as abrasive, to the system and rather, the transitional intension, into a multidimensional experience, that ascension brings.

LESSON~306:
"THE MORE EXPANDED INTO CONSCIOUSNESS I BE AND COMPREHENSIVE TO RECOGNIZE AS REAL FROM ALL THAT I DESIRE"

When the construct, of the mind starts, to change; so does the construct, of its physical reality. Eventually, the world did change, externally and in just the same, the self could not have; however, did play with the illusion, long enough, and to claim responsibility, of that, which it was not. Reality cannot be forced back, into a box; the self found how disabling, it could be, (trying/crying and for over twenty years). Insisting on external history, to be the only way, of looking at itself; had trapped it, within a box, of disillusion, for its existence. The near death experiences, that the unconscious mind, did bring and up, to the subconscious; so that it may, be given the option, for a suicide and it did not? The self physically, could not have tolerated, very well, these blockages; just how would it, escape from all this density? Awakening, to death, for its experience, to feel its existence, again as; but a dream and for, a brief moment, within the illusion, that death was real.

LESSON~306:
"THE MORE EXPANDED INTO CONSCIOUSNESS I BE AND COMPREHENSIVE TO RECOGNIZE AS REAL FROM ALL THAT I DESIRE"

The consciousness, is huge and over fills, its finite cup; to barely understand, as human and that, its mentality, creates realities. Instead, it relied upon, the many, to conform and compromise; those parts and into contractual agreements. The disconnect, from its very life force, was this dominating struggle; abusive power, might have been enough, to harness. The enforcements, to comply with, an external system; was, as synthetic, as the LSD experience and that lead back, into inner vision. The unknown, is magical and like a freaky lucid dream, not made, to be feared.
From the heart, the self had given up, the mind chatter; to be still and quiet. The peace was felt, within the open heart, of Love's expansion. From this compassion, a higher mind was birthed. From the higher heart, united and came on line, the third eye; to help the self, this time around, enlightened, to its function, of creator source, incarnate.

The purpose, is to be relaxed enough, within the physical body; to allow, for as many levels, of the states, of consciousness, to reintegrate and into the center, of beingness, that is "I".
The consciousness, of the self, is all around and that the self, is able, to travel within, its dream time; so why not include it, within the waking state, as well?

(Day 352)

15. WHAT IS IT LIKE WITH NO ILLUSION ?

Within a collapsed state, of awareness, is the neutral nothingness and from which, all stillness can be found, an unyielding force, of darkness. Like the splitting, of an atom, dark energy, can cause all things, to implode and/or explode. Imagination, can imprint upon, this source, within the same way, as it would, a photon, with intent. The self must learn, to trust, on how it feels; rather than, what it sees.

LESSON~307:
"WHEN MY EXTERNAL LIFE IS ALIGNED
WITH MY INNER SELF IMAGINATION
THE FOCUSSED IMAGES COME FROM THIS FORCE
CALLED MY INTENT"

Nothing is really true, when it is kept, for too long and made, to core belief; because core beliefs are fixed concepts, that do eventually misalign, creating illusions and misrepresentations. Feelings are electro magnetic and can hold memory, within the cell and outer plasma field, of self. The quality, of feelings, open physical sensations, in that the self, can relate, to them, on a physical level. With how a feeling, is projected out and with the imagination, of its consciousness, is the truth, of all existence (quantum shifting into another illusion to solidify as real). For what might be held as truth, in one moment, might not resonate the same, in the next, evolving self awareness.

LESSON~307:
"WHEN MY EXTERNAL LIFE IS ALIGNED
WITH MY INNER SELF IMAGINATION
THE FOCUSSED IMAGES COME FROM THIS FORCE
CALLED MY INTENT"

By thinking it, the self can manifest and to step into the integrity of honouring; that it is responsible, for everything created, in its life and thus, of its experiences, as reality.
The higher being, goes beyond creation, to understand its essence, better. All probable, possibilities, await to be impressed upon, through its awareness; from being waveforms and thus reality appears, from floating particles. When the power, of the self, is found through love; its breath will cause it, to expand and from the heart, as wholesome, in its being. The self care, will connect deeply, to reveal, the certain mastering and creating, of its own realities, at will. The reverence, for all life; is the same respect, it holds, for itself and while building, on integrity.
Today, make it a habit, to hold on, into the next and then, from here on forth: Stay present and in tune, within the moment. Once the body, of the self, has found its tune; the rest of its world, will tune(tone) in, with it.

The purpose, is to understand, that as soon as, the observer looks into a wave and with its belief, in the knowing it(will form it); already it collapses, into matter and through, this observation, it can create reality..

From atoms and molecules, as well, as empty space, to vibrate in between; this mind over matter process, is the game changer, of reality and for the way, the self might interpret it, as so.

THE INTERMISSION :

Take a day to take it in

CONGRATULATIONS ...!!!

FOR MAKING IT

THROUGH TO THE 307th Lesson

(This is a rest period to take the lessons independently as a review)

TAKE THIS DAY TO RECALIBRATE;

MAKE NOTES AND REVIEW..................

(Day 354)

15. WHAT IS IT LIKE WITH NO ILLUSION ?

Within, this physical and/or spiritual awareness; the self, will shine through, in luminosity and from the Soul, the infinite wisdom, of its Divine reflection. Within atonement, there is no individuation; because the moment individuation, is present to exist, fractals(geometric figure, each part of which has the same statistical character as the whole)will appear.

LESSON~308:
"WHEN ALL THE EGOIC PROGRAMS ARE RELEASED I CAN MOVE INTO MORE OF MY DIVINE SELF"

When the self, has yet to be cleared, from its many carbon figurines; the shadows will cast the spells, upon the splitting fragments, from the Soul, to deflect back(Bardo stages).
 The choice, to serve and worship, this diffraction, must be sought out and for the integrating lessons, they will offer. The diffraction, comes from the aperture, "of little me perspective" and that of "Ego self Identity". A constricted perspective, allows for the narrow minded, to perceive and go over, the many details, it can grasp, from that perspective. Now it can be seen, much clearly, from hence before, of having the preposterous idea, to fit in this narrow field, and truly, how dense, is that? Trust in the Universal flow and in the self; to build it, through discernment, of what resonates, with it and what does not. This is, what it means, to clear away and integrate. From Here On, Now Than, to clear the illuminating field of the self (crystalline) and anointed, by its own oils, of activation; to enlightenment and self atonement. This is, the rapture and the experience, of the self, coming home again, to itself.

LESSON~308:
"WHEN ALL THE EGOIC PROGRAMS ARE RELEASED I CAN MOVE INTO MORE OF MY DIVINE SELF"

All that resonates, is the truth and while it might be the truth, right now; is due, to change and through the self expansion; from the changing, of perspective, while exploring its options. Never truly, be locked into any given belief, unless that is, what is preferred, to be explored and further recognized. Step out of (universal concept of a disk for just a while(to find); that through memory, which holds it in, and by its electro magnetic attachment to its physical. The nervous system, of its parasympathetic needs, become the master and then, reintegrate back in, with such connection. During these changes, the body needs lots of rest, because the kidneys, can give out; that also, can help, to aid with, nerve signals and muscle function. Once the old structures, clear out, the bones too, can become depleted; needing phosphate and they too become less dense; as it leaves, the more denser realities, of its external world. The Soul too, holds memory and that, of past lives; that attract, from a magnetic component. To create a reflection, from an unresolved illusion; held in place, waiting for integration and/or discernment, to take place. The self, must deal with, its illusions and move through, or simultaneously allow, for them, to move through it; to be released and transmuted. With every transmutation, the "Sovereign Light", it will illuminate, the "plasmic" field. Illusions, are those, painful experiences, trapped inside the self and with emotions, that the thoughts, can help, to release; when it can translate them, with the "Sovereign Light", of its awareness.

LESSON~308:
"WHEN ALL THE EGOIC PROGRAMS ARE RELEASED I CAN MOVE INTO MORE OF MY DIVINE SELF"

The same illusions can exist and as unresolved, as from within, the self. These creations, were not made from, a place where, the self could understand, itself. From these unaware illusions, the experiences manifested, to teach the self and trap it, into thinking, only as its image would; rather than, that of its connection, to the clarity, of its imagination.

The purpose, is to build upon the internal connection, with the self enough, to trust. The old way, of control and authority, over that, of the self and others; was the biggest illusion, into separation. The synthetic, painful reenactment; to be, in a hive mind and working, from the unconscious level, of external existence, so that, a few may thrive.

Where as before, within the field, the self was only responsible, for its vibrational essence and the Universe, would bring it, its reflection. Can the light body, now of the self, become the Universal plasma field, to playfully and create at will, any reflection, that it chooses, to experience?

This, is the heartfelt intent, so pay attention!

(Day 355)
15. WHAT IS IT LIKE WITH NO ILLUSION ?

The more curious, that the self, can be and open to explore; it can then recognize, that the physical reality, does not have, any bearing and instead, the self, can dictate the outcome.
Sometimes the self can witness, for its density, this thing called Hell; when the outer world collides, to enter through it and as the many, will detect, it will unknowingly become(vacuum), to this cosmic portal.
At first, it felt, as an aggravated assault; because the self was disrespected. At every line up, it had to be, the one, that parted, to make way, for all, to use, as a passageway. In this way, it can create, the void or lose, from it, the energy, at every encountering, collision.
LESSON~309:
"I AM SO VERY GRATEFUL OF THIS PLACE
THAT PEACE HAS BROUGHT ME TO EXPERIENCE
FOR AN UNCOMPROMIZING EXISTENCE"

The self, was always thrown, to move in every direction, so to allow, for all to pass on, through and from behind it, too, it kept getting knocked, into and at its body, physically forcing it, to move. The self, was never allowed, to fight back; nor defend, from the many, brief and ruthless, passersby. The invasions, from behind, to takeover, its space and move in front of it, so that the self, can step, out of the way, for this illusion; was so very real, indeed. Safety and security, were once, of great importance to the self; who liked, to stand its ground, on very firmly.
The self valued the need, of these fixed realities and yet, the very same thing, that made it miserable and feeling stuck.

LESSON~309:
"I AM SO VERY GRATEFUL OF THIS PLACE THAT PEACE HAS BROUGHT ME TO EXPERIENCE FOR AN UNCOMPROMIZING EXISTENCE"

It hid inside, its prisoned fantasy and the cloak, of invisibility, was its protection, from all the judgments, of its world; that had nurtured it, into a broken adult, being.
Eventually, the authenticity, of the self, was exactly what created, the very crisis, to break it, from its hell, once and for all; the sabotage, had freed it up and out, from the collapsing, of this, its obsoleted world. A horrifying experience, to think, that the self, would have gone down, for ever and instead, it saw everything it loved; close and dear, to have had, the fall of death, take over.
The illusion, can appear, to be very real; with a catch phrase, from within an old mindset. Now reconstructed, with added choice, in the next:
"IT IS WHAT IT IS" ~ "AND THEN IT IS NOT"
as the alternative reality, it changes, for the self.

Enter the self now, into all kinds, of different realities; however never to return, to the way things were, in their settled off distortions and where, its time line might still be?
Never, for a billion years, would it ever want, to be and for all the riches, in the world, to have this misconception, of turning into man made stone(concrete); the compromise, nor can it, to go back, into that concrete safety net, of existence.

The purpose, is to make the choice, to walk completely within faith and no safety mechanisms, to awaken; from a survival existence and become, that of its very own vibrational realities.

(Day 356)
15. WHAT IS IT LIKE WITH NO ILLUSION ?
Descend into the embodiment, of the self and without needing to come out, of the body, stand in the stillness; while allowing everything to come to it. There is, what it does and what it holds, but nothing, that is, to seek for.

LESSON~310:
"I AM THAT PART OF LIFE_LONGING FOR ITSELF AND THE UNIVERSE_WANTS ME TO BE HERE"

Whatever it is, that the self might thirst for long enough, will be of purpose and that, the universe will help guide in, the accomplishment. Fear is the indication, to let go, of judgment. Support follows the self, that can hold onto its vision and the faith, to step into the purpose, of its dreams. Then again, the illusion, of another dream and that can diffract from it; the seeking out and another fragment, of its soul, to interact with. The only thing, that is left and that it thinks it knows; because it feels it, from the heart, so strongly and as to not make sense of it completely. This encounter it might also find within a situation and/or a circumstance and from the following to reinterpret from its lucid dream: always to be chasing in its dream and then finds itself traveling along and with all its luggage lost from all its travels. It does not know of its destination by name and asked a mother with her son for directions. These characters were, from the morphogenic field, combining of; religious fragments, to believe the assimilation with and that of recycled, foster parents, from the soul and reflecting back, to the self, the story(within a lucid dream). They too, did not know, how to help, on their way about, to exit, from the elevator and that the self had chose, instead of hiking it, up the mountain.

LESSON~310:
"I AM THAT PART OF LIFE
LONGING FOR ITSELF AND
THE UNIVERSE WANTS ME TO BE HERE"

Within dream space, all can be revealed and the clearing, of much lineage; how the become lucid into memory is from intensely feeling. Feelings make everything much more vivid to impress upon the Soul; that it too may hold long enough the unified consciousness to grasp this way of being. The electricity, that created the energy, to motion it; also created its hologram and in this field, must be, yet another and another, that the self can manage, to come out of and by going deep, within itself. This is how, it can unify, to bring together and by dissolving the membranes, of separation, that formed them. It can also pass, through its field, of light; to move, into the darker, plasmic fields (that were mentioned in previously) and all, from a cellular level component. Sometimes the creation, might be enough, to recognize; from within, its blood and that rushes, to the many cells, to activate and reunite. From extra terrestrial terrain and the star system to create for; given recognition as public figurine, to be so close and yet so far away again. Why does it chase it away like it was not to trust in its relations with it, always in such a hurried rush to leave, why not just let it go? It always lets it go enough, too soon and on another time line, it comes back again; for the self to feel, it needs to keep it, or just simply, be annoyed by it, being there.

LESSON~310:
"I AM THAT PART OF LIFE LONGING FOR ITSELF AND THE UNIVERSE WANTS ME TO BE HERE"

From the capillaries, to the heart and lungs and back again. Yes, it is true, that the self can work out, mostly all, of its far distant realities and from up close, the very intimate too, will come to it, in dream time. Eventually the self can become, more connected to the dream state, that it can be, more conscious. The higher state, of consciousness, can be, when the higher self, including all, of its dimensional aspects. To integrate and embody, to descend and expand and outward; from the physical, that is, the self embodiment.

The purpose, is to understand, just how important purpose is and to materialize, all that the self wishes; from within its universe, to come to it. By travelling down, it transcends upward and outward; by going deep within, its outer world, expands. Any part and by choice, to focus on, will come to it. From far and wide, to near enough; all can be made possible, to recognize and further explore.

(Day 357)

15. WHAT IS IT LIKE WITH NO ILLUSION ?

Everything, but the fitting in; was set into motion, from the heart, it was, and from a very unconscious level, for a quarter, of a lifetime. As the self kept replacing, all the broken and collapsed, to find its place, for sustenance and for a moment, to connect itself, it thought it had achieved. Yet, with not the same of tongue, preferred to speaketh with; all it had accomplished, was to stay on track enough, to keep up; with the selective many, of its system.
The disconnection, will cost; because the inner child, was never allowed, to join in, with its licensed worthy contribution, to the whole and to afford the membership, from its achievements.

LESSON~311:
"THE ILLUSION WILL MAKE THE MONSTER AND
OUT OF THE CHILD_THAT FEELS IT IS
THIS MONSTER WILL GROW INTO"

It is okay to feel the separation and know it, from the grief, it really is. Crying can help so much, to alleviate and yet, the panic can take hold, that makes the self, really feel it; however, it will recede again, just breathe and take hold, to reclaim it, from its suffocating death. Good thing, it does not last, for very long and the illusion; the self, it must go through, this grief and like any other monster, it must face. During another reality ago; it could relate, with a similar and much longer, lasting emotion, of separation(depression); until the manic side became, its victor, to prefer and from it, the longer lasting frequency, became its normal.

LESSON~311:
"THE ILLUSION WILL MAKE THE MONSTER AND OUT OF THE CHILD THAT FEELS IT IS THIS MONSTER WILL GROW INTO"

The illusions, have their way, with the self, for as long, as the self will require, to sort out, the mix up, with its "Authenticity" and lack, of support; that it might face, to value, for itself, in the becoming. The trappings, of its world; it cannot possibly make, of and that, of, what it could have been?

Religion? Sexuality? Gender? The tongue, it speaks in?

NO, It could never understand, the fitting in process.

The purpose, is to understand, that just because the self, is at a higher frequency; does not mean, that it has completely cleared out, all its monsters, from its closet and such is "Grief".

(Day 358)
15. WHAT IS IT LIKE WITH NO ILLUSION ?

Enforcing a judgment, takes a lot, of time and effort; because, of its great falsehood, it holds the highest rank, right next to fear, shame, guilt, and punishment, for wrongdoings. The dualistic side, that dictates, from a perspective, to hate and separate off, that which is not good. It is about, invested energy, with the biggest lie, of all and that would be, money. Abundance can be materialized; however, so can the blocks, that manifest enforcement. It is in, the right way, of obtaining such creations and through, the proper enslavement channels; that the procedures, of the game, must be played and within the hierarchy's system. Sovereignty, is the life force, of every beings inheritance and the biggest gift, to become aware, of this Light, as its own, to function with responsibly.

LESSON~312:
"TODAY I WILL EXPLORE ALL OF THE JUDGMENTS THAT WILL RISE TO SURFACE_FROM THE ILLUSIONS OF MY SEPARATION TO THE ONENESS"

Sometimes it is necessary, to take in the old structure, so to move into the new; Otherwise, it could get, way too overwhelming. When the collective, of the hive mind, cannot accept, individually responsibility and in creating, who will, step in and stand up, to fear; that hold the walls, of separation and holds that, of holding back, the self, from expression. Boundaries can ensure the judgments, to the very things, that is worth, fighting for, and is this not, the very same game, of competition?
Energy, can be taken, from the judgment, of closed mindedness and that had created, the resistance; instead, why not invest, in it, for greater ideas, to innovate and build something new and to expand the self with, a different perspective.

LESSON~312:
"TODAY I WILL EXPLORE ALL OF THE JUDGMENTS THAT WILL RISE TO SURFACE_FROM THE ILLUSIONS OF MY SEPARATION_TO THE ONENESS"

Take a moment, here and there, throughout the day, to notice the process, of forming an opinion; or evaluation, by discerning and comparing, of and for the things observed.
Passersby, that when the self sees briefly, for the first time and maybe, when out, for a walk, or going, for a drive; or even having, to interact, in with background and well, the given situations, persons, places and things. Maybe a limping, while walking; or wearing funny colours; dressed or style; or even, anything that will, formulate a judgment; very subtle, less pronounced; or strongly and shorter lasting. Do not even bother, with the why, the judgment came, to be, by others; just describe, the feeling and how it might have reacted, a response has triggered; perhaps laughter; anger; just feel it, with no further questioning, the why.

These are the judgments, that the self, might hold for, to its standard's; or societal expectations, of itself, projected on the many and who reflect, the awkwardness. Whatever the self might be, to hold with judgment, of another and that, of the other, onto it? What Expectations ? Maybe a little of resentment; because comparisons, are never accurate opinions and amount to, only that, of judgments.

The purpose, is to clear all, of the judgments, that the self, might have, still keeping it, in realities, it might not wish to be in; until it can clear, those separations, of illusions, from itself, it will be met, with fear and opposition.

(Day 359)
15. WHAT IS IT LIKE WITH NO ILLUSION ?

The new system, still needs time, to gather, from the old and enough charity, to co-exist; while at the same time, accepting the tainted energy; that will not permit, the self, to volunteer its services, just yet. The self must let go, eventually.

LESSON~313:
"I AM NOT MY STORIES_AS THEY RISE UP TO HEAL FROM MY EXTERNAL ENVIRONMENT AND
I AM NOT THE LIMITATION OF MY FEARS"

The new groups, that the self, might be trying, to engage with; can and will, have the influence, of its tainted past; by the older, corrupted structure, that was built in, before it and that, they both can co-exist. The Self, during this time, can do, by getting back, into its energy, to reset and expand; it must gift, itself the moment, of support and through its aloneness, will come self care.
The work, is in the self, to free up the buildup, of all external energies. To untangle, from the cords, of others "Ego mind" and driven lower vibrations; emotions, feelings, expectations and self inflicted traumas; from having to accept, those energies, in the first place, as its own. Just observe, how more insane, their expectations, to pay up and to play upon, their platform must become?
This kind of popularity, will never be obtainable; the less insidious it will become, to show up, for them, the parasitical environment, will decompose, the very thought (financially).

LESSON~313:
"I AM NOT MY STORIES_AS THEY RISE UP TO HEAL
FROM MY EXTERNAL ENVIRONMENT AND
I AM NOT THE LIMITATION OF MY FEARS"

The best thing, that the self, can do, for its world, is nothing. Today, any moment, that it comes, face on and with its "Ego mind", it musn't crumble, like a cookie; instead, It will be asked, "are you working?" "Why are you not contributing?" "Where is your voice?" "You have some explaining to do." "Stand up for yourself."
Just let it all, drop away like down-pouring rainfall; do not get entangled, by the friction and from the pressure, just feel the lightning and hear the thunder. Feel the laughter, from the lightness, of the heart and when these clouds, do part, the Sun will show them up, like rainbows.
Today, just enjoy the company, of the self and/or; come back, to this lesson and for when, it can be taken in a day, to retreat. Connect with its intuitiveness, again; so it can once more, be able to cope, with its external world. The lower energies, can be very draining, to the self. It might need, to take breaks, throughout the day; so to retreat, from the lower realities and of the world, in power, while they are still, transitioning out, of the self. When it is time for the rest of the self; it too can to catch up and from the many, of the world. Where hell might to decide, on an alternate path of a spiritual journey; so many changes and revelations, can occur, that it can feel so isolating.
The purpose, is to grasp the disconnection, that is, the grand illusion, of the money trap and see it, as a spiritual growth, of opportunities and to release the stuff, that held it down; because it is, no longer, obligated, to lift dead weight, above itself.

15. WHAT IS IT LIKE WITH NO ILLUSION ?

Hell, is a very expensive place, to be in; because it just, does not, fit right and is, another's dream, from which, the self, must be a backdrop drone, in co-creating. Now isn't this, a grand illusion? It could never really stay, within its body and always found a means, from which, to exit, from it. A formal disobedience, to its cause; in that, it could never really, play and by the same rules; just how could they possibly apply?

LESSON~314:
"I DO NOT EXPECT THE HOOKS FROM DENSITY
THAT WEIGH ME DOWN TO CARE_INSTEAD I WILL RISE
UP_TO CUT THESE CORDS AND ONLY CARE FOR ME"

"I WILL NOT SETTLE WITH THE SWARM_THAT DOES
NOT DRAW TO PERSUADE_IN THAT OF MY DIRECTION"

I HAVE FELT THE LOSS AND LOST SO MANY TIMES
BEFORE AND SOMEHOW_SOMEWHERE THE
PHERMONES JUST MIGHT NOT BE MEANT
FOR SUCH RECRUITING"

Intoxicated and asleep, is the unconscious, irresponsible and needing, to be told, exactly what to do; because there is no independent thinking, to be outside, of the hive mind. Everything must be, in submission, to follow through, the order; because hell, could not have agreed, to the self existence and in any other kind, of way, when refusing, to abide, by its restrictions.

LESSON~314:
"I DO NOT EXPECT THE HOOKS FROM DENSITY
THAT WEIGH ME DOWN TO CARE
INSTEAD I WILL RISE UP_TO CUT THESE CORDS
AND ONLY CARE FOR ME"

To compromise the well being, over money, is a contradiction, to its very, life force? It was unable, to remain, for long enough, in such a falsehood and to bear, with any self sobriety, in this way, of expression and to, contribute to, for others. To please others, at the detriment, of its self; was like the undertow, that would have taken it, only to eject it, right back out. The illusion, does not have to be and yet, everything does derive, into reality, from first, being an illusion. Illusion, can exist, be made real and for the self, through consciously, aware decisions; to choose and/or create, with not having to, compromise for any. Yes, well that, it does..it holds truth and that reality comes, in many levels before, it can impresses upon, the physical; eventually the illusion, does not have to be, at all and as part of the equation; to create and have materialize, within the physical reality, for itself.

The purpose, is to wake up and from the nightmare, of dysfunction; for having to be compromised, in such a way and that actually, had once before, disabled the self completely.

Only compromise, creates illusions; because what the self, might prefer,... another part,... might not and for that other part,.. it holds for an illusion, to accept, such compromise.

(Day 361)

15. WHAT IS IT LIKE WITH NO ILLUSION ?

All that is materialized and makes up for the reality, of the physical world, had to have come, from somewhere?
The "Ego mind", will have the self believe; that the physical and the Spiritual, are two different worlds: this systematic program, not to postulate, for its existence, as solid piece, of clay, that it had created it, from and breathe into awareness.
This, is how religion branded, in for many years, taking down the spiritual and moulding it, into the physical standards; that must have had enough, to follow with, obedience, to it. So too, accepted with the whole, the self, could have sustained and as the contribution; to that currency, of energy and that thrived, over its survival, of the fittest.

LESSON~315:
"METAPHYSICALLY I CAN EXIST WITHIN A SPIRITUAL REALITY PERSPECTIVE AND WHERE ILLUSION HAS NO PLACE THAT IT CAN BE PERCEIVED FROM"

Nothing really makes any sense, within the physical, flat/dull existence, that is, the persona, of reality; yet, when the masks fall off and the programs are removed, what is there left?
Beyond the field, that holds collectively, the records, of all thoughts, is that, of multidimensional existence. Everything, that has mocked, or made fun of, to assimilate and within the physical reality, as real; was in fact, the multitasking lie, of another existence and that, is the real, when the self awakens, from the physical illusion, of the sleeping dream.

LESSON~315:
"METAPHYSICALLY I CAN EXIST WITHIN A SPIRITUAL REALITY PERSPECTIVE AND WHERE ILLUSION HAS NO PLACE THAT IT CAN BE PERCEIVED FROM"

The pretense of a world, in action; that can only blame another, for its finite perception and to overcome the process, of its trapped experiences, yet to overcome. Why was the self rejected, from all it wanted, to contribute in; because it did not have the currency, to be accepted, as authentic? So many things, the self could do, but the illusions, would oppose, to buying into skill sets; waiting its turn; fighting for its limitations and to compete, for a position....was it never good enough? Was it maybe branded, by the many, in ways it could not possibly and secretly imagine; just by association, the liability, from its fame, became very apparent. The way to show for all, to experience and change the world, through its perspective; yet, it was not supposed to be, a real, existing being. How did it get caught up, in all, of this and within the lack, of the physical illusion; to experience itself, within a body, that was not respected, by religion? The self, can decode reality, by impacting on it, from self awareness. It does not require, much more, from it and in any other kind, of way. The choice, to vibrate forth and out, in space; that which it feels to and not by the absorption, of reinforced external perspectives; nor to believe, when tasting, feeling, seeing, and/or hearing. Through the electrical signals, of its neurons and to how, the self will interact, with its environment, as real; will all depend on, for its holographic preference, to experience and not those imposed, by other's standards.

The purpose, is for the self, to discern and in that of, how much it relies upon, for this illusion; can only be, when it thinks, of it, as real.

(Day 362)

16. WHAT IS TIME ?

The relationship, to future and past, have no longer, the strangle hold in place; those systems now held in, only when the self believes, in having to follow, those rules and regulations. Everything within a certain space, is made, of electrons, vibrating in circular patterns and at different frequencies.

LESSON~316:
"THE SPACE THAT PULLS GRAVITY IN AND REPELS IT OUT_REVOLVES AROUND ME"

The present moment, is the only space, that time, really has with the self and the ability, to bring all, of this, into the present moment. Repeat the following, throughout the day and activate the thought, for this main idea and with the following affirmations; whenever the stresses, of this illusion, called "time" feels, to pinch the self off, from its connection, to itself and repeat the following:

"THE EMOTIONAL_ INTELECTUAL AND PHYSICAL EXPERIENCE IN MY SPACE DOES NOT HAVE TO BE A PUSH PULL_LOVE HATE DISTANCE OF DISCOMFORT"

"I DO NOT REQUIRE A FAIL SAFE MECHANISM OF PROTECTION TO CIRCLE AROUND ME IN MY SPACE AND WITHIN MY HEART'S CENTER I CAN CONNECT TO CLOSE THIS GAP OF THE MANY DIVISIONS I HAVE CREATED BETWEEN OPPOSING POLES"

LESSON~316:
"THE SPACE THAT PULLS GRAVITY IN AND REPELS IT OUT, REVOLVES AROUND ME"

Feel the newness, of every moment and that, of re identifying, with the self; how does it feel? This will be the indication, of how far it has taken and/or, take, for the self adjustments.
Learning this, could be so much faster; than of bringing with it, the attachment, from the old prejudices and into the present moment with, for support. Accept the moment, in its becoming and that, it is always, to benefit the self with. Nothing, that will reflect back to it, from the illusion, of its time, can come, from anywhere else; but from within the self, as its origin. The tools or application, are insignificant. Without the self, to use them and with imagination; allowing them to also use it, in the process of learning about them. The most challenging thing, this author has ever faced, was with, how to become its very own generator and not rely, on the falsehood, of another system, to provide, for its economy.

Time, what is, its purpose ? With it, the reflection, in it, of a moment's capture and to record, as being ready; in comparison, to something else, to match with and then, mismatch again, to another, of its variable potential, of probabilities.

(Day 363)
17. WHAT IS METAPHYSICAL SIRITUALITY ?

From, all the special points, along the way, that define the self, of where, it has been; where it is going and all that was discussed before. To summarize, that Source, is this pure energy; that had required, for the self, to create reference points and as markers, to remember, of those parts, that had impressed upon and mostly from it.

LESSON~317:
"BEYOND MY MIND AND THROUGH THE ENERGETIC INFORMATION FIELD OUTSIDE THE WALLS OF SPACE/TIME ILLUSION_IS WHERE MY HEART PROVIDES A FIELD DIRECTLY TO INVOLVE
WITH MY INTUITIVE PERCEPTION"

All around the self, is an energetic field; a database, of information; projected outwardly, from this giant, physical embodiment.
This essence, that is self, as an organic computer, it can tap into and from its field; through its breath, this field exists.
The Metaphysical world, is from a macroscopic universal awareness, coexisting with, a microscopic one. From the inner workings, of the mitochondria, that travel to reveal, from its very own genesis; the very DNA(the coding system, to physical existence; structures, for the mental/emotional configuration and for the software, of the personality), that it is, for everything, around the self, to change. From this book, the self, by now, has learned, how to touch the DNA and impress upon it, what it seeks, to manifest.
The genetic configuration, right down and as far back, tracing the entire lineage; of how life must be, for the self, to grow up and under such an influence, susceptible to attach, in with, as its system, for beliefs.

LESSON~317:
"BEYOND MY MIND AND THROUGH THE ENERGETIC INFORMATION FIELD OUTSIDE THE WALLS OF SPACE/TIME ILLUSION_IS WHERE MY HEART PROVIDES A FIELD DIRECTLY TO INVOLVE WITH MY INTUITIVE PERCEPTION"

These programs can be made, to block or conflict, with newer intention, to set in motion and in part, from a magnetic stranded, structure, when decoded as. The clearing away, of the old, to make room, for the new and all that once before, were seen, as Miracles; to readjust as and at the very least, acknowledge such empowerment, for thyself. This is where the interruption, must occur, to break up, these old beliefs; that were mostly, not even applicable, to serve the self, in this timeline, or any other, that it has evolved from, to choose, to be, in the here and now, for its experience. This, is the junk, that needs, to be cleared and transmuted, for the DNA, to "transfigure", into something else and that could resonate, with its transcendence, in the now.

To influence and impress upon, its consciousness with and transform, for its reality, to what is known, as "manifesting miracles". Look to the metaphysics, of such distance and of that connection, to the subtle, bio-electric energy field. The etheric, that surrounds, the self and can hold such a map, of its feelings.

Today's lesson, is all about, the following affirmation:

"I CHANGE EVERYTHING I TOUCH AND EVERYTHING I TOUCH CHANGES"

This, is not about motivation, to diversify; rather it is, about inspiration and from it, the purpose, to feel the expression, for its awareness. Look for the opportunities, that can bring out the Spirit, of home, in all things, (include the self); they are often disguised, as challenges, within diversity.

(Day 364)

17. WHAT IS METAPHYSICAL SIRITUALITY ?

Consciousness, is spirit, the spirit, created the soul and the Soul the self; to replay back, with and in such incremental steps, all the way down, as consciousness, wanting to know itself, better.

The purpose, of these affirmations, is always, to practice, in the forming, of the will, the strength and with it, the concentration, to come out, of the daily distractions; that would have it, play in anything, other than itself, to be routine.

LESSON~318:
"IN THE EVER EXPANDING OF AWARENESS
 I WISH TO KNOW MYSELF"

The very attraction, of the unknown, to the known and from it, the very fear, of the self. The "Ego mind", has always expressed, in many other ways, to channel through; from some external entity, that can excuse, the self, from doing and that, it in fact, is the messenger directly, for these lessons and this course. Spirituality, is all about the consciousness, of the self, wishing to know itself; through this dance, of evolution, that it has grown and through, such relations. Through the experiences, of consciousness, whilst the self, is aware, from its level, of existence; then the soul too, can grow and expand outward. Evolved, from its slumber, to once more, awaken and rise, from its religions; the enlightened state, of metaphysical spirituality, is once more, expressing, as creation.

LESSON~318:
"IN THE EVER EXPANDING OF AWARENESS
I WISH TO KNOW MYSELF"

Failure, had much, to do with the lack, of understanding, to appreciate and accept, the unlimited abundance, it deserves, to dare, to dream of, imaginably so. From out of, its own choice, steps out, of the box; with a platform, to stand on, to create and play with other, like minded parts, of itself. These are the days, of "<u>Peerless Moments</u>"; where all, is welcomed, to play with(that do not oppress or overpower, from their own disconnect, to overthrow with lack and scarcity). There is nothing, to be compared, nor compete with, in such a world; where there is only, that of atonement and nothing else, less worthy of. By waking up, to notice the choices and varieties, from the richness, of its diversity and from this depth, the many opportunities; that can embrace the self, for its experience. Unavailable as separate and divided, to oppose, as contrast, for the self; from this magnetic field, of poles and that changed, the like attracting like, for the experience.

Consciousness, is the playing field and everything, that exists in consciousness, the self might want, or not want, to place attention to, for its reality and to be impressed upon, its consciousness with, for its experience.

(Day 365)

17. WHAT IS METAPHYSICAL SIRITUALITY ?

Remember, to take a few moments, throughout the day; away from all distractions and hand held gadgetry, to recalibrate and with it, this affirmation.

LESSON~319:
"IN THE EVER EXPANDING OF AWARENESS
I WISH TO KNOW MYSELF"

When many things, are going on, the self, must stop and get clear, with what it wants, to experience. From the "I am" an interruption, must occur and break up, the old beliefs and no longer applicable, in this timeline; and/or any other, that it has evolved from, to choose to be, in the here and now. From its experience, there is much junk, that has cleared and transmuted; the DNA, has transfigured, into something more, of resonance and with its transcendence, in the now. This is the influence, to impress upon, its consciousness with and transform, for its reality, to what is known, as "manifesting miracles".
The metaphysical perspective, does not have to be perceived, from within a timeline and especially, that of its prehistoric, linear one . Instead, it can be, an outcome, of many possible predictions, within this practice; to be an observer, for the many boundaries and levels, of structures collectively. Still hanging on, to such beliefs, for their control mechanisms and with that point, of decision making, for the self, to get to a place, where it can let it go.

LESSON~319:
"IN THE EVER EXPANDING OF AWARENESS I WISH TO KNOW MYSELF"

To bring about, the reality suited, with these levels, of awareness; the self can play with and transcend accordingly and in the preference, of the reality, that it already wishes forth, to have an experience with.

Evolution, is an ongoing event, that includes the earth, along with the offset, of alignment, to the magnetism, it can hold resistance, to and from the many structures, of these fields, in place, it will be creating, to explore and expand from.

The purpose of this course is: to open the self up, to the level, of removing the "Ego mind"; so the God within, can fully be expressed.

Congratulations, divine, authentic spark, of existence and welcome, to the <u>Sovereign Light</u> !

<u>NOTE FROM MASTER:</u> Metaphysical Spirituality, is transcendence and as an alchemical process, to experience; in the here and now, moment. When shifting, the process does involve: transmuting energy, to transcend;
then with intent, to transfigure and transform, back into form. This is how, change can be witnessed,
within, the self and that, of its world.

© 1156121
2019 copyright ®

COME SAMPLE THE AUDIO/VISUAL VERSION
AND SUBSCRIBE TO MY U-TUBE CHANNEL:
https://www.youtube.com/channel/UCT6OYgr_DgZUm0LJY2tjKYA
AT LOVE'S CREATION UNLIMITED

To start From The Beginning of This book Come Join me on my creator's channel on Patreon -→ https://www.patreon.com/TheSovereignLight

For more useful information and on how to purchase the complete package:
-→ https://thesovereignlightministry.blogspot.com/

https://ugetube.com/@The_Sovereign_Light_Ministry

FEARLESS
ARE WE
IN LOVE
WITH LOVE
RmA

www.ingramcontent.com/pod-product-compliance
Lightning Source LLC
Chambersburg PA
CBHW070122080526
44586CB00015B/1525